# COMLEX-USA®
# LEVEL 1
## Lecture Notes
## 2015

## Immunology and Microbiology

COMLEX-USA is a registered trademark of the National Board of Osteopathic Medical Examiners, Inc., which neither sponsors nor endorses this product.

This publication is designed to provide accurate information in regard to the subject matter covered as of its publication date, with the understanding that knowledge and best practice constantly evolve. The publisher is not engaged in rendering medical, legal, accounting, or other professional service. If medical or legal advice or other expert assistance is required, the services of a competent professional should be sought. This publication is not intended for use in clinical practice or the delivery of medical care. To the fullest extent of the law, neither the Publisher nor the Editors assume any liability for any injury and/or damage to persons or property arising out of or related to any use of the material contained in this book.

© 2015 by Kaplan, Inc.

Published by Kaplan Medical, a division of Kaplan, Inc.
395 Hudson Street
New York, NY 10014

All rights reserved. The text of this publication, or any part thereof, may not be reproduced in any manner whatsoever without written permission from the publisher. This book may not be duplicated or resold, pursuant to the terms of your Kaplan Enrollment Agreement.

Printed in the United States of America

10 9 8 7 6 5 4 3 2 1

Course ISBN: 978-1-62523-035-5 Item Number: CM4021M

## Editor

Kim Moscatello, Ph.D.
*Professor of Microbiology and Immunology*
*Lake Erie College of Osteopathic Medicine*
*Erie, PA*


## Contributors

Thomas F. Lint, Ph.D.
*Professor of Immunology and Microbiology*
*Rush Medical College*
*Chicago, IL*

Christopher C. Keller, Ph.D.
*Associate Professor of Microbiology and Immunology*
*Lake Erie College of Osteopathic Medicine*
*Erie, PA*

Previous contributions by Mary Ruebush, Ph.D.

# Contents

Preface . . . . . . . . . . . . . . . . . . . . . . . . . . . . . . . . . . . . . . . . . . vii

## Section I: Immunology

**Chapter 1:** Overview of the Immune System . . . . . . . . . . . . . . . . . . . . . . 3

**Chapter 2:** Cells of the Immune System . . . . . . . . . . . . . . . . . . . . . . . 7

**Chapter 3:** The Selection of Lymphocytes . . . . . . . . . . . . . . . . . . . . . . 23

**Chapter 4:** Lymphocyte Recirculation and Homing . . . . . . . . . . . . . . . . . 33

**Chapter 5:** The First Response to Antigen . . . . . . . . . . . . . . . . . . . . . . 39

**Chapter 6:** The Processing and Presentation of Antigen . . . . . . . . . . . . . . 51

**Chapter 7:** The Generation of Humoral Effector Mechanisms . . . . . . . . . . 67

**Chapter 8:** The Generation of Cell-Mediated Effector Mechanisms . . . . . . 89

**Chapter 9:** The Generation of Immunologic Memory . . . . . . . . . . . . . . . 101

**Chapter 10:** Vaccination and Immunotherapy . . . . . . . . . . . . . . . . . . . . 107

**Chapter 11:** Immunodeficiency Diseases . . . . . . . . . . . . . . . . . . . . . . . 117

**Chapter 12:** Acquired Immunodeficiency Syndrome . . . . . . . . . . . . . . . . 131

**Chapter 13:** Diseases Caused by Immune Responses:
Hypersensitivity and Autoimmunity . . . . . . . . . . . . . . . . . . . 139

**Chapter 14:** Transplantation Immunology . . . . . . . . . . . . . . . . . . . . . . . 157

**Chapter 15:** Laboratory Techniques in Immunology . . . . . . . . . . . . . . . . 169

**Appendix I:** CD Markers . . . . . . . . . . . . . . . . . . . . . . . . . . . . . . . . . 183

**Appendix II:** Cytokines . . . . . . . . . . . . . . . . . . . . . . . . . . . . . . . . . . 185

**Appendix III:** Adhesion Molecules . . . . . . . . . . . . . . . . . . . . . . . . . . . 189

**Appendix IV:** Mechanisms of Resistance to Microbial Infections . . . 191

# Section II: Microbiology

**Chapter 1:** General Microbiology . . . . . . . . . . . . . . . . . . . . . . . . . . . . . . . . . 197

**Chapter 2:** Medically Important Bacteria . . . . . . . . . . . . . . . . . . . . . . . . . . 207

**Chapter 3:** Microbial Genetics/Drug Resistance . . . . . . . . . . . . . . . . . . . . 307

**Chapter 4:** Medically Important Viruses . . . . . . . . . . . . . . . . . . . . . . . . . . 339

**Chapter 5:** Medically Important Fungi . . . . . . . . . . . . . . . . . . . . . . . . . . . 411

**Chapter 6:** Medical Parasitology . . . . . . . . . . . . . . . . . . . . . . . . . . . . . . . . 427

**Chapter 7:** Clinical Infectious Disease . . . . . . . . . . . . . . . . . . . . . . . . . . . 449

**Chapter 8:** Comparative Microbiology . . . . . . . . . . . . . . . . . . . . . . . . . . . 475

**Appendix I:** Reference Charts and Tables . . . . . . . . . . . . . . . . . . . . . . . 491

**Index** . . . . . . . . . . . . . . . . . . . . . . . . . . . . . . . . . . . . . . . . . . . . . . . . . . . . 509

# Preface

These volumes of Lecture Notes represent the most-likely-to-be-tested material on the current COMLEX-USA Level 1 exam.

We want to hear what you think. What do you like about the Notes? What could be improved? Please share your feedback by e-mailing us at **medfeedback@kaplan.com**.

Best of luck on your COMLEX exam!

**Kaplan Medical**

SECTION I

# Immunology

# Overview of the Immune System 1

## What the COMLEX Requires You To Know

- Components of the innate and adaptive immune responses
- Attributes of innate and adaptive immune responses
- Interactions between innate and adaptive immune responses

The **immune system** is designed to produce a coordinated response to the introduction of foreign substances or **antigens** into the body. It is organizationally divided into two complementary arms: the **innate** (or **native** or **natural**) immune system and the **adaptive** (or **acquired** or **specific**) immune system.

Innate immunity provides the body's early line of defense against microbial invaders. It comprises 4 types of defensive barriers:

- **Anatomic** or physical (skin, mucous membranes)
- **Physiologic** (temperature, pH, and chemicals such as lysozyme, complement, and some interferons)
- **Phagocytic** (monocytes, neutrophils, macrophages)
- **Inflammatory** events

Innate immune defenses have in common that they:

- Are **present intrinsically** with or without previous stimulation
- Have **limited specificity** for shared structures of microbes
- Are **not enhanced** in activity by repeated exposure
- Have **limited diversity** of expression

Once the barriers of the innate immune response have been breached, the adaptive immune response is activated in an antigen-specific fashion to provide for the elimination of antigen and lasting protection from future challenge. The components of the adaptive immune system are:

- **Lymphocytes** (T cells and B cells) and plasma cells (end cells of B-lymphocyte differentiation)
- **Antigen-presenting cells** (macrophages, B cells, and dendritic cells)

Adaptive immune defenses have in common that they are:

- **Specific** for particular antigens and are specialized to provide the best protection
- **Diverse** in their specificity
- Enhanced with each repeated exposure (express **immunologic memory**)
- Capable of **self/non-self** recognition
- **Self-limiting**

## In a Nutshell

The immune system has two arms:

- Innate
- Adaptive

## In a Nutshell

The Innate Arm (Anatomic, Physiologic, Phagocytic, Inflammatory)

- Present intrinsically
- Nonspecific
- No memory
- Limited diversity

## In a Nutshell

The Adaptive Arm (Lymphocytes and Their Products)

- Inducible
- Specific
- Memory
- Extensive diversity
- Self versus non-self distinction
- Self-limiting

These features of adaptive immunity are designed to give the individual the best possible defense against disease. **Specificity** is required, along with **memory**, to protect against persistent or recurrent challenge. **Diversity** is required to protect against the maximum number of potential pathogens. **Specialization** of function is necessary so that the most effective defense can be mounted against diverse challenges. The ability to distinguish between invaders and one's own cells and tissues (**self versus non-self**) is vital in inhibiting a response to one's own cells (**autoimmunity**). **Self-limitation** allows the system to return to a basal resting state after a challenge to conserve energy and prepare for the challenge by new microbes.

**Table I-1-1.** Comparison of Innate and Adaptive Immunity

| Characteristics | Innate | Adaptive |
|---|---|---|
| Specificity | For structures shared by groups of microbes | For specific antigens of microbial and nonmicrobial agents |
| Diversity | Limited | High |
| Memory | No | Yes |
| Self-reactivity | No | No |
| **Components** | | |
| Anatomic and chemical barriers | Skin, mucosa, chemicals (lysozyme, interferons $\alpha$ and $\beta$), temperature, pH | Lymph nodes, spleen, mucosal-associated lymphoid tissues |
| Blood proteins | Complement | Antibodies |
| Cells | Phagocytes and natural killer (NK) cells | Lymphocytes (other than NK cells) |

The innate and adaptive arms of the immune response do not operate independently of one another.

- Phagocytic cells process and display antigen to facilitate stimulation of specific T lymphocytes.
- Macrophages secrete immunoregulatory molecules (**cytokines**), which help trigger the initiation of specific immune responses.
- T lymphocytes produce cytokines, which enhance the microbicidal activities of phagocytes.
- Antibodies produced by plasma cells bind to pathogens and activate the complement system to result in the destruction of the invaders.
- Antibodies produced by B lymphocytes bind to pathogens and assist with phagocytosis (**opsonization**).

## In a Nutshell

- Antibodies and complement enhance phagocytosis.
- Antibodies activate complement.
- Cytokines stimulate adaptive and innate responses.

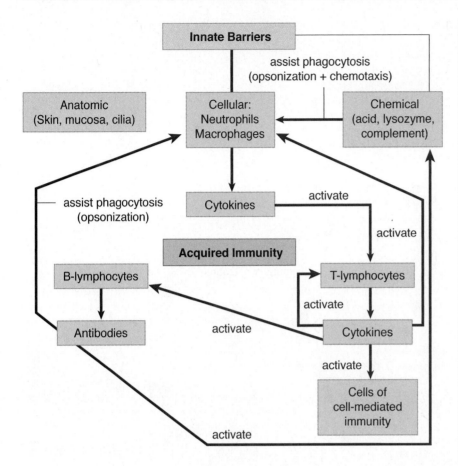

Figure I-1-1. Interaction Between Innate and Adaptive Immune Responses

## Chapter Summary

- The immune system has two arms, innate and adaptive.

- The innate arm is a barrier system consisting of anatomic, physiologic, phagocytic, or inflammatory components.

- The innate arm is present intrinsically, has limited specificity and diversity, and is not enhanced by repeated exposure.

- The adaptive arm consists of T and B lymphocytes and antigen-presenting cells.

- Adaptive immune responses are specific, diverse, self-limiting, capable of self versus non-self recognition, and display memory.

- The innate and adaptive arms interact with and augment each other through soluble substances such as antibodies, complement, and cytokines.

# 2

## What the COMLEX Requires You To Know

- The cells of the immune system, their origin, tissue distribution, and function
- The structure and function of antigen-recognition molecules of B and T lymphocytes
- The make-up of the signal transduction complex of B and T lymphocytes
- The basic mechanism of gene-segment rearrangement to generate receptor diversity

## ORIGIN

The cells of the immune system arise from a pluripotent stem cell in the bone marrow. Differentiation of this cell will occur along one of two pathways, giving rise to either a common lymphoid progenitor cell or a common myeloid progenitor cell. The common lymphoid progenitor cell gives rise to B lymphocytes, T lymphocytes, and natural killer (NK) cells. The myeloid progenitor gives rise to erythrocytes, platelets, basophils, mast cells, eosinophils, neutrophils, monocytes, macrophages, and dendritic cells.

### In a Nutshell

- The lymphoid progenitor makes B cells, T cells, and NK cells.
- The myeloid progenitor makes red blood cells, platelets, basophils, mast cells, eosinophils, neutrophils, monocytes, macrophages, and dendritic cells.

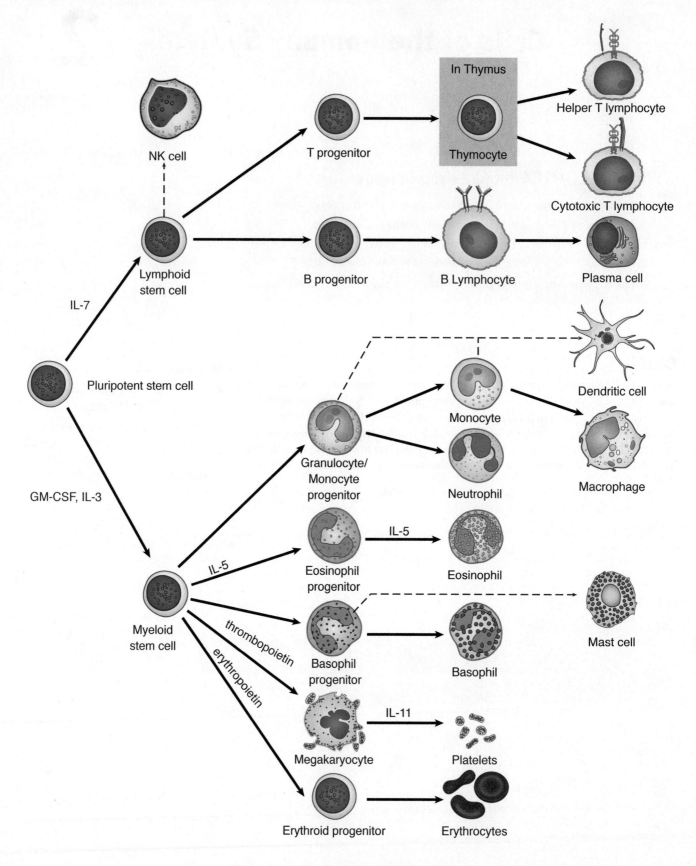

**Figure I-2-1.** The Ontogeny of Immune Cells

# FUNCTION

The white blood cells of both myeloid and lymphoid stem cell origin have specialized functions in the body once their differentiation from the bone marrow is complete. Cells of myeloid heritage perform relatively stereotyped responses and are thus considered members of the innate branch of the immune system. Cells of the lymphoid lineage perform finely tuned, antigen-specific roles in immunity.

## In a Nutshell

- Myeloid cells are in the innate branch.
- Lymphoid cells (except NK cells) are in the adaptive branch.

**Table I-2-1.** Myeloid Cells

| Myeloid Cell | Tissue Location | Identification | Function |
|---|---|---|---|
| Monocyte | Bloodstream, 0–900/μL | Kidney bean-shaped nucleus, CD14 positive | Phagocytic, differentiate into tissue macrophages |
| Macrophage | Tissues | Ruffled membrane, cytoplasm with vacuoles and vesicles, CD14 positive | Phagocytosis, secretion of cytokines |
| Dendritic cell | Epithelia, tissues | Long cytoplasmic arms | Antigen capture, transport, and presentation |
| Neutrophil | Bloodstream, 1,800–7,800/μL | Multilobed nucleus; small light pink to purple granules | Phagocytosis and activation of bactericidal mechanisms |
| Eosinophil | Bloodstream, 0–450/μL | Bilobed nucleus, large pink granules | Killing of antibody-coated parasites |

*(Continued)*

**Table I-2-1.** Myeloid Cells (*continued*)

| Myeloid Cell | Tissue Location | Identification | Function |
|---|---|---|---|
| Basophil | Bloodstream, 0-200/μL | Bilobed nucleus, large blue granules | Nonphagocytic, release pharmacologically active substances during allergic responses |
| Mast cell | Tissues, mucosa, and epithelia | Small nucleus, cytoplasm packed with large blue granules | Release of granules containing histamine, etc., during allergic responses |

Although lymphocytes in the bloodstream and tissues are nearly morphologically indistinguishable at the light microscopic level, we now know that there are several distinct but interdependent lineages of these cells: **B lymphocytes**, so called because they complete their development in the **bone marrow**, and **T lymphocytes**, so called because they pass from their origin in the bone marrow into the **thymus**, where they complete their development. Both have surface membrane–receptors designed to bind specific antigens. The third type of lymphocyte, the **natural killer (NK) cell**, is a **large, granular lymphocyte** that recognizes certain tumor and virus-infected cells (*See* Chapter 8).

**Table I-2-2.** Lymphoid Cells

| Lymphoid Cell | Location | Identification | Function |
|---|---|---|---|
| Lymphocyte | Bloodstream, 1,000–4,000/μl; lymph nodes, spleen, submucosa, and epithelia | Large, dark nucleus, small rim of cytoplasm<br>B cells – CD19, 20, 21<br>T cells – CD3<br>TH cells –CD4<br>CTLs – CD8 | B cells produce antibody<br>T helper cells regulate immune responses<br>Cytotoxic T cells (CTLs) kill altered or infected cells |
| Natural killer (NK) lymphocyte | Bloodstream, ≤10% of lymphocytes | Lymphocytes with large cytoplasmic granules<br>CD16 + CD56 positive | Kill tumor/virus cell targets or antibody-coated target cells |
| Plasma cell | Lymph nodes, spleen, mucosal-associated lymphoid tissues, and bone marrow | Small dark nucleus, intensely staining<br>Golgi apparatus | End cell of B-cell differentiation, produce antibody |

## In a Nutshell

- B lymphocytes are generated and mature in the bone marrow.
- T lymphocytes undergo maturation in the thymus.
- NK cells are large, granular lymphocytes.

# ANTIGEN RECOGNITION MOLECULES OF LYMPHOCYTES

Each of the cells of the lymphoid lineage is now clinically identified by the characteristic surface molecules that they possess, and much is known about these structures, at least for B and T cells. The B lymphocyte, in its mature ready-to-respond form (the naive B lymphocyte), wears molecules of two types of antibody or immunoglobulin called IgM and IgD embedded in its membrane. The naive T cell wears a single type of genetically related molecule, called the T-cell receptor (TCR), on its surface. Both of these types of antigen receptors are encoded within the immunoglobulin superfamily of genes and are expressed in literally millions of variations in different lymphocytes as a result of complex and random rearrangements of the cells' DNA.

### In a Nutshell

- The naive B-cell antigen receptors are IgM and IgD.

- The T-cell antigen receptor is made of α and β chains.

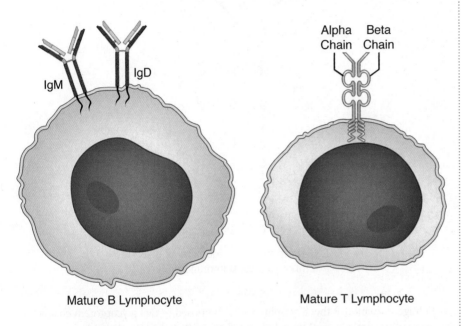

**Figure I-2-2.** Antigen Receptors of Mature Lymphocytes

The antigen receptor of the B lymphocyte, or **membrane-bound immunoglobulin**, is a 4-chain glycoprotein molecule that serves as the basic monomeric unit for each of the distinct antibody molecules destined to circulate freely in the serum. This monomer has two identical halves, each composed of a long, or **heavy chain** (μ for immunoglobulin [Ig] M and δ for IgD), and a shorter, **light chain** (κ or λ). A cytoplasmic tail on the carboxy-terminus of each heavy chain extends through the plasma membrane and anchors the molecule to the cell surface. The two halves are held together by disulfide bonds into a shape resembling a "Y," and some flexibility of movement is permitted between the halves by disulfide bonds forming a **hinge region**.

On the N-terminal end of the molecule where the heavy and light chains lie side by side, a "pocket" is formed whose 3-dimensional shape will accommodate the noncovalent binding of one, or a very small number, of related antigens. The unique 3-dimensional shape of this pocket is called the **idiotype** of the molecule, and although two classes **(isotypes)** of membrane immunoglobulin (IgM and IgD) are coexpressed (defined by amino acid sequences toward the carboxy terminus of the molecule), only one idiotype or **antigenic specificity** is expressed per cell (although in multiple copies). Each human individual is capable of producing hundreds of millions of unique idiotypes.

### In a Nutshell

- Membrane-bound Ig has two heavy and two light chains.

- A "hinge" region joins the heavy chains.

- The **idiotype** of the molecule resides in the N-terminal pocket of heavy and light chains.

- The **isotype** of the molecule is determined by domains toward the C-terminus.

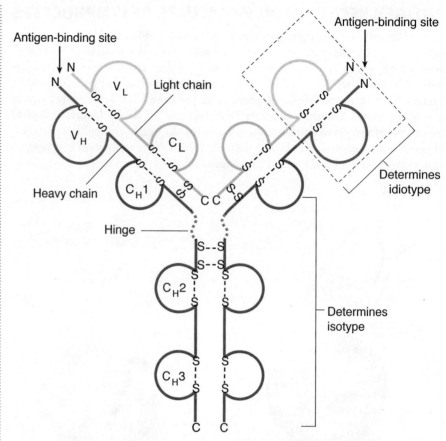

**Figure I-2-3.** B-Lymphocyte Antigen Recognition Molecule (Membrane-Bound Immunoglobulin)

**In a Nutshell**

- The T-cell receptor has α/β chains.

- It binds peptides presented by antigen-presenting cells.

- The molecule is rigid.

- The molecule is always cell-bound.

**In a Nutshell**

- B cells recognize unprocessed antigens.

- T cells recognize **cell-bound peptides**.

**In a Nutshell**

- The B-cell signal transduction complex is Ig-α, Ig-β, CD19, and CD21.

- The T-cell signal transduction complex is CD3.

The antigen receptor of the T lymphocyte is composed of two glycoprotein chains that are similar in length and are thus designated α and β chains. On the carboxy-terminus of α/β chains, a cytoplasmic tail extends through the membrane for anchorage. On the N-terminal end of the molecule, a groove is formed between the two chains, whose three-dimensional shape will accommodate the binding of a small antigenic **peptide** presented on the surface of an antigen-presenting cell (macrophage, dendritic cell, or B lymphocyte). This groove forms the idiotype of the TCR. Notice that there is no hinge region present in this molecule, and thus its conformation is quite rigid.

The membrane receptors of B lymphocytes are designed to bind **unprocessed antigens** of almost any chemical composition, whereas the TCR is designed to bind only **cell-bound peptides**. Also, although the B-cell receptor is ultimately modified to circulate freely in the plasma as secreted **antibody**, the TCR is never released from its membrane-bound location.

In association with these unique antigen-recognition molecules on the surface of B and T cells, accessory molecules are found whose function is in signal transduction. Thus, when a lymphocyte binds to an antigen complementary to its idiotype, a cascade of messages transferred through its **signal transduction complex** will culminate in intracytoplasmic phosphorylation events, which will activate the cell. In the B cell, this signal transduction complex is composed of two single-chain immunoglobulin relatives known as Ig-α and Ig-β and two other molecules designated CD (cluster of differentiation) 19 and 21. In the T cell, the signal transduction complex is a multichain structure called CD3.

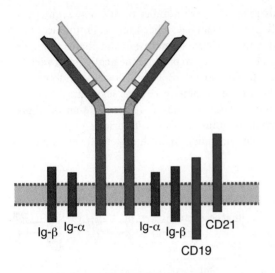

**B-Cell Signal Transduction Complex**

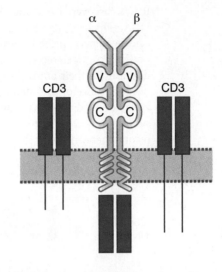

**T-Cell Signal Transduction Complex**

Figure I-2-4

**Table I-2-3.** Comparison of B- and T-Lymphocyte Antigen Receptors

| Property | B-Cell Antigen Receptor | T-Cell Antigen Receptor |
|---|---|---|
| Molecules/Lymphocyte | 100,000 | 100,000 |
| Idiotypes/Lymphocyte | 1 | 1 |
| Isotypes/Lymphocyte | 2 (IgM and IgD) | 1 ($\alpha/\beta$) |
| Is secretion possible? | Yes | No |
| Number of combining sites/molecule | 2 | 1 |
| Mobility | Flexible (hinge region) | Rigid |
| Signal-transduction molecules | Ig-$\alpha$, Ig-$\beta$, CD19, CD21 | CD3 |

## THE GENERATION OF RECEPTOR DIVERSITY

Because the body requires the ability to respond specifically to all of the millions of potentially harmful agents it may encounter in a lifetime, a mechanism must exist to generate the millions of idiotypes of antigen receptors necessary to meet this challenge. If each of these idiotypes were encoded separately in the germline DNA of lymphoid cells, it would require more DNA than is present in the entire cell. The generation of this necessary diversity is accomplished by a complex and unique set of rearrangements of DNA segments that takes place during the maturation of lymphoid cells.

### In a Nutshell

- Millions of distinct idiotypes are generated by rearranging gene segments, which code for the variable domains of the B- or T-cell receptors.

- Three gene segments (V, D, and J) are combined to create the variable domain of the B cell heavy chain or the TCR $\beta$ chain.

It was discovered that individuals inherit a large number of different segments of DNA, which may be recombined and alternatively spliced to create unique amino acid sequences in the N-terminal ends (**variable domains**) of the chains that compose their antigen recognition sites. For example, to produce the **heavy chain variable domains** of their antigen receptor, B-lymphocyte progenitors select randomly and in the absence of stimulating antigen to recombine three gene segments designated variable (V), diversity (D), and joining (J) out of hundreds of germline-encoded possibilities to produce unique sequences of amino acids in the variable domains (VDJ recombination). An analogous random selection is made during the formation of the β chain of the TCR.

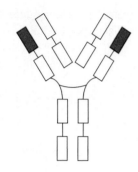

### Note

VDJ rearrangements in DNA produce the diversity of heavy chain variable domains.

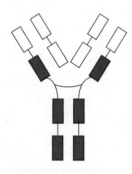

### Note

mRNA molecules are created which join this variable domain sequence to μ or δ constant domains.

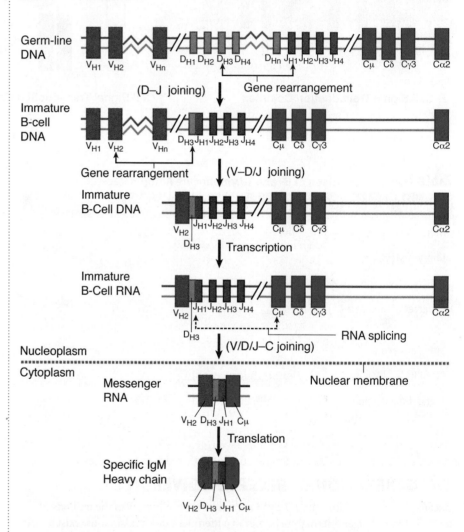

**Figure I-2-5.** Production of Heavy (B-Cell) or Beta (T-Cell) Chains of Lymphocyte Antigen Receptors

Next, the B-lymphocyte progenitor performs random rearrangements of 2 types of gene segments (V and J) to encode the **variable domain amino acids of the light chain.** An analogous random selection is made during the formation of the α chain of the TCR. The enzyme responsible for these gene rearrangements is encoded by the genes RAG1 and RAG2. Together, these genes encode the recombinase.

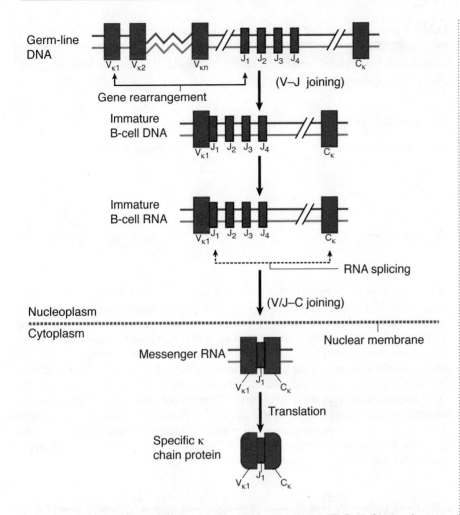

Figure I-2-6. Production of Light (B-Cell) or Alpha (T-Cell) Chain of a Lymphocyte Antigen Receptor

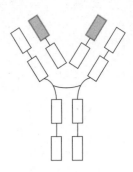

## Note

VJ rearrangements in DNA produce the diversity of light chain variable domains.

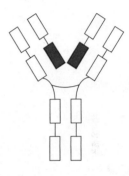

## Note

K or λ constant domains are added to complete the light chain.

## In a Nutshell

- The enzyme Tdt inserts bases randomly at the junctions of V, D, and J and creates more variability.

- Once a functional product has been made, the homologous chromosome is inactivated (allelic exclusion).

## Bridge to Pathology

Tdt is used as a marker for early stage T- and B-cell development in acute lymphoblastic leukemia.

While heavy chain gene segments are undergoing recombination, the enzyme **terminal deoxyribonucleotidyl transferase** (Tdt) randomly inserts bases (without a template on the complementary strand) at the junctions of V, D, and J segments (**N-nucleotide addition**). When the light chains are rearranged later, Tdt is not active, but it is active during the rearrangement of all gene segments in the formation of the TCR. This generates even more diversity than the random combination of V, D, and J segments alone.

Needless to say, many of these gene segment rearrangements result in the production of truncated or nonfunctional proteins. When this occurs, the cell has a second chance to produce a functional strand by rearranging the gene segments of the homologous chromosome. If it fails to make a functional protein from rearrangement of segments on either chromosome, the cell is induced to undergo **apoptosis** or programmed cell death. In this way, the cell has two chances to produce a functional heavy (or β) chain. A similar process occurs with the light or α chain. Once a functional product has been achieved by one of these rearrangements, the cell shuts off the rearrangement and expression of the other allele on the homologous chromosome—a process known as **allelic exclusion**. This process ensures that B and T lymphocytes synthesize only **one specific antigen-receptor per cell**.

Because any heavy (or β) chain can associate with any randomly generated light (or α) chain, one can multiply the number of different possible heavy chains by the number of different possible light chains to yield the total number of possible idiotypes that can be formed. This generates yet another level of diversity.

**Table I-2-4.** Summary of Mechanisms for Generating Receptor Diversity

| Mechanism | Cell in Which It Is Expressed |
|---|---|
| Existence in genome of multiple V, D, J segments | B and T cells |
| VDJ recombination | B and T cells |
| N-nucleotide addition | B cells (only heavy chain) <br> T cells (all chains) |
| Combinatorial association of heavy and light chains | B and T cells |
| Somatic hypermutation | B cells only, after antigen stimulation (*see* Chapter 7) |

Downstream on the germline DNA from the segments, which have now been rearranged to yield the variable domain that will serve as the antigen-combining site of the molecule, are encoded in sequence, the amino acid sequences of all of the remaining domains of the chain. These domains tend to be similar within the classes or isotypes of immunoglobulin or TCR chains and are thus called constant domains. The first set of constant domains for the heavy chain of immunoglobulin that is transcribed is that of IgM and next, IgD. These two sets of domains are alternatively spliced to the variable domain product at the RNA level. There are only two isotypes of light chain constant domains, named κ and λ, and one will be combined with the product of light chain variable domain rearrangement to produce the other half of the final molecule. Thus, the B lymphocyte produces IgM and IgD molecules with identical idiotypes and inserts these into the membrane for antigen recognition.

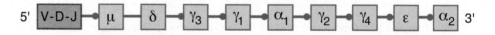

$5'$ V-D-J — $\mu$ — $\delta$ — $\gamma_3$ — $\gamma_1$ — $\alpha_1$ — $\gamma_2$ — $\gamma_4$ — $\epsilon$ — $\alpha_2$ $3'$

**Figure I-2-7.** Immunoglobulin Heavy Chain DNA

**Table I-2-5.** Clinical Outcomes of Failed Gene Rearrangement

| Clinical Syndrome | Genetics | Molecular Defect | Symptoms |
|---|---|---|---|
| Omenn syndrome | Autosomal recessive | Missense mutation in *rag* genes <br><br> The *rag* enzymes have only partial activity | Lack of B cells (below limits of detection) <br> Marked decrease in T cells <br> Characterized by early onset, failure to thrive, red rash (generalized), diarrhea, and severe immune deficiency |
| Severe combined immunodeficiency (SCID) | Autosomal recessive | Null mutations in *rag 1* or *rag 2* genes <br> No *rag* enzyme activity | Total lack of B and T cells <br> Total defects in humoral and cell-mediated immunity |

## Chapter Summary

- The cells of the immune system arise from a pluripotent stem cell in the bone marrow.

- The common lymphoid progenitor will give rise to B lymphocytes, T lymphocytes, and NK cells.

- The common myeloid progenitor will give rise to erythrocytes, platelets, basophils, mast cells, eosinophils, neutrophils, monocytes, macrophages, and dendritic cells.

- The phagocytic cells of the myeloid series include monocytes, macrophages, dendritic cells, neutrophils, and eosinophils.

- Basophils and mast cells are nonphagocytic cells, which mediate the type I hypersensitivity reaction.

- B lymphocytes secrete immunoglobulin; T cells may be helper or killer cells; and NK cells kill tumor or virus-infected target cells.

- Plasma cells are the end cells of B-lymphocyte differentiation and secrete antibody.

- The antigen receptor of the B lymphocyte is membrane-bound IgM and IgD and is designed to bind unprocessed antigens of almost any chemical composition.

- The antigen receptor of the T lymphocyte is composed of two chains ($\alpha/\beta$) and is designed to recognize cell-bound peptides.

- B-cell antigen receptors can be secreted, whereas T-cell receptors are always cell-bound.

- The antigen receptors of B and T cells are associated with signal transduction molecules: Ig$\alpha$, Ig$\beta$, CD19, and CD21 for B cells and CD3 for T cells.

- The diversity of idiotypes of antigen-combining sites is generated by rearrangements of gene segments coding for variable domain amino acids and is assisted by the action of the enzyme terminal deoxyribonucleotidyl transferase.

- There are two major points when considering gene rearrangement:

  1) The difference between the heavy and light chains is the presence of the D region in the heavy chain, and

  2) Only rearranged genes can actually be expressed; therefore, only lymphocytes express antigen receptors.

- Allelic exclusion is the process by which one chromosome of a homologous pair will be inactivated, and it ensures that only one idiotype of antigen-recognition molecule will be produced per cell.

## Review Questions

1.  A germline B lymphocyte possesses 200 distinct V region genes, 5 J region genes, and 2 isotypic possibilities to rearrange for its selection of light chain synthesis. Assuming no recombinational inaccuracies, how many distinct idiotypes could be produced by combining this coding sequence with one heavy chain?

    (A)  10

    (B)  205

    (C)  400

    (D)  1000

    (E)  2000

2.  Isotype switching during B-cell ontogeny dedicates mature B cells to production of a single heavy chain isotype, except in the case of IgM and IgD, which can be expressed concomitantly. How is this expression of both isotypes simultaneously possible?

    (A)  Allelic exclusion

    (B)  Allelic codominance

    (C)  Affinity maturation

    (D)  Alternative RNA splicing

    (E)  Somatic hypermutation

3.  A 4-year-old Caucasian boy is brought to his pediatrician with complaints of abnormal bruising and repeated bacterial infections. A blood workup reveals thrombocytopenia and neutropenia and the presence of numerous small, dense lymphoblasts with scant cytoplasm. Immunophenotyping of the abnormal cells determines them to be extremely primitive B cells, which are CD19+, HLA-DR+, and Tdt+. Which of the following best describes the status of immunoglobulin chain synthesis most likely in these cells?

    (A)  IgM monomers inserted in the membrane

    (B)  IgM monomers present in the cytoplasm

    (C)  Mu ($\mu$) chains inserted in the membrane

    (D)  Mu ($\mu$) chains present in the cytoplasm

    (E)  No immunoglobulin chain synthesis present

4. A young woman with acute myeloblastic leukemia is treated with intensive chemotherapy and achieves remission of her symptoms. Because the prognosis for relapse is relatively high, a bone marrow transplant is undertaken in her first remission. Which of the following cytokines administered with the bone marrow cells would have the beneficial result of stimulating lymphoid-cell development from the grafted stem cells?

   (A) Interleukin (IL)-1

   (B) IL-2

   (C) IL-3

   (D) IL-6

   (E) IL-7

5. A 2-year-old boy is evaluated for a severe combined immunodeficiency disease. His bone marrow has normal cellularity. Radioactive tracer studies demonstrate a normal number of T-cell precursors entering the thymus, but no mature T lymphocytes are found in the blood or peripheral organs. Cells populating the thymus are found to lack CD3. Which of the following capabilities would his cells lack?

   (A) Ability to bind cell-bound peptides

   (B) Ability to express CD4/CD8 coreceptors

   (C) Ability to produce terminal deoxyribonucleotidyl transferase

   (D) Ability to proliferate in response to specific antigen

   (E) Ability to rearrange T-cell receptor gene segments

6. A patient with advanced metastatic melanoma decides to join an experimental treatment protocol in the hope that it will cause regression of his tumor masses. Malignant cells are aspirated from several of his lesions and transfected in vitro with the gene encoding IL-3 production. The transfected tumor cells are then reinfused into the patient. Mobilization of which of the following cells from the bone marrow would be likely to result from this treatment?

   (A) Antigen-presenting cells

   (B) B lymphocytes

   (C) NK cells

   (D) Plasma cells

   (E) T lymphocytes

# Answers and Explanations

1.  **The correct answer is D.** The portion of the light chain that will be found within the antigen-combining site (idiotype) of an antibody molecule is formed by random rearrangement of V and J gene segments. Thus, given the numbers here, there are $200 \times 5$ different possible combinations. The isotypic (constant domain) possibilities do not play a part in the formation of the idiotype.

    **Choice A**, 10, is not correct. If you selected this answer, you multiplied the number of J region genes times the number of isotypes. This is not a recombination that would produce the idiotype.

    **Choice B**, 205, is not correct. If you selected this answer, you added the number of V region and J region genes together. Although you chose the correct gene segments to recombine, remember that the number of possible combinations of 200 choices and 5 choices requires that you *multiply*, not add, those figures.

    **Choice C**, 400, is not correct. If you selected this answer, you multiplied the number of V region genes times the number of isotypic possibilities. This is not a recombination that would produce the idiotype.

    **Choice E**, 2,000, is not correct. If you selected this answer, you multiplied the number of V region genes times the number of J region genes (to this point you were correct), but then further multiplied by the number of isotypic possibilities. The isotypic possibilities do not play a part in the formation of the idiotype.

2.  **The correct answer is D.** Alternative RNA splicing allows a mature B cell to attach either δ or μ constant domains on a single idiotype that has been generated by germ-line DNA rearrangements.

    Allelic exclusion (**choice A**) refers to the expression of products of either parental chromosome type, but not both. This allows lymphoid cells to express only one type of antigen receptor (one idiotype) per cell and is essential to cellular specificity of action.

    Allelic codominance (**choice B**) refers to the expression of products of both parental chromosomes simultaneously. It is found in the expression of MHC class I and II products, but not in the expression of antigen receptors.

    Affinity maturation (**choice C**) refers to the increase of affinity (binding strength) of a population of antibodies over time during the development of an immune response. Because the affinity of an antibody is dependent on the goodness-of-fit of its idiotype for its antigen, isotype switching does not affect the shape of the idiotype and does not change the affinity of the molecule.

    Somatic hypermutation (**choice E**) is the phenomenon that allows affinity maturation to occur. It is the accelerated mutation of DNA coding within the hypervariable region that occurs during B-cell proliferation in response to antigenic stimulation. Again, the isotype of the antibody does not affect the shape of the idiotype, and this term refers to a process that changes the shape of the idiotype.

3.  **The correct answer is E.** This child has acute lymphoblastic leukemia (ALL), and the malignant cells have the characteristics of early B-cell precursors. This leukemia has peak incidence at approximately 4 years of age, is twice as common in whites than in non-whites, and is slightly more frequent in boys than in girls. A leukemic cell that is positive for terminal deoxyribonucleotidyl transferase (Tdt) is in the process of rearranging the gene segments for synthesis of the heavy chain of immunoglobulin but will not yet have completed a functional product. Tdt is active for all heavy-domain gene segment rearrangements but is not used during light-chain gene segment rearrangements.

IgM monomers inserted in the membrane (**choice A**) would be found in leukemic cells that are at the mature B-cell stage. Such cells would have completed the rearrangements for both heavy and light chains and would lack Tdt as a marker. They would express surface MHC class II, CD19, and CD20 in addition to surface immunoglobulin.

IgM monomers present in the cytoplasm (**choice B**) would be found in cells that have completed the rearrangement of their variable domain gene segments. They would no longer express Tdt.

Mu (μ) chains inserted in the membrane (**choice C**) would be found in cells that have completed the rearrangement of their heavy chain variable domain gene segments, and these may transiently be expressed on the surface of a cell in association with a surrogate light chain before light chain rearrangement is complete. These cells would not be using their Tdt any more.

Mu (μ) chains in the cytoplasm (**choice D**) would be found in leukemic cells that are more highly differentiated than those described. Once the variable domain gene segments for the heavy chain have been successfully rearranged in a cell, μ chains can be found in the cytoplasm. In ALL, this is usually associated with a decreased expression of Tdt and appearance of CD10 (the common acute lymphoblastic leukemia antigen; CALLA) and CD20.

4. **The correct answer is E.** The cytokine most strongly associated with stimulation of production of lymphoid cells from the bone marrow is interleukin (IL)-7.

IL-1 (**choice A**) is the endogenous pyrogen. It is produced by macrophages and acts on the hypothalamus to raise the temperature set point. It is associated with systemic inflammatory processes, but is not known to have an effect on lymphopoiesis.

IL-2 (**choice B**) is a product of T cells that stimulates proliferation of T cells in the periphery. It is not known to have an effect on lymphopoiesis.

IL-3 (**choice C**) is the cytokine that is most strongly associated with stimulation of myeloid cell precursors in the bone marrow.

IL-6 (**choice D**) is a second endogenous pyrogen. It causes production of acute-phase proteins from hepatocytes and acts on myeloid stem cells in the bone marrow to induce differentiation.

5. **The correct answer is D.** CD3 is the signal transduction complex in T lymphocytes. When specific antigen binding has occurred on the surface of the cell, this complex is responsible for transferring the message to the cytoplasm of the cell. This culminates in intracytoplasmic phosphorylation events, which activate the cell and induce its proliferation (cloning). A cell lacking CD3 would be capable of binding specific antigen, but incapable of activation and proliferation in response to that first signal.

Ability to bind cell-bound peptides (**choice A**) would not be affected by the absence of CD3. Binding to peptides presented by antigen-presenting cells is through interaction of the T-cell receptor with major histocompatibility antigens on the surface of other cells.

Ability to express coreceptors (**choice B**) would not be affected by the absence of CD3, although cells would not be able to complete their differentiation in the thymus and become fully committed T cells.

Ability to produce terminal deoxyribonucleotidyl transferase (**choice C**) would not be affected by the absence of the T-cell signal transduction complex. T-cell precursors rearrange their receptor gene segments (and use terminal deoxyribonucleotidyl transferase) in the absence of antigenic stimulation and before signal transduction through CD3 becomes critical.

Ability to rearrange T-cell receptor gene segments (**choice E**) would not be affected by the absence of the T-cell signal transduction complex. T-cell precursors rearrange their receptor gene segments in the absence of antigenic stimulation and before signal transduction through CD3 becomes critical.

6. **The correct answer is A**. Tumor cells transfected with the gene encoding IL-3 would produce IL-3. This is a cytokine that acts on the bone marrow to cause production and mobilization of myeloid cells. The goal of such therapy would be to induce the production of antigen-presenting cells, which might increase the presentation of tumor-cell antigens to cells important in cell-mediated cytotoxicity.

   B lymphocytes (**choice B**) would not be mobilized by such a treatment. The cytokine that favors development of lymphoid precursors in the bone marrow is IL-7.

   NK cells (**choice C**) would not be mobilized by such a treatment. Although NK cells are granular, they are derived from lymphoid, not granulocyte/monocyte, precursors. The cytokine that favors development of lymphoid precursors in the bone marrow is IL-7.

   Plasma cells (**choice D**) are produced in the secondary lymphoid organs and submucosa. IL-7, which stimulates lymphoid precursors in the bone marrow, would have an indirect effect on plasma cell production, but they are not mobilized from the bone marrow.

   T lymphocytes (**choice E**) would not be mobilized by such a treatment. The cytokine that favors development of lymphoid precursors in the bone marrow is IL-7.

# The Selection of Lymphocytes  3

## What the COMLEX Requires You To Know

- The primary lymphoid organs: structure and function
- The ontogeny of T- and B-lymphocyte cell surface markers
- The structure and function of MHC gene products

As lymphoid progenitors develop in the bone marrow, we have seen that they make random rearrangements of their germline DNA to produce the unique idiotypes of antigen-recognition molecules that they will use throughout their lives. The bone marrow, therefore, is considered a **primary lymphoid organ** in humans because it supports and encourages these early developmental changes. B lymphocytes complete their entire formative period in the bone marrow and can be identified in their progress by the immunoglobulin chains they produce.

### In a Nutshell

Primary lymphoid organs are sites of lymphoid-cell development (lymphopoiesis).

- Bone marrow
- Thymus

Secondary lymphoid organs are sites of antigen exposure.

- Spleen
- Lymph nodes
- Mucosal-associated lymphoid tissues

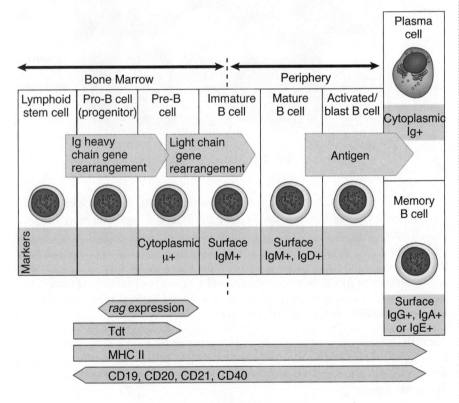

**Figure I-3-1.** B-Cell Differentiation

Because these gene segment rearrangements occur randomly and in the absence of stimulation with foreign antigen, it stands to reason that many of the idiotypes of

**In a Nutshell**

Clonal anergy and clonal deletion produce self-tolerance.

receptors produced could have a binding attraction or **affinity** for normal body constituents. These cells, if allowed to develop further, could develop into self-reactive lymphocytes that could cause harm to the host. Therefore, one of the key roles of the bone marrow stroma and interdigitating cells is to remove such potentially harmful products. Cells whose idiotype has too great an affinity for normal cellular molecules are either deleted in the bone marrow (**clonal deletion**) or inactivated in the periphery (**clonal anergy**). In such a way, only those cells that are **selectively unresponsive** (**tolerant**) to self-antigens are allowed to leave the bone marrow.

**In a Nutshell**

T-cell precursors leave the bone marrow to undergo selection and maturation in the thymus.

Immature lymphocytes destined to the T-cell lineage leave the bone marrow and proceed to the **thymus**, the second **primary lymphoid organ** dedicated to the maturation of T cells. The thymus is a bilobed structure located above the heart that consists of an outer **cortex** packed with immature T cells and an inner **medulla** into which cells pass as they mature. Both the cortex and medulla are laced with a network of epithelial cells, dendritic cells, and macrophages, which interact physically with the developing thymocytes.

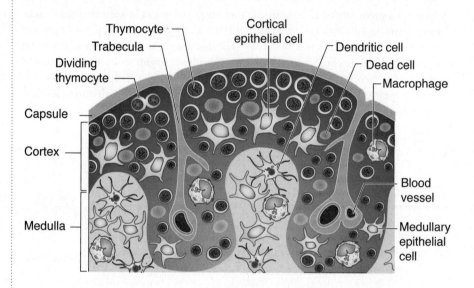

Figure I-3-2. The Structure of the Thymus

**In a Nutshell**

Thymocytes are exposed to MHC class I and II antigens.

As the developing thymocytes begin to express their TCRs, they are subjected to a rigorous two-step selection process. Because the TCR is designed to bind antigenic peptides presented on the surface of **antigen-presenting cells** (APCs) in the body, a selection process is necessary to remove those cells that would bind to normal self antigens and cause **autoimmunity,** as well as those that have no attraction whatsoever for the surfaces of APCs. This is accomplished by exposure of developing thymocytes to high levels of a unique group of membrane-bound molecules known as **major histocompatibility complex** (MHC) antigens.

The MHC is a collection of highly polymorphic genes on the short arm of chromosome 6 in the human. There are two classes of cell-bound MHC gene products (classes I and II). Both class I and class II molecules are expressed at high density on the surface of cells of the thymic stroma.

**In a Nutshell**

**MHC Class I**

- α chain plus β$_2$-microglobulin

- Codominantly expressed

- All nucleated cells of the body

**Table I-3-1.** Class I and II Gene Products

| Class I Gene Products | | | Class II Gene Products | | | |
|---|---|---|---|---|---|---|
| HLA-A | HLA-B | HLA-C | HLA-DM* | HLA-DP | HLA-DQ | HLA-DR |

*HLA-DM is not a cell surface molecule but functions as a molecular chaperone to promote proper peptide loading.

Class I molecules are expressed on all nucleated cells in the body, as well as platelets. They are expressed in **codominant** fashion, meaning that each cell expresses two A, two B, and two C products (one from each parent). The molecules (A, B, and C) consist of an $\alpha$ heavy chain with three extracellular domains and an intracytoplasmic carboxy-terminus. A second light chain, $\beta_2$-microglobulin, is not encoded within the MHC and functions in transport of the class I antigen to the cell surface. A groove between the first two extracellular domains of the $\alpha$ chain is designed to accommodate small peptides to be presented to the TCR.

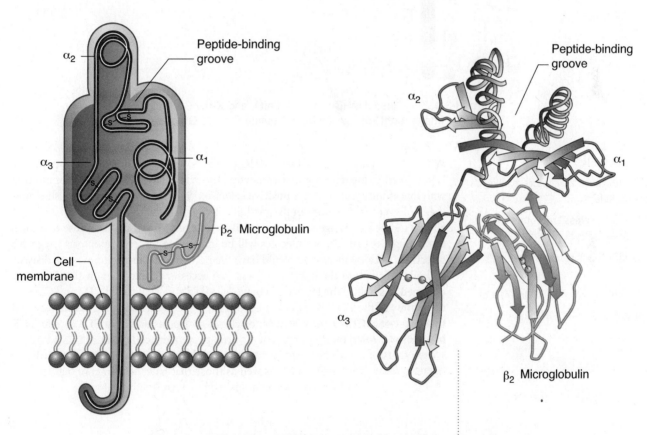

**Figure I-3-3.** The Class I MHC Molecule (left), and X-Ray Crystallographic Image (right) of Class I MHC Peptide-Binding Groove

**Class II MHC molecules** are expressed (also codominantly) on the antigen-presenting cells of the body (macrophages, B lymphocytes, dendritic cells, and Langerhans cells). The molecules are two chain structures of similar length, called $\alpha$ and $\beta$, and each possesses two extracellular domains and one intracytoplasmic domain. A groove that will accommodate peptides to be presented to the TCR is formed at the N-terminal end of both chains.

### In a Nutshell

Class II MHC

- $\alpha$ and $\beta$ chains
- Expressed codominantly
- Present on APCs

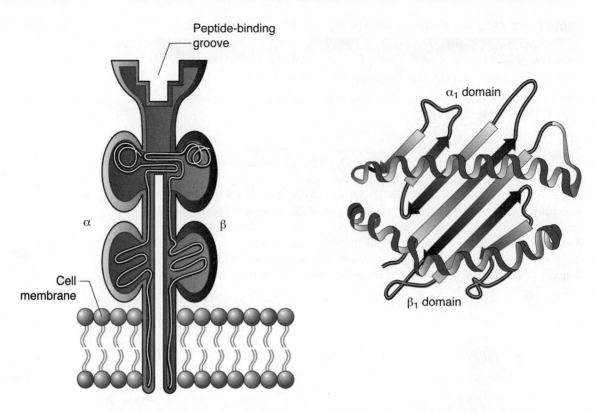

**Figure I-3-4.** The Class II MHC Molecule (left), and X-ray Crystallographic Image (right) of Class II MHC Peptide-Binding Groove

## In a Nutshell

- Cells with "good" receptors receive positive selection.

- Cells with "useless" receptors receive no positive selection.

- Cells with "bad" receptors receive negative selection.

- CD4 stabilizes MHC II/TCR interaction.

- CD8 stabilizes MHC I/TCR interaction.

Within the thymus, each of these MHC products, loaded with normal self-peptides, is presented to the developing thymocytes. Those that have TCRs capable of binding with low affinity will receive a **positive selection** signal to divide and establish clones that will eventually mature in the medulla. Those that fail to recognize self-MHC at all will not be encouraged to mature (**failure of positive selection**). Those that bind too strongly to self MHC molecules will be induced to undergo apoptosis (**negative selection**) because these cells would have the potential to cause autoimmune disease. Although immature thymocytes express two accessory molecules on their surfaces designed to stabilize the interaction between MHC and TCR called **CD4** and **CD8**, as the affinity of the TCR for class I or class II MHC is "evaluated," the cells are directed to express only CD8 if their TCR binds class I molecules and only CD4 if their TCR binds class II molecules.

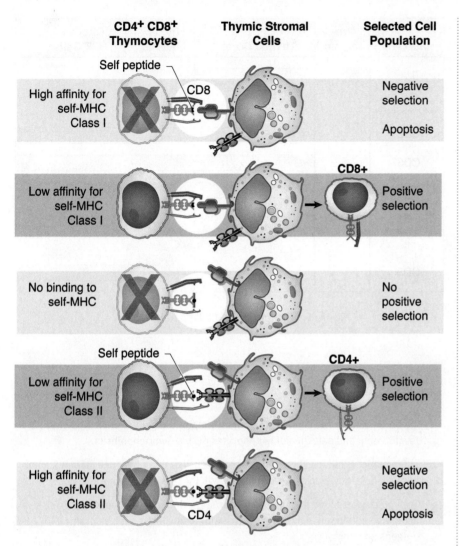

| CD4+ CD8+ Thymocytes | Thymic Stromal Cells | Selected Cell Population |
|---|---|---|

**Figure I-3-5. T-Cell Selection in the Thymus**

This selection process is an extraordinarily rigorous one. A total of 95 to 99% of all T-cell precursors entering the thymus are destined to die there. Only those with TCRs appropriate to protect the host from foreign invaders will be permitted to leave to the periphery: CD4+ cells that recognize class II MHC are destined to become **"helper" T cells** (TH), and CD8+ cells that recognize class I MHC are destined to become **cytotoxic T cells** (CTLs).

## In a Nutshell

CD4+ cells that recognize class II MHC = TH cells.

CD8+ cells that recognize class I MHC = CTLs.

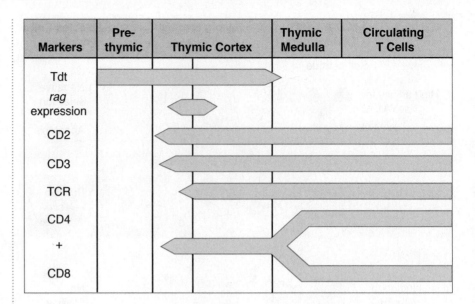

**Figure I-3-6.** Human T-Cell Differentiation

## Chapter Summary

- The bone marrow and thymus are primary lymphoid organs in which the early development and selection of lymphocytes occurs (lymphopoiesis).

- Self-tolerance is induced by deletion of self-reactive cells in the bone marrow (clonal deletion) or inactivation of self-reactive cells in the periphery (clonal anergy).

- T-cell precursors move from the bone marrow to the thymus where they are selected for self-tolerance by exposure to major histocompatibility complex (MHC) antigens on stromal cells.

- Class I MHC products are two chain structures: the $\alpha$ chain is encoded within the MHC and $\beta_2$-microglobulin is not.

- Class I MHC products are expressed on all nucleated cells of the body in a codominant fashion.

- Class II MHC products are two chain structures of which both $\alpha$ and $\beta$ chains are encoded within the MHC.

- Class II MHC products are expressed on antigen-presenting cells in a codominant fashion.

- Thymocytes with antigen receptors that bind self-peptides presented in the groove of MHC I or II molecules will be induced to undergo apoptosis (negative selection).

- Thymocytes with antigen receptors that have no binding affinity whatsoever for classes I or II MHC are not directed to mature further (failure of positive selection).

- Thymocytes with antigen receptors that can recognize "altered" self are encouraged to clone themselves and mature (positive selection) and express CD4 molecules if their affinity is for MHC class II. These will become helper T cells.

- Thymocytes with antigen receptors that can recognize "altered" self are encouraged to clone themselves and mature (positive selection) and express CD8 molecules if their affinity is for MHC class I. These will become cytotoxic T cells.

## Review Questions

1.  An 8-year-old boy is diagnosed with acute lymphoblastic leukemia. Flow cytometry is used to determine the immunophenotype of the malignant cells. The patient's cells are evaluated with monoclonal antibodies for MHC class II, CD19, and CD34, and are found to have high levels of fluorescence with all of these markers. They also possess cytoplasmic μ heavy chains. What is the developmental stage of these cells?

    (A)  Immature B cell

    (B)  Lymphoid progenitor cell

    (C)  Mature B cell

    (D)  Pre-B cell

    (E)  Pro-B cell

2.  The blood from an 8-year-old boy was analyzed by flow cytometry. The cells were treated with fluorescent-labeled antibodies to various cell surface markers before they were evaluated by flow cytometry. Which of the following markers would identify the B lymphocytes in the sample?

    (A)  CD3

    (B)  CD4

    (C)  CD8

    (D)  CD19

    (E)  CD56

3.  An 18-year-old member of a college soccer team is seen by a physician because of chest tightness and dyspnea on exertion. A 15-cm mediastinal mass is detected radiographically. Eighty percent of the white blood cells in the peripheral blood are small, abnormal lymphocytes with lobulated nuclei and scant cytoplasm. Immunophenotyping of the abnormal cells shows them to be CD4+ and CD8+. Where would such cells normally be found in the body?

    (A)  Bone marrow

    (B)  Peripheral blood

    (C)  Thymic cortex

    (D)  Thymic medulla

    (E)  Splenic periarteriolar lymphoid sheaths

4. A 12-year-old child is diagnosed with a T-cell lymphoma. The phenotype of the malignant cell matches that of normal progenitor cells that leave the bone marrow to enter the thymus. What cell surface markers would you expect to find on the malignant cells?

(A) CD4–, CD8–, TCR–

(B) CD4–, CD8–, TCR+

(C) CD4–, CD8+, TCR+

(D) CD4+, CD8–, TCR+

(E) CD4+, CD8+, TCR+

5. Herpes simplex viruses are extremely successful pathogens because they have a variety of immunologic evasion mechanisms. For example, both HSV 1 and 2 depress the expression of MHC class I molecules on the surface of infected cells. Which coreceptor's binding would be inhibited by this technique?

(A) CD2

(B) CD4

(C) CD8

(D) CD16

(E) CD56

6. A patient with a B-cell lymphoma is referred to an oncology clinic for the analysis of his condition. The malignant cells are found to be producing IgM monomers. Which of the following therapeutic regimens is most likely to destroy the malignant cells and no others?

(A) Anti-CD3 antibodies plus complement

(B) Anti-CD19 antibodies plus complement

(C) Anti-CD20 antibodies plus complement

(D) Anti-idiotype antibodies plus complement

(E) Anti-μ chain antibodies plus complement

## Answers and Explanations

1. **The correct answer is D.** The leukemic cells are pre-B cells. They have rearranged their immunoglobulin genes to encode a μ heavy chain. MHC class II antigens are expressed beginning at the pro-B cell stage, as are CD19 and CD20. CD34 is a marker for early lymphohematopoietic stem and progenitor cells, and it functions as a cell–cell adhesion molecule. These cells would also have expressed CD10, the common acute lymphoblastic leukemia antigen (CALLA), which functions as a metalloendopeptidase.

Immature B cells (**choice A**) have accomplished both and heavy and light immunoglobulin chain rearrangements and therefore express IgM molecules on their cell surface. They would be Tdt-negative, CD19- and CD20-positive, MHC class II-positive, and CD34-negative.

Lymphoid progenitor cells (**choice B**) would not have completed any of the gene rearrangements necessary to create an immunoglobulin molecule. They would be Tdt-negative, MHC class II–negative, CD19- and CD20-negative, and CD34-positive.

Mature B cells (**choice C**) possess surface IgM and IgD molecules and are capable of responding to foreign antigen. They are Tdt-negative, MHC class II-positive, CD19- and CD20-positive, CD34-negative, and may express CD40.

Pro-B cells (**choice E**) are rearranging their immunoglobulin heavy chain gene segments but have not yet completed the process. Therefore, they have no completed chains either cytoplasmically or on their cell surfaces. They would be positive for Tdt, MHC class II, CD19, and CD20.

2.  **The correct answer is D.** The best markers for identification of B lymphocytes are CD19, CD20, and CD21. CD19 and CD21 form a coreceptor complex during B-cell activation. The role of CD20 in B-cell activation is unclear, although it forms a calcium-ion channel. CD21 is also a receptor for the C3d component of complement and the Epstein-Barr virus.

    CD3 (**choice A**) is the signal transduction complex of T cells. It is found on all T cells in association with the T-cell antigen receptor.

    CD4 (**choice B**) is found on all helper T lymphocytes.

    CD8 (**choice C**) is found on all cytotoxic T lymphocytes.

    CD56 (**choice E**) is a marker for human natural killer cells.

3.  **The correct answer is C.** This patient has a T-cell lymphoblastic lymphoma. In his case, the malignant cell is "double-positive": it possesses both CD4 and CD8. In a normal individual, these would only be found as an early developmental stage in the cortex of the thymus. Once cells have rearranged their receptor genes and been subjected to positive and negative selection, the cells leaving the thymus will express one coreceptor or the other but never both.

    Bone marrow (**choice A**) would contain T lymphocyte precursors that are double negative: They will lack both CD4 and CD8.

    Peripheral blood (**choice B**) would have mature T cells that have differentiated into either helper (CD4+) or cytotoxic (CD8+) cells. There should be no double-positive T cells in the peripheral blood.

    Thymic medulla (**choice D**) is the location of maturing T cells ready to circulate into the bloodstream and peripheral lymphoid organs. It would have only single-positive cells.

    Splenic periarteriolar lymphoid sheaths (**choice E**) are the T-cell–dependent areas of the spleen. They would have fully committed helper (CD4+) or cytotoxic (CD8+) cells.

4.  **The correct answer is A.** T-lymphocyte precursors that leave the bone marrow and move to the thymus have neither CD4 nor CD8 coreceptors, and they have not rearranged the DNA of the variable domains of their antigen receptor, the TCR.

    CD4–, CD8–, and TCR+ (**choice B**) is not a possible T-cell phenotype. Once the TCR gene segments are rearranged and the TCR is expressed, the cells will bear both CD4 and CD8 coreceptors.

    CD4–, CD8+, and TCR+ (**choice C**) is the phenotype of cytotoxic T cells that would be in the circulation, not in the thymus, unless it were immediately prior to their release into the circulation following the thymic selection process.

    CD4+, CD8–, and TCR+ (**choice D**) is the phenotype of helper T cells that would be in the circulation, not in the thymus, unless it were immediately prior to their release into the circulation following thymic selection processes.

    CD4+, CD8+, and TCR+ (**choice E**) is the phenotype of cells in the thymic cortex. These are the cells that have rearranged their receptor genes and bear both CD4 and CD8 coreceptors. As the specificity of their TCR is tested, they will be directed to express either CD4 (and become a helper T cell) or CD8 (and become a cytotoxic T cell).

5. **The correct answer is C.** The interaction between the TCR and MHC class I/peptide conjugates is stabilized by the CD8 coreceptor. By downregulating the expression of MHC class I antigens on the surface of infected cells, the virus protects the infected host cell from killing by cytotoxic T lymphocytes.

   CD2 (**choice A**), also known as LFA-2, is an adhesion molecule within the immunoglobulin superfamily of genes. Its ligand is the integrin LFA-3. It is found on T cells and mediates attachment to other lymphocytes and antigen-presenting cells. It does not have a coreceptor role that would impact MHC class I–restricted killing.

   CD4 (**choice B**) is the coreceptor that stabilizes the interaction between MHC class II antigens and the TCR. It is thus important for helper T cells, not cytotoxic T cells.

   CD16 (**choice D**) is the Fc receptor involved in binding to immune complexes and promoting antibody-dependent cell-mediated cytotoxicity. It is not involved in the MHC class I–restricted killing by cytotoxic T cells.

   CD56 (**choice E**) is a cell surface marker found on NK cells. Its function is unknown. However, since NK activity is enhanced in the absence of MHC class I antigen expression, the downregulation of these molecules by herpes simplex 1 and 2 actually makes infected cells more susceptible to the NK cell form of lysis.

6. **The correct answer is D.** Because malignant cells are clonal in origin, all the cells in this patient's lymphoma should be producing IgM monomers of a single idiotype. Treatment with anti-idiotype antibodies plus complement, therefore, would specifically kill only malignant cells, and leave all other B lymphocytes unharmed.

   Anti-CD3 antibodies plus complement (**choice A**) would kill all T lymphocytes in the body. This lymphoma is clearly of B-cell origin because it is bearing IgM monomers.

   Anti-CD19 antibodies plus complement (**choice B**) would kill all B lymphocytes in the body. It would not specifically target malignant cells.

   Anti-CD20 antibodies plus complement (**choice C**) would kill all B lymphocytes in the body. It would not specifically target malignant cells.

   Anti-$\mu$ chain antibodies plus complement (**choice E**) would kill all mature and naive B cells and immature B cells that had completed VDJ rearrangement of their heavy chain genes. It would not be specific for malignant cells.

# Lymphocyte Recirculation and Homing

**4**

## What the COMLEX Requires You To Know

- The structure and function of the secondary lymphoid organs
- The areas in which B and T lymphocytes localize in the peripheral lymphoid organs
- The role of chemokines and adhesion molecules in lymphocyte trafficking

Lymphocytes of the B- and T-cell lineages that have completed their selection in the bone marrow and thymus respectively are now **mature, naive lymphocytes** ready to begin their role in the surveillance of the body against invaders. These mature, naive lymphocytes will begin the process of **recirculation** through the body, which is essential for ensuring that the limited number of cells with receptors for a specific antigen is enabled to search for that antigen throughout the body. Naive cells preferentially recirculate through the **peripheral (secondary) lymphoid organs**, the **lymph nodes, spleen, and mucosal-associated lymphoid tissue (MALT)** to maximize the chances of encounter with foreign antigen and thereby initiate specific immune responses.

**Lymph nodes** are the small nodular aggregates of secondary lymphoid tissue found along the lymphatic channels of the body and are designed to initiate immune responses to **tissue-borne antigens**. Each lymph node is surrounded by a fibrous capsule that is punctured by **afferent lymphatics,** which bring lymph into the **subcapsular sinus**. The fluid percolates through an outer **cortex** area that contains aggregates of cells called **follicles**. The lymph then passes into the inner **medulla** and the **medullary sinus** before leaving the node through the **hilum** in an efferent lymphatic vessel. Ultimately, lymph from throughout the body is collected into the **thoracic duct**, which empties into the vena cava and returns it to the blood.

## In a Nutshell

Peripheral (Secondary) Lymphoid organs

- Lymph nodes, spleen, and MALT
- Sites of foreign antigen exposure

## In a Nutshell

- Lymph nodes filter tissue fluids.
- Outer cortex contains follicles (B-cell areas).
- Paracortex is a T-cell area.
- Inner medulla contains macrophages.

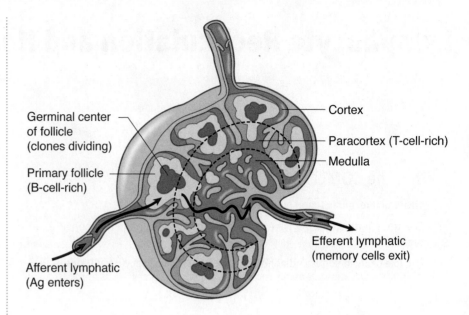

**Figure I-4-1.** Compartmentalization of a Lymph Node

### In a Nutshell

- The spleen filters blood.
- PALS are T-cell areas.
- Follicles are B-cell areas.

The **spleen** is the secondary lymphoid organ designed to initiate immune responses to **blood-borne antigens**. A single splenic artery enters the capsule at the hilum and branches into arterioles, which become surrounded by cuffs of lymphocytes, the **peri-arteriolar lymphoid sheaths** (PALS). **Lymphoid follicles** surrounded by a rim of lymphocytes and macrophages are attached nearby. This constitutes the **white pulp**. The arterioles ultimately end in vascular **sinusoids,** which make up the **red pulp**. From here, venules collect blood into the splenic vein, which empties into the portal circulation.

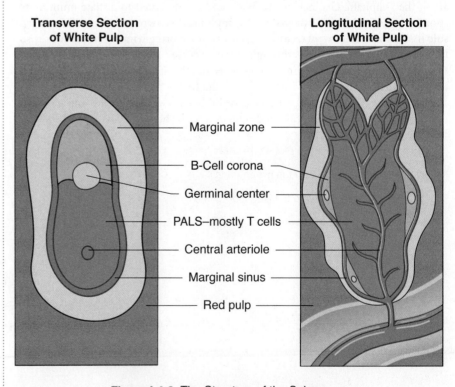

**Figure I-4-2.** The Structure of the Spleen

Naive lymphocytes enter the lymph nodes from the blood through **high endothelial venules** (HEVs). This migration involves a multistep sequence of interactions between the lymphocyte and adhesion molecules on the endothelium. The initial low-affinity interaction is mediated by homing receptors, called **L-selectins**, present on the lymphocytes, which bind to **addressins** present on the HEVs.

Naive T cells migrate into the **paracortical** areas under the influence of a chemokine gradient. Naive B cells are guided along a chemokine gradient into the **lymphoid follicles**.

Less is known about lymphocyte recirculation through the spleen. Naive T cells home to the **periarteriolar lymphoid sheaths** (PALS), whereas naive B cells create **lymphoid follicles** outside of the T cell area.

The rate of recirculation of naive lymphocytes through the body by this system is quite high. It is estimated that each lymphocyte passes through each lymph node in the body once a day and through the spleen once every two days on average. This high rate of **trafficking** maximizes the possibility that the very small number of cells having a specific antigen receptor have the maximum possibility of encountering that antigen when it is present.

## In a Nutshell

- Naive lymphocytes leave the blood through HEVs.
- L-selectins on lymphocytes bind to addressins on HEVs.
- Naive T cells home to the lymph node paracortex or the splenic PALS.
- Naive B cells create a corona outside the T cell area.

## Chapter Summary

- Mature naive lymphocytes recirculate through the peripheral lymphoid organs (lymph nodes and spleen) to search for antigen.
- Lymph nodes are designed to filter antigens from the tissue fluids.
- Lymph enters through afferent lymphatics and percolates through an outer cortex and inner medulla before leaving through the efferent lymphatic in the hilus.
- The spleen is designed to filter antigens from blood. Blood enters through a single splenic artery, which branches into arterioles that become surrounded by cuffs of lymphocytes (periarteriolar lymphoid sheaths) with follicles and macrophages nearby.
- Lymphocytes leave the bloodstream to enter lymph nodes through high endothelial venules.
- L-selectins on lymphocytes bind to addressins on the high endothelial venules, and chemokine receptors mediate the homing of specific cells to specific areas.
- T lymphocytes migrate into the lymph node paracortical areas.
- B lymphocytes migrate into the lymph node follicles.
- In the spleen, T lymphocytes are attracted to the periarteriolar lymphoid sheaths.
- B cells entering the spleen form a corona outside the T cell area.
- Every lymphocyte passes through every lymph node once per day and through the spleen once every two days on average.

## Review Questions

1. A lymph node biopsy of a 6-year-old boy shows markedly decreased numbers of lymphocytes in the paracortical areas. Analysis of his peripheral blood leukocytes is likely to show normal to elevated numbers of cells expressing surface

   (A) CD2

   (B) CD3

   (C) CD4

   (D) CD8

   (E) CD19

2. A 65-year-old woman was involved in an automobile accident that necessitated the removal of her spleen. To which of the following pathogens would she have the most increased susceptibility?

   (A) *Babesia microti*

   (B) *Bordetella pertussis*

   (C) *Corynebacterium diphtheriae*

   (D) Enteroaggregative *Escherichia coli*

   (E) Human papilloma virus

3. A 4-year-old boy is referred to a specialist for the diagnosis of a possible immunologic problem. The child has extremely elevated white blood cell counts, with a profound lymphocytosis. A biopsy performed on a cervical lymph node reveals extreme hypocellularity in both cortical and paracortical areas. Absence of which of the following leukocyte surface molecules could result in this clinical picture?

   (A) Addressins

   (B) Chemokines

   (C) Immunoglobulin family cell adhesion molecules

   (D) Integrins

   (E) L-selectins

4. A 6-year-old child is taken to his pediatrician because the parents are alarmed about an indurated fluctuant mass on the posterior aspect of his neck. The mass is nontender and shows no signs of inflammation. The child is examined carefully, and no other masses are found. The pediatrician decides to submit a biopsy of this area to a pathologist. The pathologist reports back that the mass is a lymph node with markedly increased numbers of cells in the cortical area. Fluorescent antisera to which of the cell surface markers is most likely to bind to cells in this area?

   (A) CD2

   (B) CD3

   (C) CD4

   (D) CD16

   (E) CD19

5.  A radioactive tracer dye is injected subcutaneously into the forearm of an experimental subject. What is the first area of the first draining lymph node that would develop significant radioactivity?

    (A) Cortex

    (B) Medulla

    (C) Paracortex

    (D) Primary follicle

    (E) Subcapsular sinus

## Answers and Explanations

1.  **The correct answer is E.** The paracortex of a lymph node is a T-cell–dependent area. If this area is lacking cellularity, then the patient has a deficiency of T lymphocytes. B-lymphocyte numbers could be normal or even elevated. The only B-cell marker on this list is CD19, the marker which is used clinically to enumerate B cells in the body.

    CD2 (**choice A**), also known as LFA-2, is an adhesion molecule found on T cells, thymocytes, and NK cells. In a person with a T-cell deficiency, there would be decreased numbers of cells bearing this marker.

    CD3 (**choice B**) is found on all T cells. It is also called the "pan-T" cell marker. In a person with a T-cell deficiency, there would be decreased numbers of cells bearing this marker.

    CD4 (**choice C**) is found on all helper T lymphocytes. In a person with a T-cell deficiency, there would be decreased numbers of cells bearing this marker.

    CD8 (**choice D**) is found on all cytotoxic T lymphocytes. In a person with a T-cell deficiency, there would be decreased numbers of cells bearing this marker.

2.  **The correct answer is A.** The spleen is the secondary lymphoid organ that is responsible for primary surveillance against blood-borne antigens. *Babesia microti* is an intraerythrocytic parasite of humans, transmitted by the same vector tick as Lyme disease. Red blood cells (and their parasites) are filtered by the spleen, so splenectomy is a predisposing factor in development of serious disease with this parasite.

    *Bordetella pertussis* (**choice B**) is a mucosal surface pathogen that attaches to the upper airways. Although its toxin becomes blood-borne, the organism itself is confined to the respiratory tree.

    *Corynebacterium diphtheriae* (**choice C**) is a mucosal surface pathogen that attaches to the upper airways. Although its toxin becomes blood-borne, the organism itself is confined to the respiratory tree.

    Enteroaggregative *Escherichia coli* (**choice D**) is an organism that causes diarrhea by producing a biofilm-like aggregation of organisms on the surface of the colonic mucosa, which impedes absorption. It is not likely to be a blood-borne pathogen.

    Human papilloma virus (**choice E**) produces localized infections in epithelial cells where it is transferred by human-to-human or human-to-fomite contact. It is not likely to be a blood-borne pathogen.

3.  **The correct answer is E.** L-selectins are the molecules found on the surfaces of lymphocytes that mediate their binding to the high endothelial venules of lymph nodes. This is the means by which lymphocytes enter lymph nodes; without these molecules, they would be unable to leave the blood. Thus, they would rise in the blood to extreme levels and be absent from their appropriate areas in the secondary lymphoid organs.

Addressins (**choice A**) are the molecules complementary to L-selectins, which are found on endothelial cells. Although their absence could also cause similar signs, the question asks about a leukocyte surface molecule, and addressins are not found on leukocytes.

Chemokines (**choice B**) are not cell surface molecules, but do play a role in the homing of lymphocytes to specific regions of the secondary lymphoid organs. An absence of chemokine receptors on leukocytes could have caused similar signs, but chemokines themselves are soluble substances, not surface molecules.

Immunoglobulin family cell adhesion molecules (**choice C**), or IgCAMs, are adhesion molecules found on various cells of the immune system. They mediate cell-to-cell interactions, as well as binding to the extracellular matrix. Their ligands are the integrins. If these molecules were absent, cell-cell interactions would be diminished, but movement of lymphocytes out of the circulation and into the secondary lymphoid organs would not be affected.

Integrins (**choice D**) are the ligands for the IgCAMs. They are involved in cell-to-cell interactions, as well as binding to the extracellular matrix. If these molecules were absent, cell-cell interactions would be diminished, but movement of lymphocytes out of the circulation and into the secondary lymphoid organs would not be affected.

4. **The correct answer is E.** The cortex of lymph nodes is a B-lymphocyte area. Thus, cells in this area would stain with fluorescent antibodies against CD19, the molecule that serves as a portion of the B-cell signal transduction complex. This molecule would be found on all B cells, but would be absent from T cells, macrophages, and NK cells.

   CD2 (**choice A**) is a T-cell marker. T cells will be found in the paracortical areas of lymph nodes.

   CD3 (**choice B**) is a T-cell marker. It is the signal transduction complex of the T cell and will be found on all T cells. T cells will be found in the paracortical areas of lymph nodes.

   CD4 (**choice C**) is a marker for helper T cells. These cells would be found in the paracortical areas of lymph nodes.

   CD16 (**choice D**) is the Fc receptor for IgG antibodies. It would be found on natural killer and phagocytic cells, which would not be numerous in the cortex of the lymph nodes. Phagocytic cells typically are found in the medullary cords.

5. **The correct answer is E.** Lymph nodes are designed to filter tissue fluids. Fluids entering the lymph nodes do so through the afferent lymphatics and are released into the subcapsular sinus. From there, fluids percolate through the cortex, into the medulla, through the medullary cords, and finally exit through the efferent lymphatics in the hilum.

   The cortex (**choice A**) of the lymph node is directly beneath the subcapsular sinus. It would be the second region of the lymph node to be exposed to the radioactive tracer. The cortex is a B-lymphocyte–rich area.

   The medulla (**choice B**) of the lymph node is rich in macrophages. It would not receive the radioactive fluid until it had passed through the cortex and paracortex.

   The paracortex (**choice C**) of the lymph node is a T-cell area. It lies between the cortex and the medulla and thus would receive the radioactive fluid after the cortical areas.

   Primary follicles (**choice D**) are found in the cortex of the lymph node. These are areas of active B-lymphocyte proliferation and cloning. They would receive the radioactivity after it left the subcapsular sinus.

## What the COMLEX Requires You To Know

- The sequence of inflammatory events and their role in the initial response to invasion
- The mechanism and chemoattractive molecules involved in phagocyte extravasation
- The steps of phagocytosis and mechanisms of intracellular killing
- The meaning of opsonization and the molecules involved
- The clinical sequelae of defects in chemotaxis and phagocytosis (LAD and CGD)

## DEFINITIONS

Historically, the word **antigen** was meant to designate a substance capable of inducing the formation of a specific antibody: an **anti**body-**gen**erating substance. Today the word is used almost interchangeably with the word **immunogen**—an **immune** response–**gen**erating substance—to encompass any substance capable of activating and generating a response from any committed lymphocyte. For a molecule to be an immunogen, it needs to fit 3 basic criteria:

- It must be recognized as **foreign**.
- It must have a certain degree of **chemical complexity**.
- It must have a **molecular weight** of at least 5,000 to 10,000 Kd.

B lymphocytes are capable of recognizing molecules of almost any chemical composition. The portion of the foreign molecule that actually fits into the idiotype of the B-cell receptor is quite small: 5 to 6 amino acids in the case of a protein or 4 to 5 hexose units in the case of a carbohydrate. This portion of the molecule that has 3-dimensional complementarity with the idiotype is called the **epitope** or **antigenic determinant** of the immunogen. Because most of the microbes that challenge the immune system are quite large, most naturally occurring antigens have many copies of the same epitopes.

The size of a molecule is a critical factor in its immunogenicity because B lymphocytes can only be activated when their antigen receptors are **crosslinked** by the accommodation of more than one identical epitope. This serves as the first signal to then send the message through the signal transduction complex to activate the cell. Molecules that possess only one epitope are called **haptens** because they can occupy only one combining site of the double-armed B-cell receptor. T lymphocytes recognize peptides of 10 to 20 amino acids in length only when presented to them in the groove of an MHC molecule on the surface of an antigen-presenting cell.

### In a Nutshell

- An immunogen is a substance that can elicit an immune response.
- It must be foreign, chemically complex, and large.

### Note

The idiotype of a cell receptor fits the epitope (antigenic determinant) of the antigen.

### Note

Haptens are single antigenic determinants.

## Clinical Correlate

Drug allergies to penicillin and other agents such as streptomycin, aspirin, sulfa drugs, succinyl choline, and some opiates can be induced by small doses of the drug and are not consequences of the pharmacologic or physiologic effects of the drugs. Typically, an allergic response occurs 7 to 14 days following exposure, and the first symptoms may be mild. Subsequent drug exposures can result in severe and life-threatening anaphylaxis (*see* Chapter 13). Most drugs are low molecular weight compounds that are not capable of inducing immune responses by themselves—they act as **haptens**. Inside the body, however, these agents can become conjugated to body proteins (the **carrier**), and the hapten-carrier conjugate serves as the immunogen for the ensuing allergic response.

## ACUTE INFLAMMATORY RESPONSE

Antigens are normally introduced into the body across the mucosa or the epithelia. The **acute inflammatory response** is often the first response to this invasion and represents a response of the innate immune system to block the challenge. The first step in the acute inflammatory response is activation of the vascular endothelium in the breached epithelial barrier. **Cytokines** and other inflammatory mediators released in the area as a result of tissue damage induce expression of **selectin-type adhesion molecules** on the endothelial cells. **Neutrophils** are the first cells to bind to the inflamed endothelium and extravasate into the tissues, peaking within 6 hours. Monocytes, macrophages, and even eosinophils may arrive 5 to 6 hours later in response to neutrophil-released mediators.

## Steps in Extravasation

The extravasation of phagocytes into the area requires 4 sequential, overlapping steps:

### Step 1: Rolling

Phagocytes attach **loosely** to the endothelium by low-affinity, selectin-carbohydrate interactions. E-**selectin** molecules on the endothelium bind to mucin-like adhesion molecules on the phagocyte membrane and bind the cell briefly, but the force of blood flow into the area causes the cell to detach and reattach repeatedly, rolling along the endothelial surface until stronger binding forces can be elicited.

### Step 2: Activation by chemoattractants

Chemokines released in the area during inflammation, such as interleukin 8 (IL-8), complement split product C5a, and N-formyl peptides produced by bacteria bind to receptors on the phagocyte surface and trigger a G-protein–mediated activating signal. This signal induces a conformational change in integrin molecules in the phagocyte membrane that increases their affinity for immunoglobulin-superfamily adhesion molecules on the endothelium.

### Step 3: Arrest and adhesion

Interaction between **integrins** and **Ig-superfamily cellular adhesion molecules** (Ig-CAMs) mediates the **tight binding** of the phagocyte to the endothelial cell. These integrin-IgCAM interactions also mediate the tight binding of phagocytes and their movement through the extracellular matrix.

### Step 4: Transendothelial migration

The phagocyte extends pseudopodia through the vessel wall and extravasates into the tissues.

## In a Nutshell

- The acute inflammatory response is a first response to invasion.
- Cytokines increase expression of selectin-type adhesion molecules.

## In a Nutshell

Extravasation of phagocytes involves rolling, activation by chemoattractants, arrest/adhesion, and transendothelial migration.

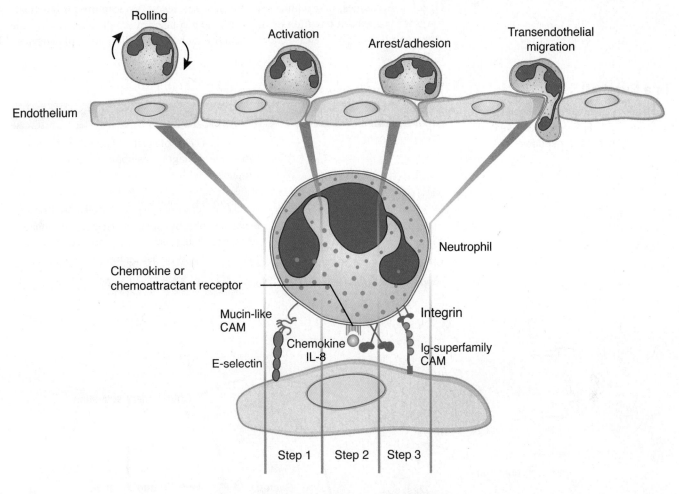

**Figure I-5-1.** Steps of Phagocyte Extravasation
(CAM, cellular adhesion molecule)

## Clinical Correlate

**Leukocyte adhesion deficiency** is a rare autosomal recessive disease in which there is an absence of **CD18,** which is the common $\beta_2$ chain of a number of integrin molecules. A key element in the migration of leukocytes is integrin-mediated cell adhesion; these patients suffer from an inability of their leukocytes to undergo adhesion-dependent migration into sites of inflammation. The first indication of this defect is often omphalitis, a swelling and reddening around the stalk of the umbilical cord. These patients are no more susceptible to virus infection than are normal controls, but they suffer recurrent, chronic bacterial infections. Patients frequently have abnormally high numbers of granulocytes in their circulation, but migration into sites of infection is not possible, so **abscess and pus formation do not occur.**

One method of diagnosing LAD involves evaluating expression (or lack) of the $\beta$ chain (CD18) of the integrin by flow cytometry.

Bacterial infections in these patients can be treated with antibiotics, but they recur. If a suitable bone marrow donor can be found, the hematopoietic system of the patient is destroyed with cytotoxic chemicals and a bone marrow transplant is performed.

Once in the tissues, neutrophils express increased levels of receptors for chemoattractants and exhibit **chemotaxis** migrating up a concentration gradient toward the attractant. Neutrophils release chemoattractive factors that call in other phagocytes.

### In a Nutshell

Substances chemoattractive to neutrophils include IL-8, C5a, leukotriene B$_4$, and formyl methionyl peptides.

**Table I-5-1.** Chemoattractive Molecules

| Chemoattractive Molecule | Origin |
| --- | --- |
| Chemokines (IL-8) | Tissue mast cells, platelets, neutrophils, **monocytes**, **macrophages**, eosinophils, basophils, lymphocytes |
| Complement split product C5a | Classical or alternative pathways |
| Leukotriene B$_4$ | Membrane phospholipids of macrophages, monocytes, neutrophils, mast cells → arachidonic acid cascade → lipoxygenase pathway |
| Formyl methionyl peptides | Released from microorganisms |

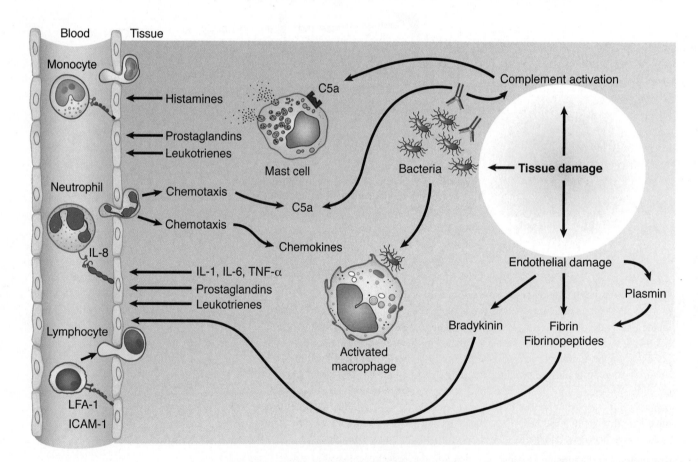

Figure I-5-2. The Acute Inflammatory Response

# Phagocytosis

Once chemotaxis of phagocytic cells into the area of antigen entry is accomplished, these cells ingest and digest particulate debris, such as microorganisms, host cellular debris, and activated clotting factors. This process, called **phagocytosis**, involves:

- Extension of pseudopodia to engulf attached material
- Fusion of the pseudopodia to trap the material in a phagosome
- Fusion of the phagosome with a lysosome to create a phagolysosome
- Digestion
- Exocytosis of digested contents

**In a Nutshell**

Phagocytosis involves:

- Extension of pseudopodia
- Formation of phagosome
- Fusion with lysosome to form phagolysosome
- Digestion
- Exocytosis

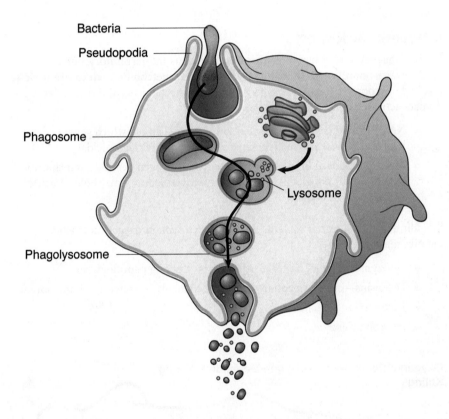

**Figure I-5-3. Phagocytosis**

# Opsonization

Both macrophages and neutrophils have membrane receptors for certain types of antibody (**IgG**) and certain complement components (**C3b**). If an antigen is coated with either of these materials, adherence and phagocytosis may be enhanced by up to 4,000-fold. Thus, antibody and complement are called **opsonins**, and the means by which they enhance phagocytosis is called **opsonization**.

**In a Nutshell**

Opsonization is enhancement of phagocytosis with:

- IgG
- C3b

### Bridge to Microbiology

Protein A of *Staphylococcus aureus* impedes opsonization by binding to the Fc component of IgG.

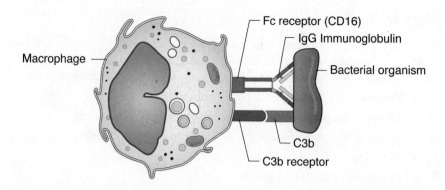

**Figure I-5-4.** Opsonization of Bacteria with Antibody and Complement C3b

## Intracellular Killing

During phagocytosis, a metabolic process known as the respiratory burst activates a membrane-bound oxidase that generates oxygen metabolites, which are toxic to ingested microorganisms. Two oxygen-dependent mechanisms of intracellular digestion are activated as a result of this process.

- **NADPH oxidase** reduces oxygen to superoxide anion, which generates hydroxyl radical and hydrogen peroxide, which are microbicidal.
- **Myeloperoxidase** in the lysosomes acts on hydrogen peroxide and chloride ions to produce hypochlorite (the active ingredient in household bleach), which is microbicidal.

In addition, the lysosomal contents of phagocytes contain oxygen-independent degradative materials:

- Lysozyme—digests bacterial cell walls by cleaving peptidoglycan
- Defensins—circular peptides that form channels in bacterial cell membranes
- Lactoferrin—chelates iron
- Hydrolytic enzymes

### In a Nutshell

Intracellular killing mechanisms include:

- Toxic oxygen metabolites
- Toxic halide radicals
- Lysosomal contents:
    - Lysozyme
    - Defensins
    - Lactoferrin
    - Hydrolytic enzymes

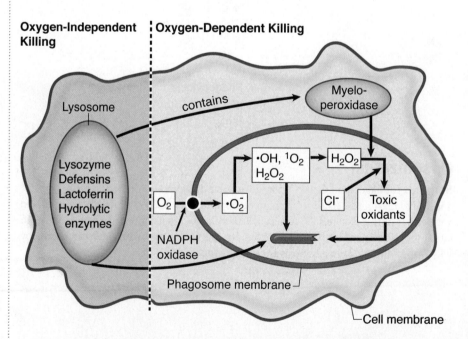

**Figure I-5-5.** Metabolic Stimulation and Killing Within the Phagocyte

# Clinical Correlate

## Chronic Granulomatous Disease

When defects occur in the ability of phagocytes to perform their critical functions as first responders and intracellular destroyers of invading antigens, clinically important pathologic processes ensue. Such defects tend to make the patient susceptible to severe infections with **extracellular bacteria and fungi.**

Chronic granulomatous disease (CGD) is an inherited deficiency in the production of one of several subunits of **NADPH oxidase.** This defect eliminates the phagocyte's ability to produce many critical oxygen-dependent intracellular metabolites ($\cdot O_2^-$, $\cdot OH$, $^1O_2$, and $H_2O_2$). The two other intracellular killing mechanisms remain intact (myeloperoxidase $+ H_2O_2 \rightarrow HOCl$ and lysosomal contents). If the patient is infected with a catalase-negative organism, the $H_2O_2$ waste product produced by the bacterium can be used as a substrate for myeloperoxidase, and the bacterium is killed. If, however, the person is infected with a catalase-positive organism (e.g., *Staphylococcus, Klebsiella, Serratia, Aspergillus*), the myeloperoxidase system lacks its substrate (because these organisms destroy $H_2O_2$), and the patient is left with the oxygen-independent lysosomal mechanisms that prove inadequate to control rampant infections. Thus, CGD patients suffer from chronic, recurrent infections with **catalase-positive** organisms.

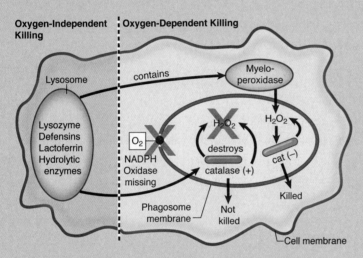

Figure I-5-6. Intracellular Killing in CGD

Failures of phagocytic cells to generate oxygen radicals are easily detected by the nitroblue tetrazolium (NBT) reduction test or neutrophil oxidative index (NOI; a flow cytometric assay).

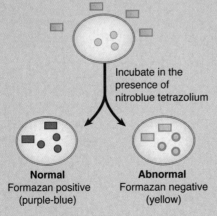

Figure I-5-7. Nitroblue Tetrazolium Reduction

## Chapter Summary

- An antigen or immunogen is a substance capable of activating or generating a response from any committed lymphocyte.

- To be immunogenic, a substance must be recognized as foreign and have chemical complexity and sufficient size.

- The portion of an antigen that fits into the idiotype of an antigen receptor is called the epitope or antigenic determinant.

- Haptens are single antigenic determinants that can only generate immune responses if they are linked to larger carrier proteins. This is the mechanism of elicitation of many drug allergies.

- After antigen is introduced across an anatomic barrier, phagocytes (first neutrophils and then monocytes) will extravasate into the area of injury by
1) rolling, 2) activation with chemoattractants, 3) arrest/adhesion, and
4) transendothelial migration.

- Important chemoattractants include IL-8, C5a, leukotriene $B_4$, and N-formyl methionyl peptides.

- Integrins on the phagocyte membrane bind to Ig-CAMs on endothelia to mediate adhesion.

- Once through the endothelium, phagocytes are attracted to the area of injury by chemokines of the IL-8 family, complement split products, leukotriene $B_4$, and formyl methionyl peptides.

- Phagocytosis involves: the formation of pseudopodia that trap particulate material in a phagosome; addition of lysosomes to cause intracellular digestion within the phagolysosome; and exocytosis of the digested materials.

- Opsonization is the coating of particles with IgG or C3b (or both) to enhance engulfment.

- Ingestion is accompanied by a respiratory burst, which generates the toxic metabolites necessary to destroy intracellular materials.

- NADPH oxidase produces toxic oxygen radicals, and myeloperoxidase generates hypochlorite.

- Lysosomal contents (lysozyme, defensins, lactoferrin, and hydrolytic enzymes) are also toxic to ingested material.

- Patients with chronic granulomatous disease (CGD; an inherited deficiency of NADPH oxidase) are susceptible to chronic, recurrent infections with catalase-positive organisms.

# Review Questions

1.  A rabbit hunter in Arkansas is diagnosed with ulceroglandular tularemia and treated with streptomycin. Within a week, he returns to the hospital. The tularemic papule, lymphadenopathy, and bacteremia have resolved, but he has now developed a raised, itching skin rash and a fever. The drug was discontinued, and the symptoms subsided. What was the role of streptomycin in this case?

    (A) It acted as a B-cell mitogen

    (B) It acted as a hapten

    (C) It acted as a provider of costimulatory signals

    (D) It acted as a superantigen

    (E) It acted as an immunogen

2.  During World War II, when quinine was used as a prophylactic against malaria infections in U.S. personnel on long-term assignment to the South Pacific, a small proportion of soldiers developed blackwater fever (chronic kidney damage from the autoimmune effects of complement-mediated hemolysis of quininized red blood cells). In this case, the quinine played the role of

    (A) autoantigen

    (B) carrier

    (C) hapten

    (D) immunogen

    (E) reagin

3.  A two-year-old child who has suffered recurrent bacterial infections is evaluated for immunologic deficiency. The child has age-normal numbers of CD19+ and CD3+ cells in the peripheral blood and an extreme neutrophilia. The nitroblue tetrazolium dye reduction test is normal. What is the most likely defect in this child?

    (A) Absence of CCR4

    (B) Absence of CD18

    (C) Absence of interleukin-1

    (D) Absence of interleukin-4

    (E) Absence of tumor necrosis factor-$\alpha$

4. A 2-year-old boy is admitted to the hospital for workup of a possible immunologic disorder. His history is remarkable for the occurrence of multiple skin infections involving *Staphylococcus, Pseudomonas,* and *Candida.* On examination the child has cervical lymphadenopathy and mild hepatosplenomegaly. Blood tests reveal an elevated erythrocyte sedimentation rate and neutrophilia. The nitroblue tetrazolium dye reduction test and neutrophil oxidative index are negative. What is the most likely defect in this child?

   (A) C3 deficiency

   (B) Deficiency of CD18

   (C) Deficiency of myeloperoxidase

   (D) NADPH oxidase deficiency

   (E) Phagocyte granule structural defect

5. It has been learned in animal experiments that there are advantages to eliciting nonspecific inflammation at the site of inoculation of antigen toward the ultimate development of a protective immune response to that immunogen. Which of the following substances, if introduced with a vaccine, would serve the purpose of attracting a neutrophilic infiltrate into the area?

   (A) Complement component 3b

   (B) Immunoglobulin G

   (C) Interleukin-8

   (D) Myeloperoxidase

   (E) Tumor necrosis factor-α

## Answers and Explanations

1. **The correct answer is B.** Many drug allergies, such as the one described here, are hapten-carrier immune responses. The drug is not large enough by itself to elicit an immune response (it is a hapten), but when it becomes covalently coupled to the body's own proteins (which act as carriers), the combined molecule becomes immunogenic, and a response against one's own tissues is elicited.

   Acting as a B-cell mitogen (**choice A**) is not correct. B-cell mitogens, such as pokeweed mitogen and lipopolysaccharide, cause polyclonal proliferation of B cells and elaboration of IgM antibodies. The drug allergy described here is not a polyclonal response, but a specific anti–altered-self response generated by T and B lymphocytes and production of antibodies.

   Acting as a provider of costimulatory signals (**choice C**) is not correct. The costimulatory signals required to activate B and T lymphocytes include CD28/B7 and CD40/CD40L interactions. These are additional interactions (beyond the specific recognition of antigen) required for the activation of B and T lymphocytes. Although these costimulatory signals would be involved in the evolution of this allergic response, the streptomycin does not serve as a costimulatory signal.

   Acting as a superantigen (**choice D**) is not correct. Superantigens are materials that crosslink the variable β domain of the T-cell receptor and the α-chain of class II MHC molecules. They induce activation of all T cells that express receptors with a particular Vβ domain. The resulting T-cell mitogenesis causes overproduction of T-cell and macrophage cytokines and system-wide pathology. Toxic shock syndrome toxin-1 and *Streptococcus pyogenes* erythrogenic exotoxins act as superantigens.

Acting as an immunogen (**choice E**) is not correct because streptomycin is not large enough to be immunogenic. Immunogens must be large enough to have at least two epitopes. It is only through binding to a larger carrier protein (the patient's own tissue proteins) that a hapten such as a drug can become immunogenic.

2.  **The correct answer is C.** This is a case of autoimmune hemolytic anemia generated during a hapten-carrier immune response. The drug is not large enough by itself to elicit an immune response (it is a hapten), but when it becomes covalently coupled to the red blood cell proteins (which act as carriers), the combined molecule becomes immunogenic. Antibodies are generated and bind to the drug–RBC complex, complement is activated, and the red blood cells are lysed.

    Autoantigen (**choice A**) is not correct because the immune response is being generated against an "altered-self" component. The RBCs of the patient are not themselves the immunogen: It is the complex of drug–RBC protein that elicits the response. The effect is certainly similar to an autoimmune response: The patient destroys his own tissues. However, the eliciting immunogen is altered-self, so this is not a case where failure of self-tolerance causes disease.

    Carrier (**choice B**) is not correct because carriers must be protein molecules. The carrier component of a hapten-carrier complex is recognized by T lymphocytes. Because T lymphocytes are only capable of recognizing peptides presented in the groove of major histocompatibility complex antigens, a molecule such as quinine is "invisible" to T cells.

    Immunogen (**choice D**) is not correct because quinine is not large enough to be immunogenic. Immunogens must be large enough to have at least two epitopes. It is only through binding to a larger carrier protein (the patient's own tissue proteins) that a hapten such as a drug can become immunogenic.

    Reagin (**choice E**) is a word that is used to denote an immunogen that elicits an IgE-antibody response. Although some drug allergies are indeed IgE-mediated immediate hypersensitivity responses, this one is not. The antibodies that activate complement are IgM and IgG. IgE does not activate complement.

3.  **The correct answer is B.** This child has leukocyte adhesion deficiency (LAD), which is a genetic deficiency of CD18. CD18 is an essential component of a number of integrins, and absence of these molecules causes the inability of WBCs to migrate into sites of inflammation. Thus in this patient, the blood contained abnormally high numbers of neutrophils, but they were unable to extravasate. CD18 is a component of LFA-1, CR3, and CR4.

    Absence of CCR4 (**choice A**) would cause difficulties in extravasation and migration of activated T cells and monocytes. This chemokine receptor is not found on neutrophils and therefore would have no effect on neutrophil migration.

    Absence of interleukin-1 (**choice C**) might cause difficulties in producing the acute and chronic inflammatory responses. This cytokine, frequently referred to as the endogenous pyrogen, produces fever, acute phase protein production, and many other results critical to inflammation. However, the actions of IL-1 are extremely redundant with those of IL-6 and tumor necrosis factor-$\alpha$, so such a condition might have no clinically observable effects.

    Absence of interleukin-4 (**choice D**) would result in defects in the ability to mount a normal IgE antibody response. This cytokine also serves as the major stimulus for the development of TH2 cells from naive helper T cells, so its absence would be likely to have profound effects on all aspects of the secondary antibody response.

Absence of tumor necrosis factor-α (**choice E**) might cause difficulties in producing the acute and chronic inflammatory responses. This cytokine has many functions that are redundant with those of IL-1 and IL-6, so such a condition might have no clinically observable effects.

4. **The correct answer is D.** This child has chronic granulomatous disease (CGD). The history indicates he has had recurrent infections with catalase-positive organisms and has a defect in generating oxygen radicals intracellularly in his phagocytic cells (the negative nitroblue tetrazolium test and neutrophil oxidative index). This genetic defect arises from a failure to produce one of the subunits of NADPH oxidase, which makes the individual incapable of producing intracellular oxygen radicals. Redundant intracellular killing mechanisms (myeloperoxidase and lysosomal contents) are still functional in these patients, but when they are infected with catalase-positive organisms, the substrate for myeloperoxidase (hydrogen peroxide) is destroyed, and the only remaining intracellular killing mechanism (lysosomes) is insufficient to protect from infection.

   C3 deficiency (**choice A**) would cause increased susceptibility to pyogenic infections because C3b is an important opsonin that enhances phagocytosis of extracellular organisms. All extracellular bacteria would be included in this list, not simply catalase-positive ones, as mentioned here. The NBT and NOI would not be negative in this case.

   Deficiency of CD18 (**choice B**) is the cause of leukocyte adhesion deficiency (LAD). Because CD18 is the common β chain of the $\beta_2$ integrins, its absence compromises leukocyte function antigen (LFA)-1, as well as complement receptors 3 and 4. Patients with LAD suffer recurrent infections with extracellular pathogens (not just catalase-positive ones) because of defective opsonization, mobilization, adhesion, and chemotaxis. The NBT and NOI would be positive.

   Deficiency of myeloperoxidase (**choice C**) results from a deficiency of an important granule enzyme in phagocytic cells. However, because there are so many redundant mechanisms of intracellular killing, these patients generally have mild symptoms or none at all.

   A phagocyte granule structural defect (**choice E**) is responsible for the Chediak-Higashi syndrome. These patients have chemotactic and degranulation defects, lack NK activity, and have partial albinism.

5. **The correct answer is C.** The only substance on the list that is chemotactic for neutrophils is IL-8. Other neutrophil chemotactic factors that might have been mentioned would include C5a, leukotriene B4, and formyl methionyl peptides.

   Complement component 3b (**choice A**) is not chemotactic for neutrophils. It acts as an opsonin, enhancing the phagocytosis of coated particles.

   Immunoglobulin G (**choice B**) is not chemotactic for neutrophils. It acts as an opsonin, enhancing the phagocytosis of coated particles.

   Myeloperoxidase (**choice D**) is not chemotactic for neutrophils. It is an enzyme in the lysosomes of phagocytic cells that generates toxic halide radicals intracellularly when exposed to its substrate, hydrogen peroxide.

   Tumor necrosis factor-α (**choice E**) is not chemotactic for neutrophils. It is produced by macrophages and is involved with the production of chronic inflammation and cytotoxicity.

# The Processing and Presentation of Antigen

## What the COMLEX Requires You To Know

- How the grooves of class I and II MHC are loaded with peptides
- The 3 signals required for T-cell activation (TCR binding, costimulatory molecules, and cytokines)
- How superantigens act
- The subclasses of T helper (TH) cells, their functions, and regulation

MHC molecules are designed to bind small peptides and present them to T cells. The class I molecule is synthesized in the endoplasmic reticulum of the cell and proteins are loaded there by an **endogenous pathway**. Proteins synthesized in the cell cytosol are routinely degraded in proteasomes, and the peptides from these proteins are transported through a peptide transporter, known as the TAP complex, into the endoplasmic reticulum, where they have the opportunity to bind to freshly synthesized MHC class I proteins. These are then transported to the cell membrane where they may be presented to **CD8+ T lymphocytes** (*see* Chapter 8).

### In a Nutshell

- MHC I molecule is loaded with peptides via the endogenous pathway.
- CD8+ T cells recognize MHC I/peptide.

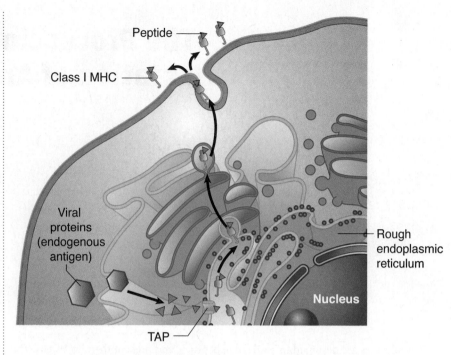

**Figure I-6-1.** The Endogenous Pathway of Binding Peptides to Class I MHC Molecules

## In a Nutshell

MHC class II molecules are loaded with peptides by the endosomal (exogenous) pathway.

## Note

The invariant chain prevents any normal cellular peptides from being bound.

Although some small, easily digestible antigens are almost totally degraded and exocytosed by phagocytes, as we saw in the last chapter, the critical first step in the elicitation of the adaptive immune response to a first antigenic challenge is the processing of such antigen for the presentation to naive T lymphocytes. Professional antigen-presenting cells (dendritic cells, macrophages) load partially degraded peptides they have ingested into the groove of the class II MHC molecule, so that this can be presented to T cells with idiotypes complementary to that structure. This is accomplished by the **endosomal (exogenous) pathway** of MHC loading.

When MHC class II molecules are produced in the endoplasmic reticulum of an antigen-presenting cell (APC), in addition to the α and β chains, a third chain called the **invariant chain** is synthesized at the same time. This blocks the peptide-binding groove so **no** normal cellular peptides can accidentally be attracted there. As the molecule is completed, it is transported in a vesicle to the location of endocytic vesicles containing the ingested internalized peptides. As these vesicles fuse, the invariant chain is degraded, and peptides in the vacuole are loaded into the MHC II groove. The MHC class II–peptide complex is then transported to the cell surface where it will be accessible for interaction with any T lymphocyte with a complementary TCR.

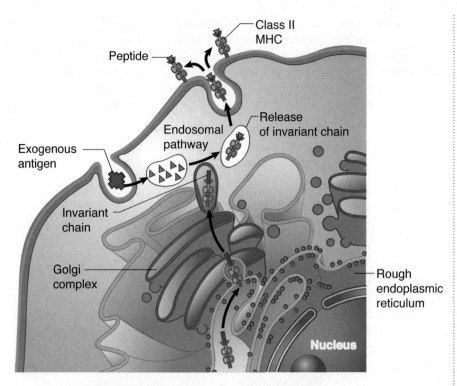

**Figure I-6-2.** The Exogenous Pathway of Binding Peptides to Class II MHC Molecules

**Table I-6-1.** Human MHC Summary

|  | MHC Class I | MHC Class II |
|---|---|---|
| Names | HLA-A, -B, and -C | HLA-DP, -DQ, -DR, HLA-DM* |
| Tissue distribution | All nucleated cells, platelets | **B lymphocytes, monocytes, macrophages, dendritic cells,** Langerhans cells, activated T cells, activated endothelial cells |
| Recognized by | Cytotoxic T cells (CD8+) | TH cells (CD4+) |
| Peptides bound | Endogenously synthesized | Exogenously processed |
| Function | Elimination of abnormal (infected) host cells by cytotoxic T cells | Presentation of foreign antigen to TH cells |
| Invariant chain | No | Yes |
| $\beta_2$ microglobulin, TAP | Yes | No |

*Not expressed on cell surface

Within a few hours of the initiation of the acute inflammatory response by the breaching of the mucosa or epithelia, the professional APCs that have phagocytosed and processed the invading antigen begin to leave the area via lymphatic vessels. Dendritic cells, with their long, finger-like processes, are probably the most efficient of these cells and retract their membranous processes to round up and begin the journey to the closest lymph node. Thus, phagocytes with MHC class II molecules

**In a Nutshell**

APCs with MHC class II/peptide molecules travel to the secondary lymphoid organs.

loaded with peptides digested from the invading antigen enter the lymph node through the afferent lymphatics and become trapped in the meshwork of the organ. If the initial tissue damage is sufficient, these cells can also be flushed into blood vessels, ultimately to become trapped in the vascular sinusoids of the spleen. Regardless, the secondary lymphoid organs (lymph nodes and spleen) are the sites where naive, recirculating lymphocytes will first be exposed to their specific antigen.

## Bridge to Microbiology

Absence of spleen or functional asplenia (sickle cell anemia) makes patients exceptionally susceptible to encapsulated bacteria or blood-borne pathogens.

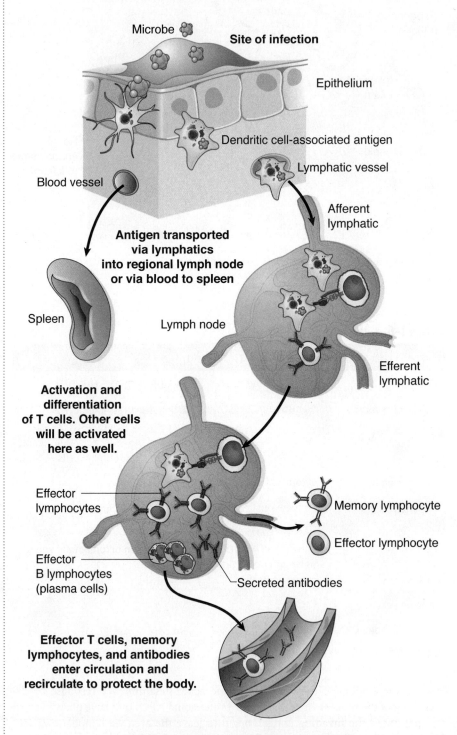

**Figure I-6-3.** The Transportation of Antigen to the Secondary Lymphoid Organs

The binding of the TCR of the naive T cell to the MHC class II–peptide complex of the APC provides the first signal to the T cell to begin its activation. This provides the antigenic specificity of the response. Costimulatory molecules on APC provide the second signal, and cytokines secreted by APC and the activating T cells themselves induce the proliferation (**clonal expansion**) and differentiation of the T cells into **effector cells** and **memory cells**.

Several costimulatory molecules are involved in the activation of naive T lymphocytes:

- **CD4 and CD8** (coreceptors for MHC classes II and I, respectively) transduce activating signals to the T cells.
- **Integrins** on T cells (LFA-1) bind to IgCAMs on APCs (ICAM-1) to increase cell–cell adherence.
- Pathogen binding to innate receptors (e.g., TLR molecules) along with antigen recognition triggers upregulation of B7.
- **IgCAMs** on T cells (CD2) bind to integrins (LFA-3) on APCs to increase cell–cell adherence.
- **CD28** on T cells binds to B7 on APCs and triggers the transcription of several cytokine genes.

The proliferation of naive T cells in response to antigen recognition is mediated principally by an autocrine growth pathway, in which the responding T cell secretes its own growth-promoting cytokines and also expresses receptor molecules for these factors. IL-2 is the most important growth factor for T cells and stimulates the proliferation of clones of T cells specific to that antigen.

### In a Nutshell

T-cell activation—first signal = binding TCR to MHC II/peptide complex

### In a Nutshell

Second Signal (Costimulatory Molecules)

- CD4 binds MHC II.
- CD8 binds MHC I.
- CD28 binds B7.

### In a Nutshell

Third Signal (Cytokines)

- IL-2
- IL-1
- IL-6
- TNF-α

## In a Nutshell

- Stimulation of TH cells in the absence of costimulatory signals produces anergy.

- CTLA-4 (CD152) competes with CD28 for binding B7 and acts as a down-regulator

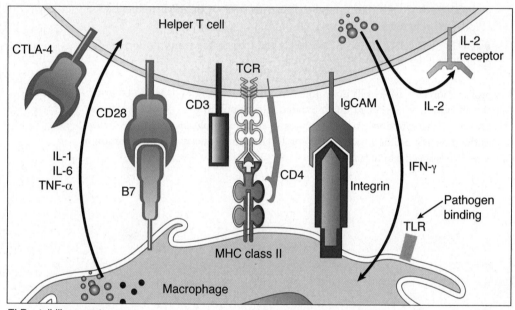

TLR = toll-like receptor

**Figure I-6-4.** Helper T Cell and Macrophage Adhesion
(TLR = toll-like receptor)

## Clinical Correlate

**Superantigens** are viral or bacterial proteins that cross-link the variable β domain of a T-cell receptor to an α chain of a class II MHC molecule outside the normal peptide-binding groove. This cross-linkage provides an activating signal that induces T-cell activation and proliferation, in the absence of antigen-specific recognition of peptides in the MHC class II groove. Because superantigens bind outside of the antigen-binding cleft, they activate any clones of T cells expressing a particular variable β sequence and thus cause polyclonal activation of T cells, resulting in the overproduction of IFN-γ. This, in turn, activates macrophages, resulting in overexpression of proinflammatory cytokines (IL-1, IL-6 and TNF-α). Excess amounts of these cytokines induce systemic toxicity. Molecules produced during infectious processes and known to act as superantigens include staphylococcal enterotoxins, toxic-shock syndrome toxin-1 (TSST-1), and streptococcal pyrogenic exotoxins.

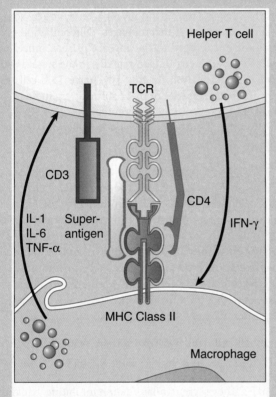

**Figure I-6-5.** Superantigen Activation. Notice that there is no complementarity between the TCR and the MHC/peptide complex.

## In a Nutshell

TH cells control effector mechanisms of immunity (antibody, macrophage activation, CTL killing, and NK killing).

## In a Nutshell

- TH1 cells arise from precursor when a strong innate immune response is stimulated.
- TH2 cells arise in the absence of such responses.
- $T_{Reg}$ cells inhibit TH1 cell function.
- TH17 cells increase inflammation.

## In a Nutshell

- TH1 cells produce IFN-γ, TNF-β, and IL-2.
- TH2 cells produce IL-4, IL-5, IL-6, IL-10, IL-13 and TGFβ.
- IFN-γ produced by TH1 inhibits TH2.
- IL-4 and IL-10 produced by TH2 inhibit TH1.

The activated CD4+ (helper) T lymphocytes, which have thus been generated in the lymph nodes and spleen following antigen administration, are now ready to serve as the orchestrators of virtually all the possible **effector mechanisms** that will arise to destroy the antigenic invaders. The effector mechanisms that are controlled totally or at least in part by TH cells include antibody synthesis, macrophage activation, cytotoxic T-cell killing, and NK cell killing. The "decision" as to which of these mechanisms should be encouraged is a function of the characteristics of the invading pathogen and is controlled by the differentiation of specialized classes of helper cells.

There are two major and two minor classes of helper T (TH) cells, both of which arise from the same precursor, the naive TH lymphocyte, sometimes called the TH0 cell. The pattern of differentiation is determined by the stimuli present early in the immune response, at the site of antigen introduction. Differentiation of a TH0 cell into a TH1 cell seems to be stimulated by microbes that stimulate a strong initial innate immune response with the resultant production of **IL-12** by macrophages or **IFN-γ** by NK cells. The differentiation of TH1 cells is stimulated by many intracellular bacteria, such as *Listeria* and mycobacteria, and by some parasites such as *Leishmania*—all of which infect macrophages. Differentiation of a TH0 cell into a TH2 cell seems to be encouraged in the absence of such innate immune stimuli, perhaps by default when persistent antigen remains in the system without significant macrophage or NK-cell stimulation. In this way, naive TH0 cells seem to produce IL-4 constitutively, and in the absence of IL-12 stimulation, these cells will upregulate their production of IL-4 to encourage differentiation into TH2 cells. The differentiation into the TH2 subset seems to be favored in infections with helminths and in response to allergens.

These classes of TH cells are distinguished almost entirely on the basis of the cytokines they produce. IFN-γ, TNF-β, and IL-2 are produced by TH1 cells, and IL-4, IL-5, IL-6, IL-10, IL-13 and TGFβ are the cytokines produced by TH2 cells. These cytokines not only determine the stimulatory pathways that the cells will employ, but they also expand and develop the cells of the respective subset. For example, **IFN-γ produced by TH1 cells promotes further TH1 development and inhibits the proliferation of TH2 cells. IL-4 and IL-10 produced by TH2 cells promote TH2 differentiation and inhibit the activation of TH1 cells**. Thus, each subset amplifies itself and cross-regulates the other set so that immune responses become increasingly polarized over time, reaching extremes in cases where antigen exposure becomes chronic.

A third population of T cells which arises from the TH0 is called the $T_{Reg}$ (T regulatory cell). These cells regulate (inhibit) TH1 cell function. They are identified by their constitutive expression of CD25 on their surface and by the expression of the transcription factor FoxP3. They secrete inflammation inhibiting cytokines such as IL-10 and have been shown to be critical for the prevention of autoimmunity.

The final population of TH cells which arises from the TH0 is called the TH17 cell. These cells are identified by the expression of transcription factor RORgammat and by their production of the proinflammatory cytokine IL-17. They are believed to play a role in the tissue damage associated with some autoimmune diseases.

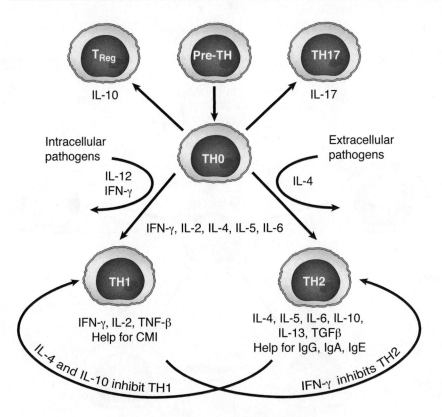

**Figure I-6-6.** Subsets of Helper T Cells

The effector mechanisms stimulated by the different classes of TH cells are specialized to optimally destroy different classes of invading antigens and are roughly (and somewhat artificially) divided into **cell-mediated** or **humoral** effector mechanisms.

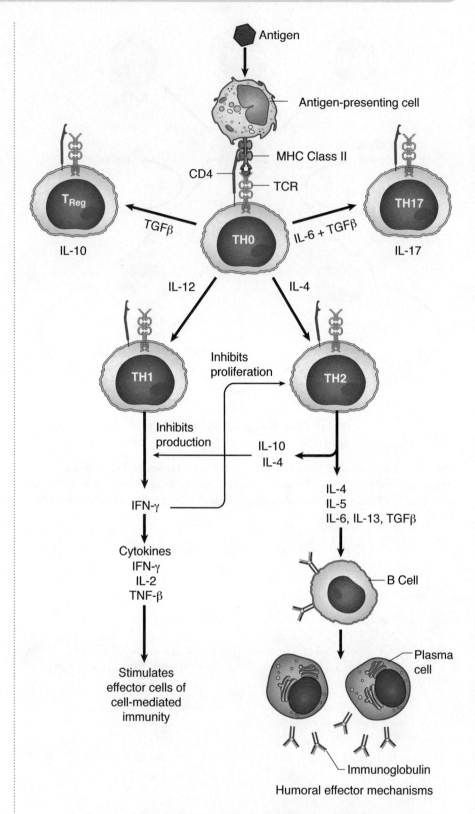

**Figure I-6-7.** Overview of T-Helper Cell Regulation of the Adaptive Immune Response

## Clinical Correlate

**Tuberculoid Versus Lepromatous Leprosy**

The progression of disease with *Mycobacterium leprae* in humans is a well-documented example of the crucial balance between TH1 and TH2 subsets. Leprosy is not a single clinical entity, but presents as a spectrum of diseases, with tuberculoid and lepromatous forms being at the far poles. In **tuberculoid** leprosy, the patient has a **strong TH1** response, which eradicates the intracellular pathogens by granuloma formation. There is some damage to skin and peripheral nerves, but the disease progresses slowly, if at all, and the patient survives. In **lepromatous** leprosy, the **TH2 response is turned on**, and because of reciprocal inhibition, the cell-mediated response is depressed. These patients develop antibodies to the pathogen that are not protective, and the mycobacteria multiply inside macrophages, sometimes reaching levels of $10^{10}$ per gram of tissue. Hypergammaglobulinemia may occur, and these cases frequently progress to disseminated and disfiguring infections.

## Chapter Summary

- MHC Class I molecules are loaded with peptides via the endogenous pathway.

- Partially digested peptides are loaded into the groove of class II MHC molecules on antigen-presenting cells by the endosomal (exogenous) pathway.

- APCs migrate to the secondary lymphoid organs, where they present this processed antigen to recirculating naive lymphocytes.

- The binding of the TCR to the peptide/MHC class II complex provides the first signal in T-cell activation.

- Costimulatory molecule interactions (e.g., CD28 binds to B7, CD4 binds to MHC II, CD8 binds to MHC I, LFA-1 binds to ICAM-1, and CD2 binds to LFA-3) serve as the second signal in T-cell activation.

- Cytokines (IL-2, IL-1, IL-6, and TNF-$\alpha$) serve as the final signal in T-cell activation.

- Superantigens are viral or bacterial proteins that cross-link the variable $\beta$ domain of a T-cell receptor to an $\alpha$ chain of a class II MHC molecule and thereby cause polyclonal activation of T cells, overproduction of cytokines, and systemic toxicity.

- Activated TH cells act as the orchestrators of the effector mechanisms of the immune response (antibody synthesis, macrophage activation, cytotoxic T cell killing, and NK cell killing).

- Naive TH cells (TH0) differentiate into TH1 cells when IL-12 from macrophages or IFN-$\gamma$ from NK cells is present. TH1 cells secrete IFN-$\gamma$, IL-2, and TNF-$\beta$.

- Naive TH0 cells differentiate into TH2 cells when there is extracellular attack. TH2 cells secrete IL-4, IL-5, IL-6, IL-10, IL-13 and TGF$\beta$.

- The cytokines produced by TH subsets are cross-regulatory: IFN-$\gamma$ produced by TH1 cells inhibits TH2 cells, and IL-4 and IL-10 produced by TH2 cells inhibit TH1 cells.

- $T_{Reg}$ cells are CD25$^+$ and express the FoxP3 transcription factor. They develop from TH0 cells and are believed to be important in the prevention of autoimmunity.

- TH17 cells are identified by the transcription factor RORgammat and their production of IL-17. They play a role in the tissue damage associated with some autoimmune diseases.

## Review Questions

1. Human infections with *Mycobacterium leprae* express a spectrum of clinical presentations depending on the extent and expression of their immune response to the intracellular organism. On one end of the spectrum, patients with tuberculoid leprosy produce an effective cell-mediated immune response, which is successful at killing the intracellular organisms and, unfortunately, produces tissue damage. Patients with tuberculoid leprosy have granulomas that have elevated amounts of IL-2, IFN-γ, and TNF-β. The immune cell responsible for this pattern of cytokine production is the

   (A) Cytotoxic T lymphocyte

   (B) Epithelioid cell

   (C) Macrophage

   (D) TH1 cell

   (E) TH2 cell

2. There is evidence that the immunologic pathway that distinguishes the selection between the two polar forms of leprosy depends on the initial means of antigen presentation, as well as individual human differences in response. If early events of antigen recognition elicit production of IL-4, IL-5, IL-6, and IL-10, lepromatous leprosy is more likely to result, with the outcome of failure to mount a protective delayed-type hypersensitivity response. What differential characteristic of the lepromatous form is predicted based on the fact of overproduction of IL-4, IL-5, IL-6, IL-10, IL-13 and TGFβ in lepromatous lesions?

   (A) Autoimmunity

   (B) Granuloma formation

   (C) Hypergammaglobulinemia

   (D) Immediate hypersensitivity

   (E) Inflammation

3. An elderly man with diabetes develops a blister on the heel of his foot, which becomes infected. Although nursing staff in the home where he is a resident clean and treat the wound with topical antibiotic ointment, he develops a fever and hypotension, and a desquamating rash spreads from the site of the original blister. How does the toxin responsible for his symptoms cause these signs?

   (A) It acts as an IL-1 homologue

   (B) It activates B lymphocytes polyclonally

   (C) It activates complement

   (D) It cross-links MHC class II molecules to TCRs polyclonally

   (E) It stimulates neutrophils

4. It has been learned in several experimental systems that proliferation and differentiation of T lymphocytes in response to tumor cells is low because tumor cells lack the necessary costimulatory molecules for lymphocyte activation. If melanoma cells from a patient were induced to express these costimulatory molecules by transfection, production of an effective antitumor response might occur. Which of the following molecules would be the best candidate for transfection of tumor cells to achieve this end?

    (A) B7

    (B) CD2

    (C) CD4

    (D) CD28

    (E) LFA-1

5. A 50-year-old woman with severe rheumatoid arthritis is started on infliximab (anti-tumor necrosis factor-alpha). This therapy has been shown to increase the production of CD25-positive T cells. Which of the following is likely, therefore, to become elevated in this patient?

    (A) Interferon-gamma

    (B) Interleukin-1

    (C) Interleukin-2

    (D) Interleukin-10

    (E) Transforming growth factor-beta

## Answers and Explanations

1. **The correct answer is D**. IL-2, IFN-$\gamma$, and TNF-$\beta$ are all elaborated by the TH1 cell. TNF-$\beta$ can also be made by NK cells. In tuberculoid leprosy, the TH1 arm of the immune response is most active, resulting in a protective (but also damaging) cell-mediated response and a dampening of the antibody response. In lepromatous leprosy, the patient has an overabundance of TH2 responses, causing the production of a nonprotective antibody response.

   Cytotoxic T lymphocytes (**choice A**) are an effector cell in the cell-mediated immune response. They do not elaborate many cytokines but produce cytotoxic molecules, which cause the destruction of specific target cells.

   Epithelioid cells (**choice B**) are modified macrophages. They are extremely secretory and may produce IL-1, IL-6, TNF-$\alpha$, IFN-$\gamma$, and GM-CSF. They are prominent in granulomas, and their cytokines would be elevated in a patient with tuberculoid leprosy, but that was not the question.

   Macrophages (**choice C**), once activated, may produce IL-1, IL-6, TNF-$\alpha$, IFN-$\gamma$, and GM-CSF. They are prominent in granulomas, and their cytokines would be elevated in a patient with tuberculoid leprosy, but again, that was not the question.

   TH2 cells (**choice E**) would be elevated during lepromatous leprosy. The cytokines they secrete include IL-4, IL-5, IL-6, IL-10, IL-13 and TGF$\beta$. These cells are stimulators of the humoral immune response.

2. **The correct answer is C.** In lepromatous leprosy, the activation of the TH2 arm of the immune response results in elicitation of those cytokines that stimulate production of antibody (IL-4, IL-5, IL-6, IL-10, IL-13 and TGF$\beta$) and those that inhibit the development of the protective cell-mediated immune response (IL-4 and IL-10). Therefore, hypergammaglobulinemia is a frequent finding in lepromatous leprosy.

Autoimmunity (**choice A**) may develop after infectious processes, but there is no evidence that stimulation of TH2 cells, by itself, causes autoimmune disease.

Granuloma formation (**choice B**) would be decreased after exposure to these cytokines. Granulomas are an expression of the delayed-type hypersensitivity response, which is a function of TH1 cells. IL-10 and IL-4 would depress the TH1 response.

Immediate hypersensitivity (**choice D**) requires sensitized mast cells and IgE antibodies. Although this result could occur in persons predisposed to atopic allergy, it is not the most likely result of stimulation with TH2 cytokines.

Inflammation (**choice E**) is primarily mediated by substances released during tissue injury (leukotrienes, histamine, etc.) and the cytokines of activated macrophages (IL-1, IL-6, and TNF-α). It is not enhanced by TH2 cytokines.

3. **The correct answer is D**. This patient is showing signs of toxic shock syndrome, caused by infection of the blister with *Staphylococcus aureus* and the resultant elaboration of the exotoxin TSST-1. This toxin acts as a superantigen, cross-linking the variable β region of the TCR to the α chain of the class II MHC molecule. This binds TH cells and APC together without the specificity of antigen recognition, and so clonal proliferation of T cells and production of IFN-γ leads to activation of macrophages. As a result, the macrophages overproduce the cytokines IL-1, IL-6, and TNF-α, which are toxic at high levels.

It acts as an IL-1 homologue (**choice A**) is not true. IL-1 is produced by macrophages as a result of T-cell activation, but TSST-1 does not itself act as an IL-1 homologue.

It activates B lymphocytes polyclonally (**choice B**) is not true. TSST-1 acts on TH cells to stimulate macrophage cytokines. It does not have a direct effect on B-cell proliferation.

It activates complement (**choice C**) is not correct. TSST-1 does not have an effect on complement.

It stimulates neutrophils (**choice E**) is not correct. Although neutrophils are stimulated during *Staphylococcus aureus* infection and produce IL-1, which causes fever, the mechanism of action of TSST-1 and other superantigens is not through neutrophil activation.

4. **The correct answer is A.** The B7 molecule on antigen-presenting cells binds to the CD28 molecule on T lymphocytes and serves as a costimulatory signal for their activation. If the tumor cells could be induced to express this costimulatory molecule, they would provide the important activating signal to the T cells.

CD2 (**choice B**) is the molecule on T lymphocytes that binds to LFA-3 on antigen-presenting cells. If the tumor cell were induced to express CD2, it would bind to the complementary structure on macrophages and not activate the T cells.

CD4 (**choice C**) is the molecule on T lymphocytes that stabilizes the interaction of MHC class II and the TCR. If the tumor cell were induced to express CD4, it would not increase the tumor-specific response.

CD28 (**choice D**) is the molecule on T cells that binds to B7. If the tumor cell were induced to express CD28, it would bind to the complementary structure on macrophages and not activate the T cells.

LFA-1 (**choice E**) is the molecule on T cells that binds ICAM-1 on the antigen-presenting cells. If the tumor cells were induced to express LFA-1, it would bind to the complementary structure on macrophages and not activate the T cells.

5. **The correct answer is D.** CD25-positive $T_{Reg}$ cells have been shown to have a role in maintenance of self-tolerance, and therefore, defects in these cells are being blamed in many cases of autoimmune disease. $T_{Reg}$ cells secrete interleukin-10 which is an anti-inflammatory cytokine.

Interferon-gamma (**choice A**) is a product of TH1 which activates macrophages and amplifies pro-inflammatory pathways in the body. It is not a product of $T_{Reg}$ cells and would cause additional damage in a case of rheumatoid arthritis, so it would not be a logical goal of therapy.

Interleukin-1 (**choice B**) is endogenous pyrogen which is responsible for the setting of the hypothalamic temperature point. It is a product of macrophages which activates TH1 cells, and therefore would be considered a pro-inflammatory cytokine rather than an anti-inflammatory one.

Interleukin-2 (**choice C**) is a product of TH0 and TH1 cells which causes the proliferation of T cells and the effector cells of cell-mediated immunity. Although IL-2 is required for natural $T_{Reg}$ development, it would not be expected to be increased with the therapy mentioned here.

Transforming growth factor-beta (**choice E**) is a product of T cells and macrophages which is required for natural $T_{Reg}$ development, but with this artificial therapy to increase $T_{Reg}$ numbers, it would not be expected to be elevated.

# The Generation of Humoral Effector Mechanisms

**7**

## What the COMLEX Requires You To Know

- The humoral responses to thymus-independent and -dependent antigens
- The cell surface molecules that contribute to production of T- and B-cell conjugates
- The basic structures and effector functions of the 5 antibody isotypes
- The characteristics and function of secretory IgA
- The role of somatic hypermutation in affinity maturation
- How the alternative and classical complement cascades are initiated
- The biologic functions of complement components

## GOALS OF HUMORAL IMMUNITY

**Humoral** immunity is mediated by antibodies synthesized by B lymphocytes and secreted by their fully differentiated end cell, the **plasma cell**. This arm of the immune response is directed toward the defense against **extracellular** microbes or toxins and may culminate in the extracellular degradation of such materials or the enhancement of their destruction via phagocytosis.

As mature naive B lymphocytes leave the bone marrow following successful rearrangement of their membrane immunoglobulin receptor genes, they recirculate throughout the body, attracted to **follicular areas** of the lymph nodes and spleen. If antigen entering these secondary lymphoid organs binds to and cross-links the idiotypes of these membrane receptors, this provides the first signal for the activation of the B lymphocyte.

Most antigens introduced into the body fall into the category of **thymus-dependent antigens**. Response to such molecules requires the direct contact of B cells with TH cells and their **cytokines**. After the cross-linking of receptors on the B-cell surface with antigen, the material is endocytosed and processed via the endocytic (exogenous) pathway to generate MHC class II/peptide conjugates, which are then inserted in the membrane, just as we have seen during phagocytosis and processing in the professional phagocyte lineages. Simultaneously, expression of costimulatory molecules such as B7 is upregulated on the B lymphocyte, making them effective presenters of antigen to TH cells in the area. Once a TH cell recognizes a processed antigenic peptide displayed with MHC class II molecules on the membrane of the B cell, the two cells form a **conjugate**, and the TH cell is activated and induced to become a TH2 cell. TH2 cells in conjugates rearrange their Golgi apparatus toward the junction with the B cell leading to the directional release of cytokines toward the B cell. In addition, expression of a molecule known as CD40L on the surface of the TH2 cell is upregulated, and this molecule interacts with CD40 on the B cell to provide the second signal for B-cell activation. The B cells are encouraged to proliferate after this interaction. The final signal delivered by the TH2 cell is the release of cytokines, which will induce the differentiation of B cells into fully differentiated, antibody-secreting cells and memory cells (*see* Chapter 9) and induce **class switching**.

## In a Nutshell

- Humoral immunity = antibodies
- Defends against extracellular agents
- B lymphocytes are attracted to follicular areas of secondary lymphoid organs.
- Pathogens are thymus-dependent antigens.

## In a Nutshell

B-cell contact with TH cells requires:
- MHC II/peptide presentation
- Costimulatory molecules (B7)
- CD40/CD40L binding

## In a Nutshell

TH2 cytokines induce B-cell:

- Differentiation
- Memory
- Class switching

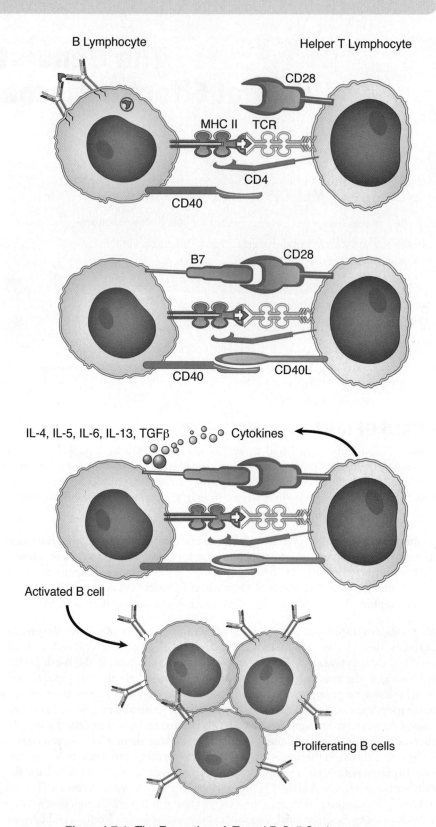

**Figure I-7-1.** The Formation of T- and B-Cell Conjugates

T cells recognize peptides bound to MHC molecules. Therefore, antigens that possess no peptide structure cannot be recognized by T cells. These antigens are called **thymus-independent antigens** and include lipopolysaccharide from the cell envelope of gram-negative bacteria and polysaccharide capsular antigens. These antigens may directly stimulate B cells to cause proliferation and secretion of antibody, or they may act as B-cell **mitogens**, directly causing mitosis regardless of the cell's antigenic specificity. The response to thymus-independent antigens is generally **weaker** than the response to other classes of antigens, resulting in the **secretion of IgM antibodies only** and the **absence of immunologic memory**.

Although all of the antibody molecules secreted by a clone of B lymphocytes will have identical idiotypes (*see* Chapter 2), the B cell is induced to make new classes, or **isotypes**, of immunoglobulin in response to cytokine-directed instruction from the TH2 cell. The progression of new antibody isotypes produced by B cells is defined by the sequence of constant domain coding in the B-lymphocyte DNA, and each isotype of immunoglobulin is designed with a different effector function in mind. Just as the three-dimensional structure of the **idiotype defines antigen specificity**, the sequence of amino acids in the constant domains of the immunoglobulin molecule (**isotype**) **dictates the effector functions** that will be expressed.

The biologic function of segments of the antibody molecule was first elucidated by digestion of these molecules with proteolytic enzymes. If an antibody molecule is digested with **papain**, cleavage occurs above the disulfide bonds that hold the heavy chains together. This generates three separate fragments, two of which are called Fab (fragment antigen binding), and one is called Fc (fragment crystallizable). Cleavage of the antibody molecule with **pepsin** generates one large fragment called F(ab′)$_2$ and a digested Fc fragment. The **bridging of antigens** by antibody molecules is required for **agglutination of particulate antigens** or the **precipitation of soluble antigens**.

## In a Nutshell

Thymus-independent antigens:

- contain no peptides.
- stimulate only IgM.
- create no memory.

## Note

Mitogens activate many clones of B cells and are used clinically to assess lymphocyte function.

## In a Nutshell

- Isotype switching is directed by TH2 cells.
- Isotypes dictate effector function of the antibody molecule.

## In a Nutshell

- Papain generates 2 Fab + 1 Fc.
  - Fab (monovalent): capable of binding
- Pepsin generates 1 F(ab')₂.
  - F(ab')₂ (divalent): capable of binding and bridging

## Note

- IgG and F(ab')₂ fragments both have a valence of 2 and can bridge between antigens.
- Soluble antigens will then **precipitate**
- Particulate antigens (RBC and latex beads) will then clump together **(agglutinate)**

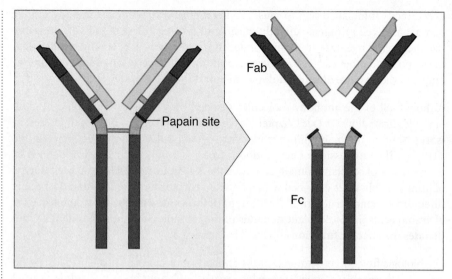

**Proteolytic Cleavage with Papain**

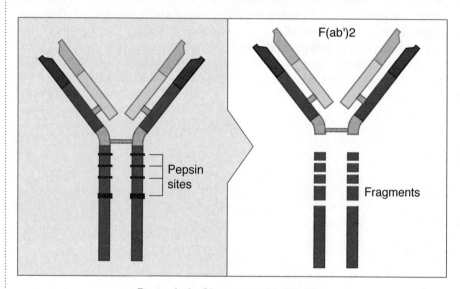

**Proteolytic Cleavage with Pepsin**

**Figure I-7-2.** Proteolytic Cleavage of Immunoglobulin by Papain/Pepsin

# THE PRIMARY HUMORAL RESPONSE

The first isotype of immunoglobulin that can be produced by a B cell with or without T-cell help is IgM. This is because coding for the constant domains of the heavy chain of IgM (μ chains) are the first sequences downstream from the coding for the idiotype of the molecule. The IgM molecule on the surface of the B cell is a monomer, but the secreted form of this molecule is a **pentamer**, held together in an extremely compact form by a **J chain** synthesized by the cell.

## In a Nutshell

- IgM is the first isotype produced.
- Plasma IgM exists as a pentamer.
- J chain joins the monomer units.

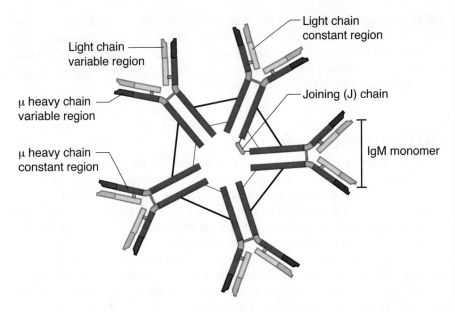

Light chain constant region

Light chain variable region

μ heavy chain variable region

Joining (J) chain

μ heavy chain constant region

IgM monomer

**Figure I-7-3.** The IgM Pentamer

The design of the IgM pentamer maximizes the effector functions critical to the body early during antigenic challenge. Because of its multimeric structure (5 of the Y-shaped monomers joined into one unit), plasma IgM has 5 times the capacity for binding antigenic epitopes as any monomeric immunoglobulin unit. The valence of the molecule is therefore 10: In other words, 10 identical epitopes can be simultaneously bound, as compared with 2 for the monomeric structure. This makes IgM the most effective immunoglobulin isotype at "sponging" the free antigen out of the tissues and proves critical, as the humoral response evolves, in trapping antigen so that it can be presented to the lymphocytes that will ultimately refine the choice of effector mechanism. Although the binding strength (affinity) of the idiotype for the epitope may not be strong early in the immune response, the IgM molecule possesses the highest avidity (number of combining sites available to bind epitopes) of any immunoglobulin molecule produced in the body.

**In a Nutshell**

IgM

● Plasma IgM valence = 10

● Functions in trapping free antigen

● Affinity (binding strength) may be low

● Avidity (multipoint binding) highest of all isotypes

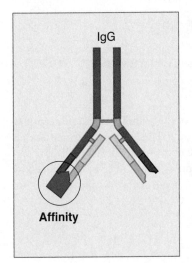

IgG

Affinity

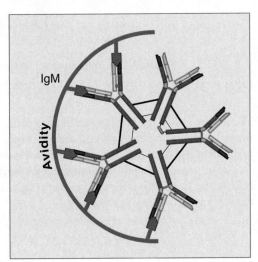

IgM

Avidity

**Figure I-7-4.** Affinity and Avidity

**In a Nutshell**

- IgM is most effective isotype at activating complement.

- It is not an opsonin.

- It does not mediate ADCC.

**Clinical Correlate**

- IgM is used as a measure of a primary response (acute infection).

- Convalescent serum will have mostly IgG with subthreshold levels of IgM.

**Note**

Isotype switching is induced by TH2 cells.

The multimeric structure of IgM also makes it the most effective antibody at activating complement, a set of serum proteases important in mediating inflammation and antigen removal. Serum IgM is incapable of binding to cellular Fc receptors and thus cannot act as an opsonin (*see* Chapter 5) or a mediator of antibody-dependent cell-mediated cytotoxicity (ADCC) (*see* Chapter 8).

## ISOTYPE SWITCHING

As the B lymphocyte receives cytokine signals from the activated TH2 cells in the secondary lymphoid organs, it is induced to undergo **isotype switching**, changing the heavy-chain constant domains to classes of antibodies with new and different effector functions. It does this by rearranging the DNA encoding the constant region of the heavy chain by activating switch regions that cause the intervening DNA to be looped out, excised, and degraded. The idiotype is then joined to a new constant region domain coding, and an antibody molecule with identical antigenic specificity but a new effector function is produced. This isotype switch is **one-way**: Because the excised DNA is degraded, a cell that has begun to produce an isotype downstream from IgM coding can never produce IgM again.

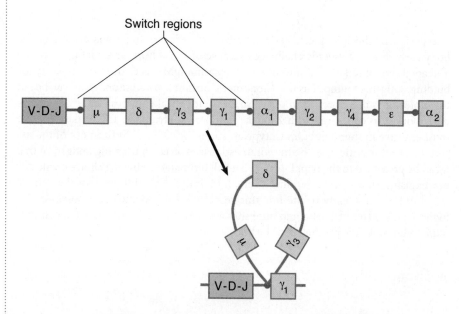

**Figure I-7-5.** Immunoglobulin Heavy Chain Switching

This is why IgM is the principal immunoglobulin of the **primary immune response** when antigen is first encountered, and it is replaced in later responses by antibodies of different isotypes. Although IgM antibodies are occasionally produced at low levels during secondary and later immunologic responses, they are always produced by cells seeing that antigen for the first time; namely, naive cells newly emerging from the bone marrow (*see* Chapter 9).

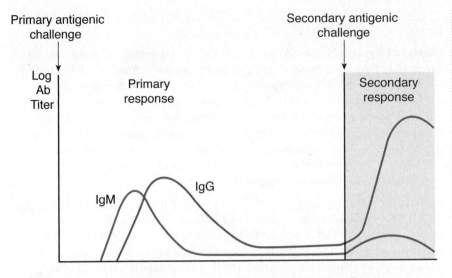

**Figure I-7-6.** Primary and Secondary Antibody Responses

During the activation of B lymphocytes by TH2 cells, intense proliferation of the B cells results in the formation of **germinal centers** in the follicles of the lymph nodes and spleen. These are clones of proliferating, antigen-specific cells. During the intense proliferative response of the B cell, random mutations in the coding of the variable domain region may occur. This is called **somatic hypermutation** and creates single point mutations in the antibody idiotype. If these slightly altered idiotypes have increased affinity for the antigen, then the cell expressing them will be at a selective advantage in competing to bind antigen. Because binding antigen serves as the first signal for proliferation, over time, clones of cells with higher receptor affinity will begin to predominate in the germinal center. This **clonal selection** results in the predominance of clones capable of producing antibodies with increasing affinity for the antigen, a process known as **affinity maturation**. This means that although isotype switching will necessarily **decrease the avidity** of the preponderance of antibody molecules as the immune response evolves, this will be substituted by an **increase in antibody affinity** over time.

The choice of activation of particular switch regions in the B-cell DNA sequence is apparently dictated by the release of specific cytokines by activated TH2 cells.

## In a Nutshell

- Germinal centers are clones of proliferating antigen-specific B cells.

- Somatic hypermutation may cause minor idiotype changes.

- Clonal selection by competition for antigen causes affinity maturation.

## In a Nutshell

TH2 cytokines dictate switch region activation.

**Memory Tool**

**5** = **A**lways +

**4** = **E**ver

(IL-5 → IgA)

(IL-4 → IgE)

## Clinical Correlate

**X-Linked Hyper-IgM Syndrome** is characterized by a deficiency of IgG, IgA, and IgE and elevated levels of IgM. IgM levels can reach 2000 mg/dL (normal is 45–250 mg/dL). It is most commonly inherited as an X-linked recessive disorder, but some forms seem to be acquired and can be seen in both sexes. The peripheral blood of infected individuals has high numbers of IgM-secreting plasma cells, as well as autoantibodies to neutrophils, platelets, and red blood cells. These patients fail to make germinal centers during a humoral immune response. Children with this condition suffer recurrent respiratory infections, especially those caused by *Pneumocystis jirovecii*.

The defect in this syndrome is in the gene encoding the CD40 ligand, which maps to the X chromosome. Therefore, TH cells from these patients will fail to express functional CD40L on their membrane and will thereby fail to give the costimulatory signal necessary for the B-cell response to T-dependent antigens, so only IgM antibodies are produced. The B-cell response to T-independent antigens is unaffected.

**In a Nutshell**

- IgG is the major antibody produced after IgM.

- IgG exists in 4 subisotypes.

- IgG activates complement, opsonizes, and mediates ADCC.

- IgG is actively transported across the placenta.

## ANTIBODIES OF SECONDARY IMMUNE RESPONSES

The preponderant isotype of immunoglobulin that begins to be produced after IgM during the primary immune response is IgG. IgG is a monomeric molecule with a γ **heavy chain** and a new set of effector functions. IgG exists in 4 different **subisotypes** (subclasses) in humans—IgG1, -2, -3 and -4, each of which exhibits slightly different capacity in effector functions. But in general, IgG activates complement, acts as an opsonin, and mediates ADCC. It is also actively transported across the placenta by receptor-mediated transport and thus plays a crucial role in protection of the fetus during gestation.

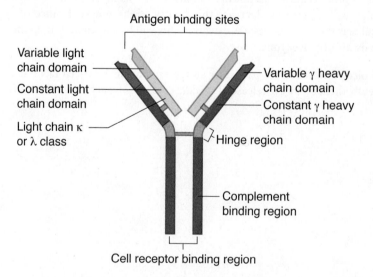

**Figure I-7-7.** The Basic Structure of IgG

Another isotype of antibody that can be produced following class switching is IgA, although this isotype is much more commonly produced in the submucosa than in the lymph nodes and spleen. IgA generally exists as a **dimer**, held together by a J chain similar to that produced with IgM, and serves as a major protective **defense of**

**the mucosal surfaces of the body**. Its sole function appears to be the inhibition of binding of toxins or adhesive microbial components to the mucosa of the digestive, respiratory, and urogenital systems, and it does not activate complement or act as an opsonin.

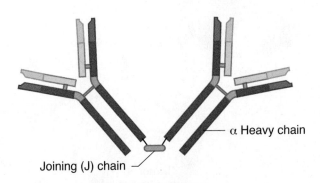

**Figure I-7-8.** The IgA Dimer

The homing of specific memory cells to epithelial and mucosal surfaces leads to the production of specialized lymphoid aggregations along these barriers. Collectively referred to as **mucosal-associated lymphoid tissues**, or **MALT**, they include the tonsils and Peyer patches, as well as numerous less well-organized lymphoid accumulations in the lamina propria. TH2 cells in these sites are dedicated to providing help for class switching to IgA. Most IgA-secreting B lymphocytes and plasma cells in the body will be found in these locations. **Secretory IgA** (that which is released across the mucosa of the respiratory, digestive, and urogenital tracts) differs from serum IgA in an important fashion. As the IgA dimer is produced by plasma cells and B lymphocytes, it becomes bound to receptors on the abluminal side of the epithelia, is endocytosed, and is released into the lumen wearing a secretory piece that is the residue of the epithelial-cell receptor. The **secretory component** thus serves an important function in transepithelial transport, and once in the lumen of the tract, has a function in protecting the molecule from proteolytic cleavage.

## In a Nutshell

- Most IgA is produced in the submucosa.

- IL-5 and TGFβ cause isotype switching to IgA

- IgA is a dimer with a J chain.

- IgA inhibits binding of adhesive substances to mucosal surfaces.

- IgA is an important component in breast milk.

## In a Nutshell

- MALT contains TH2 cells assisting IgA production.

- Secretory IgA is a dimer with secretory component.

- Secretory component:
  - Transepithelial transport
  - Protection from proteolytic cleavage

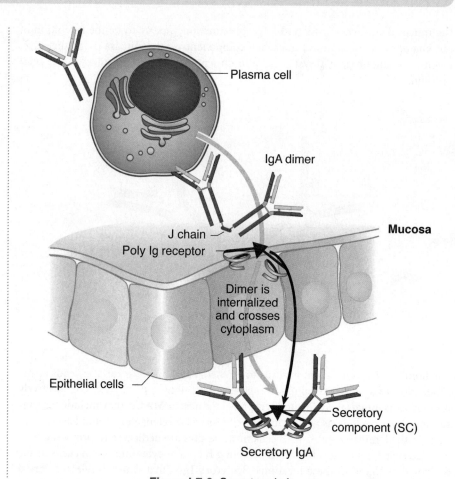

**Figure I-7-9.** Secretory IgA

IgE is the so-called homocytotropic antibody because it binds to directly to Fcε receptors present on mast cells and basophils (without binding antigen) and is involved in elicitation of protective immune responses against helminth parasites and many allergic responses (*see* Chapter 13). It does not activate complement or act as an opsonin. Its heavy chain is called an ε chain.

## In a Nutshell

- IL-4 and IL-13 cause isotype switching to IgE

- IgE is bound to mast cells and basophils.

- IgE mediates immediate type I allergic reactions.

- IgE protects against parasites.

**Table I-7-1.** Summary of the Biologic Functions of the Antibody Isotypes

| | IgM | IgG | IgA | IgD | IgE |
|---|---|---|---|---|---|
| Heavy chain | μ | γ | α | δ | ε |
| Adult serum levels (in mg/dL) | 45–250 | 620–1,400 | 80–350 | Trace | Trace |
| **Functions** | | | | | |
| Complement activation, classic pathway | + | + | – | – | – |
| Opsonization | – | + | – | – | – |
| Antibody-dependent cell-mediated cytotoxicity (ADCC) | – | + | – | – | – |
| Placental transport | – | + | – | – | – |
| Naive B-cell antigen receptor | + | – | – | + | – |
| Memory B-cell antigen receptor (one only) | – | + | + | – | + |
| Trigger mast cell granule release | – | – | – | – | + |

## Clinical Correlate

### Immunodeficiencies Involving B Lymphocytes

Patients with B-cell deficiencies usually present with recurrent pyogenic infections with extracellular pathogens. The absence of immunoglobulins for opsonization and complement activation is a major problem (*see* Chapter 11). The T-cell immune system is intact, and T-cell activities against intracellular pathogens, delayed-type hypersensitivity, and tumor rejection are normal (*see* Chapter 8).

# COMPLEMENT

The **complement system** is a set of interacting proteins released into the blood after production in the liver. The components act together as zymogens, activating one another in cascade fashion after initiation from a variety of stimuli. Two different pathways of activation occur in the body and culminate similarly in the production of important split products that mediate **inflammation**, enhance phagocytosis by **opsonization**, and cause **lysis** of particles by membrane pore formation.

## In a Nutshell

The Complement System

- Has two pathways of activation
- Enhances inflammation
- Enhances phagocytosis
- Causes lysis

## Note

C3a, C4a & C5a are all anaphylatoxins while only C5a is also chemotactic.

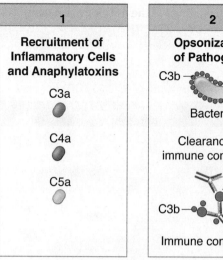
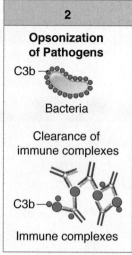
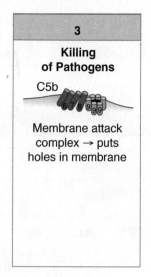

| 1 | 2 | 3 |
|---|---|---|
| **Recruitment of Inflammatory Cells and Anaphylatoxins** | **Opsonization of Pathogens** | **Killing of Pathogens** |

**Figure I-7-10.** Three Functions of the Complement System

## In a Nutshell

The alternative pathway is initiated by surfaces of pathogens.

The **alternative pathway** of complement activation is probably the more primitive of the two pathways because it is initiated by simple attraction of the early factors to the surfaces of microbes. Bacterial polysaccharides and the lipopolysaccharide of the cell envelope of gram-negative bacteria both serve as potent, initiating stimuli.

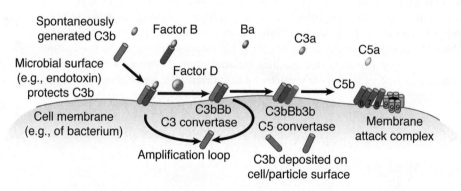

**Figure I-7-11.** The Alternative Complement Pathway

## Note

The classical pathway is activated by Ag/Ab complexes.

The **classical pathway** is activated by antigen-antibody complexes and is probably the more phylogenetically advanced system of activation. Both IgG and IgM can activate the system by this pathway, although IgM is the most efficient.

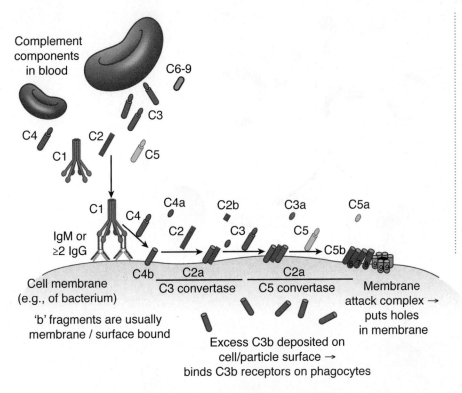

**Figure I-7-12.** The Classical Complement Pathway

Although the complement cascade is considered a component of the innate immune response, its overlapping stimulation of effector functions of cells of the adaptive immune response, as well as its role in enhancement of inflammation, make it a critical effector system for removal of extracellular invaders and concentration of antigens into the secondary lymphoid organs, where the adaptive immune responses are elicited.

When uncontrolled activation of complement occurs in certain disease states (*see* Chapters 11 and 13), damage to host tissues can ensue. Physiologic controls on complement activation occur at the level of C1 (classical pathway) and C3 and C5 (both pathways).

**In a Nutshell**

Physiologic controls on complement activation act at level of C1, C3, and C5.

## Clinical Correlate

### Complement Deficiencies

Genetic deficiencies have been described for each of the components of complement and their regulatory proteins (*see* Chapter 11). These deficiencies highlight the critical role of the early components of complement in generating C3b and the essential role of C3b for clearance of immune complexes from the body. Furthermore, even though gram-positive bacteria may be resistant to the membrane attack complex of complement, the early components of the cascade mediate localized inflammation and opsonize the bacteria. In a great number of cases then, it is the complement cascade that converts immunoglobulins into powerful effectors of bacterial destruction.

When deficiencies of complement regulatory components occur, then the uncontrolled activation of the complement cascade can have dangerous results in the body's own innocent bystanders. In hereditary angioedema, uncontrolled complement activation at the mucosal surfaces causes edema and pain. In paroxysmal nocturnal hemoglobinuria, the absence of regulatory proteins causes paroxysms of hemolysis of RBCs and the resultant hemoglobinuria.

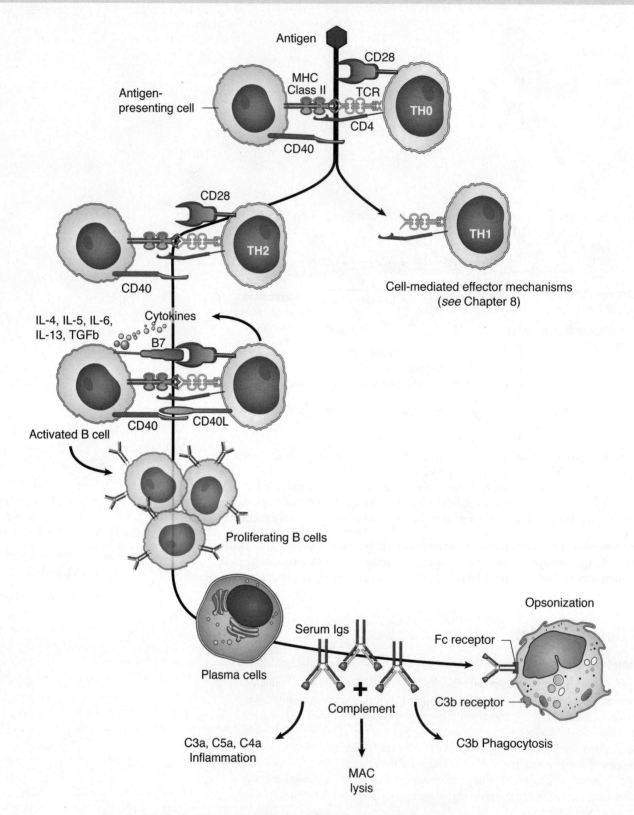

**Figure I-7-13.** Overview of the Generation of Humoral Effector Mechanisms

## Chapter Summary

- Humoral immunity is mediated by antibodies synthesized by B cells and secreted by plasma cells.

- Humoral immunity is the major defense mechanism against extracellular microbes and toxins.

- Most naturally occurring antigens are thymus-dependent: They require collaboration of TH and B cells.

- Contact between specific B and TH cells involves MHC class II/peptide presentation, costimulatory molecules (B7/CD28), CD40/CD40L binding, and cytokine production (IL-2, IL-4, IL-5,and IL-6).

- TH2 cells direct isotype switching by B cells, which changes the effector function of the antibody produced.

- Thymus-independent antigens, such as bacterial lipopolysaccharide, cross-link the receptors of B lymphocytes and cause them to proliferate and secrete IgM antibodies. These antigens *do not* create "immunologic memory."

- IgM is the first isotype of antibody that can be produced. It exists in serum as a pentamer held together by a joining (J) chain.

- The functions of IgM are (as a monomer) receptor on B cells, antigen capture in the secondary lymphoid organs, and (as a pentamer) in plasma, activation of complement.

- TH2 activation of B lymphocytes causes intense proliferation in the germinal centers, and somatic hypermutation may cause slight variation in the shape of the idiotype. Clonal selection of the idiotype with the highest affinity for antigen results in "affinity maturation": a general improvement in the "goodness-of-fit" for the antigen as the immune response progresses.

- IgG is the major isotype produced after IgM. It exists in 4 subisotypes. It activates complement, opsonizes, mediates ADCC, and is actively transported across the placenta.

- IgA is the major isotype produced in the submucosa, colostrum, and breast milk. It is a dimer with a J chain holding it together. It functions in inhibiting the binding of substances to cells or mucosal surfaces. It does not activate complement or mediate opsonization.

- Secretory IgA is transported into the lumen of the gastrointestinal, respiratory, or genitourinary tracts by binding to a polyimmunoglobulin receptor.

- This receptor (now called a secretory component) is retained for protection of IgA from proteolytic cleavage.

- IgE is the antibody that binds to mast cells and is responsible for antihelminthic and allergic responses.

- Complement is a set of interacting serum proteins that enhance inflammation (C3a, C4a, C5a) and opsonization (C3b) and cause lysis of particulate substances (C5b-9).

- The alternative pathway of complement is activated by interaction with microbial surfaces.

- The classical pathway is activated by antigen–antibody complexes.

- Inappropriate activation of the complement cascade is controlled at the level of C1, C3, and C5.

## Review Questions

1. An antibody preparation is being used in a laboratory protocol to study B lymphocytes. The preparation does not activate the cells or cause capping. It does not cause precipitation of its purified ligand, and it does not cause agglutination of latex beads covalently coupled to its ligand. Which of the following is the most likely antibody preparation?

    (A) Monoclonal anti-CD19 IgG

    (B) Monoclonal anti-CD56 IgG

    (C) Papain-treated anti-CD19 IgG

    (D) Papain-treated anti-CD56 IgG

    (E) Pepsin-treated anti-CD19 IgG

    (F) Pepsin-treated anti-CD56 IgG

2. IgM isohemagglutinins from an individual of blood group A are treated with pepsin. When the product of this reaction is added to group B erythrocytes, they will be

    (A) agglutinated

    (B) lysed

    (C) phagocytized

    (D) precipitated

    (E) unaffected

3. A 26-year-old obstetric patient becomes ill during the first trimester of pregnancy with fever and lymphadenopathy. She is found to have a rising titer of anti-*Toxoplasma gondii* antibodies. She delivers a full-term baby with no apparent signs of in utero infection. The best test to diagnose acute infection in the neonate would be a parasite-specific ELISA for which isotype of immunoglobulin?

    (A) IgA

    (B) IgD

    (C) IgE

    (D) IgG

    (E) IgM

4. A 4-year-old boy is evaluated for a possible immunologic deficiency. He has suffered repeated infections of mucosal-surface pathogens and has shown delayed development of protective responses to the standard childhood vaccinations. Immunoelectrophoresis of his serum demonstrates absence of a macroglobulin peak, and his sputum is devoid of secretory IgA. Normal numbers of B lymphocytes bearing monomeric IgM are found by flow cytometry, and serum levels of monomeric IgA, IgE, and each of the 4 subisotypes of IgG are normal. Which of the following deficiencies could account for these findings?

    (A) Absence of CD40

    (B) Absence of J chains

    (C) Absence of IL-4

    (D) Absence of Tdt

    (E) Absence of TH2 cells

5. A 56-year-old homeless, alcoholic, and febrile man is brought to the emergency department after a difficult night during which his coughing kept everyone at the shelter awake. On arrival his pulse is rapid, and his breathing is labored with diffuse rales. Endotracheal aspirates produce a mucopurulent discharge containing numerous gram-positive cocci in chains. His serum contains high titers of IgM antibodies specific for the polysaccharide capsule of *Streptococcus pneumoniae*. The effector mechanism most likely to act in concert with this early IgM production to clear infection is

   (A) ADCC

   (B) complement-mediated opsonization

   (C) cytotoxic T lymphocytes

   (D) LAK cells

   (E) NK cells

6. A 3-year-old boy has had several bouts with pneumonia. *Streptococcus pneumoniae* was isolated and identified in each of the cases. The child was treated with penicillin each time, and the condition resolved. He is now being evaluated for a potential immunologic deficiency. Serum electrophoresis shows age-normal values for all isotypes of immunoglobulin, but serum levels of some components of complement are depressed. Which of the following deficiencies could explain his problem?

   (A) C1

   (B) C2

   (C) C3

   (D) C4

   (E) C5

7. Up until the 1970s, tonsillectomies were routinely performed on children with swollen tonsils. This procedure has lost its widespread appeal as we have learned the important role of mucosal-associated lymphoid tissue (MALT) in the protective immune response. What is the major immunoglobulin produced by the MALT?

   (A) A dimeric immunoglobulin with secretory component

   (B) A monomeric immunoglobulin that crosses the placenta

   (C) A monomeric immunoglobulin bound by mast cells

   (D) A monomeric immunoglobulin that opsonizes

   (E) A pentameric immunoglobulin that activates complement

8. A 64-year-old man undergoes surgery to excise 18 inches of bowel with adenocarcinoma. When the tissue and draining mesenteric lymph nodes are sent for pathologist's examination, the Peyer patches are noted to be hyperplastic with IgA-secreting plasma cells, but there is no secretory IgA found in the lumen of the colon. Which of the following changes in the bowel epithelium could explain this finding?

   (A) Failure of isotype switching

   (B) Failure of variable domain gene-segment rearrangement

   (C) Loss of J chain synthesis

   (D) Loss of the polyimmunoglobulin receptor

   (E) Loss of TH2 cells

# Answers and Explanations

1.  **The correct answer is C.** The cell surface marker which is typically used to identify B lymphocytes is CD19. This is a component of the B-cell/signal transduction complex and thus will be found on all B cells. Treatment of IgG with papain yields two monovalent antigen binding (Fab) fragments and destroys the function of the Fc portion of the molecule. Immunoglobulin molecules that are disrupted this way lose their ability to cross-link the receptors on cells, to promote precipitation or agglutination, and to activate cells by providing a first stimulatory signal.

    Monoclonal anti-CD19 IgG (**choice A**) is a divalent antibody molecule that recognizes the signal transduction complex on B cells. Monoclonal antibodies can cross-link cell-surface receptors and cause capping, cell activation, and precipitation. Agglutination is usually accomplished using IgM because a very large molecule is needed to overcome the zeta potential (repulsive charge) of erythrocytes. If IgG is used, a second developing antibody must be added.

    Monoclonal anti-CD56 IgG (**choice B**) is a divalent antibody molecule that recognizes a molecule found on NK cells. Because both arms of the molecule are intact, it is capable of causing capping, cell activation, precipitation, and agglutination if a developing antiserum is added.

    Papain-treated anti-CD56 IgG (**choice D**) would not be used for the study of B lymphocytes because CD56 is a marker for NK cells.

    Pepsin-treated anti-CD19 IgG (**choice E**) is a divalent molecule possessing two Fab fragments joined together ($F[ab']_2$), and a fragmented Fc region. The $F(ab')_2$ portion of the antibody is capable of causing capping, cell activation, precipitation, and, with a developing antiserum, agglutination.

    Pepsin-treated anti-CD56 IgG (**choice F**) is a divalent molecule possessing two Fab fragments joined together ($F[ab']_2$) and a fragmented Fc region. Its specificity is for NK cells. Additionally, the $F(ab')_2$ portion of the antibody is capable of causing capping, cell activation, precipitation, and, with a developing antiserum, agglutination.

2.  **The correct answer is A.** Isohemagglutinins are IgM antibodies that will agglutinate the RBCs of individuals with another blood type. They are believed to be made due to exposure to cross-reactive antigens found on the surface of normal gut flora organisms. Thus, a person of blood group A will produce isohemagglutinins that will agglutinate type B cells. If these antibodies are pretreated with pepsin, a divalent $F(ab')_2$ fragment and destruction of the Fc will result. A divalent fragment is capable of causing agglutination.

    Lysed (**choice B**) is not correct because it would require the integrity of the complement-binding regions of the IgM, which are found in the Fc, and the question stem does not provide complement in the mix.

    Phagocytized (**choice C**) is not correct because it would require an intact cell-binding region in the Fc, and the question stem does not provide phagocytic cells in the mix.

    Precipitated (**choice D**) would be the correct answer if the antigen in question were a soluble protein. Proteins precipitate when treated with specific antibodies, particles agglutinate. The two particles used in laboratory medicine are latex beads and erythrocytes. If neither of these is mentioned, then the student can assume that treatment would result in precipitation, not agglutination. Precipitation has exactly the same requirements as agglutination: a divalent antigen-binding molecule.

    Unaffected (**choice E**) would be the correct answer if papain had been used to treat the isohemagglutinins. Because papain produces two monovalent Fab fragments, these are incapable of cross-linking antigen (whether soluble protein or particle), so neither agglutination nor precipitation would be possible.

3. **The correct answer is E.** The only way to identify a neonatal infection serologically is by detection of pathogen-specific IgM antibodies. This is because the fetus receives IgG antibodies from the mother by active transport across the placenta. Because you cannot identify the source of the antibodies, IgG detection in the child can simply reflect this natural passive type of protection. Because IgM does not cross the placenta, any IgM detected in the neonate is being produced in the child and is reflective of a response to infection. In this way, all children born to HIV-infected mothers will be seropositive by both ELISA and Western blot, but only 20% will actually be infected in utero, even in the absence of antiviral therapy.

   IgA (**choice A**) does not usually begin to be produced by a child until one to two years after birth. At the end of the first year, most children have no more than 20% of adult values, so it would not be a useful diagnostic in the neonate. Additionally, because *Toxoplasma gondii* is an intracellular parasite, IgA would not be the most effective immune response in any individual.

   IgD (**choice B**) will be produced by an infected neonate along with IgM because of alternative RNA splicing, but this is not a useful diagnostic. IgD rarely reaches levels easily detected by serology, and the immunoglobulin has the shortest half-life of all the immunoglobulins. The function of secreted IgD, if any, is not clear, so it is not a useful serologic test.

   IgE (**choice C**) does not usually begin to be produced by a child until well into the second year after birth. Additionally, because *Toxoplasma gondii* is an intracellular parasite, IgE would not be the most effective immune response in any individual.

   IgG (**choice D**) is not a useful serologic test in a neonate because it is impossible to determine the origin of such molecules. Children infected in utero will begin to produce IgG due to isotype switching late in gestation, but because the placenta is actively transporting all maternal IgG into the fetus, it is not possible to distinguish whether the child is actually infected or simply passively protected using this technique.

4. **The correct answer is B.** IgM and secretory IgA are similar in that they are held together by a J chain synthesized by the B cell or plasma cell. Without the presence of the J chain, IgM would exist only in monomeric form, and the macroglobulin peak would be absent on electrophoresis. Because pentameric IgM is important for capturing newly introduced foreign antigen and thus beginning the immune response, the child is delayed in his development of protective responses to vaccination. Because secretory IgA is a dimer that protects the mucosal surfaces, such a child would be especially susceptible to infectious agents crossing the mucosal surfaces.

   Absence of CD40 (**choice A**) would affect the production of IgG, IgA, and IgE, but would not prevent macroglobulin synthesis. Indeed, most patients with this defect have hyper-macroglobulinemia because the CD40/CD40L interaction is necessary for isotype switching.

   Absence of IL-4 (**choice C**) would cause problems with the ability to produce IgG, IgA, and IgE. This cytokine, produced by TH2 cells, is necessary for the differentiation and development of most antibody responses other than IgM. Thus, IgM levels either would not be affected or would be increased in a compensatory fashion.

   Absence of Tdt (**choice D**) would cause problems with the patient's ability to perform the genetic rearrangements necessary to form the idiotype of the antibody molecule. They would not affect the isotype of antibody produced.

   Absence of TH2 cells (**choice E**) would affect the production of IgG, IgA, and IgE, but would not affect IgM production.

5. **The correct answer is B.** One of the most effective protective responses to infections with extracellular, encapsulated bacteria, such as *Streptococcus pneumoniae*, is complement-mediated opsonization. Because IgM is the most effective antibody at activating complement, generation of C3b fragments during this process coats the bacteria and makes them more susceptible to ingestion and intracellular killing by cells of the phagocytic system.

   ADCC (**choice A**), or antibody-dependent cell-mediated cytotoxicity, is a mechanism by which NK cells, neutrophils, macrophages, and eosinophils can use their Fc receptor to bind specific antibody and target an agent for lysis. No cells have Fc receptors for IgM, so this is not a mechanism that could act in concert with early IgM production.

   Cytotoxic T lymphocytes (**choice C**) identify altered-self/MHC class I molecule conjugates on the surfaces of cells that are malignantly transformed or infected with intracellular pathogens. They are not a protective mechanism that acts in concert with any antibody molecule.

   LAK cells (**choice D**), or lymphokine-activated killer cells, are NK cells that have been stimulated in vitro with cytokines that enhance their killing activity. These cells have a function in early surveillance against altered-self cells, but are not believed to play a role in protection against extracellular pathogens, such as this one.

   NK cells (**choice E**) are members of the innate immune system and are believed to play a role in surveillance against tumor cells and other altered-self cells that fail to express MHC class I antigens on their surfaces. They would not act in concert with IgM production, and they would not be effective against an extracellular pathogen, such as this one.

6. **The correct answer is C.** The component of complement that is most important in clearance of extracellular pathogens such as *Streptococcus pneumoniae* is C3b. This fragment acts as an opsonin and enhances the ingestion and intracellular killing of the bacteria by phagocytic cells.

   C1 (**choice A**) is the first component of the complement cascade activated in the classic pathway. Although it is critical to initiating those events that can culminate in the production of the membrane attack complex, it is not the most important component for the clearance of infections such as this one.

   C2 (**choice B**) is the third component of the complement cascade activated in the classic pathway. Although it is critical to initiating those events that can culminate in the production of the membrane attack complex, it is not the most important component for the clearance of infections such as this one.

   C4 (**choice D**) is the second component of the complement cascade activated during the classic pathway. Although it is critical to initiating those events that can culminate in the production of the membrane attack complex, it is not the most important component for the clearance of infections such as this one.

   C5 (**choice E**) is the fifth component of the complement cascade activated during the classic pathway and the first step in the formation of the membrane attack complex (C5b–9). It is not the most important component for the clearance of infections such as this one.

7. **The correct answer is A.** The mucosal-associated lymphoid tissues (MALT) are the major sites of synthesis of IgA. IgA is a dimeric molecule held together by a J chain similar to that used in IgM. As IgA is transported across the epithelial surface, it acquires the secretory component, which functions both in transepithelial transport and protection from proteolytic cleavage.

A monomeric immunoglobulin that crosses the placenta (**choice B**) describes IgG. IgG is the major immunoglobulin of the blood and is produced in lymph nodes and spleen, but less commonly in the MALT.

A monomeric immunoglobulin bound by mast cells (**choice C**) describes IgE. IgE is the immunoglobulin that causes immediate hypersensitivity by virtue of its attraction to the Fc receptors of mast cells. It is not the major immunoglobulin produced in the MALT, although it may be produced there.

A monomeric immunoglobulin that opsonizes (**choice D**) describes IgG. IgG is the major immunoglobulin of the blood and is produced in lymph nodes and spleen, but less commonly in the MALT.

A pentameric immunoglobulin that activates complement (**choice E**) describes IgM. IgM is the major immunoglobulin of the primary immune response and is produced in lymph nodes and spleen, but less commonly in the MALT.

8.  **The correct answer is D**. The transport of IgA dimers from the abluminal side of the mucosa to the lumen is mediated via attachment to polyimmunoglobulin receptors on mucosal cells. This allows endocytosis of IgA into the mucosal cell and secretion onto the other side. Secretory IgA found in the lumen of the bowel retains a residue of this receptor, secretory component, which further protects it from proteolytic cleavage inside the intestine. If this receptor were lacking, transport of IgA across the mucosa would not be possible, and the IgA dimers would be trapped on the abluminal side of the mucosa.

    Failure of isotype switching (**choice A**) is not a potential cause of such a condition because isotype switching occurs in secondary lymphoid organs and not in epithelial cells. Because the IgA dimers were present, isotype switching had been successful, but transepithelial transport was not occurring.

    Failure of variable domain gene segment rearrangement (**choice B**) is not a potential cause of such a condition because variable domain gene-segment rearrangement occurs in the primary lymphoid organs and not in epithelial cells. Because immunoglobulin was being produced, these gene segment rearrangements had occurred successfully, but transepithelial transport was not occurring.

    Loss of J chain synthesis (**choice C**) would result in the inability of an individual to join dimers of IgA and pentamers of IgM. Because the question states that the individual was making IgA dimers, J chain is clearly being made successfully by the B cell.

    Loss of TH2 cells (**choice E**) would cause the patient to be unable to switch isotypes. These persons could make only IgM, and this patient clearly has successfully produced IgA.

# The Generation of Cell-Mediated Effector Mechanisms

# 8

## What the COMLEX Requires You To Know

- The biologic function of cell-mediated immunity (CMI)
- The effector cells of CMI, their targets, and mechanisms of killing
- The means of regulation of CMI responses

The cell-mediated arm of the immune response (CMI) is designed to identify and eradicate antigenic stimuli that arise from **inside** the cells of the body. This occurs when cells of the host become infected with intracellular pathogens, such as viruses, some parasites and bacteria, or when malignant transformation causes cells to express aberrant surface molecules. In such cases, TH1 cells primed in the lymph nodes and spleen serve to provide the cytokine stimuli to activate the three potential effector cells to destroy the infected or altered cells: **cytotoxic CD8+ T lymphocytes (CTLs)**, **macrophages**, and **NK cells**.

One example of a cell-mediated effector mechanism that is enhanced by the action of TH1 cells is macrophage killing. This is a critical protective mechanism in the defense against organisms invading macrophages and attempting to live there (mycobacteria, *Leishmania*) or in the case where phagocytosed microbes have protective mechanisms that make them resistant to intracellular digestion (*Listeria*). In CMI against phagocytosed microbes, the specificity of the response arises from T cells, but the actual effector function is mediated by the phagocytes. This provides an important link between the adaptive and innate immune responses, and in essence, converts phagocytes into agents of the adaptive immune response. The most important cytokine elaborated by TH1 cells and CD8+ T lymphocytes to enhance the microbicidal capabilities of phagocytes is IFN-γ. In addition, production of TNF-α and TNF-β by T cells enhances inflammation and provides other stimuli that activate phagocytic cells. Macrophages and other phagocytes kill microbes intracellularly (as discussed in Chapter 6) in contrast to the mechanism observed with CTLs and NK cells.

When TH1 cytokines activate macrophages and cause tissue damage, the result is **delayed-type hypersensitivity (DTH)** (*see* Chapter 13). Assay of DTH by skin testing is often used as a measure of the patient's ability to mount a CMI response (e.g., Mantoux test, Lepromin test).

The CTL recognizes the cell it will ultimately kill by interaction between its TCR and MHC class I antigens on the surface of the target cell. If the cell in question is performing normal functions and therefore producing normal "self" peptides, there should be no CD8+ T cells that have a complementary TCR structure. If the cell is infected with an intracellular parasite or is expressing neoantigens reflective of tumor transformation, however, some small proportion of those CD8+ cells generated from the thymus should be capable of binding their TCRs to this MHC class I/non-self peptide combination. Unfortunately, because of the extreme polymorphism of the HLA system in humans, when tissues are transplanted between nonidentical individuals, cells of the transplant are often targeted by CTLs as abnormal. In spite of the

## In a Nutshell

- CMI protects against intracellular pathogens.
- TH1 cells stimulate:
  - Macrophages
  - CTLs
  - NK cells

## In a Nutshell

- Macrophages kill intracellularly.
- Killing is enhanced by IFN-γ, TNF-α, and TNF-β.
- The DTH skin test measures TH1 function.

## In a Nutshell

CTL stimulation requires:

- Non-self peptide/class I MHC

- IL-2

- IFNs increase MHC expression

## In a Nutshell

CTLs kill by:

- Perforins

- Cytokines (TNF)

- Granzymes

fact that they may only be presenting normal cellular peptides, in these cases the HLA molecules themselves are different enough to turn on the system (*see* Chapter 14).

CTLs are capable of differentiation and cloning by themselves in the presence of the appropriate non-self peptide/class I MHC antigen stimulus, but are much more effective in so doing if they are assisted by signals from TH1 cells. The TH1 cell secretes IL-2 which acts on CD8+ cells to enhance their differentiation and cloning. Interferons produced in the area will increase the expression of MHC molecules to make targets more susceptible to killing.

CTLs kill their target by the delivery of toxic granule contents that induce the apoptosis of the cell to which they attach. This process occurs in 4 phases:

- **Attachment** to the target (mediated by TCR, CD8, and LFA-1 integrin)
- **Activation** (cytoskeletal rearrangement to concentrate granules against attached target)
- **Exocytosis** of granule contents (perforin and granzymes)
- **Detachment** from the target

The death of the target may be mediated in distinct fashions. First, **perforin** present in the CTL granules creates pores in the membrane of the target cell through which **granzymes** (serine proteases) enter the target, inducing the activation of caspases, which activate the "death domain". Second, cytokines such as IFN-γ with TNF-α or TNF-β can induce apoptosis. Furthermore, activated CTLs express a membrane protein called **Fas ligand** (FasL), which may bind to its complementary structure on the target, Fas. When this occurs, caspases are induced and death results.

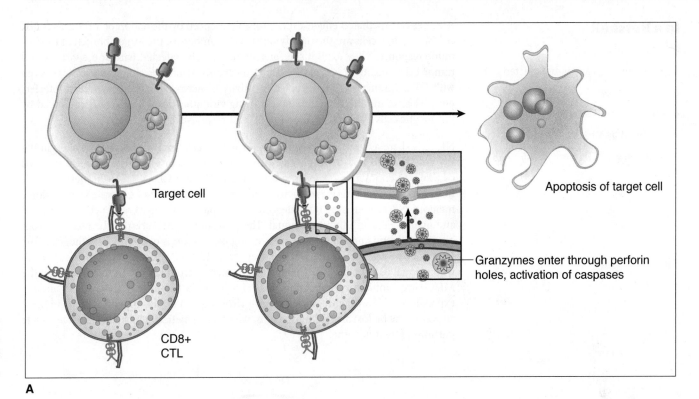

**Figure I-8-1.** Mechanisms of Cytotoxic T-Cell Killing. A: Perforin and Granzymes, and B: Fas/FasL Interaction

## In a Nutshell

NK Cells

- Kill tumor cells and virus-infected cells

- Kill by granzymes and perforin

- Enhanced by IFN-α, IFN-β, and IL-12

- Inhibited by MHC class I

- Counted with CD16 and CD56

Another cell-mediated effector mechanism enhanced by the action of TH1 cells is NK cell killing. NK cells are the only lymphocyte members of the innate branch of the immune response. They exhibit the capacity to kill cells infected with some viruses and tumor cells, and they kill via the same mechanisms of inducing apoptosis observed with CTLs (granzymes, perforin). NK activity is increased in the presence of interferons (IFNs) α and β (IFNs stimulated during viral infections) and IL-12 (produced by phagocytic cells during the induction of TH1 responses).

NK cells share a common early progenitor with T cells, but they do not develop in the thymus. They do not express antigen-specific receptors or CD3. The markers are used clinically to enumerate NK cells and include CD16 and CD56 (CD3–). Their recognition of targets is not MHC-restricted, and their activity does not generate immunologic memory. NK cells employ two categories of receptors: One delivers an activation signal, and one delivers an inhibitory signal. The activation signals seem to be received from binding of lectins possibly conserved among many groups of common pathogens. The inhibitory molecules on the NK cell seem to bind MHC class I antigens: Thus, a cell with normal MHC class I antigens will be protected from killing. In the absence of the MHC class I inhibitory signal, the NK cell will kill the target cell. MHC class I antigen expression may be downregulated during virus infections (*see* Appendix IV), and these antigens may be lost among tumor cells, which are genetically unstable and may delete portions of their genome.

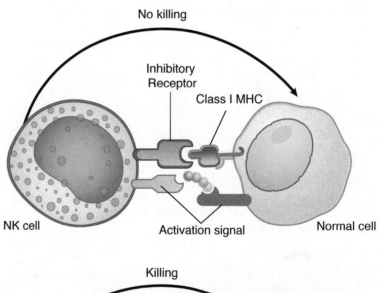

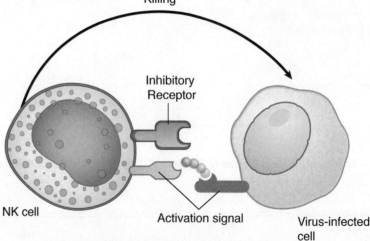

**Figure I-8-2. Activation of NK Cells**

A final mechanism of cell-mediated cytotoxicity that bridges humoral and cell-mediated effector systems in the body is **antibody-dependent cell-mediated cytotoxicity (ADCC)**. A number of cells with cytotoxic potential (NK cells, macrophages, monocytes, neutrophils, and eosinophils) have membrane receptors for the Fc region of IgG. When IgG is specifically bound to a target cell, the cytotoxic cells can bind to the free Fc "tail" and subsequently cause lysis of the target cell. Although these effectors are not specific for antigen, the specificity of the idiotype of the antibody directs their cytotoxicity. The mechanism of target cell killing in these cases may involve

- Lytic enzymes
- Tumor necrosis factor
- Perforin

**In a Nutshell**

ADCC

- NK cells
- Macrophages and monocytes
- Neutrophils
- Eosinophils
- Target recognition via IgG
- Killing by lytic enzymes, TNF, and perforin

**Note**

IgE can mediate ADCC in one special case: when the target is a parasitic worm.

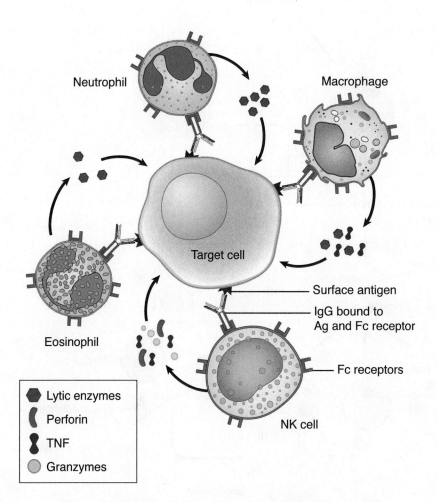

**Figure I-8-3.** Antibody-Dependent Cell-Mediated Cytotoxicity

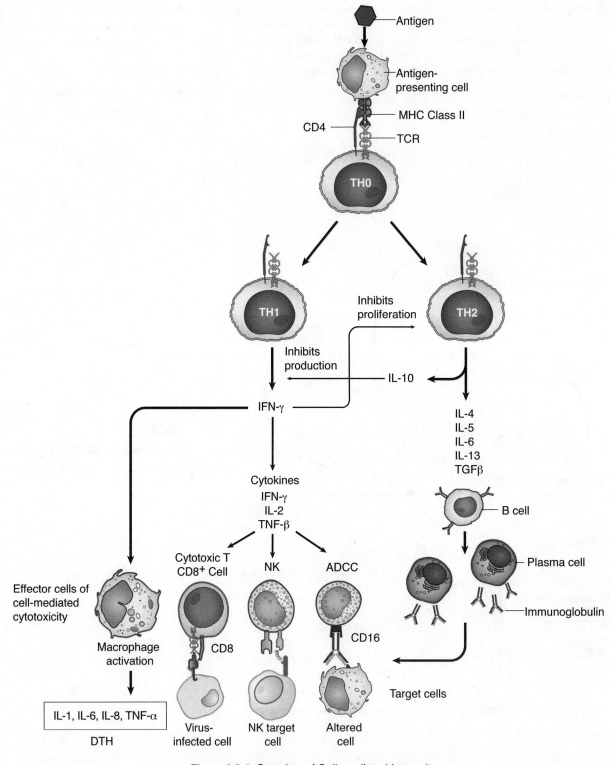

**Figure I-8-4.** Overview of Cell-mediated Immunity

**Table I-8-1.** Effector Cells in Cell-Mediated Immunity

| Effector Cell | CD Markers | Antigen Recognition | MHC Recognition Required for Killing | Effector Molecules |
|---|---|---|---|---|
| CTL | TCR, CD3, CD8, CD2 | Specific, TCR | Yes, class I | Perforin, granzymes, cytokines (TNF-β, IFN-γ) |
| NK cell | CD16, CD56, CD2 | ADCC: specific by IgG; otherwise, recognizes lectins | No, MHC I recognition inhibits | Perforin, granzymes, cytokines (TNF-β, IFN-γ) |
| Macrophage | CD14 | Nonspecific | No | TNF-α, enzymes, NO, oxygen radicals |

## Clinical Correlate

### Viral Strategies for Evasion of the Cell-Mediated Immune Response

- In the struggle for survival inside the human host, viruses have developed several strategies for evasion of protective cell-mediated immune responses. In viruses that replicate quickly, as do most RNA viruses, CTLs are the major protective response. These viruses will replicate until the TH1 response turns on CTLs and destroys all infected cells. The virus is eradicated in this host, but the rate of viral replication has ensured that a new nonimmune host is now infected to continue the cycle.

- In viruses that replicate slowly and cannot out-race the CTL response, a different strategy is necessary. Many such viruses block host cell protein synthesis, specifically MHC class I synthesis, transport, and expression (*see* Appendix IV). With this molecule downregulated, infected cells become "immune" to CTL recognition and killing. The downregulation of class I MHC, however, makes most of these viruses susceptible to the second cell-mediated immune mechanism, NK killing. Therefore, in most cases, the conjunction of CTL and NK mechanisms is sufficient to eradicate viral infections.

- The exception to this rule is cytomegalovirus (CMV). CMV downregulates the class I MHC molecule like many other viruses, but also produces a "decoy" MHC class I–like molecule. This virally encoded decoy molecule is too different from the host's to be recognized by CTLs, but it is sufficient to fool the NK cell, so CMV escapes both of these killing mechanisms. The reason humans are not all overwhelmed by this pathogen is that CMV can be successfully killed by the third cell-mediated immune response, ADCC. IgG molecules with specificity for the surface-expressed CMV antigens, such as the decoy molecule, will bind to virus-infected cells and be recognized by Fc receptor–bearing effector cells, like NK cells, which will then kill the target.

## Chapter Summary

- The cell-mediated immune response protects against intracellular pathogens.

- TH1 cells activate macrophages, CTLs, and NK cells.

- Macrophages kill intracellularly in response to TNF-$\alpha$, TNF-$\beta$, and IFN-$\gamma$ activation.

- The DTH skin test measures TH1 function.

- CTLs kill targets wearing MHC class I/altered-self peptides, using perforin, cytokines, granzymes, and Fas ligand.

- CTLs are stimulated by IL-2 from TH1 cells. IFNs increase MHC expression on targets.

- NK cells kill tumor and virus-infected cells using granzymes and perforin.

- NK cells are stimulated by IFN-$\alpha$, IFN-$\beta$, and IL-12, and kill targets lacking MHC I.

## Review Questions

1.  A 62-year-old accountant develops a solid tumor that is unresponsive to chemotherapy. He elects to participate in an experimental treatment protocol to stimulate his own immune effector cells to recognize and kill the malignant cells. The tumor cells are found to have no expression of MHC class I antigens. Which of the following in vitro treatments of his tumor cells is likely to stimulate the most effective immune response when reinfused into the patient?

    (A) IFN-γ

    (B) IL-2

    (C) IL-8

    (D) IL-10

    (E) TNF-β

2.  *Toxoplasma gondii* is an intracellular parasite that lives inside phagocytic and nonphagocytic cells by generating its own intracellular vesicle. This may allow it to avoid recognition and killing by CD8+ lymphocytes, which require the presentation of foreign peptides transported into the endoplasmic reticulum and loaded onto MHC molecules that have

    (A) a $\beta_2$ domain instead of a $\beta_2$ microglobulin

    (B) invariant chains

    (C) a peptide-binding groove

    (D) a single transmembrane domain

    (E) two similar chains

3.  Before 1960, children with enlarged thymus glands were frequently irradiated to functionally ablate this organ, whose role was not yet known. Over the lifetime of such individuals, which of the following conditions was likely to develop?

    (A) Depressed immune surveillance of tumors

    (B) Depressed oxygen-dependent killing by neutrophils

    (C) Depressed primary response to soluble antigens

    (D) Increased cellularity of lymph node paracortical areas

    (E) Increased tendency toward atopy

4.  A 42-year-old Nigerian man who is in the United States visiting with his brother comes into the hospital clinic. He complains of several months of weight loss, night sweats, mild sputum production, and the spitting up of blood. You run a PPD skin test and the results are positive. What can you conclude from this result?

    (A) A cell-mediated immune response has occurred

    (B) A humoral immune response has occurred

    (C) The B-cell system is functional

    (D) The B- and T-cell systems are functional

    (E) The neutrophilic phagocyte system is functional

5. A woman with advanced metastatic breast cancer undergoes a radical mastectomy, followed by irradiation and chemotherapy. After a 2-year remission, a metastatic focus appears, and she enrolls in an experimental treatment protocol. In it, a sample of her aspirated bone marrow is treated with GM-CSF, TNF-α, and IL-2, then pulsed with membrane fragments of her tumor cells and reinfused. Which of the following cell subpopulations is the most directly targeted by this treatment?

(A) B lymphocytes

(B) Cytotoxic T lymphocytes

(C) NK cells

(D) TH1 cells

(E) TH2 cells

## Answers and Explanations

1. **The correct answer is A.** The killer cells cytotoxic to targets lacking MHC class I antigens are NK cells. These cells are members of the innate immune response, and as such their response is not enhanced over time. The most specific, inducible cytotoxic cells in the body are cytotoxic T lymphocytes (CTLs), which depend on MHC class I recognition of their target. Because this question asks how the tumor cells can be altered to make them better stimulators of an immune response, one approach would be to increase their expression of MHC class I molecules. This can be accomplished by treatment of the tumor cells with interferon (IFN)-γ. IFN-γ increases expression of both class I and II MHC products on cells.

IL-2 (**choice B**) is a product of TH1 lymphocytes and induces proliferation of antigen-primed TH and cytotoxic T cells. It also supports their long-term growth. It would not have an effect on this patient's tumor cells.

IL-8 (**choice C**) is a product of macrophages and endothelial cells and acts on neutrophils to cause their chemotaxis and extravasation into tissues. It would not have an effect on this patient's tumor cells.

IL-10 (**choice D**) is a product of TH2 cells and acts on macrophages to suppress their cytokine production. It therefore indirectly reduces cytokine production by TH1 cells and dampens the activation of the cell-mediated arm of the immune response. It would not have an effect on this patient's tumor cells.

TNF-β (**choice E**) is a product of macrophages and NK cells and acts on tumor cells to cause direct cytotoxicity. It acts on inflammatory cells to induce cytokine secretion and causes the cachexia associated with chronic inflammation. It would not cause the patient's tumor cells to stimulate better immunity.

2. **The correct answer is D.** CD8+ lymphocytes, or cytotoxic T lymphocytes recognize their target cells by binding to MHC class I molecules containing altered-self peptides. The class I molecule is a two-chain structure, with one long α chain that passes through the cellular membrane and a shorter chain called $\beta_2$ microglobulin that becomes associated with the α chain.

A $\beta_2$ domain instead of a $\beta_2$ microglobulin (**choice A**) describes the class II MHC molecule. It is loaded with peptides by the endosomal (exogenous) pathway and is recognized by CD4+ T cells.

Invariant chains (**choice B**) are found blocking the peptide-binding groove of the class II MHC molecule immediately after synthesis. These chains are digested away when the class II MHC is exposed to the contents of the phagocytic vesicles of macrophages, and the groove is loaded with peptides from the ingested particle.

A peptide-binding groove (**choice C**) would be found in both class I and II MHC molecules and is therefore not the best answer.

Two similar chains (**choice E**) would be found in the class II MHC molecule. It is composed of an α and a β chain of similar lengths, both of which have transmembrane domains. The class II MHC molecule is loaded with peptides by the endosomal (exogenous) pathway and is recognized by CD4+ T cells.

3.  **The correct answer is A.** Although the ablation of the thymus in early child-hood will ultimately have far-reaching consequences in the development of many immune responses, the immune surveillance of tumors is performed only by cytotoxic T cells and NK cells, and thus would be profoundly affected by this treatment. Although NK cell numbers would not be affected by loss of the thymus, in the absence of TH1 cell cytokines, they would not be able to increase in number in response to challenge. Other parameters that could be depressed include immune responses to intracellular pathogens and secondary antibody responses.

    Depressed oxygen-dependent killing by neutrophils (**choice B**) would not be expected in this case because neutrophils are components of the innate immune response and function in the absence of T-cell help.

    Depressed primary response to soluble antigens (**choice C**) would not be expected in this case because the IgM response to many antigens is T-cell inde-pendent. It is class switching that would be impossible without T-cell help.

    Increased cellularity of lymph node paracortical areas (**choice D**) would not be expected in this case because the paracortex of lymph nodes is a T-cell area. Therefore, following thymic irradiation, decreased cellularity of these regions would occur.

    Increased tendency toward atopy (**choice E**) would not be expected in this case because atopic allergies are those that involve IgE antibodies and mast cells. IgE cannot be produced without T-cell help, so athymic individuals will have decreased tendency toward atopy.

4.  **The correct answer is A.** The Mantoux test, or tuberculin test (or simply the TB skin test), is the classic clinical demonstration of the function of the delayed-type hypersensitivity response. This is a cell-mediated reaction caused by sensitization of TH1 cells and demonstrated by the influx and activation of macrophages in response to the cytokines that they elaborate.

    That a humoral immune response has occurred (**choice B**) is not true. Antibodies are not involved in the production of a DTH response, and they are not important products during infections with most intracellular pathogens.

    That the B-cell system is functional (**choice C**) is not true. B cells do not play a role in the DTH response, and they do not play a major role in defense during infections with most intracellular pathogens.

    That the B- and T-cell systems are functional (**choice D**) is not true. The DTH response certainly demonstrates that the TH1 response is functional, but it says nothing about the function of B cells.

    That the neutrophilic phagocyte system is functional (**choice E**) is not true. Neutrophils do not play a role in the elicitation of the DTH response. Neutrophils are the important cells in abscess formation, not granuloma formation.

5.  **The correct answer is D.** The goal of this therapy is to provide an increased pop-ulation of activated antigen-presenting cells primed with tumor cell antigens

so that these can be presented to the TH cells involved in stimulation of cell-mediated immunity. The TH1 cell is the first cell listed which would be activated by such a treatment.

B lymphocytes (**choice A**) would not be stimulated by such treatment. B lymphocytes bind to and are activated by unprocessed (not cell-bound) antigens.

Cytotoxic T lymphocytes (**choice B**) would be indirectly stimulated by this treatment. Cytokines secreted by the activated TH1 cells would have the effect of increasing the number and cytotoxic activity of killer cells.

NK cells (**choice C**) would be indirectly stimulated by this treatment. Cytokines secreted by the activated TH1 cells would have the effect of increasing the number and cytotoxic activity of killer cells.

TH2 cells (**choice E**) would be stimulated by this treatment, but this is not the major goal of such therapy. TH2 cells stimulate humoral immunity, which is not the most important protective mechanism against tumor cells.

# The Generation of Immunologic Memory

**9**

## What the COMLEX Requires You To Know

- The recirculation patterns of memory B and T lymphocytes
- The comparative attributes of the primary and secondary immune responses

As long as foreign antigen is present in the system, the activation, proliferation, and differentiation of lymphocytes into effector cells will continue in the secondary lymphoid organs. As the effector mechanisms generated are successful in destroying or causing clearance of the invader, however, the system will slowly return to its baseline quiescent state, and **immunologic memory** will be generated. This is important because it avoids expending energy on the generation of cells and molecules that are no longer needed and may be potentially harmful in the absence of the invading stimulus. It also "resets" the baseline homeostatic function of the immunologic organs so that they can efficiently respond to new and emerging challenges.

Both B- and T-lymphocyte populations will respond to a primary antigenic challenge by the production of long-lived memory cells. In B lymphocytes, this is primarily accomplished by the fact that their differentiation into plasma cells is antigen-dependent, and as that antigen disappears, the stimulus for that differentiation is removed. Plasma cells, which function only as factories for immunoglobulin synthesis, are relatively short-lived (two weeks) and as they die and are not replaced from the differentiating B-cell pool, the response wanes. Memory B lymphocytes differ from naive B cells in that they have undergone isotype switching; will bear membrane immunoglobulin of IgG, IgA, or IgE isotype; and enter a resting stage of the cell cycle.

The body's mechanism of dampening T-cell activity after the primary immune response is more active, presumably because the cytokines they produce can have harmful effects if they are generated unnecessarily. These cells no longer benefit the host and can be potentially harmful, so apoptosis is induced in all but a few, which will become quiescent in a resting stage of the cell cycle. This is called **activation-induced cell death (AICD)** and is mediated through the Fas pathway. In this way, trimerization of the Fas molecule expressed on the surface of activated T cells with the Fas ligand molecule on neighboring cells initiates a signal-transduction cascade that leads to apoptosis of the Fas-bearing cell.

Although the memory cells generated during the waning stages of the primary immune response are small and relatively quiescent, they exhibit high-level expression of adhesion molecules, which will help them to recirculate throughout the body and home to areas of new antigen introduction. In this way, a response that was initiated in a single draining lymph node will become generalized throughout the body and available to initiate a rapid and powerful secondary response if that challenge is reintroduced.

**In a Nutshell**

As pathogens are eliminated, immunologic memory is generated.

**In a Nutshell**

Memory B cells have surface IgG, IgA, or IgE.

**In a Nutshell**

AICD removes activated T cells after the primary response.

**In a Nutshell**

Memory cells home to inflamed tissues.

**Table I-9-1.** Characteristics of Naive, Effector, and Memory Lymphocytes

| | Naive Lymphocytes | Activated or Effector Lymphocytes | Memory Lymphocytes |
|---|---|---|---|
| **T lymphocytes** | | | |
| Migration | To peripheral lymph nodes | To inflamed tissues | To inflamed tissues or mucosa |
| Effector functions | None | Cytokine secretion, cytotoxicity | None |
| Cell cycling | Absent | Present | +/− |
| IL-2 receptor | Low | High | Low |
| **B lymphocytes** | | | |
| Isotype of membrane Ig | IgM and IgD | IgG, IgA, or IgE | IgG, IgA, or IgE |
| Affinity of Ig | Low | Increasing | High |
| Effector function | None | Antibody secretion | None |
| Morphology | Small, little cytoplasm | Large, more cytoplasm | Small |

## In a Nutshell

Memory cells return to the tissue where they first encountered antigen.

## Clinical Correlate

### Dissemination of Immunologic Memory

The vaccine used by the military against adenovirus types 4 and 7 is an enteric-coated, live, nonattenuated virus preparation. This vaccine produces an asymptomatic intestinal infection and thereby induces mucosal IgA memory cells. These cells then populate the mucosal immune system throughout the body. Vaccine recipients are thus protected against adenovirus acquired by aerosol, which could otherwise produce pneumonia.

The trafficking patterns of memory lymphocytes are different than those of either naive or effector lymphocytes. As discussed in Chapter 4, naive cells tend to home to regions of the secondary lymphoid organs specific for their cell type (T cells to paracortical areas, etc.). Effector cells tend to home to areas of active inflammation because of their expression of cell adhesion molecules such as LFA-1. Memory cells tend to home in a tissue-specific fashion, presumably returning to the type of tissue in which they first encountered antigen. In this way, some memory cells express adhesion molecules that direct them to a protective location along the digestive tract, whereas others express different adhesion molecules that tend to direct them to protective sites in the dermis of the skin.

When an antigen is introduced into the system a second time, the response of lymphocytes is accelerated and the result amplified over that of the primary immune response. The increased speed of response is due to the presence of the memory-cell progeny of the first response throughout the body, and the increased amplitude of effector production is due to the fact that activation and cloning now begin from a much larger pool of respondents.

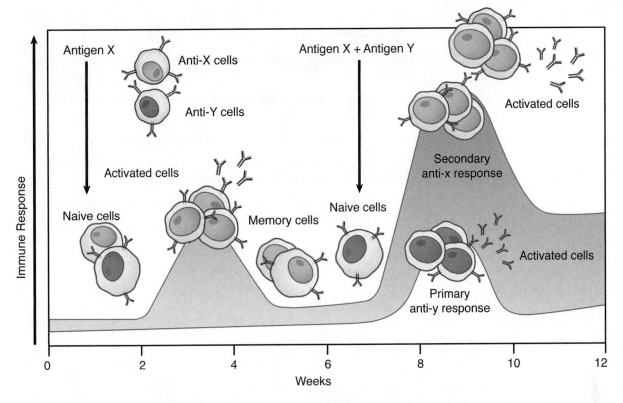

**Figure I-9-1.** The Primary and Secondary Immune Responses

**Table I-9-2.** Comparison of the Primary and Secondary Immune Responses

| Feature | Primary Response | Secondary Response |
|---|---|---|
| Time lag after immunization | 5–10 days | 1–3 days |
| Peak response | Small | Large |
| Antibody isotype | IgM, then IgG | Increasing IgG, IgA, or IgE |
| Antibody affinity | Variable to low | High (affinity maturation) |
| Inducing agent | All immunogens | **Protein** antigens |
| Immunization protocol | High dose of antigen (often with adjuvant) | Low dose of antigen (often without adjuvant) |

## Chapter Summary

- Immunologic memory is generated as pathogens are eliminated by the immune response.

- Long-lived B and T memory cells are generated and recirculate through the body in surveillance for the antigen.

- Memory B lymphocytes express IgG, IgA, or IgE molecules as antigen receptors.

- The secondary immune response is more rapid, is larger, has higher affinity, and requires less antigenic stimulation than the primary response.

- The immunoglobulins of the secondary immune response are IgG, IgA, and IgE.

# Review Questions

1. A patient is suffering from lymphadenopathy and splenomegaly. He has greatly increased numbers of lymphocytes, reduced numbers of platelets, and auto-immune anemia. When his peripheral blood leukocytes are exposed to T-cell mitogens, they proliferate wildly, even for weeks after the mitogenic stimulus is removed. Which of the following is most likely to be the genetic defect?

    (A) Absence of complement

    (B) Absence of Fas

    (C) Absence of interferon-γ

    (D) Absence of perforin

    (E) Absence of TNF

2. In a lifetime, a person may receive a dozen or more tetanus toxoid inoculations. When boosters are administered at 10-year intervals, which of the following would be true of the B lymphocytes that respond?

    (A) Their receptors would have high avidity

    (B) They would be large and highly metabolic

    (C) They would have low levels of adhesion molecules

    (D) They would have surface IgG, IgA, or IgE

    (E) They would have surface IgM

3. An immunologic laboratory is studying the migration patterns of different lymphocyte subpopulations. One population of small, nondividing lymphocytes, which are CD3+ and CD4+ and express low levels of IL-2 receptors but high levels of LFA-1, are labeled with a radioactive marker and traced as they migrate through the body. What type of cell has been labeled in this case?

    (A) A blast cell

    (B) A memory T cell

    (C) An activated T cell

    (D) A naive T cell

    (E) An effector T cell

# Answers and Explanations

1. **The correct answer is B.** This patient has Canale-Smith syndrome, a condition in which a mutant Fas protein is produced. This mutant protein competes with the normal proteins essential for the Fas-mediated death pathway. For this reason, these patients develop a progressively increasing and ultimately unsustainable number of lymphocytes of specific clones and the inability to mount any new protective response.

    Absence of complement (**choice A**) is not a condition that would result in a failure of homeostasis in immune cells. Complement is activated by invasion of foreign pathogens or by the complexes of antigen and antibody. Neither of these is believed to play a role in the dampening of specific immune responses when they are no longer necessary.

Absence of interferon-γ (**choice C**) would tend to promote immune deviation toward the TH2 arm of the immune response and promote antibody synthesis. It would not cause uncontrolled cell proliferation or an inability to remove unnecessary cells. This cytokine is a product of TH1 cells, which then inhibits the function of TH2 cells.

Absence of perforin (**choice D**) would inhibit the ability of cytotoxic T lymphocytes or NK cells to kill their specific targets. It is not a major mechanism involved in homeostasis of lymphocyte populations in the body.

Absence of tumor necrosis factor (TNF) (**choice E**) would cause decreased killing of some tumor cell targets and decreased phagocytosis. Neither TNF-α nor TNF-β is believed to be involved in the homeostasis of lymphocyte populations in the body.

2.  **The correct answer is D.** The protective response to the tetanus toxoid depends on production of antibodies that prevent the binding of the toxin. After repeated immunizations, the population of memory B cells is stimulated, which is the goal of such prophylaxis. Memory B cells may have IgG, IgA, or occasionally IgE on their surfaces serving as antigen receptors.

    That their receptors would have high avidity (**choice A**) is not true because avidity decreases with repeated booster inoculations. This is because IgM, which is the immunoglobulin of the primary immune response and is the receptor on mature naive B lymphocytes, is replaced in secondary and subsequent responses by isotype switching to other isotypes such as IgG or IgA or IgE. All of these molecules have less avidity than IgM because they have fewer combining sites than IgM. The secondary and subsequent responses should have increased affinity (goodness-of-fit of idiotype for epitope), but decreased avidity.

    That they would be large and highly metabolic (**choice B**) is not true because memory lymphocytes are usually small and in a resting phase of the cell cycle. Activated lymphocytes are large and highly metabolic.

    That they would have low levels of adhesion molecules (**choice C**) is not true because memory lymphocytes express high levels of adhesion molecules. This allows them to migrate to areas of active inflammation where they can have maximum benefit in protection of the host.

    That they would have surface IgM (**choice E**) is not true because this would describe mature, naive B lymphocytes that have not met their antigen before. As soon as the primary response begins, isotype switching to other classes of immunoglobulin is directed by TH cells.

3.  **The correct answer is B.** This is a population of memory T lymphocytes (small, nonmitotic cells rich in adhesion molecules).

    A blast cell (**choice A**) is a cell undergoing blastogenesis (rapid proliferation or cloning). These cells would be large and highly mitotic and possess high levels of adhesion molecules.

    An activated T cell (**choice C**) would be large and highly mitotic and possess high levels of adhesion molecules.

    Naive T cells (**choice D**) would be small with scant cytoplasm. They would be nonmitotic and express low levels of adhesion molecules.

    An effector T cell (**choice E**) would be large and highly mitotic and express high levels of adhesion molecules on its surface.

# Vaccination and Immunotherapy 10

## What the COMLEX Requires You To Know

- The immunologic rationales for standard vaccination protocols
- The ontogeny of the immune response in children as it relates to vaccination, diagnosis of prenatal infection, and detection of immunodeficiency diseases
- The role of adjuvants in vaccination

Immunity to infectious organisms can be achieved by **active** or **passive immunization**. The goal of passive immunization is transient protection or alleviation of an existing condition, whereas the goal of active immunization is the elicitation of protective immunity and immunologic memory. Active and passive immunization can be achieved by both **natural** and **artificial** means.

**In a Nutshell**

Immunization

- Active
- Passive
- Natural
- Artificial

**Table I-10-1.** Types of Immunity

| Type of Immunity | Acquired Through | Examples |
|---|---|---|
| Natural | Passive means | Placental IgG transport, colostrum |
| Natural | Active means | Recovery from infection |
| Artificial | Passive means | Horse antivenin against black widow spider bite, snake bite |
| | | Horse antitoxin against botulism, diphtheria |
| | | Pooled human immune globulin versus hepatitis A and B, measles, rabies, varicella zoster or tetanus |
| | | "Humanized" monoclonal antibodies versus RSV* |
| Artificial | Active means | Hepatitis B component vaccine |
| | | Diphtheria, tetanus, pertussis toxoid vaccine |
| | | *Haemophilus* capsular vaccine |
| | | Polio live or inactivated vaccine |
| | | Measles, mumps, rubella attenuated vaccine |
| | | Varicella attenuated vaccine |

*Monoclonal antibodies prepared in mice but spliced to the constant regions of human IgG

## In a Nutshell

Passive immunotherapy can cause:

- IgE production
- Type III hypersensitivity
- Anti-allotype antibodies

Passive immunotherapy may be associated with several risks:

- Introduction of antibodies from other species can generate IgE antibodies, which may cause systemic anaphylaxis (*see* Chapter 13).

- Introduction of antibodies from other species can generate IgG or IgM anti-isotype antibodies, which form complement-activating immune complexes, which can lead to type III hypersensitivity reactions (*see* Chapter 13).

- Introduction of antibodies from humans can elicit responses against minor immunoglobulin polymorphisms or **allotypes.**

Persons with selective IgA deficiency (1:700 in population, *see* Chapter 11) are at risk to develop reactions against infused IgA (a molecule they have not seen before).

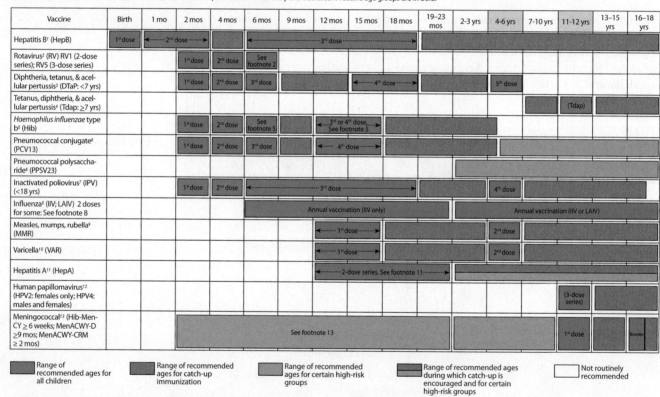

**Recommended immunization schedule for persons aged 0 through 18 years – United States, 2014.**
**(FOR THOSE WHO FALL BEHIND OR START LATE, SEE THE CATCH-UP SCHEDULE).**
These recommendations must be read with the footnotes that follow. For those who fall behind or start late, provide catch-up vaccination at the earliest opportunity as indicated by the green bars. To determine minimum intervals between doses, see the catch-up schedule. School entry and adolescent vaccine age groups are in bold.

This schedule includes recommendations in effect as of January 1, 2014. Any dose not administered at the recommended age should be administered at a subsequent visit, when indicated and feasible. The use of a combination vaccine generally is preferred over separate injections of its equivalent component vaccines. Vaccination providers should consult the relevant Advisory Committee on Immunization Practices (ACIP) statement for detailed recommendations, available online at http://www.cdc.gov/vaccines/hcp/acip-recs/index.html. Clinically significant adverse events that follow vaccination should be reported to the Vaccine Adverse Event Reporting System (VAERS) online (http://www.vaers.hhs.gov) or by telephone (800-822-7967). Suspected cases of vaccine-preventable diseases should be reported to the state or local health department. Additional information, including precautions and contraindications for vaccination, is available from CDC online (http://www.cdc.gov/vaccines/recs/vac-admin/contraindications.htm) or by telephone (800-CDC-INFO [800-232-4636]).

This schedule is approved by the Advisory Committee on Immunization Practices (http://www.cdc.gov/vaccines/acip), the American Academy of Pediatrics (http://www.aap.org), the American Academy of Family Physicians (http://www.aafp.org), and the American College of Obstetricians and Gynecologists (http://www.acog.org).

**Figure I-10-1.** Recommended Vaccination Schedule in the United States

# IMMUNOPROPHYLAXIS

Active immunization (**vaccination**) has played an important role in the reduction of morbidity and mortality from various infectious diseases, especially among children, and is currently recommended on the following schedule:

**Table I-10-2.** Summary of Bacterial Vaccines

| Organism | Vaccine | Vaccine Type |
|----------|---------|--------------|
| C. diphtheriae | **D**TaP | Toxoid |
| B. pertussis | DTa**P** | Toxoid plus filamentous hemagglutinin |
| C. tetani | D**T**aP | Toxoid |
| H. influenzae | Hib | Capsular polysaccharide and protein |
| S. pneumoniae | PCV Pediatric | 13 capsular serotypes and protein |
| | PPV Adult | 23 capsular serotypes |
| N. meningitidis | MCV-4 | 4 capsular serotypes (Y, W-135, C, A) and protein |

**Table I-10-3.** Viral Vaccines

| | Attenuated (Live) | Killed | Component |
|---|-------------------|--------|-----------|
| Can it revert to a pathogenic form? | Possibly | No | No |
| Can it cause infections in immunocompromised hosts? | Sometimes | No | No |
| Immunogenicity? | High (CMI & HMI) | Lower (HMI) | Middle |
| Special storage? | Yes; viable organisms | No | No |
| Potential for contamination with other viruses? | Yes; high | Reduced | No |

Abbreviations: CMI – cell-mediated immunity; HMI – humoral-mediated immunity

# Active Immunization—Killed Vaccines

RIP-A (Rest In Peace Always—the killed viral vaccines):

 <u>R</u>abies (killed human diploid cell vaccine)

 <u>I</u>nfluenza

 <u>P</u>olio (Salk)

 <u>A</u> Hepatitis

**Note**

- Vaccines contraindicated in pregnancy:
  – Rubella [MMR]
- Vaccines contraindicated in patients with egg allergies:
  – Influenza
  – Yellow fever

## Active Immunization—Live Viral Vaccines

All but adenovirus are attenuated

(mnemonic: Mrr. V.Z. Mapsy)

Mumps

Rotavirus

Rubella

Varicella - Zoster

Measles

Adenovirus (pathogenic [not attenuated] respiratory strains given in enteric coated capsules)

Polio (Sabin)

Small Pox

Yellow Fever

Live viral vaccines are dangerous for immunocompromised patients because even attenuated live viruses could cause significant pathology in these individuals.

**Note**

Live viral vaccines are dangerous for immunocompromised patients.

## Active Immunization—Component Vaccines

Hepatitis B

HPV (human papilloma virus)

The hepatitis B and human papilloma virus vaccines are produced by recombinant DNA technology. In the hepatitis B vaccine, the gene coding for the HBsAg is inserted into yeast cells, which then release this molecule into the culture medium. The molecule is then purified and used as the immunogen in the vaccine. The new vaccine against human papilloma virus is also a recombinant DNA vaccine which includes 4 capsid proteins (serotypes 6, 11, 16 & 18).

Many vaccinations require multiple booster inoculations in children to achieve maximal protection. Live attenuated virus vaccines are only given after 12 months of age because residual maternal antibodies would inhibit replication and the vaccine would fail. In cases where children are at exceptionally high risk for exposure to a pathogen, this rule is sometimes broken, but administration of vaccines earlier than 6 to 9 months of age is almost always associated with the need for repeated booster inoculations.

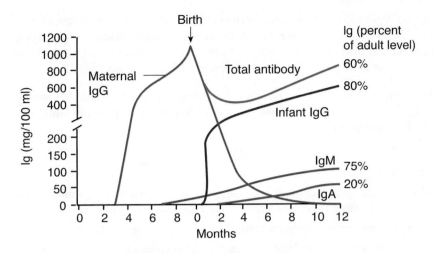

**Figure I-10-2.** Immunoglobulins in the Serum of the Fetus and Newborn Child

## Clinical Correlate

- Persistence of maternal Ab affects vaccinations.

- Infant has 20% of adult IgA at 12 months, so colostrum is important.

- IgM is the only isotype useful in diagnosing infections in neonate.

- Normal infants have few infections during first few months because of maternal IgG.

- Children with immune deficiencies don't become ill until maternal IgG is low.

One of the key factors for consideration in the design of vaccines is the arm of the immune response that needs to be stimulated to produce a protective response. Thus, although humoral responses are usually adequate to neutralize bacterial toxins or block virus or bacterial binding, if TH cells are not elicited during this process, the immune response generated will display no immunologic memory. For this reason, the pediatric vaccines for *Haemophilus influenzae* type B, *Streptococcus pneumoniae, and Neisseria meningitidis* were engineered in such a way that the capsular polysaccharide of the organism was covalently coupled to a protein carrier (either *Neisseria meningitidis* outer-membrane proteins or the diphtheria toxoid), so that T-cell recognition of the protein carrier would serve to provide the activated TH cells necessary for the generation of IgA and IgG antibodies and immunologic memory. In general, vaccines administered to children under age 5 must contain protein to achieve protective benefit.

## In a Nutshell

- Hib vaccine is a T-cell–dependent vaccine.

- Living viral vaccines elicit CMI and HMI.

- Killed viral vaccines elicit antibodies.

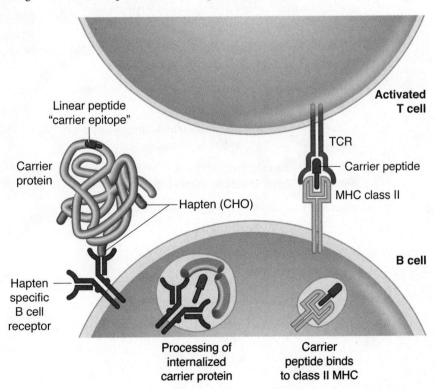

**Figure I-10-3.** Pediatric vaccines for *Haemophilus influenzae, Streptococcus pneumoniae,* and *Neisseria meningitidis* include capsular polysaccharides from the bacteria (hapten, carbohydrate) conjugated to a carrier protein.

Two other polysaccharide capsular vaccines used in older age groups, against *Streptococcus pneumoniae* and *Neisseria meningitidis*, are not administered with a protein component, but may elicit protective immunity by stimulating previously existing reactive cells formed in response to previous infection or normal flora cross-reactivities.

**As a general rule, viral vaccines that are living strains elicit both cell-mediated and humoral immunity, whereas killed viral vaccines elicit predominantly an antibody response.**

**In a Nutshell**

Hepatitis B and HPV vaccines are produced by recombinant DNA.

**In a Nutshell**

Adjuvants increase immunogenicity nonspecifically.

### Adjuvants

**Adjuvants** are substances that increase the immunogenicity of an antigen when administered with it. They may exert one or more of the following effects:

- Prolonging antigen persistence (aluminum potassium sulfate)
- Enhancing costimulatory signals (muramyl dipeptide)
- Inducing granuloma formation
- Inducing nonspecific lymphocyte proliferation (lipopolysaccharide and synthetic polyribonucleotides)

## Chapter Summary

- Active immunization occurs when an individual is exposed (naturally or artificially) to a pathogen.

- Passive immunization occurs when an individual receives preformed immune products (antibodies, cells) against a pathogen (naturally or artificially).

- Passive immunotherapy is useful in postexposure prophylaxis but runs the risk of eliciting adverse immune responses (hypersensitivity).

- Childhood vaccination protocols must take into account risk of exposure, presence of maternal antibodies, and the type of protective immune response needed.

- Only killed or component vaccines are safe for use in immunocompromised patients.

- Live viral vaccines elicit both cellular and humoral responses, whereas killed viral vaccines elicit primarily antibody responses.

- The hepatitis B and human papilloma virus vaccines are component vaccines produced by recombinant DNA technology.

- Adjuvants increase immunogenicity nonspecifically.

# Review Questions

1. A 10-year-old child was bitten by a stray dog. The child is started on a course of anti-rabies post-exposure prophylaxis, beginning with inoculation of pooled human antirabies immunoglobulin. What would repeated inoculation of this antirabies immunoglobulin preparation be likely to induce?

   (A) Anti-allotype antibodies

   (B) Anti-epitope antibodies

   (C) Anti-idiotype antibodies

   (D) Anti-isotype antibodies

   (E) Anti-rabies antibodies

2. All residents of a Chicago nursing home are inoculated intramuscularly with an H3N2 influenza A preparation. The goal of this protocol is to stimulate which of the following types of immunity?

   (A) Adaptive

   (B) Artificial active

   (C) Artificial passive

   (D) Natural active

   (E) Natural passive

3. A city sanitation worker is struck by a car and his leg is crushed against his sanitation truck. The extreme trauma to the leg necessitates amputation above the knee. Although the patient's health records reflect a tetanus booster 6 years ago, the man is revaccinated and human, pooled antitetanus immunoglobulin is injected around the macerated tissue. Administration of immunoglobulin is an example of which of the following forms of immunization?

   (A) Adaptive

   (B) Artificial active

   (C) Artificial passive

   (D) Natural active

   (E) Natural passive

4. A 28-year-old man was brought into court for nonpayment of child support. A 20-year-old woman insists that he is the father of her child. The court suggests before hearing the paternity case that various genetic tests be performed on the man, woman, and child. One of the sets of tests was for genetic immunoglobulin identification. Which immunoglobulin marker would be useful in this case?

   (A) Allotype

   (B) Idiotype

   (C) IgA2

   (D) IgM

   (E) Isotype

5. In 1988 a new childhood vaccine was developed to protect against epidemic meningitis by mixing *Haemophilus influenzae* type B capsular polysaccharide with whole, killed *Bordetella pertussis* bacteria. The function of the whole, killed bacteria in this vaccine was as a(n)

(A) carrier

(B) hapten

(A) mitogen

(D) adjuvant

(E) immunogen

## Answers and Explanations

1. **The correct answer is A.** Because rabies antitoxin is a pooled, human immunoglobulin product, repeated inoculation will cause a patient to produce anti-allotype antibodies. Allotypes are minor amino-acid sequence variations in the constant domains of heavy and light immunoglobulin chains. Their expression is genetically determined, and repeated exposure to molecules of foreign allotype can cause antibodies to be produced which recognize these sequence variations.

   Anti-epitope antibodies (**choice B**) would be produced by repeated inoculation of an immunogen. The epitope of the antigen has a three-dimensional complementarity with the idiotype of the antibody molecule. In this case, anti-epitope antibodies would be generated by rabies vaccination, but the question asks what the result of repeated exposure to immunoglobulins would be.

   Anti-idiotype antibodies (**choice C**) would be generated in a human if a monoclonal antibody preparation were repeatedly inoculated. The idiotype of an antibody is the three-dimensional shape of its antigen-combining site. It is unique to the antibodies produced by a clone of cells. Because the material mentioned in this case is a pooled human immunoglobulin, it would contain many different idiotypes and would be unlikely to elicit any one specific anti-idiotype antibody.

   Anti-isotype antibodies (**choice D**) are usually raised across species barriers. For example, to produce anti-human IgG, IgG pooled from many humans is repeatedly injected into rabbits, goats, or sheep. These animals will recognize the human determinants in the constant domains of the heavy and light chains (the isotypes) and will produce antibodies that specifically recognize those determinants.

   Anti-rabies antibodies (**choice E**) are generated during vaccination. When the killed virus is administered, the patient makes an active, artificial response to the immunogen and produces immunoglobulins, which will protect against virus attachment. In this case, anti-rabies antibodies were inoculated, so there is no possibility that more of the same will be generated.

2. **The correct answer is B.** In this case, high-risk individuals are vaccinated with the serotype of influenza virus that is predicted to be most common in this flu season. This elicits an active immunologic response in the patient and is artificial by definition because it is being administered in a medical setting. This sort of immunization causes the development of memory in the patient that will protect for the whole season, but it requires approximately two weeks for development of protection.

Adaptive (**choice A**) immunity describes all immune responses that have specificity and memory. These immune responses are produced by specific B and T lymphocytes. Although adaptive immunity will be elicited in these patients, this is not the best answer because it is imprecise.

Artificial passive (**choice C**) immunity is achieved when preformed immunologic products (immune cells or antibodies) are given to a patient. These procedures provide passive protection that is rapid but lacks immunologic memory. Because it is administered in a medical setting, it is, by definition, artificial.

Natural active (**choice D**) immunity would result following recovery from an infection.

Natural passive (**choice E**) immunity is acquired across the placenta and in the colostrum and breast milk, from mother to child. The child receives preformed antibodies (IgG across the placenta and IgA in milk) that protect the child until a natural active immune response can be mounted.

3. **The correct answer is C.** In this case, an attempt at postexposure prophylaxis against tetanus is made by inoculating antitetanus immunoglobulin into the patient. When preformed immunologic products (immune cells or antibodies) are given to a patient, the procedure provides passive protection that is rapid but lacks immunologic memory. Because it is being administered in a medical setting, it is by definition artificial.

Adaptive (**choice A**) immunity describes all immune responses that have specificity and memory. These immune responses are produced by specific B and T lymphocytes. Because this patient is being given a product of the adaptive immune response (antibodies), there will be no elicitation of an adaptive immune response in this individual.

Artificial active (**choice B**) immunity is produced during the process of vaccination. The patient is exposed to a modified pathogen or product. As a result, an active immune response to that inoculation is made. This sort of immunization causes the development of memory in the patient.

Natural active (**choice D**) immunity would result after a recovery from an infection.

Natural passive (**choice E**) immunity is acquired across the placenta and in the colostrum and breast milk, from mother to child. The child receives preformed antibodies (IgG across the placenta and IgA in milk), which serve to protect the child until a natural active immune response can be mounted.

4. **The correct answer is A.** Allotypes are minor amino-acid sequence variations in the constant domains of heavy and light immunoglobulin chains. Their expression is genetically determined, and variations can be used as evidence in favor of paternity in some cases. Allotypic markers are most frequently used in studies of population genetics, as certain ethnic groups are likely to have similar allotypic markers on their immunoglobulins. Allotypic markers do not affect the biologic function of the immunoglobulin molecule.

The term "idiotype" (**choice B**) describes the 3-dimensional shape of the antigen-combining site of an antibody or T-cell receptor molecule. Because each human is capable of producing many millions of different idiotypic sequences, these would not be useful in paternity cases.

IgA2 (**choice C**) is an isotype of immunoglobulin. Because all normal human beings produce some amount of this immunoglobulin, it would not be useful in paternity cases.

IgM (**choice D**) is an isotype of immunoglobulin. Because all normal human beings produce some amount of this immunoglobulin, it would not be useful in paternity cases.

An isotype (**choice E**) is found in the heavy- or light-chain constant domains of an immunoglobulin. Thus, there are 5 heavy-chain isotypes (A, E, G, M, and D) and two light-chain isotypes (κ and λ). Because all human beings produce heavy- and light-chain isotypes, this would not be useful in paternity testing.

5.  **The correct answer is D.** Although this vaccine is no longer in use because of the possible side effects of *Bordetella pertussis* inoculation, in this case the whole, killed bacteria served as an adjuvant. They increased local inflammation, thus calling inflammatory cells to the site and prolonging exposure to the immunogen, the capsular polysaccharide of *Haemophilus*.

    A carrier (**choice A**) is not correct because a carrier is a protein covalently coupled to a hapten to elicit a response. There is no mention in the question stem here that the polysaccharide is chemically coupled to the bacteria; it is stated that they are only mixed together.

    A hapten (**choice B**) is not correct because a hapten is a single antigenic epitope, and a whole, killed bacterium such as *Bordetella* has many epitopes.

    A mitogen (**choice C**) is not correct because mitogens are substances that cause the polyclonal activation of immune cells. The mitogens most commonly used in clinical laboratory medicine are lipopolysaccharide, concanavalin A, and pokeweed mitogen.

    An immunogen (**choice E**) is not correct because the immunogen in a vaccine is the substance to which the immune response is being made. Because the object of the Hib vaccine is to immunize against *Haemophilus influenzae*, *Bordetella pertussis* bacteria cannot be the immunogen.

# Immunodeficiency Diseases 11

## What the COMLEX Requires You To Know

The molecular defects, signs, and symptoms associated with defects of phagocytic cells, complement, and B and T cells.

If individuals experience defects in the functioning of any of the components of the immune system, clinical manifestations are common. These **immunodeficiency diseases** are favorite topics of COMLEX vignettes and are reviewed here in their totality, although many have been discussed previously in the Clinical Correlates spread throughout the chapters.

## DEFECTS OF PHAGOCYTIC CELLS

**Table I-11-1.** Defects of Phagocytic Cells

| Disease | Molecular Defect(s) | Symptoms |
|---|---|---|
| **Chronic granulomatous disease** (CGD) | Deficiency of **NADPH oxidase** (any one of 4 component proteins); failure to generate superoxide anion, other $O_2$ radicals | Recurrent infections with **catalase-positive** bacteria and fungi |
| **Leukocyte adhesion deficiency** | Absence of **CD18**—common β chain of the leukocyte integrins | Recurrent and chronic infections, fail to form pus, and do not reject umbilical cord stump |
| Chediak-Higashi syndrome | Granule structural defect | Recurrent infection with bacteria: chemotactic and degranulation defects; absent NK activity, partial **albinism** |
| Glucose-6-phosphate dehydrogenase (G6PD) deficiency | Deficiency of essential enzyme in hexose monophosphate shunt | Same as CGD, with associated **anemia** |
| Myeloperoxidase deficiency | Granule enzyme deficiency | Mild or none |
| Job's syndrome | TH1 cells cannot make IFN-γ, Neutrophils do not respond to chemotactic stimuli | Coarse facies, cold abscesses, retained primary teeth, ↑ IgE, eczema |

# DEFECTS OF HUMORAL IMMUNITY

**Table I-11-2.** Defects of Humoral Immunity

| Disease | Molecular Defect | Symptoms/ Signs | Treatment |
|---|---|---|---|
| **Bruton X-linked hypogamma-globulinemia** | Deficiency of a **tyrosine kinase** blocks B-cell maturation | Low immunoglobulin of all classes, no circulating B cells, B-cell maturation in bone marrow stopped at **pre-B stage** normal cell-mediated immunity | Monthly gamma-globulin replacement, antibiotics for infection |
| **X-linked hyper-IgM syndrome** | Deficiency of **CD40L** on activated T cells | **High serum titers of IgM without other isotypes,** normal B and T-cell numbers, susceptibility to extracellular bacteria and opportunists | Antibiotics and gammaglobulins |
| **Selective IgA deficiency** | Deficiency of IgA (most common) | Repeated **sinopulmonary and gastrointestinal** infections, ↑**atopy** | Antibiotics, not immunoglobulins |
| Common variable Immunodeficiency | Unknown | Onsets in **late teens,** early twenties; B cells present in peripheral blood, immunoglobulin levels decrease with time; ↑ autoimmunity | Antibiotics |
| Transient hypogam-maglob-ulinemia of infancy | Delayed onset of normal IgG synthesis | Detected in 5th to 6th month of life, resolves by 16–30 months; susceptibility to pyogenic bacteria | Antibiotics and in severe cases, gamma-globulin replacement |

# DEFICIENCIES OF COMPLEMENT OR ITS REGULATION

**Table I-11-3.** Deficiencies of Complement or Its Regulation

| Deficiencies in Complement Components | Deficiency | Signs/Diagnosis |
|---|---|---|
| Classic pathway | C1q, C1r, C1s, C4, C2 | Marked increase in immune complex diseases, increased infections with pyogenic bacteria |
| Both pathways | C3 | Recurrent bacterial infections, immune complex disease |
| | C5, C6, C7, C8, or C9 | Recurrent **meningococcal and gonococcal infections** |
| Deficiencies in complement regulatory proteins | C1-INH **(hereditary angio-edema)** | Overuse of C1, C4, or C2 Edema at mucosal surfaces |

# DEFECTS OF T LYMPHOCYTES AND SEVERE COMBINED IMMUNODEFICIENCIES

Although patients with defects in B lymphocytes can deal with many pathogens adequately, defects in T lymphocytes are observed globally throughout the immune system. Because of the central role of T cells in activation, proliferation, differentiation, and modulation of virtually all naturally occurring immune responses, abnormalities in these cell lines send shock waves throughout the system. It is often a Herculean clinical effort to dissect the cause-and-effect relationships in such inherited diseases, and their diagnosis is often one of trial-and-error, which takes years to unravel. Although in some cases both B- and T-lymphocyte defects may occur, the initial manifestation of these diseases is almost always infection with agents such as **fungi and viruses** that are normally destroyed by T-cell–mediated immunity. The B-cell defect, if any, is usually not detected for the first few months of life because of the passive transfer of immunoglobulins from the mother through the placenta or colostrum. The immune system is so compromised that even attenuated vaccine preparations can cause infection and disease.

**Table I-11-4.** B- and T-Cell Deficiencies

| Category | Disease | Defect | Clinical Manifestations |
|---|---|---|---|
| Selective T-cell deficiency | **DiGeorge Syndrome** | Failure of formation of **3rd and 4th pharyngeal pouches**, thymic aplasia | Facial abnormalities, hypoparathyroidism, cardiac malformations, depression of T-cell numbers, and absence of T-cell responses |
| | **MHC class I deficiency** | Failure of TAP 1 molecules to transport peptides to endoplasmic reticulum | **CD8+ T cells deficient, CD4+ T cells normal**, recurring viral infections, normal DTH, normal Ab production |
| | Bare Lymphocyte Syndrome/**MHC class II deficiency** | Failure of MHC class II expression, defects in transcription factors | T cells present and responsive to nonspecific mitogens, no GVHD, **deficient in CD4+ T cells**, hypogammaglobulinemia. Clinically observed as a severe combined immunodeficiency |
| Combined partial B- and T-cell deficiency | **Wiskott-Aldrich Syndrome** | Defect in cytoskeletal glycoprotein, X-linked | Defective responses to bacterial polysaccharides and depressed IgM, gradual **loss of humoral and cellular responses, thrombocytopenia, and eczema**<br><br>IgA and IgE may be elevated<br><br>thrombocytopenia<br>eczema ⟷ immunodeficiency |
| | **Ataxia telangiectasia** | Defect in kinase involved in the cell cycle | **Ataxia** (gait abnormalities), **telangiectasia** (capillary distortions in the eye), **deficiency of IgA and IgE** production |
| Complete functional B- and T-cell deficiency | Severe combined immunodeficiency (SCID) | Defects in common γ chain of IL-2 receptor (present in receptors for IL-4, −7, −9, −15), X-linked | Chronic diarrhea; skin, mouth, and throat lesions; opportunistic (**fungal**) infections; low levels of circulating lymphocytes; cells unresponsive to mitogens |
| | | Adenosine deaminase deficiency (results in toxic metabolic products in cells) | See above |
| | | *rag*1 or *rag*2 gene nonsense mutations | Total absence B+ T cells |

## Clinical Correlate

### MHC Class I Deficiency

A recessively inherited deficiency in the production of MHC class I molecules has been described in rare individuals. Some of these cases result from the failure of TAP molecules to transport MHC I molecules to the surface of the cell, and others are due to the production of aberrant or nonfunctional MHC I molecules themselves. These patients, as anticipated, suffer from profound deficiencies of CD8+ T cells, although numbers of CD4+ T cells are normal. This is because MHC class I expression in the thymus is essential to the development of committed CD8+ cells.

Patients are susceptible to multiple, recurrent viral infections, but interestingly, not all viral infections appear to be involved. It may be that they are able to compensate in the case of some specific viral infections, by using NK cells to control those infections, whereas other viruses require killing by CD8+ cells alone. Patients with this defect will possess a normal ability to mount CD4+ cell responses such as delayed-type hypersensitivity (DTH) and antibody production, and indeed their antibody responses may be higher than usual, presumably because of the absence of inhibitory feedback signals (IFN-γ) from CD8+ cells directed toward TH2 responses. Thus, they are not very efficient at terminating antibody responses and tend to overproduce them as a result.

## Clinical Correlate

### Bare Lymphocyte Syndrome

Rare cases of MHC class II molecule deficiency (also known as **bare lymphocyte syndrome**) inherited in an autosomal-recessive fashion have been observed in humans. Immune problems tend to appear early in infancy and present as a mild form of severe combined immunodeficiency (SCID) with increased susceptibility to pyogenic and opportunistic infections. However, these defects can be distinguished from true SCID in that these patients will have T cells that can respond to nonspecific T-cell mitogens, such as phytohemagglutinin, and also to stimuli with allogeneic cells (cells from genetically nonidentical human beings). They do not develop graft-versus-host disease when given HLA-mismatched bone marrow transplants (*see* Chapter 14) because they do not express the MHC class II molecules against which such grafted cells can react.

Patients with MHC class II deficiency are deficient in CD4+ cells due to failure of positive selection in the thymus, and they have moderate to severe hypogamma-globulinemia. This defect results from defects in the transcription factors required to coordinate their expression on the cell surface. Because MHC class I antigens are expressed normally, they do have CD8+ cells, although their function is diminished by the absence of TH1 cell cytokines.

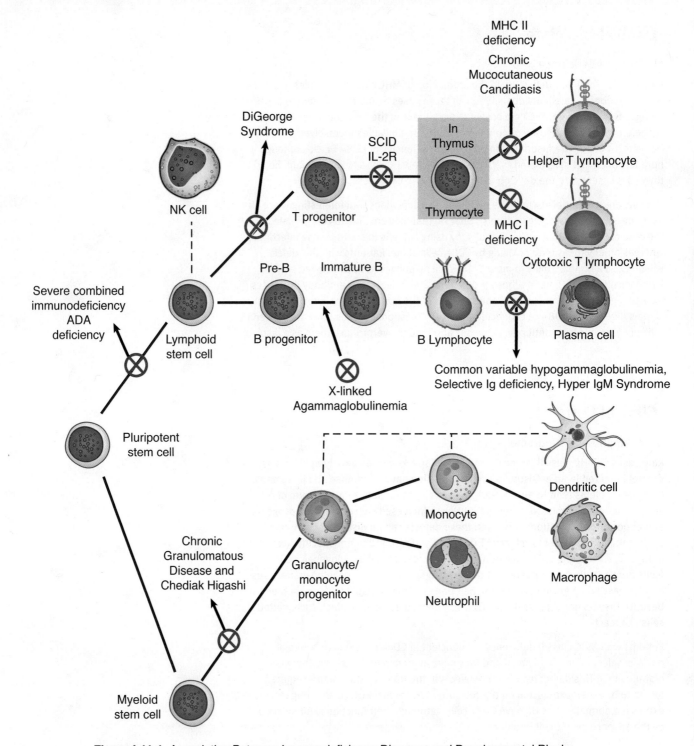

**Figure I-11-1.** Association Between Immunodeficiency Diseases and Developmental Blocks

## Chapter Summary

- B-cell, phagocyte, and complement defects predispose to infections with extra-cellular pathogens.

- T-cell defects predispose to infections with intracellular pathogens.

- Severe combined immunodeficiencies tend to manifest first as T-cell defects (especially fungal infections).

# Review Questions

1. A newborn is evaluated for immunologic function. He has a distortion of the shape of his mouth, low-set and malformed ears, and widely spaced eyes. Radiographically, there is evidence of cardiac malformation and absence of a thymic shadow. Which of the following parameters would be normal in this child?

   (A) Antibody-dependent cell-mediated cytotoxicity of parasite targets

   (B) Cellularity of splenic periarteriolar lymphoid sheaths

   (C) Cytotoxic killing of virus-infected targets

   (D) Generation of oxygen metabolites in phagocytic cells

   (E) Proliferative response to concanavalin A


2. A 14-month-old male infant is referred to a specialist for diagnosis of a potential immunologic deficiency. For the past 4 months, the child has suffered repeated episodes of bacterial infections and attempts to induce immunity using the pneumococcal vaccine have failed. Studies of peripheral blood indicate an absence of cells responsive to pokeweed mitogen. Bone marrow aspirates are remarkable for hypercellularity of pre-B cells. What is the most likely diagnosis?

   (A) Bruton agammaglobulinemia

   (B) Common variable hypogammaglobulinemia

   (C) DiGeorge syndrome

   (D) Selective immunoglobulin deficiency

   (E) Wiskott-Aldrich syndrome


3. A 31-year-old man is treated for a fourth episode of disseminated *Neisseria gonorrhoeae* infection in the last 5 years. He had no previous history of unusual or recurrent infections. If he has an immunologic defect, which of the following is most likely?

   (A) Common variable immunodeficiency

   (B) C8 deficiency

   (C) DiGeorge syndrome

   (D) Selective IgA deficiency

   (E) Severe combined immunodeficiency


4. A patient has been hospitalized 3 times for painful abdominal edema and is complaining now of swollen lips. What will laboratory findings in this patient most likely include?

   (A) Abnormal superoxide anion production by neutrophils

   (B) Abnormal T-cell function

   (C) Abnormal T-cell numbers

   (D) Defective neutrophil chemotaxis

   (E) Reduced C4 levels

5.  A 4-year-old girl presents with a severe *Staphylococcus aureus* abscess. Her history is significant for a previous infection with *Serratia marcescens*. If she has an enzyme deficiency, which of the following is most likely?

    (A) Adenosine deaminase

    (B) C1 inhibitor

    (C) Myeloperoxidase

    (D) NADPH oxidase

    (E) Superoxide dismutase

6.  A new pediatrician has just opened his office next to the hospital, and one of his first patients is a small, 4-year-old boy. His mother brings him into the office because he has several boil-like lesions on his arm. His mother told the physician that the boy has had these lesions on several different occasions. His other physician had prescribed antibiotics, and the lesions resolved. His records indicate he has had all of his immunizations. The pediatrician orders several different laboratory tests, and the following results are reported:

    | | |
    |---|---|
    | Immunoglobulin levels | normal |
    | B-cell and T-cell counts | normal |
    | Complement levels | normal |
    | Calcium and parathyroid hormone levels | normal |
    | Nitroblue tetrazolium test | negative |

    The mother told the physician that she was not aware of any eczema or bleeding problems. Which disease is indicated by these findings?

    (A) Bruton X-linked agammaglobulinemia

    (B) Chronic granulomatous disease

    (C) DiGeorge syndrome

    (D) Severe combined immunodeficiency disease

    (E) Wiskott-Aldrich syndrome

7.  An acutely ill, 2-year-old boy is hospitalized with *Staphylococcus aureus* pneumonia, which is treated appropriately. The patient's history indicates similar bouts of bacterial infections in the past. He had recovered uneventfully from measles 6 months ago. Physical examination discloses scant tonsillar tissue and no palpable lymphadenopathy. Immunoelectrophoresis reveals subnormal levels of gammaglobulins. The nitroblue tetrazolium and chemiluminescence assays indicate normal phagocytic killing. Which of the following disorders is most likely responsible for this child's condition?

    (A) Adenosine deaminase deficiency

    (B) Defect of the *Btk* gene

    (C) Defect of the *SAP* gene

    (D) Defect of the *WAS* gene

    (E) ICAM-1 deficiency

8. A 2-year-old boy suffering from repeated painful bouts of inflammation of mucosal surfaces, especially affecting the lips, is brought to the pediatrician's office. The mother remembers similar symptoms in previous generations of her family and fears a heritable tendency toward food allergy. What laboratory finding would best support the physician's suspicion?

    (A) Depressed C3

    (B) Depressed C4

    (C) Depressed C5

    (D) Elevated C1

    (E) Elevated C1, C4, and C2

9. A 10-month-old infant girl is admitted to the hospital with signs of *Pneumocystis jirovecii* pneumonia. Studies of her peripheral blood demonstrate age-normal counts of CD19+ cells, but CD3+ and CD4+ cell numbers are depressed. Immunoelectrophoresis of her serum reveals a moderate hypogammaglobulinemia. Her peripheral blood lymphocytes proliferate normally in response to phytohemagglutinin and MHC class I mismatched allogeneic cells. In a one-way mixed lymphocyte reaction using her cells as the stimulator cells, allogeneic T lymphocytes did not proliferate. Which of the following best describes the molecule most likely lacking from her lymphocytes?

    (A) It is designed to bind endogenously produced peptides

    (B) It is designed to bind exogenously processed peptides

    (C) It possesses $\beta_2$ microglobulin

    (D) It possesses two chains of unequal length

    (E) It should be present on all nucleated cells in the body

## Answers and Explanations

1. **The correct answer is D.** This is a case of DiGeorge syndrome, which is a congenital failure in the formation of the third and fourth pharyngeal pouches. As a result, individuals with this defect have aplastic thymus and parathyroids and facial, esophageal, and cardiac malformations. Immunologically, the absence of the thymus will ultimately have global effects on the development of all T-cell–mediated immune responses. At birth, the child will have IgG antibodies that have been transplacentally transferred from the mother, but by 9 months or so after birth, these will be gone and IgM will be the only isotype of immunoglobulin present. Phagocytic killing will be normal until that point, although after all the maternal IgG is gone, opsonization of bacteria will no longer be possible.

   Antibody-dependent cell-mediated cytotoxicity of parasite targets (**choice A**) will be depressed in this child because eosinophil-mediated ADCC requires IgE antibodies, and these cannot be produced without T-cell help.

   Cellularity of splenic periarteriolar lymphoid sheaths (**choice B**) will be decreased in this child because these are T-cell–dependent areas of the spleen.

   Cytotoxic killing of virus-infected targets (**choice C**) will be depressed in this child because cytotoxic T cells will be absent, and only NK cells will be available for antiviral protection.

   The proliferative response to concanavalin A (**choice E**) will be depressed in this child because concanavalin A is a T-cell mitogen. If there are no T cells, there will be no proliferation in response to this mitogen.

2. **The correct answer is A.** This is a case of X-linked agammaglobulinemia, or Bruton agammaglobulinemia. It is caused by a mutation in a tyrosine kinase gene, which is important in B-cell maturation. The bone marrow becomes hypercellular with cells that cannot progress beyond the pre-B stage, while the peripheral blood lacks mature B lymphocytes. There will be no proliferative response to B-cell mitogens (pokeweed mitogen), and CD19+ cells will be absent from the blood. Persons with this condition are unable to mount a normal antibody response; therefore, symptoms appear after the disappearance of maternal antibodies. Susceptibility to extracellular, encapsulated pathogens is profound.

   Common variable hypogammaglobulinemia (**choice B**) is a condition that usually appears in the late teens or early twenties. It is believed to be an autoimmune disease and is associated with the disappearance of immunoglobulin isotypes over time.

   DiGeorge syndrome (**choice C**), or congenital thymic aplasia, is a condition in which there is failure of formation of the third and fourth pharyngeal pouches. These infants have facial abnormalities, failure of formation of the parathyroids, and cardiac defects, as well as absence of T-lymphocyte development.

   Selective immunoglobulin deficiency (**choice D**) would not be manifested by a failure of B-cell development in the bone marrow. Selective IgA deficiency is most common of these and would manifest as increased susceptibility to mucosal-surface pathogens.

   Wiskott-Aldrich syndrome (**choice E**) is a complex immune deficiency with a triad of symptoms: eczema, thrombocytopenia, and immunodeficiency. It is inherited in an X-linked recessive fashion. These patients are prone to development of malignant lymphomas and have inability to respond to polysaccharide antigens.

3. **The correct answer is B.** Unusual frequency or severity of *Neisseria* infections should always lead to a suspicion of a terminal complement component deficiency (C5, C6, C7, or C8). *Neisseria* seem to be highly susceptible to

complement-mediated lysis, so any failure of production of the membrane attack complex predisposes the patient to recurrent bacteremias with these organisms.

Common variable immunodeficiency (**choice A**) is a condition that usually appears in the late teens or early twenties. It is believed to be an autoimmune disease and is associated with the disappearance of immunoglobulin isotypes over time.

DiGeorge syndrome (**choice C**) is a condition in which there is failure of formation of the third and fourth pharyngeal pouches. Diagnosed in infancy, these individuals have facial abnormalities, failure of formation of the parathyroids, and cardiac defects, as well as an absence of T-lymphocyte development. This condition predisposes to early viral and fungal infections.

Selective IgA deficiency (**choice D**) would be expected to result in respiratory and gastrointestinal tract infections, autoimmune disease, and allergies.

Severe combined immunodeficiency (**choice E**) typically presents with early susceptibility to viral and fungal agents. It is most frequently diagnosed in infancy, after the disappearance of maternally derived IgG antibodies.

4.  **The correct answer is E.** The description of painful abdominal edema and edema in the oral mucosa are typical of hereditary angioedema. This is a genetic deficiency of complement C1 inhibitor. When this important control protein is missing, there is excessive use of the classic complement pathway components, especially C4. This causes abnormal inflammation along the mucosal surfaces.

    Abnormal superoxide anion production by neutrophils (**choice A**) would result in predisposition to infections with extracellular pathogens.

    Abnormal T-cell function (**choice B**) would result in predisposition to infections with viral and fungal pathogens, not edema of the mucosal surfaces.

    Abnormal T-cell numbers (**choice C**) would result in predisposition to infections with viral and fungal pathogens, not edema of the mucosal surfaces.

    Defective neutrophil chemotaxis (**choice D**) would result in neutrophilia and failure to produce pus and abscesses in response to extracellular bacterial invasion.

5.  **The correct answer is D.** The infections of this child with catalase-positive bacteria are characteristic of chronic granulomatous disease (CGD). While two thirds of CGD patients are male, one third has the autosomal recessive form of NADPH oxidase deficiency and can be female.

    Adenosine deaminase deficiency (**choice A**) produces a severe combined immunodeficiency. The infections seen are likely to be the result of T-cell deficiency (viral and fungal agents). In the absence of adenosine deaminase, deoxyadenosine phosphate builds up in T cells and is toxic to them.

    C1 inhibitor (**choice B**) is not an enzyme, and its absence does not predispose to infections. It is absent in the condition known as hereditary angioedema, represented by recurrent, painful bouts of mucosal edema.

    Myeloperoxidase (**choice C**) deficiency is normally without clinical symptoms. This is an enzyme that is important in intracellular killing in phagocytes because it causes formation of toxic halide radicals. However, because oxygen radicals are more important in intracellular killing, MPO deficiency will present without symptoms.

    Superoxide dismutase (**choice E**) deficiency has not been described in leukocytes, and its absence would not be likely to predispose to infection.

6. **The correct answer is B.** The negative result on the nitroblue tetrazolium dye reduction test indicates a failure of oxygen radical generation inside phagocytic cells. It is a common diagnostic, along with the neutrophil oxidative index, to diagnose chronic granulomatous disease. This is a genetic defect in the production of a subunit of NADPH oxidase and is usually diagnosed when children develop recurrent infections with catalase-positive organisms.

Bruton X-linked agammaglobulinemia (**choice A**) is caused by a mutation in a tyrosine kinase gene, which is important in B-cell maturation. The bone marrow becomes hypercellular with cells that cannot progress beyond the pre-B stage, while the peripheral blood lacks mature B lymphocytes. Because the child in this case has normal immunoglobulin levels, this diagnosis is not possible.

DiGeorge syndrome (**choice C**) is a condition in which there is failure of formation of the third and fourth pharyngeal pouches. Children with this defect are diagnosed in infancy and would have an absence of T lymphocytes and deficiencies of calcium and parathyroid hormone.

Severe combined immunodeficiency disease (**choice D**) usually manifests first as a T-lymphocyte defect. The child would be susceptible to viral and fungal pathogens and have depressed levels of immunoglobulins, decreased counts of both B and T lymphocytes, and normal nitroblue tetrazolium dye reduction.

Wiskott-Aldrich syndrome (**choice E**) is a complex immune deficiency with a triad of symptoms: eczema, thrombocytopenia, and immunodeficiency. Because the mother in this case is not aware of any bleeding dyscrasias or eczema, this would be an unlikely diagnosis.

7. **The correct answer is B.** This is a case of X-linked agammaglobulinemia, or Bruton agammaglobulinemia. During the early 1990s, the gene responsible for this condition was cloned. The normal counterpart of the mutant gene encodes a protein tyrosine kinase (Bruton tyrosine kinase, *Btk*), which is important in B-cell signaling. When it is absent or altered, B lymphocytes are unable to progress beyond the pre-B cell stage in the bone marrow. Thus, the bone marrow becomes hypercellular, while the peripheral blood is lacking mature B lymphocytes. Persons with this condition are unable to mount a normal antibody response; therefore, symptoms appear after the disappearance of maternal antibodies, and susceptibility to extracellular, encapsulated pathogens such as *Streptococcus pneumoniae* and *Haemophilus influenzae* is profound.

Adenosine deaminase deficiency (**choice A**) is an example of a severe combined immunodeficiency disease (SCID). When this enzyme is absent, toxic metabolites build up in B and T lymphocytes and cause a general failure of the immune response. It would have clinical manifestations of both B- and T-lymphocyte defects, and not exclusively B lymphocytes, as described in this case history.

A defect of the *SAP* gene (**choice C**) is believed to cause X-linked proliferative disease, in which uncontrolled T-cell proliferation follows infection with Epstein-Barr virus. *SAP* stands for SLAM-associated protein, and SLAM (signaling lymphocytic activation molecule) is a potent T-cell coactivator.

Defect of the *WAS* gene (**choice D**) causes Wiskott-Aldrich syndrome, in which a defect in CD43 (a cytoskeletal protein) causes defects in T cells and platelets. Patients with Wiskott-Aldrich syndrome display a triad of signs: thrombocytopenia, eczema, and immunodeficiency.

ICAM-1 deficiency (**choice E**) would cause defects of antigen recognition and activation of lymphocytes. ICAM-1 is an adhesion molecule in the immunoglobulin superfamily of genes and is bound by LFA-1 integrin.

8.  **The correct answer is B.** This is a case of hereditary angioedema, caused by a deficiency in an important complement regulatory protein, C1-INH. When it is absent, the early components of the classical complement cascade are over-used. It is normally diagnosed by the finding of depressed levels of complement component C4 in the blood.

    Depressed C3 (**choice A**) would not be a correlate of C1-INH deficiency. There are separate regulatory controls on abnormal complement activation that operate at the C3 level, so this condition is rarely found.

    Depressed C5 (**choice C**) would not be a correlate of C1-INH deficiency. There are separate regulatory controls on abnormal complement activation that operate at the C5 level, so this condition is rarely found.

    Elevated C1 (**choice D**) would not be found in this case because the condition results in the overuse of early components of the classical complement cascade. Therefore, serum levels of C1, C4, and C2 would be decreased from normal values.

    Elevated C1, C4, and C2 (**choice E**) would not be found in this case because the condition results in the overuse of early components of the classical complement cascade. Therefore, serum levels of C1, C4, and C2 would be decreased from normal values.

9.  **The correct answer is B**. This child has bare lymphocyte syndrome, a rare autosomal-recessive disease in which there is absence of MHC class II molecules on cells. Thus, her cells can recognize other cells as foreign and proliferate to T-cell mitogens, but they cannot be recognized by allogeneic lymphocytes because they do not express class II MHC antigens on their surface. The phrase which best describes the MHC class II molecule on this list is that it is designed to bind exogenously processed peptides. Other descriptions that could apply would be that it has two chains of similar length, is produced with an invariant chain, and is designed to present foreign peptides to TH cells.

    It is designed to bind endogenously produced peptides (**choice A**) is a description that fits the class I MHC molecule. If this were a case of class I MHC deficiency, she would not have made a normal proliferative response to mismatched allogeneic cells.

    It possesses $\beta_2$ microglobulin (**choice C**) is a description that fits the class I MHC molecule.

    It possesses two chains of unequal length (**choice D**) is a description of the class I MHC molecule. It has an $\alpha$ chain with 3 domains, and a smaller chain, $\beta_2$ microglobulin, becomes associated with the $\alpha$ chain.

    It should be present on all nucleated cells in the body (**choice E**) describes the class I MHC molecule. Class II MHC will be found on all antigen-presenting cells in the body.

# Acquired Immunodeficiency Syndrome 12

## What the COMLEX Requires You To Know

- The receptors and coreceptors of HIV
- The immunologic results of systematic TH-cell eradication
- The mechanisms through which HIV evades the immune response

Of all the newly emerging pathogens of the past century, none so efficiently and inexorably eradicates the functioning of the immune system as the **human immunodeficiency virus** (HIV). This D-type retrovirus attaches to CD4 receptors on host cells (TH cells, macrophages, and microglia) and utilizes several chemokine receptors on these cells as coreceptors. Early in the infection, the virus uses the **CCR5 chemokine receptor** and is thus predominantly **macrophage-tropic**, whereas late in the infection, the virus uses the **CXCR4 chemokine receptor** and becomes **T cell-tropic.**

HIV infection ultimately results in impaired function of both adaptive and innate immune systems. The most prominent defects arise in cell-mediated immunity, but because TH cells and macrophages are infected and destroyed, all aspects of immunity are eventually affected.

**In a Nutshell**

- HIV infects CD4+ cells.
- CXCR4 and CCR5 chemokine receptors are coreceptors.

**Table I-12-1.** Mechanisms of Immune System Destruction by the Human Immunodeficiency Virus

| Virus Characteristic | Immunologic Result |
|---|---|
| Multiplication in activated lymphocytes and macrophages | Reproduces virus<br>Increases viral load |
| Direct cytopathic effect on lymphocytes and macrophages | Eliminates cell- and antibody-mediated immunity |
| Destruction of TH cells | Eliminates immune enhancement |
| Immune deviation toward TH2 response | Inhibits potentially protective CMI responses and produces antibodies that can mediate ADCC, resulting in further elimination of TH cells |
| *Nef* gene product downregulates class I MHC expression | Makes infected cells less susceptible to CTL killing |
| *Tat* gene product | Inhibits cytokine synthesis in both infected and uninfected cells |
| Antigenic drift of gp120 | Evades antibody-mediated effector mechanisms and exhausts individual's immune capacity |
| Heavy glycosylation of gp120 | Hides potentially protective epitopes from immune recognition |

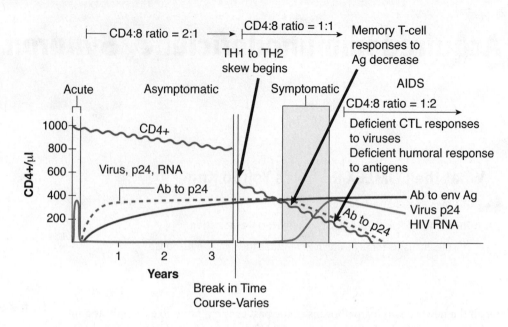

**Figure I-12-1.** The Course of Untreated HIV Infection and the Sequence of Immune Response Destruction

**In a Nutshell**

- Macrophages serve as reservoirs of infection.

- The immune response to the virus kills infected cells, but thereby eradicates all help.

**In a Nutshell**

- CCR5 mutation:
  - homozygote = immune
  - heterozygote = slows clinical course

Macrophages and dendritic cells are infected with HIV, but they are resistant to its cytopathic effects. Nevertheless, they serve as reservoirs of infection, delivering virus particles into the secondary lymphoid organs and throughout the body, and their antigen-presenting function may be impaired by the infection.

HIV-infected patients exhibit both cell-mediated and humoral responses to the pathogen, but these responses are unable to eradicate the virus, and the infection eventually overwhelms the immune response. CD8+ cytotoxic cells are generated to kill infected CD4+ cells, and antibodies are generated to many viral antigens within 6 to 9 weeks after infection. These antibodies are used as the basis of the diagnostic tests for the infection (ELISA and Western blot, *see* Chapter 15), but there is no evidence that they play a protective role in the infection. The initial, massive CD8+ response may be responsible for the control of viremia and transition into clinical latency, but ultimately, because CD4+ cells are important in amplifying the cytotoxic response as helper numbers diminish, the amplification loop for stimulation of CD8+ cytotoxicity will be eliminated.

The speed of progression to full-blown AIDS has now been linked to certain chemokine receptors and their mutations. An individual who is homozygous for a mutation to the CCR5 receptor cannot be infected with the virus. A person who is heterozygous for this mutation will exhibit a slow progression to AIDS.

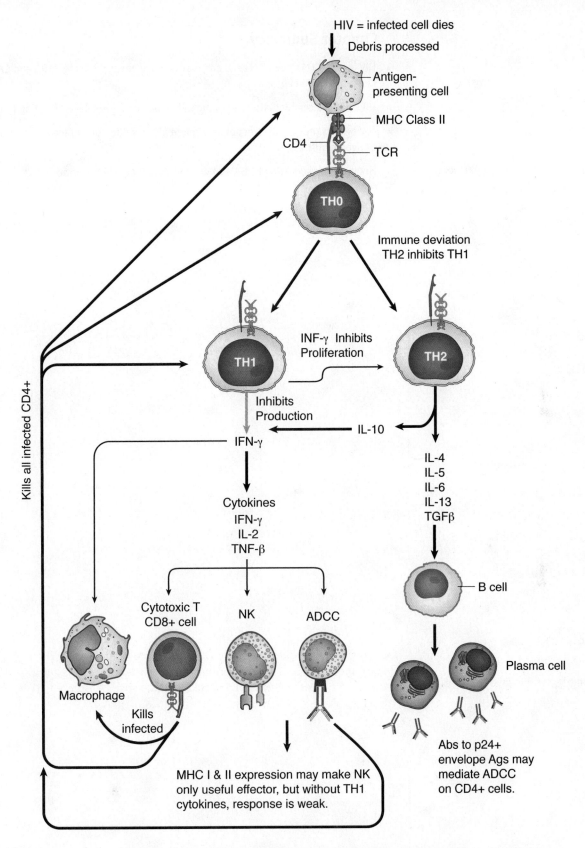

**Figure I-12-2.** The Global Effects of HIV on the Immune Response

## Chapter Summary

- HIV infects CD4+ cells (TH cells and macrophage lineages) using CCR5 and CXCR4 chemokine coreceptors.

- HIV destroys cell-mediated and humoral immune responses by eradicating TH cells.

- HIV evades the immune response through glycosylation of surface antigens and antigenic drift.

- HIV is diagnosed using ELISA and Western blot for anti-HIV antibodies.

# Review Questions

1. A 27-year-old woman who was 5 months pregnant presented for prenatal care. A routine evaluation was performed, which included testing for HIV antibody. The patient was reported to be negative for RPR but positive for HIV antibody by the EIA assay. The HIV Western blot only demonstrated the presence of an antibody to the HIV p24 antigen. How should this patient be counseled?

   (A) That she and her baby are both infected with HIV

   (B) That she is negative for HIV because the RPR is more specific

   (C) That she is positive for the HIV virus

   (D) That she should have an HIV polymerase chain reaction (PCR) test performed

   (E) That this is a confirmed false-positive HIV result

2. A neonate born to a known HIV-positive mother is evaluated for HIV status. What would be the assay of choice?

   (A) CD4 cell count

   (B) EIA for the detection of HIV antibody

   (C) Polymerase chain reaction (PCR) for the detection of HIV DNA

   (D) gp120 antigen assay

   (E) Western blot

3. The attachment of HIV to a TH cell is initiated by the binding of the HIV gp120 molecule to the CD4 receptor. Then gp120 undergoes a conformational change and binds to a second molecule. What is the second molecule on the surface of the CD4 lymphocyte that acts as a coreceptor and binds with the lymphotropic HIV?

   (A) The chemokine receptor CCR5 expressed on dendritic cells

   (B) The chemokine receptor CXCR4 expressed on T cells

   (C) The chemokine receptor CXCR5 expressed on T cells

   (D) The complement receptor CR2 (CD21) on B cells

   (E) The cytokine receptor CCR5 expressed on T cells

4. A male exotic dancer in San Francisco has been HIV-positive for 10 years. Because of his low income, he can only irregularly afford the antiretroviral drugs prescribed to him at the AIDS clinic. When he presents to the clinic for a checkup, his CD4 cell count is found to be $390/mm^3$. Which of the following immunologic parameters is likely to be most profoundly depressed at this stage of his infection?

   (A) Cell proliferation in response to pokeweed mitogen

   (B) Delayed-type hypersensitivity to *Candida* antigens

   (C) IgA production

   (D) Intracellular killing of bacteria

   (E) Rejection of allogeneic skin grafts

5. Patients with HIV infection begin to display an immunologic deviation toward TH2 responses relatively early in the course of their disease. Which of the following cytokines would be increased in a patient with a CD4 count of 500/mm$^3$?

(A) IFN-γ

(B) IL-1

(C) IL-2

(D) IL-10

(E) TNF-β

## Answers and Explanations

1. **The correct answer is D.** A patient who is HIV EIA-positive must always have the result confirmed by a confirmatory assay, e.g., HIV Western blot. The HIV Western blot is considered positive when the patient demonstrates the presence of antibody to at least 2 of 3 important HIV antigens, which are gp120, gp41, and p24. If no reaction is observed, then the patient is considered negative, but any reaction that is not consistent with a positive is reported as indeterminate. This patient is considered indeterminate. The physician can wait 6 months and retest by the EIA assay, with a reflex to the Western blot assay if the EIA result is positive. If the Western blot results are identical to the previous, then the patient is reported as negative or the patient can be tested by another confirmatory test such as the PCR assay. A negative PCR in this situation would classify this patient as negative; however, it would be wise to retest the patient in 3 to 6 months if she has risk factors.

That she and her baby are both infected with HIV (**choice A**) is not correct. Approximately 30% of the babies from untreated and <8% from treated HIV-positive mothers will be infected.

That she is negative for HIV because the RPR is more specific (**choice B**) is not correct because RPR is not a test for HIV but a test for syphilis.

That she is positive for the HIV virus (**choice C**) is not correct because her Western blot was indeterminate, and a confirmatory test (e.g., Western blot or PCR) must confirm the EIA assay before the patient can be reported positive.

That this is a confirmed false-positive HIV result (**choice E**) may eventually be proven to be correct, but with the present data one does not know if the patient has been detected in the early stages of seroconversion or is simply a patient who is false positive.

2. **The correct answer is C.** The neonate could not be tested for anti-HIV antibodies because the known HIV-positive mother passively transmits anti-HIV IgG antibodies to the baby through the placenta. All babies born to HIV-positive mothers will be anti-HIV antibody-positive. Because of the sensitivity of HIV antibody testing, an HIV antibody test on a specimen from a baby born to an HIV-positive mother should not be believed until 15 months of age. The test of choice is to detect the DNA of the virus by PCR.

CD4 cell count (**choice A**) is not correct because this assay is used to measure the progression of the disease and the destruction of the target CD4+ cells. It is not a diagnostic test for the presence of the virus or antiviral antibodies.

EIA for the detection of HIV antibody (**choice B**) is incorrect because maternal antibodies can be detected in babies who are from known HIV-positive mothers for up to 12 months after birth. The HIV EIA assay is an antibody-screening test, whereas the HIV Western blot is a confirmatory test for the presence of anti-HIV antibody.

p120 antigen assay (**choice D**) is incorrect because there is no such test as an HIV gp120 antigen assay. The ELISA (EIA) tests for p24 antibody.

Western blot (**choice E**) is incorrect because maternal antibodies can be detected in babies who are from known HIV-positive mothers for up to 12 months after birth. The HIV EIA assay is an antibody-screening test, whereas the HIV Western blot is a confirmatory test for the presence of anti-HIV antibody.

3.  **The correct answer is B.** The HIV envelope, derived from the host-cell membrane, displays viral glycoproteins gp120 and gp41. The gp120 glycoprotein has a high affinity for CD4 and is thus important in the attachment of the virus to the cell. All cells expressing CD4 are potential targets for infection with HIV. After the gp120 of the HIV binds to the CD4, it undergoes a conformational change and must then bind to a second molecule, a coreceptor, on the surface of the target cell. The variation of the gp120 molecule determines the tropism of the HIV and thus dictates which CD4+ cell can be infected. Lymphotropic HIV virions use the CXCR4 chemokine receptor (coreceptor) expressed on T cells and require a high density of CD4 on the surface of the cell. Macrophage-tropic HIV uses the CCR5 chemokine receptor and requires only a low level of CD4 expression on the target cell.

    The CCR5 chemokine receptor expressed on dendritic cells (**choice A**) is not correct. The question is addressing the infection of TH, not dendritic, cells.

    The CXCR5 chemokine receptor expressed on T cells (**choice C**) is not correct. The chemokine receptor on T cells is CXCR4, not CXCR5.

    The complement receptor CR2 (CD21) on B cells (**choice D**) is not correct. CR2 (CD21) is found on B cells and is not the coreceptor on TH cells for the attachment of HIV. CR2 is the receptor for EBV.

    The CCR5 cytokine receptor expressed on T cells (**choice E**) is not correct. Chemokines are small cytokines of relatively low molecular weight released from a variety of cells involved in inflammatory responses; however, the receptor on the T cells is CXCR4. The CCR5 is found on macrophages and dendritic cells.

4.  **The correct answer is B.** At this stage of this patient's infection, TH cell numbers are depressed to the point that TH-dependent immune responses will be depressed. Because delayed-type hypersensitivity is a purely TH1-mediated response, it will be impaired at this stage of infection.

    Cell proliferation in response to pokeweed mitogen (**choice A**) is incorrect because pokeweed mitogen is a B-cell mitogen. These responses will remain within normal limits until the end of life in an HIV-positive patient.

    IgA production (**choice C**) is not correct because these antibodies will not begin to fall until later in the infection. IgA is a TH2-dependent antibody, but at this stage of infection, there should still be B memory cells capable of mounting this response.

    Intracellular killing of bacteria (**choice D**) is mediated by phagocytic cells. Although TH1 cytokines contribute to phagocyte activation, the intracellular killing mechanisms themselves should be unaffected in this patient.

    Rejection of allogeneic skin grafts (**choice E**) is a CD8+ cell–mediated response and should not begin to be depressed until later in the course of HIV infection. Although cytotoxic T lymphocytes are stimulated by the cytokines of TH1 cells, this response should remain relatively normal at this stage of the disease.

5.  **The correct answer is D.** Most patients will begin to show immune deviation of TH responses toward the TH2 arm around 600 CD4+ cells/mm$^3$. As the TH2 response is augmented, IL-4 and IL-10 will be produced, which further inhibit

the TH1 response. Over time this leads to more and more profound skewing of the immune response toward a humoral response and more and more production of TH2 cytokines, such as IL-10 and IL-4.

Interferon-γ (**choice A**) is a product of TH1 cells that stimulates the effector cells of cell-mediated immunity and inhibits the TH2 cell. This cytokine would be decreasing in the patient at this point.

IL-1 (**choice B**) is a product of activated macrophages. Macrophages are activated by TH1 cytokines, so interferon-γ production should begin to decrease at this time.

IL-2 (**choice C**) is a product of TH0 and TH1 cells. Its levels would probably be unaffected at this point in an infection.

Tumor necrosis factor-β (**choice E**) is a product of TH1 cells that stimulates the effector cells of cell-mediated immunity. This cytokine would be decreasing in the patient at this point.

# Diseases Caused by Immune Responses: Hypersensitivity and Autoimmunity

# 13

## What the COMLEX Requires You To Know

- The immunologic mechanisms involved in the 4 types of hypersensitivity reactions
- The molecule, cell, or tissue targeted in the major autoimmune diseases

**Hypersensitivity diseases** are conditions in which tissue damage is caused by immune responses. They may result from uncontrolled or excessive responses against **foreign** antigens or from a **failure of self-tolerance**, in which case they are called **autoimmune diseases**. The two principal factors that determine the clinical and pathologic consequences of such conditions are the type of immune response elicited and the nature and location of the inciting antigen.

Hypersensitivity diseases are classified on the basis of the effector mechanism responsible for tissue injury, and 4 types are commonly recognized.

**In a Nutshell**

Hypersensitivity Diseases

- Excessive responses to foreign antigens
- Failure of self-tolerance (autoimmunity)

**Table I-13-1.** Classification of Immunologic Diseases

| Type of Hypersensitivity | Immune Mechanisms | Mechanisms of Tissue Injury |
|---|---|---|
| **Immediate (type I)** | **IgE** | **Mast cells** and their mediators |
| **Antibody-mediated (type II)** | **IgM and IgG** Abs against cell or tissue Ags | Opsonization and phagocytosis of cells; complement- and Fc receptor–mediated recruitment and activation of neutrophils and macrophages; abnormalities in cellular functions (hormone/receptor signaling) |
| **Immune complex– mediated (type III)** | **Immune complexes** of circulating Ags and IgM or IgG Abs | Complement- and Fc-receptor–mediated recruitment and activation of leukocytes |
| **Delayed-type hypersensitivity (type IV)** | **CD4+ TH1 and TH17 cells,** their cytokines, and the cells of CMI that they stimulate | **Macrophage** activation, cytokine-mediated inflammation (granuloma formation) |
| | **CD8+ CTLs** (T-cell-mediated cytolysis) | Direct target cell killing, cytokine-mediated inflammation |

## In a Nutshell

In all hypersensitivity reactions:

- First exposure sensitizes.
- Subsequent exposures damage.
- Reaction is Ag-specific

## In a Nutshell

Type I Hypersensitivity

- IgE-mediated
- Protective response to helminths
- Atopic/allergic individuals develop this response to inappropriate stimuli

What the hypersensitivity reactions have in common:

- The first exposure to the antigen "sensitizes" lymphocytes.
- Subsequent exposures elicit a damaging reaction.
- The response is specific to a particular antigen or a cross-reacting substance.

# TYPE I (IMMEDIATE) HYPERSENSITIVITIES

This is the only type of hypersensitivity mediated by IgE antibodies and mast cells. It is manifested within minutes of the reexposure to an antigen. The IgE response is the normal protective response against many metazoan parasites, which are too large to be phagocytized or killed by other cytopathic mechanisms. Twenty percent of all individuals in the United States, however, display this immune response against harmless environmental antigens, such as pet dander or pollen: We call these responses **atopic** or **allergic** responses.

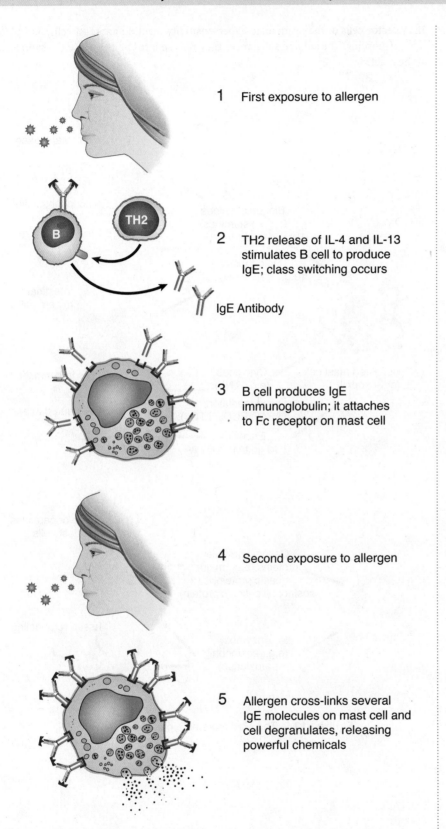

1 First exposure to allergen

2 TH2 release of IL-4 and IL-13 stimulates B cell to produce IgE; class switching occurs

IgE Antibody

3 B cell produces IgE immunoglobulin; it attaches to Fc receptor on mast cell

4 Second exposure to allergen

5 Allergen cross-links several IgE molecules on mast cell and cell degranulates, releasing powerful chemicals

**Figure I-13-1. Development of the Immediate-Hypersensitivity Reaction**

## In a Nutshell

Type I Effector Cells

- Mast cells
- Basophils
- Eosinophils

The effector cells of the immediate hypersensitivity reaction are mast cells, basophils, and eosinophils. The soluble substances they release into the site cause the symptoms of the reaction.

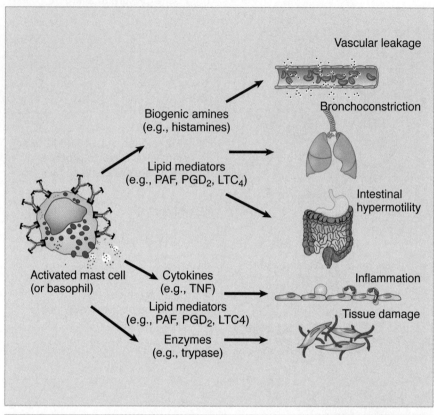

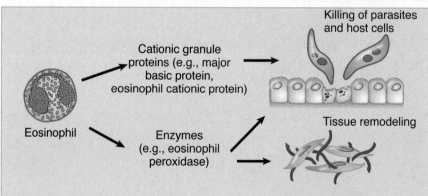

**Figure I-13-2.** The Mediators of Type I Hypersensitivity

Two to 4 hours after the immediate response to release of these mediators, a **late-phase reaction** is mediated by products of the arachidonic acid cascade.

**In a Nutshell**

Late-phase reaction—arachidonic acid cascade

**Table I-13-2.** Mast Cell Mediators

| Mediators Stored and Released | Effect |
|---|---|
| Histamine | Smooth muscle contraction; increased vascular permeability |
| Heparin | Anticoagulant |
| Eosinophil chemotactic factor A (multiple chemokines) | Chemotactic |
| **Mediators Newly Synthesized from Arachidonic Acid** | **Effect** |
| Prostaglandin $D_2$, $E_2$, $F_{2\alpha}$ | Increased smooth muscle contraction and vascular permeability |
| Leukotrienes $C_4$, $D_4$, $E_4$ (lipoxygenase pathway) | Increased smooth muscle contraction and vascular permeability |
| Leukotriene $B_4$ | Chemotactic for neutrophils |

**Table I-13-3.** Allergic Diseases Due to Specific Allergens and Their Clinical Manifestations

| Allergic Disease | Allergens | Clinical Findings |
|---|---|---|
| **Allergic rhinitis** (hay fever) | Trees, grasses, dust, cats, dogs, mites | Edema, irritation, mucus in nasal mucosa |
| **Systemic anaphylaxis** | **Insect stings, drug reactions** | Bronchial and tracheal constriction, complete vasodilation and death |
| Food allergies | Milk, eggs, fish, cereals, grains | Hives and gastrointestinal problems |
| Wheal and flare | In vivo skin testing for allergies | Local skin edema, reddening, vasodilation of vessels |
| Asthma | Inhaled materials | Bronchial and tracheal constriction, edema, mucus production, massive inflammation |

**In a Nutshell**

Type II Hypersensitivities

- Tissue-specific autoantibodies
- Opsonize or activate complement
- Recruit inflammatory cells
- Interfere with cellular function

# TYPE II (ANTIBODY-MEDIATED) HYPERSENSITIVITIES

Antibodies against cell or matrix antigens cause diseases that are **specific to the tissues** where those antigens are present and are usually not systemic. In most cases, these antibodies are **autoantibodies**, but they may be produced against a foreign antigen that is cross-reactive with self components of tissues. These antibodies can cause tissue damage by 3 main mechanisms:

- The antibodies may opsonize cells or activate the complement system.
- The antibodies may recruit neutrophils and macrophages that cause tissue damage.
- The antibodies may bind to normal cellular receptors and interfere with their function.

**Table I-13-4.** Type II Hypersensitivities

| Disease | Target Antigen | Mechanism of Pathogenesis | Clinical Manifestations |
|---|---|---|---|
| **Cytotoxic** | | | |
| **Autoimmune hemolytic anemia (HDNB)** | RBC membrane proteins (Rh, I Ags) | Opsonization, phagocytosis, and complement-mediated destruction of RBCs | Hemolysis, anemia |
| **Acute rheumatic fever** | **Streptococcal cell-wall Ag;** Ab cross-reacts with myocardial Ag | Inflammation, macrophage activation | **Myocarditis, arthritis** |
| **Goodpasture syndrome** | **Type IV collagen** in basement membranes of kidney glomeruli and lung alveoli | Complement- and Fc-receptor–mediated inflammation | **Nephritis,** lung hemorrhage, **linear Ab deposits** |
| Transfusion reaction | ABO blood glycoproteins | IgM isohemagglutinins formed naturally in response to normal bacterial flora cause opsonization + complement activation | Hemolysis |
| Autoimmune thrombocytopenic purpura | Platelet membrane proteins | Ab-mediated platelet destruction through opsonization and complement activation | Bleeding |
| **Non-cytotoxic** | | | |
| **Myasthenia gravis** | **Acetylcholine receptor** | Ab inhibits acetylcholine binding, downmodulates receptors | **Muscle weakness, paralysis** |
| **Graves disease** | **TSH receptor** | Ab-mediated stimulation of TSH receptors | **Hyperthyroidism followed by hypothyroidism** |
| Type II (insulin-resistant) diabetes | Insulin receptor | Ab inhibits binding of insulin | Hyperglycemia |
| Pernicious anemia | Intrinsic factor of gastric parietal cells | Neutralization of intrinsic factor, decreased absorption of vitamin $B_{12}$ | Abnormal erythropoiesis, anemia |

In some types of type II hypersensitivities, complement is activated and/or ADCC is active (e.g., hemolytic disease of the newborn [HDNB]). In other types of type II hypersensitivities, cell function is altered in the absence of complement activation and ADCC (e.g., myasthenia gravis and Graves disease). Eventually, as these diseases progress, complexes of antigen and antibody may cause localized damage, but these complexes **do not circulate** so the damage is localized to the specific tissue.

An important example of type II hypersensitivity is HDNB, also known as erythroblastosis fetalis. In the fetus, this disease is due to transport of IgG specific for one of the Rhesus (Rh) protein antigens (RhD) across the placenta. About 85% of people are Rh+. If a pregnant woman is Rh− and the father is Rh+, there is a chance that the fetus will also be Rh+. This situation will pose no problem in the first pregnancy, as the mother's immune system will not usually encounter fetal blood cell antigens until placental separation at the time of birth. At that time, however, Rh+ fetal red blood cells will enter the maternal circulation and stimulate a T-dependent immune response, eventually resulting in the generation of memory B cells capable of producing IgG antibody against RhD. In a subsequent pregnancy with another Rh+ fetus, this maternal IgG can be transported across the placenta, react with fetal Rh+ red cells, and activate complement, producing hemolytic disease. Hemolytic disease of the newborn can be prevented by treating the Rh− mother with RhoGAM™, a preparation of human anti-RhD antibody, at 28 weeks of gestation and again within 72 hours after birth. This antibody effectively eliminates the fetal Rh+ cells before they can generate RhD-specific memory B cells in the mother. Anti-RhD antibody should be given to any Rh− individual following any termination of pregnancy.

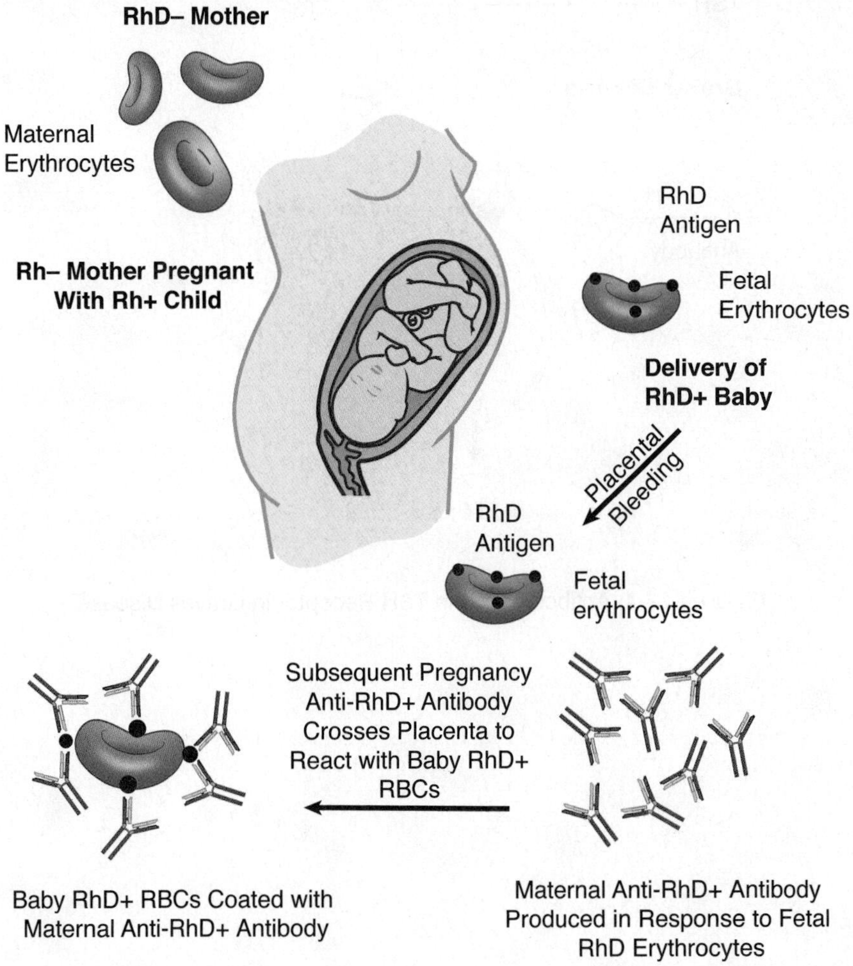

## In a Nutshell
Hemolytic Disease of the Newborn (HDNB)

- Erythroblastosis fetalis
- Anti-RhD+ IgG formed in Rh− mother carrying Rh+ child
- First pregnancy sensitizes
- Ab crosses placenta and injures subsequent fetuses
- Prevent with RhoGAM™

**RhD− Mother**

Maternal Erythrocytes

**Rh− Mother Pregnant With Rh+ Child**

RhD Antigen

Fetal Erythrocytes

**Delivery of RhD+ Baby**

Placental Bleeding

RhD Antigen

Fetal erythrocytes

Subsequent Pregnancy Anti-RhD+ Antibody Crosses Placenta to React with Baby RhD+ RBCs

Maternal Anti-RhD+ Antibody Produced in Response to Fetal RhD Erythrocytes

Baby RhD+ RBCs Coated with Maternal Anti-RhD+ Antibody

Figure I-13-3. Hemolytic Disease of the Newborn

## In a Nutshell

Graves Disease

- Anti-TSH receptor antibodies
- Hyperthyroidism early
- Hypothyroidism late

**Normal**

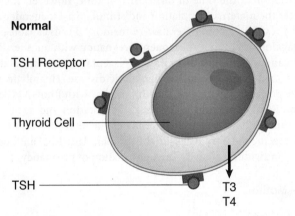

**Graves Disease**

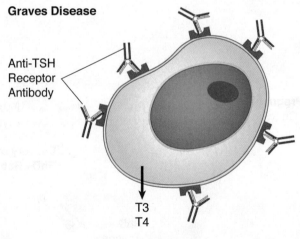

**Figure I-13-4.** Antibodies to the TSH Receptor in Graves Disease

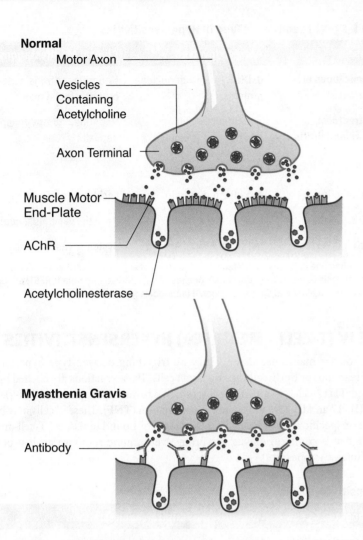

**Figure I-13-5.** Antibodies Against Acetylcholine Receptors in Myasthenia Gravis

# TYPE III (IMMUNE COMPLEX) HYPERSENSITIVITIES

The immune complexes that cause disease may either involve self or foreign antigens bound to antibodies. These immune complexes are filtered out of the circulation in the small vasculature, so their sites of ultimate damage do not reflect their sites of origin. These diseases tend to be **systemic**, with little tissue or organ specificity.

## In a Nutshell

Type III Hypersensitivities

- Systemic damage
- Immune complexes activate complement
- Self or foreign Ags

**Table I-13-5.** Examples of Type III Hypersensitivities

| Disease | Antigen Involved | Clinical Manifestations |
|---|---|---|
| **Systemic lupus erythematosus**[+] | **dsDNA,** Sm, other nucleoproteins | Nephritis, arthritis, vasculitis, **butterfly facial rash** |
| **Poststreptococcal glomerulonephritis** | Streptococcal cell wall Ags (may be "planted" in glomerular basement membrane) | Nephritis, **"lumpy-bumpy" deposits** |
| Arthus reaction | Any injected protein | Local pain and edema |
| Serum sickness | Various proteins | Arthritis, vasculitis, nephritis |
| Polyarteritis nodosa | Hepatitis B virus Ag | Systemic vasculitis |

+Other autoimmune diseases correlated with production of antinuclear antibodies include diffuse systemic sclerosis (antibodies to DNA topoisomerase 1), limited scleroderma (CREST; antibodies to centromeric proteins) and Sjögren syndrome (antibodies to ribonucleoproteins).

## In a Nutshell

Type IV Hypersensitivities

- Delayed-type (48 to 72 hours)
- CD4+ TH1 cells mediate
- Activate macrophages
- Cause inflammation
- Common in chronic intracellular infections

# TYPE IV (T-CELL–MEDIATED) HYPERSENSITIVITIES

T lymphocytes may cause tissue injury by triggering delayed-type hypersensitivity (DTH) reactions or by directly killing target cells. These reactions are elicited by CD4+ TH1 and TH17 cells, and CD8+ cells, which activate macrophages (IFN-γ), recruit PMNs (IL-17 and IL-23), and induce inflammation (TNF). These T cells may be autoreactive or specific against foreign protein antigens bound to tissues. T-cell–mediated tissue injury is common during the protective immune response against persistent intracellular microbes.

**Table I-13-6.** Examples of Type IV Hypersensitivities

| Disease | Specificity of Pathogenic T Cells | Clinical Manifestations |
|---|---|---|
| **Tuberculin test** | PPD (tuberculin & mycolic acid) | Indurated skin lesion (granuloma) |
| **Contact dermatitis** | **Nickel, poison ivy/oak catechols, hapten/carrier** | Vesicular skin lesions, pruritus, rash |
| **Hashimoto thyroiditis*** | Unknown Ag in thyroid | **Hypothyroidism** |
| **Multiple sclerosis** | Myelin Basic Protein | Progressive demyelination, blurred vision, paralysis |
| **Rheumatoid arthritis*** | Unknown Ag in joint synovium (type II collagen?) | Rheumatoid factor (IgM against Fc region of IgG), alpha-cyclic citrullinated peptide (α-CCP) antibodies, chronic arthritis, inflammation, destruction of articular cartilage and bone |
| Insulin-dependent diabetes mellitus (type I)* | Islet-cell antigens, insulin, glutamic acid decarboxylase, others | Chronic inflammation and destruction of β cells, polydipsia, polyuria, polyphagia, ketoacidosis |
| Guillain-Barré syndrome* | Peripheral nerve myelin or gangliosides | Ascending paralysis, peripheral nerve demyelination |
| Celiac disease | CD4+ cells—gliadin, CD8+ cells—HLA class I-like molecule expressed during stress | Gluten-sensitive enteropathy |
| Crohn disease | Unknown Ag, commensal bacteria? | Chronic intestinal inflammation due to TH1 and TH17 cells, obstruction |

*Diseases classified at type IV pathologies in which autoantibodies are present and used as clinical markers

**Table I-13-7.** Hypersensitivity Summary

| Type | Antibody | Complement | Effector Cells | Examples* |
|---|---|---|---|---|
| I (Immediate) | IgE | No | Basophil, mast cell | **Hay fever,** atopic dermatitis, **insect venom sensitivity, anaphylaxis** to drugs, some food allergies, allergies to animals and animal products, asthma |
| II (Cytotoxic) | IgG, IgM | Yes | PMN, macrophages, NK cells | Autoimmune or drug-induced hemolytic anemia, transfusion reactions, **HDNB,** hyperacute graft rejection, **Goodpasture disease, rheumatic fever** |
| II (Noncytotoxic) | IgG | No | None | **Myasthenia gravis, Graves disease,** type 2 diabetes mellitus |
| III (Immune complex) | IgG, IgM | Yes | PMN, macrophages | **SLE,** polyarteritis nodosa, **poststreptococcal glomerulonephritis,** Arthus reaction, serum sickness |
| IV (Delayed, DTH) | None | No | CTL, TH1, macrophages | **Tuberculin test,** tuberculosis, **MS,** leprosy, **Hashimoto thyroiditis,** poison ivy **(contact dermatitis),** acute graft rejection, **GVHD,** IDDM, **RA,** Crohn disease, celiac disease |

*Most high-yield diseases are bolded.

*Abbreviations:* HDNB, hemolytic disease of the newborn; SLE, systemic lupus erythematosus; RA, rheumatoid arthritis; GVHD, graft-versus-host disease; IDDM, insulin-dependent diabetes mellitus; MS, multiple sclerosis

# THE PATHOGENESIS OF AUTOIMMUNITY

The key factor in the development of autoimmunity is the recognition of self-antigens by autoreactive lymphocytes, which then become activated, proliferate, and differentiate to produce effector cells and cytokines that cause tissue injury. Autoimmunity must initially result from a failure of mechanisms of **self-tolerance,** as cells are "educated" in the bone marrow and thymus. Genetic factors contribute to this susceptibility, as well as environmental and hormonal triggers. Infections and tissue injury may alter the way that self-antigens are presented to lymphocytes and serve as an inciting factor in the development of disease. Because autoimmune reactions against one self-antigen may injure other tissues, exposing other potential self-antigens for recognition, autoimmune diseases tend to be chronic and progressive.

**In a Nutshell**

Autoimmunity

- Failure of self-tolerance
- Genetics (class II MHC)
- Environment (infections)
- Hormones

Among the strongest genetic associations with the development of autoimmune disease are the **class II MHC genes**.

**Table I-13-8.** Examples of HLA-Linked Immunologic Diseases

| Disease | HLA Allele |
|---|---|
| Rheumatoid arthritis | DR4 |
| Insulin-dependent diabetes mellitus | DR3/DR4 |
| Multiple sclerosis, Goodpasture's | DR2 |
| Systemic lupus erythematosus | DR2/DR3 |
| Ankylosing spondylitis, psoriasis, inflammatory bowel disease, Reiter's syndrome | B27 |
| Celiac disease | DQ2 or DQ8 |
| Graves disease | B8 |

**In a Nutshell**

Infections can trigger autoimmunity through:

- Activating bystanders
- Molecular mimicry
- Inflammatory damage

**In a Nutshell**

Therapies for immune diseases:

- Inhibit T cell proliferation
- Inhibit T cell function
- Kill T cells
- Antagonize damaging products

Infections may trigger autoimmune responses by:

- **Bystander activation**—immune responses may recruit leukocytes and increase expression of costimulators, which activate T lymphocytes that are not specific for the infectious pathogen.
- **Molecular mimicry**—antigens of a microbe cross-react with or mimic self antigens.
- **Inflammation** and associated damage may expose self antigens that are normally concealed from immune cells.

## Strategies for the Therapy of Hypersensitivity and Autoimmune Diseases

The mainstay of therapy for hypersensitivity diseases is directed at **modification of T-cell function:**

- Inhibit proliferation (cyclosporine)
- Inhibit function (corticosteroids)
- Kill T cells (cyclophosphamide)
- Antagonists to proinflammatory cytokines or costimulatory molecules (monoclonals or binding proteins)

# Clinical Correlate

Monclonal antibodies are produced by fusing antigen-specific spleen cells with myeloma cells. This causes the production of identical, monospecific antibodies because they are all produced by a single, cloned, parent cell. At present, the following monoclonal antibodies (mabs) are in clinical use:

**Table I-13-9.** Clinical Uses of Monoclonal Antibodies

| Mab | Clinical Uses |
| --- | --- |
| **Abciximab** | Antiplatelet—antagonist of IIb/IIIa receptors |
| **Infliximab** | Rheumatoid arthritis and Crohn disease—binds TNF |
| **Trastuzumab** | Breast cancer—antagonist to ERB-B2 |
| Dacliximab | Kidney transplants—blocks IL-2 receptors |
| Muromonab | Kidney transplant—blocks allograft rejection—blocks CD3 |
| Palivizumab | Respiratory syncytial virus—blocks RSV fusion protein |
| Rituximab | Non-Hodgkin lymphoma—binds CD20 |

## Chapter Summary

- There are 4 types of hypersensitivities: immediate, antibody-mediated (cytotoxic, blocking, enhancing), immune complex–mediated and T cell–mediated.

- Hypersensitivity reactions require initial sensitization, and subsequent exposures to the same or cross-reactive antigens cause the damage.

- Type I hypersensitivities (immediate) involve IgE antibodies and mast cells, show symptoms in minutes, and are mounted against harmless environmental antigens in atopic or allergic individuals.

- Initial tissue damage in immediate hypersensitivities is due to release of mast cell mediators, and late-phase reactions involve products of the arachidonic acid cascade.

- Examples of type I hypersensitivities include hay fever, asthma, food allergies, and systemic anaphylaxis.

- Type II (antibody-mediated) hypersensitivities are tissue specific and involve autoantibodies that opsonize or activate complement. Some noncytotoxic forms (myasthenia gravis, Graves disease, type II diabetes) cause interference with cellular function.

- Examples of cytotoxic type II hypersensitivities include autoimmune hemolytic anemia, hemolytic disease of the newborn, autoimmune thrombocytopenic purpura, Goodpasture syndrome, rheumatic fever, and pernicious anemia.

- Type III (immune complex) hypersensitivities cause systemic damage by activating complement wherever immune complexes of antibodies against self or foreign antigens are filtered from the circulation.

- Examples of type III hypersensitivities include systemic lupus erythematosus, polyarteritis nodosa, poststreptococcal glomerulonephritis, serum sickness, and the Arthus reaction.

- Type IV hypersensitivities are delayed-type (manifesting symptoms in 48 to 72 hours after reexposure); are caused by TH1 and TH17 cells, CD8+ cells, and macrophages; and are common results of infection with persistent intracellular microbes.

- Examples of type IV hypersensitivities include the tuberculin test, insulin-dependent diabetes mellitus, celiac disease, contact dermatitis, Guillain-Barré syndrome, RA, Crohn disease and Hashimoto thyroiditis.

- Autoimmune diseases may associate with specific class II MHC haplotypes, environmental factors, hormonal factors, or be triggered by infections.

- Therapies for immune diseases involve inhibition of proliferation or function of T cells, killing of T cells, or antagonism of the damaging products of T cells.

## Review Questions

1.  A 43-year-old woman is seen by her physician with complaints of painful, swollen joints. On examination, her hands appear to be disfigured at the joints with apparent subcutaneous nodule formation. Her left knee is grossly enlarged, and 100 mL of fluid is withdrawn from the joint capsule. An examination of this fluid should reveal which of the following?

    (A) Activated T lymphocytes

    (B) Antibodies against type IV collagen

    (C) Antibodies against double-stranded DNA

    (D) Antibodies against microsomal antigens

    (E) IgM antibodies reactive with the Fc region of IgG

2.  A 36-year-old farmer has been exposed to poison ivy on several different occasions, and he usually gets very severe skin lesions. A pharmaceutical company is developing cytokines by recombinant DNA technology and formulating them in a fashion that they are readily absorbed through the skin. Which of the following cytokines administered topically could inhibit the severity of this reaction?

    (A) γ-Interferon

    (B) IL-2

    (C) IL-3

    (D) IL-8

    (E) IL-10

3.  In the 1960s, it was quickly ascertained that Peace Corps workers sent to schistosome-endemic areas were exposed to massive initial doses of cercariae before any protective immunity existed. In these individuals, IgG antibodies developed in response to the developing worms, and when the adults began their prodigious release of eggs into the circulation, the patients suffered acute and potentially life-threatening symptoms of fever, edema, arthralgia, and rash. Which of the following is another condition that arises by a similar immunologic mechanism?

    (A) Arthus reaction

    (B) Atopic allergy

    (C) Goodpasture syndrome

    (D) Tuberculin reaction

    (E) Transfusion reaction

4. A young, newly married woman goes to her physician with concerns about a "hereditary problem" described to her by her mother that was associated with her own birth in 1968. Her family was poor, and her mother received no medical prenatal care before she was born "blue" and covered with "splotches" and "bruises." Although an earlier sibling had been born apparently normal, the patient required multiple transfusions before her condition stabilized, and two further pregnancies of her mother ended in stillbirths. The patient is concerned about the potential for development of similar problems in her own pregnancies. Blood tests ordered by the physician confirm his suspicions. How should he advise this patient?

(A) Her husband should be tested for Rh incompatibility

(B) She is RhD– and should be treated postpartum with RhoGAM™

(C) She is RhD–; there is no risk to a fetus

(D) She is RhD+ and should be treated postpartum with RhoGAM™

(E) She is RhD+; there is no risk to a fetus

5. In native Egyptian populations, children are exposed to the cercariae of the fluke *Schistosoma mansoni* in early childhood when they wade in irrigation ditches throughout the Nile Delta. On first exposure, the cercariae penetrate the skin and become schistosomula, which enter the circulation and eventually mature in the mesenteric veins. On subsequent exposures, schistosomula are frequently killed within minutes by an immune response in the skin manifested by intense itching, stinging, and urticaria. What is this protective immune response a manifestation of?

(A) Arthus reaction

(B) Contact dermatitis

(C) Passive cutaneous anaphylaxis

(D) Serum sickness

(E) Type I hypersensitivity

## Answers and Explanations

1. **The correct answer is E.** This woman has the signs of rheumatoid arthritis (RA), an autoimmune disease diagnosed by the finding of IgM antibodies against one's own IgG (rheumatoid factor). These antibodies complex with their antigen (IgG) and are filtered out of the blood in joints where they cause complement activation. RA has been recently reclassified as a type IV hypersensitivity because the disease is initiated by TH1 and TH17 cells and their mediators.

Activated T lymphocytes (**choice A**) would be found in the nodules and synovium of RA but would be less likely in the joint fluid. In multiple sclerosis, which is a T-cell–mediated autoimmune disease, activated T lymphocytes sensitized to myelin can be found in the cerebrospinal fluid.

Antibodies against type IV collagen (**choice B**) would be found in Goodpasture disease. This is an example of a type II (cytotoxic antibody) hypersensitivity. In this disease, linear deposition of IgG and complement occurs in the alveolar and glomerular basement membranes and causes destruction of the underlying tissues.

Antibodies against double-stranded DNA (**choice C**) occur in the plasma of patients with systemic lupus erythematosus. This is a type III hypersensitivity disease, so immune complexes and complement play a role in pathogenesis, but patients with lupus have a characteristic facial rash, and symptoms would have their onset between 20 and 40 years of age. Although SLE can be associated with arthritis, it is not generally disfiguring as described here.

Antibodies against microsomal antigens (**choice D**) and thyroglobulin would be found in Hashimoto thyroiditis. In addition, T cells sensitized to thyroid antigens are found, so this disease is generally categorized as a type IV (delayed-type) hypersensitivity response. The age group and sex of the patient are correct for this diagnosis, but the symptoms would include hypothyroidism, not joint inflammation.

2. **The correct answer is E.** IL-10 is produced by TH2 cells and inhibits TH1 cells. Because the response to poison ivy is a delayed-type hypersensitivity response and therefore is mediated by TH1 cells and macrophages, inhibiting their activity would minimize the severity of the reaction.

γ-Interferon (**choice A**) is a product of TH1 cells, CTLs, and NK cells. It inhibits the proliferation of TH2 cells and therefore would skew the immune response toward a more potent cell-mediated arm. This is not a cytokine that would help this patient: It would make his condition worse.

IL-2 (**choice B**) is a product of TH cells that induces the proliferation and enhances the activity of antigen-primed TH cells and CTLs. It would tend to increase the symptoms of this patient, not ameliorate them.

IL-3 (**choice C**) is a product of TH cells and NK cells. It acts on hematopoietic cells to encourage myeloid cell development. It would neither hinder nor help this man's condition.

IL-8 (**choice D**) is a product of macrophages and endothelial cells and acts on neutrophils to attract them to areas of inflammation. It would increase inflammation in the area.

3. **The correct answer is A.** The condition described here is an immune complex–mediated pathology. When large amounts of antigen are added into a situation where there is pre-existence of a large amount of antibody, the precipitation of those complexes in the small vasculature causes a type III hypersensitivity response. The only syndrome on this list that also has a type III etiology is the Arthus reaction.

Atopic allergy (**choice B**) is a type I hypersensitivity, mediated by IgE antibodies and mast cells. Although many parasitic diseases elicit IgE and ADCC by eosinophils, the question stem clearly stipulates the presence of IgG antibodies, so a type I hypersensitivity reaction is ruled out.

Goodpasture syndrome (**choice C**) and transfusion reaction (**choice E**) are examples of a type II, cytotoxic antibody hypersensitivity response. In these cases, antibody binds to cells or tissues of the body and elicits complement activation in those locations. The result is a tissue- or organ-specific pathology, and not a systemic problem as described here.

The tuberculin reaction (**choice D**) is a type IV hypersensitivity response. Delayed-type hypersensitivities are mediated by TH1 and TH17 cells and their mediators and have no contribution whatsoever from antibodies.

4. **The correct answer is E.** From the description, this patient was born with hemolytic disease of the newborn, or erythroblastosis fetalis. This occurs when an Rh– woman becomes pregnant with an Rh+ fetus. During a first pregnancy

(the patient's older sibling), no problems are encountered, but the mother is sensitized against the RhD antigens. In all subsequent pregnancies, anti-Rh IgG antibodies from the mother can cross the placenta and cause hemolysis of the child's RBCs. This means that the patient is RhD+. It is irrelevant what the Rh type of any fetus she would carry is: She will make no immunologic response.

That her husband should be tested for Rh incompatibility (**choice A**) is not correct because the patient is Rh+. She will not recognize any Rh product as foreign.

That she is RhD– and should be treated postpartum with RhoGAM™ (**choice B**) is not true because she is RhD+. Women who are RhD– should be treated with RhoGAM (IgG anti-Rh antibodies) during and following the termination of any pregnancy.

That she is RhD–; there is no risk to a fetus (**choice C**) is not true because she is RhD+. Women who are RhD– should be treated with RhoGAM (IgG anti-Rh antibodies) during and following the termination of any pregnancy.

That she is RhD+ and should be treated postpartum with RhoGAM (**choice D**) is not true because there is no need to treat RhD+ women in any way following termination of pregnancies.

5.  **The correct answer is E.** The description in the vignette is a type I hypersensitivity reaction—the only type of hypersensitivity that can be manifested in minutes. These are IgE-mediated responses and are an important protective response against helminth parasites that migrate through the tissues.

    The Arthus reaction (**choice A**) is an example of a type III (immune complex–mediated) pathology. These hypersensitivities develop when antigen is added to pre-existing antibody and immune complexes are filtered out of the circulation in the small vasculature. Complement is activated in these locations, and the underlying tissue is damaged. In this vignette, the killing is occurring in the skin and is associated within minutes with stinging, itching, and urticaria.

    Contact dermatitis (**choice B**) is an example of a type IV (delayed-type) hypersensitivity response. After the sensitizing exposure, symptoms of this type of hypersensitivity will occur in 48 to 72 hours (not minutes, as described here).

    Passive cutaneous anaphylaxis (**choice C**) is an example of a type I hypersensitivity reaction, but it is used to diagnose these conditions using passive transfer of serum. It is not a mechanism of protection, but a diagnostic technique.

    Serum sickness (**choice D**) is an example of a type III (immune complex-mediated) pathology. These hypersensitivities develop when antigen is added to pre-existing antibody and immune complexes are filtered out of the circulation in the small vasculature. Complement is activated in these locations, and the underlying tissue is damaged. In this vignette, the killing is occurring in the skin and is associated within minutes with stinging, itching, and urticaria.

# Transplantation Immunology 14

## What the COMLEX Requires You To Know

- The different types of tissue transplantation performed in medicine
- The mechanisms and timing of graft rejection phenomena
- The pathogenesis of graft-versus-host disease
- The techniques for tissue compatibility testing
- The therapeutic strategies to inhibit graft rejection

## DEFINITIONS

**Transplantation** is the process of taking cells, tissues, or organs (a **graft**) from one individual (the **donor**) and implanting them into another individual or another site in the same individual (the **host** or **recipient**). **Transfusion** is a special case of transplantation and the most frequently practiced today, in which circulating blood cells or plasma are infused from one individual into another. As we have seen in previous chapters, the immune system is elaborately evolved to recognize minor differences in self antigens that reflect the invasion of harmful microbes or pathologic processes, such as cancer. Unfortunately, it is this same powerful mechanism of self-protection that thwarts tissue transplantation because tissues derived from other individuals are recognized as **"altered-self"** by the educated cells of the host's immune system.

Several different types of grafts are used in medicine:

- Autologous grafts (or **autografts**) are those where tissue is moved from one location to another in the same individual (skin grafting in burns or coronary artery replacement with saphenous veins).
- **Isografts (or syngeneic grafts)** are those transplanted between genetically identical individuals (monozygotic twins).
- **Allogeneic** grafts are those transplanted between genetically different members of the same species (kidney transplant).
- **Xenogeneic** grafts are those transplanted between members of different species (pig heart valves into human).

## MECHANISMS OF GRAFT REJECTION

The recognition of transplanted cells as self or foreign is determined by the extremely polymorphic genes of the major histocompatibility complex, which are expressed in a **codominant** fashion. This means that each individual inherits a complete set or **haplotype** from each parent and virtually assures that two genetically unrelated individuals will have distinctive differences in the antigens expressed on their cells. The

**In a Nutshell**

Transplantation

- Tissues taken from donor given to host
- Transfusion most common

**In a Nutshell**

Types of Grafts

- Autografts
- Isografts
- Allogeneic grafts
- Xenogeneic grafts

**Note**

MHC alleles are expressed codominantly.

**In a Nutshell**

Graft Rejection Effectors

- CTLs
- Macrophages
- Antibody

**In a Nutshell**

Graft Rejection

- Hyperacute
- Accelerated
- Acute
- Chronic

net result is that all grafts except autografts are ultimately identified as foreign invading proteins and destroyed by the process of **graft rejection**. Even syngeneic grafts between identical twins can express recognizable antigenic differences due to somatic mutations that occur during the development of the individual. For this reason, all grafts except autografts must be followed by some degree of lifelong immunosuppression of the host to attempt to avoid rejection reactions.

The time sequence of allograft rejection differs depending on the tissue involved but always displays specificity and memory. As the graft becomes vascularized, CD4+ and CD8+ cells that migrate into the graft from the host become sensitized and proliferate in response to both major and minor histocompatibility differences. In the **effector phase** of the rejection, TH cytokines play a critical role in stimulating macrophage, cytotoxic T cell, and even antibody-mediated killing. Interferons and TNF-$\alpha$ and -$\beta$ all increase the expression of class I MHC molecules in the graft, and IFN-$\gamma$ increases the expression of class II MHC as well, increasing the susceptibility of cells in the graft to MHC-restricted killing.

Four different classes of allograft rejection phenomena are classified according to their time of activation and the type of effector mechanism that predominates.

**Table I-14-1.** Type and Tempo of Rejection Reactions

| Type of Rejection | Time Taken | Mechanism & Pathogenesis |
|---|---|---|
| **Hyperacute rejection** | Minutes to hours | Endothelial cell / Blood vessel / Alloantigen (e.g., blood group antigen) / Circulating alloantigen specific antibody (pre-formed) — Complement activation, endothelial damage, inflammation and thrombosis |
| Acute rejection | Days to weeks | Parenchymal cells / Alloreactive antibody / Endothelial cell — Parenchymal cell damage, interstitial inflammation; Endothelialitis |
| Accelerated acute rejection | Days | As above, but mediated by memory cell responses |
| Chronic rejection | Months to years | Macrophage / Vascular smooth muscle cell / Cytokines / Alloantigen-specific CD4+ T cell — Causes unclear: Chronic DTH reaction in vessel wall, intimal smooth muscle cell proliferation, vessel occlusion |

## In a Nutshell

Graft-Versus-Host Disease

● Bone marrow transplant

● Grafted T cells attack host

● Rash, jaundice, diarrhea, gastrointestinal hemorrhage

A special case of tissue transplantation occurs when the grafted tissue is bone marrow. Because the bone marrow is the source of pluripotent hematopoietic stem cells, it can be used to reconstitute myeloid, erythroid, and lymphoid cells in a recipient who has lost these cells as a result of malignancy or chemotherapeutic regimens. Because the bone marrow is a source of some mature T lymphocytes, it is necessary to remove these cells before transplantation to avoid the appearance of **graft-versus-host disease** in the recipient. In this special case of rejection, any mature T cells remaining in the bone marrow inoculum can attack allogeneic MHC-bearing cells of the recipient and cause widespread epithelial cell death accompanied by rash, jaundice, diarrhea, and gastrointestinal hemorrhage.

## TESTING FOR TISSUE COMPATIBILITY

Several clinical laboratory tests are used to reduce the risk of immunologic rejection during transplantation. These include ABO blood typing, HLA matching (tissue typing), screening for preformed antibodies, and crossmatching.

## In a Nutshell

Tissue Compatibility Testing

● ABO blood typing

● Cross matching

● Mixed lymphocyte reaction (class II)

● Microcytotoxicity test (class I)

ABO blood typing is a uniform first step in all tissue transplantation because ABO incompatibilities will cause hyperacute graft rejection in the host. The ABO blood group antigens are a group of glycoprotein molecules expressed on the surface of erythrocytes and endothelial cells. Natural isohemagglutinins (IgM antibodies that will agglutinate the glycoprotein molecules on the red blood cells of nonidentical individuals) are apparently produced in response to similar molecules expressed on the intestinal normal flora. A person is protected (by self-tolerance) from producing antibodies that would agglutinate his own red blood cells, but will produce those agglutinins that will react with the red cells from other individuals.

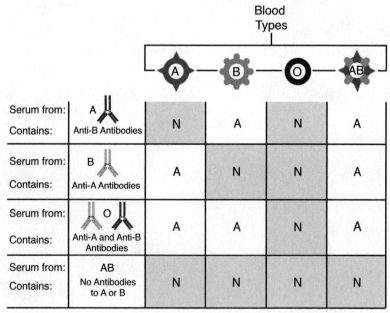

Figure I-14-1. Agglutination Test for Blood Typing

In cases where a living donor may be used for tissue transplantation (kidney and bone-marrow transplants), **tissue typing** to match the HLA antigens of recipient and donor is the next step. In general, the larger the number of matched MHC alleles between donor and recipient, the better the graft survival. In heart, lung, and liver transplantation, this step is often not considered because recipients are often in critical condition, and these organs cannot be stored indefinitely while tests are performed. Routine HLA typing focuses only on **HLA-A, HLA-B, and HLA-DR** because these are the only loci that appear to predict the likelihood of rejection of the transplant.

Two different laboratory techniques may be used to identify the histocompatibility antigens of donor and recipient. To identify class I antigens, a microcytotoxicity test using antisera against specific class I antigens is performed. In this test, lymphocytes from the donor or recipient are mixed with different antisera. If the antibodies recognize their specific epitope on the cells, they will be bound there, and addition of complement will result in cell lysis. The lysis of cells is monitored by adding a dye that will penetrate cells whose membranes have become leaky from the actions of complement.

### In a Nutshell

Routine HLA Typing

- HLA-A
- HLA-B
- HLA-DR

### In a Nutshell

Class I compatibility testing— microcytotoxicity test

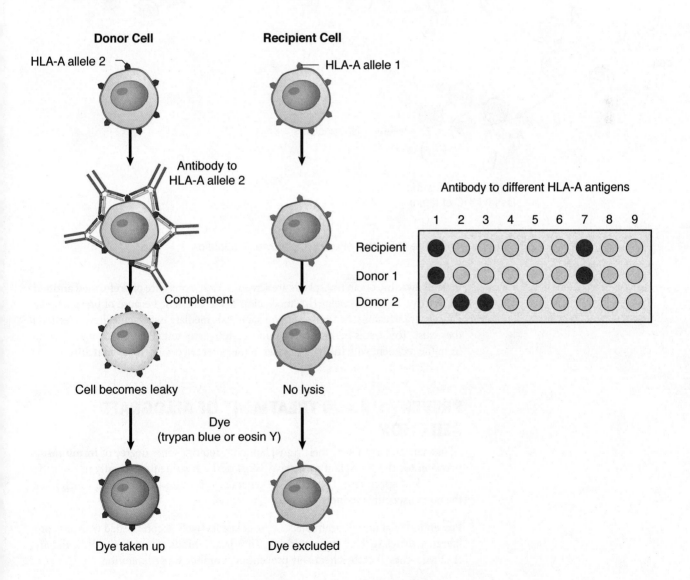

**Figure I-14-2. Microcytotoxicity Assay**

**In a Nutshell**

Class II compatibility testing— mixed lymphocyte reaction

To identify **class II antigens**, a microcytotoxicity test (*see* Figure I-14-2) or the **mixed lymphocyte reaction** (MLR) may be performed. In the MLR, lymphocytes from one individual being tested are irradiated so that they cannot proliferate, but will act as **stimulator cells** for the presentation of MHC antigens. The other individual's cells are added to the culture, and uptake of tritiated thymidine is used as an indicator of cell proliferation. If the MHC class II antigens are different, proliferation will occur. If they are the same, no proliferation will occur.

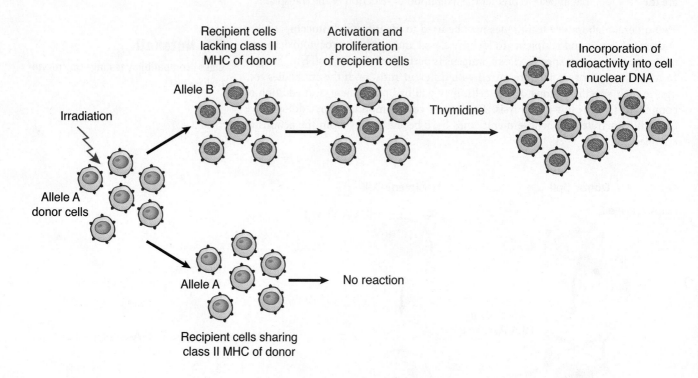

**Figure I-14-3. The One-Way Mixed Lymphocyte Response**

Patients awaiting organ transplants are screened for the presence of **preformed antibodies** reactive with allogeneic HLA molecules. These can arise because of previous pregnancies, transfusions, or transplantations and can mediate hyperacute graft rejection if they exist. This test is performed as a microcytotoxicity test (Fig I-14-2) mixing serum from the recipient with the lymphocytes of the potential donor (**cross-matching**).

## PREVENTION AND TREATMENT OF ALLOGRAFT REJECTION

Allogeneic and even syngeneic transplantation require some degree of **immunosuppression** for the transplant to survive. Most of the treatments currently in use suffer from lack of specificity: They result in generalized immunosuppression, which leaves the host susceptible to increased risk of infection.

Prevention of acute allograft rejection is most effectively accomplished with anti-proliferative drugs such as **cyclosporin A**. This drug inhibits expression of IL-2 and also IL-2 receptors, thereby effectively preventing lymphocyte proliferation.

## Chapter Summary

- In transplantation, tissues are taken from a donor and given to a host or recipient.

- Autografts are grafts transplanted from one location to another in the same individual.

- Isografts are grafts transplanted between monozygotic twins.

- Allogeneic grafts are grafts transplanted between nonidentical members of the same species.

- Xenogeneic grafts are grafts transplanted from one species to another.

- During graft rejection, MHC allele products are recognized as foreign by CTLs, macrophages, and antibodies, and the graft is destroyed.

- Graft rejection is hyperacute when preformed antidonor antibodies and complement destroy the graft in minutes to hours.

- Graft rejection is accelerated when sensitized T cells are reactivated to destroy the graft in days.

- Graft rejection is acute when T cells are activated for the first time and destroy the graft in days to weeks.

- Graft rejection is chronic when antibodies, immune complexes, or cytotoxic cells destroy the graft in months to years.

- Graft-versus-host disease occurs when mature T cells inside bone marrow transplants become activated against the MHC products of the graft recipient.

- Tissue compatibility testing involves ABO blood typing, cross-matching, the mixed lymphocyte reaction (for class II compatibility), and the microcytotoxicity test (for class I compatibility).

- Immunosuppression is required to ensure the survival of all grafts, except autografts.

- The goal of immunosuppression is to block cell proliferation.

## Review Questions

1. A 42-year-old auto mechanic has been diagnosed with end-stage renal disease. His twin brother is HLA identical at all MHC loci and volunteers to donate a kidney to his brother. What type of graft transplant terminology is correct in this situation?

   (A) Allograft

   (B) Autograft

   (C) Heterograft

   (D) Isograft

   (E) Xenograft

2. A patient with acute myelogenous leukemia (AML) undergoes irradiation and chemotherapy for his malignancy while awaiting bone marrow transplantation from a closely matched sibling. Six months after the transplant, the immune response appears to be reconstituting itself well—until 9 months postinfusion, when symptoms of generalized rash with desquamation, jaundice, and bloody diarrhea begin to appear. A second, more closely matched bone marrow donor is sought unsuccessfully, and 10 months after the transfer, the patient dies. What is the immunologic effector mechanism most closely associated with this rejection reaction?

   (A) Activated macrophages

   (B) Antibodies and complement

   (C) CD8+ lymphocytes

   (D) LAK cells

   (E) NK cells

3. A 45-year-old welder develops a severe corneal ulcer, which requires treatment with corneal transplantation. A suitable cadaver cornea is available and is successfully engrafted. What is the appropriate postsurgical treatment for this patient?

   (A) Corticosteroids, such as prednisone, for life

   (B) Fungal metabolites, such as cyclosporin A, for life

   (C) Mitotic inhibitors, such as cyclophosphamide, for life

   (D) Monoclonal anti–IL-2 receptor for life

   (E) No treatment required

4. A child who requires a kidney transplant has been offered a kidney by both parents and 3 siblings. A one-way mixed lymphocyte reaction between prospective donors and recipient is performed, and the stimulation indices are shown. The stimulation index is the ratio of proliferation (measured by $[^3H]$-thymidine incorporation) of the experimental group versus the negative control group. Which of the prospective donors would be the best choice?

| Responder Cells | Irradiated Stimulator Cells | | | | | |
|---|---|---|---|---|---|---|
| | Recipient | Father | Mother | Sibling 1 | Sibling 2 | Sibling 3 |
| Recipient | 1.0 | 4.1 | 2.3 | 1.1 | 8.3 | 8.5 |
| Father | 5.3 | 1.0 | 12.3 | 5.6 | 4.9 | 5.9 |
| Mother | 3.2 | 12.6 | 1.0 | 4.5 | 3.9 | 4.8 |
| Sibling 1 | 1.6 | 6.5 | 5.5 | 1.0 | 4.4 | 6.0 |
| Sibling 2 | 7.6 | 5.9 | 4.9 | 4.4 | 1.0 | 7.8 |
| Sibling 3 | 9.0 | 5.7 | 4.4 | 7.0 | 8.9 | 1.0 |

(A) Father

(B) Mother

(C) Sibling 1

(D) Sibling 2

(E) Sibling 3

5. In heart–lung transplantation, where the critical illness of the transplant recipient and the inability to preserve tissues from brain-dead donors often precludes tissue typing prior to transplantation surgery, a variety of experimental immunosuppressive protocols are under study. In one such experimental protocol, patients are treated with anti-CD28 antibody Fab fragments at the time of transplantation and at monthly intervals thereafter. What would be the goal of such therapy?

(A) To destroy T cells

(B) To induce anergy to transplanted tissues

(C) To inhibit mitosis in B cells

(D) To inhibit mitosis in T cells

(E) To stop inflammation

6. A 6-year-old child from Zimbabwe is admitted to a U.S. oncology center for treatment of an advanced case of Burkitt lymphoma. Analysis of the malignant cells reveals that they are lacking MHC class I antigens on their surface. Which of the following cytokines produced by recombinant DNA technology could be injected into his solid tumor to increase this tumor cell's susceptibility to CD8+-mediated killing?

(A) IFN-γ

(B) IL-1

(C) IL-2

(D) IL-10

(E) TNF-α

## Answers and Explanations

1. **The correct answer is D.** An isograft is performed between genetically identical individuals. In human medicine, these are performed between monozygotic twins. In reality, even these "identical" individuals are not identical because minor mutations can occur during development. These sorts of grafts still require immunosuppression for success. They are, however, the best chance for success other than autografts.

   An allograft (**choice A**) is a transplant between two members of the same species who are not genetically identical. These are the most common types of transplants used in medicine, but in this vignette, the twins are described as having identical MHC haplotypes.

   An autograft (**choice B**) is a transplant from one location in the body to another. This is the only form of transplantation that will succeed without immunosuppression.

   "Heterograft" (**choice C**) is not a word that is used in transplantation immunology.

   A xenograft (**choice E**) is a transplant that is performed across species barriers.

2. **The correct answer is C.** Graft-versus-host disease (GVHD) is primarily a manifestation of sensitization of transplanted T cells against recipient tissues. The killing of mucosal and other epithelial cells is largely mediated through recognition of MHC class I incompatibility by transferred cytotoxic cells or their precursors. However, eventually, continuous priming by the host's own tissues will elicit immune responses at the level of all the cells of the immune system.

   Activated macrophages (**choice A**) are involved in the delayed-type hypersensitivity response, but are not stimulated by MHC incompatibility, so if they become involved in pathology, it has to be secondary to TH stimulation.

   Antibodies and complement (**choice B**) are not involved in GVHD. Because bone marrow is a cellular transplant, it is the cells inside it that start the problem, not accidentally transferred antibodies or complement.

   LAK (lymphokine-activated killer) cells (**choice D**) are believed to be involved in the rejection of bone marrow transplants by the recipient (host-versus-graft), but not in GVHD.

   NK cells (**choice E**) are believed to be involved in the rejection of bone marrow transplants by the recipient (host-versus-graft), but not in GVHD.

3.  **The correct answer is E.** Because the eye is an immunoprivileged site, corneal transplantation is unique amongst allogeneic transplantation techniques practiced in human medicine in that it does not require immunosuppression. Other immunoprivileged sites in the human include the uterus, the testes, the brain, and the thymus. What these sites have in common is that they do not possess lymphatic vessels. For this reason, the alloantigens of the graft are not able to sensitize the recipient's lymphocytes, and the graft has an increased likelihood of acceptance.

    Corticosteroids, such as prednisone, for life (**choice A**) are required for most types of transplantation. Corticosteroids act as broad-spectrum antiinflammatories, which are particularly important in treatment of episodes of acute graft rejection.

    Fungal metabolites, such as cyclosporin A, for life (**choice B**) would be necessary for most types of transplantation. These agents act by blocking proliferation of TH cells and production of their cytokines.

    Mitotic inhibitors, such as cyclophosphamide, for life (**choice C**) would be necessary for most types of transplantation. These agents act by blocking proliferation of cells.

    Monoclonal anti–IL-2 receptor for life (**choice D**) is an experimental protocol that would inhibit T-cell proliferation. It would not be necessary in the case of corneal transplantation.

4.  **The correct answer is C.** The lowest stimulation index (and the lowest amount of proliferation) is shown between sibling 1 and the prospective recipient, both when the donor cells are used as stimulators and as responders. This means (most importantly) that the recipient will make little response to the graft and (less importantly, except in graft-versus-host disease) that the donor will make little response against the recipient.

    The father (**choice A**) is not the best choice of donors because the recipient makes 4 times the proliferative response to his cells as to those of sibling 1.

    The mother (**choice B**) is not the best choice of donors because the recipient makes twice the proliferative response to her cells as to those of sibling 1. She would be the second-best choice, unless sibling 1 had an incompatible ABO blood group.

    Sibling 2 (**choice D**) is not the best choice of donors because the recipient makes 8 times the proliferative response to his cells as to those of sibling 1.

    Sibling 3 (**choice E**) is not the best choice of donors because the recipient makes 8 times the proliferative response to his cells as to those of sibling 1.

5.  **The correct answer is B.** If a patient were treated with the Fab portions of antibodies to the CD28 molecule, this would block the binding of CD28 (on T cells) to B7 on antigen-presenting cells. Because this costimulatory signal is necessary as a second signal following TCR binding, the cell receives no second signal and becomes unresponsive (anergic) to that antigen.

    To destroy T cells (**choice A**) is the goal of treatment with experimental monoclonals such as anti-CD3 antibodies. These bind to and deplete T cells, but act in a nonspecific fashion, so there is increased susceptibility to infection.

    To inhibit mitosis in B cells (**choice C**) is not a goal of any of the therapies against graft rejection. T cells are at the root of all types of graft rejection, with the possible exception of hyperacute rejection based on ABO blood group incompatibilities.

    To inhibit mitosis in T cells (**choice D**) is the goal of agents such as cyclophosphamide and methotrexate.

To stop inflammation (**choice E**) is the goal of corticosteroids such as prednisone and dexamethasone. These are broad-spectrum antiinflammatories used during periods of acute graft rejection.

6.  **The correct answer is A.** IFNs of all types increase cellular expression of MHC class I and II products. Because CD8+ cells recognize their targets by MHC class I–dependent mechanisms, increases in the amount of these antigens on tumor-cell targets would increase susceptibility to cytotoxic killing.

    IL-1 (**choice B**) does not increase MHC class I molecule expression. The endogenous pyrogen is responsible for alteration of the hypothalamic temperature set point during acute inflammatory events.

    IL-2 (**choice C**) does not increase MHC class I molecule expression. It is produced by TH cells and causes proliferation of many classes of lymphocytes.

    IL-10 (**choice D**) does not increase MHC class I molecule expression. It is a product of TH2 cells and inhibits TH1 cells; thus, it inhibits the cell-mediated arm of the immune response.

    TNF-α (**choice E**) does not increase MHC class I molecule expression. It may act directly on tumor cells to cause their necrosis and decrease angiogenesis. It is a product of TH1 cells that stimulates the effector cells of cell-mediated immunity.

# Laboratory Techniques in Immunology 15

## What the COMLEX Requires You To Know

- The procedures for quantification of antigen–antibody complexes
- The general procedures and applications of agglutination, fluorescent antibody, radioimmunoassay, ELISA, Western blot, and flow cytometry
- How to interpret data from these tests to diagnose immunologic or microbial diseases

Many diagnoses in infectious disease and pathology would not be possible without laboratory procedures that identify antibodies or antigens in the patient. This chapter will illustrate the most commonly used techniques.

## ANTIGEN–ANTIBODY INTERACTIONS

Interaction of antigen and antibody occurs in vivo, and in clinical settings it provides the basis for all serologically based tests. The formation of immune complexes produces a visible reaction that is the basis of precipitation and agglutination tests. Agglutination and precipitation are maximized when multiple antibody molecules share the binding of multiple antigenic determinants, a condition known as **equivalence**. In vivo, the precipitation of such complexes from the blood is critical to the trapping of invaders and the initiation of the immune response in the secondary lymphoid organs, as well as the initiation of the pathologic phase of many immune complex–mediated diseases. In vitro, the kinetics of such reactions can be observed by titration of antigen against its specific antibody.

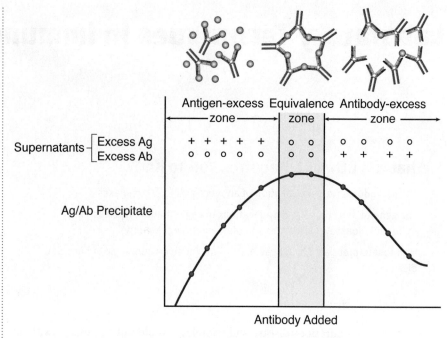

**Figure I-15-1.** Precipitation of Ag–Ab Complexes during Titration of Ag with Ab

### In a Nutshell

- Ag excess—early in infection
- Equivalence—all available Ag complexed with Ab = window period
- Ab excess—late in infection

Figure I-15-1 demonstrates the normal progression of the antibody response during many infectious diseases. At the start of the infection, the patient is in a state of **antigen excess** because the pathogen is proliferating in the host and the development of specific antibodies has not yet begun. As the patient begins to make an adequate antibody response, he enters the **equivalence zone**, when all available antigen is complexed with antibody, and neither free antigen nor free antibody can be detected in the serum. Finally, as the infection is resolved, the patient enters the **antibody excess** zone, when more antibody is being produced than is necessary to precipitate all available antigen. The clinical demonstration of this phenomenon is most elegantly seen in our use of the serologic diagnosis of hepatitis B infection. Early in the course of this infection, HBsAg and HBeAg are easily detectable in the blood. The patient is in the antigen excess zone for those two antigens. As the patient enters the **window period** (the equivalence zone), the HBsAg disappears from the circulation because it is being removed by antibody precipitation. Finally antibody titers (HBsAb and HBeAb) rise in the serum as the patient enters the antibody excess zone and resolves the infection. Although the "window period" in the hepatitis B infection is used exclusively to connote the absence of HBsAg and HBsAb from the serum (because it is the only antigen–antibody response that has a clinical significance in the prognosis of disease), an equivalence zone is a universal stage in the development of any antibody–antigen interaction.

## AGGLUTINATION

Agglutination tests are widespread in clinical medicine and are simply a variation on precipitation reactions in which the antigen is a particle and not a soluble material. The two particles most commonly used in medicine for this purpose are RBCs and latex beads, and both will clump up to form of a carpet of antibody-bound particles in the presence of appropriate antibodies. Latex bead agglutination tests are available for the diagnosis of cerebrospinal infections such as *Haemophilus*, pneumococcus, meningococcus, and *Cryptococcus neoformans*. In each of these cases, antibodies against these organisms are conjugated to latex beads, and the presence of pathogen antigens in the CSF is detected by the subsequent agglutination of those beads. RBC agglutination reactions are important in defining ABO blood groups (*see* Chapter 14), diagnosing Epstein-Barr virus infection (the monospot test), and the Coombs test for Rh incompatibility.

Two variations of the Coombs test exist. The direct Coombs is designed to identify maternal anti-Rh antibodies already bound to infant RBCs or antibodies bound to RBCs in patients with autoimmune hemolytic anemia. The indirect Coombs test is used to identify Rh-negative mothers who are producing anti-Rh antibodies of the IgG isotype, which may be transferred across the placenta to harm Rh-positive fetuses.

**In a Nutshell**

Direct Coombs—detect antibodies bound to RBC

Indirect Coombs—detect production of anti-RBC antibodies

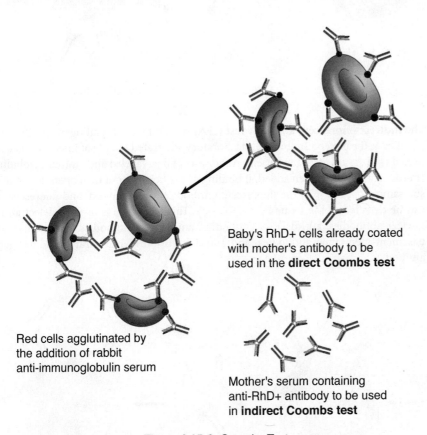

Baby's RhD+ cells already coated with mother's antibody to be used in the **direct Coombs test**

Red cells agglutinated by the addition of rabbit anti-immunoglobulin serum

Mother's serum containing anti-RhD+ antibody to be used in **indirect Coombs test**

**Figure I-15-2.** Coombs Test

# FLUORESCENT ANTIBODY TESTS

The direct fluorescent antibody test (DFA) is used to detect and localize antigen in the patient. The tissue sample to be tested is treated with antibodies against that particular antigen that have been labeled with a fluorescent dye. If the antigen is present in the tissues, the fluorescent-labeled antibodies will bind, and their binding can be detected with a fluorescence microscope. Variations of this test are used to diagnose respiratory syncytial virus, herpes simplex-1 and -2, and *Pneumocystis* infections.

**In a Nutshell**

DFA identifies Ag in tissues.

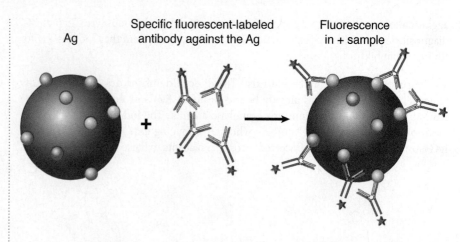

**Figure I-15-3.** Direct Fluorescent Antibody (DFA) Test

**In a Nutshell**

IFA detects Abs in the patient.

The **indirect fluorescent antibody test (IFA)** is used to detect pathogen-specific antibodies in the patient. In this case, a laboratory-generated sample of infected tissue is mixed with serum from the patient. A fluorescent dye–labeled anti-immunoglobulin (raised in animals) is then added. If binding of antibodies from the patient to the tissue sample occurs, then the fluorescent antibodies can be bound, and fluorescence can be detected in the tissue by microscopy. This technique is used to detect antinuclear antibodies, anti-dsDNA antibodies, antithyroid antibodies, antiglomerular basement-membrane antibodies, and anti–Epstein-Barr virus viral-capsid antigen antibodies.

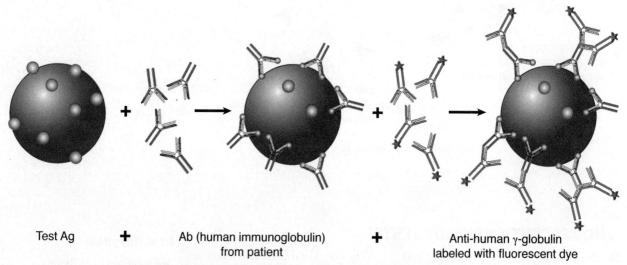

Test Ag   +   Ab (human immunoglobulin)   +   Anti-human γ-globulin
from patient                                labeled with fluorescent dye

If the test Ag is fluorescent following these steps, then the
patient had antibody against this antigen in their serum.

**Figure I-15-4.** Indirect Fluorescent Antibody (IFA) Test

# RADIOIMMUNOASSAY (RIA) AND ENZYME-LINKED IMMUNOABSORBENT ASSAY (EIA OR ELISA)

RIA and ELISA are extremely sensitive tests (as little as $10^{-9}$ g of material can be detected) that are common in medical laboratories. They can be used to detect the presence of hormones, drugs, antibiotics, serum proteins, infectious disease antigens, and tumor markers. Both tests are conducted similarly, but the RIA uses the detection of a radiolabeled product and the ELISA detects the presence of enzyme-mediated color changes in a chromogenic substrate.

In the screening test for HIV infection, the ELISA is used, with the p24 capsid antigen from the virus coated onto microtiter plates. The serum from the patient is then added, followed by addition of an enzyme-labeled antihuman immunoglobulin. Finally, the enzyme substrate is added, and the production of a color change in the well can be observed if all reagents bind one another in sequence.

**In a Nutshell**

ELISA and RIA

● Extremely sensitive

● ELISA is screening test for HIV

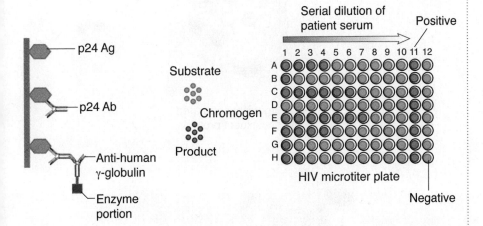

**Figure I-15-5.** ELISA Test

**In a Nutshell**

Western blot is a confirmatory test for HIV.

# WESTERN BLOT OR IMMUNOBLOT

The Western blot is primarily used in medicine for confirmation of HIV infection in a patient who has seroconverted and is thus positive by the ELISA test. Because the ELISA suffers from the detection of some false-positives, this follow-up step is essential for the diagnosis of HIV infection. In this test, the antigens of the virus are separated in an electric field and blotted onto nitrocellulose paper. The serum of the patient is then added and allowed to bind to any antigens that it recognizes. Next, antihuman immunoglobulin antibodies conjugated to either enzyme or radioactive labels are added, to bind to the previously bound patient's antibodies (if any). The result of color change in the case of an enzyme system or radioactivity in the case of radiolabeling can then be visualized. An HIV Western blot is judged to be "reactive" if the patient has reacted to at least 2 of 3 gene products (p24, gp41, gp120).

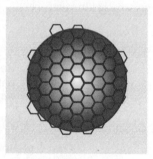

Viral organism separated
into constituent proteins

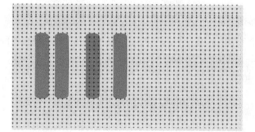

Proteins separated in SDS-PAGE (sodium dodecyl
sulfate-polyacrylamide gel electrophoresis)

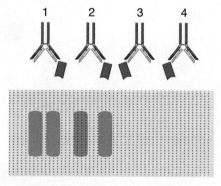

Separated proteins are transferred to nitrocellulose sheet and reacted
with patient's serum. Next, antihuman γ-globulin labeled with an enzyme
is reacted for color development and identification. Four different
antibodies were identified from this patient.

**Figure I-15-6.** Western Blot Test

# FLUORESCENCE-ACTIVATED CELL SORTER

This procedure is used to rapidly analyze cell types in a complex mixture and sort them into different populations based on their binding to specific fluorescent dyes. By using antibodies against specific cell-surface markers conjugated to different fluorescent dyes, it is possible to analyze the relative numbers of cells present in a specific tissue location. As cells pass through the apparatus in a single file, a computer-generated graph is produced, plotting the intensity and color of fluorescence of each cell along the axes. Each dot on the graph reflects the passage of a cell with a certain level and color of fluorescence, so the darkly dotted areas of the graph reflect the presence of many cells of similar attributes. Cells with high fluorescence from both dyes will therefore be found in the top right quadrant.

## In a Nutshell

Flow cytometry analyzes cell populations in a complex mixture.

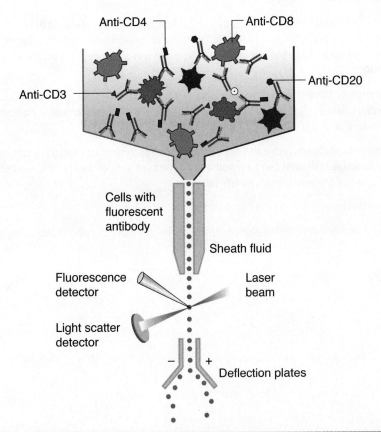

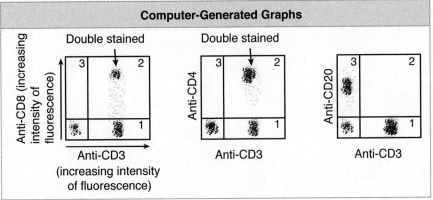

**Figure I-15-7.** Flow Cytometric Analysis

## Chapter Summary

- Antigen–antibody interactions can be visualized in vitro and serve as the basis of many medical diagnostic tests.

- Early in infection when antigen is in excess, only the pathogen's antigens can be detected in patient serum. As antibodies begin to be produced, complexes are formed that precipitate out of the circulation, and the patient enters the equivalence zone. Rising titers of antibody are measured as the patient progresses into the antibody excess zone, and convalescence.

- Agglutination tests are used to measure antibodies that can cause clumping of particles (RBCs and latex beads).

- The direct Coombs test is an agglutination test that detects infants at risk for developing erythroblastosis fetalis. The indirect Coombs test is used to diagnose the presence of antibody in mothers who are at risk of causing this condition in their children.

- The direct fluorescent antibody test is used to detect and localize antigen in patient tissues. The indirect fluorescent antibody test is used to detect antibody production in a patient.

- The radioimmunoassay and enzyme-linked immunoabsorbent assay are extremely sensitive tests that can be modified to detect antigens or antibodies. The ELISA is used as a screening test for HIV infection.

- The Western blot is the confirmatory test for HIV infection.

- Flow cytometry is used to analyze and separate cell types out of complex mixtures.

## Review Questions

1. A 16-year-old runaway heroin user visits a family planning/STD clinic irregularly to receive birth control pills. In April 2004, the standard HIV screen performed by this clinic reports back that her test was positive. What does the primary test for HIV infection use?

   (A) Electrophoresis of HIV antigens in polyacrylamide gel

   (B) HIV antigen covalently coupled to RBC, patient serum, and anti-immunoglobulin

   (C) HIV antigen covalently coupled to RBC, patient serum, and complement

   (D) HIV antigen, patient serum, anti-immunoglobulin serum, and enzyme-substrate ligand

   (E) HIV antigen, patient serum, anti-immunoglobulin serum, and radioactive ligand

2. A direct Coombs test was performed on a baby in its seventh month of gestation. The mother has had trouble with two earlier pregnancies, and she has never received RhoGAM™. The physician is concerned about the possibility of erythroblastosis fetalis. What ingredients would be necessary to perform this procedure?

   (A) Mother's serum plus RhoGAM plus Coombs reagent

   (B) Mother's serum plus Rh– RBCs plus Coombs reagent

   (C) RhoGAM plus Rh+ RBCs from the baby

   (D) Rh+ RBCs from the baby plus Coombs reagent

   (E) Rh+ RBCs plus mother's serum plus Coombs reagent

3.  A patient with Chediak-Higashi syndrome is analyzed for ability to mobilize NK cells into the peripheral blood. His peripheral blood leukocytes are treated with fluorescent-labeled antibodies to CD3, CD56, and CD20 before they are passed through a fluorescence-activated cell sorter. The computer-generated results of this process are shown. In which quadrant of which panel would the natural killer cells be found?

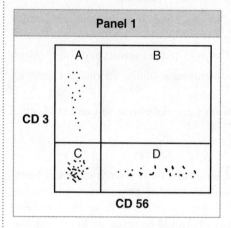 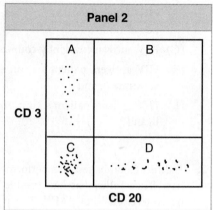

(A)  Panel 1, quadrant A

(B)  Panel 1, quadrant B

(C)  Panel 1, quadrant C

(D)  Panel 1, quadrant D

(E)  Panel 2, quadrant A

(F)  Panel 2, quadrant B

(G)  Panel 2, quadrant C

(H)  Panel 2, quadrant D

4.  In both ABO blood typing and the Coombs test for detection of hemolytic disease of the newborn, agglutination of coated erythrocytes is a positive test result. Why is addition of Coombs reagent not a necessary step in ABO blood typing?

(A)  All antibodies made in response to blood glycoproteins are IgG

(B)  Complement-mediated lysis is not important in ABO incompatibilities

(C)  Coombs serum identifies only anti-Rh antibodies

(D)  IgM pentamers are large enough to agglutinate erythrocytes directly

(E)  The high titer of natural isohemagglutinins makes Coombs reagent unnecessary

5. A young woman is in the care of an infertility specialist for evaluation of her inability to conceive since her marriage 5 years ago. As a first step in her examination, cervical scrapings are tested for the possibility of undiagnosed infection with *Chlamydia trachomatis*, which could cause fallopian tube scarring. Which of the following diagnostic tests could be used to identify chlamydial antigens in this specimen?

    (A) Direct fluorescent antibody test

    (B) Enzyme-linked immunosorbent assay (ELISA)

    (C) Indirect fluorescent antibody test

    (D) Radioimmunoassay

    (E) Western blot

6. An experimental treatment for melanoma involves in vitro stimulation of tumor-specific killer cells with tumor cells transfected with a gene for production of altered-self MHC class I molecules. As a first step, peripheral blood leukocytes from the patient are incubated with fluorescent-labeled antibodies against CD4, CD8, and CD20. The cells are then subjected to flow cytometry and separated into different populations based on their expression of these cell surface markers. In which quadrant would you find the cell subpopulation most likely to produce a beneficial anti-tumor response in this protocol?

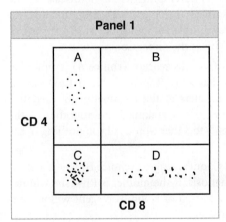 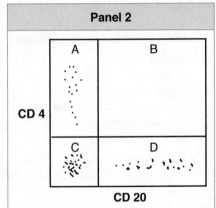

    (A) Panel I, quadrant A

    (B) Panel I, quadrant B

    (C) Panel I, quadrant C

    (D) Panel I, quadrant D

    (E) Panel II, quadrant A

    (F) Panel II, quadrant B

    (G) Panel II, quadrant C

    (H) Panel II, quadrant D

# Answers and Explanations

1. **The correct answer is D.** The standard screening test for HIV infection is the enzyme-linked immunosorbent assay, or ELISA. In this test, the virus p24 antigen is coated onto microtiter plates. Serum from the test subjects is added, followed by antihuman-immunoglobulin, which is labeled with an enzyme. When the substrate for the enzyme is added, if the antibodies listed have bound in sequence, there will be a color change in that microtiter well.

   Electrophoresis of HIV antigens in polyacrylamide gel (**choice A**) describes the Western blot, which is used as a confirmatory test of HIV infection.

   HIV antigen covalently coupled to RBC, patient serum, and anti-immunoglobulin (**choice B**) describes an erythrocyte agglutination test. There is no such test in use for diagnosis of HIV. The indirect Coombs test, which is used to detect Rh– mothers who have become sensitized to the Rh antigens of their fetuses, operates on this principle, however.

   HIV antigen covalently coupled to RBC, patient serum, and complement (**choice C**) describes either a complement-fixation or complement-mediated hemolysis assay. There is no such test in use for the diagnosis of HIV.

   HIV antigen, patient serum, anti-immunoglobulin serum, and radioactive ligand (**choice E**) describes a radioimmunoassay. This is not used in the standard screening for HIV.

2. **The correct answer is D.** If the child is developing hemolytic disease of the newborn, then his erythrocytes will already be coated with maternal anti-Rh antibodies. Adding Coombs serum (antihuman gammaglobulin) to the baby's RBCs then will cause agglutination. This is the direct Coombs test.

   Mother's serum plus RhoGAM plus Coombs reagent (**choice A**) is not a set of reagents that will accomplish any diagnosis. RhoGAM is anti-RhD immunoglobulin, which is given to Rh– mothers at the termination of any Rh+ pregnancy. If the mother is sensitized, she is making IgG antibodies of the same specificity. Adding these 3 reagents together would tell you nothing of the baby's condition.

   Mother's serum plus Rh– RBCs plus Coombs reagent (**choice B**) is not a set of reagents that will accomplish any diagnosis. If the mother is Rh–, she will not make a response to Rh– RBCs, and addition of Coombs reagent will accomplish nothing.

   RhoGAM plus Rh+ RBCs from the baby (**choice C**) is not a set of reagents that will accomplish any diagnosis. RhoGAM will bind to Rh+ RBCs from the baby by definition, but adding these reagents together would tell you nothing of the baby's condition.

   Rh+ RBCs plus mother's serum plus Coombs (**choice E**) is the set of reagents necessary for the performance of the indirect Coombs test. This is a test used to determine if the mother is making IgG anti-Rh antibodies, which could cross the placenta and harm a fetus. The question asks about the direct Coombs test, not the indirect.

3. **The correct answer is D.** The cell surface marker that would be useful to identify NK cells is CD56. The cells that have the highest fluorescence with antibodies to CD56 are found in quadrant D of panel 1.

   Panel 1, quadrant A (**choice A**) contains the cells with maximum fluorescence with antibodies to CD3. These would be T lymphocytes.

   Panel 1, quadrant B (**choice B**) contains the cells double-labeled with CD3 and CD56. Because CD3 is the pan-T-cell marker and CD56 is an NK-cell marker, there are no double-labeled cells in this case.

Panel 1, quadrant C (**choice C**) contains the cells that have background fluorescence with both CD3 and CD56. These are non-T, non-NK cells, so they could be B lymphocytes or any other leukocyte.

Panel 2, quadrant A (**choice E**) contains the cells with maximum fluorescence with antibodies to CD3. These are T lymphocytes.

Panel 2, quadrant B (**choice F**) contains double-labeled cells, which fluoresce with both antibody to CD3 and antibody to CD20. Because CD3 is a T-cell marker and CD20 is a B-cell marker, there are no cells in this quadrant.

Panel 2, quadrant C (**choice G**) contains the cells with background fluorescence with both antibodies to CD3 and CD20. These would be non-B, non-T cells and would contain some NK cells, but other leukocytes would be included here, so this is not the best choice.

Panel 2, quadrant D (**choice H**) contains the cells with maximum fluorescence with antibody to CD20, which is a B-cell marker.

4.  **The correct answer is D.** Coombs reagent is antihuman IgG. It is necessary in the direct and indirect Coombs tests because in those cases, one is looking for IgG antibodies that could be transported across the placenta to harm an unborn child. IgG is a much smaller molecule than IgM, and is not capable of agglutinating erythrocytes without the addition of a "developing" antibody. In the ABO blood typing test, the important isohemagglutinins are of the IgM variety, capable of agglutinating erythrocytes by themselves because of their sheer size.

The statement that all antibodies made in response to blood glycoproteins are IgG (**choice A**) is not true because isohemagglutinins against ABO blood group antigens are IgM.

The statement that complement-mediated lysis is not important in ABO incompatibilities (**choice B**) is not true because isohemagglutinins of the IgM variety are extremely powerful activators of complement-mediated lysis. The agglutination tests here, however, do not use complement-mediated lysis as the indicator system.

That Coombs serum identifies only anti-Rh antibodies (**choice C**) is not true. Coombs serum is antihuman IgG. It will bind to the Fc portion of any human IgG molecule, regardless of its antigenic specificity.

The statement that the high titer of natural isohemagglutinins makes Coombs reagent unnecessary (**choice E**) is not true. It is the isotype of these antibodies (IgM) and the size of that molecule that allows agglutination to proceed without a developing antibody.

5.  **The correct answer is A.** The direct fluorescent antibody test is used to detect antigens in the tissues of a patient.

The enzyme-linked immunosorbent assay (**choice B**) is a test usually used to detect antibody production. It can be modified to detect antigen, but not from a tissue specimen such as this one.

The indirect fluorescent antibody test (**choice C**) is used to detect antibodies being produced in a patient. It is not used for detection of microbial antigens.

Radioimmunoassay (**choice D**) is generally used to detect antibodies in a patient.

Western blot (**choice E**) is used to detect antibodies in a patient, not antigen.

6.  **The correct answer is D.** To generate tumor-specific killer cells in vitro that would kill tumor cells transfected with an altered-self MHC class I gene, one would need to start with potential killer cells that use MHC I as a stimulatory

signal. The only cytotoxic cell in the body that meets these criteria is the cytotoxic T lymphocyte (CTL). In panel I, increasing levels of fluorescence with antibody to CD8 are plotted as one moves to the right, and increasing levels of fluorescence with antibody to CD4 are plotted as one moves upward. Thus, the cells most strongly positive with CD8 are found the farthest to the right in quadrant D of panel I.

Panel I, quadrant A (**choice A**) would contain cells that are CD4+ and CD8–. These would be helper cells, and they would not be cytotoxic to transfected tumor cells.

Panel I, quadrant B (**choice B**) would contain cells that are double-positive for CD4 and CD8. These cells would be found as immature thymocytes in the thymus and not in the blood; thus, there are no double-labeled cells shown in this quadrant.

Panel I, quadrant C (**choice C**) contains the cells that have only background levels of fluorescence with antibodies to CD4 and CD8. These would be nonhelper, noncytotoxic cells, so they could be B lymphocytes, NK cells, or any other peripheral blood leukocyte.

Panel II, quadrant A (**choice E**) would contain cells which are strongly CD4+ and CD20–. These are helper T lymphocytes.

Panel II, quadrant B (**choice F**) would contain cells positive for CD4 and CD20. Because CD4 is a TH cell marker, and CD20 is a B-cell marker, such cells do not exist and thus this quadrant is empty.

Panel II, quadrant C (**choice G**) contains the cells that have only background levels of fluorescence with antibodies to CD4 and CD20. These would be nonhelper, non-B cells, so they could be cytotoxic T lymphocytes, NK cells, or any other peripheral blood leukocyte. Although this quadrant clearly contains some of the cytotoxic cells that this question asks about, there are other cells present, so this is not the best answer.

Panel II, quadrant D (**choice H**) contains the cells strongly positive for CD20 and negative for CD4. These are B lymphocytes.

| CD Designation | Cellular Expression | Known Functions |
|---|---|---|
| CD2 (LFA-2) | T cells, thymocytes, NK cells | Adhesion molecule |
| CD3 | T cells, thymocytes | Signal transduction by the TCR |
| CD4 | TH cells, thymocytes, monocytes, and macrophages | Coreceptor for TCR-MHC II interaction, receptor for HIV |
| CD8 | CTLs, some thymocytes | Coreceptor for MHC class I–restricted T cells |
| CD14 (LPS receptor) | Monocytes, macrophages, granulocytes | Binds LPS |
| CD16 (Fc receptor) | NK cells, macrophages, neutrophils | Opsonization ADCC |
| CD18 | Leukocytes | Cell adhesion molecule (missing in leukocyte adhesion deficiency) |
| CD19 | B cells | Coreceptor with CD21 for B-cell activation (signal transduction) |
| CD20 | Most or all B cells | Unknown role in B-cell activation |
| CD21 (CR2, C3d receptor) | Mature B cells | Receptor for complement fragment C3d, forms coreceptor complex with CD19, Epstein-Barr virus receptor |
| CD25 | Activated TH cells and $T_{Reg}$ | Alpha chain of IL-2 receptor |
| CD28 | T cells | T-cell receptor for costimulatory molecule B7 |
| CD34 | Precursors of hematopoietic cells, endothelial cells in HEV | Cell–cell adhesion, binds L-selectin |
| CD40 | B cells, macrophages, dendritic cells, endothelial cells | Binds CD40L, role in T-cell–dependent B cell, macrophage, dendritic cell and endothelial cell activation |
| CD56 | NK cells | Not known |
| CD152 (CTLA-4) | Activated T cells | Negative regulation: competes with CD28 for B7 binding |

| Cytokine | Secreted by | Target Cell/Tissue | Activity |
|---|---|---|---|
| Interleukin (IL)-1 | Monocytes, macrophages, B cells, dendritic cells, endothelial cells, others | TH cells | Costimulates activation |
| | | B cells | Promotes maturation and clonal expansion |
| | | NK cells | Enhances activity |
| | | Endothelial cells | Increases expression of ICAMs |
| | | Macrophages and neutrophils | Chemotactically attracts |
| | | Hepatocytes | Induces synthesis of acute-phase proteins |
| | | Hypothalamus | Induces fever |
| IL-2 | TH cells | Antigen-primed TH and CTLs | Induces proliferation, enhances activity |
| IL-3 | TH cells, NK cells | Hematopoietic cells (myeloid) | Supports growth and differentiation |
| IL-4 | TH2 cells | Antigen-primed B cells | Costimulates activation |
| | | Activated B cells | Stimulates proliferation and differentiation, induces class switch to IgE |
| IL-5 | TH2 cells and mast cells | Activated B cells | Stimulates proliferation and differentiation, induces class switch to IgA |
| | | Bone marrow cells | Induces eosinophil differentiation |

*(Continued)*

| Cytokine | Secreted by | Target Cell/Tissue | Activity |
|---|---|---|---|
| IL-6 | Monocytes, macrophages, TH2 cells, bone marrow stromal cells | Proliferating B cells | Promotes terminal differentiation into plasma cells |
| | | Plasma cells | Stimulates Ab secretion |
| | | Myeloid stem cells | Helps promote differentiation |
| | | Hepatocytes | Induces synthesis of acute-phase proteins |
| IL-7 | Bone marrow, thymic stromal cells | Lymphoid stem cells | Induces differentiation into progenitor B and T cells |
| IL-8 | Macrophages, endothelial cells | Neutrophils | Chemokine, induces adherence to endothelium and extravasation into tissues |
| IL-10 | TH2 cells $T_{Reg}$ cells | Macrophages | Suppresses cytokine production by TH1 cells |
| IL-11 | Bone marrow stroma | Bone marrow | ↑ platelet count |
| IL-12 | Macrophages, B cells | Activated CD8+ cells | Acts synergistically with IL-2 to induce differentiation into CTLs |
| | | NK and LAK cells and activated TH1 cells | Stimulates proliferation |
| IL-13 | TH2 cell | B cells | Induces isotype switch to IgE |
| IL-17 | TH17 cells | Fibroblasts, endothelial cells, macrophages | Increases inflammation. Attracts PMNs, induces IL-6, IL-1, TGFβ, TNFα, IL-8 Role in autoimmune disease & allergy |
| Interferon-α (type I) | Leukocytes | Uninfected cells | Inhibits viral replication |

(Continued)

| Cytokine | Secreted by | Target Cell/ Tissue | Activity |
|---|---|---|---|
| Interferon-β (type I) | Fibroblasts | Uninfected cells | Inhibits viral replication |
| Interferon-γ (type II) | TH1, CTLs, NK cells | Macrophages | Enhances activity |
| | | Many cell types | Increases expression of classes I and II MHC |
| | | Proliferating B cells | Induces class switch to IgG2a, blocks IL-4–induced class switch to IgE and IgG1 |
| | | TH2 cells | Inhibits proliferation |
| | | Phagocytic cells | Mediates effects important in DTH, treatment for CGD |
| Transforming growth factor-β | Platelets, macrophages, lymphocytes, mast cells | Proliferating B cells | Induces class switch to IgA |
| Tumor necrosis factor-α | Macrophages, NK cells | Tumor cells | Has cytotoxic effect |
| | | Inflammatory cells | Induces cytokine secretion, causes cachexia of chronic inflammation |
| Tumor necrosis factor-β | TH1 and CTL | Tumor cells | Has cytotoxic and other effects, like TNF-α |
| | | Macrophages and neutrophils | Enhances phagocytic activity |
| Granulocyte colony-stimulating factor (G-CSF) | Macrophages and TH cells | Bone marrow granulocyte precursors | Induce proliferation, used clinically to counteract neutropenia following ablative chemotherapy |
| Granulocyte–macrophage colony-stimulating factor (GM-CSF) | Macrophages and TH cells | Bone marrow granulocyte and macrophage precursors | Induces proliferation; used clinically to counteract neutropenia following ablative chemotherapy |

# CYTOKINES AVAILABLE IN RECOMBINANT FORM

| Cytokine | Clinical Uses |
| --- | --- |
| Aldesleukin (IL-2) | ↑ Lymphocyte differentiation and ↑ NKs—used in renal cell cancer and metastatic melanoma |
| Interleukin-11 | ↑ Platelet formation—used in thrombocytopenia |
| Filgrastim (G-CSF) | ↑ Granulocytes—used for marrow recovery |
| Sargramostim (GM-CSF) | ↑ Granulocytes and macrophages—used for marrow recovery |
| Erythropoietin | Anemias, especially associated with renal failure |
| Thrombopoietin | Thrombocytopenia |
| Interferon-$\alpha$ | Hepatitis B and C, leukemias, melanoma |
| Interferon-$\beta$ | Multiple sclerosis |
| Interferon-$\gamma$ | Chronic granulomatous disease →↑ TNF |

# Adhesion Molecules

| Family | Figures | Name | Tissue Distribution | Ligand |
|---|---|---|---|---|
| **Selectins** (bind carbohydrates, **initial binding** leukocyte– endothelia) | L-selectin | L-selectin | Leukocytes | Addressins |
| | | P-selectin | Endothelium and platelets | Addressins |
| | | E-selectin | Activated endothelium | Addressins |
| Mucin-like vascular **addressins** (bind to L-selectin, initiate leukocyte endothelial interaction) | CD34 | CD34 | Endothelial venules | L-selectin |
| | | GlyCAM-1 | High endothelial venules | L-selectin |
| | | MAdCAM-1 | Mucosal lymphoid tissue venules | L-selectin |
| **Integrins** (bind to cell-adhesion molecules and extracellular matrix; **strong adhesion**) | LFA-1 | LFA-1 | Monocytes, T cells, macrophages, neutrophils, dendritic cells | ICAMs |
| | | CR3 | Neutrophils, monocytes, macrophages | ICAM-1, iC3b, fibrinogen |
| | | CR4 | Dendritic cells, macrophages, neutrophils | iC3b |

*(Continued)*

| Family | Figures | Name | Tissue Distribution | Ligand |
|---|---|---|---|---|
| **Immunoglobulin super-family** (various roles in cell adhesion, ligand for integrins) | CD2 | CD2 | T cells | LFA-3 |
| | | ICAM-1 | Activated vessels, lymphocytes, dendritic cells | LFA-1, CR3 |
| | | ICAM-2 | Resting vessels, dendritic cells | LFA-1 |
| | | ICAM-3 | Lymphocytes | LFA-1 |
| | | LFA-3 | Lymphocytes, antigen-presenting cells | CD2 |
| | | VCAM-1 | Activated endothelium | VLA-4 |

*Note:* Early adhesion = selectin–addressin; late, strong adhesion = integrin–ICAM.

# Mechanisms of Resistance to Microbial Infections

| Category | Pathogen | Protective Mechanism | Evasive Mechanism | Immune Pathology |
|---|---|---|---|---|
| Prion | CJD, kuru, etc. | No immune response | None | None |
| Viruses | Naked capsid (all) | Antibody blocks receptor binding, CMI destroys infected cells | | |
| | Rhinovirus | See above | Antigenic drift | |
| | Adenovirus | See above | Decreases MHC I expression | |
| | Enveloped (all) | Antibody blocks receptor binding, C lyses envelope, Ab and C enhances phagocytosis, TH1 cells stimulate CTLs and NK | | |
| | Hepatitis C | | Blocks IFN-$\alpha$ and -$\beta$ | |
| | Hepatitis B | | | Immune complexes cause vasculitis |
| | All Herpesviridae | | Nuclear membrane envelope is nonimmunogenic | |
| | Herpes simplex 1 and 2 | | Block TAP function (inhibits MHC I expression), viral glycoprotein $\downarrow$ C activation | |
| | Cytomegalovirus | | Generalized immuno-suppression, $\downarrow$ MHC I and II expression, produces chemokine receptor and MHC I homologues | |
| | Epstein-Barr virus | | Generalized immuno-suppression, produces molecule homologous to IL-10 (shuts down TH1) | Activates B cells, causes production of heterophile Abs |
| | Paramyxoviruses | | Generalized immuno-suppression | |

*(Continued)*

| Category | Pathogen | Protective Mechanism | Evasive Mechanism | Immune Pathology |
|---|---|---|---|---|
| | Human Immuno-deficiency virus | | Infects and kills immuno-competent cells, antigenic drift | |
| | Rubeola | | ↓ MHC II expression | |
| | Influenza | | Antigenic shift and drift | |
| Extracellular bacteria | All | Ab or C enhance phagocytosis or block toxin binding | | |
| Gram-negative extracellular bacteria | All | Ab or C enhance phagocytosis or block toxin binding | | LPS activates macrophages → IL-1 and TNF-α |
| | *Neisseria gonorrhoeae* | MAC lyses | Antigenic variation of pili and OMPs | |
| | *Pseudomonas* | Ab or C enhance phagocytosis or block toxin binding | Inactivates C3a, C5a | |
| | *Borrelia burgdorferi* | | | Immune complexes cause rash, arthritis, neurologic symptoms |
| Encapsulated bacteria | All | Opsonization with Ab and C, spleen is critical | Resist phagocytosis | Abscess formation |
| IgA protease producers | *Streptococcus pneumoniae, Haemophilus influenzae, Neisseria meningitidis* and *Neisseria gonorrhoeae* | | Destroy IgA | |
| Coagulase-positive bacteria | *Staphylococcus aureus Yersinia pestis* | | Inhibit phagocytosis | |
| Gram-positive, extracellular bacteria | *Streptococcus pyogenes* | Opsonization with Ab and C | | Exotoxins act as superantigens, nonsuppurative sequelae: types II and III hypersensitivities |
| Catalase-positive bacteria | All | | Catalase destroys reactive oxygen intermediates | Serious in CGD patients |
| | *Staphylococcus aureus* | | Protein A binds Fc of IgG and inhibits opsonization | Exotoxins act as superantigens |

*(Continued)*

| Category | Pathogen | Protective Mechanism | Evasive Mechanism | Immune Pathology |
|---|---|---|---|---|
| Intracellular bacteria | All | TH1 cells activate NK, macrophages, and CTLs | | |
| | *Mycobacterium tuberculosis* | TH1 produces IFN-γ to make angry macrophages | Sulfatides inhibit phagolysosome formation | Granuloma formation is CMI-mediated |
| | *Mycobacterium leprae* | TH1 stimulation is protective (tuberculoid form) | TH2 stimulation results in lepromatous form | Nerve damage in tuberculoid form is DTH-mediated |
| | *Listeria monocytogenes* | DTH and CTL | Hemolysin disrupts phagosome membrane, allows escape into cytoplasm | |
| | *Chlamydia trachomatis* | DTH and CTLs | | Scarring of fallopian tubes is DTH-mediated |
| Extracellular protozoa | All | Abs to surface molecules plus C cause lysis or opsonize | | |
| | *Trypanosoma brucei rhodesiense* and *gambiense* | | Antigenic variation of variable surface glycoprotein | |
| | *Entamoeba histolytica* | | Antigen shedding | |
| Intracellular protozoa | All | TH1 cells stimulate macrophages, CTLs | | |
| | *Plasmodium* spp. | Antibodies plus C plus above; spleen is critical | Maturational stages change antigens, antigenic variation | |
| | *Trypanosoma cruzi* | Amastigotes killed by CMI, trypomastigotes (extracellular) killed by Ab and C | | |
| | *Leishmania* spp. | TH1 cells stimulate macrophages, CTLs | | |
| Helminth parasites | All | ADCC-mediated by eosinophils, macrophages | | |
| | Filarial nematodes | | Immunosuppression secondary to lymphatic obstruction | |
| | *Schistosoma* spp. | | Adult envelops itself in host self glycoproteins (ABO and MHC antigens) | Granulomas in liver due to DTH response to egg antigens |

*(Continued)*

| Category | Pathogen | Protective Mechanism | Evasive Mechanism | Immune Pathology |
|---|---|---|---|---|
| Fungi | Most | Phagocytosis by PMNs and macrophages, Abs not protective | | Calcifying lesions due to indigestibility of cell-wall carbohydrates |
| | *Cryptococcus neoformans* | As above | Inhibits TH1, stimulates TH2, capsule protects against phagocytosis | |
| | *Histoplasma capsulatum* | TH1 cell stimulates macrophages and CTLs | | Granulomas, calcifications |

# Microbiology

# General Microbiology  (1)

## What the COMLEX Requires You To Know

- Differences among viruses, fungi, bacteria, and parasites
- Differences between eukaryotic and prokaryotic cells
- Important normal flora
- Major mechanisms of pathogenicity

## EPIDEMIOLOGY

### Normal Flora

- Is found on body surfaces contiguous with the outside environment
- Is semi-permanent, varying with major life changes
- Can cause infection
  - if misplaced, e.g., fecal flora to urinary tract or abdominal cavity, or skin flora to catheter
  - or, if person becomes compromised, normal flora may overgrow (oral thrush)
- Contributes to health
  - protective host defense by maintaining conditions such as pH so other organisms may not grow
  - serves nutritional function by synthesizing: K and B vitamins
  - competition for space

### In a Nutshell

**Definitions**

**Carrier:** person colonized by a potential pathogen without overt disease.

**Bacteremia:** bacteria in bloodstream without overt clinical signs.

**Septicemia:** bacteria in bloodstream (multiplying) with clinical symptoms.

**Table II-1-1.** Important Normal Flora

| Site | Common or Medically Important Organisms | Less Common but Notable Organisms |
|---|---|---|
| Blood, internal organs | None, generally sterile | |
| Cutaneous surfaces including urethra and outer ear | *Staphylococcus epidermidis* | *Staphylococcus aureus*, Corynebacteria (diphtheroids), streptococci, anaerobes, e.g., peptostreptococci, yeasts (*Candida* spp.) |
| Nose | *Staphylococcus aureus* | *S. epidermidis*, diphtheroids, assorted streptococci |
| Oropharynx | **Viridans streptococci** including *Strep. mutans*[1] | Assorted streptococci, **nonpathogenic *Neisseria*, nontypeable[2] *Haemophilus influenzae*, *Candida albicans*** |
| Gingival crevices | Anaerobes: *Bacteroides, Prevotella, Fusobacterium, Streptococcus, Actinomyces* | |
| Stomach | None | |
| Colon (microaerophilic/ anaerobic) | Babies; breast-fed only: *Bifidobacterium* | *Lactobacillus*, streptococci |
| | Adult: ***Bacteroides**/Prevotella* (Predominant organism) *Escherichia* *Bifidobacterium* | *Eubacterium, Fusobacterium, Lactobacillus*, assorted Gram-negative anaerobic rods, *Enterococcus faecalis* and other streptococci |
| Vagina | ***Lactobacillus***[3] | Assorted streptococci, gram-negative rods, diphtheroids, yeasts, *Veillonella* |

[1] **S. mutans** secretes a biofilm that glues it and other oral flora to teeth, producing **dental plaque**.

[2] Nontypeable for *Haemophilus* means no capsule.

[3] Group B streptococci colonize vagina of 15–20% of women and may infect the infant during labor or delivery, causing septicemia and/or meningitis (as may *E. coli* from fecal flora).

## COMLEX Note

The COMLEX will require you to know major virulence factors. Toxins, capsules and pili are high yield.

# PATHOGENICITY (INFECTIVITY AND TOXICITY) MAJOR MECHANISMS

## Colonization

(Important unless organism is traumatically implanted.)

**Adherence** to cell surfaces involves

- **Pili/fimbriae:** primary mechanism in most gram-negative cells.
- **Teichoic acids:** primary mechanism of gram-positive cells.
- **Adhesins:** colonizing factor adhesins, pertussis toxin, and hemagglutinins.
- **IgA proteases:** make it easier for pathogens to colonize.

**Partial adherence** to inert materials, **biofilms**: *Staph. epidermidis, Streptococcus mutans, Pseudomonas aeruginosa*

# Avoiding Immediate Destruction by Host Defense System:

- **Anti-phagocytic surface components** (inhibit phagocytic uptake):
  - **Capsules**/slime layers:

    *Streptococcus pyogenes* M protein

    *Neisseria gonorrhoeae* pili

    *Staphylococcus aureus* A protein

- **IgA proteases,** destruction of mucosal IgA: *Neisseria, Haemophilus, S. pneumoniae*

# "Hunting and Gathering" Needed Nutrients:

- **Siderophores** steal (chelate) and import iron.

# Antigenic Variation

- Changing surface antigens to avoid immune destruction
- *N. gonorrhoeae*—pili and outer membrane proteins
- *Trypanosoma brucei rhodesiense* and *T. b. gambiense*—phase variation
- Enterobacteriaceae: capsular and flagellar antigens may or may not be expressed
- HIV, influenza—antigenic drift

# Ability to Survive Intracellularly

- **Evading intracellular killing by professional phagocytic cells** allows intracellular growth:
  - *M. tuberculosis* survives by inhibiting phagosome-lysosome fusion.
  - *Listeria* quickly escapes the phagosome into the cytoplasm **before** phagosome-lysosome fusion.
- **Invasins**: surface proteins that allow an organism to bind to and invade normally non-phagocytic human cells, escaping the immune system. Best studied invasin is on *Yersinia pseudotuberculosis* (an organism causing diarrhea).
- Damage from viruses is largely from intracellular replication, which either kills cells, transforms them or, in the case of latent viruses, may do no noticeable damage.

# Type III Secretion Systems

- Tunnel from the bacteria to the host cell (macrophage) that delivers bacterial toxins directly to the host cell
- Have been demonstrated in many pathogens: *E. coli, Salmonella* species, *Yersinia* species, *P. aeruginosa*, and *Chlamydia*

## Note

**Mnemonic**

**S**treptococcus pneumoniae
**K**lebsiella pneumoniae
**H**aemophilus influenzae
**P**seudomonas aeruginosa
**N**eisseria meningitidis
**C**ryptococcus neoformans

(**S**ome **K**illers **H**ave **P**retty **N**ice **C**apsules)

## Note

**Intracellular organisms**

- Elicit different immune responses
- Different pathology
- Different antibiotics
- Different culture techniques

## Inflammation or Immune-Mediated Damage

### Examples

- **Cross-reaction of bacteria-induced antibodies with tissue antigens** causes disease. Rheumatic fever is one example.

- **Delayed hypersensitivity and the granulomatous response** stimulated by the presence of intracellular bacteria is responsible for neurological damage in leprosy, cavitation in tuberculosis, and fallopian tube blockage resulting in infertility from *Chlamydia* PID (pelvic inflammatory disease).

- **Immune complexes** damage the kidney in post streptococcal acute glomerulonephritis.

- **Peptidoglycan-teichoic acid** (large fragments) of gram-positive cells:
  - Serves as a structural toxin released when cells die.
  - Chemotactic for neutrophils.

## Physical Damage

- Swelling from infection in a fixed space damages tissues; examples: meningitis and cysticercosis.

- Large physical size of organism may cause problems; example: *Ascaris lumbricoides* blocking bile duct.

- Aggressive tissue invasion from *Entamoeba histolytica* causes intestinal ulceration and releases intestinal bacteria, compounding problems.

# TOXINS

Toxins may aid in invasiveness, damage cells, inhibit cellular processes, or trigger immune response and damage.

## COMLEX Note

Be able to differentiate between endotoxins (LPS) and exotoxins. Know the mechanism of actions for the toxins listed in Table II-1-3.

## Structural Toxins

- **Endotoxin** (Lipopolysaccharide = LPS)
  - LPS is part of the **gram-negative outer membrane.**
  - **Toxic portion is lipid A:** generally not released (and toxic) until death of cell. Exception: *N. meningitidis,* which over-produces outer membrane fragments.
  - **LPS is heat stable** and not strongly immunogenic so it **cannot be converted to a toxoid.**
  - Mechanism
    - **LPS activates macrophages,** leading to release of TNF-alpha, IL-1, and IL-6.
    - IL-1 is a major mediator of fever.
    - Macrophage activation and products lead to tissue damage.
    - Damage to the endothelium from **bradykinin-induced vasodilation leads to shock.**
    - **Coagulation** (DIC) is mediated through the **activation of Hageman factor.**

- **Peptidoglycan, Teichoic Acids**

# Exotoxins

- Are **protein toxins,** generally **quite toxic** and **secreted by** bacterial **cells** (some gram +, some gram –)
- **Can be modified** by chemicals or heat to produce a **toxoid** that still is **immunogenic, but no longer toxic** so can be used as a vaccine
- **A-B** (or "two") **component** protein toxins
    - **B** component **binds** to specific cell receptors to facilitate the internalization of A.
    - **A** component is the **active (toxic) component** (often an enzyme such as an ADP ribosyl transferase).
    - Exotoxins may be subclassed as enterotoxins, neurotoxins, or cytotoxins.
- **Cytolysins:** lyse cells from outside by damaging membrane.
    - *C. perfringens* **alpha toxin** is a **lecithinase.**
    - *Staphylococcus aureus* **alpha toxin** inserts itself to form **pores** in the membrane.

**Table II-1-2.** Major Exotoxins

| | Organism (Gram) | Toxin | Mode of Action | Role in Disease |
|---|---|---|---|---|
| Inhibitors of Protein Synthesis | *Corynebacterium diphtheriae* (+) | Diphtheria toxin | ADP ribosyl transferase; inactivates eEF-2; 1´ targets: heart/nerves/epithelium | Inhibits eukaryotic cell protein synthesis |
| | *Pseudomonas aeruginosa* (−) | Exotoxin A | ADP ribosyl transferase; inactivates eEF-2; 1´ target: liver. | Inhibits eukaryotic cell protein synthesis |
| | *Shigella dysenteriae* (−) | Shiga toxin | Interferes with 60S ribosomal subunit | Inhibits protein synthesis in eukaryotic cells. Enterotoxic, cytotoxic, and neurotoxic |
| | Enterohemorrhagic *E. coli* (EHEC) (−) | Verotoxin (a shiga-like toxin) | Interferes with 60S ribosomal subunit | Inhibits protein synthesis in eukaryotic cells |
| Neurotoxins | *Clostridium tetani* (+) | Tetanus toxin | Blocks release of the inhibitory transmitters glycine and GABA | Inhibits neurotransmission in inhibitory synapses |
| | *Clostridium botulinum* (+) | Botulinum toxin | Blocks release of acetylcholine | Inhibits cholinergic synapses |
| Super-antigens | *Staphylococcus aureus* (+) | TSST-1 | Superantigen | Fever, increased susceptibility to LPS, rash, shock, capillary leakage |
| | *Streptococcus pyogenes* (+) | Exotoxin A, a.k.a.: erythrogenic or pyrogenic toxin | Similar to TSST-1 | Fever, increased susceptibility to LPS, rash, shock, capillary leakage, cardiotoxicity |
| cAMP Inducers | Enterotoxigenic *Escherichia coli* (−) | Heat labile toxin (LT) | LT stimulates an adenylate cyclase by ADP ribosylation of GTP binding protein | Both LT and ST promote secretion of fluid and electrolytes from intestinal epithelium |
| | *Vibrio cholerae* (−) | Cholera toxin | Similar to *E. coli* LT | Profuse, watery diarrhea |
| | *Bacillus anthracis* (+) | Anthrax toxin (3 proteins make 2 toxins) | EF = edema factor = adenylate cyclase LF = lethal factor PA = protective antigen (B component for both) | Decreases phagocytosis; causes edema, kills cells |
| | *Bordetella pertussis* (−) | Pertussis toxin | ADP ribosylates G$_i$, the negative regulator of adenylate cyclase → increased cAMP | Histamine-sensitizing Lymphocytosis promoting Islet activating |
| Cytolysins | *Clostridium perfringens* (+) | Alpha toxin | Lecithinase | Damages cell membranes; myonecrosis |
| | *Staphylococcus aureus* (+) | Alpha toxin | Toxin intercalates forming pores | Cell membrane becomes leaky |

## Review Questions

1.  A 21-year-old student was seen by his family physician with complaints of pharyngitis. Examination of the pharynx revealed patchy erythema and exudates on the tonsillar pillars. Throat smear showed gram-positive cocci in chains and gram-negative diplococci. He admitted to having been sexually active. What is the significance of the Gram stain smear in this case?

    (A)  It provides a rapid means of diagnosing the infection

    (B)  It indicates laboratory contamination

    (C)  It is not useful as it is not possible to make a diagnosis this way

    (D)  It strongly suggests gonococcal pharyngitis

    (E)  It is evidence of infection with hemolytic streptococci and *Neisseriae*

2.  Your laboratory isolates an entirely new and unknown pathogen from one of your patients, which has all the characteristics of an aerobic filamentous fungus except that the ribosomes are prokaryotic. Unfortunately, your patient with this pathogen is very ill. Which agent would most likely be successful in treating your patient?

    (A)  Third generation of cephalosporins

    (B)  Isoniazid

    (C)  Metronidazole

    (D)  Careful limited usage of Shiga toxin

    (E)  Tetracycline

3.  Mitochondria are missing in

    (A)  Filamentous fungi

    (B)  Protozoan parasites

    (C)  Viruses

    (D)  Yeasts

    (E)  Cestodes

4.  A culture isolate from a patient with subacute endocarditis is reported to be gram positive and possess a complex carbohydrate cell wall. What is the most likely taxonomic group of the causal agent?

    (A)  Fungus

    (B)  Parasite

    (C)  Prion

    (D)  Prokaryot

    (E)  Virus

5.  A patient with a non-healing skin lesion has that lesion biopsied to determine its cause. The pathology lab reports back that the lesion has the characteristics of a stellate granuloma. Which of the following is most likely to be true of the causal agent?

    (A)  It has lipopolysaccharide.

    (B)  It has pili.

    (C)  It is an exotoxin producer.

    (D)  It is a superantigen.

    (E)  It is intracellular.

6. A cancer chemotherapy patient has to have her intravenous port revised after it becomes blocked and the catheter is found to contain bacterial contaminants. Which of the following attributes is most likely to be a factor in this pathogenesis?

   (A) Biofilm production
   (B) Ergosterol containing membrane
   (C) Peptidoglycan layer
   (D) Possession of IgA protease
   (E) Possession of pili

7. A 45-year-old female executive goes to a cosmetic surgeon with the complaint of frown lines on her forehead which she feels are negatively affecting her appearance. Rather than undergoing surgery, she opts to try injection of BOTOX. What is the mechanism of action of this toxin?

   (A) It blocks release of acetylcholine.
   (B) It inhibits glycine and GABA.
   (C) It is a lecithinase.
   (D) It is a superantigen.
   (E) It ribosylates eukaryotic elongation factor-2.
   (F) It ribosylates Gs.

# Answers and Explanations

1. **Answer: C.** Gram-positive cocci (alpha hemolytic streptococci) and gram-negative cocci (*Neisseriae*) are normally present in the throat. There is no way to differentiate pathogens from non-pathogens by the Gram stain.

2. **Answer: E.** The cephalosporin that inhibits prokaryotic cell peptidoglycan cross linkage will not likely be effective against the complex carbohydrate cell wall. Isoniazid, which appears to inhibit mycolic acid synthesis, also would not likely work. Metronidazole would not work on an aerobic organism. Shiga toxin is only effective against eukaryotic ribosomes. Tetracycline (the correct answer) would have the greatest chance of success. However, it may not be taken up by the cell, or the cell could have an effective pump mechanism to get rid of it quickly.

3. **Answer: C.** Mitochondria are found only in eukaryotic organisms so both viruses and bacteria lack them.

4. **Answer: A.** The clue of a complex carbohydrate cell wall (chitin, glucan or mannan) defines the organism as a fungus. The mention that the organism was gram positive was a tricky clue, because of course, the gram stain is used diagnostically to differentiate between the two major categories of bacteria (prokaryots; **choice D**). The student should remember that some fungi will stain gram positive, however, because their thick cell wall makes them retain the gram stain just as a gram positive bacterium would. Parasites (**choice B**) do not possess a cell wall, prions (**choice C**) are infectious proteins, prokaryots (**choice D**) have a peptidoglycan cell wall, and viruses (**choice E**) are acellular.

5. **Answer: E.** The attribute of microorganisms which associates most strongly with the causation of granulomas is the fact that they live intracellularly. This

causes stimulation of the TH1 arm of the immune response, and the production of the cytokines of cell-mediated immunity, with the net result of the formation of granulomas in the infected tissues. Some organisms which are extracellular will also produce granulomas, but in those cases it is generally the chronic persistence and indigestibility of the pathogen which cause that result. Lipopolysaccharide (**choice A**) is a synonym for endotoxin, which causes gram negative shock, but not granuloma formation. Pili (**choice B**) are surface structures of some bacteria which mediate attachment to cellular surfaces. Exotoxins (**choice C**) are secreted toxins which may cause cell damage in a number of ways, and superantigens (**choice D**) cause stimulation of large numbers of clones of T lymphocytes and macrophages to cause symptoms similar to endotoxin shock.

6.  **Answer: A.** Catheters, shunts and prosthetic devices which are left in the body long-term, are almost always coated with Teflon which is extremely slippery. Organisms which are capable of adherence to Teflon (or the enamel of teeth), do so by creation of a biofilm, which allows them to change the surface tension of the liquid around them and thereby "glue" themselves to the material. Ergosterol (**choice B**) is the major sterol in the cell wall of fungi, and is important in membrane integrity, but not adherence. Peptidoglycan (**choice C**) is the cell wall material of bacteria, and is responsible for the shape of bacteria, but not their adherence. IgA proteases (**choice D**) can assist in the adherence of bacteria to mucosal surfaces, but would not be important in adherence to an intravenous catheter, and although pili (**choice E**) mediate attachment of bacteria to human cells, they would not be important in adherence to Teflon.

7.  **Answer: A.** Botulinum toxin (in BOTOX) inhibits release of acetylcholine and results in a flaccid paralysis. Inhibition of glycine and GABA (**choice B**) describes the action of Tetanus toxin which causes a rigid paralysis. The toxin of *Clostridium perfringens* is a lecithinase (**choice C**) which directly disrupts cell membranes. Toxic shock syndrome toxin-1 and the pyrogenic exotoxins of *Streptococcus pyogenes* act as superantigens (**choice D**) which cause systemic inflammatory response syndrome. Ribosylation of eukaryotic elongation factor-2 (**choice E**) is the mechanism of action of the diphtheria toxin and *Pseudomonas* exotoxin A. Ribosylation of Gs (**choice F**) is the mechanism of action of the cholera toxin and the labile toxin of Enterotoxigenic *Escherichia coli*.

# Medically Important Bacteria

**2**

## What the COMLEX Requires You To Know

**The type of major disease from presenting symptoms**

- Determine the causal agent from case clues.

- No distinguishing clues given? Know most common agent(s).

- Epidemiologic clues, symptomatic clues, or organism information given? Know the specific agent.

- Be able to answer basic science questions about disease or organism, predisposing conditions, epidemiology, mechanisms of pathogenicity, complications, standard preventive measures, and major tests used in identification.

**The basic science used as clues or tested directly**

- Morphology (Gram reaction, basic morphology, motility, spore formation)

- Physiology (obligate aerobes/anaerobes; a few specific fermentations; oxidase, urease, catalase, coagulase, superoxide dismutase, hemolysins; and how bacterial cells grow, divide, and die

- Bacterial structures (composition, function, and role in disease)

- Determinants of pathogenicity (toxins; factors aiding in invasiveness, pathogenicity or immune evasion; and obligate and facultative intracellular pathogens)

- Epidemiology/transmission (arthropod vectors; and how each major disease is acquired)

- Laboratory diagnosis (serologic/skin tests: specific serology for syphilis; acid fast and Gram stains; specific media; and unusual growth requirements)

- Treatment (drug of choice and prophylaxis where regularly used)

## Note

**Nomenclature**

Latin bacterial **family** names have **"-aceae,"** e.g., Enterobacteriaceae.

**Genus and species** names are **italicized** and **abbreviated**, e.g., *Enterobacter aerogenes = E. aerogenes*.

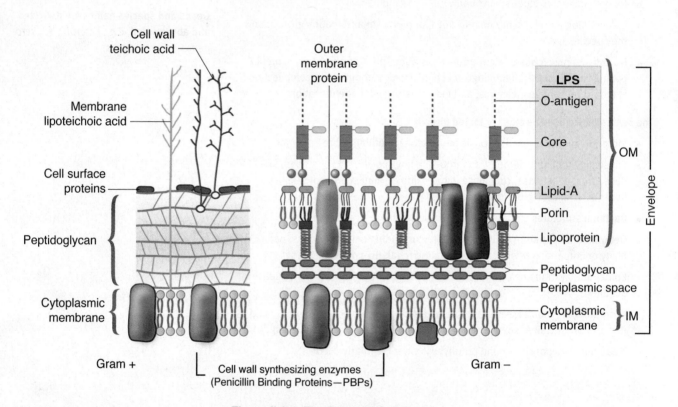

**Figure II-2-1.** The Bacterial Cell Envelope

# ENDOSPORES

## Organisms: *Bacillus* and *Clostridium*

### Function

- Survival not reproductive (1 bacterium → 1 spore)
- Resistance to chemicals, dessiccation, radiation, freezing, and heat

### Mechanism of resistance

- New enzymes (i.e., dipicolinic acid synthetase, heat-resistant catalase)
- Increases or decreases in other enzymes
- Dehydration: calcium dipicolinate in core
- Keratin spore coat

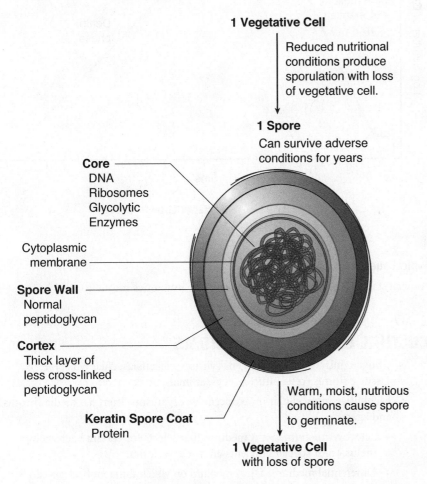

**1 Vegetative Cell**

Reduced nutritional conditions produce sporulation with loss of vegetative cell.

**1 Spore**
Can survive adverse conditions for years

**Core**
DNA
Ribosomes
Glycolytic
Enzymes

Cytoplasmic membrane

**Spore Wall**
Normal peptidoglycan

**Cortex**
Thick layer of less cross-linked peptidoglycan

**Keratin Spore Coat**
Protein

Warm, moist, nutritious conditions cause spore to germinate.

**1 Vegetative Cell**
with loss of spore

**Figure II-2-2.** Endospore

### Note

Spores of fungi have a reproductive role.

**COMLEX Note**

The COMLEX does not require you to calculate bacterial growth curves, whereas the USMLE might require them.

# BACTERIAL GROWTH AND DEATH

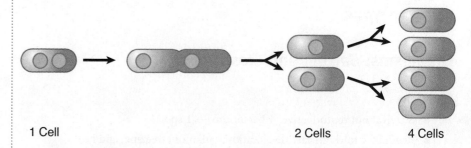

1 Cell      2 Cells      4 Cells

**Figure II-2-3.** Exponential Growth by Binary Fission

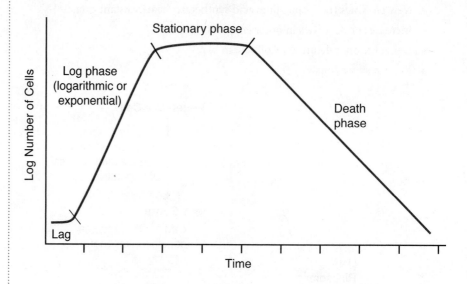

**Figure II-2-4.** Bacterial Growth Curve

**In a Nutshell**

**Lag Phase**

- Initial Phase (only 1 lag phase)

- Detoxifying medium

- Turning on enzymes to utilize medium

- For exam, number of cells at beginning equals number of cells at end of lag phase.

**Log Phase**

- Rapid exponential growth

- Generation time = time it takes one cell to divide into two. This is determined during log phase.

**Stationary Phase**

- Nutrients used up

- Toxic products like acids and alkali begin to accumulate.

- Number of new cells equals the number of dying cells.

**Typical question:**

At what stage of the bacterial growth curve are antibiotics most effective?

# CULTURE OF MICROORGANISMS

- Obligate intracellular pathogens (viruses, rickettsias, chlamydias, etc.): Tissue cultures (cell cultures), eggs, animals, or not at all

- Facultative intracellular or extracellular organisms: Inert lab media (broths and agars)

    - Selective medium (S): A medium that selects for certain bacteria by inclusion of special nutrients and/or antibiotics.

    - Differential medium (D): A medium on which different bacteria can be distinguished by differences in colonial morphology or color.

**Table II-2-1.** Special Media for Selected Organisms

| Organism | Medium |
|---|---|
| Anaerobes | Thioglycolate |
| *Corynebacterium* | Löffler's coagulated serum medium (S)<br>Tellurite agar (D) |
| Enteric bacteria | Eosin methylene blue (D)<br>MacConkeys (D and S) |
| Enteric pathogens | Hektoen enteric agar (D)<br>Xylose-lysine-deoxycholate agar |
| *Vibrio cholerae* (likes alkaline growth medium) | TCBS (Thiosulfate Citrate Bile Salts Sucrose agar) (S) |
| *Legionella* | Charcoal-yeast extract agar (CYE agar) (S) |
| *Mycobacterium* | Löwenstein-Jensen medium (S) |
| *Neisseria* from normally sterile sites, *Haemophilus* | Chocolate agar |
| *Neisseria* from sites with normal flora | Thayer-Martin selective medium* (S) |

*Thayer-Martin media is a chocolate agar supplemented with vancomycin, nystatin and colistin to inhibit the normal flora, including nonpathogenic *Neisseria*.

**Table II-2-2.** Miscellaneous Growth Requirements

| | |
|---|---|
| Cholesterol and purines and pyrimidines | *Mycoplasma* |
| Cysteine* | *Francisella, Brucella, Legionella, Pasteurella* |
| X (protoporphyrin) and V (NAD) | *Haemophilus* (*influenzae* and *aegypticus* require both) |

*The 4 Sisters Ella and the Cysteine Chapel.

## Note

**Mnemonic**

The 4 sisters "Ella" worship in the "Cysteine" chapel:

- *Francisella*
- *Brucella*
- *Legionella*
- *Pasteurella*

**Table II-2-3.** Oxygen Requirements and Toxicity

| Classification | Characteristics | Important Genera |
|---|---|---|
| Obligate aerobes | Require oxygen<br>Have no fermentative pathways<br>Generally produce superoxide dismutase | *Mycobacterium*<br>*Pseudomonas*<br>*(Bacillus)* |
| Microaerophilic | Require low but not full oxygen tension | *Campylobacter*<br>*Helicobacter* |
| Facultative anaerobes | Will respire aerobically until oxygen is depleted and then ferment | Most bacteria,<br>e.g., *Enterobacteriaceae* |
| Obligate anaerobes | • Lack superoxide dismutase<br>• Generally lack catalase<br>• Are fermenters<br>• Cannot use $O_2$ as terminal electron acceptor | *Actinomyces**<br>*Bacteroides*<br>*Clostridium* |

*ABCs of anaerobiosis = *Actinomyces*, *Bacteroides*, and *Clostridium*.

# STAINS

**Table II-2-4.** Gram Stain

| Reagent | Gram-Positive | Gram-Negative |
|---|---|---|
| Crystal Violet (a very intense purple, small dye molecule) | Purple/Blue | Purple/Blue |
| Gram's Iodine | Purple/Blue (a large dye complex) | Purple/Blue (a large dye complex) |
| Acetone or Alcohol | Purple/Blue | Colorless |
| Safranin (a pale dye) | Purple/Blue | Red/Pink |

All cocci are gram-positive except *Neisseria*, *Moraxella* and *Veillonella*.
All spore formers are gram-positive.
Background in stain modified for tissues will be pale red.

**Table II-2-5.** Ziehl-Neelsen Acid Fast Stain (or Kinyoun)

| Reagent | Acid Fast | Non-Acid Fast* |
|---|---|---|
| Carbol Fuchsin with heat** | Red (Hot Pink) | Red (Hot Pink) |
| Acid Alcohol | Red | Colorless |
| Methylene Blue*** | Red | Blue |

\* *Mycobacterium* is acid fast. *Nocardia* is partially acid fast. All other bacteria are non-acid fast. Two protozoan parasites (*Cryptosporidium* and *Isospora*) have acid fast oocysts.

\*\* Without the heat, the dye would not go in the mycobacterial cells.

\*\*\* Sputa and human cells will be blue.

# GRAM-STAINING REACTIONS

## Table II-2-6. Gram-Positive Bacteria

| Cocci |
|---|
| Staphylococcus[†] |
| Streptococcus[†] |

| Rods |
|---|
| **Aerobic or facultative anaerobic** |
| Bacillus |
| Listeria |
| Corynebacterium[†] |
| Nocardia |
| Mycobacterium[†] |
| **Anaerobic** |
| Clostridium[†] |
| Actinomyces |
| Eubacterium |
| Propionibacterium |
| Lactobacillus |

Note: Spore formers are *Bacillus* and *Clostridium*.

## Table II-2-7. Non-Gram–staining Bacteria*

| Mycoplasmataceae |
|---|
| Mycoplasma[†] |
| Ureaplasma |

*Note:

**Poorly visible** on traditional Gram stain: ***Mycobacterium*** does not stain well with the Gram stain due to its waxy cell wall. It is considered gram-positive.

Most **spirochetes, chlamydiae,** and **rickettsias** are so thin that the color of the Gram stain cannot be seen. All have gram-negative cell walls.

*Legionella* (gram-negative) also does not stain well with the traditional Gram stain unless counterstain time is increased.

## Table II-2-8. Gram-Negative Bacteria

| Aerobic | | |
|---|---|---|
| **Cocci** | Neisseria[†] | |
| | Moraxella | |
| **Rods** | | |
| | Pseudomonas | Eikenella |
| | Legionella | Kingella |
| | Brucella | |
| | Bordetella[†] | |
| | Francisella | |

| Helical or curved (and microaerophilic) |
|---|
| Campylobacter |
| Helicobacter |

| Facultative anaerobic rods | | |
|---|---|---|
| **Enterobacteriaceae[†]** | | **Also:** |
| | Escherichia[†] | Capnocytophaga |
| | Shigella | Actinobacillus |
| | Salmonella[†] | Cardiobacterium |
| | Citrobacter | Gardnerella |
| | Klebsiella | |
| | Enterobacter | |
| | Serratia | |
| | Proteus | |
| | Yersinia[†] | |
| **Vibrionaceae** | | |
| | Vibrio | |
| **Pasteurellaceae** | | |
| | Pasteurella | |
| | Haemophilus[†] | |

| Anaerobic straight to helical rods |
|---|
| Bacteroides/Prevotella |
| Fusobacterium |

| Spirochetes | |
|---|---|
| | Treponema[†] |
| | Borrelia |
| | Leptospira |
| **Rickettsiaceae and relatives** | Rickettsia[†] |
| | Bartonella |
| | Ehrlichia |

| Chlamydiaceae | |
|---|---|
| | Chlamydia[†] |
| | Chlamydophila |

([†]Marked organisms have high numbers of questions in the pool.)

# GRAM-POSITIVE COCCI

- *Staphylococcus*
- *Streptococcus*

**Table II-2-9.** Major Species of *Staphylococcus* and *Streptococcus* and Identifying Features*

| | Catalase | Coagulase | Hemolysis† | Distinguishing Features | Disease Presentations |
|---|---|---|---|---|---|
| **_Staphylococcus_ Species** | | | | | |
| *S. aureus* | + | + | β | Ferments mannitol<br>Salt tolerant | Infective endocarditis (acute)<br>Abscesses<br>Toxic shock syndrome<br>Gastroenteritis<br>Suppurative lesions, pyoderma, impetigo<br>Osteomyelitis |
| *S. epidermidis* | + | − | γ | Novobiocin$^S$<br>Biofilm producer | Endocarditis in IV drug users<br>Catheter and prosthetic device infections |
| *S. saprophyticus* | + | − | γ | Novobiocin$^R$ | UTIs in newly sexually active females |
| **_Streptococcus_ Species (Grouped by analysis of C carbohydrate)** | | | | | |
| *S. pyogenes* (Group A) | − | − | β | Bacitracin$^S$<br>PYR† | Pharyngitis<br>Scarlet fever<br>Pyoderma/impetigo<br>Suppurative lesions<br>Rheumatic fever<br>Acute glomerulonephritis |
| *S. agalactiae* (Group B) | − | − | β | Bacitracin$^R$<br>CAMP$^+$ | Neonatal septicemia and meningitis |
| *S. pneumoniae* (not groupable) | − | − | α | Optochin$^S$ | Pneumonia (community acquired)<br>Adult meningitis<br>Otitis media and sinusitis in children |
| Viridans group (not groupable) | − | − | α | Optochin$^R$ | Infective endocarditis<br>Dental caries |
| *Enterococcus* sp. (Group D) | − | − | α, β, or γ | PYR†<br>Esculin agar | Infective endocarditis<br>Urinary and biliary infections |
| *S. bovis* | − | − | γ | Bile esculin† | Endocarditis, especially in patients with colon cancer |

† β hemolysis = clear; α hemolysis = partial; γ hemolysis = no hemolysis

*Definition of abbreviations:* PYR, pyrrolidonyl arylamidase; $^S$, sensitive; $^R$, resistant

*Many of the diseases caused by *Staphylococcus* and *Streptococcus* are similar (i.e., skin infections, endocarditis). Therefore, laboratory tests are extremely important in differentiating between these organisms.

## Key Vignette Clues

**S. epidermidis**

- Coagulase (–); gram (+) cocci
- Novobiocin sensitive
- Infections of catheters/shunts

**S. saprophyticus**

- Coagulase (–), gram (+) cocci
- Novobiocin resistant
- "Honeymoon cystitis"

## Key Vignette Clues

**Staphylococcus aureus**

- Coagulase (+), gram (+) cocci in clusters
- Gastroenteritis: 2–6 h onset, salty foods, custards
- Endocarditis: acute
- Toxic shock syndrome: desquamating rash, fever, hypotension
- Impetigo: bullous
- Pneumonia: nosocomial, typical, acute
- Osteomyelitis: #1 cause unless HbS mentioned

# GENUS: *STAPHYLOCOCCUS*

## Genus Features

- Gram-positive cocci in clusters
- **Catalase positive** (streptococci are catalase negative)

## Species of Medical Importance

- *S. aureus*
- *S. epidermidis*
- *S. saprophyticus*

## *Staphylococcus aureus*

### Distinguishing Features

- Small, yellow colonies on blood agar
- β-hemolytic
- **Coagulase positive** (all other *Staphylococcus* species are negative)
- **Ferments mannitol** on mannitol salt agar

### Reservoir

- Normal flora
  - Nasal mucosa (25% of population are carriers)
  - Skin

### Transmission

- Hands
- Sneezing
- Surgical wounds
- Contaminated food
  - Custard pastries
  - Potato salad
  - Canned meats

### Predisposing Factors for Infection

- Surgery/wounds
- Foreign body (tampons, surgical packing, sutures)
- Severe neutropenia (<500/μL)
- Intravenous drug abuse
- Chronic granulomatous disease
- Cystic fibrosis

## Pathogenesis

- Protein A binds Fc component of IgG, inhibits phagocytosis
- **Enterotoxins:** fast acting, heat stable
- **Toxic shock syndrome toxin-1 (TSST-1):** superantigen (see Chapter 6 of Immunology for further explanation of a superantigen)
- Coagulase: converts fibrinogen to fibrin clot
- Cytolytic toxin (α toxin): pore-forming toxin, Panton-Valentine leukocidin (PVL), forms pores in infected cells and is acquired by bacteriophage; associated with increased virulence, MRSA strains
- Exfolatins: skin-exfoliating toxins (involved in scalded skin syndrome [SSS]) and bullous impetigo

## Diseases

**Table II-2-10.** *Staphylococcus aureus*

| Diseases | Clinical Symptoms | Pathogenicity Factors |
|---|---|---|
| Gastroenteritis (food poisoning)— toxin ingested preformed in food | **2–6 hours** after ingesting toxin: nausea, abdominal pain, vomiting, followed by diarrhea | Enterotoxins A–E preformed in food |
| Infective endocarditis (acute) | Fever, malaise, leukocytosis, heart murmur (may be absent initially) | Fibrin-platelet mesh, cytolytic toxins |
| Abscesses and mastitis | Subcutaneous tenderness, redness and swelling; hot | Coagulase, cytolysins |
| Toxic shock syndrome | Fever, hypotension, **scarlatiniform rash that desquamates (particularly on palms and soles)**, multiorgan failure | TSST-1 |
| Impetigo | Erythematous papules to **bullae** | Coagulase, exfoliatins |
| Scalded skin syndrome | Diffuse epidermal peeling | Coagulase, exfoliatins |
| Pneumonia | Productive pneumonia with rapid onset, high rate of necrosis, and high fatality; nosocomial, ventilator, postinfluenza, IV drug abuse, CF, CGD, etc. Salmon-colored sputum | Coagulase, cytolysins |
| Surgical infections | Fever with cellulitis and/or abscesses | Coagulase, exfoliatins, ± TSSTs |
| Osteomyelitis (most common cause) | Bone pain, fever, ±tissue swelling, redness; lytic bone lesions on imaging | Cytolysins, coagulase |

*Definition of abbreviations:* CF, cystic fibrosis; CGD, chronic granulomatous disease.

## Differential Diagnosis

- Gastroenteritis
  - *Bacillus cereus*
  - *Clostridium perfringens*
  - Norovirus
- Skin infections—group A streptococci
- Pneumonia
- Cystic fibrosis
  - *Haemophilus influenzae*
  - *Pseudomonas aeruginosa*
- Post viral infection
  - S. pneumoniae
- Endocarditis
  - *S. epidermidis*
  - *Enterococcus* species
  - Viridans streptococci
  - HACEK group
- Osteomyelitis
  - Group A streptococci
  - *P. aeruginosa*
  - *H. influenzae*
  - *Salmonella* species

## COMLEX Note

*Staphylococcus* and *Streptococcus* may be heavily tested on boards. They often cause similar disease presentations, especially in the skin. The simplest method to differentiale *Staphylococcus* from *Streptococcus* is the *catalase test.*

## Treatment

- Gastroenteritis is self-limiting.
- Nafcillin/oxacillin are drugs of choice because of widespread antibiotic resistance.
- For methicillin-resistant *Staphylococcus aureus* (MRSA): vancomycin
- For vancomycin-resistant *Staphylococcus aureus* (VRSA) or vancomycin-intermediate *S. aureus* (VISA): quinupristin/dalfopristin

# GENUS: *STREPTOCOCCUS*

## Genus Features

- **Gram-positive cocci in chains**
- **Catalase negative**
- Serogrouped using known antibodies to the cell wall carbohydrates (Lancefield groups A–O)
  - *S. pneumoniae* serotyped via capsule
  - *S. pyogenes* serotyped via M protein

## Species of Medical Importance

- *S. pyogenes*
- *S. agalactiae* (group B streptococci; GBS)
- *S. pneumoniae*
- Viridans streptococci
- *Enterococcus faecalis/Enterococcus faecium*
- *Streptococcus bovis*

# *Streptococcus pyogenes* (Group A Streptococcus; GAS)

## Distinguishing Features

- **β hemolytic**
- **Bacitracin sensitive**
- **Pyrrolidonyl arylamidase (PYR) positive**

## Reservoir

- Human throat
- Skin

## Transmission

- Direct contact
- Respiratory droplets

## Pathogenesis

- **Hyaluronic acid: is non-immunogenic**
- **M-protein: antiphagocytic, M12 strains** associated with **acute glomerulonephritis**
- Streptolysin O: immunogenic, hemolysin/cytolysin
- Streptolysin S: not immunogenic, hemolysin/cytolysin

## Spreading Factors

- Streptokinase: breaks down fibrin clot
- Streptococcal DNAse: liquefies pus, extension of lesion
- Hyaluronidase: hydrolyzes the ground substances of the connective tissues
- Exotoxins A–C (pyrogenic or erythrogenic exotoxins)
  - Phage-coded (i.e., the cells are lysogenized by a phage.)
  - Cause **fever and rash** of scarlet fever
    - ° **Superantigens**

## Diseases

**Table II-2-11.** Acute Suppurative Group A Streptococcal Infections*

| Diseases | Symptoms |
|---|---|
| Pharyngitis | Abrupt onset of sore throat, fever, malaise, and headache; tonsillar abscesses and tender anterior cervical lymph nodes |
| Scarlet fever | Above followed by a blanching **"sandpaper" rash** (palms and soles are usually spared), circumoral pallor, **strawberry tongue**, and nausea/vomiting |
| Pyoderma/impetigo | Pyogenic skin infection (honey-crusted lesions) |

*Also, cellulitis/necrotizing fasciitis, puerperal fever, lymphangitis, erysipelas

**Table II-2-12.** Nonsuppurative Sequelae to Group A Streptococcal Infections

| Disease | Sequelae of | Mechanisms/Symptoms |
|---|---|---|
| Rheumatic fever | Pharyngitis with group A strep | Antibodies to heart tissue/2 weeks post pharyngitis, fever, joint inflammation, carditis, erythema marginatum (chorea later)—type II hypersensitivity |
| Acute glomerulonephritis (M12 serotype) | Pharyngitis or skin infection | Immune complexes bound to glomeruli/pulmonary edema and hypertension, "smoky" urine (type III hypersensitivity) |

## Laboratory Diagnosis

- The rapid strep test (ELISA-based) misses approximately 25% of infections. Culture all negatives.
- Antibodies to streptolysin O (ASO) titer of >200 is significant for rheumatic fever.

## Key Vignette Clues

**Group A *Streptococcus***

- Catalase (–), β hemolytic, bacitracin sensitive, gram (+) cocci
- Pharyngitis: abrupt onset, tonsillar abscesses
- Scarlet fever: blanching, sandpaper rash, strawberry tongue
- Impetigo: honey-crusted lesions

## Key Vignette Clues

- Rheumatic fever: after streptococcal pharyngitis, ↑ ASO titer
- AGN: after streptococcal skin or throat infection, hypertension, edema, smoky urine

## Differential Diagnosis

- Pharyngitis
  - *C. pneumoniae*
  - *M. pneumoniae*
  - *N. gonorrhoeae*
  - Adenovirus
  - Influenza
  - Coronavirus
  - Respiratory syncytial virus
- Scarlet fever
  - EBV
  - B19
  - Measles
  - Rubella
  - HHV-6

## Differential Diagnosis (*Cont'd*)

- Pyoderma/impetigo
  - *S. aureus*
  - *C. albicans*
  - *Trichophyton, Microsporum, Epidermophyton*
- Rheumatic fever
  - *S. epidermidis*
  - *S. aureus*
  - *Enterococcus* species
  - Viridans streptococci
  - HACEK group

## Key Vignette Clues

**S. agalactiae**

- Gram (+), catalase (−), β hemolytic, bacitracin resistant, CAMP test (+)
- Neonatal meningitis and septicemia: #1 cause, especially in prolonged labors

## Differential Diagnosis

- *Escherichia coli* (second most common cause of neonatal meningitis)
- *Listeria monocytogenes*
- Herpes simplex virus 1 or 2

**Figure II-2-5.** *Streptococcus pneumoniae*

## Treatment

- Beta lactam drugs
- Macrolides are used in the case of penicillin allergy.

## Prevention

- Prophylactic antibiotics should be considered in patients for at least 5 year post acute rheumatic fever.
- Beta lactams and macrolides

# *Streptococcus agalactiae* (Group B Streptococci; GBS)

## Distinguishing Features

- β hemolytic
- **Bacitracin resistant**
- **Hydrolyze hippurate**
- **CAMP test positive** (CAMP factor is a polypeptide that "complements" the sphingomyelinase of *S. aureus* to create an enhanced hemolytic pattern in the shape of an arrowhead)

## Reservoir

- Human vagina (15–20% of women)
- Gastrointestinal tract

**Transmission**—newborn infected during birth (increased risk with **prolonged labor after rupture of membranes**)

## Pathogenesis

- Capsule
- β hemolysin and CAMP factor

**Diseases**—neonatal septicemia and meningitis; most common causal agent

**Treatment**—ampicillin with an aminoglycoside or a cephalosporin

## Prevention

- Prophylaxis during delivery in women with a positive vaginal or rectal culture of GBS, a history of recent infection with GBS, or prolonged labors after membrane rupture
- Ampicillin or penicillin drugs of choice
- Clindamycin or erythromycin for penicillin allergies

# *Streptococcus pneumoniae*

## Distinguishing Features

- α **hemolytic**
- **Optochin sensitive**
- **Lancet-shaped diplococci**
- **Lysed by bile**

**Reservoir**—human upper respiratory tract

**Transmission**

- Respiratory droplets
  - Not considered highly communicable
  - Often colonizes the nasopharynx without causing disease

**Predisposing Factors**

- Antecedent influenza or measles infection
- Chronic obstructive pulmonary disease (COPD)
- Congestive heart failure (CHF)
- Alcoholism
- Asplenia predisposes to septicemia

**Pathogenesis**

- **Polysaccharide capsule** is the major virulence factor
- IgA protease
- Teichoic acid
- Pneumolysin O: hemolysin/cytolysin
  - Damages respiratory epithelium
  - Inhibits leukocyte respiratory burst and inhibits classical complement fixation

**Diseases**

- Typical pneumonia
  - **Most common cause** (especially in sixth decade of life)
  - Shaking chills, high fever, lobar consolidation, **blood-tinged, "rusty" sputum**
- Adult meningitis
  - **Most common cause**
  - Peptidoglycan and teichoic acids are highly inflammatory in the CNS.
  - CSF reveals high WBCs (neutrophils) and low glucose, high protein
- Otitis media and sinusitis in children—**most common cause**

**Laboratory Diagnosis**

- Gram stain of CSF
- PCR of CSF
- Quellung reaction: positive (swelling of the capsule with the addition of type-specific antiserum, no longer used but still tested!)
- Latex particle agglutination: test for capsular antigen in CSF

**Treatment**

- Bacterial pneumonia—macrolides
- Adult meningitis—Ceftriaxone or cefotaxime. Vancomycin is added if penicillin-resistant *S. pneumoniae* has been reported in the community
- Otitis media and sinusitis in children—amoxicillin, erythromycin for allergic individuals

**Prevention**

- Antibody to the capsule (over 80 different capsular serotypes) provides type-specific immunity

## Key Vignette Clues

*Streptococcus pneumoniae*

- Gram (+), catalase (−), α hemolytic, soluble in bile, optochin sensitive
- Pneumonia—typical, most common cause, rusty sputum
- Meningitis—many PMNs, ↓ glucose, ↑ protein in CSF, most common adult cause
- Otitis media and sinusitis—most common cause

## COMLEX Note

It is important to be able to differentiate between the bacterial pneumonias. Pay attention to "buzz words" and the age and condition of the patient.

- rust colored sputum = *S. pneumoniae*
- "current jelly" sputum = *K. pneumoniae*
- salmon colored sputum = *S. aureus*
- For an elderly smoker, if none of the above clues are present, then *Legionella pneumophilus*

## In a Nutshell

**Typical Pneumonia**

Bacterial pneumonia such as *Streptococcus pneumoniae* elicits neutrophils; arachidonic acid metabolites (acute inflammatory mediators) cause pain and fever. *Pneumococcus* produces a lobar pneumonia with a productive cough, grows on blood agar, and usually responds well to penicillin treatment.

## Differential Diagnosis

- Bacterial pneumonia
  - **Typical**
    - *K. pneumoniae*
    - *H. influenzae*
    - *S. aureus*
  - **Atypical**
    - *L. pneumophila*
    - *M. pneumoniae*
    - *C. pneumoniae*

## Differential Diagnosis (*Cont'd*)

- Adult (bacterial) meningitis
  - *N. meningitidis*
  - *H. influenzae*
  - *Streptococcus* species
  - *L. monocytogenes*
- Otitis media and sinusitis in children
  - *H. influenzae*
  - *M. catarrhalis*
  - *S. pyogenes*
  - RSV

## Key Vignette Clues

### Viridans Streptococci

- Gram (+), catalase (–), α hemolytic, optochin resistant, bile insoluble
- Plaque and dental caries
- Subacute bacterial endocarditis—pre-existing damage to the heart valves; follows dental work

- Vaccine
  - Pediatric (PCV, pneumococcal conjugate vaccine)
    - Thirteen of the most common serotypes
    - Conjugated to diphtheria toxoid
    - Prevents invasive disease
  - Adult (PPV, pneumococcal polysaccharide vaccine)
    - 23 of the most common capsular serotypes
    - Recommended for all adults ≥65 years of age and any at-risk individuals

# Viridans Streptococci (*S. sanguis, S. mutans*)

### Distinguishing Features

- **α hemolytic**
- **Optochin resistant**

**Reservoir**—human oropharynx (normal flora)

**Transmission**—endogenous

**Pathogenesis—dextran (biofilm)–mediated adherence** onto tooth enamel or damaged heart valve and to each other (vegetation); growth in vegetation protects organism from immune system.

### Diseases

- Dental caries—*S. mutans* dextran–mediated adherence glues oral flora onto teeth, forming plaque and causing dental caries.
- Infective endocarditis (subacute)
  - Malaise, fatigue, anorexia, night sweats, weight loss, splinter hemorrhages
  - Predisposing conditions: damaged (or prosthetic) heart valve *and* dental work without prophylactic antibiotics or extremely poor oral hygiene

**Treatment**—penicillin G with aminoglycosides for endocarditis

**Prevention**—prophylactic antibiotics prior to dental work for individuals with damaged heart valve

# GENUS: *ENTEROCOCCUS*

**Genus Features**

- **Catalase negative**
- **PYR+**

**Species of Medical Importance**

- *Enterococcus faecalis*
- *Enterococcus faecium*

## *Enterococcus faecalis/faecium*

**Distinguishing Features**

- **Group D gram-positive cocci in chains**
- **PYR test positive**
- Catalase-negative, varied hemolysis
- **Hydrolyze esculin in 40% bile and 6.5% NaCl** (bile esculin agar turns black)

**Reservoir**—human colon, urethra ± and female genital tract

**Transmission**—endogenous

**Pathogenesis**

- Bile/salt tolerance allows survival in bowel and gall bladder.
- During medical procedures on GI or GU tract: *E. faecalis* → **bloodstream** → **previously damaged heart valves** → **endocarditis**

**Diseases**

- Urinary and biliary tract infections
- Infective (subacute) endocarditis—in persons (often elderly) with damaged heart valves

**Diagnosis**

- Culture on blood agar
- Antibiotic sensitivities

**Treatment**

- All strains carry some drug resistance.
- Some **vancomycin-resistant strains of *Enterococcus faecium*** or ***E. faecalis*** have no reliably effective treatment. In general for low-level resistance, use ampicillin, gentamicin, or streptomycin.
- VanA strains have UDP-N-acetylmuramyl pentapeptide with the terminal D-alanyl-D-alanine replaced with D-alanyl-D-lactate, which functions in cell wall synthesis but does not bind to vancomycin.

**Prevention**—prophylactic use of penicillin and gentamicin in patients with damaged heart valves prior to intestinal or urinary tract manipulations

## Key Vignette Clues

*Enterococcus faecalis/faecium*

- Gram (+), catalase (–), variable hemolysis, hydrolyzes esculin
- Urinary/biliary tract infections—elderly males
- Subacute bacterial endocarditis—elderly males, follows GI/GU surgery, preexisting heart valve damage

## Differential Diagnosis

- *S. epidermidis* (endocarditis)
- *S. aureus*
- Viridans strep
- HACEK organisms

# GRAM-POSITIVE RODS

**Table II-2-13.** Summary of Gram-Positive Rods

| Genus | Spore | Aerobic Growth | Exotoxin | Facultative Intracellular | IC Hosts* | Acid Fast | Branching Rods |
|---|---|---|---|---|---|---|---|
| *Bacillus* | + | + | + | − | − | − | − |
| *Clostridium* | + | − | + | − | − | − | − |
| *Listeria* | − | + | + | + | + | − | − |
| *Corynebacterium* | − | + | + | − | − | − | − |
| *Actinomyces* | − | − | − | − | − | − | + |
| *Nocardia* | − | + | − | − | + | +† | + |
| *Mycobacterium* | − | + | − | + | + | + | − |

*Definition of abbreviation:* IC, immunocompromised.

*Column defines whether the organism a significant problem in IC hosts.

†*Nocardia* is considered partially acid fast.

# GENUS: *BACILLUS*

**Genus Features**

- Gram-positive rods
- **Spore forming**
- **Aerobic**

**Species of Medical Importance**

- *Bacillus anthracis*
- *Bacillus cereus*

## *Bacillus anthracis*

**Distinguishing Features**

- **Large,** boxcar-like, gram-positive, **spore-forming rods**
- **Capsule is polypeptide (poly-D-glutamate)**
- **Potential biowarfare agent**

**Reservoir**—animals, skins, soils

**Transmission**—contact with infected animals or inhalation of spores (bioterrorism)

**Pathogenesis**

- Capsule—polypeptide, antiphagocytic, immunogenic
- **Anthrax toxin** includes 3 protein components:
  - **Protective antigen** (B component)—mediates entry of LF or EF into eukaryotic cells
  - **Lethal factor**—kills cells
  - **Edema factor** is an adenylate cyclase (calmodulin-activated like pertussis adenylate cyclase)

**Diseases**

- Cutaneous anthrax—papule → papule with vesicles (malignant pustules) → central necrosis (eschar) with erythematous border often with painful regional lymphadenopathy; fever in 50%
- Pulmonary (wool sorter's disease)
  - Life-threatening **pneumonia**; cough, fever, malaise, and ultimately facial edema, dyspnea, diaphoresis, cyanosis, and shock with **mediastinal hemorrhagic lymphadenitis**
- Gastrointestinal anthrax
  - Rare
  - Edema and blockage of gastrointestinal tract can occur, vomiting and bloody diarrhea, high mortality

**Diagnosis**

- Gram stain and culture of blood, respiratory secretions or lesions
- Serology
- PCR

**Treatment**—ciprofloxacin or doxycycline. (Genes encoding resistance to penicillin and doxycycline have been transferred to *B. anthracis*.)

## Key Vignette Clues

***Bacillus anthracis***

- Gram (+), spore forming, aerobic rods
- Contact with animal hides or postal worker; eschar or life-threatening pneumonia

## COMLEX Note

Biowarfare scenarios are becoming increasingly popular. Some likely agents include:

*B. anthracis*

*Y. pestis*

*F. talarensis*

*Brucella*

Smallpox virus

## Differential Diagnosis

- *C. immitis*
- *S. pneumoniae/K. pneumoniae*
- *M. tuberculosis*

**Prevention**

- Toxoid vaccine (AVA, acellular vaccine adsorbed)
- Given to individuals in high risk occupations (military)

## Key Vignette Clues

**Bacillus cereus**

- Rapid-onset gastroenteritis
- Fried rice, Chinese restaurants

# *Bacillus cereus*

**Distinguishing Feature**—spores

**Reservoir**—found in nature

**Transmission**

- Foodborne, intoxication
- Major association with fried rice from Chinese restaurants
- Associated with food kept warm, not hot (buffets)

**Pathogenesis—two possible toxins:**

- **Emetic toxin: preformed fast (1–6 hours)**, similar to *S. aureus* with vomiting and diarrhea; associated with **fried rice**
- Diarrheal toxin produced in vivo (meats, sauces): 18 hours, similar to *E. coli*; LT: increasing cAMP → watery diarrhea

## Differential Diagnosis

- *S. aureus*
- *C. perfringens*

**Diseases**

- Gastroenteritis
  - −Nonbloody
  - −± Vomiting

**Diagnosis**

- Clinical grounds
- Culture and Gram stain of implicated food

**Treatment**—self-limiting

# GENUS: *CLOSTRIDIUM*

Genus Features

- **Gram-positive rods**
- **Spore forming**
- **Anaerobic**

Species of Medical Importance

- *Clostridium tetani*
- *Clostridium botulinum*
- *Clostridium perfringens*
- *Clostridium difficile*

## *Clostridium tetani*

Distinguishing Features

- **Large gram-positive, spore-forming rods**
- Anaerobes
- Produces tetanus toxin

Reservoir—soil

Transmission

- Puncture wounds/trauma (human bites)
- Requires low tissue oxygenation ($E_h$)

Pathogenesis

- Spores germinate in the tissues, producing **tetanus toxin** (an exotoxin also called **tetanospasmin**).
- Carried intra-axonally to CNS
- **Binds to ganglioside receptors**
- **Blocks release of inhibitory mediators (glycine and GABA) at spinal synapses**
- Excitatory neurons are unopposed → extreme muscle spasm
- One of the most toxic substances known

Disease—**tetanus**

- Risus sardonicus
- Opisthotonus
- Extreme muscle spasms

## Key Vignette Clues

*Clostridium tetani*

- Dirty puncture wound
- Rigid paralysis

## Differential Diagnosis

- Rabies virus
- *N. meningitidis*
- *S. pneumoniae*
- *H. influenzae*

**Diagnosis**—primarily a clinical diagnosis; organism is rarely isolated.

**Treatment of Actual Tetanus**

- **Hyperimmune human globulin (TIG) to neutralize toxin plus metronidazole or penicillin**
- **Spasmolytic drugs** (diazepam); debride; delay closure

**Prevention**

- Toxoid is formaldehyde-inactivated toxin.
- Important because disinfectants have poor sporicidal action
- Care of wounds: proper wound cleansing and care plus treatment

**Table II-2-14.** Wound Management

| Patient | Not Tetanus Prone | Tetanus Prone |
|---|---|---|
|  | Linear, 1 cm deep cut, without devitalized tissue, without major contaminants, less than 6 hours old | Blunt/missile, burn, frostbite, 1 cm deep; devitalized tissue present + contaminants (e.g., dirt, saliva); any wound 6 hours old |
| Not completed primary or vaccination history unknown | Vaccine | Vaccine and TIG* |
| Completed primary series | Vaccine if more than 10 years since last booster | Vaccine if more than 5 years since last booster |

*TIG = tetanus immunoglobulin (human).

# Clostridium botulinum

**Distinguishing Features**

- **Anaerobic**
- **Gram-positive spore-forming rods**

**Reservoir**—soil/dust

**Transmission**—foodborne/traumatic implantation

Pathogenesis

- **Spores** survive in soil and dust; **germinate** in moist, warm, nutritious but **nonacidic and anaerobic conditions**
- **Botulinum toxin**
  - **A-B polypeptide neurotoxin** (actually a series of 7 antigenically different; type A and B most common)
  - **Coded for by a prophage** (lysogenized *Clostridium botulinum*).
  - Highly toxic
  - **Heat labile** (unlike staph), 10 minutes 60.0°C
  - **Mechanism of action**
    - **Absorbed by gut** and carried by blood to peripheral nerve synapses
    - **Blocks release of acetylcholine** at the myoneuronal junction resulting in a reversible **flaccid paralysis**

## Key Vignette Clues

*Clostridium botulinum*

- Home-canned alkaline vegetables
- Floppy baby syndrome (infant with flaccid paralysis)
- Reversible flaccid paralysis

## COMLEX Note

- Food intoxications

  S. aureus

  B. cereus

  C. perfringens

  C. botulinum

- generally fast acting (ex. *C. botulinum*)

## Differential Diagnosis

- Polio virus
- *C. diphtheriae*

Disease(s)

**Table II-2-15.** Forms of Botulism

| Disease | Adult | Infant |
|---|---|---|
| Acquisition | **Preformed toxin ingested (toxicosis)** | **Spores ingested: household dust, honey** |
| | Poorly canned alkaline vegetables (green beans), smoked fish | Toxin produced in gut (toxi-infection) |
| Symptoms | 1–2 day onset of weakness, dizziness, blurred vision, flaccid paralysis (reversible); ± diarrhea, nausea or vomiting | Constipation, limpness/flaccid paralysis (reversible): diplopia, dysphagia, weak feeding/crying; may lead to respiratory arrest |
| Toxin demonstrated in | Suspected food or serum | Stool or serum |
| Treatment | Respiratory support | Respiratory support in monitored intensive care; hyperimmune human serum |
| | Trivalent (A-B-E) antitoxin | Antibiotics generally not used as may worsen or prolong |
| Prevention | **Proper canning; heat all canned foods** | **No honey first year** |

## *Clostridium perfringens*

**Distinguishing Features**

- Large **gram-positive, spore-forming** rods (spores rare in tissue), nonmotile
- **Anaerobic: "stormy fermentation" in milk media**
- **Double zone of hemolysis**

**Reservoir**—soil and human colon

**Transmission—foodborne and traumatic implantation**

### Key Vignette Clues

*Clostridium perfringens*

- Contaminated wound
- Pain, edema, gas, fever, tachycardia
- Food poisoning: reheated meats, non-inflammatory diarrhea

## COMLEX Note

- Food intoxications

  *S. aureus*

  *B. cereus*

  *C. perfringens*

  *C. botulinum*

- generally fast acting (ex. *C. botulinum*)

## Differential Diagnosis

- Gangrene
  - Group A *Streptococcus* (necrotizing fasciitis)
- Food poisoning
  - Salmonella species
  - ETEC
  - Vibrio cholerae/V. parahaemolyticus
  - Norwalk virus
  - Rotavirus

### Pathogenesis

- **Spores** germinate under anaerobic conditions in tissue.
- Vegetative cells produce:
  - **Alpha toxin** (phospholipase C) is a **lecithinase.** It disrupts membranes, damaging RBCs, platelets, WBCs, endothelial cells → massive hemolysis, tissue destruction, hepatic toxicity.
- Identified by **Nagler reaction:** egg yolk agar plate—one side with anti-α-**toxin**; lecithinase activity is detected on side with no antitoxin.
- Twelve other toxins damage tissues.
- **Enterotoxin** produced in intestines in food poisoning: disrupts ion transport → watery diarrhea, cramps (similar to *E. coli*); resolution <24 hours.

### Disease(s)

- Gas gangrene (myonecrosis)
  - Contamination of **wound with soil or feces**
  - **Acute** and **increasing pain** at wound site
  - **Tense tissue** (edema, gas) and exudate
  - Systemic symptoms include **fever** and **tachycardia** (disproportionate to fever), diaphoresis, pallor, etc.
  - **Rapid, high mortality**
- Food poisoning
  - **Reheated meat dishes,** organism grows to high numbers; 8–24 hour incubation
  - **Enterotoxin** production in gut; self-limiting noninflammatory, watery diarrhea

### Diagnosis—clinical

### Treatment

- Gangrene
  - Debridement, delayed closure, clindamycin and penicillin, hyperbaric chamber
- Food poisoning
  - Self-limiting

### Prevention—extensive **debridement** of the wound plus administration of penicillin.

# *Clostridium difficile*

**Reservoir**—human colon/gastrointestinal tract

**Transmission**—endogenous

**Pathogenesis**

- Toxin A: enterotoxin damaging mucosa leading to fluid increase; granulocyte attractant
- Toxin B: cytotoxin: cytopathic

**Disease(s)—antibiotic-associated (clindamycin, cephalosporins,** amoxicillin, ampicillin) **diarrhea, colitis, or pseudomembranous colitis** (yellow plaques on colon)

**Diagnosis**

- Culture is not diagnostic because organism is part of normal flora
- Stool exam for toxin production

**Treatment**

- Severe disease—**metronidazole**: use vancomycin only if no other drug available; to avoid selecting for vancomycin-resistant normal flora
- Mild disease—discontinue other antibiotic therapy

**Prevention**

- Caution in overprescribing broad-spectrum antibiotics (limited-spectrum drugs should be considered first)
- In the nursing home setting, patients who are symptomatic should be isolated.
- Autoclave bed pans (treatment kills spores)

## Key Vignette Clues

*Clostridium difficile*

- Hospitalized patient on antibiotics
- Develops colitis, diarrhea

## Differential Diagnosis

- *Salmonella* species
- ETEC
- *V. cholerae*
- Norwalk virus
- Rotavirus

## Key Vignette Clues

*Listeria monocytogenes*

- Gram (+), β hemolytic bacilli, cold growth
- Facultative intracellular
- Foodborne (deli foods)
- Transplacental—granulomatosis infantiseptica
- Neonatal septicemia and meningitis (third most common cause)
- Meningitis in renal transplant or cancer patients (most common cause)

# GENUS: *LISTERIA*

## Genus Features

- **Gram-positive, non–spore forming rods**
- **Facultative intracellular**
- **Tumbling motility**

**Species of Medical Importance**—*Listeria monocytogenes*

## *Listeria monocytogenes*

### Distinguishing Features

- Small gram-positive rods
- Beta hemolytic, nonspore-forming rod on blood agar, CAMP positive
- **Tumbling motility** in broth; actin jet motility in cells
- **Facultative intracellular parasite**
- **Cold growth**

### Reservoir

- Widespread: animals (gastrointestinal and genital tracts), **unpasteurized milk products**, plants, and soil
- Cold growth: soft cheeses, deli meats, cabbages (coleslaw), hotdogs

### Transmission—foodborne, vertical, or across the placenta

### Pathogenesis

- **Listeriolysin O, a β-hemolysin:** facilitates rapid egress from phagosome into cytoplasm, thus evading killing when lysosomal contents are dumped into phagosome; "jets" directly (by actin filament formation) from cytoplasm to another cell
- **Immunologic immaturity predisposes to serious infection.**

### Disease(s)

- Listeriosis (human, peaks in summer)
  - Healthy adults and children: generally asymptomatic or diarrhea with low % carriage
  - Pregnant women: symptomatic carriage, septicemia characterized by fever and chills; can cross the placenta in septicemia.
- Neonatal disease
  - **Early-onset:** (granulomatosis infantisepticum) in utero transmission; sepsis with high mortality; disseminated granulomas with central necrosis
  - **Late-onset:** 2–3 weeks after birth from fecal exposure; meningitis with septicemia
- In immunocompromised patients
  - **Septicemia and meningitis** (most common clinical presentation)
  - *Listeria* meningitis—most common cause of meningitis in **renal transplant patients and adults with cancer**

**Diagnosis**

- Blood or CSF culture
- CSF wet mount or Gram stain

**Treatment**—ampicillin with gentamicin added for immunocompromised patients

**Prevention**—pregnant women or immunocompromised patients should not eat cold deli foods

## COMLEX Note

The differential diagnosis for neonatal meningitis is a perfect example of where knowing the gram reaction and shape will help you immensely.

## Differential Diagnosis

- Neonatal meningitis
  - *S. agalactiae*
  - *E. coli*
  - *H. influenzae*
  - HSV-2

## Key Vignette Clues

*Corynebacterium diphtheriae*

- Gram (+), aerobic, non–spore forming rods
- Bull neck, myocarditis, nerve palsies
- Gray pseudomembrane → airway obstruction
- Toxin produced by lysogeny
- Toxin ribosylates eEF-2; heart, nerve damage

# GENUS: *CORYNEBACTERIUM*

**Genus Features**

- Gram-positive rods
- Non–spore forming
- Aerobic

**Species of Medical Importance**

- *Corynebacterium diphtheriae*
- Diphtheroids (normal flora)

## *Corynebacterium diphtheriae*

**Distinguishing Features**

- Gray-to-black colonies of **club-shaped** gram-positive rods arranged in V or L shapes on **Gram stain**
- **Granules (volutin)** produced on Loeffler coagulated serum medium stain metachromatically
- Aerobic, non–spore forming
- **Toxin-producing strains have β-prophage** carrying genes for the toxin (**lysogeny, β-corynephage**). The phage from one patient with diphtheria can infect the normal nontoxigenic diphtheroid of another person and cause diphtheria.

**Reservoir**—throat and nasopharynx

**Transmission**—bacterium or phage via respiratory droplets

**Pathogenesis**

- Organism **not invasive**; colonizes epithelium of oropharynx or skin in cutaneous diphtheria
- **Diphtheria toxin (A-B component)—inhibits protein synthesis by adding ADP-ribose to eEF-2**
- Effect on oropharynx: **Dirty gray pseudomembrane** (made up of dead cells and fibrin exudate, bacterial pigment)
- **Extension into larynx/trachea → obstruction**
- Effect of systemic circulation → **heart** and **nerve** damage

**Disease**—diphtheria (sore throat with **pseudomembrane, bull neck**, potential respiratory obstruction, **myocarditis**, cardiac dysfunction, **recurrent laryngeal nerve palsy**, and lower limb polyneuritis)

## Differential Diagnosis

- *H. influenzae* (epiglottitis)
- *S. pyogenes* (pharyngitis)
- EBV
- *S. pneumoniae/K. pneumoniae*

**Diagnosis**

- Elek test to document toxin production (ELISA for toxin is now the frontline)
- Toxin produced by toxin-producing strains diffuses away from growth.
- Antitoxin diffuses away from the strip of filter paper.
- Precipitin lines form at zone of equivalence.

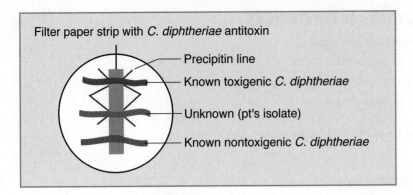

**Figure II-2-6.** Elek Test

**Treatment**

- Erythromycin and antitoxin
- For endocarditis, intravenous penicillin and aminoglycosides for 4–6 weeks

**Prevention**—toxoid vaccine (formaldehyde-modified toxin is still immunogenic but with reduced toxicity), part of DTaP, DTP, or Td, boosters 10-year intervals

# GENUS: *ACTINOMYCES*

### Genus Characteristics

- **Anaerobic**
- Gram-positive **branching** rods
- **Non–acid fast**

**Species of Medical Importance**—*Actinomyces israelii*

## *Actinomyces israelii*

### Distinguishing Features

- Anaerobic
- Branching rods
- Non–acid fast

**Reservoir**—human; normal flora of **gingival crevices** and **female genital tract**

**Transmission**—endogenous

**Pathogenesis**—invasive growth in tissues with compromised oxygen supply

**Disease—actinomycosis**

- Generally not painful but **very invasive**, penetrating all tissues, including bone
- **Tissue swelling → draining abscesses** (sinus tracts) with **"sulfur" granules** (hard yellow microcolonies) in exudate that can be used for microscopy or culture
- Only in tissues with low oxygenation ($E_h$)
    - **Cervicofacial (lumpy jaw): dental trauma or poor oral hygiene**
    - **Pelvic: from thoracic or sometimes IUDs**
    - Abdominal: surgery or bowel trauma
    - Thoracic: aspiration with contiguous spread
    - CNS: **solitary brain abscess** (*Nocardia* will produce multiple foci)

### Diagnosis

- Identify gram-positive branching bacilli in "sulfur granules"
- Colonies resemble molar tooth

**Treatment**—ampicillin or penicillin G and surgical drainage

## Key Vignette Clues

- Patient with mycetoma on jaw line or spread from IUD
- Sulfur granules in pus grow anaerobic, gram (+), non-acid fast branching rods

## Differential Diagnosis

- Thoracic
    - *H. capsulatum*
    - *B. dermatitidis*
    - *M. tuberculosis*
- CNS
    - *M. tuberculosis*
    - *H. capsulatum*
    - *C. neoformans*
    - *B. dermatitidis*
    - *Nocardia* species
- Cervical
    - *S. aureus*

# GENUS: *NOCARDIA*

**Genus Features**

- Gram-positive filaments breaking up into rods
- Aerobic
- Partially acid fast (some areas of smear will be blue and some red)

**Species of Medical Importance**

- *N. asteroides*
- *N. brasiliensis*

## *Nocardia asteroides* and *Nocardia brasiliensis*

**Distinguishing Features**

- Aerobic
- Gram-positive branching rods
- Partially acid fast

**Reservoir**—soil and dust

**Transmission**—airborne or traumatic transplantation

**Pathogenesis**

- No toxins or virulence factors known
- **Immunosuppression and cancer predispose** to pulmonary infection

**Disease(s)**

- Nocardiosis
  - **Cavitary bronchopulmonary nocardiosis**
  - Mostly *N. asteroides*
  - Can be acute, subacute, chronic
  - Symptoms: cough, fever, dyspnea, localized or diffuse pneumonia with cavitation
  - May spread hematogenously to brain (**brain abscesses**)
- Cutaneous/subcutaneous nocardiosis
  - Mostly *N. brasiliensis*
  - Starts with traumatic implantation
  - Symptoms: **cellulitis** with swelling → **draining subcutaneous abscesses** with **granules** (mycetoma)

**Diagnosis**—culture of sputum or pus from cutaneous lesion

**Treatment**—sulfonamides (high dose) or trimethoprim/sulfamethoxazole (TMP-SMX)

## Key Vignette Clues

*Nocardia asteroides* and
*Nocardia brasiliensis*

- Gram (+) filamentous bacilli, aerobic, partially acid fast
- Cavitary bronchopulmonary disease, mycetomas

## Differential Diagnosis

- Pulmonary
  - *M. tuberculosis*
  - *A. fumigatus*
  - *H. capsulatum*
  - *B. dermatitidis*
  - *C. immitis*
  - *P. jiroveci*
- Cutaneous
  - *M. tuberculosis*
  - *M. marinum*
  - *S. schenckii*
  - *A. israelii*

## GENUS: *MYCOBACTERIUM*

**Genus Features**

- **Acid fast rods** with a waxy cell wall
- **Obligate aerobe**
- Cell wall
  - Unique: **high concentration of lipids** containing long chain fatty acids called mycolic acids
  - Wall makes **mycobacteria highly resistant to:**
    - **Desiccation**
    - **Many chemicals** (including NaOH used to kill other bacteria in sputa before neutralizing and culturing)
- **Sensitive to UV**

**Species of Medical Importance**

- *M. tuberculosis*
- *M. leprae*
- *M. avium-intracellulare*
- *M. kansasii*
- *M. scrofulaceum*
- *M. marinum*

## *Mycobacterium tuberculosis*

**Distinguishing Features**

- **Auramine-rhodamine staining bacilli** (fluorescent apple green); no antibody involved (sensitive but not specific)
- **Acid fast**
- **Aerobic, slow growing** on **Lowenstein-Jensen** medium; new culture systems (broths with palmitic acid) faster
- **Produces niacin**
- **Produces a heat-sensitive catalase**
  - Catalase negative at 68.0°C (standard catalase test)
  - Catalase active at body temperature

## Key Vignette Clues

*Mycobacterium tuberculosis*

- High-risk patient (poverty, HIV+, IV drug user)
- Chronic cough, weight loss
- Ghon complex
- Auramine-rhodamine staining, acid fast bacilli in sputum
- Produce niacin, heat-sensitive catalase
- Positive PPD
- Facultative intracellular

**Reservoir**—human lungs

**Transmission**—respiratory droplets

**Pathogenesis**

- **Facultative intracellular organism** (most important)
- **Sulfatides (sulfolipids** in cell envelope)
  - **Inhibit phagosome-lysosome fusion,** allowing intracellular survival (if fusion occurs, waxy nature of cell envelope reduces killing effect)
- **Cord factor (trehalose dimycolate)**
  - Causes **serpentine growth** in vitro
  - **Inhibits leukocyte migration; disrupts mitochondrial respiration and oxidative phosphorylation**
- **Tuberculin** (surface protein) along with mycolic acid → delayed hypersensitivity and **cell-mediated immunity** (CMI)
  - Granulomas and caseation mediated by CMI
  - No exotoxins or endotoxin; damage done by immune system

**Disease(s)**

- Primary pulmonary tuberculosis
  - Organisms replicate in naive alveolar macrophages, killing the macrophages until CMI is set up (Ghon focus)
  - Macrophages transport the bacilli to the regional lymph node (**Ghon complex**) and most people heal without disease
  - Organisms that are walled off within the Ghon complex remain viable unless treated
- Reactivational tuberculosis
  - Erosion of granulomas into airways (high oxygen) later in life under conditions of reduced T-cell immunity leads to mycobacterial replication and disease symptoms
  - Complex disease with the potential of infecting any organ system
  - May disseminate (miliary TB)

**Diagnosis**

- Microscopy of sputum: screen with auramine-rhodamine stain (fluorescent apple-green); no antibody involved; very sensitive; if positive, confirm with acid fast stain
- **PPD skin test** (Mantoux): measure **zone of induration at 48–72 hours; positive if:**
  - ≥5 mm in HIV+ or anyone with recent TB exposure; AIDS patients have reduced ability to mount skin test.
  - ≥10 mm in high-risk population: IV drug abusers, people living in poverty, or immigrants from high TB area
  - ≥15 mm in low-risk population
- **Positive skin test indicates** only **exposure but not necessarily active disease.**
- Quantiferon-TB Gold Test: measures interferon-gamma production when leukocytes exposed to TB antigens
- Slow-growing (3–6 weeks) colonies on Lowenstein-Jensen medium (faster new systems)
- Organisms produce **niacin** and are **catalase-negative** (68°C).
- **No serodiagnosis**

**Figure II-2-7.**
Cord Factor

## COMLEX Note

- ACID FAST
  - *M. tuberculosis*
  - atypical Mycobacteria
  - *M. leprae*
  - *Nocardia*
  - *Cryptosporidium*
  - *Isospora*
- Many of these organisms will show up in AIDS patients - ACID FAST IS A BIG CLUE!

## Differential Diagnosis

- *A. israelii*
- *A. fumigatus*
- *H. capsulatum*
- Atypical mycobacteria
- *Nocardia* species
- *B. dermatitidis*

**Treatment**

- **Multiple drugs critical** to treat infection
- Standard observed short-term therapy for uncomplicated pulmonary TB (rate where acquired resistance <4%):
  - First 2 months: rifampin + isoniazid + pyrazinamide + ethambutol (RIPE)
  - Next 4 months: rifampin and isoniazid
- Ethambutol or streptomycin added for possible drug-resistant cases until susceptibility tests are back (if area acquired has >4% drug-resistant mycobacteria)

**Prevention**

- **Isoniazid** taken for 9 months can prevent TB in persons with infection but no clinical symptoms.
- Bacille Calmette-Guérin (BCG) **vaccine** containing live, attenuated organisms may prevent disseminated disease; not used in U.S.
- UV lights or HEPA filters used to treat potentially contaminated air.

# Mycobacteria Other than Tuberculosis (MOTTS)

**Distinguishing Features**

- Atypical mycobacteria
- **Noncontagious**
- Found in surface waters, soil, cigarettes
- Commonly found in southeastern U.S.

**Table II-2-16.** Summary of MOTTS

| Organism | Disease | Transmission | Clinical Presentation | Treatment |
|---|---|---|---|---|
| *M. avium-intra-cellulare*<br><br>*M. kansasii* | Pulmonary, Gastrointestinal, Disseminated | Respiratory, Ingestion | AIDS patients, cancer, chronic lung disease | AIDS patients prophylaxis <50 CD4+ cells/mm$^3$<br>Macrolide plus ethambutol |
| *M. scrofulaceum* | Lymphadenitis | Contaminated water sources | Solitary cervical LN in kids | Surgery |
| *M. marinum* | Soft tissue infections "fish tank granuloma" | Abrasions | Cutaneous granulomas in tropical fish enthusiasts | INH<br>Rifampin or ethambutol |

*Definition of abbreviation:* INH, isonazid; LN, lymph node.

# Mycobacterium leprae

**Distinguishing Features**

- **Acid fast rods** (seen in punch biopsy)
- **Obligate intracellular parasite** (cannot be cultured in vitro)
- Optimal growth at less than body temperature

**Reservoir**

- **Human** mucosa, skin, and nerves are only significant reservoirs
- Some infected armadillos in Texas and Louisiana

**Transmission**—nasal discharge from untreated lepromatous leprosy patients

**Pathogenesis**

- **Obligate intracellular parasite**
- Cooler parts of body, e.g., skin, mucous membranes, and peripheral nerves

**Disease(s)**—leprosy: a continuum of disease, which usually starts out with an indeterminate stage called "borderline"

**Table II-2-17.** Two Extreme Forms of Leprosy

| | Tuberculoid | | Lepromatous |
|---|---|---|---|
| Cell-mediated immune system | Strong CMI (TH1) | | Weak CMI (TH2) |
| Lepromin skin test | Lepromin test + | | Lepromin test – |
| Number of organisms in tissue | Low | | High (foam cells totally filled) |
| Damage from | Immune response (CMI killing infected cells) Granuloma formation → nerve enlargement/ damage Loss of sensation → burns and trauma | B o r d e r l i n e | Large number of intracellular organisms Nerve damage from overgrowth of bacteria in cells Loss of sensation → burns and trauma |
| Number of lesions and other symptoms | Fewer lesions: macular; nerve enlargement, paresthesia | | Numerous lesions becoming nodular; loss of eyebrows; destruction of nasal septum Paresthesia Leonine facies |

**Diagnosis**

- **Punch biopsy or nasal scrapings; acid fast stain**
- **Lepromin skin test** is positive in the tuberculoid but not in the lepromatous form
- No cultures

**Treatment**—multiple-drug therapy with dapsone and rifampin, with clofazimine added for lepromatous

**Prevention**—dapsone for close family contacts

## Note

- *M. tuberculosis* in HIV patient with normal count or low CD4 count (disseminated)
- MAI only in late HIV patient with low CD4 count

## Key Vignette Clues

**Leprosy**

- Acid fast bacilli in punch biopsy
- Immigrant patient with sensory loss in extremities

## Differential Diagnosis

- *Leishmania* species
- *T. pallidum*
- *M. furfur*

# GRAM-NEGATIVE COCCI

## GENUS: *NEISSERIA*

**Genus Features**

- Gram negative
- Diplococci with flattened sides
- Oxidase positive

**Species of Medical Importance**

**Table II-2-18.** Medically Important *Neisseria* Species

| Organism | Capsule | Vaccine | Portal of Entry | Glucose Fermentation | Maltose Fermentation | β-Lactamase Production |
|---|---|---|---|---|---|---|
| *N. meningitidis* | Yes | Yes | Respiratory | Yes | Yes | Rare |
| *N. gonorrhoeae* | No | No | Genital | Yes | No | Common |

## Note

### Oxidase

- *Oxidase (cytochrome C oxidase) test:* flood colony with phenylenediamine; in presence of oxidase, phenylenediamine turns black. Rapid test.
- Major oxidase-negative gram-negative group is Enterobacteriaceae.

## Key Vignette Clues

### Meningococcal Meningitis

- Gram (–) diplococcus in CSF
- Young adults with meningitis
- Abrupt onset with signs of endotoxin toxicity

## *Neisseria meningitidis*

**Distinguishing Features**

- **Gram-negative, kidney bean–shaped diplococci**
- **Large capsule; latex particle agglutination** (or CIE, counter immunoelectrophoresis) **to identify *N. meningitidis* capsular antigens in CSF**
- Grows on **chocolate (not blood) agar in 5% $CO_2$** atmosphere
- **Ferments maltose** in contrast to gonococci

**Reservoir**—human nasopharynx (5–10% carriers)

**Transmission**

- Respiratory droplets; oropharyngeal colonization, spreads to the meninges via the bloodstream
- Disease occurs in only small percentage of colonized individuals.

**Pathogenesis**

- Important virulence factors
  - Polysaccharide **capsule:** antiphagocytic, antigenic, 5 common serogroups: B is not strongly immunogenic (sialic acid); B strain is most common strain in U.S.; Used for serogrouping, detection in CSF, and vaccine
  - **IgA protease** allows oropharynx colonization.
  - **Endotoxin** (lipo**oligo**saccharide): fever, septic shock in meningococcemia, **overproduction of outer membrane**
  - Pili and outer membrane proteins important in ability to colonize and invade
  - Deficiency in late complement components (C5–C9) predisposes to bacteremia

**Disease(s)**

- Meningitis and meningococcemia
  - **Abrupt onset with fever, chills, malaise, prostration, and a rash that is generally petechial;** rapid decline
  - Fulminant cases: ecchymoses, DIC, shock, coma, and death (Waterhouse-Friderichsen syndrome)

**Diagnosis**

- Gram stain of the CSF
- PCR
- Latex agglutination

**Treatment**

- Neonates/infants: ampicillin and cefotaxime
- Older infants, children, and adults: cefotaxime or ceftriaxone with or without vancomycin

**Prevention**

- **Vaccine:** capsular polysaccharide of strains **Y, W-135, C, and A**
  - Type B (50% of the cases in U.S.) capsule not a good immunogen
- Prophylaxis of close contacts: **rifampin** (or ciprofloxacin)

## *Neisseria gonorrhoeae*

**Distinguishing Features**

- **Gram-negative,** kidney bean–shaped **diplococci**

**Reservoir**—human genital tract

**Transmission**

- Sexual contact, birth
- Sensitive to drying and cold

**Pathogenesis**

- Pili
  - **Attachment** to mucosal surfaces
  - **Inhibit phagocytic uptake**
  - **Antigenic** (immunogenic) **variation:** >1 million variants
- **Outer membrane proteins**
  - OMP I: structural, antigen used in serotyping
  - Opa proteins (opacity): **antigenic variation,** adherence
  - **IgA protease:** aids in colonization and cellular uptake
- **Organism invades mucosal surfaces and causes inflammation.**

**Disease—gonorrhea**

- Male: **urethritis,** proctitis
- Female: **endocervicitis,** PID (contiguous spread), arthritis, proctitis
- Infants: **ophthalmia** (rapidly leads to **blindness if untreated**)

### Differential Diagnosis

- *S. pneumoniae*
- Picornaviruses (enteroviruses)
- Arboviruses
- HSV
- Measles virus

### Key Vignette Clues

**Neisseria gonorrhoeae**

- Sexually active patient
- Urethral/vaginal discharge (leukorrhea)
- Arthritis possible
- Neonatal ophthalmia
- Gram (–) diplococcus in neutrophils

### COMLEX Note

*N. gonorrhoeae* is high yield. You should be able to recognize an image of *gonorrhoeae* in a urethral smear. If PMN's are seen without organism—think *C. trachomatis*!

## Differential Diagnosis

- *Chlamydia trachomatis*
- *Gardnerella vaginalis*
- *Trichomonas vaginalis*

### Diagnosis

- Intracellular **gram-negative diplococci in PMNs** from urethral smear from symptomatic male are suggestive of *N. gonorrhoeae.*
- Commonly: diagnosis by **genetic probes** with amplification
- Culture (when done) on **Thayer-Martin medium**
  - Oxidase-positive colonies
  - Maltose not fermented
  - No capsule

### Treatment

- Ceftriaxone
- Test for *C. trachomatis* or treat with a doxycycline
- Penicillin-binding protein mutations led to gradual increases in penicillin resistance from the 1950s to the 1970s.
- Plasmid-mediated β-**lactamase** produces **high-level penicillin resistance.**

### Prevention

- Adult forms: no vaccine; condoms
- Neonatal: silver nitrate or erythromycin ointment in eyes at birth

## *Moraxella catarrhalis*

### Distinguishing Features

- Gram-negative diplococcus
- Close relative of *Neisseria*

**Reservoir**—normal upper respiratory tract flora

**Transmission**—respiratory droplets

**Pathogenesis**—endotoxin may play role in disease

### Disease(s)

- Otitis media
- Sinusitis
- Bronchitis and bronchopneumonia in elderly patients with COPD

### Treatment

- Drug resistance is a problem; most strains produce a β-lactamase.
- Amoxicillin + clavulanate, second or third generation cephalosporin or TMP-SMX

## Differential Diagnosis

- *S. pneumoniae*
- *H. influenzae*

# GRAM-NEGATIVE BACILLI

## GENUS: *PSEUDOMONAS*

**Genus Features**

- Gram-negative rod
- Oxidase-positive
- Aerobic (nonfermenting)

**Species of Medical Importance**—*Pseudomonas aeruginosa*

## *Pseudomonas aeruginosa*

**Distinguishing Features**

- Oxidase-positive, **Gram-negative rods, nonfermenting**
- Pigments: **pyocyanin (blue-green)** and fluorescein
- Grape-like odor
- Slime layer
- **Non–lactose fermenting** colonies on EMB or MacConkey
- Biofilm

**Reservoir**—ubiquitous in water

**Transmission**—water aerosols, raw vegetables, flowers

**Pathogenesis**

- **Endotoxin** causes inflammation in tissues and gram-negative shock in septicemia.
- ***Pseudomonas* exotoxin A ADP ribosylates eEF-2,** inhibiting protein synthesis (like diphtheria toxin)
- **Liver is the primary target.**
- **Capsule/slime layer:** allows formation of pulmonary **microcolonies**; difficult to remove by phagocytosis

**Disease(s)**

- Healthy people
  - Transient gastrointestinal tract colonization: loose stools (10% population)
  - Hot tub folliculitis
  - Eye ulcers: trauma, coma, or prolonged contact wear
- Burn patients
  - Gastrointestinal tract colonization → skin → colonization of eschar → **cellulitis (blue-green pus)** → **septicemia**
- Neutropenic patients
  - **Pneumonia** and **septicemias**—often **superinfections** (infections while on antibiotics)
- Chronic granulomatous disease (CGD)
  - Pneumonias, septicemias (*Pseudomonas* is catalase positive)
- Otitis externa
  - Swimmers, diabetics, those with pierced ears

## Key Vignette Clues

*Pseudomonas*

- Gram (–), oxidase (+), aerobic bacillus
- Blue-green pigments, fruity odor
- Burn infections—blue-green pus, fruity odor
- Typical pneumonia—CGD or CF
- UTI—catheterized patients

## Note

*Pseudomonas* **Medical Ecology**

Pseudomonas aeruginosa is a **ubiquitous water** and soil organism that grows to very high numbers overnight in standing water (distilled or tap).

Sources for infections include:

- Raw vegetables, respirators, humidifiers, sink drains, faucet aerators, cut and potted flowers, and, if not properly maintained, whirlpools.
- Transient colonization of colons of about 10% of people. Bacteria get on skin from fecal organisms. Requires exquisitely careful housekeeping and restricted diets in burn units.

## Differential Diagnosis

- *S. aureus*
- Gram-negative rods
- *Klebsiella pneumoniae*

## Note

**Drug Resistance in *P. aeruginosa***

**Susceptibilities important.**

Drug resistance very common:

Intrinsic resistance (missing high affinity porin some drugs enter through); Plasmid-mediated β-lactamases and acetylating enzymes.

- Septicemias
  - Fever, shock ± skin lesions (black, necrotic center, erythematous margin, **ecthyma gangrenosum**)
- Catheterized patients
  - Urinary tract infections (UTIs)
- Cystic fibrosis
  - Early pulmonary colonization, recurrent pneumonias; **always** high **slime-producing strains**

**Diagnosis**—Gram stain and culture

**Treatment**—antipseudomonal penicillin and an aminoglycoside

**Prevention**

- Pasteurization or disinfection of water-related equipment, hand washing; prompt removal of catheters
- No flowers or raw vegetables in burn units

# GENUS: *LEGIONELLA*

**Genus Features**

- Weakly gram-negative
- Pleomorphic rods requiring cysteine and iron
- Water organisms

**Species of Medical Importance**—*Legionella pneumophila*

## *Legionella pneumophila*

**Distinguishing Features**

- **Stain poorly** with standard Gram stain; **gram-negative**
- **Fastidious** requiring increased **iron and cysteine** for laboratory culture (CYE, charcoal yeast extract)
- **Facultative intracellular**

**Reservoir**—rivers/streams/amebae; air-conditioning water cooling tanks

**Transmission**

- Aerosols from contaminated **air-conditioning**
- **No human-to-human transmission**

**Predisposing Factors**

- **Smokers over 55 years with high alcohol intake**
- **Immunosuppressed patients, e.g.,** renal transplant patients

**Pathogenesis**

- **Facultative intracellular** pathogen
- **Endotoxin**

**Disease(s)**

- Legionnaires disease ("atypical pneumonia")
  - Associated with air-conditioning systems, now routinely decontaminated
  - Pneumonia
  - Hyponatremia
  - Mental confusion
  - Diarrhea (no *Legionella* in gastrointestinal tract)
- Pontiac fever
  - Pneumonitis
  - No fatalities

**Diagnosis**

- Diagnosis: **DFA** (direct fluorescent antibody) on biopsy, (+) by Dieterle silver stain
- Fourfold increase in antibody

**Treatment**

- Fluoroquinolone or azithromycin or erythromycin with rifampin for immunocompromised patients
- Drug must penetrate human cells.

**Prevention**—routine decontamination of air-conditioner cooling tanks

## Key Vignette Clues

*Legionella pneumophila*

- Elderly smoker, heavy drinker, or Immunosuppressed
- Exposure to aerosols of water
- Atypical pneumonia
- Triad of atypical pneumonia, diarrhea, and hyponatremia

## Differential Diagnosis

- *S. pneumoniae/K. pneumoniae*
- *M. pneumoniae*
- *C. pneumoniae*

## Key Vignette Clues

***Francisella tularensis***

- Hunter with ulceroglandular disease, atypical pneumonia, or gastrointestinal disease
- Arkansas/Missouri
- Exposure to rabbits, deer, ticks

# GENUS: *FRANCISELLA*

**Genus Features**

- **Gram-negative small rods**
- **Facultative intracellular pathogen**

**Species of Medical Importance**—*Francisella tularensis*

# *Francisella tularensis*

**Distinguishing Features**

- Small gram-negative rod
- **Potential biowarfare agent**
- **Zoonosis**

**Reservoir**—many species of wild **animals**, especially rabbits, deer, and rodents

**Transmission**

- **Tick bite** *(Dermacentor)* → **ulceroglandular** disease, characterized by **fever**, ulcer at bite site, and regional lymph node enlargement and necrosis
- **Traumatic implantation** while skinning rabbits → ulceroglandular disease
- Aerosols (skinning rabbits) → pneumonia
- Ingestion (of undercooked, infected meat or contaminated water) produces typhoidal tularemia.

**Pathogenesis**

- **Facultative intracellular pathogen (localizes in reticuloendothelial cells)**
- Granulomatous response

## Differential Diagnosis

- *Brucella abortus*
- *Chlamydophila psittaci*
- *Coxiella burnetii*
- *Bartonella henselae*

**Disease**

- Tularemia
  - Endemic in every state of the U.S.
  - Highest in Arkansas and Missouri

**Diagnosis**

- Serodiagnosis; culture is hazardous.
- DFA

**Treatment**—streptomycin

**Prevention**

- Protect against tick bites, gloves while butchering rabbits
- Live, attenuated vaccine for persons in high risk

# GENUS: *BORDETELLA*

**Genus Features**

- **Gram-negative small rods**
- **Strict aerobes**

**Species of Medical Importance**—*Bordetella pertussis*

## *Bordetella pertussis*

**Distinguishing Features**

- Small **gram-negative,** aerobic **rods**
- Encapsulated organism

**Reservoir—human** (vaccinated)

**Transmission**—respiratory droplets

**Pathogenesis**

- ***B. pertussis* is a mucosal surface pathogen.**
- **Attachment** to nasopharyngeal ciliated epithelial cells is via:
  - Filamentous hemagglutinin
  - Pertussis toxin (on outer membrane) aids in attachment.
- **Toxins** damage respiratory epithelium.
  - **Adenylate cyclase toxin:** impairs leukocyte chemotaxis → inhibits phagocytosis and causes local edema
  - **Tracheal cytotoxin:** interferes with ciliary action; kills ciliated cells
  - Endotoxin
  - **Pertussis toxin** (A and B component, OM protein toxin): **ADP ribosylation of $G_i$** (inhibiting negative regulator of adenylate cyclase) interferes with transfer of signals from cell surface to intracellular mediator system.
    - Lymphocytosis
    - Islet-activation → hypoglycemia
    - Blocks immune effector cells (decreased chemotaxis)
    - Increased histamine sensitivity

## Key Vignette Clues

***Bordetella pertussis***

- Unvaccinated child (immigrant family or religious objections)
- Cough with inspiratory "whoop"

## In a Nutshell

***B. pertussis* Immunity**

- Vaccine immunity lasts 5–10 years (and is primarily IgA)
- Babies born with little immunity.
- Vaccinated humans >10 yrs serve as reservoir.
- 12–20% of afebrile adults with cough >2 weeks have pertussis.
- New vaccines (DTaP)
- Acellular
- Components:
  - Immunogens vary by manufacturer
  - Pertussis toxoid
  - Filamentous hemagglutinin
  - Pertactin (OMP)
  - 1 other

**Table II-2-19.** Stages of Whooping Cough (Pertussis) vs. Results of Bacterial Culture

|  | Incubation | Catarrhal | Paroxysmal | Convalescent |
|---|---|---|---|---|
| **Duration** | 7-10 days | 1-2 weeks | 2-4 weeks | 3-4 weeks (or longer) |
| **Symptoms** | None | Rhinorrhea, malaise, sneezing, anorexia | Repetitive cough with whoops, vomiting, leukocytosis | Diminished paroxysmal cough, development of secondary complications (pneumonia, seizures, encephalopathy) |
| **Bacterial Culture** | | | | |

## Differential Diagnosis

- *C. pneumoniae*
- *M. pneumoniae*
- RSV
- Adenovirus

### Diagnosis

- Fastidious/delicate: **Regan-Lowe** or Bordet-Gengou media; either direct cough plates or nasopharyngeal cultures
- Difficult to culture from the middle of paroxysmal stage on
- Direct immunofluorescence (**DFA**) on nasopharyngeal smear
- PCR and serologic tests available

### Treatment

- Supportive care; hospitalization if <6 months old, erythromycin for 14 days including all household contacts
- Macrolides can also be given.

### Prevention

- Vaccine: DTaP (acellular pertussis: filamentous hemagglutin plus pertussis toxoid); immunity wanes 5–7 years
- Babies are born with little or no immunity (IgA) from mother.

# GENUS: *BRUCELLA*

## Genus Features

- Gram-negative rods, aerobic
- **Zoonosis**
- Facultative intracellular pathogen
- **Potential biowarfare agent**

## Species of Medical Importance

- *Brucella abortus*: cattle
- *Brucella melitensis*: goats
- *Brucella suis:* pigs

# *Brucella* Species

## Distinguishing Features

- Small **gram-negative** rods, aerobic
- Facultative intracellular
- Serological confirmation of disease most common
- Culture is hazardous.
- Potential biowarfare agent

**Reservoir**—domestic livestock

## Transmission

- **Unpasteurized dairy products** (California and Texas highest number of cases; most associated with travel to Mexico)
- **Direct contact with the animal,** work in slaughterhouse

## Pathogenesis

- **Endotoxin**
- **Facultative intracellular parasite** (localizes in cells of the RES, reticuloendothelial system) → **septicemia**
- **Granulomatous response** with central necrosis

## Disease

- Brucellosis (undulant fever)
  - Acute septicemias
  - Fever 100–104°F (often in evening)
  - Influenza-like symptoms, including arthralgias, anorexia, myalgia, back pain
  - Sweating (profuse)
  - Hepatomegaly

## Key Vignette Clues

### *Brucella*

- Patient with acute septicemia
- Exposure to animals or unpasteurized dairy
- California/Texas or travel to Mexico

## Note

### Zoonotic Organisms

- *Brucella*
- *Bacillus anthracis*
- *Listeria monocytogenes*
- *Salmonella enteritidis*
- *Campylobacter*
- *Chlamydophila psittaci*
- *Francisella tularensis*
- *Yersinia pestis*

## Differential Diagnosis

- *Coccidioides immitis*
- *Histoplasma capsulatum*
- Influenza
- *Mycobacterium tuberculosis*
- *F. tularensis*

### Diagnosis

- Culture is hazardous.
- Serum agglutination test, fourfold increase in titer
  - Antibodies against *Brucella* >1:160 considered positive

### Treatment

- Adults: rifampin and doxycycline minimum of 6 weeks
- Children: rifampin and cotrimoxazole

### Prevention

- Vaccinate cattle.
- Pasteurize milk, especially goat milk.

# GENUS: *CAMPYLOBACTER*

**Genus Features**

- Gram-negative curved rods with polar flagella ("gulls' wings")
- Oxidase-positive

**Figure II-2-8.**
Campylobacter

**Species of Medical Importance—***Campylobacter jejuni*

## *Campylobacter jejuni*

**Distinguishing Features—microaerophilic, grows well at 42.0°C** on selective media (Campy medium or Skirrow agar)

**Reservoir—**intestinal tracts of humans, cattle, sheep, dogs, cats, **poultry**

**Transmission—**fecal-oral, primarily from **poultry**

**Pathogenesis**

- **Low infectious dose (as few as 500)**
- **Invades** mucosa of the colon, destroying mucosal surfaces; blood and **pus** in stools (inflammatory diarrhea)
- Rarely penetrates to cause septicemia

**Disease**

- Gastroenteritis
  - Common cause of infectious diarrhea worldwide
  - In U.S., *Campylobacter* enteritis > *(Salmonella* plus *Shigella)*
  - **Ten or more stools/day, may be frankly bloody**
  - Abdominal pain, fever, malaise, nausea, and vomiting
  - Generally **self-limiting in 3–5 days** but may last longer
  - Complications
    - **Guillain-Barré syndrome (GBS)** → 30% of the GBS in the U.S. Serotype O:19, antigenic cross-reactivity between *Campylobacter* oligosaccharides and glycosphingolipids on neural tissues
    - Reactive arthritis

**Diagnosis**

- Culture on Campylobacter or Skirrow agar at 42°C

**Treatment**

- Mostly supportive via fluid and electrolyte replacement
- Erythromycin, fluoroquinolones, penicillin resistant

**Key Vignette Clues**

*Campylobacter jejuni*

- Patient with inflammatory diarrhea
- Gram (–), curved rod, microaerophilic, oxidase (+), grows at 42°C

**Differential Diagnosis**

- *C. difficile*
- *Salmonella* species
- *Shigella* species
- *Yersinia enterocolitica*

# GENUS: *HELICOBACTER*

## Genus Features

- Gram-negative spiral gastric bacilli with flagella
- **Microaerophilic**, 37.0°C growth (Campy medium or Skirrow agar); oxidase positive

**Species of Medical Importance**—*Helicobacter pylori*

## Key Vignette Clues

### *Helicobacter pylori*

- Patient with gastritis, ulcers, stomach cancer
- Gram (–), helical bacilli, oxidase (+), microaerophilic, urease (+)

# *Helicobacter pylori*

**Distinguishing Feature—urease positive**

**Reservoir**—humans

## Transmission

- Fecal-oral
- Oral-oral

## Pathogenesis

- **Motile**
- **Urease-positive:** ammonium cloud neutralizes stomach acid, allowing survival in stomach acid during transit to border.
- **Mucinase** aids in penetration of mucous layer (rapid shift down to neutral as it penetrates).
- **Invasive** into stomach lining where pH is neutral
- Inflammation is prominent.
- Two biotypes (I and II); type I produces vacuolating cytotoxin.

## Differential Diagnosis

No specific organisms associated with similar symptoms

## Diseases

- Chronic gastritis and duodenal ulcers
    - Associated with several forms of **stomach cancer** (gastric adenocarcinoma, gastric mucosa-associated lymphoid tissue lymphoma [MALT-oma], B-cell lymphomas)
    - Now classed by WHO as **type I carcinogen**

## Diagnosis

- Biopsy with culture; histology with Giemsa or silver stain
- Breath test: $^{13}$C-urea swallowed; ammonia+$^{13}$C-CO$_2$ exhaled
- Serology

## Treatment

- Myriad of regimens
    - Omeprazole + amoxicillin + clarithromycin is one example of triple therapy.
    - Treat for 10–14 days.
    - Quadruple therapy is used in areas where clarithromycin resistance is ≥15%, e.g., PPI + bismuth + 2 antibiotics (metronidazole + tetracycline)

# GENUS: *VIBRIO*

## Genus Features

- **Gram-negative curved rod with polar flagella**
- Oxidase positive
- Vibrionaceae
- Growth on **alkaline,** but not acidic, media (**TCBS, t**hiosulfate **c**itrate **b**ile salt **s**ucrose medium)

## Species of Medical Importance

- *Vibrio cholerae*
- *Vibrio parahaemolyticus*
- *Vibrio vulnificus*

# *Vibrio cholerae*

## Distinguishing Features

- "Shooting star" motility inactivated by specific serum

## Reservoir

- Human colon; **no vertebrate animal carriers** (copepods or shellfish may be contaminated by water contamination)
- Human carriage may persist after untreated infection for months after infection; permanent carrier state is rare.

## Transmission

- Fecal-oral spread; sensitive to stomach acid
- Requires high dose (>$10^7$ organisms), if stomach acid is normal

## Pathogenesis

- Motility, mucinase, and toxin coregulated pili (TCP) aid in attachment to the intestinal mucosa.
- **Cholera enterotoxin (choleragen) similar to *E. coli* LT; ADP ribosylates (G$_s$ alpha) activating adenylate cyclase → increased cAMP → efflux of Cl$^-$ and H$_2$O (persistent activation of adenylate cyclase)**

## Disease

- Cholera
  - Rice water stools, **tremendous fluid loss**
  - Hypovolemic shock if not treated

## Diagnosis

- Culture stool on TCBS
- **Oxidase positive**

## Key Vignette Clues

*Vibrio cholerae*

- Patient with noninflammatory diarrhea
- Rice-water stool
- Dehydration
- Travel to endemic area
- Gram (–) curved rods, polar flagellae, oxidase (+)
- Alkaline growth

## Differential Diagnosis

- ETEC
- Norwalk virus

Treatment

- **Fluid and electrolyte replacement**
- Doxycycline or ciprofloxacin shorten disease and reduce carriage
- Resistance to tetracycline reported

**Prevention**—proper sanitation; new vaccine

## Other *Vibrio* Species

**Table II-2-20.** Additional *Vibrio* Species

| Species | Reservoir | Transmission | Disease | Symptoms | Treatment |
|---|---|---|---|---|---|
| *V. parahaemolyticus* | Marine life | Consumption of undercooked or raw seafood | Gastroenteritis | Watery diarrhea with cramping and abdominal pain | Self-limiting |
| *V. vulnificus* | Brackish water, oysters | Consumption of undercooked or raw seafood | Gastroenteritis | As above | As above |
| | | Swimming in brackish water, shucking oysters | Cellulitis | Rapidly spreading; difficult to treat | Tetracycline; third-generation cephalosporins |

# FAMILY: ENTEROBACTERIACEAE

## Family Features

- **Gram-negative rods**
- **Facultative anaerobes**
- Ferment glucose
- **Cytochrome C oxidase negative**
- **Reduce nitrates to nitrites**
- Catalase positive

## Family Pathogenesis

- **Endotoxin**
- Some also produce **exotoxins.**
- **Antigens**
  - O= cell envelope or O antigen
  - H= flagellar (motile cells only) antigen
  - K = capsular polysaccharide antigen
  - Vi (virulence) = *Salmonella* capsular antigen

## Lab Diagnosis

- Blood agar
- Eosin methylene blue or MacConkey agar (differentiate lactose fermentation)
- **Lactose fermenters** (colored colonies)
- **Non–lactose fermenters** (colorless colonies)

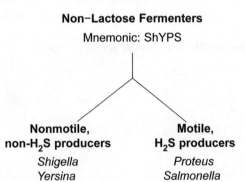

**Lactose Fermenters**

Mnemonic: CEEK

*Citrobacter*

*Enterobacter*

**Escherichia**

**Klebsiella**

**Non–Lactose Fermenters**

Mnemonic: ShYPS

**Nonmotile,
non-H₂S producers**
*Shigella*
*Yersina*

**Motile,
H₂S producers**
*Proteus*
*Salmonella*

**Figure II-2-9**

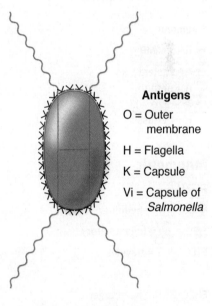

**Antigens**

O = Outer
  membrane

H = Flagella

K = Capsule

Vi = Capsule of
  *Salmonella*

**Figure II-2-10.** Antigens
of Enterobacteriacae

## Note

*E. coli* identification from stool

- **Isolation of *E. coli* from feces is not by itself significant.**
- **Sorbitol MacConkey screen**
- Most *E. coli* ferment sorbitol.
- Most EHEC do not (colorless)

*E. coli* from normal flora are more commonly:

- **Immunoassay** looking for specific protein antigens (on or excreted by the bacterium)
- **Serotyping** since certain serotypes are more often pathogenic
- **DNA probes** for specific genes in a culture
- **PCR** on clinical specimen

### Mnemonic

Toxins ↑cAMP

    c = cholera
    A = anthrax
    ∑ = *E. coli* LT
    P = pertussis

### Mnemonic

**PITcH**

| | |
|---|---|
| EPEC | P = pediatric |
| EIEC | I = inflammatory |
| ETEC | T = traveler |
| | C = coli |
| EHEC | H = hamburger |

# GENUS: *ESCHERICHIA*

## Genus Features

- **Gram-negative rods**
- **Enterobacteriaceae**
- **Ferments lactose**

**Species of Medical Importance**—*Escherichia coli*

## *Escherichia coli*

### Distinguishing Features

- **Gram-negative rod**
- **Facultative anaerobic, oxidase negative**
- *E. coli* is a **lactose fermenter:** colonies with iridescent green sheen on EMB

### Reservoir

- **Human colon;** may colonize vagina or urethra
- Contaminated crops where human fecal fertilizer is used
- **Enterohemorrhagic strains: bovine feces**

### Transmission

- Endogenous
- Fecal-oral
- Maternal fecal flora
- Enterohemorrhagic strains: bovine fecal contamination (raw or undercooked beef, milk, apple juice from fallen apples)

**Pathogenesis**—listed under specific diseases

**Table II-2-21.** Disease Syndromes Caused by *Escherichia coli*

| Transmission | Mechanism of Pathogenesis | Clinical Clues | Treatment |
|---|---|---|---|
| **UTI (most common cause)** | | | |
| Endogenous fecal flora contaminate and ascend | Motility<br><br>Adherence to uroepithelium— pyelonephritis associated pili, X-adhesins, β hemolytic (many) | Gram (–) bacilli, $\geq 10^5$ CFU/ml | Fluoroquinolone or sulfonamides |
| **Neonatal septicemia/ meningitis (second most common cause)** | | | |
| Maternal fecal flora contaminate during parturition | Capsule—K1 serotype, endotoxin | Blood, CSF culture, gram (–) bacilli | Ceftriaxone |
| **Septicemia** | | | |
| Indwelling IV lines, cytotoxic drugs damage intestinal mucosa, allow escape | Endotoxin | Blood culture, gram (–) bacilli, oxidase (–) | Fluoroquinolones, third-generation cephalosporins |
| **Gastroenteritis** | | | |
| ETEC (travelers' diarrhea)<br>Fecal/oral | LT—heat-labile toxin stimulates adenylate cyclase by ADP ribosylation of Gs<br><br>ST—stimulates guanylate cyclase; capsule impedes phagocytosis; colonizing factor adhesins bind to mucosa | Noninflammatory diarrhea, identify enterotoxin by immunoassay, bioassay, DNA probe | Rehydration, TMP/SMX may shorten symptoms |
| EPEC (second most common infantile diarrhea)<br>Fecal/oral | Adherence to M cells → rearrangement of actin and effacement of brush border microvilli | Noninflammatory diarrhea in babies in developing countries | Beta-lactams |
| EIEC<br>Fecal/oral | Invades large bowel<br><br>Inflammatory diarrhea; similar to shigellosis, induces formation of actin jet trails | Inflammatory diarrhea, blood, pus, fever, abdominal pain | |
| EHEC (VTEC)—O157:H7 most common<br><br>Bovine feces, petting zoos | Verotoxin—Shigella-like toxins 1 and 2, ↓ protein synthesis by interfering with 60S ribosomal subunit | No fever, no PMNs, blood in stool, nonfermenters of sorbitol; may progress to hemorrhagic colitis and HUS; most common in children <5 years | Antibiotics ↑ risk of HUS |

*Definition of abbreviations:* CSF, cerebrospinal fluid; EIEC, enteroinvasive *E. coli*; EHEC, enterohemorrhagic *E. coli*; EPEC, enteropathogenic *E. coli*; HUS, hemolytic uremic syndrome; UTI, urinary tract infection

## GENUS: *KLEBSIELLA*

**Genus Features**

- **Gram-negative rods**
- **Enterobacteriaceae**
- **Major capsule**

**Species of Medical Importance**

- *Klebsiella pneumoniae*

## *Klebsiella pneumoniae*

**Distinguishing Features**

- **Gram-negative rods** with **large** polysaccharide **capsule**
- **Mucoid, lactose-fermenting** colonies on MacConkey agar
- Oxidase negative

**Reservoir**—human colon and upper respiratory tract

**Transmission**—endogenous

**Pathogenesis**

- **Capsule:** impedes phagocytosis
- **Endotoxin:** causes fever, inflammation, and shock (septicemia)

**Disease(s)**

- Pneumonia
  - Community-acquired, most often in older males; most commonly in **patients with either chronic lung disease, alcoholism, or diabetes** (but this is not the most common cause of pneumonia in alcoholics; *S. pneumoniae* is.)
  - Endogenous; assumed to reach lungs by inhalation of respiratory droplets from upper respiratory tract
  - Frequent **abscesses** make it hard to treat; fatality rate high
  - **Sputum is generally thick and bloody (currant jelly)** but not foul smelling as in anaerobic aspiration pneumonia.
- Urinary tract infections—**catheter-related (nosocomial)** from fecal contamination of catheters
- Septicemia—in immunocompromised patients, may originate from bowel defects or invasion of IV lines

**Diagnosis**

- Culture of sputum or clean catch urine sample
- Lactose fermenter

**Treatment**

- Third-generation cephalosporin with or without an aminoglycoside
- Fluoroquinolones may also be used.

**Prevention**—good catheter care, limit use

## Key Vignette Clues

*Klebsiella pneumoniae*

- Elderly patient with typical pneumonia: currant-jelly sputum
- UTI (catheter associated)
- Septicemia: immunocompromised or nosocomial
- Gram (–) bacilli, oxidase (–), encapsulated, lactose fermenters

## In a Nutshell

**Comparative Microbiology:**

**Major encapsulated organisms**

**S**ome **K**illers **H**ave **P**retty **N**ice **C**apsules:

**S**trep pneumoniae

**K**lebsiella pneumoniae

**H**aemophilus influenzae Type b (a-d)

**P**seudomonas aeruginosa

**N**eisseria meningitidis

**C**ryptococcus neoformans (the yeast)

(Not a complete list, just the big ones.)

## Differential Diagnosis

- Pneumonia
  - *S. pneumoniae*
  - *H. influenzae*
  - *S. aureus*
  - *L. pneumophila*
- Urinary tract infections
  - *E. coli*
  - *S. saprophyticus*
  - *Proteus* species
  - *P. aeruginosa*

# GENUS: *SHIGELLA*

## Genus Features

- **Gram-negative rod**
- **Enterobacteriaceae**
- **Non–lactose fermenters** (colorless colonies on EMB or MacConkey)
- **Nonmotile**

## Species of Medical Importance

- *Shigella sonnei* (**most common in U.S.**)
- *Shigella flexneri*
- *Shigella dysenteriae* (**most severe disease**)
- *Shigella boydii*

## *Shigella* Species

### Distinguishing Features

- **Gram-negative rods**, nonmotile

**Reservoir—human colon only (no animal carriers)**

**Transmission—fecal-oral spread,** person to person

### Pathogenesis

- **Endotoxin** triggers inflammation.
- No H antigens
- Shigellae **invade M cells** (membrane ruffling and macropinocytosis), get into the cytoplasm, replicate, and then **polymerize actin jet trails to go laterally** without going back out into the extracellular milieu. This produces **very shallow ulcers** and rarely causes invasion of blood vessels.
- **Shiga toxin:**
  - Produced by *S. dysenteriae,* type 1
  - Three activities: **neurotoxic, cytotoxic, enterotoxic**
  - **AB component toxin** is internalized in human cells; **inhibits protein synthesis by clipping 60S ribosomal subunit**

### Disease(s)

- Enterocolitis/shigellosis (most severe form is dysentery)
  - Few organisms required to start infection (1–10) (extremely acid resistant)
  - 1–4 day incubation
  - Organisms invade, producing bloody diarrhea.
  - **Fever (generally >101.0°F); lower abdominal cramps; tenesmus; diarrhea first watery, then bloody; invasive but rarely causes septicemia; shallow ulcers**
  - Severity depends on the age of patient and the strain; *S. dysenteriae* type 1 with toxin most severe

**Diagnosis—isolation from stool during illness and culture on selective media**

## Note

### Comparative Microbiology

- Invasive bacteria: PMN in stool: *Shigella, Salmonella, Campylobacter,* EIEC.
- Toxigenic bacteria: ETEC, *V. cholera, Cl. perfringens,* EHEC.

## Key Vignette Clues

### *Shigella*

- Patient with acute bloody diarrhea and fever
- Gram (–) bacilli, which are nonmotile, nonlactose fermenters, do not produce $H_2S$

## Differential Diagnosis

- *C. jejuni*
- *Salmonella* species
- EIEC
- *E. histolytica*

**Treatment**

- Mild cases: fluid and electrolyte replacement only
- Severe cases: antibiotics
- Resistance is mediated by plasmid-encoded enzymes.
- Many strains are ampicillin resistant.

**Prevention**—proper sanitation (sewage, clean drinking water, hand washing)

# GENUS: *YERSINIA*

## Genus Features
- **Gram-negative rods**
- **Enterobacteriaceae**

## Species of Medical Importance
- *Yersinia pestis*
- *Yersinia enterocolitica*

# *Yersinia pestis*

## Distinguishing Features
- Small **gram-negative** rods with **bipolar staining**
- **Facultative intracellular parasite**
- **Coagulase positive**

## Reservoir
- **Zoonosis**
- **U.S. desert southwest: rodents** (e.g., prairie dogs, chipmunks, squirrels)
- **Potential biowarfare agent**

## Transmission
- Wild rodents **flea bite** → sylvatic plague
- Human-to-human transmission by **respiratory droplets**

## Pathogenesis
- **Coagulase**-contaminated mouth parts of flea
- **Endotoxin** and exotoxin
- **Envelope antigen (F-1) inhibits phagocytosis.**
- Type III secretion system suppresses cytokine production and resists phagocytic killing

## Disease(s)
- Bubonic plague
  - Flea bites infected animal and then later uninfected human
  - Symptoms
    - **Rapidly increasing fever**
    - **Regional buboes**
    - **Conjunctivitis**
    - Leads to septicemia and death if untreated
- Pneumonic plague
  - Arises from septic pulmonary emboli in bubonic plague or **inhalation of organisms from infected individual**
  - **Highly contagious!**

## Key Vignette Clues
### *Yersinia pestis*
- Patient with high fever, buboes, conjunctivitis, pneumonia
- Exposure to small rodents, desert Southwest

## Differential Diagnosis

- *B. henselae*
- *C. perfringens*
- *S. pneumoniae/K. pneumoniae*
- *S. pyogenes* (scarlet fever)
- *Rickettsia rickettsii*

## Key Vignette Clues

### *Yersinia enterocolitica*

- Patient with inflammatory diarrhea or pseudoappendicitis
- Cold climates
- Unpasteurized milk, pork
- Gram (–) bacilli, non–lactose fermenters, non–$H_2S$ producers

## Differential Diagnosis

- *C. jejuni*
- *C. difficile*
- *Salmonella* species
- *Shigella* species

## Diagnosis

- Clinical specimens and **cultures are hazardous.**
- **Serodiagnosis** or direct **immunofluorescence**
- **"Safety pin" staining**

## Treatment—aminoglycosides

## Prevention

- Animal control; avoid sick and dead animals.
- **Killed vaccine** (military)

# *Yersinia enterocolitica*

## Distinguishing Features

- Motile at 25.0°C, nonmotile at 37.0°C
- Cold growth

## Reservoir—zoonotic

## Transmission

- Unpasteurized milk, pork
- Prominent in northern climates (Michigan, Scandinavia)

## Pathogenesis

- Enterotoxin, endotoxin
- **Multiplies in the cold**

## Disease(s)

- Enterocolitis
  - Presentations may vary with age
    - Very young: febrile diarrhea (blood and pus)
    - Older kids/young adults: **pseudoappendicitis** (also caused by *Yersinia pseudotuberculosis*)
    - Adults: enterocolitis with postinfective sequelae like reactive arthritis
- Blood transfusion–associated infections

## Diagnosis—stool culture, 25°C, cold enrichment

## Treatment

- Usually supportive care
- For immunocompromised: fluoroquinolones or third-generation cephalosporins

# GENUS: *PROTEUS*

## Genus Features

- **Gram-negative rod**
- **Enterobacteriaceae**
- **Peritrichous flagella**/highly motile/"swarming motility"
- **Non–lactose-fermenting**
- **Urease positive**

## Species of Medical Importance

- *Proteus mirabilis* (90% of infections)
- *Proteus vulgaris*

# Proteus mirabilis/Proteus vulgaris

## Distinguishing Features

- Gram-negative rods
- **Highly motile;** "swarming" motility on surface of blood agar
- **Urease** produced
- Facultative anaerobe (Enterobacteriaceae), oxidase negative

## Reservoir—human colon and environment (water and soil)

## Transmission—endogenous

## Pathogenesis

- **Urease raises urine pH to cause kidney stones** (staghorn renal calculi).
- **Motility** may aid entry into bladder.
- Endotoxin causes fever and shock when septicemia occurs.

## Disease(s)

- Urinary tract infections
- Septicemia

## Diagnosis—culture of blood or urine for lactose-negative organisms with swarming motility.

## Treatment

- Fluoroquinolones, TMP-SMX, or third-generation cephalosporin for uncomplicated UTIs
- Remove stones, if present.

## Prevention—promptly remove urinary tract catheters.

## Key Vignette Clues

*Proteus mirabilis/Proteus vulgaris*

- Patient with UTI or septicemia
- Swarming motility
- Staghorn renal calculi (struvite stones)
- Gram (–), non–lactose fermenting, urease (+)

## Differential Diagnosis

- *E. coli*
- *K. pneumoniae*
- *S. saprophyticus*

## COMLEX Note

*Proteus* and *Helicobacter* are the main urease positive organisms.

## Note

Weil-Felix test: antigens of OX strains of *Proteus vulgaris* cross-react with rickettsial organisms.

# GENUS: *SALMONELLA*

## Genus Features

- **Gram-negative rods (Enterobacteriaceae)**
- **Non–lactose fermenters**
- **Motile**
- More than 2,400 serotypes of salmonellae

## Species of Medical Importance

- *S. typhi*
- *S. enteritidis*
- *S. typhimurium*
- *S. choleraesuis*
- *S. paratyphi*
- *S. dublin*

# *Salmonella typhi*

## Distinguishing Features

- **Gram-negative rods,** highly motile with the **Vi capsule**
- Facultative anaerobe, **non–lactose fermenting**
- **Produces H$_2$S**
- Species identification with biochemical reactions
- **Sensitive to acid**

## Reservoir

- **Humans only; no animal reservoirs**

## Transmission

- **Fecal-oral** route from **human carriers (gall bladder)**
- **Decreased stomach acid or** impairment of mononuclear cells such as in **sickle cell disease predisposes** to *Salmonella* infections

## Pathogenesis and Disease

- Typhoid fever (enteric fever), **S. typhi** (milder form: paratyphoid fever; *S. paratyphi*)
  - Organism ingested (requires large number if stomach acid is normal)
  - **Infection begins in ileocecal region**; constipation common
  - Host cell membranes "ruffle" from *Salmonella* contact.
  - *Salmonella* reach basolateral side of M cells, then **mesenteric lymph nodes and blood** (transient 1′ septicemia)
  - At 1 week: patients have 80% **positive blood cultures**; 25% have **rose spots** (trunk/abdomen)
  - **Liver and spleen** are infected with additional release of bacteria to bloodstream → signs of **septicemia** (mainly fever).

## Key Vignette Clues

*Salmonella typhi*

- Patient with fever, abdominal pain
- Travel to endemic area
- Gram (–), encapsulated, nonlactose fermenter, produces H$_2$S gas
- Widal test

– *S. typhi* survives intracellularly and replicates in macrophages; **resistant to macrophage killing due to:**

  ◦ Decreased fusion of lysosomes with phagosomes

  ◦ Defensins (proteins) allow it to withstand oxygen-dependent and oxygen-independent killing.

– Released from the macrophages; the Vi capsular antigen (*S. typhi* only) withstands complement-mediated killing.

– **Biliary system** (liver, gallbladder) is infected, organisms enter intestinal tract in bile.

– **By week 3: 85% of stool cultures** are positive.

– Symptoms: **fever,** headache, abdominal pain, constipation more common than diarrhea

– Complications if untreated: **necrosis of Peyer patches** with perforation (local endotoxin triggered damage), thrombophlebitis, cholecystitis, pneumonia, abscess formation, etc.

**Diagnosis**—organisms can be isolated from blood, bone marrow, urine, and tissue biopsy from the rose spots if present.

**Treatment**—fluoroquinolones or third-generation cephalosporins

**Prevention**

- Sanitation
- Three vaccines: attenuated oral vaccine of *S. typhi* strain 21 (Ty21a), parenteral heat-killed *S. typhi* (no longer used in the U.S.), and parenteral ViCPS polysaccharide capsular vaccine

# *Salmonella* Subspecies Other Than *typhi* (*S. enteritidis, S. typhimurium*)

## Distinguishing Features

- Facultative gram-negative rods, non–lactose-fermenting on EMB, MacConkey medium
- Produces $H_2S$, **motile** (unlike *Shigella*)
- Speciated with biochemical reactions and serotyped with O, H, and Vi antigens
- **Antibodies** to O, Vi, and H antigens **in patient's serum** can be detected by agglutination (**Widal test**)

**Reservoir**—enteric tracts of humans and domestic animals, e.g., **chickens** and turtles

## Transmission

- Largely through chicken products (raw chicken and eggs) in the kitchen
- Reptile pets—snakes, turtles

## Pathogenesis

- Sensitive to stomach acid (infectious dose $10^5$ organisms)
- Lowered stomach acidity (antacids or gastrectomy) increases risk.
- Endotoxin in cell wall; no exotoxin

## Key Vignette Clues

**Salmonella enterica Subspecies Other Than *typhi***

- Enterocolitis—inflammatory, follows ingestion of poultry products or handling pet reptiles
- Septicemia—very young or elderly
- Osteomyelitis—sickle cell disease
- Gram (–) bacillus, motile, non–lactose fermenter, produces $H_2S$
- Widal test

- **Invades** the mucosa in the ileocecal region, invasive to lamina propria → inflammation → increased PG → increased cAMP → loose diarrhea; shallow ulceration
- Spread to septicemia not common with *S. enterica* subsp. *enteritidis* (the most common) but may occur with others

**Disease(s)**

- Enterocolitis/gastroenteritis
  - Second most common bacterial cause after *Campylobacter:* **6–48 hour incubation; nausea; vomiting; only occasionally bloody, loose stools; fever; abdominal pain; myalgia; headache**
- Septicemia
  - *S. enterica* subsp. *choleraesuis, S. enterica* subsp. *paratyphi,* and *S. enterica* subsp. *dublin*
  - When it occurs, it is usually in very young or elderly.
  - Endocarditis or arthritis complicates about 10% of cases.
- Osteomyelitis
  - Sickle cell disease predisposes to osteomyelitis. ***Salmonella*** is the **most common causal agent of osteomyelitis in sickle cell disease** (not trait) **patients (>80%).**

**Diagnosis**—culture on Hektoen agar, $H_2S$ production

**Treatment**

- For gastroenteritis self-limiting, antibiotics are contraindicated
- For invasive disease, ampicillin, third-generation cephalosporins, fluoroquinolones, or TMP-SMX

**Prevention**—properly cook foods and wash hands, particularly food handlers

# GENUS: *HAEMOPHILUS*

## Genus Features

- **Gram-negative, pleomorphic rod**
- **Requires growth factors factors X (hemin) and V (NAD)** for growth on nutrient or blood agar (BA)
- Grows near *S. aureus* on BA = "satellite" phenomenon
- Chocolate agar provides both X and V factors.

## Species of Medical Importance

- *Haemophilus influenzae*
- *Haemophilus ducreyi*

# *Haemophilus influenzae*

## Distinguishing Features

- Encapsulated, **gram-negative rod; 95%** of invasive disease caused by capsular type b
- Fastidious: requires factors X and V

**Reservoir**—human nasopharynx

**Transmission**—respiratory droplets, shared toys

## Pathogenesis

- **Polysaccharide capsule (type b capsule is polyribitol phosphate)** most important virulence factor
- Capsule important in diagnosis; **antigen screen on CSF** (e.g., latex particle agglutination); serotype all isolates by quellung.
- **IgA protease** is a mucosal colonizing factor.

## Diseases

- Meningitis
  - **Epidemic in unvaccinated children ages 3 months to 2 years**
  - After maternal antibody has waned and before the immune response of the child is adequate
  - *H. influenzae* **was** most common cause of meningitis in 1- to 5-year-old children (mainly younger than 2) up to 1990.
  - Still a problem if child is <2 years and is not vaccinated
- Otitis media
  - Usually nontypeable strains
- Bronchitis
  - Exacerbations of acute bronchitis in smokers with COPD
- Pneumonia
  - 1–24 months; rare in vaccinated children; smokers
- Epiglottitis
  - Rare in vaccinated children; seen in unvaccinated toddlers; *H. influenzae* was the major causal agent.

## Key Vignette Clues

### *Haemophilus influenzae*

- 3 mo–2 y unvaccinated child—meningitis, pneumonia, epiglottitis
- Smokers with COPD—bronchitis, pneumonia
- Gram (–) rod, requires factors X and V

## Differential Diagnosis

- Meningitis
  - *S. pneumoniae*
  - *N. meningitidis*
  - HSV
- Otitis media/pneumonia/bronchitis
  - *S. pneumoniae*
  - *M. pneumoniae*
  - RSV
  - Influenza
  - Parainfluenza virus
- Epiglottitis
  - *S. pneumoniae*
  - *M. catarrhalis*
  - Beta hemolytic streptococci

## Differential Diagnosis

- *T. pallidum*
- *K. granulomatis*
- HSV

**Diagnosis**

- Blood or CSF culture on chocolate agar
- PCR
- Antigen detection of capsule (latex particle agglutination)

**Treatment**—cefotaxime or ceftriaxone for empirical therapy of meningitis; check nasal carriage before releasing; use rifampin if still colonized.

**Prevention**

- **Conjugate capsular polysaccharide-protein vaccine**
- **Vaccination effective** to prevent type b disease
  - **Polyribitol capsule conjugated to protein:** (diphtheria toxoid or *N. meningitidis* outer membrane proteins), making it a **T-cell dependent vaccine**
  - Vaccine: 2, 4, 6 months; booster 15 months; 95% effective
- Rifampin reduces oropharynx colonization and prevents meningitis in unvaccinated, close contacts <2 years of age.

## *Haemophilus ducreyi*

**Reservoir**—human genitals

**Transmission**—sexual transmission and direct contact

Diseases

- Chancroid
- Genital ulcers: **soft, painful chancre** ("You do cry with ducreyi.")
- **Slow to heal without treatment**
- **Open lesions increase transmission of HIV.**

**Diagnosis**—DNA probe

**Treatment**—azithromycin, ceftriaxone, or ciprofloxacin

# GENUS: *GARDNERELLA*

**Genus Features**

- **Gram-negative (pleomorphic) rods**
- Catalase and oxidase negative

**Species of Medical Importance**—*Gardnerella vaginalis*

**Distinguishing Features**

- Gram-variable rod
- Facultative anaerobe

**Reservoir**—human vagina

**Transmission**—endogenous (normal flora gets disturbed, increased pH)

**Pathogenesis**

- Polymicrobial infections
- Works synergistically with other normal flora organisms including *Lactobacillus, Mobiluncus, Bacteroides, Peptostreptococcus*
- Thought to flourish when the vaginal pH increases, reduction of vaginal *Lactobacillus*
- Follows menses or antibiotic therapy

**Disease**

- bacterial vaginosis
    - **Vaginal odor, increased discharge (thin, gray fluid)**

**Diagnosis**—pH >4.5, **clue cells** (epithelial cells covered with bacteria) on vaginal saline smears. Whiff test: add KOH to sample → "fishy" amine odor

**Treatment**—metronidazole or clindamycin

## Key Vignette Clues

*Gardnerella*

- Female patient with thin vaginal discharge
- Post antibiotic or menses
- Clue cells
- Whiff test

## COMLEX Note

The COMLEX requires you to identify an image of a clue cell.

## Differential Diagnosis

- *Candida albicans*
- *C. trachomatis*
- *N. gonorrhoeae*
- *T. vaginalis*
- HSV

# GENUS: *PASTEURELLA*

**Genus Features**

- **Small gram-negative rods**
- **Facultative anaerobic rods**

**Species of Medical Importance**—*Pasteurella multocida*

## *Pasteurella multocida*

**Reservoir**—mouths of many animals, especially cats and dogs

**Transmission**—animal bites; **particularly from cat bites**

**Pathogenesis**—**endotoxin, capsule;** spreads rapidly within skin, no exotoxins known

**Disease**

- Cellulitis with lymphadenitis
  - Wound infections, rapidly spreading
  - Frequently polymicrobial infections

**Diagnosis**—rarely cultured because routine prophylaxis is common

**Treatment**

- Amoxicillin/clavulanate for cat bites
- Resistant to macrolides

**Prevention**—amoxicillin/clavulanate is standard prophylaxis and treatment for most bites (human included), along with thorough cleaning.

## Key Vignette Clues

*Pasteurella multocida*

- Patient with animal (cat) bite
- Cellulitis/lymphadenitis

## Differential Diagnosis

- *B. henselae*
- *Capnocytophaga canimorsus*
- *S. aureus*

**Table II-2-22.** Additional Organisms Associated with Animal/Human Bites

| Organism | Characteristics | Reservoir/Trans-mission | Disease | Treatment |
|---|---|---|---|---|
| *Eikenella corrodens* | Gram-negative rods **"corrodes" agar; bleach-like odor** | Human oropharynx **human bites or fist fight injuries** | Cellulitis | Third-generation cephalosporins; fluoroquinolones |
| *Capnocytophaga canimorsus* | Gram-negative filamentous rods | Dog oropharynx/ **dog bite wounds** | Cellulitis splenectomy → overwhelming sepsis | Third-generation cephalosporins; fluoroquinolones resistant to amino-glycosides |
| *Bartonella henselae* | Gram-negative rods | Cats and dogs/ bites, scratches, fleas | Cat scratch fever; **bacillary angioma-tosis (AIDS)** | Azithromycin; doxycycline |

## HACEK Group Infections

- Group of gram-negative fastidious rods
  - *Aggregatibacter aphrophilus* (formerly *Haemophilus aphrophilus*)
  - *Actinobacillus actinomycetemcomitans*
  - *Cardiobacterium hominis*
  - *Eikenella corrodens*
  - *Kingella kingae*
- HACEK organisms responsible for 5–10% of cases of infective endocarditis (usually subacute)
- Most common cause of gram-negative endocarditis in non–IV drug users
- All part of normal oral flora
- Difficult to diagnose with a mean diagnosis time of 3 months
- Treated with third-generation cephalosporins or fluoroquinolones

# GENUS: *BACTEROIDES*

**Genus Features**

- **Gram-negative rod**
- **Anaerobic**
- Modified LPS with reduced activity

**Species of Medical Importance**—*Bacteroides fragilis*

## *Bacteroides fragilis*

**Reservoir**—human **colon; the genus** *Bacteroides* **is the predominant anaerobe.**

**Transmission**—**endogenous** from bowel defects (e.g., from cytotoxic drug use, cancer), surgery, or trauma

Pathogenesis

- Modified LPS (missing heptose and 2-keto-3 deoxyoctonate) has reduced endotoxin activity.
- Capsule is antiphagocytic.

**Diseases**—**septicemia, peritonitis (often mixed infections), and abdominal abscess**

**Diagnosis**—anaerobes are identified by biochemical tests and gas chromatography.

**Treatment**

- Metronidazole, clindamycin, or cefoxitin; **abscesses should be surgically drained.**
- **Antibiotic resistance** is common (penicillin G, some cephalosporins, and aminoglycosides).
- 7–10% of all strains are now clindamycin resistant

**Prevention**—prophylactic antibiotics for gastrointestinal or biliary tract surgery

## Key Vignette Clues

*Bacteroides fragilis*

- Patient with abdominal trauma, emergency abdominal surgery
- Septicemia, peritonitis, abscess
- Gram (–) bacilli, anaerobic

## Differential Diagnosis

- Other *Bacteroides* species
  - *B. thetaiotaomicron*
- *Prevotella melaninogenica*
- *Fusobacterium* species

# SPIROCHETES

## GENUS: *TREPONEMA*

**Genus Features**

- Spirochetes: spiral with axial filament (endoflagellum)
- Poorly visible on Gram stain but gram-negative envelope

**Species of Medical Importance**—*Treponema pallidum*

## *Treponema pallidum*

**Distinguishing Features**

- **Thin spirochete,** not reliably seen on Gram stain
- Basically a gram-negative cell envelope
- Outer membrane has endotoxin-like lipids.
- Axial filaments = endoflagella = periplasmic flagella
- Cannot culture in clinical lab; serodiagnosis
- Is an **obligate pathogen (but not intracellular)**

**Reservoir**—human genital tract

**Transmission**—transmitted **sexually** or **across the placenta**

**Pathogenesis**

- Disease characterized by **endarteritis resulting in lesions.**
- Strong tendency to chronicity

### Key Vignette Clues

*Treponema pallidum*

- Sexually active patient or neonate of IV drug–using female
- Primary—nontender, indurated genital chancre
- Secondary—maculopapular, copper-colored rash, condylomata lata
- Tertiary—gummas in CNS and cardiovascular system
- Spirillar, gram (–) bacteria visualized by dark-field or fluorescent antibody
- Specific and nonspecific serologic tests

**Table II-2-23.** Stages of Syphilis

| Stage | Clinical | Diagnosis |
|---|---|---|
| Primary (10 d to 3 mo after exposure) | Nontender chancre; clean, indurated edge; contagious; heals spontaneously 3–6 weeks | **Dark-field or fluorescent microscopy of lesion** 50% of patients will be negative by nonspecific serology |
| Secondary (1 to 3 mo later) | Maculopapular (copper-colored) rash, diffuse, includes palms and soles, patchy alopecia Condylomata lata: flat, wartlike perianal and mucous membrane lesions; highly infectious | **Serology nonspecific and specific;** both positive |
| Latent | None | Positive serology |
| Tertiary (30% of untreated, years later) | Gummas (syphilitic granulomas), aortitis, CNS inflammation | **Serology: specific tests** Nonspecific may be negative |
| Congenital (babies of IV drug–using) | Stillbirth, keratitis, 8th nerve damage, notched teeth; most born asymptomatic or with rhinitis → widespread desquamating maculopapular rash | Serology: should revert to negative within 3 mo of birth if uninfected |

**COMLEX Note**

Lab tests with a screening step and a confirmatory step are high yield.

- Syphillis
  screen—nontreponemal antibody
  confirmation—FTA-ABS
- HIV
  screen—ELISA
  confirmation—Western blot
- TB
  screen—auramine-rhodamine
  confirmation—Acid fast

## Differential Diagnosis

- *H. ducreyi*
- *C. trachomatis*
- HSV

## Diagnosis

- **Visualize organisms by immunofluorescence or dark-field microscopy.**
- **Serology** important—two types of antibody:
  1. **Nontreponemal antibody (= reagin) screening tests**
     - **Ab binds to cardiolipin**
       ° An antigen found in mammalian mitochondrial membranes and in treponemes
       ° Cheap source of antigen is cow heart, which is used in screening tests (VDRL, RPR, ART).
       ° Very sensitive in primary (except early) and secondary syphilis; titer may decline in tertiary and with treatment.
       ° But not specific; confirm with FTA-ABS
     - **Examples:**
       ° Venereal disease research lab (VDRL)
       ° Rapid plasma reagin (RPR)
       ° Automated reagin test (ART)
       ° Recombinant antigen test (ICE)
  2. **Specific tests for treponemal antibody (more expensive)**
     - **Earliest** antibodies; **bind to spirochetes**
       ° These tests are more specific and positive earlier; usually remain positive for life—but positive in patients with other treponemal diseases (bejel) and may be positive in Lyme disease.
       ° Fluorescent treponemal antibody-absorption (**FTA-ABS; most widely used test**)
       ° *Treponema pallidum* microhemagglutination (MHA-TP)

## Treatment

- **Benzathine penicillin** (long-acting form) for primary and secondary syphilis (no resistance to penicillin); penicillin G for congenital and late syphilis
- Jarisch-Herxheimer reaction
  - Starts generally during the first 24 hours of antibiotic treatment
  - Increase in temperature, decrease in blood pressure; rigors, leukopenia
  - May occur during treatment of **any of the spirochete diseases**

**Prevention**—benzathine penicillin is given to contacts; no vaccine is available.

# GENUS: *BORRELIA*

**Genus Features**

- Larger spirochetes
- Gram negative
- Microaerophilic
- Difficult to culture

**Species of Medical Importance**—*Borrelia burgdorferi* (10 species responsible for human disease)

## *Borrelia burgdorferi*

**Reservoirs**—white-footed mice (nymphs) and **white-tailed deer (adult ticks)**

**Transmission**

- By *Ixodes* (deer) ticks and nymphs; worldwide but in 3 main areas in the U.S.:
  - *Ixodes scapularis* (*I. dammini*) in Northeast (e.g., Connecticut), Midwest (e.g., Wisconsin)
  - *Ixodes pacificus* on West Coast (e.g., California)
  - Late spring/early summer incidence

**Pathogenesis**

- *B. burgdorferi* **invades skin and spreads via the bloodstream to involve primarily the heart, joints, and central nervous system.**
- Arthritis is caused by immune complexes.

**Disease**

- Lyme disease (#1 tick-borne disease in the U.S.)

| Stage 1: Early localized (3 days to 1 month) | Target rash |
|---|---|
| Stage 2: Early disseminated (days to weeks later) <br><br> Organism spreads hematogenously | Fatigue <br> Chills and fever <br> Headache <br> Muscle and joint pain <br> Swollen lymph nodes <br> Secondary annular skin lesions |
| Stage 3: Late persistent (months to years) | Bell palsy, headache, meningitis, extreme fatigue, conjunctivitis, palpitations, arrhythmias, myocarditis, pericarditis <br><br> Arthritis, most common in knees, immune complex-mediated |

**Diagnosis**

- **Serodiagnosis** by ELISA—negative early
- Western blot for confirmation

## Key Vignette Clues

*Borrelia burgdorferi*

- Patient with influenza-like symptoms and erythema migrans
- Spring/summer seasons
- Northeast, Midwest, West Coast
- Later—neurologic, cardiac, arthritis/arthralgias

## COMLEX Note

Co-infections with Lyme disease

- *Babesia*
- *Erlichia*

- think about co-infection (*Babesia*) when treatment for Lyme disease does not alleviate symptoms.

## Differential Diagnosis

- *Babesia microti*
- *Ehrlichia* species
- *C. burnetii*
- *R. rickettsii*
- *F. tularensis*

**Treatment**

- Doxycycline, amoxicillin, or azithromycin/clarithromycin (primary)
- Ceftriaxone for secondary
- Doxycycline or ceftriaxone for arthritis

**Prevention**

- DEET; avoid tick bites
- Vaccine (OspA flagellar antigen) not used in the U.S.

# GENUS: *LEPTOSPIRA*

**Genus Features**

- Spirochetes: thin, with hooks
- Too thin to visualize, but gram-negative cell envelope

**Species of Medical Importance**—*Leptospira interrogans*

## *Leptospira interrogans*

**Distinguishing Features**

- Spirochetes with tight terminal hooks
  - Seen on **dark-field microscopy** but not light microscopy
  - Can be cultured in vitro; aerobic
- Generally diagnosed by serology

**Reservoir**—wild and domestic animals (zoonosis)

**Transmission**

- **Contact with animal urine in water. Organism penetrates mucous membranes or enters small breaks in epidermis**
- **In U.S., via dog, livestock, and rat urine** through contaminated **recreational waters (jet skiers)** or occupational exposure (sewer workers)
- **Hawaii highest incidence state**

**Pathogenesis**—no toxins or virulence factors known

**Disease**

- Leptospirosis (swineherd's disease, swamp or mud fever)
  - **Influenza-like disease ± gastrointestinal tract symptoms (Weil disease)**
  - Progressing on to hepatitis and renal failure if not treated

**Diagnosis**

- Serodiagnosis (agglutination test)
- Culture (blood, CSF, urine) available in few labs
- Dark-field microscopy insensitive

**Treatment**—penicillin G or doxycycline

**Prevention**

- Doxycycline effective for short-term exposure
- Vaccination of domestic livestock and pets; rat control

## Key Vignette Clues

*Leptospira interrogans*

- Patients with influenza-like symptoms ± GI symptoms
- Occupational or recreational exposure to water aerosols
- Hawaii
- Spirochetes with terminal hook

## Differential Diagnosis

- Dengue virus
- Hantavirus
- EBV
- *N. meningitidis*
- *S. pneumoniae*
- Aseptic meningitis

# UNUSUAL BACTERIA

**Table II-2-24.** Comparison of the *Chlamydiaceae, Rickettsiaceae,* and *Mycoplasmataceae* with Typical Bacteria

|  | Typical Bacteria (*S. aureus*) | Chlamydiaceae | Rickettsiaceae | Mycoplasmataceae |
|---|---|---|---|---|
| Obligate intracellular parasite? | Mostly no | Yes | Yes | No |
| Make ATP? | Normal ATP | No ATP | Limited ATP | Normal ATP |
| Peptidoglycan layer in cell envelope? | Normal peptidoglycan | Modified* peptidoglycan | Normal peptidoglycan | No peptidoglycan |

*Chlamydial peptidoglycan lacks muramic acid and is considered by some as modified, by others as absent.

## FAMILY: CHLAMYDIACEAE

**Family Features**

- **Obligate intracellular bacteria**
- **Elementary body/reticulate body**
- **Not seen on Gram stain**
- **Cannot make ATP**
- **Cell wall lacks muramic acid**

**Genera of Medical Importance**

- *Chlamydia trachomatis*
- *Chlamydophila pneumoniae* (formerly *Chlamydia pneumoniae*)
- *Chlamydophila psittaci* (formerly *Chlamydia psittaci*)

## *Chlamydia trachomatis*

**Distinguishing Features**

- Obligate intracellular bacterium; cannot make ATP
- Found **in cells as metabolically active, replicating reticulate bodies**
- **Infective form:** inactive, extracellular **elementary body**
- Not seen on Gram stain; peptidoglycan layer lacks muramic acid.

**Reservoir—human** genital tract and eyes

**Transmission—sexual contact** and **at birth;** trachoma is transmitted by **hand-to-eye contact** and flies.

**Pathogenesis—infection of nonciliated columnar or cuboidal epithelial cells of mucosal surfaces** leads to **granulomatous response and damage.**

## Key Vignette Clues

*Chlamydia trachomatis*

- Sexually active patient or neonate
- Adult: urethritis, cervicitis, PID, inclusion conjunctivitis
- Neonate: inclusion conjunctivitis/pneumonia
- Immigrant from Africa/Asia, genital lymphadenopathy
- Cytoplasmic inclusion bodies in scrapings

**Diseases**

- STDs in U.S.
  - **Serotypes D-K** (This is the most common **bacterial** STD in the U.S., although overall, herpes and HPV are more common.)
  - **Nongonococcal urethritis, cervicitis, PID,** and major portion of infertility (no resistance to reinfection)
  - **Inclusion conjunctivitis**
  - **Inclusion conjunctivitis** and/or **pneumonia in neonates/infants (staccato cough)**
- Lymphogranuloma venereum
  - Serotypes L1, 2, 3
    - ° This STD is prevalent in Africa, Asia, and South America.
    - ° Painless ulcer at the site of contact
    - ° Swollen lymph nodes leading to genital elephantiasis in late stage
    - ° Tertiary: ulcers, fistulas, genital elephantiasis
- Trachoma
  - Leading cause of preventable infectious blindness: **serotypes A, B, Ba, and C**
  - **Follicular conjunctivitis** leading to **conjunctival scarring,** and **inturned eyelashes** leading to **corneal scarring** and **blindness**

**Diagnosis**

- DNA probes in U.S. (rRNA) and PCR
- **Cytoplasmic inclusions seen on Giemsa-, iodine-, or fluorescent-antibody-stained smear or scrapings**
- **Cannot be cultured on inert media**
- Is cultured in **tissue cultures or embryonated eggs**
- Serodiagnosis: DFA, ELISA

**Treatment**—doxycycline or azithromycin

**Prevention**

- Erythromycin is effective in infected mothers to prevent neonatal disease.
- Treat neonatal conjunctivitis with systemic erythromycin to prevent pneumonia.

## COMLEX Note

In order to differentiate between the STD's and/or vaginal infections, recognize the discharge.

*gonorrhoeae/chlamydia* = purulent/mucoid

Trichomonas = frothy yellow-green, malodorous

*Candida* = cottage cheese

*Gardnerella* = thin, greyish fluid, malodorous

## Differential Diagnosis

- Nongonococcal urethritis, cervicitis, PID
  - *N. gonorrhoeae*
  - *Ureaplasma urealyticum*
  - *T. vaginalis*
- Lymphogranuloma venereum
  - *K. granulomatis*
  - *Mycobacterial* infections
- Trachoma
  - Adenovirus
  - HSV
  - *H. influenzae*
  - *S. pneumoniae*

## Key Vignette Clues

*Chlamydophila*

- *C. pneumoniae:* atypical pneumonia
  - Sputum with intracytoplasmic inclusions
- *C. psittaci:* atypical pneumonia
  - Exposure to parrots

# GENUS: *CHLAMYDOPHILA*

**Table II-2-25.** Diseases Caused by *Chlamydophila* Species

| Organism | *C. pneumoniae* | *C. psittaci* |
|---|---|---|
| **Distinguishing characteristics** | Potential association with atherosclerosis | No glycogen in inclusion bodies |
| **Reservoir** | Human respiratory tract | Birds, **parrots,** turkeys (major U.S. reservoir) |
| **Transmission** | Respiratory droplets | Dust of dried bird secretions and feces |
| **Pathogenesis** | Intracellular growth; infects smooth muscle, endothelial cells, or coronary artery and macrophages | Intracellular growth |
| **Disease** | Atypical "walking" pneumonia; single lobe; bronchitis; scant sputum, prominent dry cough and hoarseness; sinusitis | Psittacosis (ornithosis); atypical pneumonia with hepatitis; cough may be absent, when present, nonproductive at first, then scant mucopurulent; CNS and GI symptoms may be present. |
| **Diagnosis** | Serology (complement fixation or microimmunofluorescence) | Serology (fourfold rise in antibody titer), complement fixation |
| **Treatment** | Macrolides and tetracycline | Doxycycline |
| **Prevention** | None | Avoid birds |

# GENUS: *RICKETTSIA*

**Table II-2-26.** Infections Caused by Rickettsiae and Close Relatives

| Group Disease | Bacterium | Arthropod Vector | Reservoir Host |
|---|---|---|---|
| Rocky Mountain Spotted Fever | *R. rickettsii* | Ticks | Ticks, dogs, rodents |
| Epidemic Typhus | *R. prowazekii* | Human louse | Humans |
| Endemic Typhus | *R. typhi* | Fleas | Rodents |
| Scrub Typhus | *Orientia tsutsuga-mushi* | Mites | Rodents |
| Ehrlichiosis | *E. chafeensis* *E. phagocytophila* | Tick | Small mammals |

## Genus Features

- **Aerobic, gram-negative bacilli (too small to stain well with Gram stain)**
- **Obligate intracellular bacteria (do not make sufficient ATP for independent life)**

## Species of Medical Importance

- *Rickettsia rickettsii*
- *Rickettsia prowazekii*
- *Rickettsia typhi*
- *Orientia tsutsugamushi* (formerly *R. tsutsugamushi*)
- *Ehrlichia spp.*

## Rickettsia rickettsii

**Reservoir**—small wild rodents and larger wild and domestic animals (dogs)

**Transmission—hard ticks:** *Dermacentor* (also **reservoir hosts** because of transovarian transmission)

**Pathogenesis**—invade endothelial cells lining capillaries, causing vasculitis in many organs including brain, liver, skin, lungs, kidney, and gastrointestinal tract.

**Disease**

- Rocky Mountain spotted fever (RMSF)
  - Prevalent on **East Coast (OK, TN, NC, SC)**; 2–12 day incubation
  - **Headache, fever (102°F)**, malaise, myalgias, toxicity, vomiting, and confusion
  - **Rash** (maculopapular → **petechial) starts** (by day 6 of illness) **on ankles and wrists** and then spreads to the trunk, **palms, soles, and face (centripetal rash).**
  - **Ankle and wrist swelling** also occur.
  - Diagnosis may be confused by gastrointestinal symptoms, periorbital swelling, stiff neck, conjunctivitis, and arthralgias.

### Key Vignette Clues

*Rickettsia rickettsii*

- Patient with influenza-like symptoms and petechial rash that begins on ankles and wrists and moves to trunk
- East Coast mountainous areas
- Spring/summer seasons
- Outdoor exposure
- Weil-Felix (+)

## Differential Diagnosis

- *B. burgdorferi*
- *N. meningitidis*
- Rubeola virus
- Dengue virus

Diagnosis

- Clinical symptoms (above) and tick bite
- **Start treatment without laboratory confirmation.**
- **Serological IFA test is most widely used; fourfold increase in titer is diagnostic**
- Weil-Felix test (cross-reaction of *Rickettsia* antigens with OX strains of *Proteus vulgaris*) is no longer used (but may still be asked!)

**Treatment**—doxycycline

**Prevention**—tick protection and prompt removal; doxycycline effective in exposed persons

# GENUS: *EHRLICHIA*

**Genus Features**

- Gram-negative bacilli
- Obligate intracellular bacteria of mononuclear or granulocytic phagocytes

**Species of Medical Importance**

- *Ehrlichia chaffeensis*
- *Anaplasma phagocytophila*

## *Ehrlichia chaffeensis/Anaplasma phagocytophila*

**Table II-2-27.** Summary of Diseases Caused by *Ehrlichia* Species

| Organism | Reservoir | Transmission | Pathogenesis | Disease | Diagnosis | Treatment |
|----------|-----------|--------------|--------------|---------|-----------|-----------|
| *E. chaffeensis* | Ticks and deer | Lone star tick (*Amblyomma*) | Infects monocytes and macrophages | Ehrlichiosis (monocytic) similar to RMSF without rash; leukopenia, low platelets, morulae | IFA PCR Blood film | Doxycycline |
| *A. phagocytophila* | Ticks, deer, mice | *Ixodes* ticks Coinfection with *Borrelia* | Infects neutrophils | Ehrlichiosis (granulocytic) similar to RMSF without rash; leukopenia, low platelets, morulae | IFA PCR Blood film | Doxycycline |

**Disease**

- Similar to Rocky Mountain spotted fever but generally without rash
- Leukopenia
- Thrombocytopenia
- Morulae—mulberry-like structures inside infected cells

**Diagnosis**

- Giemsa-stained blood film (morulae)
- Serology
- DNA probe

**Treatment**—doxycycline (begin before laboratory confirmation)

**Prevention**—no vaccine, avoid ticks

## Key Vignette Clues

*Ehrlichia chaffeensis/Anaplasma phagocytophila*

- Patient with influenza-like symptoms, no rash, leukopenia, thrombocytopenia
- Same geographic range as Lyme disease
- Spring/summer seasons
- Exposure to outdoors
- Morulae inside monocytes or granulocytes

# FAMILY: MYCOPLASMATACEAE

## Family Features

- **Smallest free-living (extracellular) bacteria**
- **Missing peptidoglycan (no cell wall)**
- **Sterols in membrane**
- **Require cholesterol for in vitro culture**
- **"Fried-egg" colonies on *Mycoplasma* or Eaton's media (all *Mycoplasma*, except *M. pneumoniae*)**

## Genera of Medical Importance

- *Mycoplasma pneumoniae*
- *Ureaplasma urealyticum*

# *Mycoplasma pneumoniae*

## Distinguishing Features

- Extracellular, tiny, flexible
- No cell wall; not seen on Gram-stained smear
- Membrane with cholesterol but **does not synthesize cholesterol**
- Requires cholesterol for in vitro culture

**Reservoir**—human respiratory tract

**Transmission**—respiratory droplets; close contact: families, military recruits, medical school classes, college dorms

## Pathogenesis

- Surface parasite: not invasive
- **Attaches to respiratory epithelium via P1 protein**
- **Inhibits ciliary action**
- **Produces hydrogen peroxide, superoxide radicals, and cytolytic enzymes,** which damage the respiratory epithelium, leading to necrosis and a bad, hacking cough (walking pneumonia)
- *M. pneumoniae* functions as superantigen, elicits production of IL-1, IL-6, and TNF-α

## Disease

- Walking pneumonia
  - **Pharyngitis**
  - **May develop into an atypical pneumonia with persistent hack (little sputum produced)**
  - **Most common atypical pneumonia (along with viruses) in young adults**

## Diagnosis

- Primarily clinical diagnosis; PCR/nucleic acid probes
- **ELISA and immunofluorescence sensitive and specific.**
- **Mulberry-shaped colonies on sterol-containing media, 10 days**
- **Positive cold agglutinins** (autoantibody to red blood cells) test is nonspecific and is positive in only 65% of cases.

## Key Vignette Clues

***Mycoplasma pneumoniae***

- Young adult with atypical pneumonia
- Mulberry-shaped colonies on media containing sterols
- Positive cold agglutinin test

## COMLEX Note

*M. pneumoniae* is most common bacterial agent of "walking pneumonia"

## Differential Diagnosis

- *C. pneumoniae*
- *L. pneumophila*
- Influenza

**Treatment**—erythromycin, azithromycin, clarithromycin; **no cephalosporins or penicillins**

**Prevention**—none

## *Ureaplasma urealyticum*

**Distinguishing Features**

- Member of family Mycoplasmataceae

**Pathogenesis**

- Urease positive

**Diseases**

- Urethritis, prostatitis, renal calculi

**Diagnosis**

- Non-Gram-staining, urease(+)

**Treatment**

- Erythromycin or tetracycline

## Key Vignette Clues

*Ureaplasma urealyticum*

- Adult patient with urethritis, prostatitis, renal calculi
- Alkaline urine
- Non–Gram-staining, urease (+)

## Differential Diagnosis

- *C. trachomatis*
- *N. gonorrhoeae*
- *P. vulgaris/mirabilis*

## Review Questions

1. A 4-year-old boy develops several honey-crusted lesions behind his ears and on his face. The simplest test for the physician to determine the genus of bacteria responsible for this child's illness is the

   (A) catalase test

   (B) coagulase test

   (C) growth of the organism in 6.5% sodium chloride

   (D) hemolysis pattern on blood agar

   (E) polymerase chain reaction

2. An atherosclerotic 80-year-old man develops a pelvic abscess following a ruptured appendix. What is/are the most likely causal agent(s)?

   (A) *Bacteroides* species and microaerophilic streptococci

   (B) *Candida albicans*

   (C) *Enterobacter aerogenes*

   (D) *Haemophilus influenzae* group B

   (E) *Streptococcus viridans*

3. A homeless, malnourished chronic alcoholic presents with severe headache and dyspnea. Physical examination reveals a disheveled male with poor hygiene. His temperature is 41°C, blood pressure is 110/78 mm Hg, and his pulse is 96/minute and regular. Auscultation of the chest reveals absence of breath sounds over the left middle lung fields. A chest x-ray confirms left lobar pneumonia. Sputum stain reveals partially acid-fast bacilli with branching rods. Which of the following agents is the most likely cause?

   (A) *Mycobacterium avium-intracellulare*

   (B) *Mycobacterium kansasii*

   (C) *Mycobacterium leprae*

   (D) *Mycobacterium tuberculosis*

   (E) *Nocardia asteroides*

4. A 70-year-old man presents to the emergency department with a fever of 103.5°F, a dry cough, tachypnea, and chest pain. History reveals he has been smoking since he was a teen. He mentions that several people at the assisted living community where he resides have had similar symptoms. A sputum sample isolated organisms that grew on buffered charcoal yeast extract agar and stained weakly gram-negative. Which of the following properties is consistent with the above organism?

   (A) Capsule

   (B) No cell wall

   (C) Optochin sensitive

   (D) Requires iron and cysteine for growth

   (E) Serpentine growth in vitro

5.  A 33-year-old man presents to the emergency department with a fever of 102.5°F, facial palsy, headache, and malaise. A circular maculopapular rash was identified on the patients left shoulder; the patient was unaware of the rash. The patient likely acquired the above infection via which of the following routes?

    (A) Consumption of contaminated food

    (B) Direct contact with fomite

    (C) Arthropod vector

    (D) Respiratory route

    (E) Sexual contact

6.  A 25-year-old man develops a high fever and swelling in the armpits and groin. Aspirates from the lymph nodes reveal gram-negative rods with bipolar staining. The patient is most likely

    (A) a farmer

    (B) from the southwestern U.S.

    (C) in the military

    (D) living in a dormitory

    (E) sexually promiscuous

7.  A previously healthy 5-month-old infant presents with apparent upper body weakness including droopy eyes, head lag, drooling, and inability to sit unassisted. The most likely infectious form is

    (A) elementary body

    (B) endospore

    (C) exotoxin

    (D) reticulate body

    (E) vegetative cell

8.  Sixteen residents in a retirement home have fever, malaise, and anorexia. These residents have taken their meals prepared by the same kitchen. Blood cultures from 11 of these residents grow *Salmonella enterica* subsp. *typhi*. The primary reservoir of this organism is

    (A) hen's egg

    (B) dogs and cats

    (C) turkeys

    (D) people

    (E) water

9. If a culture is inoculated to a density of $5 \times 10^2$ cells/mL at time 0 and has both a generation time and lag time of 10 minutes, how many cells/mL will there be at 40 minutes?

   (A) $1.5 \times 10^3$

   (B) $2 \times 10^3$

   (C) $4 \times 10^3$

   (D) $6 \times 10^3$

   (E) $4 \times 10^6$

10. A 6-year-old girl had crashed on a toboggan ride and complained of pain in the perineal area. Exam showed only bruising of the area. Two days later, she develops fever, prostration, discoloration of the buttock, and blebs of the skin in the area. After admission to the hospital, she develops progressive involvement of the leg, thigh, and buttock with extension to the lower abdomen. She goes into shock and dies before surgery could be performed. At autopsy, a 1-inch piece of wood is found in the perineum, which had perforated the anus. The most likely causal agent

    (A) requires an elevated oxidation reduction potential

    (B) is a gram-negative coccobacillus

    (C) is a marked lecithinase producer

    (D) is nonhemolytic on blood agar

    (E) is nonfermentative

11. A 71-year-old man is admitted from his extended care facility (nursing home) because of recent aggravation of an exfoliative skin condition that has plagued him for several years. He had been receiving a variety of topical antibiotic regimens over the last year or two. He now has a temperature of 38.9°C (102°F). The skin of upper chest, extremities, and neck shows erythema with diffuse epidermal peeling and many pustular lesions. Cultures obtained from these lesions were reported back from the laboratory as yielding a gram-positive organism that is highly salt (NaCl) tolerant. What lab result is used to confirm the species of the causal agent?

    (A) Bacitracin sensitivity

    (B) Bile solubility

    (C) Catalase production

    (D) Coagulase production

    (E) Optochin sensitivity

12. Eight of 10 family practice residents who had a potluck 4 days ago now have diarrhea with abdominal cramps, general malaise, and fever ranging from 37.5° to 38.7°C. Stools from 3 residents are blood tinged. Laboratory studies revealed the causal agent was a microaerophilic gram-negative, curved rod with polar flagella often in pairs to give a "seagull" appearance. It grew on special media at 42°C. The original contamination probably was found in

    (A) poultry

    (B) improperly canned food

    (C) fried rice

    (D) fish

    (E) vegetables

13. A 19-year-old man was brought to the emergency department by his dorm mate with a petechial rash, headache, nuchal rigidity, and vomiting. Which of the following describes the most likely causal agent?

    (A) Gram-negative coccus, capsule, ferments maltose

    (B) Gram-negative coccus, ferments glucose only

    (C) Gram-negative coccobacillus, capsular serotype b

    (D) Gram-positive coccus, alpha hemolytic, optochin sensitive

    (E) Gram-positive rods, growth at 4°C

14. A 70-year-old woman is brought to the emergency department by her spouse with complaints of shortness of breath and fever. Physical examination revealed a fever of 103°F, hypotension, and a diastolic murmur. History revealed a cardiac valve replacement 5 years earlier. Three consecutive blood cultures taken during febrile periods revealed gram-positive cocci that were catalase-positive and coagulase-negative. Which of the following organisms is the most likely cause?

    (A) *Enterococcus faecalis*

    (B) *Kingella kingae*

    (C) *Staphylococcus aureus*

    (D) *Staphylococcus epidermidis*

    (E) *Staphylococcus saprophyticus*

15. What is the structure that is found in gram-negative but not in gram-positive bacteria?

    (A) Capsule

    (B) Cell wall

    (C) Cytoplasmic membrane

    (D) Endospore

    (E) Outer membrane

16. A tourist who recently returned from a trip to Peru goes to her physician complaining of persistent high fever, malaise, and constipation that persisted over a week. She recalls that the fever began slowly and climbed to 41°C. A physical exam reveals an enlarged spleen and tender abdomen with rose-colored spots. Laboratory isolation of a bacterium that produces $H_2S$ and is motile is revealed. Which organism is the most likely cause of her condition?

    (A) EHEC

    (B) ETEC

    (C) *Salmonella enterica* subsp. *enteritidis*

    (D) *Salmonella enterica* subsp. *typhi*

    (E) *Shigella dysenteriae*

17. A 5-year-old child of an Eastern European immigrant family is brought to your pediatric clinic. The child is afebrile, but weak and exhausted from a week of paroxysmal coughing with inspiratory whoops, frequently associated with vomiting. The parents profess religious objections to childhood vaccinations, but permit withdrawal of a blood sample, which reveals a lymphocytosis of 44,000/mm³. Production of lymphocytosis, insulin secretion, and histamine sensitization are all results of which attribute of this organism?

    (A) Motility

    (B) Adenylate cyclase toxin

    (C) Beta-hemolysin

    (D) Anaerobic growth

    (E) Pertussis toxin

    (F) Filamentous hemagglutinin

18. The clinical laboratory reports the presence of 0157:H7 strains of *E. coli* in the bloody stools of 6 children ages 3–5 who attended a local petting zoo. These young children would be at an increased risk for developing

    (A) buboes

    (B) hemolytic uremic syndrome

    (C) infant botulism

    (D) renal stones

    (E) rice water stools

19. A 65-year-old man develops pneumonia. The organisms isolated from the sputum are gram-positive cocci that are alpha hemolytic on blood agar and sensitive to optochin. Which structure of the causal agent provides protection against phagocytosis?

    (A) Capsule

    (B) Catalase

    (C) Coagulase

    (D) M protein

    (E) Teichoic acid

20. A 68-year-old woman on chemotherapy for leukemia has developed sepsis due to an infection with *Escherichia coli*. The following day the patient develops septic shock and dies. The structure on the bacterium most likely responsible for causing septic shock in this patient is

    (A) capsule
    (B) lipopolysaccharide
    (C) pili
    (D) spore
    (E) teichoic acid

21. A 12-year-old boy from North Carolina presents to the emergency department with rash, fever, and severe headache that began 3 days ago. The rash began on his arms and legs and then spread to the trunk. The pediatrician notes conjunctival redness, and lab tests reveal proteinuria. Which of the following events likely led to the child's illness?

    (A) Cutting himself while butchering rabbits
    (B) Eating undercooked meat
    (C) Hiking in the woods
    (D) Kissing
    (E) Not washing his hands

22. A 10-year-old child develops glomerulonephritis a week after he was treated for a sore throat. The causal agent is identified by serotyping of the

    (A) capsule
    (B) M proteins
    (C) outer membrane proteins
    (D) pili
    (E) teichoic acids

23. An 8-year-old boy presents to the emergency department with vomiting and a severe cough in which he can't catch his breath. His vaccination history is incomplete. Physical exam reveals fever and conjunctival injection. A nasopharyngeal aspirate grew gram-negative coccobacilli on Bordet-Gengou media. What is the mechanism of action of the toxin involved?

    (A) ADP ribosylation of eukaryotic elongation factor 2 (eEF-2)
    (B) ADP ribosylation of $G_i$
    (C) ADP ribosylation of GTP-binding protein
    (D) Blocks release of acetylcholine
    (E) Blocks release of inhibitory transmitters GABA and glycine

24. What is the typical means of transmission of a toxin that blocks the release of inhibitory transmitters GABA and glycine?

    (A) Eating home-canned foods

    (B) Fecal-oral, travel to foreign country

    (C) Infant given honey during the first year of life

    (D) Puncture wound

    (E) Respiratory, with incomplete vaccination history

25. An infant presents to the emergency department due to difficulty breathing, constipation, and anorexia. Upon examination, the physician notes flaccid paralysis. A toxin screen of the stool identified the agent. What is the mechanism of action of the toxin?

    (A) ADP ribosylation of eukaryotic elongation factor 2 (eEF-2)

    (B) ADP ribosylation of $G_i$

    (C) ADP ribosylation of GTP-binding protein

    (D) Blocks release of acetylcholine

    (E) Blocks release of inhibitory transmitters GABA and glycine

26. A 10-year-old girl with an incomplete vaccination history presents to her pediatrician with a fever of 101.5°F, sore throat, malaise, and difficulty breathing. Physical examination reveals cervical lymphadenopathy and a gray, leathery exudate in the rear of the oropharynx. The area bleeds profusely when disturbed with a tongue depressor. Which of the following correctly describes the causal agent?

    (A) Gram-negative rod; toxin that inhibits protein synthesis

    (B) Gram-negative rod; toxin that increases cAMP

    (C) Gram-positive aerobic rod; toxin that inhibits protein synthesis

    (D) Gram-positive anaerobic rod; toxin that inhibits protein synthesis

    (E) Gram-positive aerobic rod; toxin that increases cAMP

27. A 38-year-old man who recently visited India on business presents to the emergency department with profuse watery diarrhea flecked with mucus, and severe dehydration. Which of the following correctly describes the causal agent?

    (A) Gram-negative curved rod; toxin that increases cAMP

    (B) Gram-negative curved rod; toxin that inhibits protein synthesis

    (C) Gram-negative rod; toxin that increases cAMP

    (D) Gram-negative rod; toxin that inhibits protein synthesis

    (E) Intoxication with a heat labile toxin that blocks the release of acetylcholine

28. A 30-year-old man presents to his physician with complaints of midepigastric pain. He describes the pain as moderate, occasionally waking him at night, and improving immediately following meals. A urease breath test was positive. Which of the following correctly describes the causal agent?

    (A) Gram-negative curved rod; microaerophilic

    (B) Gram-negative rod; aerobic

    (C) Gram-negative rod; facultative anaerobe

    (D) Gram-positive rod; aerobic

    (E) Gram-positive rod; microaerophilic

29. A 13-year-old girl presents to her pediatrician with fever, malaise, and a sore throat. Physical examination reveals a fever of 103°F, cervical lymphadenopathy, and pharyngeal erythema. A swab is taken from some of the tonsillar exudate and cultured on blood agar. Culture reveals beta hemolytic, gram-positive cocci, and a rapid antigen test is positive. What is the major component that protects the causal agent from osmotic damage?

    (A) Lipopolysaccharide

    (B) Peptidoglycan

    (C) Phospholipids

    (D) Polysaccharide

    (E) Teichoic acid

30. A 27-year-old woman, after returning home from her honeymoon, has developed urinary frequency, dysuria, and urgency. Her urine is grossly bloody. Which lab data are most likely to define the causal agent?

    (A) A gram-negative diplococcus, which is oxidase positive but does not ferment maltose

    (B) A gram-positive coccus, which is catalase positive and coagulase negative

    (C) An optochin-resistant, catalase-negative, gram-positive coccus

    (D) A gram-positive bacillus grown on a low oxidation-reduction medium

    (E) A gram-negative bacterium capable of reducing nitrates to nitrites

31. Two days after eating a meal that included home-canned green beans, 3 people developed various degrees of visual problems, including double vision and difficulties focusing. Describe the Gram reaction of the organism most likely to be isolated from the leftover beans and lab findings which would be used in its identification.

    (A) A gram-positive coccus which is catalase-positive and grows in a high salt environment

    (B) A gram-positive aerobic bacillus which sporulates

    (C) A gram-positive coccus which is catalase-negative and optochin-resistant

    (D) A gram-positive bacillus grown on a low oxidation-reduction medium

    (E) A gram-negative bacillus capable of reducing nitrates to nitrites

32. A 16-year-old has pneumonia with a dry, hacking cough. The x-ray pattern shows a light, diffuse infiltrative pattern. The most likely organism producing these symptoms is

    (A) A non-Gram–staining bacterium requiring sterols

    (B) A bacillus showing granules when stained with methylene blue

    (C) A bacitracin-sensitive, catalase-negative gram-positive coccus

    (D) A coagulase positive, gram-positive, catalase positive coccus in clusters

    (E) A gram-positive bacillus grown on a low oxidation-reduction medium

33. A 7-day-old infant presents to the emergency department with a fever, poor feeding, and a bulging fontanelle. During her physical examination, she begins to convulse. A Gram stain of the CSF reveals gram-positive rods. Which of the following organisms is the most likely causal agent?

    (A) *Escherichia coli*

    (B) *Haemophilus influenzae*

    (C) *Listeria monocytogenes*

    (D) *Neisseria meningitidis*

    (E) *Streptococcus agalactiae*

34. A 55-year-old woman had her rheumatic heart valve replaced with a prosthetic valve. Six blood cultures became positive after 3 days of incubation. An optochin-resistant, catalase-negative gram-positive coccus that was alpha-hemolytic was isolated. What was the most likely causal agent?

    (A) *Streptococcus viridans*

    (B) *Pseudomonas aeruginosa*

    (C) *Serratia marcescens*

    (D) *Staphylococcus aureus*

    (E) *Streptococcus pneumoniae*

35. A surgical patient develops an abdominal abscess. The abscess was drained, and culture reveals a polymicrobial infection. The predominant organism identified is a gram-negative anaerobic rod. Which of the following is the most likely causal agent?

    (A) *Bacteroides fragilis*

    (B) *Escherichia coli*

    (C) *Pseudomonas aeruginosa*

    (D) *Staphylococcus aureus*

    (E) *Staphylococcus epidermidis*

36. A 40-year-old homeless man presents to the emergency department with fever and night sweats, coughing up blood. Acid-fast bacilli are identified in his sputum. Which of the following virulence factors allows the causal agent to inhibit phagosome-lysosome fusion to survive intracellularly?

    (A) Cord factor

    (B) Calcium dipicolinate

    (C) Peptidoglycan

    (D) Sulfatides

    (E) Tuberculin

37. A 28-year-old woman presents to her gynecologist with complaints of a malodorous vaginal discharge. Upon examination the physician notes a thin, gray vaginal discharge with no vaginal redness. A whiff test was positive for an amine odor. Which of the following is consistent with this case?

    (A) Clue cells

    (B) Gram-negative diplococci in PMNs

    (C) Koilocytic cells

    (D) Owl-eye inclusions

    (E) Tzanck smear

38. Several postal workers come down with symptoms of dyspnea, cyanosis, hemoptysis, and chest pain. Chest x-ray reveals mediastinal widening. Sputum cultures are negative for all routine respiratory pathogens. Serology correctly identifies the causal agent. Which of the following structures is possessed by the causal agent?

    (A) Elementary body

    (B) Endotoxin

    (C) Periplasmic space

    (D) Reticulate body

    (E) Spore

39. A 25-year-old man gets into a fight at the local bar and punches another patron in the mouth. The following day his fist becomes infected and he visits a local urgent care center. Exudate from the wound is cultured on blood and chocolate agar and reveals gram-negative rods that have a bleach-like odor. Which of the following agents is the most likely cause?

    (A) *Actinobacillus actinomycetemcomitans*

    (B) *Cardiobacterium hominis*

    (C) *Eikenella corrodens*

    (D) *Pseudomonas aeruginosa*

    (E) *Kingella kingae*

40. A 45-year-old woman presents to the emergency department with intense pain in her lower back and a burning sensation upon urination. A urine culture was taken and plated on MacConkey agar. Gram-negative rods that did not ferment lactose were identified. Which virulence factor of the causal agent is most important to pathogenesis?

    (A) Capsule
    (B) Catalase
    (C) Coagulase
    (D) Exotoxin
    (E) Urease

41. A 70-year-old man is hospitalized for an infection and treated with clindamycin. The patient improves and returns to his nursing home. Two weeks later he is rushed to the emergency room with fever and loose, mucoid green stools. The diarrhea is voluminous, and he is having severe abdominal pain. Sigmoidoscopy of his colon reveals yellow-white plaques. What is the single most likely event/factor that contributed to this patient's current illness?

    (A) Administration of antibiotics
    (B) Advanced age
    (C) Drinking unpasteurized milk
    (D) Eating contaminated cold cuts
    (E) Living in nursing home

42. A 15-day-old boy presents with conjunctivitis. Iodine staining bodies are seen in conjunctival scrapings. The most likely infectious form is a(n)

    (A) elementary body
    (B) reticulate body
    (C) endospore
    (D) exotoxin
    (E) vegetative cell

43. A 45-year-old man presents to the emergency department with shortness of breath and a productive cough. His sputum was gelatinous and bloody. Gram stain of the sputum revealed numerous PMNs and gram-negative rods. Which of the following descriptions is most likely to fit the patient?

    (A) Alcoholic
    (B) Homeless
    (C) Hiker
    (D) IV drug user
    (E) Veterinarian

44. An infant presents with fever, convulsions, and nuchal rigidity during the first month of life. Which of the following agents is the most likely cause?

    (A) *Escherichia coli*

    (B) *Haemophilus influenzae*

    (C) *Listeria monocytogenes*

    (D) *Streptococcus agalactiae*

    (E) *Streptococcus pneumoniae*

45. A 60-year-old woman is hospitalized following a stroke and develops a high-grade fever with chills. She is catheterized due to urinary incontinence and receives cephalosporin for treatment of pneumonia. Blood cultures and Gram stain are performed by the laboratory. The organisms isolated are gram-positive cocci that are catalase-negative and capable of growth in 6.5% sodium chloride. Which of the following is the most likely causal agent?

    (A) *Enterococcus faecalis*

    (B) *Staphylococcus aureus*

    (C) *Staphylococcus epidermidis*

    (D) *Streptococcus pyogenes*

    (E) Viridans streptococci

46. A 35-year-old man who is positive for HIV develops sepsis with the subsequent development of a necrotic lesion on the buttock that has a black center and an erythematous margin. Which of the following is the most likely causal agent?

    (A) *Bacillus anthracis*

    (B) *Clostridium perfringens*

    (C) *Enterococcus faecalis*

    (D) *Pseudomonas aeruginosa*

    (E) *Staphylococcus aureus*

47. A 15-year-old girl develops a sore throat, fever, and earache of approximately 1 week duration. Upon examination by her physician, an erythematous rash is noted covering most of her body and her tongue appears bright red. Which of the following is the description of the causal agent?

    (A) Gram-positive coccus, alpha hemolytic, catalase negative

    (B) Gram-positive coccus, beta hemolytic, catalase negative

    (C) Gram-positive coccus, alpha hemolytic, catalase positive

    (D) Gram-positive coccus, beta hemolytic, catalase positive

    (E) Gram-positive coccus, gamma hemolytic, catalase negative

48. A patient is admitted to the hospital because of a bleeding duodenal ulcer. Culture at 37°C reveals a urease-positive, gram-negative, curved rod. Which of the following is a likely complication due to infection with the causal agent?

    (A) Diarrhea

    (B) Kidney stones

    (C) Pseudomembranous colitis

    (D) Stomach cancer

    (E) Vomiting

49. Roommates of a 19-year-old college student become alarmed when he does not get up to go to swim practice in the morning and they are unable to wake him for his 11 AM class (he had complained of a headache and not feeling well the night before). The rescue squad finds a febrile, comatose young man with a petechial rash. In the emergency room, Kernig and Brudzinski signs are present. No papilledema is seen, so a spinal tap is done. Protein is high, glucose low. CSF WBC count is 9,000 (mainly PMNs) with few RBCs. The characteristics of the most likely causal agent are

    (A) An enveloped dsDNA virus

    (B) A naked (+)ssRNA virus

    (C) A Gram-negative bacillus with a polyribitol capsule

    (D) A Gram-negative, oxidase-positive diplococcus

    (E) A Gram-positive, lancet-shaped, alpha-hemolytic diplococcus

## Answers and Explanations

1.  **Answer: A.** The easiest way to differentiate between *Staphylococcus* and *Streptococcus* is the catalase test (**choice A**). This is important because they can have similar presentations. Coagulase (**choice B**) differentiates between members of the genus *Staphylococcus*. Hemolysis pattern (**choice D**) is inconclusive. Growth of organism in sodium chloride (**choice C**) can be useful for *Enterococcus*. PCR (**choice E**) is currently used to identify organisms that are difficult to culture.

2.  **Answer: A.** Atherosclerosis leads to poor circulation to the lower extremities, which in turn lowers the oxidation-reduction potential of the tissues. All this predisposes to infections caused by anaerobic microorganisms, in this case, *Bacteroides* and streptococci. The patient is suffering from anaerobic cellulitis or possibly myonecrosis.

3.  **Answer: E.** Partially acid-fast branching rods in a patient with lobar pneumonia suggests *Nocardia*. All the other agents listed are acid-fast bacilli, not branching rods.

4.  **Answer: D.** The causal agent is *Legionella pneumophila*. The clues are dry cough, smoking, weakly gram-negative, and growth on buffered charcoal yeast agar. Remember that *Legionella* is one of the 4 sisters **ELLA** that worship in the **cysteine** chapel. Other sisters include *Francisella*, *Brucella*, and *Pasteurella*. A capsule (**choice A**) would identify agents such as *Streptococcus pneumoniae*. No cell wall (**choice B**) describes *Mycoplasma*. Optochin-sensitive (**choice C**) also describes *Streptococcus pneumoniae*. Serpentine growth in vitro (**choice E**) describes *Mycobacterium tuberculosis*.

5. **Answer: C.** The causal agent is *Borrelia burgdorferi*, and the disease is known as Lyme disease. The clues are facial palsy, rash, fever and malaise. *Borrelia* is spread by ticks.

6. **Answer: B.** The causal agent is *Yersinia pestis*. The clues are high fever, swelling in the armpits and groin, and gram-negative rods with bipolar staining. *Yersinia pestis* is endemic in the U.S. in the desert southwest.

7. **Answer: B.** Infant botulism is an infection started by the ingestion of *Clostridium botulinum* endospores from the environment. The spores germinate in the alkaline pH of the immature gastrointestinal tract and the toxin is produced *in vivo*. In adult botulism, the preformed toxin is ingested.

8. **Answer: D.** The reservoir for *S. enterica* subsp. *typhi* is humans. Other subspecies of *Salmonella* have animals as their reservoirs.

9. **Answer: C.** Each cell divides into two at each generation following the single lag phase. So at the end of the first 10 minutes there are still $5 \times 10^2$, and then at the end of the first 20 minutes (total) there are $10 \times 10^2$. At the end of 30 minutes total time there will be $20 \times 10^2$, and at the end of the total time, $40 \times 10^2$, which is written $4 \times 10^3$ in proper scientific notation.

10. **Answer: C.** The description strongly suggests that she has myonecrosis. Therefore, the causal agent (at least one) is *C. perfringens*. *C. perfringens* is an anaerobe; therefore **choice A** is wrong. *Clostridia* are all gram-positive; therefore, **choice B** is wrong. *C. perfringens* produces concentric areas of hemolysis; therefore, **choice D** is wrong. *C. perfringens* is a marked lecithinase producer; therefore, **choice C** is correct.

11. **Answer: D.** The patient has "scalded skin" syndrome caused by *S. aureus*. The genus *Staphylococcus* would be distinguished from *Streptococcus* by staphylococcal production of catalase. But the species (*S. aureus*) would be distinguished from *S. epidermidis* on the basis of *S. aureus* production of coagulase. Bacitracin sensitivity is characteristic of *Streptococcus pyogenes*, and bile solubility is characteristic of *Streptococcus pneumoniae*.

12. **Answer: A.** The clue is gram-negative curved rods with polar flagella often in pairs to give a "seagull" appearance, microaerophilic on special media and growing at 42°C. That description is most compatible with *Campylobacter jejuni*. Poultry are the most important reservoirs, so **choice A** is the correct response.

13. **Answer: A.** The causal agent is *Neisseria meningitidis*. The clues are age, dorm room, petechial rash, and nuchal rigidity. *Neisseria meningitidis* is a gram-negative diplococcus and can ferment maltose. Remember that *Neisseria* **men**ingitidis can ferment **m**altose. Gram-negative coccus, ferments glucose only (**choice B**) describes *Neisseria gonorrhoeae*. Gram-negative coccobacillus, capsular serotype b (**choice C**) describes *Haemophilus influenzae*. Gram-positive coccus, alpha hemolytic, optochin-sensitive (**choice D**) describes *Streptococcus pneumoniae*. Gram-positive rods, growth at 4°C (**choice E**) describes *Listeria monocytogenes*.

14. **Answer: D.** The clues are endocarditis, heart valve replacement, and gram-positive cocci that are catalase-positive and coagulase-negative. Many times *Staphylococcus epidermidis* can be a contaminant, but the fact that it was present in 3 consecutive blood cultures identifies it as the causal agent. *Enterococcus faecalis* (**choice A**) is catalase-negative. *Kingella kingae* (**choice B**)

is a gram-negative rod. *Staphylococcus aureus* (**choice C**) is coagulase-positive. *Staphylococcus saprophyticus* (**choice E**) is the causal agent of UTIs, not endocarditis.

15. **Answer: E.** Capsules, cell wall, and cytoplasmic membranes are found in both gram-positive and gram-negative bacteria. Endospores (**choice D**) occur with certain gram-positive bacteria, e.g., *Bacillus* and *Clostridium*. Only gram-negatives have an outer membrane.

16. **Answer: D.** The clues are travel, constipation, which is more common than diarrhea, enlarged spleen, and rose-colored spots on the abdomen. It also is an $H_2S$ producer and motile. Remember, salmon(ella) swim upstream (are motile). EHEC (**choice A**) does not produce $H_2S$ and produces bloody diarrhea. ETEC (**choice B**) does not produce $H_2S$ and produces watery diarrhea. *Salmonella enterica* subsp. *enteritidis* (**choice C**) diarrhea (watery, can be bloody) is associated with consumption of raw or undercooked poultry. *Shigella dysenteriae* (**choice E**) does not produce $H_2S$ and causes bloody diarrhea.

17. **Answer: E.** The disease here is whooping cough, caused by *Bordetella pertussis*. The pertussis toxin (also known as the lymphocytosis-promoting toxin) is not believed to be directly cytotoxic, but stimulates adenylate cyclase by ribosylating regulatory proteins. It causes a variety of effects depending on the cell type involved: insulin secretion, lymphocytosis, and alteration of immune effector cells. Of the distractors: the filamentous hemagglutinin (**choice F**) mediates attachment; the adenylate cyclase toxin (**choice B**) stimulates local edema; the organism produces only a small zone of hemolysis around its colonies, so **choice C** is not true; it is an aerobe and does not grow anaerobically (**choice D**). All systemic manifestations of the disease arise from the circulation of the toxins, not the organism itself (**choice A**).

18. **Answer: B.** In children younger than age 5, the most serious complication of EHEC is hemolytic uremic syndrome, or HUS. This is because the toxin (which inhibits protein synthesis) can also bind to the glomerular epithelial cells. Also, because this toxin is Shiga-like, it is important to remember that *Shigella* can also lead to HUS.

19. **Answer: A.** The causal agent is *Streptococcus pneumoniae*. It is a gram-positive coccus, which is alpha hemolytic and optochin-sensitive, and it is the most common cause of pneumonia in the elderly. It is the capsule of *S. pneumoniae* which protects it against phagocytosis. That is why asplenic individuals have a difficult time clearing infections with *S. pneumoniae*, because a major antibody-producing organ is missing and phagocytosis is inhibited in organisms with capsules. Coagulase (**choice C**) is an anti-phagocytic attribute of *Staphylococcus aureus*. M protein (**choice D**) of *Streptococcus pyogenes* is anti-phagocytic. Catalase (**choice B**) breaks down $H_2O_2$, and teichoic acids (**choice E**) mediate adherence. Neither protects against phagocytosis.

20. **Answer: B.** The causal agent *E. coli* is gram-negative, and the primary means of developing septic shock with gram-negative organisms is via lipopolysaccharide (endotoxin).

21. **Answer: C.** The causal agent is *Rickettsia rickettsiae*, the disease is Rocky Mountain spotted fever. The clues are North Carolina (located in the tick belt of U.S.), rash that spread from extremities to trunk, conjunctivitis, and proteinuria. Rocky Mountain spotted fever is spread via a tick vector.

22. **Answer: B.** The case diagnosis is poststreptococcal glomerulonephritis caused by group A strep. The Lancefield group is determined by the C carbohydrate and the serotype is determined via the M proteins. This is particularly important in post streptococcal glomerulonephritis, as certain strains, such as the M12 serotype, are more commonly associated with this type of nonsuppurative sequela.

23. **Answer: B.** The causal agent is *Bordetella pertussis*. The clues are severe cough, can't catch breath, vomiting, incomplete vaccination history, conjunctival redness, and gram-negative coccobacilli on Bordet-Gengou medium. Pertussis toxin works by ADP ribosylation of $G_i$. ADP ribosylation of elongation factor 2 (**choice A**) describes toxins found in *Corynebacterium diphtheriae* and *Pseudomonas aeruginosa*. ADP ribosylation of a GTP-binding protein (**choice C**) describes the toxins found in ETEC and *Vibrio cholerae*. Blocks release of acetylcholine (**choice D**) describes the toxin found in *Clostridium botulinum*. Blocks release of inhibitory transmitters GABA and glycine (**choice E**) describes the toxin found in *Clostridium tetani*.

24. **Answer: D.** The toxin described is tetanus toxin, which would be acquired via some type of penetrating wound. Eating home-canned foods (**choice A**) describes transmission of adult botulism. Fecal-oral, travel to foreign country (**choice B**) describes ETEC, *Vibrio cholerae*, etc. Infant given honey during the first year of life (**choice C**) describes infant botulism. Respiratory, with incomplete vaccination history (**choice E**) describes *Bordetella pertussis*, for example.

25. **Answer: D.** The diagnosis is infant botulism caused by *Clostridium botulinum*. The clues are flaccid paralysis, constipation, difficulty breathing, tox screen of stool, and age. The flaccid paralysis is due to a toxin that blocks the release of acetylcholine. ADP ribosylation of eukaryotic elongation factor 2 (eEF-2; **choice A**) describes toxins found in *Corynebacterium diphtheriae* and *Pseudomonas aeruginosa*. ADP ribosylation of $G_i$, an inhibitory subunit of the G protein (**choice B**), describes *Bordetella pertussis*. ADP ribosylation of GTP-binding protein (**choice C**) describes the toxins found in ETEC and *Vibrio cholerae*. Blocks release of inhibitory transmitters GABA and glycine (**choice E**) describes the toxin found in *Clostridium tetani*.

26. **Answer: C.** The causal agent is *Corynebacterium diphtheriae*. The clues are incomplete vaccination history and (dirty gray pseudomembrane which causes bleeding when displaced). *C. diphtheriae* are gram-positive rods, and the toxin functions by inhibition of protein synthesis.

27. **Answer: A.** The causal agent is *Vibrio cholerae*. The clues are history of travel and voluminous "rice water" diarrhea. *Vibrio* are gram-negative curved rods, and the toxin functions by increasing intracellular cAMP.

28. **Answer: A.** The causal agent is *Helicobacter pylori*. The clues are midepigastric pain, relief after meals, positive urease test. *H. pylori* is a gram-negative curved rod that is microaerophilic. Gram-negative rod, aerobic (**choice B**) describes *Pseudomonas aeruginosa*, for example. Gram-negative rod, facultative anaerobe (**choice C**) describes *Escherichia coli*, for example. Gram-positive rod, aerobic (**choice D**) describes *Bacillus*, for example. Gram-positive rod, microaerophilic (**choice E**) does not describe a medically relevant genus.

29. **Answer: B.** The causal agent is *Streptococcus pyogenes*. The clues: sore throat, beta hemolytic, gram-positive cocci. To answer this question, you have to know that the agent is gram-positive and that gram-positive organisms have a thick peptidoglycan layer that protects them from osmotic damage. Lipopolysaccharide (**choice A**) is only found on gram-negative organisms and is associated with shock. Phospholipids (**choice C**) are found in the membranes

of gram-positive and gram-negative organisms. Polysaccharide (**choice D**) can be found on gram-positive and gram-negative organisms. Teichoic acid (**choice E**) is only found on gram-positives and is used for attachment.

30. **Answer: E.** *Escherichia coli* is the most common cause of cystitis overall and should be assumed to be the cause of any case of cystitis unless contrary culture characteristics are described. It generally reduces nitrates and is also a lactose fermenter. **Choice A** identifies *Neisseria gonorrhoeae*; **choice B**, *Staphylococcus saprophyticus*; **choice C**, *Streptococcus viridans*; **choice D**, *Clostridium*.

31. **Answer: D.** This case history describes botulism (key words: home-canned green beans and visual problems). Foods classically associated are those with a neutral or alkaline pH. *C. botulinum,* the agent of botulism, is an anaerobe and thus has a low oxidation-reduction requirement. **Choice A**, *Staph aureus*; **choice B**, *Bacillus cereus*; **choice C**, *S. viridans*; **choice D**, *C. botulinum*; **choice E**, *E. coli*.

32. **Answer: A.** The disease is most likely *Mycoplasma* pneumonia caused by *Mycoplasma pneumoniae*, which is non-Gram staining and requires cholesterol for growth. **Choice B**, *C. diphtheriae*; **choice C**, *Streptococcus pyogenes*; **choice D**, *Staph aureus*; **choice E**, *Clostridium*.

33. **Answer: C.** The causal agent is *Listeria monocytogenes*. The clues are neonatal meningitis (age), gram-positive rods. The only organism in the list that is a gram-positive rod is *Listeria*. *Escherichia coli* (**choice A**) is a gram-negative rod. *Haemophilus influenzae* (**choice B**) is a gram-negative coccobacillus. *Neisseria meningitidis* (**choice D**) is a gram-negative diplococcus. *Streptococcus agalactiae* (**choice E**) is a gram-positive coccus.

34. **Answer: A.** The agent is viridans streptococcus. The clues are heart valve replacement, gram-positive cocci, alpha hemolytic, and optochin resistant. *Pseudomonas aeruginosa* and *Serratia marcescens* (**choices B and C**) are gram-negative rods. *Staphylococcus aureus* (**choice D**) is a catalase-positive, gram-positive coccus. *Streptococcus pneumoniae* (**choice E**) is a gram-positive, catalase-negative coccus, but it is optochin-sensitive.

35. **Answer: A.** The clues are abscess, polymicrobial, gram-negative anaerobe. *Bacteroides* is the only anaerobe listed.

36. **Answer: D.** The causal agent is *Mycobacterium tuberculosis*. The clues are coughing up blood, acid-fast bacilli, and homeless. Sulfatides are sulfolipids which hydrolyze to form sulfuric acid. The acidic pH of the *M. tuberculosis*-containing phagosome acts to stop lysosomal fusion. Cord factor (**choice A**) is responsible for serpentine growth in vitro. Calcium dipicolinate (**choice B**) is a component of endospores. Peptidoglycan (**choice C**) is a cell wall component. Tuberculin (**choice E**) is a surface protein, which is not involved in protection from phagosome-lysosome fusion.

37. **Answer: A.** The causal agent is *Gardnerella vaginalis*. The clues are malodorous discharge, positive whiff test, thin gray discharge. Gram-negative diplococci in PMNs (**choice B**) is consistent with *Neisseria gonorrhoeae*. Koilocytic cells (**choice C**) is consistent with human papilloma virus. Owl-eye inclusions (**choice D**) are consistent with cytomegalovirus. Tzanck smears (**choice E**) are diagnostic for herpes simplex virus.

38. **Answer: E.** The causal agent is *Bacillus anthracis*. The clues are postal workers, hemoptysis and mediastinal widening. Elementary body and reticulate

body (**choices A and D**) are consistent with *Chlamydia*. Endotoxin and periplasmic space (**choices B and C**) are consistent with gram-negative bacteria.

39. **Answer: C.** The clues are fist fight wound, gram-negative rods with bleach-like odor.

40. **Answer: E.** The causal agent is *Proteus vulgaris*. The clues are lower back pain (kidney stones), gram-negative rods, lactose nonfermenter, UTI. Capsules (**choice A**) are antiphagocytic, and *Proteus* does not have a capsule. Catalase (**choice B**) is produced by *Proteus*, but is not a major mechanism of pathogenesis. Coagulase (**choice C**) is produced by *Staphylococcus aureus*. Exotoxins (**choice D**) are secreted toxins.

41. **Answer: A.** The causal agent is *Clostridium difficile*. The clues are clindamycin, loose, mucoid, stools, yellow plaques. Clindamycin and other broad-spectrum antibiotics are associated with pseudomembranous colitis, as they kill off the normal gut flora and *C. difficile* flourishes without competition.

42. **Answer: A.** The patient has inclusion conjunctivitis caused by *Chlamydia trachomatis*. The only form of this bacterium that has the ability to bind to the membranes and infect is the elementary body.

43. **Answer: A.** The causal agent is *Klebsiella pneumoniae*. The clues are gelatinous and bloody sputum, PMNs, and gram-negative rods identified in the sputum. The most likely patient to present with *K. pneumoniae* would be elderly with a preexisting condition, like chronic obstructive pulmonary disease, or an alcoholic.

44. **Answer: D.** Group B *Streptococcus* (GBS) is the most common cause of neonatal meningitis, followed by *E. coli*. *S. pneumoniae* is most common in adults.

45. **Answer: A.** The clues are elderly, catheter, gram-positive cocci, catalase-negative, growth in 6.5% sodium chloride. *Staphylococcus aureus* and *Staphylococcus epidermidis* (**choices B and C**) are catalase-positive. *Streptococcus pyogenes* and viridans streptococci (**choices D and E**) would not grow in a high concentration of salt.

46. **Answer: D.** The clues are immunosuppressed (HIV+), necrotic lesion with black center and erythematous margin (ecthyma gangrenosum). *Bacillus anthracis* (**choice A**) is close because a black eschar can resemble ecthyma gangrenosum, but it usually would appear at the point of contact (probably not on the buttock). *Clostridium perfringens*, *Enterococcus faecalis*, and *Staphylococcus aureus* (**choices B, C**, and **E**) do not fit the case description.

47. **Answer: B.** The causal agent is *Streptococcus pyogenes*; the disease is scarlet fever. The clues are sore throat for 1 week, rash, red tongue (strawberry tongue). Gram-positive coccus, alpha hemolytic, catalase-negative (**choice A**) is descriptive of *Streptococcus pneumoniae*. Gram-positive coccus, alpha hemolytic, catalase-positive (**choice C**) does not describe an important medical pathogen. Gram-positive coccus, beta hemolytic, catalase positive (**choice D**) is descriptive of *Staphylococcus aureus*. Gram-positive coccus, gamma hemolytic, catalase negative (**choice E**) is descriptive of some strains of *Enterococcus*.

48. **Answer: D.** The causal agent is *Helicobacter pylori*. The clues are ulcer, urease positive, gram-negative curved rod. It is important to know all organisms that are associated with an increased risk of developing cancer.

49. **Answer: D.** The most likely causal agent here is a bacterium. Viral meningitis is usually mild and would not fit the CSF values. Both the age of the patient and the petechial rash suggest it is most likely to be *Neisseria meningitidis*, which is a Gram-negative diplococcus that is oxidase-positive. The overproduction of outer-membrane fragments is what leads to the petechial rash, even prior to antibiotic treatment.

# Microbial Genetics/Drug Resistance

**3**

## What the COMLEX Requires You To Know

- Mechanisms by which microbes perform replication, transcription, and translation
- Mechanisms by which bacteria can exchange genes (transformation, conjugation, and transduction)
- Mechanisms by which multi-drug-resistant plasmids arise (transposition)
- Important mechanisms of drug resistance (e.g., MRSA)
- Common hospital techniques for drug-sensitivity testing
- Common methods of sterilization and disinfection

# THE BACTERIAL GENETIC MATERIAL

Three different types of DNA may be found in a bacterial cell: bacterial chromosomal DNA, plasmid DNA, or bacteriophage DNA.

## Bacterial Chromosome (Genome)

- Most bacteria have only **one chromosome but often multiple copies** of it in the cell.
- Most bacterial chromosomes are a **large, covalently closed, circular DNA molecule** (about 1,000 times the diameter of the cell).
- The chromosome is **organized into loops** around a proteinaceous center. A single-stranded topoisomerase (1 nick) will relax only the nicked loop, allowing DNA synthesis or transcription.
- Most have **around 2,000 genes**. (*E. coli* has about 4,500 kbases.)
- All **essential genes** are on the bacterial chromosome.

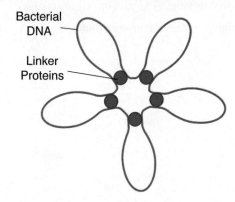

**Figure II-3-1.** The Bacterial Chromosome

## Plasmids

- Are **extrachromosomal genetic elements** found in bacteria (and eukaryotes)
- Are generally covalently closed, **circular DNA**
- Are **small** (1.5–400 kB)
- Can **replicate autonomously** in bacterial cells
- One subclass of plasmids, called **episomes**, may be integrated into the bacterial DNA. Episomes have insertion sequences matching those on the bacterial chromosome.
- Plasmids carry the genetic material for a variety of genes, e.g., the **fertility genes** directing conjugation (*tra* operon), many of the genes for **antibiotic resistance**, and most **bacterial exotoxins**.
- They contain genes that are **nonessential** for bacterial life.

## Bacteriophage ( = Phage = Bacterial Virus) Genome

- **Stable pieces of bacteriophage DNA** may be present in the bacterial cell.
- These are **generally repressed temperate phage (called prophage)** inserted into the bacterial chromosome.
- Besides the repressor protein, prophage DNA may also direct synthesis of other proteins. Most notable are gene products that make bacteria more pathogenic. This enhanced virulence is called **lysogenic conversion.**

# REARRANGEMENT OF DNA WITHIN A BACTERIUM

## Homologous Recombination

- Homologous recombination is a gene exchange process that may **stabilize genes** introduced into a cell by transformation, conjugation, or transduction.
- Imported bacterial DNA (transferred into a cell by transformation, conjugation, or transduction) is on short linear pieces of DNA called **exogenotes**. Most linear DNA is not stable in cells because it is broken down by exonucleases.
- Homologous recombination produces an **"exchange"** of DNA between the linear exogenote of DNA and a homologous region on the stable (circular) bacterial chromosome.
- Homologous recombination requires:
  - Several genes worth of **homology or near homology** between the DNA strands.
  - A series of recombination **enzymes**/factors coded for by the recombination genes *recA*, *recB*, *recC*, and *recD* (with *recA* generally an absolute requirement).

### In a Nutshell

There are two processes available to stabilize "new" DNA:

- Homologous recombination
- Site-specific recombination

### In a Nutshell

**Homologous Recombination**

- Is a mechanism to incorporate **short, linear** pieces of DNA into the chromosome.
- There must be **some sequence homology**.
- **Recombinase A** is required.
- There is a **one-to-one exchange** of DNA.

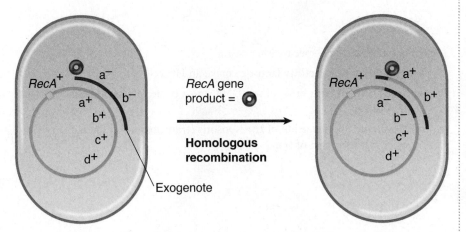

Genes ending up on the linear piece of DNA are lost. Those on the circular molecule become part of the cell's permanent genetic make up.

**Figure II-3-2.** Homologous Recombination

# Site-Specific Recombination

Site-specific recombination is the integration of one DNA molecule into another DNA molecule with which it has **no homology** except for a small site on each DNA (called an **attachment, integration, or insertion site**).

- Requires **restriction endonucleases** and restriction endonuclease sites on each DNA
- Because this process **integrates** rather than exchanges pieces of DNA, the end result is a molecule the **sum of the two original molecules**.

## In a Nutshell

### Site-Specific Recombination

- Is the mechanism used to combine **circular pieces** of DNA:
  - Plasmids
  - Temperate phage
  - Transposons
- It requires **no homology**.
- **No DNA is lost**.
- It **requires restriction endonucleases**.

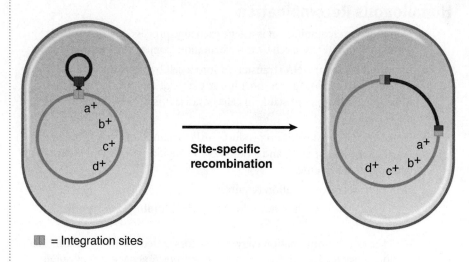

■■ = Integration sites

**Figure II-3-3.** Site-Specific Recombination

Three major roles of site-specific integration

- Integration of a **fertility factor** to make an Hfr cell
- Integration of **temperate phage** DNA into a bacterial chromosome to create a prophage
- Movement and insertion of **transposons** (transposition is the name of site-specific integration of transposons)

# GENE TRANSFER

## Overview

**Bacterial reproduction is asexual,** so progeny are identical to parent cell with only rare mutations.

**How do you get new genetic combinations in bacteria?**

Answer: Gene transfer followed by stabilization of genes (recombination)

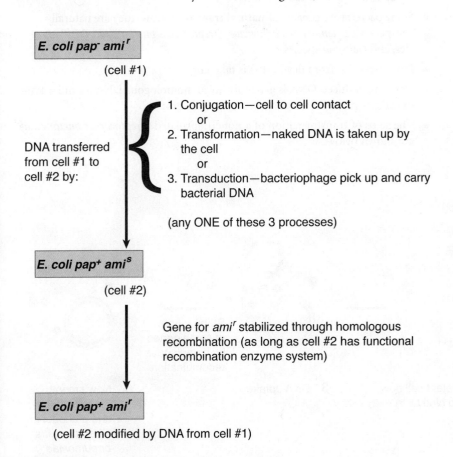

*E. coli pap⁻ ami^r*

(cell #1)

DNA transferred from cell #1 to cell #2 by:

1. Conjugation—cell to cell contact
   or
2. Transformation—naked DNA is taken up by the cell
   or
3. Transduction—bacteriophage pick up and carry bacterial DNA

(any ONE of these 3 processes)

*E. coli pap⁺ ami^s*

(cell #2)

Gene for *ami^r* stabilized through homologous recombination (as long as cell #2 has functional recombination enzyme system)

*E. coli pap⁺ ami^r*

(cell #2 modified by DNA from cell #1)

- Now *pap⁺* (initially linked to *ami^s*) is linked to *ami^r* instead, producing a new combination of genes and more significantly, a cell that can cause pyelonephritis and is amikacin resistant.
- (Could also have yielded *E. coli* that was *pap⁻ ami^s* or *pap⁻ ami^r* or the cell could have stayed *pap⁺ ami^s*.)

**Figure II-3-4.** The Classic Experiment Demonstrating That Bacteria Are Capable of Genetic Exchange

Any DNA that is transferred between bacterial cells must be stabilized by recombination or it will be lost.

**In a Nutshell**

**DNA can be transferred** from bacterium to bacterium by:

- **Conjugation**
- **Transformation**
- **Transduction**

## In a Nutshell

**Competent:** capable of binding and importing free DNA from the environment

**Transformation:**

- Requires free DNA
- Requires **competent cells**
- Captured DNA is incorporated by homologous recombination

# MECHANISMS OF DNA EXCHANGE

## Transformation

**Transformation is the uptake of naked DNA from the environment by competent cells.**

- Cells become **competent (able to bind short pieces of DNA to the envelope and import them into the cell)** under certain environmental conditions (which you do not need to know).
- Some bacteria are capable of **natural transformation** (they are naturally competent): *Haemophilus influenzae, Streptococcus pneumoniae, Bacillus* species, and *Neisseria* species.
- DNA (released from dead cells) is taken up.
- Newly introduced DNA is generally linear, homologous DNA a similar type of cell but perhaps one that is genetically diverse.
- The steps of transformation of a nonencapsulated *Streptococcus pneumoniae* are shown below.

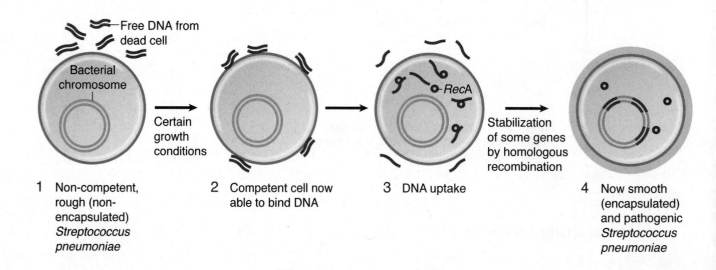

Figure II-3-5. Transformation

# Conjugation

**Conjugation is gene transfer from one bacterial cell to another involving direct cell-to-cell contact.**

- **Fertility factors control** conjugation.
- **Sex pili** (genes on F factor) play a role in establishing cell-to-cell contact.
- A **single strand** (or a portion thereof) of the double helix of DNA is transferred from the donor (or male) cell to the recipient or female cell.
- Chromosomal genes transferred in by conjugation have to be stabilized by **homologous recombination** (in an Hfr × F⁻ cross). Plasmid genes transferred by conjugation circularize and are stable without recombination (in an F⁺ × F⁻ cross).
- Conjugation with recombination may produce new genetic combinations.

## Donor (male) cells

- All have fertility plasmids known as **F factors**. F factors have a series of important plasmid "fertility" genes called the transfer or *tra region*, which code for:
  - **Sex pili**
  - Genes whose products **stabilize mating pairs**
  - Genes that **direct conjugal DNA transfer**, and other genes.
- Have a region called *oriT* (**origin of transfer**) where a single strand break in the DNA will be made and then *oriT* begins the transfer of one strand of the double helix.
- Many have **insertion sequences** where the plasmid can be inserted into the bacterial chromosome combining to make one larger molecule of DNA.
- A genetic map of an F factor is shown below.

## In a Nutshell

- **Conjugation:** gene transfer from donor (F⁺ or Hfr cell) to recipient (F⁻ cell) during cell-to-cell contact
- **Fertility factors** (in plasmid or episome form) **control conjugation**.
- A single strand of DNA is transferred to recipient from donor.

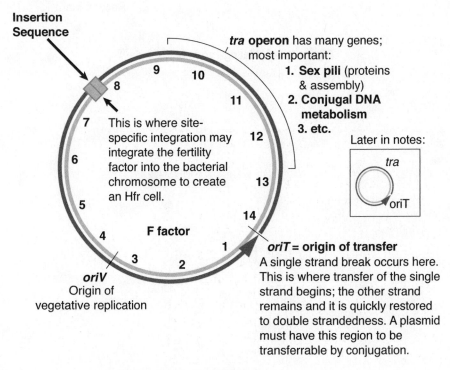

**Figure II-3-6. Fertility Factor**

- Donor cells in which the **fertility plasmid** is in its **free state** are called **F⁺ cells**.
- Donor cells in which the **fertility factor has inserted** itself into the bacterial chromosome are called **Hfr cells**. An integrated plasmid is called an episome.

### Recipient (female) cells: F⁻ cells

- Recipient cells **lack fertility factors**.
- In every cross, one cell must be an F⁻ cell.

### Mating types of bacterial cells

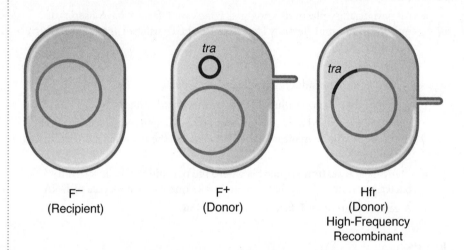

| F⁻ (Recipient) | F⁺ (Donor) | Hfr (Donor) High-Frequency Recombinant |

**Figure II-3-7.** Mating Types of Bacteria

# CONJUGAL CROSSES

There are two major types of crosses:

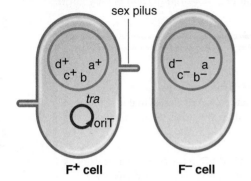

F⁺ cell    F⁻ cell

**1** Important points: In the male or F⁺ parent, the fertility factor is present but free from the bacterial chromosome. Transfer is uni-directional from male to female. *OriT*, as in every cross, will be transferred first and then the rest of the plasmid genes.

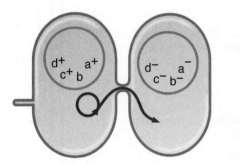

**2** Only a single strand of the plasmid DNA duplex is transferred. The area that is lost is reduplicated so that the donor always stays the same genotype. The last genes to be transferred are the *tra* region.

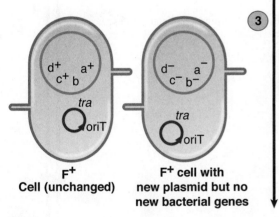

F⁺
Cell (unchanged)    F⁺ cell with
new plasmid but no
new bacterial genes

**3** The transfer of the plasmid is fairly quick so assume it is transferred in its entirety 100% of the time unless otherwise told. Note that the F⁻ cell undergoes a sex change, becoming F⁺ (male). These two F⁺ cells can no longer mate, but no BACTERIAL genes are transferred.

**Figure II-3-8.** The F⁺ by F⁻ Conjugal Cross

## In a Nutshell

In the F⁺ × F⁻ cross:

- One strand of the entire plasmid is transferred
- Recipient becomes F⁺

## *Integrated Fertility Factor*

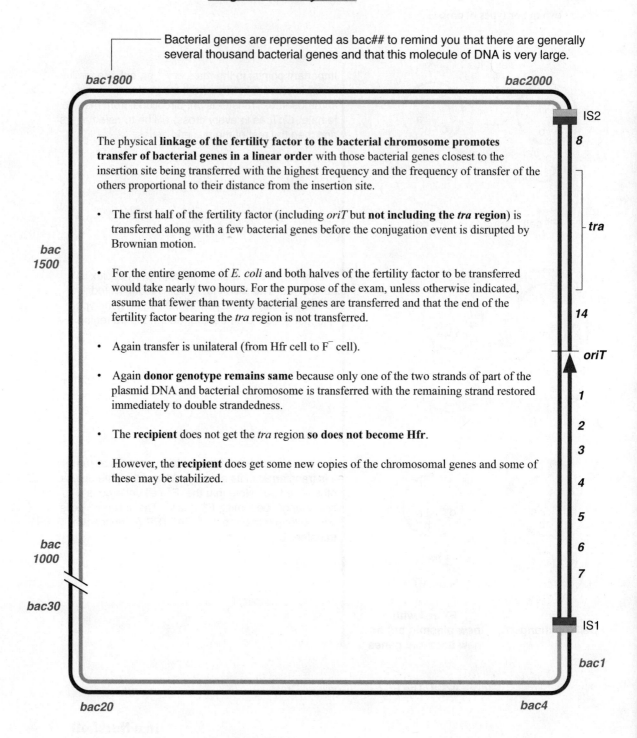

Bacterial genes are represented as bac## to remind you that there are generally several thousand bacterial genes and that this molecule of DNA is very large.

The physical **linkage of the fertility factor to the bacterial chromosome promotes transfer of bacterial genes in a linear order** with those bacterial genes closest to the insertion site being transferred with the highest frequency and the frequency of transfer of the others proportional to their distance from the insertion site.

- The first half of the fertility factor (including *oriT* but **not including the *tra* region**) is transferred along with a few bacterial genes before the conjugation event is disrupted by Brownian motion.

- For the entire genome of *E. coli* and both halves of the fertility factor to be transferred would take nearly two hours. For the purpose of the exam, unless otherwise indicated, assume that fewer than twenty bacterial genes are transferred and that the end of the fertility factor bearing the *tra* region is not transferred.

- Again transfer is unilateral (from Hfr cell to F⁻ cell).

- Again **donor genotype remains same** because only one of the two strands of part of the plasmid DNA and bacterial chromosome is transferred with the remaining strand restored immediately to double strandedness.

- The **recipient** does not get the *tra* region **so does not become Hfr.**

- However, the **recipient** does get some new copies of the chromosomal genes and some of these may be stabilized.

**Figure II-3-9.** The Hfr Chromosome (Bacterial Chromosome with Integrated F Factor)

## Conjugation: 2nd type of cross Hfr × F⁻

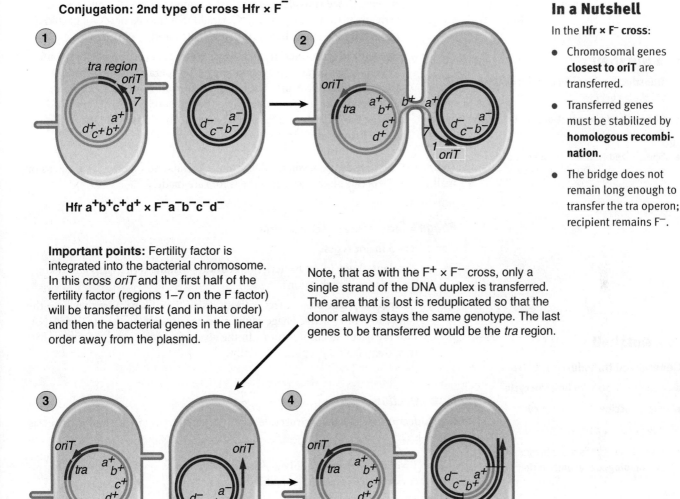

Hfr a⁺b⁺c⁺d⁺ × F⁻a⁻b⁻c⁻d⁻

**In a Nutshell**

In the **Hfr × F⁻ cross**:

- Chromosomal genes **closest to oriT** are transferred.

- Transferred genes must be stabilized by **homologous recombination**.

- The bridge does not remain long enough to transfer the tra operon; recipient remains F⁻.

**Important points:** Fertility factor is integrated into the bacterial chromosome. In this cross *oriT* and the first half of the fertility factor (regions 1–7 on the F factor) will be transferred first (and in that order) and then the bacterial genes in the linear order away from the plasmid.

Note, that as with the F⁺ × F⁻ cross, only a single strand of the DNA duplex is transferred. The area that is lost is reduplicated so that the donor always stays the same genotype. The last genes to be transferred would be the *tra* region.

It takes approximately two hours for a complete transfer to occur. Because the cytoplasmic bridge and DNA strand is so fine, mating is normally interrupted before the transfer is complete. For the purpose of exam, assume that mating is interrupted and the recipient gets some new genes but does not become Hfr.

**Hfr cell (unchanged)**

**F⁻ cell with new bacterial genes: a⁺ and b⁺ (no sex change)**

Figure II-3-10. The Hfr by F⁻ Conjugal Cross

# Transduction

- **Transduction** is the transfer of bacterial DNA by a phage vector.
- During transduction, the phage picks up the bacterial DNA through an error in phage production.
- There are **two types of transduction: generalized and specialized**.
  - A **generalized transducing phage** is produced when the phage **with a lytic life cycle** puts a piece of bacterial DNA into its head. All bacterial genes have an equal chance of being transduced.
  - **Specialized transduction** may occur when an error is made in the life cycle of a temperate (lysogenic) phage. **Temperate phage introduce their genomic DNA into the bacterial chromosome** at a specific site and then excise it later to complete their life cycle. If errors are made during the excision process, then bacterial chromosomal DNA can be carried along into the next generation of viruses.

To understand transduction, you need first to understand how a phage replicates normally so that you can understand how the errors are made.

***Phage*** = bacteriophage = bacterial virus

Come in two major types:

- **Virulent phage** infect bacterial cells, always making more virus and lysing the cells (lytic replication).
- **Temperate phage** often infect without lysing the cells because they have the ability to repress active phage replication and to stably integrate their DNA into the bacterial chromosome. In the absence of functional repressor protein, they also may replicate lytically.

## Lytic infection

Lytic infection, by phage or viruses, leads to production of viruses and their release by cell lysis.

- **Virulent viruses can only go into lytic life cycles and can accidentally carry out generalized transduction.**
- The lytic (or productive) life cycle of virulent phage is shown below. It is entirely normal except for a mistaken incorporation of bacterial DNA into one phage head, creating a transducing virus, shown at the bottom of the next page. Transduction of another bacterial cell is shown following that.

**In a Nutshell**

- **Transduction:** transfer of bacterial DNA via phage vector
- **Generalized transduction:** error of **lytic virus** life cycle
- **Specialized transduction:** error of **temperate virus** life cycle

**In a Nutshell**

**Generalized transduction**

- Requires virus with **lytic life cycle**
- It is an **accident** of the life cycle
- **Any** genes can be transferred
- Transferred genes must be stabilized by **homologous recombination**

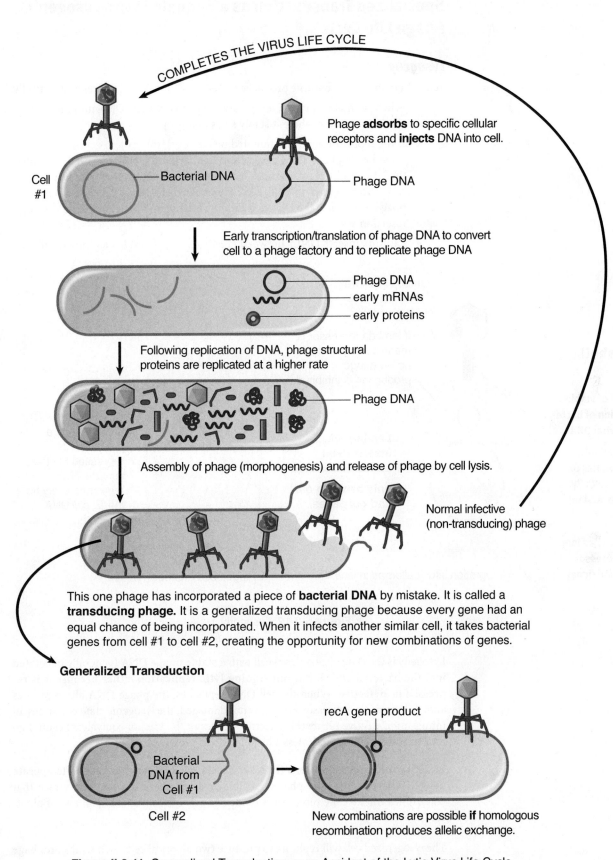

COMPLETES THE VIRUS LIFE CYCLE

Phage **adsorbs** to specific cellular receptors and **injects** DNA into cell.

Cell #1

Bacterial DNA

Phage DNA

Early transcription/translation of phage DNA to convert cell to a phage factory and to replicate phage DNA

Phage DNA
early mRNAs
early proteins

Following replication of DNA, phage structural proteins are replicated at a higher rate

Phage DNA

Assembly of phage (morphogenesis) and release of phage by cell lysis.

Normal infective (non-transducing) phage

This one phage has incorporated a piece of **bacterial DNA** by mistake. It is called a **transducing phage.** It is a generalized transducing phage because every gene had an equal chance of being incorporated. When it infects another similar cell, it takes bacterial genes from cell #1 to cell #2, creating the opportunity for new combinations of genes.

**Generalized Transduction**

recA gene product

Bacterial DNA from Cell #1

Cell #2

New combinations are possible **if** homologous recombination produces allelic exchange.

**Figure II-3-11.** Generalized Transduction as an Accident of the Lytic Virus Life Cycle

# Specialized Transduction as a Sequela to the Lysogenic Phage Life Cycle

## *Lysogeny*

Temperate phage may become prophage (DNA stably integrated) or replicate lytically.

- When repressor is made, temperate phage insert their DNA into the bacterial chromosome where it stably stays as a **prophage**.

- If the repressor gene gets mutated or the repressor protein gets damaged then the prophage gets excised from the bacterial DNA and is induced into the lytic production of virus. On rare occasions these temperate phage can produce either specialized or generalized transducing viruses. Lambda phage of *E. coli* is the best studied. Most temperate phages have only a single insertion site.

- **Lambda inserts ONLY between *E. coli* genes *gal* and *bio* as shown below.**

## In a Nutshell

### Lysogeny

- Is a state of **stable association of bacterial and viral DNA**
- May impart **new characteristics to bacterial cells (lysogenic conversion)**
- **COBEDS**
- It **continues as long as the repressor gene is functional**

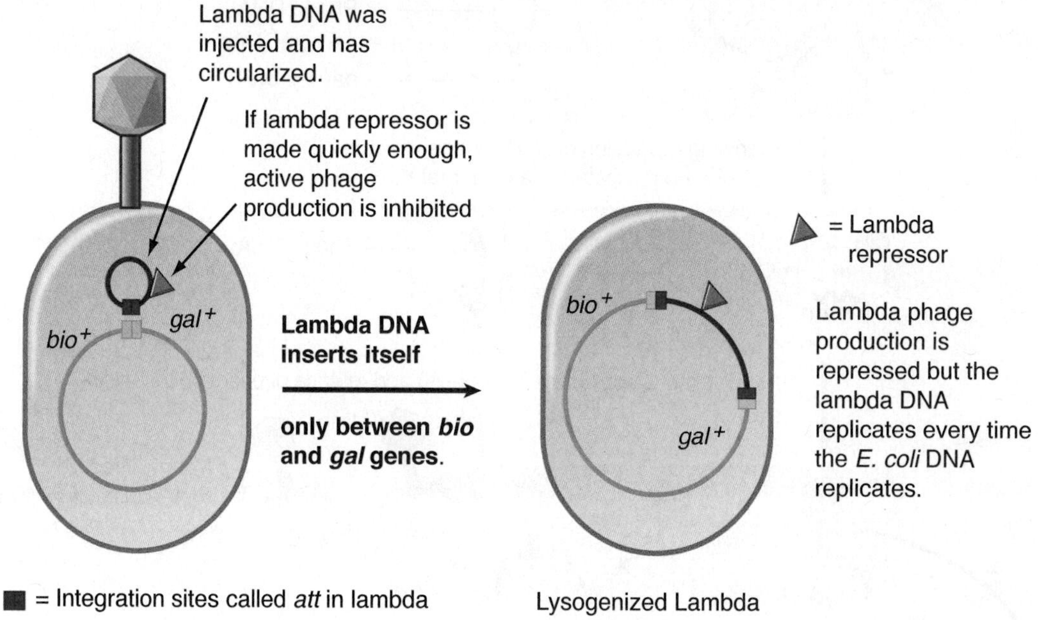

Lambda DNA was injected and has circularized.

If lambda repressor is made quickly enough, active phage production is inhibited

*bio⁺*   *gal⁺*

**Lambda DNA inserts itself**

**only between *bio* and *gal* genes.**

■ = Integration sites called *att* in lambda

▲ = Lambda repressor

Lambda phage production is repressed but the lambda DNA replicates every time the *E. coli* DNA replicates.

*bio⁺*   *gal⁺*

Lysogenized Lambda

**Figure II-3-12.** Lysogeny

Lysogeny is the state of a bacterial cell with a **stable phage DNA** (generally integrated into the bacterial DNA), **not undergoing lytic replication either because it is repressed or defective.** When the cell DNA replicates, the phage DNA also replicates and, as long as the repressor protein is not damaged, the lysogenic state continues ad infinitum. Defective phage (or defective viruses in the human equivalent) cannot go into an active replication unless a helper virus is present.

**Phage that have both options (lytic replication or lysogeny) are called temperate phage.** When a temperate phage first infects a cell there is a regulatory race that determines whether the repressor is made fast enough to prevent synthesis of phage components.

The lysogenized cell will replicate to produce two identical cells each with a prophage as long as the repressor gene product is present.

Lysogeny can confer new properties on a genus such as toxin production or antigens (**lysogenic conversion**):

    C:  Cholera toxin

    O:  Presence of specific prophage in *Salmonella* can affect **O** antigens.

    B:  Phage CE β or DE β cause *Clostridium botulinum* to produce **B**otulinum toxin.

    E:  **E**xotoxins A–C (erythrogenic or pyogenic) of *Streptococcus pyogenes*

    D:  Prophage beta causes *Corynebacterium diphtheriae* to make **D**iphtheria toxin.

    S:  Shiga toxin

- (Mnemonic for phage-mediated pathogenic factors = COBEDS)
- Model for retrovirus provirus
- Allows specialized transduction

## In a Nutshell

### Lysogenic Conversion

- C = Cholera toxin
- O = O antigen of *Salmonella*
- B = Botulinum toxin
- E = Erythrogenic exotoxins of *S. pyogenes*
- D = *Diphtheria* toxin
- S = Shiga toxin

COBEDS = when 2 people share a bed, someone gets a little bit pregnant (with phage)

## Induction

If the repressor is damaged (by UV, cold, or alkylating agents), then the prophage is excised and the cell goes into lytic replication phase. This process is called **induction**.

Most of the time this process is carried out **perfectly**, recreating the figure 8 of DNA that was the product of viral site-specific recombination, and normal (**nontransducing**) **phage** are produced.

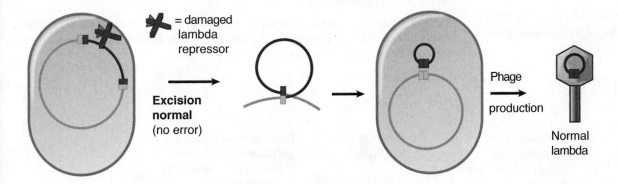

**Figure II-3-13.** Normal Excision of a Lysogenic Phage

Rarely, in the excision process, an **excisional error** is made and **one of the bacterial genes next to the insertion site is removed attached to the lambda DNA, and a little bit of lambda DNA is left behind**. Only genes on one side *or* the other side of the virus insertion site can be incorporated by excisional error.

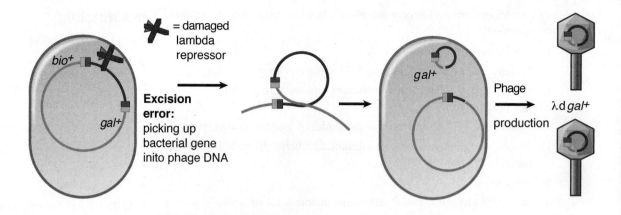

**Figure II-3-14.** Excision Error of a Lysogenic Phage

## In a Nutshell

**Specialized Transduction**

- Requires a **temperate phage and lysogeny**

- Requires an **error in excision**

- Only genes **near the virus insertion site** can be transferred.

- Any transferred genes must be stabilized by **homologous recombination.**

Because lambda has only one insertion site (between *gal* or *bio*), only *gal* <u>or</u> *bio* can be incorporated by excisional error.

Because all of the phage genes are still in the cell, phage are still made with the circular defective phage genome copied and put in each phage head. These are **specialized transducing phage** (only able to transduce *bio* or *gal*).

### Specialized Transduction

Bacterial genes picked up by error in the excision process are transferred to another closely related but often genetically distinct cell. If any genes on the exogenote are stabilized by recombinational exchange, then new genetic combinations occur.

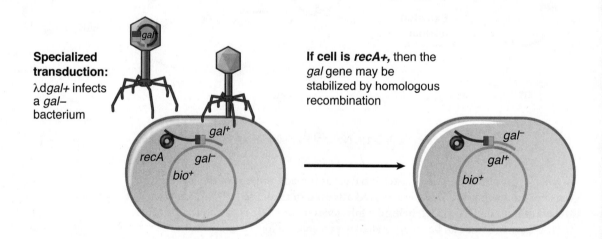

**Figure II-3-15.** Specialized Transduction

Only those genes next to the phage insertion site can be transduced by specialized transduction.

**Table II-3-1.** Comparison of Transformation, Conjugation, and Transduction

| Requirement | Transformation | Conjugation | Transduction |
|---|---|---|---|
| Is cell-to-cell contact required? | No | Yes | No |
| Does it require an antecedent phage infection? | No | No | Yes |
| Is competency required? | Yes | No | No |
| Is naked (free) DNA involved? | Yes | No | No |
| Is recombination required to stabilize new genes? | Yes | No for F⁺ × F⁻  Yes for Hfr × F⁻ | Yes |

**Table II-3-2.** Comparison of Generalized and Specialized Transduction

| | Generalized | Specialized |
|---|---|---|
| Mechanism | **Error in assembly** | **Error of excision**  Requires stable insertion of prophage DNA (lysogeny) |
| What genes may be transferred? | **Any** | Only **genes next to the insertion site** |

# DRUG RESISTANCE

## Overall Problem

- Drug resistance is becoming such a significant problem that there are bacteria for which most antibiotics no longer work. We are entering a "post-antibiotic era."
- Drug resistance can be transferred from one genus of bacteria to another, e.g., from normal flora to a pathogen.
- Three general types of antibiotic resistance exist: intrinsic, chromosome-mediated, and plasmid-mediated.

## Intrinsic Drug Resistance

Bacteria are intrinsically resistant to an antibiotic if they lack the target molecule for the drug or if their normal anatomy and physiology makes them refractory to the drug's action.

- Bacteria that lack mycolic acids are intrinsically resistant to isoniazid.
- Bacteria such as *Mycoplasma* that lack peptidoglycan are intrinsically resistant to penicillin.

**In a Nutshell**

Drug resistance may be:

- **Intrinsic**
- **Chromosomal**
- **Plasmid mediated**

**Intrinsic mechanisms:**

innate to organism

**In a Nutshell**

**Chromosomal Mechanisms**

- Alter target for drug
- Usually low level
- MRSA

# Chromosome-Mediated Antibiotic Resistance

The genes that determine this resistance are located on the bacterial chromosome.

- Most commonly these genes modify the **receptor for a drug** so that the drug can no longer bind (e.g., a mutation in a gene for a penicillin binding protein).
- In general, causes **low-level drug resistance** rather than high
- In methicillin-resistant *Staphylococcus aureus* a major penicillin-binding protein was mutated.
- Even low-level resistance may be clinically significant, e.g., in *Streptococcus pneumoniae* meningitis.

**In a Nutshell**

**Plasmid-Mediated Mechanisms**

- Enzymes modify the drug
- Transposition has produced multiple drug–resistance plasmids.

# Plasmid-Mediated Drug Resistance

The genes that determine this resistance are located on plasmids.

- Plasmid-mediated resistance is created by a variety of mechanisms but often genes code for **enzymes that modify the drug**.
- R factors are conjugative plasmids carrying genes for drug resistance.
  - One section of the DNA (containing *oriT* and the *tra* gene region) mediates conjugation.
  - The other section (**R determinant**) carries genes for drug resistance. Multiple genes seem to have been inserted through **transpositional insertion** into a "hot spot."

**In a Nutshell**

**Transposable Elements**

- Have **indirect repeats** on each end
- **Create mutations** with insertion into unrelated genes
- Create **direct repeats** where they land
- Create multiple drug–resistant plasmids

# How Do Multiple Drug-Resistance Plasmids Arise?

Gene cassettes/integrons/transposons:

- Are mobile genetic elements (DNA) that can move themselves or a copy from one molecule of DNA to another ("jumping genes")
- Are found in eukaryotic and bacterial cells and viruses
- Have at least one gene for a **transposase** (enzyme involved in the movement)
- Create additional **mutations** with their insertion into another totally unrelated gene

A typical genetic map of an R factor (a conjugative drug-resistant plasmid) is shown:

R factor = R-determinant + RTF

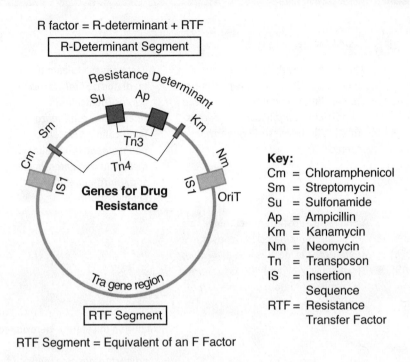

RTF Segment = Equivalent of an F Factor

**Key:**
Cm = Chloramphenicol
Sm = Streptomycin
Su = Sulfonamide
Ap = Ampicillin
Km = Kanamycin
Nm = Neomycin
Tn = Transposon
IS = Insertion Sequence
RTF = Resistance Transfer Factor

**Figure II-3-16.** A Resistance Transfer Factor

**Table II-3-3.** Plasmid-Mediated Mechanisms of Bacterial Drug Resistance

| Antimicrobial Agent | Mechanism |
|---|---|
| Penicillins and cephalosporins | Production of β-**lactamase**; cleavage of β-lactam rings |
| Aminoglycosides | Production of acetyltransferase, adenosyltransferase, or phosphotransferase; **inactivation of drug by acetylation**, adenosylation, or phosphorylation |
| Chloramphenicol | Production of acetyltransferase; **inactivation of drug by acetylation** |
| Tetracyclines | Increased **efflux** out of cell |
| Sulfonamides | Active **export** out of cell and lowered affinity of enzyme |
| Vancomycin | Ligase produces cell wall pentapeptides that terminate in D-alanine-D-lactate, which will not bind to drug |

**Table II-3-4.** Summary of Emerging Bacterial Resistances to Antimicrobial Agents

| Antimicrobic | Mechanism | | |
|---|---|---|---|
| **Inhibitors of Cell Wall Synthesis** | | | |
| | **Altered Accumulation** | **Altered Target** | **Enzymatic Inactivation** |
| β-lactams | Variable outer membranes (chromosome mediated): gram (–), e.g., *Pseudomonas aeruginosa* (ceftazidime) | Mutant and new PBPs (chromosome mediated): *Streptococcus pneumoniae* (penicillin); *Haemophilus influenzae* (ampicillin); *Staphylococcus aureus* (methicillin); *Neisseria gonorrhoeae* (penicillin) | β-lactamases* (plasmid mediated), *Staphylococcus aureus* (penicillin); *Haemophilus influenzae* (ampicillin); *Neisseria gonorrhoeae* (penicillin); *Klebsiella* and *Enterobacter* spp. (third-generation cephalosporins) |
| Glycopeptides | ↑ cell-wall thickness (chromosome mediated), vancomycin intermediate *Staphylococcus aureus* (VISA) | Amino acid substitution (chromosome- or plasmid-mediated transposon), *Enterococcus faecalis* and *E. faecium* (vancomycin); *Staphylococcus aureus* (plasmid mediated), vancomycin, VRSA† | — |
| Isoniazid | — | — | Mutation of catalase-peroxidase gene needed to activate the drug (chromosome mediated), *Mycobacterium tuberculosis* |
| Ethambutol | — | Mutation of arabinosyl transferase gene (chromosome mediated), *Mycobacterium tuberculosis* | — |
| **Inhibitors of Protein Synthesis** | | | |
| Aminoglycosides | Oxidative transport required (plasmid mediated), *Pseudomonas aeruginosa*, gentamicin | Ribosomal binding site mutations (chromosome mediated), *Enterococcus*, gentamicin | Adenylases, acetylases, phosphorylases (plasmid mediated), *Klebsiella* and *Enterobacter* spp., gentamicin |
| Macrolides, lincosamides | Minimal outer membrane penetration (chromosome mediated), gram (–); efflux pump (plasmid mediated), gram (+) cocci; erythromycin | Methylation of 23S rRNA (plasmid mediated), *Bacteroides fragilis*, *Staphylococcus aureus*, MLS resistance‡ | Phosphotransferase, esterase (plasmid mediated), gram (+) cocci |
| Chloramphenicol | — | — | Acetyltransferase (plasmid mediated), *Salmonella*, chloramphenicol |
| Tetracycline | Efflux pump (transposon in plasmid), widespread due to use in animal feed | New protein protects ribosome site (transposon in chromosome or plasmid), *Staphylococcus aureus* | — |

*(Continued)*

**Table II-3-4.** Summary of Emerging Bacterial Resistances to Antimicrobial Agents (*Cont'd*)

| Antimicrobic | | Mechanism | |
|---|---|---|---|
| **Inhibitors of Nucleic Acid Synthesis** | | | |
| | **Altered Accumulation** | **Altered Target** | **Enzymatic Inactivation** |
| Fluoroquinolones | Efflux pump (plasmid mediated), *Enterococcus*; permeability mutation (chromosomal), *Pseudomonas* | Mutant topoisomerase (chromosome mediated), *Escherichia coli* and *Pseudomonas aeruginosa*, ciprofloxacin | — |
| Rifamycins | — | Mutant RNA polymerase (chromosome mediated), *Mycobacterium tuberculosis*, *Staphylococcus* spp., and *Neisseria meningitidis*, rifampin | — |
| Folate inhibitors | — | New dihydropteroate synthetase, altered dihydrofolate reductase (chromosome mediated), Enterobacteriaceae sulfonamides | — |

* Gram (+) β-lactamases are exoenzymes with little activity against cephalosporins, methicillin, or oxacillin. Gram (–) β-lactamases act in the periplasmic space and may have both penicillinase and cephalosporinase activity. Extended spectrum β-lactamases (ESBLs) are inducible and may not be detected by susceptibility testing. The range of ESBLs includes multiple cephalosporins. *TEM-1* is the most common of the plasmid β-lactamase genes.

† The most common vancomycin resistance genes, *vanA* and *vanB*, are found in a transposon. These have been transferred from *Enterococcus* to a multidrug resistance plasmid in *Staphylococcus aureus*. The super multidrug resistance plasmid now contains resistance genes against β-lactams, vancomycin, aminoglycosides, trimethoprim, and some disinfectants.

‡ MLS, macrolide-lincosamine-streptogramin resistance. Methylation of the 23S rRNA will impart resistance to erythromycin, lincomycin, and clindamycin.

# Transfer of Drug Resistance

## Conjugation

### Gram-negative bacilli

Plasmid mediated, transferred by conjugation.

### Staphylococcus aureus (Methicillin Resistant = MRSA)

Resistance to methicillin is chromosomal, transferred by transduction. Most of the other antibiotic resistance is transferred by plasmids.

*S. aureus* recently acquired the genes for vancomycin resistance (van A and van B) from *Enterococcus faecalis* via a transposon on a multi-drug resistant conjugative plasmid. In *S. aureus*, the transposon moved from the *E. faecalis* plasmid to a multi-drug resistant plasmid in S. aureus. The new *S. aureus* super multi-drug resistant plasmid now contains resistance genes against β-lactams, vancomycin, aminoglycosides, trimethoprim, and some disinfectants and can be transferred to other strains via conjugation.

### Enterococcus faecalis and faecium

Resistance to vancomycin is carried on a multi-drug–resistant conjugative plasmid.

## Note

- **Conjugation is the most common means of exchange of drug resistance genes (DRGs), which are encoded in plasmids.**

- Accumulation of DRGs into multiple drug resistance plasmids can be detected by the identification of characteristic flanking sequences (direct and indirect repeats).

- Plasmids can be easily exchanged between members of the same or different species, or even different genera (between normal flora in the intestine).

- Although it is the most rapid and efficient means of transfer in any bacteria, it is most common in gram (–) bacilli.

### Neisseria gonorrhoeae

In *Neisseria gonorrhoeae*, two plasmids are required to transfer drug resistances. In this bacterial species, drug resistance genes are located on **nonconjugative plasmids**. These are plasmids that have lost their *tra* operon but retained *oriT*. Nonconjugative plasmids may be transferred by conjugation as long as there is another fertility factor in the same cell with a functional *tra* operon. The process is referred to as **mobilization**.

## Transformation

It is difficult to mark the movement of drug resistance genes through the process of transformation, but epidemiologic studies suggest that the spread of **penicillin-binding protein mutations of *Streptococcus pneumoniae* occurs via transformation**.

## Transduction

The high host cell specificity of bacteriophage limits transduction to a transfer mechanism between members of the same bacterial species. Nevertheless, in ***Staphylococcus aureus* resistance to methicillin is chromosome mediated and transferred by transduction**. In *Pseudomonas aeruginosa*, imipenem resistance is transferred from one member of the species to another during transduction by wild-type bacteriophage.

# ANTIBIOTIC SUSCEPTIBILITY TESTING

## Kirby-Bauer Agar Disk Diffusion Test

- Solid medium with patient's isolate swabbed on the entire plate surface.
- Multiple paper disks, each with a single dried drug placed on plate.
- Hydration and diffusion of drug sets up a concentration gradient during incubation and growth of the bacteria.
- The diameter of the zones of inhibition must be measured to determine significance.
- Advantages: relatively cheap, easy, can test numerous antibiotics on one plate, wealth of information based on clinical correlation.
- Disadvantage: qualitative. Bacterial isolate is classified as resistant, intermediate, or susceptible to each drug.

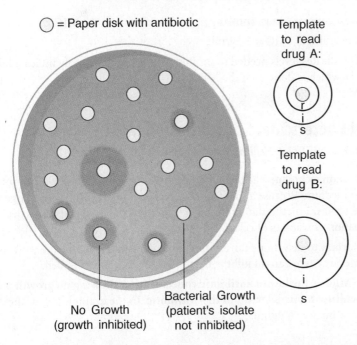

**Antibiotic Susceptibility Testing**
**Kirby Bauer Agar Diffusion Plate**

**Figure II-3-17.** The Kirby-Bauer Agar Disk Diffusion Technique

## E-Test (Agar Diffusion)

E-test uses a strip of plastic marked with a gradient unique to each antibiotic that has dried antibiotic on the underside. This is placed on an agar plate already swabbed with the patient's isolate and read after incubation. It produces a µg/ml value that is much more quantitative than the results of the Kirby-Bauer.

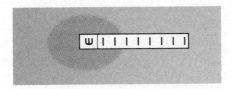

**Figure II-3-18.** The E Test

## "Rapid" Methods

Testing for specific enzymes and a very few probes for genes determining drug resistance are currently available but still require a culture of the patient's pathogen. One current example is β-lactamase testing, shown below.

| Patient's bacterial isolate (8–24 hours) | + | Chromogenic beta lactam | 5–10 min → | Color change if beta lactamase is present |
|---|---|---|---|---|

## Minimal Inhibitory Concentration (MIC)

MIC measures antibiotic inhibition of bacterial multiplication.

- This is a dilution technique where **each container** (well of microtiter plate, test tube, or automated system bottle) **has one concentration of an antibiotic** with the patient's isolate. Always one control container has just the patient's isolate and growth medium with no antibiotic to make sure the inoculum is viable.

- **Lowest concentration showing no visible growth is the MIC.**

- In the example, MIC = 2 μg/ml.

- This indicates levels needed to inhibit; it does not necessarily indicate killing levels, which is done with the MBC.

## Minimal Bactericidal Concentration (MBC)

This measures the antibiotic killing (bactericidal activity).

- A dilution technique starting with the MIC containers and subplating onto solid medium. Because a small inoculum is used on the plate with a large volume of medium, this dilutes the drug way below the MIC and allows determination of viability of cells.

- Important to determine for treating immunocompromised patients whose immune system cannot kill the bacteria while they are inhibited.

- **The MBC is the lowest antibiotic concentration showing no growth on subculture to media without the antibiotic.** In the example below, the MBC would be 4 μg/ml.

**Minimal Inhibitory Concentration = MIC**
1. Each container has one concentration of a drug.
2. Each container has identical inoculum of the patient's bacterial isolate
3. Must run a no drug control.
4. Lowest concentration showing no visible growth = MIC
   (in example, MIC = 2 µg/ml)

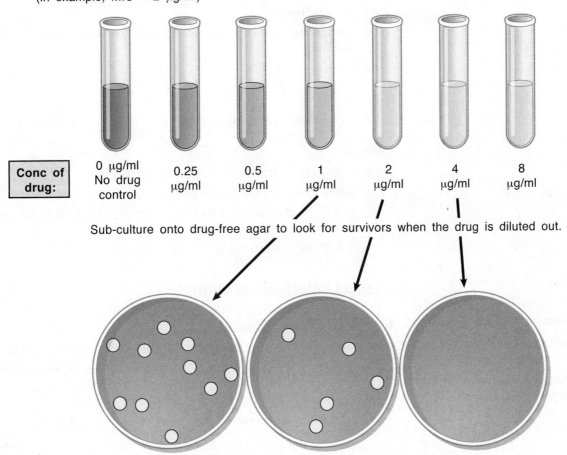

| Conc of drug: | 0 µg/ml No drug control | 0.25 µg/ml | 0.5 µg/ml | 1 µg/ml | 2 µg/ml | 4 µg/ml | 8 µg/ml |

Sub-culture onto drug-free agar to look for survivors when the drug is diluted out.

**Minimal Bactericidal Concentration (MBC)**
(Not routinely done in many hospitals but ordered when necessary)

The lowest drug concentration showing no growth on sub-culture to media without drugs = MBC
MBC in example would be 4 µg/ml.

**Figure II-3-19.** The Minimal Inhibitory Concentration (MIC) and
the Minimal Bactericidal Concentration (MBC) for a Drug

# Sterilization, Disinfection, Pasteurization

**Sterilization:** complete removal or killing of all viable organisms.

**Disinfection:** the removal or killing of disease-causing organisms. Compounds for use on skin: antiseptics.

**Pasteurization:** the rapid heating and cooling of milk designed to kill milk-borne pathogens such as *Mycobacterium bovis*, *Brucella*, and *Listeria*.

# Physical Methods of Control

Heat = saturated steam

- **Autoclaving (steam under pressure): 15 lbs pressure → 121°C 15–20 min** (sterilizing)
- Dry heat—2 hr 180°C

Radiation

- UV: formation of thymine–thymine pairs on adjacent DNA bases

Filtration

- HEPA (High Efficiency Particulate Air) filters for air
- Nitrocellulose or other known pore-size filters
  - 0.45 μm filters out most bacteria except mycoplasmas and other cell-wall–less forms.
  - 0.22 μm will filter out all bacteria and spores.

# Chemical Methods of Control

## *Agents damaging membranes*

- **Detergents:** surface active compounds—most notable the quaternary ammonium compounds like benzalkonium chloride—interact with membrane through hydrophobic end disrupting membrane.
- **Alcohols:** disrupt membrane and denature proteins.
- **Phenols** and derivatives: damage membrane and denature proteins.

## *Agents modifying proteins*

- **Chlorine:** oxidizing agent inactivating sulfhydryl-containing enzymes
- **Iodine and iodophors** (that have reduced toxicity): also oxidation of sulfhydryl-containing enzymes
- **Hydrogen peroxide:** oxidizing agent (sulfhydryl groups); catalase inactivates
- **Heavy metals:** (silver and mercury)—bind to sulfhydryl groups inhibiting enzyme activity
- **Ethylene oxide:** alkylating agent (sterilizing agent)
- **Formaldehyde** and glutaraldehyde: denatures protein and nucleic acids and alkylates amino and hydroxyl groups on both

## *Modification of nucleic acids*

- **Dyes:** like crystal violet and malachite green whose positively charged molecule binds to the negatively charged phosphate groups on the nucleic acids

---

**In a Nutshell**

The choice of disinfectant depends on the **outer surface** of the infectious agent.

- Use **membrane-denaturing** compounds on **enveloped** viruses
- Use **protein-denaturing** compounds on **naked capsid** viruses

# Review Questions

1.  What type of genetic material is created by repeated transpositional recombination events?

    (A) Chromosomal drug resistance genes

    (B) Genetic operon

    (C) Hfr chromosome

    (D) Insertion sequences

    (E) Multiple drug resistance plasmids

2.  Which genetic material is found in pathogenic *Corynebacterium diphtheriae* but not in nonpathogenic normal flora diphtheroids?

    (A) A diphthamide on eEF-2

    (B) An episome

    (C) An F factor

    (D) An integrated temperate phage

    (E) Highly repetitive bacterial DNA

3.  How is a prophage created?

    (A) Through activation of the *recA* gene product of an exogenote

    (B) Through infection of a bacterial cell with a virulent bacteriophage

    (C) Through site-specific recombination of a temperate phage and bacterial DNA

    (D) Through infection of a bacterial cell with lambda phage, lacking the lambda repressor

    (E) Through excision of bacterial DNA and active lytic replication of a bacteriophage

4.  If one cell of type one (figure below) is mixed into a culture of 100 cells of type two (below), and culture conditions are optimized for conjugation BUT NOT for cell division, the cellular genotype that would predominate after overnight incubation would be that of

    (A) Cell #1

    (B) Cell #1 with new a, b, c, and d alleles

    (C) Cell #2 with new A, B, C, and D alleles

    (D) Cell #1 with a new a allele

    (E) Cell #2 with a new A allele

    (F) Cell #1 with new a and b alleles

    (G) Cell #1 with new A and B alleles

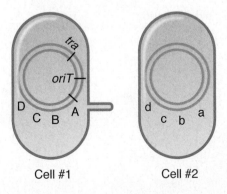

Cell #1          Cell #2

5. Assume the following cells have no plasmids other than those mentioned. Which cell type would contain two molecules of DNA?

   (A) F$^+$

   (B) F$^-$

   (C) Hfr

6. Assume the cells whose genotype is listed below have no other plasmids than those indicated by the indicated genotype. Which bacterial cell is most likely to transfer chromosomal genes in linear order?

   (A) F$^+$

   (B) F$^-$

   (C) Hfr

7. What bacterial gene transfer process is most sensitive to extracellular nucleases?

   (A) Conjugation

   (B) Generalized transduction

   (C) Homologous recombination

   (D) Site-specific recombination

   (E) Specialized transduction

   (F) Transformation

8. Following specialized transduction, if any of the bacterial genes transferred in are to be stabilized, what process must occur?

   (A) Conjugation

   (B) Generalized transduction

   (C) Homologous recombination

   (D) Site-specific recombination

   (E) Specialized transduction

   (F) Transformation

9. The ability of a cell to bind DNA to its surface and import it is required for which genetic process?

   (A) Conjugation

   (B) Generalized transduction

   (C) Homologous recombination

   (D) Site-specific recombination

   (E) Specialized transduction

   (F) Transformation

10. The process by which bacterial or plasmid DNA may be mistakenly incorporated (during assembly) into one phage being produced by the lytic life cycle and then that DNA-transferred to another bacterial cell which may acquire some new genetic traits is called

    (A) Conjugation

    (B) Generalized transduction

    (C) Homologous recombination

    (D) Site-specific recombination

    (E) Specialized transduction

    (F) Transformation

11. Recombination is required for stabilization of genetic material newly transferred by all of the following processes EXCEPT

    (A) Movement of a transposon

    (B) Integration of a temperate bacteriophage

    (C) Transduction of a chromosomal gene

    (D) Conjugal transfer of an R factor

    (E) Transformation of a chromosomal gene

12. Lysogenic conversion

    (A) is a change in pathogenicity due to the presence of a prophage.

    (B) is the induction of a prophage to its virulent state.

    (C) is the conversion of a virulent phage into a temperate phage.

    (D) refers to the incorporation of a prophage into the chromosome.

    (E) is the immunity that a prophage confers on a bacterium.

13. Which of the following events is most likely due to bacterial transformation?

    (A) A formerly non-toxigenic strain of *Corynebacterium diphtheriae* becomes toxigenic.

    (B) A non-encapsulated strain of *Streptococcus pneumoniae* acquires a gene for capsule formation from the extract of an encapsulated strain.

    (C) A strain of *Neisseria gonorrhoeae* starts producing a plasmid-encoded β-lactamase similar to that another Gram-negative strain.

    (D) A gene for gentamicin resistance from an *Escherichia coli* chromosome appears in the genome of a bacteriophage that has infected it.

14. Which of the following mechanisms is most likely to be involved in multiple drug resistance transfer from one cell to another?

    (A) Specialized transduction of a chromosomal gene for drug resistance

    (B) Transformation of chromosomal genes

    (C) Transposition

    (D) Conjugation with a cell with a free plasmid carrying drug resistance

    (E) Conjugation with a cell with chromosomal drug resistance

15. Which of the following agents, if introduced into a growing culture of bacteria, would halt growth but, if then removed, would allow growth to resume?

    (A) Antiseptic

    (B) Bacteriocide

    (C) Bacteriostat

    (D) Disinfectant

    (E) Sterilizing Agent

16. A burn patient develops a purulent infection at the site of a skin graft. Culture of the pus is positive for *Pseudomonas aeruginosa*. The patient is started on anti-pseudomonal penicillin while a Kirby-Bauer agar disc diffusion test is requested for the isolate. The results are shown.

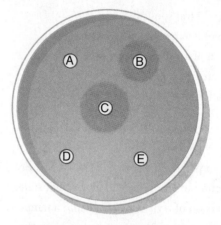

    What is the correct interpretation of these lab results?

    (A) The isolate is most sensitive to antibiotic B

    (B) The isolate is most sensitive to antibiotic C

    (C) The isolate is most sensitive to antibiotic E

    (D) The isolate is resistant to antibiotic B

    (E) Results cannot be analyzed without a key

17. A bacterial isolate from a patient with chronic sinusitis is shown to be sensitive to amoxicillin on a Kirby-Bauer agar disk diffusion test. A follow-up determination of the MIC of the drug is reported back from the laboratory at 2 µg/ml with an MBC of 1 µg/ml. What is the correct interpretation of this data?

    (A) The drug is bacteriocidal.

    (B) The drug is bacteriostatic.

    (C) The drug should be administered to the patient at 1 µg/ml.

    (D) The drug should be administered to the patient at 2 µg/ml.

    (E) There has been a laboratory error.

# Answers and Explanations

1.  **Answer: E.** Transposition or transpositional recombination is a form of site-specific recombination and is largely responsible for the creation of multiple drug resistant plasmids. Chromosomal drug resistance may arise by movement of a plasmid gene to the chromosome, but it is usually just a solitary gene and not a repetitive event. The Hfr chromosome arises through a single site-specific integration of a fertility factor with the bacterial chromosome.

2.  **Answer: D.** This question is asking what carries the genetic code for diphtheria toxin, which must be some kind of DNA, which in turn means that the protein eEF-2 can be immediately eliminated. The diphthamide on eEF-2 is actually the substrate for the ADP-ribosylation done by the diphtheria toxin. Genes expressing the diphtheria toxin originally enter *C. diphtheriae* as part of the DNA of the temperate corynephage. Integration of this temperate phage results in a stable prophage, which directs the production of the diphtheria toxin.

3.  **Answer: C.** Site-specific recombination of phage DNA into bacterial cell DNA by the process of lysogeny creates a prophage. The *recA* gene product (**choice A**) is necessary for homologous recombination with an exogenote but does not create a prophage. A virulent bacteriophage (**choice B**) causes lysis of the host cell and not the production of prophage. The lambda phage, (**choice D**), is a temperate phage, which can cause lysogeny of infected cells, but the lambda repressor is necessary in such cases to prevent the lytic life cycle. **Choice E** might be the pathway a prophage could choose to reinitiate its lytic lifestyle, but it would not be a means to create a prophage.

4.  **Answer: E.** This hypothetical condition describes the mixing of one Hfr cell with 100 F⁻ recipients. Over time, with no cell division occurring, the one Hfr cell would repeatedly conjugate with the F⁻ cells and transfer one strand of its chromosomal DNA in sequence, beginning with oriT and theoretically ending with the tra genes. The most frequently transferred bacterial genes also have the greatest likelihood of successful recombination; they are those closest to oriT; in this example, the A allele. The entire chromosome is so large that it is virtually never transferred in its entirety and thus, the tra genes would not be transferred. (Even if tra genes were transferred, oriT and tra genes have no homologous regions in the recipient cell chromosome and so would not successfully recombine within.) Thus, the recipient cell acquires only new chromosomal alleles and NOT the whole fertility factor and never changes phenotype to become an Hfr cell. Therefore, any of the answers with cell one (the Hfr parent) as the dominant type would be wrong.

    The genes are transferred in linear order, so allele A will always be transferred more frequently than any of the later genes.

    Therefore, given sufficient time for conjugation, the cell type that would be most numerous is that of the recipient genotype with a newly acquired allele close to oriT. This means that the best answer is choice F: cell two with a new A gene. The farther from oriT that the allele is, the less likely that it will be successfully transferred. The distractor, choice C, with all 4 alleles transferred in, is less likely.

5.  **Answer: A.** The F⁺ cell would contain both the bacterial chromosome and the fertility factor. The other two would just each have the bacterial chromosome (F⁻) or the single DNA molecule of the chromosome with the integrated fertility factor.

6.  **Answer: C.** Only F⁺ and Hfr can donate genes to a recipient or F⁻ cell. The F⁺ cell would transfer only plasmid genes. The Hfr would be the only one likely to transfer chromosomal genes.

7.  **Answer: F.** In transformation, free DNA from lysed cells is not protected from the environment either by a cell or by a phage coat, but is instead naked and therefore subject to nucleases.

8.  **Answer: C.** The DNA is transferred in as a linear piece and must be stabilized by homologous recombination.

9.  **Answer: F.** The statement fits the definition of competency required for transformation.

10. **Answer: B.** This is generalized transduction, but what are your clues? First, it says "one phage" rather than all the phage in the cell (as for specialized). Then it also says plasmid DNA could be picked up. For specialized transduction, only episomal plasmid DNA (incorporated into the bacterial chromosome near an attachment site) or chromosomal DNA could be picked up. Finally, it mentions a lytic virus lifecycle. Lytic viruses are only capable of generalized transduction.

11. **Answer: D.** Transpositional movement actually involves a type of recombination called transposition that is a form of site-specific recombination. Site-specific recombination is also involved in integration of a temperate bacteriophage. Both transformation and transduction require homologous recombination as would transfer of Hfr DNA by conjugation. But either F factor or R factor DNA circularizes when it enters a new cell and thus is stable without recombination since circular DNA is not subject to cellular exonucleases.

12. **Answer: A.** Choice D is a definition of lysogeny but lysogenic conversion is when lysogeny changes the characteristic of the lysogenized organism. In medicine this usually means an increased pathogenicity from the process.

13. **Answer: B.** Choice A would require phage infection with a temperate corynephage. Choice C is most likely to take place through a conjugal transfer. Choice D might occur by specialized transduction.

14. **Answer: D.** Multiple drug resistance is almost always plasmid-mediated, which rules out choices A, B, and E. Transposition is moving a piece of DNA to another molecule of DNA within the cell.

15. **Answer: C.** This is the classic description of a bacteriostatic agent.

16. **Answer: E.** The Kirby-Bauer agar disk diffusion test is a means to compare the functions of several antibiotics against one bacterial isolate. In a general sense, bacteria will be inhibited from growing in close proximity to any disk of antibiotic to which they are sensitive, so the larger the zone of inhibited growth around the filter paper disk, the more sensitive the bacteria are to that drug. Comparison between the disks cannot be accomplished without the key which comes with the kit, however, since the company which prepared the kit has done the clinical trials which correlate the in vitro results with those in human patients.

17. **Answer: E.** The MIC (Minimal Inhibitory Concentration) is the most dilute amount of drug in which no growth of a bacterial isolate will occur. The MBC (Minimal Bactericidal Concentration) of a drug is the most dilute amount of a drug in which there will be no colonial growth after the drug is removed. In some cases the MBC may be equal to the MIC, but the amount of drug necessary to kill all bacteria is never less than the amount required to inhibit their growth temporarily.

# Medically Important Viruses

**4**

## What the COMLEX Requires You To Know

- Major concepts of host and tissue specificity
- Major concepts of viral replication
- How viruses cause disease
- Basics of viral diseases (as for bacterial diseases)
- Plus, for each virus
  - Nucleic acid (and generalities about how it replicates)
  - Nucleocapsid shape
  - Whether or not it is enveloped

## COMLEX Note

The COMLEX generally does not require you to know the replication cycles for each virus. Concentrate on the age of the patient, disease presentation, transmission, tissue specificity and any diagnostic features such as "owl's eye" inclusions, koilocytic cells, etc.

## Bridge to Biochemistry

Positive-sense = coding strand

Negative-sense = template strand

*Positive-sense RNA = (+)RNA (can be used itself as mRNA)

ss = Single stranded
ds = Double stranded

*Negative-sense RNA = (−)RNA

- Complementary to mRNA
- Cannot be used as mRNA
- Requires virion-associated, RNA-dependent RNA polymerase (as part of the mature virus)

## STRUCTURE AND MORPHOLOGY

| DNA or RNA* | + | Structural proteins (capsomers, etc.) | = | Nucleocapsid | = | Naked capsid virus |

Enzymes e.g., polymerase

| Nucleocapsid | + | Host membrane with viral-specified glycoproteins (critical for infectiousness of viral progeny) | = | Enveloped virus |

**Figure II-4-1.** The Basic Virion

## VIRAL STRUCTURE

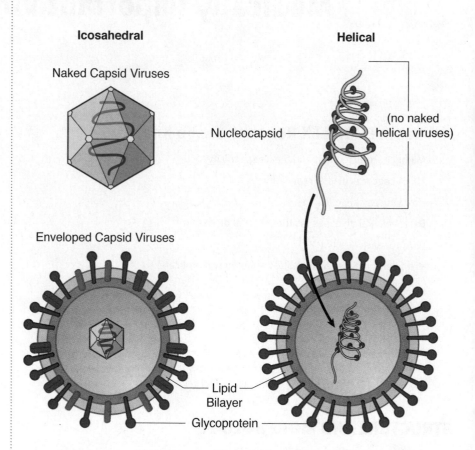

**Figure II-4-2.** Morphology of Viruses

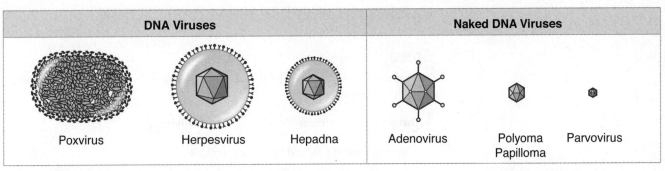

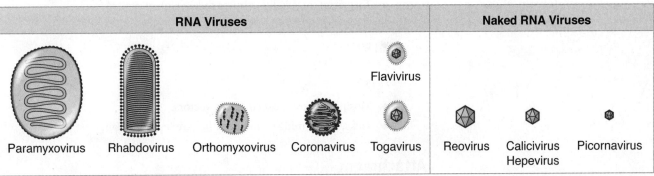

**Figure II-4-3.** Relative Sizes and Shapes of Different Viruses

# VIRAL REPLICATION

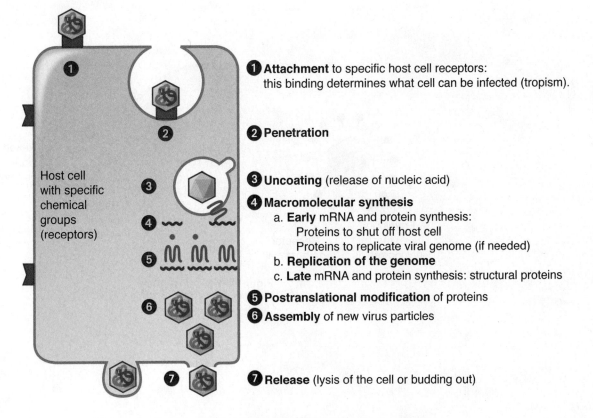

❶ **Attachment** to specific host cell receptors: this binding determines what cell can be infected (tropism).

❷ **Penetration**

❸ **Uncoating** (release of nucleic acid)

❹ **Macromolecular synthesis**
 a. **Early** mRNA and protein synthesis:
  Proteins to shut off host cell
  Proteins to replicate viral genome (if needed)
 b. **Replication of the genome**
 c. **Late** mRNA and protein synthesis: structural proteins

❺ **Postranslational modification** of proteins

❻ **Assembly** of new virus particles

❼ **Release** (lysis of the cell or budding out)

**Figure II-4-4.** Generalized Viral Replication Scheme

# IMPORTANT STEPS IN VIRAL REPLICATION

## Spread

Viruses are spread basically by the same mechanisms (e.g., respiratory droplets or sexually) as other pathogens.

**Arthropod-borne** viruses are referred to as **arboviruses**.

Most belong to 3 formal taxonomic groups

- Togavirus encephalitis viruses (a.k.a. alphaviruses)
- Flavivirus
- Bunyavirus

Vectors

- Mosquitoes are most common vectors.
- Ticks, biting midges, and sandflies are less common.

## Attachment

**Viruses bind through specific interaction with the host cell surface components <u>and</u>**

- Specific **viral surface glycoproteins** of **enveloped viruses**, or
- Specific **viral surface proteins** of **naked viruses**.

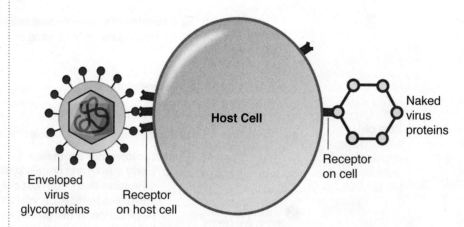

**Figure II-4-5.** Attachment

These interactions (and the distribution of the receptors) **determine viral**

1. **Host range** (e.g., horses or humans)
2. **Tissue specificity** (e.g., liver versus heart; **tropism**)

**Table II-4-1.** Specific Viral Receptors to Know

| Virus | Target Cell | Receptor on Host Cell |
|-------|-------------|----------------------|
| HIV | TH cells, macrophages, microglia | CD4 plus CCR5 or CXCR4 |
| EBV | B lymphocytes | CD21= CR2 |
| Rabies | Neurons | Acetylcholine receptor |
| Rhinovirus | Respiratory epithelial cells | ICAM-1 |

**COMLEX Note**

Knowing the viral receptors is important.

**Table II-4-2.** Difference Between Naked and Enveloped Viruses

| | Naked | Enveloped |
|---|-------|-----------|
| Inactivated by heat, detergents, acid and organic solvents like ether and alcohols? | No | Yes, since the lipid envelope holds the glycoproteins essential for attachment. Dissolving the envelope inhibits attachment and therefore uptake. |

# Viral Entry Into Host Cell

Viral entry is by

- Receptor-mediated endocytosis
- Uptake via coated pits
- Or for those enveloped viruses with fusion proteins via fusion of the cell membrane with the viral envelope

# Macromolecular Synthesis

How do the various viruses make their mRNA? mRNA production is diagrammed below.

- The major types of viral genomes are shown on the right.
- The replication intermediates necessary to make mRNA are shown in the gray area.

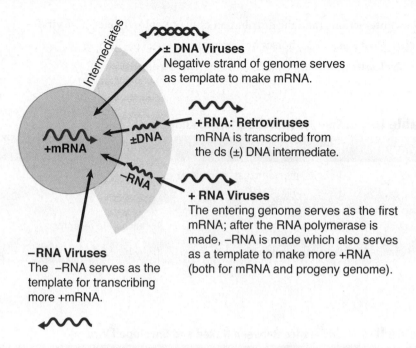

**Figure II-4-6.** Production of Viral Messenger RNA

# Replication of the Genomic Nucleic Acid (NA)

**Progeny viruses have a nucleic acid sequence identical to the parent virus.**

All single-stranded **RNA viruses replicate through a replicative intermediate**. Going back to the Simplified Imaginary Teaching Viruses:

- If the parental genomic sequence is UUUUUUUUU, then the progeny must have the same sequence.
- (Poly AAA would make a polylysine capsid instead.)
- To make more poly UUU, a replicative intermediate of AAAAAAAAA would be required.
- The replicative intermediate is used to make new poly UUU.

**Table II-4-3.** Strategy for Viral Genome Replication

| Virus Type | Parental Genome | Intermediate Replicative Form | Progeny Genome |
|---|---|---|---|
| Most dsDNA viruses | dsDNA | | dsDNA |
| Hepatitis B | dsDNA | ssRNA → | dsDNA |
| Most +ssRNA viruses | +ssRNA | −ssRNA | +ssRNA |
| Retroviruses | +ssRNA → | dsDNA | +ssRNA |
| −ssRNA viruses | −ssRNA | +ssRNA | −ssRNA |

+ means an RNA which can serve as mRNA (or for the retroviruses has the same sequence.)

→ = RNA-dependent DNA polymerase

- Called reverse transcriptase for the retroviruses.
- Called the DNA polymerase for hepatitis B.
- Both actually make the first strand of the DNA using the RNA original and then break down the RNA and use the single strand of DNA as template to make the second strand.

# Release of Viruses

Naked viruses lyse the host cells. Thus, there are **no persistent productive infections** with naked viruses (only cytolytic productive or latent infections).

Release of enveloped viruses: Budding leads to cell senescence (aging), but cells may produce a low level of virus for years as occurs in chronic hepatitis B.

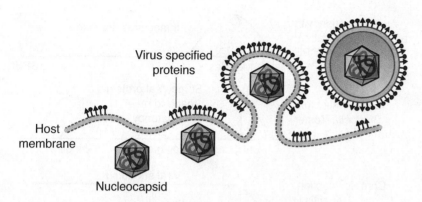

**Figure II-4-7.** Release of Enveloped Virus

The glycoproteins on the enveloped viral surface are essential for viral infectivity.

# PATTERNS OF VIRAL INFECTIONS

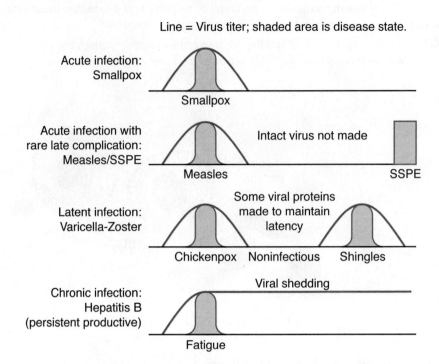

Line = Virus titer; shaded area is disease state.

**Figure II-4-8.** Time Courses of Viral Infections

## Table II-4-4. Cellular Effects

| Infection Type | Virus Production | Fate of Cell |
|---|---|---|
| **Abortive** | – | No effect: No virus is made nor is latency established; Virus is terminated |
| **Cytolytic** Naked viruses lyse host cells. Some enveloped viruses also are cytolytic, killing the cell in the process of replication. | + | Lysis of the host cell (death) |
| **Persistent** | | |
| Productive (enveloped viruses) | + | Senescence (premature aging) |
| Latent | – | No overt damage to host; no production of virus, but viral production may be turned on later. |
| Transforming | ± | Immortalization |

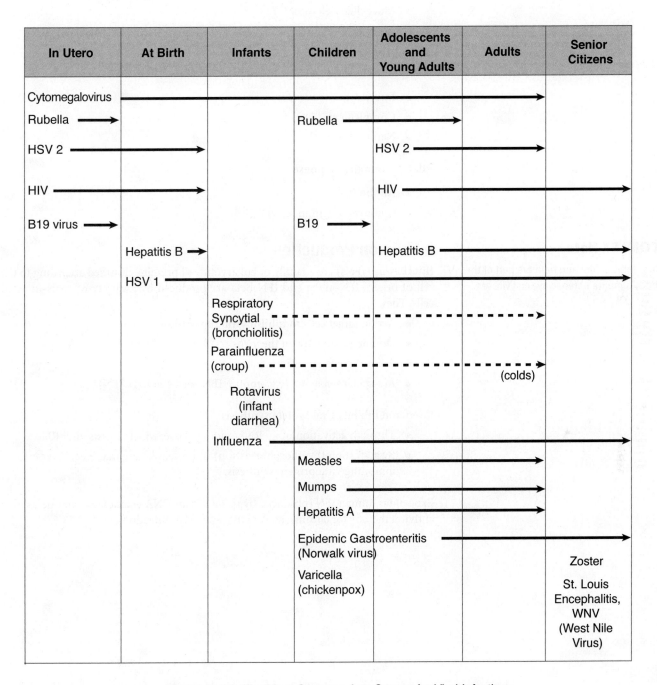

**Figure II-4-9.** The Most Common Age Groups for Viral Infections

**COMLEX Note**

Viral infections vary by age of the patient and can be a big clue in answering questions.

# HOST RESISTANCE TO VIRAL INFECTION

## Primary Defenses

- Skin barrier (dead keratinized cells impervious to viruses)
- Skin has acids and other inhibitors produced by normal bacterial flora
- Mucociliary elevator

## Immune Defense

Innate immune response

- Interferon
- Complement
- Natural killer cells

Adaptive immune response

- Antibody
- Cytotoxic T lymphocytes

**COMLEX Note**

Interferon alpha and beta are part of the body's innate defense against viruses.

## Interferon Production

**Interferons** (IFNs) are a family of eukaryotic cell proteins classified according to the cell of origin. IFN-alpha and IFN-beta are produced by a variety of virus-infected cells. They:

- Act on target cells to **inhibit viral replication.**
- Do not act directly on the virus.
- Are **not virus-specific.**
- Are **species-specific** (e.g., mouse IFN versus human IFN).

Interferon inhibits viral protein synthesis

- Through activation of an RNA endonuclease, which digests viral RNA.
- By activation (by phosphorylation) of protein kinase that inactivates eIF2, inhibiting viral protein synthesis.

Exogenous human IFN (produced by recombinant DNA technology) may be used in antiviral therapy for chronic, active HBV and HCV infections.

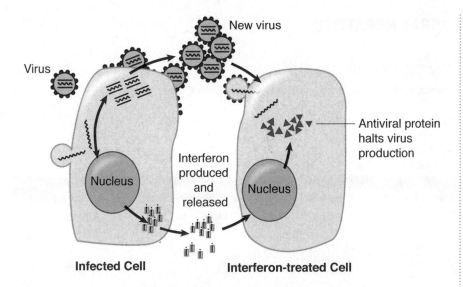

**Figure II-4-10.** Interferon Production

## Clinical Correlate

### The Therapeutic Use of Interferons

Since the first description of interferons almost 50 years ago, a multitude of dramatic immunomodulatory roles have been discovered for this group of proteins. As a group, interferons induce increases in the expression of class I and II MHC molecules and augment NK cell activity. They increase the efficiency of presentation of antigens to both cytotoxic and helper cell populations. Cloning of the genes that encode $\alpha$, $\beta$, and $\gamma$ interferons has made it possible to produce amounts of these products which makes their use clinically practical.

Interferon-$\alpha$ has well-known antiviral activity and has been used in the treatment of hepatitis B and C infections. Within cancer therapy, IFN-$\alpha$ has shown promise in treatment of hairy B-cell leukemia, chronic myelogenous leukemia, and Kaposi sarcoma.

Interferon-$\beta$ was the first drug shown to have a positive effect on young adults with multiple sclerosis. Patients treated with IFN-$\beta$ enjoy longer periods of remission and reduced severity of relapses.

Interferon-$\gamma$ is being used in the treatment of chronic granulomatous disease (CGD). This molecule is a potent inducer of macrophage activation and a promoter of inflammatory responses. Its application appears to significantly reverse the CGD patient's inability to generate toxic oxygen metabolites inside phagocytic cells.

The side effects of IFN therapy are fortunately mild and can be managed with acetaminophen. They include headache, fever, chills, and fatigue and diminish with continued treatment.

### Bridge to Biochemistry

Production of IFN and most immunologic cytokines is under the control of the transcription factor NF$\kappa$B.

**COMLEX Note**

It is essential to be able to differntiate be-tween acute, chronic active, chronic and immune persons based on the expression of viral markers (HBs As) or viral specific antibody for Hepatitis B virus.

# VIRAL HEPATITIS

## Symptoms of Hepatitis

Fever, malaise, headache, anorexia, vomiting, dark urine, jaundice.

**Table II-4-5.** Hepatitis Viruses (Hepatotropic)

|  | Hepatitis A | Hepatitis B | Hepatitis C | Hepatitis D | Hepatitis E |
|---|---|---|---|---|---|
|  | "Infectious" (HAV) | "Serum" (HBV) | "Post-transfusion Non A, Non B" (HCV) | "Delta" (HDV) | "Enteric" (HEV) |
| Family | Picornavirus | Hepadnavirus | Flavivirus | Defective | Hepevirus |
| Features | RNA<br><br>Naked Capsid | DNA<br><br>Enveloped | RNA<br><br>Enveloped | Circular RNA<br><br>Enveloped | RNA<br><br>Naked capsid |
| Transmission | Fecal-oral | Parenteral, sexual | Parenteral, sexual | Parenteral, sexual | Fecal-oral |
| Disease presentation | Mild acute<br><br>No chronic<br><br>No sequellae | Acute; occasionally severe<br><br>Chronic: 5–10% adults 90% infants<br><br>Primary hepatocellular carcinoma, cirrhosis | Acute is usually subclinical<br><br>80% become chronic<br><br>Primary hepatocellular carcinoma, cirrhosis | Co-infection with HBV: occasionally severe<br><br>Superinfection with HBV: often severe<br><br>Cirrhosis, fulminant hepatitis | Normal patients: mild<br><br>Pregnant patients: severe<br><br>No chronic |
| Mortality | <0.5% | 1–2% | 0.5–1% | High to very high | Normal patients 1–2%<br><br>Third-trimester pregnant patients 25% |
| Diagnosis | IgM to HAV | HBsAg,<br><br>IgM to HBcAg | Antibody to HCV, ELISA | Hepatitis D Ab,<br><br>HBsAg | Antibody to HEV, ELISA |

Note: Remember that hepatitis also may occur in other viral diseases (e.g., CMV and EBV infections, congenital rubella, and yellow fever).

**Table II-4-6.** Hepatitis B Terminology and Markers

| Abbreviation | Name and Description |
|---|---|
| HBV | Hepatitis B virus, a hepadnavirus (enveloped, partially double-stranded DNA virus); Dane particle = infectious HBV |
| HBsAg | Antigen found on surface of HBV; also found on spheres and filaments in patient's blood: positive during acute disease; continued presence indicates carrier state |
| HBsAb | Antibody to HBsAg; provides immunity to hepatitis B |
| HBcAg | Antigen associated with core of HBV |
| HBcAb | Antibody to HBcAg; positive during window phase; IgM HBcAb is an indicator of recent disease |
| HBeAg | A second, different antigenic determinant on the HBV core; important indicator of transmissibility |
| HBeAb | Antibody to e antigen; indicates low transmissibility |
| Delta agent | Small RNA virus with HBsAg envelope; defective virus that replicates only in HBV-infected cells |
| Window period | The period between the end of detection of HBsAg and the beginning of detection HBsAb |

**Table II-4-7.** Hepatitis B Serology

| | HBsAg HBeAg* HBV-DNA | HBcAb IgM | HBcAb IgG | HBeAb | HBsAb |
|---|---|---|---|---|---|
| Acute infection | + | + | − | − | − |
| Window period | − | +/− | + | + | − |
| Prior infection | − | − | + | + | + |
| Immunization | − | − | − | − | + |
| Chronic infection | + | − | + | +/− | − |

*HBeAg—Correlates with viral proliferation and infectivity.

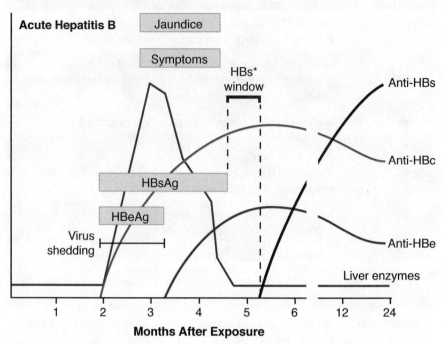

*The window is the time between the disappearance of the HBsAg and before HBsAb is detected.

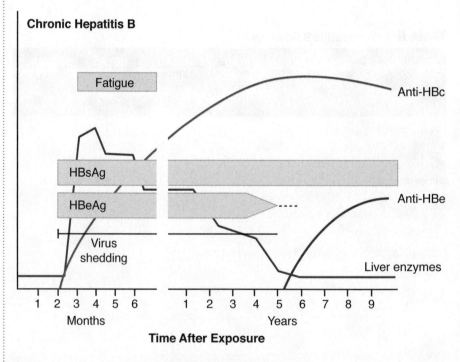

**Figure II-4-11.** Hepatitis B

# DNA VIRUSES: CHARACTERISTICS

All DNA viruses:

- Are double-stranded, except parvovirus
- Are icosahedral, except poxviruses, which are a brick-shaped "complex"
- Replicate their DNA in the nucleus, except poxvirus

**Table II-4-8.** DNA Viruses*

| Virus Family | DNA type | Virion-Associated Polymerase | Envelope | DNA Replicates in: | Major Viruses |
|---|---|---|---|---|---|
| Parvovirus | ssDNA | No | Naked | Nucleus | B19 |
| Papillomavirus Polyomavirus | dsDNA, circular | No | Naked | Nucleus | Papilloma, Polyoma |
| Adenovirus | dsDNA, linear | No | Naked | Nucleus | Adenoviruses |
| Hepadnavirus | Partially dsDNA, circular | Yes*** | Enveloped | Nucleus, RNA intermediate | Hepatitis B |
| Herpes virus | dsDNA, linear | No | Enveloped (nuclear) | Nucleus; virus assembled in nucleus | HSV, Varicella-zoster, Epstein-Barr, Cytomegalovirus |
| Poxvirus | dsDNA, linear | Yes** | Enveloped | Cytoplasm | Variola, Vaccinia, Molluscum contagiosum |

\* Mnemonic: Pardon Papa As He Has Pox

\** **Poxviruses** have a **virion-associated transcriptase** (DNA dependent RNA polymerase), so it can transcribe its own DNA in the cytoplasm and make all of the enzymes and factors necessary for replication of the poxvirus DNA in the cytoplasm.

\*** Hepadnaviruses: DNA viruses that carry a DNA polymerase with reverse transcriptase activity to synthesize an RNA intermediate that is then used to make the genomic DNA. Hepatitis B is partially double-stranded with one complete strand.

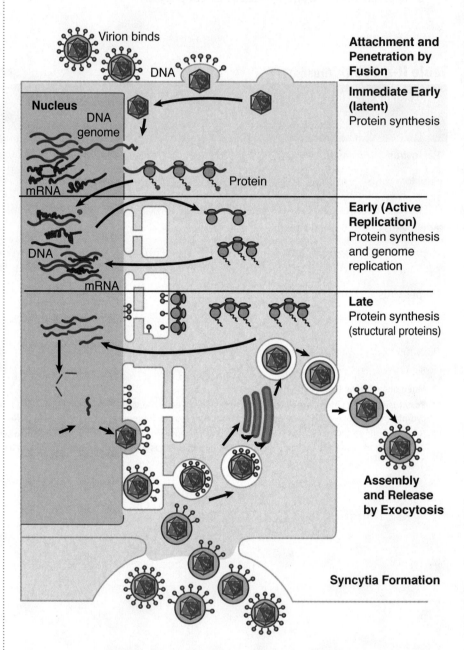

Attachment and
Penetration by
Fusion

Immediate Early
(latent)
Protein synthesis

Virion binds

DNA

Nucleus

DNA
genome

mRNA

Protein

Early (Active
Replication)
Protein synthesis
and genome
replication

DNA

mRNA

Late
Protein synthesis
(structural proteins)

Assembly
and Release
by Exocytosis

Syncytia Formation

**Figure II-4-12.** DNA Virus: Life Cycle of Herpes

# PARVOVIRIDAE

**Virus Characteristics**

- ssDNA virus, linear
- Naked, icosahedral

**Figure II-4-13.** Parvovirus

Viruses of Medical Importance—B19

# B19

**Reservoir**—human respiratory tract

**Transmission**—respiratory route, fomites, vertical transmission

**Pathogenesis**—B19 infects immature (cycling) erythroid progenitor cells, resulting in cell lysis. The resulting **anemia** is only clinically significant in patients with **sickle-cell anemia** and may result in **aplastic crisis**.

**Diseases**

- Children/adults
    - Fifth disease, erythema infectiosum, slapped cheek fever
    - 7–10 day incubation
    - Nonspecific "flu-like" symptoms followed by raised, indurated facial rash
    - Rash and arthralgias (adults predominantly) are due to immune complexes in the skin and joints
- Fetus
    - Severe anemia
    - Congestive heart failure
    - Hydrops fetalis
    - Spontaneous abortion

**Diagnosis**—serology and molecular analysis

**Treatment**—supportive care

## Key Vignette Clues

**B19**

- School-aged child with fever and indurated facial rash
- Pregnant woman with flu-like symptoms → hydrops fetalis or spontaneous abortion

## Differential Diagnosis

- Measles
- Mumps
- Rubella
- HHV-6
- Coxsackie virus A16
- *S. pyogenes*

# PAPILLOMAVIRIDAE

**Figure II-4-14.** Papillomavirus

**Virus Characteristics**

- dsDNA virus, circular
- Naked, icosahedral

**Viruses of Medical Importance**

- Human papilloma virus (HPV)

## Human Papilloma Virus (HPV)

**Distinguishing Characteristics**

- Over 75 serotypes
- Different serotypes are associated with different clinical presentations

**Reservoir**—human skin and genitals

**Transmission**—direct contact, fomites

**Pathogenesis**

- Virus infects basal layer of the skin and mucous membranes
- Hyperkeratosis leads to the formation of the "wart"
- Malignancy may result: **E6 and E7 inhibit tumor-suppressor genes p53 and Rb, respectively.**

**Diseases**

- Cutaneous warts
  - **Common warts** (serotypes 2 and 4) are predominantly found on the hands and fingers.
  - **Plantar warts** (serotype 1) are predominantly found on soles of feet and tend to be deeper and more painful.
- Anogenital warts (Condylomata acuminata)
  - Also cause laryngeal papillomas in infants and sexually active adults
  - **Over 90% of genital warts are serotypes 6 and 11 (benign)**
  - **Serotypes 16 and 18** (31 and 35) are preneoplastic (cervical intraepithelial neoplasia; CIN)
  - **95% of cases of CINs contain HPV DNA**
  - Viral genes E6 and E7 inactivate tumor-suppressor genes

## Key Vignette Clues

**HPV**

- Warts
- Cervical intraepithelial neoplasia
- Biopsy or Pap smear—koilocytic cells

## COMLEX Note

It is important to recall the infectious agents associated with cancer

**Viruses**

- HPV
- EBV
- HBV, HCV
- HHVG
- HTLV

**Bacteria**

- *H. pylori*

**Parasites**

- *S. hematobium*

**Diagnosis**

- Cutaneous—clinical grounds
- Genital—finding of koilocytic cells (cells with perinuclear cytoplasmic vacuolization and nuclear enlargement) in Pap smears
- In situ DNA probes and PCR can be used to confirm any diagnosis and type the HPV strain involved

**Treatment**

- Cryotherapy, electrocautery, or chemical means (salicylic acid)
- Imiquimod (induces proinflammatory cytokines), interferon-$\alpha$, and virus-specific cidofovir

**Prevention**

- A vaccine composed of HPV capsid proteins produced by recombinant DNA technology
- Safe sex practices

# POLYOMAVIRIDAE

**Table II-4-9.** Summary of Polyomaviridae

| Virus | Reservoir/Transmission | Pathogenesis | Disease | Diagnosis | Treatment |
|-------|------------------------|--------------|---------|-----------|-----------|
| BK | Respiratory | Latent infection in kidney | Renal disease in AIDS patients | ELISA, PCR | Supportive |
| JC | Respiratory | Infection in oligodendrocytes = demyelination | Progressive multifocal leukoencephalopathy (PML) in AIDS and transplant patients | ELISA, PCR | Supportive |

## Key Vignette Clues

### Adenovirus

- Young adults: ARD
- Swimmers and shipyard workers: nonpurulent conjunctivitis
- Daycare: viral gastroenteritis

## Differential Diagnosis

- Acute respiratory disease and pneumonia
  - Influenza
  - *S. pyogenes*
  - *S. pneumoniae/K. pneumoniae*
- Pharyngoconjunctivitis
  - *S. pneumoniae*
  - *H. influenzae*

# ADENOVIRIDAE

## Virus Characteristics

- dsDNA, nonenveloped
- Hexons, pentons, and fibers

## Viruses of Medical Importance

- Adenovirus
- ~49 serotypes

# Adenovirus

**Reservoir**—ubiquitous in humans and animals

**Transmission**—respiratory, fecal-oral, direct contact

## Pathogenesis

- Penton fibers act as hemagglutinin.
- Purified penton fibers are toxic to cells.
- Virus is lytic in permissive cells and can be chronic or oncogenic in nonpermissive hosts. The adenoviruses are the standard example of a permissive host (where virus is produced) and nonpermissive host (where the virus is not produced, but transformed).

## Disease

- Acute respiratory disease (ARD) and pneumonia
  - Spring and winter peak incidence
  - Children, young military recruits and college students serotypes 4, 7, and 21
- Pharyngoconjunctivitis
  - Swimming pool conjunctivitis, pink eye
  - Fever, sore throat, coryza, and red eyes
  - Nonpurulent
- Acute hemorrhagic cystitis
  - Boys ages 5 to 15 predominantly
  - Dysuria, hematuria
- Gastroenteritis
  - Daycare, not as common as rotavirus
  - Serotypes 40 and 41

**Diagnosis**—serology; ELISA

**Treatment**—supportive care

**Prevention**—live, nonattenuated vaccine

# HEPADNAVIRIDAE (see previous discussion)

# HERPESVIRIDAE

**Virus Characteristics**

- Large dsDNA
- Enveloped, icosahedral
- Derives envelope from nuclear membrane
- **Intranuclear inclusion bodies**
- **Establishes latency**

**Figure II-4-15.** Herpesvirus

**Viruses of Medical Importance**

- Herpes simplex virus 1 and 2 (HSV)
- Varicella-zoster virus (VZV)
- Epstein-Barr virus (EBV)
- Cytomegalovirus (CMV)
- Human herpesvirus 6 (HHV-6)
- Human herpesvirus 8 (HHV-8)

# HSV-1 and HSV-2

**Reservoir**—human mucosa and ganglia

**Transmission**—close personal contact (i.e., kissing, sexual contact)

**Pathogenesis**—HSV establishes infection in the mucosal epithelial cells and leads to the formation of vesicles. The virus travels up the ganglion to establish lifelong latent infection. Stress triggers reactivation of virus in nerve and recurrence of vesicles.

**Diseases—The rule of thumb is that HSV-1 infections generally occur above the waist and HSV-2 infections generally occur below the waist.**

**HSV-1**

- Gingivostomatitis and cold sores
    - Blister-like lesions on the oral mucosa
    - **Latent in trigeminal ganglion**
- Keratoconjunctivitis
    - Generally with lid swelling and vesicles
    - Dendritic ulcers may be seen
    - Untreated and repeat attacks may result in blindness

## COMLEX Note

It is essential to recall the sites of latency for the herpes viral infections

HSV-1—trigemial

HSV-2—sacral

VZV—dorsal

EBV—B cells

CMV—mononuclear cells

## Key Vignette Clues

**HSV-1 and HSV-2**

- Cold sores/genital vesicles
- Keratoconjunctivitis
- Meningoencephalitis/encephalitis
- Neonatal disseminated/encephalitis
- Tzanck smear, Cowdry type A inclusion bodies

- Encephalitis
  - Fever, headache, and confusion
  - **Focal temporal lesions** and perivascular cuffing
  - If untreated, 70% mortality rate
  - Most common cause of viral encephalitis in the United States

**HSV-2**

- Genital infections
  - Painful genital vesicles
  - Systemic effects can include fever, malaise, and myalgia
  - **Latency in the sacral nerve ganglia**
- Neonatal herpes
  - Infection during passage through infected birth canal
  - Infections are usually severe:
    - ° Disseminated with liver involvement and high mortality
    - ° Encephalitis, high mortality
    - ° Skin, eyes, or mouth

## Differential Diagnosis

- *C. albicans*
- Coxsackie A16 (hand, foot, and mouth)
- *T. pallidum*
- *H. ducreyi*

**Diagnosis**

- Oral lesions—clinical
- Encephalitis
  - PCR on CSF
  - Large numbers of RBCs in CSF
- Genital infections—Tzank smear to show the formation of multinucleated giant cells and Cowdry type A intranuclear inclusions has been largely replaced by immunofluorescent staining, which can distinguish HSV-1 from HSV-2

**Treatment**—Acyclovir is a nucleoside analog that is only activated in cells infected with HSV-1, HSV-2 or VZV. This is because the virus thymidine kinase is required to activate the drug by placing the first phosphate on the drug, followed by the phosphorylation via cellular enzymes. Resistance to acyclovir occurs due to a mutation in the thymidine kinase. Famciclovir, valacyclovir, and penciclovir are alternatives if resistance develops.

# Varicella Zoster Virus (VZV)

**Reservoir**—human mucosa and nerves

**Transmission**—respiratory droplets

**Pathogenesis**—VZV enters the respiratory tract → replicates in the local lymph nodes → primary viremia → spleen and liver → secondary viremia → skin (rash) → **latent in the dorsal root ganglia.** Reactivation of virus due to stress or immunocompromise causes vesicular lesions and severe nerve pain.

**Diseases**

- Chickenpox
    - Fever, pharyngitis, malaise, rhinitis
    - **Asynchronous rash**
    - One of the 5 "classic" childhood exanthems, less common due to vaccination
- Shingles
    - Zoster
    - Pain and vesicles restricted to one dermatome
    - Fifth or sixth decade of life
    - **Reactivation of latent infection**

**Diagnosis**

- Tzanck smear—Cowdry type A, intranuclear inclusions
- Antigen detection by PCR

**Treatment**

- Healthy adults with shingles—oral acyclovir
- Immunocompromised—IV acyclovir
- Aspirin contraindicated due to association with Reye syndrome

**Prevention**

- Live, attenuated vaccine, booster for 60-year-old to prevent shingles
- VZIG (varicella-zoster immunoglobulin) for postexposure prophylaxis of the immunocompromised

## Key Vignette Clues

**VZV**

- Chickenpox: unvaccinated child with asynchronous rash
- Shingles: elderly with unilateral vesicular rash that follows dermatome
- Tzank smear with Cowdry type A intranuclear inclusions and syncytia

## Differential Diagnosis

- HSV
- *S. pyogenes*/*S. aureus* (impetigo)
- Smallpox

## Key Vignette Clues

**EBV**

- Young adult with fever, lymphadenopathy, splenomegaly

- Downey type II atypical T lymphocytes reach 70% in blood

- Heterophile (monospot) positive

# Epstein-Barr Virus (EBV)

**Reservoir**—humans

## Transmission

- Saliva

- 90% of the adult population is seropositive

## Pathogenesis

- Virus infects nasopharyngeal epithelial cells, salivary and lymphoid tissues → latent infection of B cells (EBV binds to CD21 and acts as a B-cell mitogen) → results in the production of atypical reactive T cells (Downey cells), which may constitute up to 70% of the WBC count

- Heterophile antibodies are produced (due to B cell mitogenesis)

## Diseases

- Heterophile-positive mononucleosis, "kissing disease"
    - Fatigue, fever, sore throat, lymphadenopathy and splenomegaly
    - **Latency in B cells**
- Lymphoproliferative disease
    - Occurs in immunocompromised patients
    - T cells can't control the B-cell growth
- Hairy oral leukoplakia
    - Hyperproliferation of lingual epithelial cells
    - AIDS patients

## Malignancies

- Burkitt lymphoma
    - Cancer of the maxilla, mandible, abdomen
    - Africa
    - Malaria cofactor
    - AIDS patients
    - Translocation juxtaposes c-myc oncogene to a very active promoter, such as an immunoglobulin gene promoter
- Nasopharyngeal carcinoma
    - Asia
    - Tumor cells of epithelial origin
- Hodgkin lymphoma

## Differential Diagnosis

- CMV

- *T. gondii*

- HAV, HBV, HCV, etc.

- HHV-6

- HIV

## Diagnosis

- Heterophile-antibody positive (IgM antibodies that recognize the Paul-Bunnell antigen on sheep and bovine RBCs)

## Treatment

- For uncomplicated mononucleosis, treatment is symptomatic

# Cytomegalovirus (CMV)

**Reservoir**—humans

**Transmission**—saliva, sexual, parenteral, in utero

**Pathogenesis**

- CMV infects the salivary gland epithelial cells and establishes a persistent infection in fibroblasts, epithelial cells, and macrophages
- **Latency in mononuclear cells**

**Disease**

- Cytomegalic inclusion disease
  - Most common in utero infection in U.S.
  - Disease ranges from infected with no obvious defects to severe cytomegalic inclusion disease characterized by jaundice, hepatosplenomegaly, thrombocytic purpura ("blueberry muffin baby"), pneumonitis, and CNS damage to death
- Mononucleosis (children and adults)—heterophile-negative mononucleosis
- Interstitial pneumonitis to severe systemic infection—due to reactivation in a transplanted organ or in an AIDS patient
- CMV retinitis—common in AIDS patients

## Key Vignette Clues

**CMV**

- Heterophile-negative mononucleosis in children and adults
- Neonate with jaundice, hepatosplenomegaly, thrombocytic purpura
- Owl-eye intranuclear inclusion bodies in biopsy

## Differential Diagnosis

- *T. gondii*
- EBV
- Rubella

## Key Vignette Clues

**HHV-6**

Infant with fever → lacy body rash

## Differential Diagnosis

- Measles
- Rubella
- B19
- *S. pyogenes* (scarlet fever)
- Enterovirus
- HHV-7

## Key Vignette Clues

**HHV-8**

AIDS patient with sarcoma

## Differential Diagnosis

*B. henselae* (bacillary angiomatosis in AIDS patients)

**Diagnosis**

- Owl-eye inclusion ("sight-o-megalo-virus") in biopsy material and urine
- Basophilic intranuclear inclusions
- Serology, DNA detection, virus culture

**Treatment**

- In healthy—supportive
- In immuncompromised (AIDS and transplant patients)—ganciclovir/foscarnet ± human immunoglobulin. Resistance to ganciclovir through hL97 gene.

**Prevention**

- Safe sex
- Screening of blood and organ donors

# HHV-6

**Reservoir**—humans

**Transmission**—respiratory droplets

**Pathogenesis**—replicates in peripheral blood mononuclear cells

**Disease**

- Roseola (exanthema subitum)
- Fever for ~3–5 days followed by a lacy body rash

**Diagnosis**—clinical

**Treatment**—symptomatic

# HHV-8

**Reservoir**—humans

**Transmission**—sexual contact, saliva, vertical, transplantation

**Pathogenesis**—HHV-8 has a gene that turns on vascular endothelial growth factor (VEGF), which plays a direct role in the development of Kaposi sarcoma

**Disease**—Kaposi sarcoma

**Diagnosis**

- Clinical
- Serology, PCR

**Treatment**—none

**Table II-4-10.** Summary of Herpesvirus Infections

| Virus | Site of Primary Infection | Clinical Presentation of Primary Infection | Site of Latency | Clinical Presentation of Recurrent Infection |
|-------|---------------------------|--------------------------------------------|-----------------|----------------------------------------------|
| HSV-1 | Mucosa | Gingivostomatitis, keratoconjunctivitis, pharyngitis | Trigeminal ganglia | Cold sores |
| HSV-2 | Mucosa | Genital herpes, neonatal herpes | Sacral ganglia | Genital herpes |
| VZV | Mucosa | Chickenpox | Dorsal root ganglia | Shingles (zoster) |
| EBV | Mucosal epithelial cells, B cells | Mononucleosis (heterophile ⊕) | B cells | Asymptomatic shedding of virus |
| CMV | Mononuclear cells, epithelial cells | Mononucleosis (heterophile –), cytomegalic inclusion disease | Mononuclear cells | Asymptomatic shedding of virus |
| HHV-6 | Mononuclear cells | Roseola infantum | Mononuclear cells | Asymptomatic shedding of virus |
| HHV-8 | Dermis | Kaposi sarcoma | ? | ? |

# POXVIRIDAE

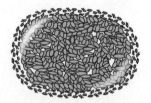

**Figure II-4-16.** Poxvirus

### Virus Characteristics

- Large dsDNA, enveloped
- Complex morphology
- Replicates in the cytoplasm
- Potential biowarfare agent

### Viruses of Medical Importance

- Variola
- Vaccinia (vaccine strain)
- Molluscum contagiosum
- Orf
- Monkeypox

## Variola/Smallpox

### Reservoir

- Humans
- Variola has 1 serotype, which made eradication (1977) possible

### Transmission—respiratory route

### Pathogenesis

- Via inhalation, the virus enters the upper respiratory tract and disseminates via lymphatics → viremia
- After a secondary viremia, the virus infects all dermal tissues and internal organs
- Classic "pocks"

### Disease

- 5–17 day incubation
- Prodrome of flu-like illness for 2–4 days
- Prodrome followed by rash, which begins in the mouth and spreads to the face, arms and legs, hands, and feet and can cover the entire body within 24 hours
- All vesicles are in the same stage of development (synchronous rash)

## Key Vignette Clues

**Variola/Smallpox**

- Virus extinct
- Synchronous rash begins in mouth → face and body
- Guarnieri bodies (intracytoplasmic inclusions)

## COMLEX Note

Do not ignore smallpox because it has been eradicated. It is atop the CDC's list of biowarfare agents.

**Diagnosis**

- Clinical
- Guarnieri bodies found in infected cells (intracytoplasmic)

**Treatment**—supportive care

**Prevention**—live, attenuated vaccine

# Molluscum contagiosum

**Reservoir**—humans

**Transmission**—direct contact (sexual) and fomites

**Pathogenesis**—replication in dermis

**Disease**

- Single or multiple (<20) benign, wart-like tumors
- Molluscum bodies in central caseous material (eosinophilic cytoplasmic inclusion bodies)

**Diagnosis**

- Clinical (warts are umbilicated)
- Eosinophilic cytoplasmic inclusion bodies

**Treatment**

- In healthy persons, self limiting
- Ritonavir, cidofovir in immunocompromised

# RNA VIRUSES: CHARACTERISTICS

**General Characteristics**

- All RNA viruses are single stranded (ss), except Reovirus.
- ss(−)RNA viruses carry RNA-dependent RNA polymerase.
- A virion-associated polymerase is also carried by:
  - Reovirus
  - Arenavirus
  - Retrovirus (reverse transcriptase)
- Most are enveloped; the **only naked ones** are:
  - Picornavirus
  - Calicivirus and Hepevirus
  - Reovirus
- Some are segmented (different genes on different pieces of RNA)
  - **Reovirus**
  - **Orthomyxovirus**
  - **Bunyavirus**
  - **Arenavirus**

**Differential Diagnosis**

VZV

**Key Vignette Clues**

**Molluscum Contagiosum**

- Young adult (wrestling, swim team)
- Umbilicated warts
- Eosinophilic cytoplasmic inclusion bodies

**Differential Diagnosis**

- HSV
- HPV
- VZV
- *S. schenckii*
- *M. marinum*

# POSITIVE-STRANDED RNA VIRUSES

**Table II-4-11.** Positive-Stranded RNA Viruses*

| Virus Family | RNA Structure | Virion-Associated Polymerase | Envelope | Shape | Multiplies in | Major Viruses |
|---|---|---|---|---|---|---|
| Calicivirus | ss(+)RNA Linear Non-segmented | No polymerase | Naked | Icosahedral | Cytoplasm | Norwalk agent<br>Noro-like virus |
| Hepevirus | ↓ | ↓ | ↓ | ↓ | ↓ | Hepatitis E |
| Picornavirus | ss(+)RNA Linear Non-segmented | No polymerase | Naked | Icosahedral | Cytoplasm | Polio**<br>ECHO<br>Enteroviruses<br>Rhino<br>Coxsackie<br>Hepatitis A |
| Flavivirus | ss(+)RNA Linear Non-segmented | No polymerase | Enveloped | Icosahedral | Cytoplasm | Yellow fever<br>Dengue<br>St. Louis encephalitis<br>Hepatitis C<br>West Nile virus |
| Togavirus | ss(+)RNA Linear Non-segmented | No polymerase | Enveloped | Icosahedral | Cytoplasm | Rubella<br>WEE, EEE<br>Venezuelan encephalitis |
| Coronavirus | ss(+)RNA Linear Non-segmented | No polymerase | Enveloped | Helical | Cytoplasm | Coronaviruses<br>SARS-CoV |
| Retrovirus | Diploid ss (+) RNA Linear Non-segmented | RNA dep. DNA polymerase | Enveloped | Icosahedral or truncated conical | Nucleus | HIV<br>HTLV<br>Sarcoma |

\*   Mnemonic:   (+)RNA Viruses: Call Henry Pico and Flo To Come Rightaway

\*\*  Mnemonic:   Picornaviruses: PEE Co Rn A Viruses
              Polio, Entero, Echo, Coxsackie, Rhino, Hep A

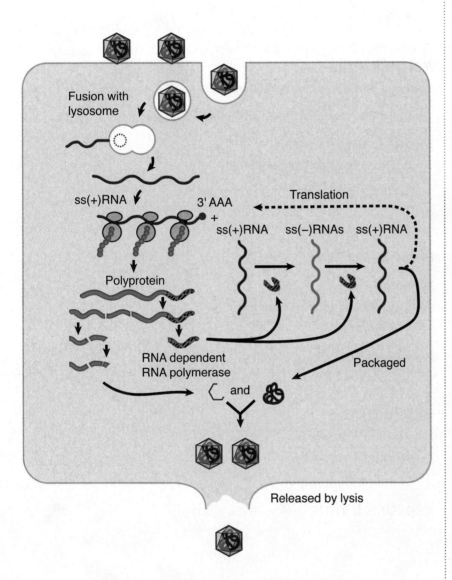

**Figure II-4-17.** Positive-Sense RNA Virus Life Cycle

## CALICIVIRIDAE

**Family Characteristics**

- Naked, icosahedral
- Positive-sense ssRNA

**Viruses of Medical Importance**

- Norwalk virus (Norovirus)
- Noro-like virus

## Norwalk Virus

**Reservoir**—human gastrointestinal tract

**Transmission**—fecal-oral route, contaminated food and water

**Disease**—acute gastroenteritis

- Watery; no blood or pus in stools
- Nausea, vomiting, diarrhea
- 60% of all nonbacterial gastroenteritis in U.S.
- Outbreak of viral gastroenteritis in cruise ships attributed to Norovirus

**Diagnosis**—RIA, ELISA

**Treatment**

- No specific antiviral treatment
- Self-limiting

**Prevention**—handwashing

## HEPEVIRIDAE

- Naked, icosahedral
- Positive-sense ssRNA

## Hepatitis E Virus (previously discussed)

### Key Vignette Clues

**Norwalk Virus**

- School-aged child → adult
- Acute viral gastroenteritis (noninflammatory)

### Differential Diagnosis

- Rotavirus
- Adenovirus
- ETEC
- *S. aureus/B. cereus* food poisoning
- *G. lamblia*
- *C. difficile*

# PICORNAVIRIDAE

**Figure II-4-18.** Picornavirus

## Family Characteristics

- Small, naked, icosahedral
- Positive-sense ssRNA
- Summer/fall peak incidence
- Resistant to alcohol, detergents (naked capsid)
- Divided into genera:

    Enteroviruses:

    - Fecal-oral transmission, do *not* cause diarrhea
    - Peak age group <9 years
    - Stable at pH 3

    Rhinoviruses:

    - Not stable under acidic conditions
    - Growth at 33°C

    Heparnavirus

## Viruses of Medical Importance

- Enteroviruses (acid stable)
    - Polio virus
    - Coxsackie virus A
    - Coxsackie virus B
    - Echoviruses
- Rhinoviruses (acid labile)
- Heparnaviruses—HAV

## COMLEX Note

You must be able to differentiate between bacterial and viral meningitis.

|  | **Bacterial** | **Viral** |
|---|---|---|
| Patient's condition | severe | less severe |
| CSF | ↑ PMN's | ↑ lymphocytes |
| glucose | decreased | normal |
| protein | increased | normal-slightly increased |

**Table II-4-12.** Summary of Picornaviridae

| Virus | Transmission | Pathogenesis | Diseases | Diagnosis | Treatment*/Prevention |
|---|---|---|---|---|---|
| **Enteroviruses** | | | | | |
| Polio | Fecal-oral | Virus targets anterior horn motor neurons | Asymptomatic to FUO; aseptic meningitis; paralytic polio (flaccid asymmetric paralysis, no sensory loss) | Serology (virus absent from CSF) | No specific antiviral/live vaccine (Sabin); killed vaccine (Salk) |
| | | Neural fatigue (?) | Post-Polio Syndrome | Patient with polio decades earlier, progressive muscle atrophy | |
| Coxsackie A | Fecal-oral | Fecal-oral spread with potential for dissemination to other organs; often asymptomatic with viral shedding | Hand, foot, and mouth (A16); herpangina; aseptic meningitis; acute lymphoglandular pharyngitis; common cold | Virus isolation from throat, stool, or CSF | No specific treatment/handwashing |
| Coxsackie B | Fecal-oral | As above | Bornholm disease (devil's grip); aseptic meningitis; severe systemic disease of newborns; **myocarditis** | As above | No specific/handwashing |
| Echoviruses | Fecal-oral | As above | Fever and rash of unknown origin; aseptic meningitis | As above | No specific/handwashing |
| **Rhinovirus** | | | | | |
| Rhinovirus | Respiratory | Acid labile; grows at 33°C; over 100 serotypes | Common cold; #1 cause, peak summer/fall | Clinical | No specific/handwashing |
| **Heparnavirus** | | | | | |
| HAV | Fecal-oral | Virus targets hepatocytes; liver function is impaired | Infectious hepatitis | IgM to HAV serology | No specific/killed vaccine and hyperimmune serum |

*Definition of abbreviations:* FUO, fever of unknown origin.

*Pleconaril (blocks uncoating by fitting into cleft in receptor-binding canyon of picornavirus capsid) is available on a limited basis. Must be administered early.

| **Differential Diagnosis** | | | | | |
|---|---|---|---|---|---|
| Polio | Coxsackie A | Coxsackie B | Echoviruses | Rhinovirus | HAV |
| *C. botulinum*, SLE, WNV, EEE, WEE, VEE | HSV, SLE, WNV, EEE, WEE, VEE, rhinovirus | VZV (reactivated, prodrome), SLE, WNV, EEE, WEE, VEE | HHV-6, B19, measles | Coronavirus, coxsackie A | HBV, HCV, HEV |

# FLAVIVIRIDAE

### Family Characteristics

- Enveloped, icosahedral
- Positive-sense ssRNA
- Arthropod-borne (arboviruses)

### Viruses of Medical Importance

- St. Louis encephalitis virus (SLE)
- West Nile encephalitis virus (WNV)
- Dengue virus
- Yellow fever virus (YFV)
- Hepatitis C virus (HCV; discussed with the hepatitis viruses)

**Table II-4-13.** Summary of Flaviviridae

| Virus | Vector | Host(s) | Disease | Diagnosis | Prevention |
|-------|--------|---------|---------|-----------|------------|
| SLE | Mosquito (*Culex*) | Birds | Encephalitis | Serology, hemagglutination inhibition, ELISA, latex particle agglutination | Vector control |
| WNV | Mosquito (*Culex*) | Birds (killed by virus) | Encephalitis | As above | Vector control |
| Dengue | Mosquito (*Aedes*) | Humans (monkeys) | Break bone fever (rash, muscle and joint pain), reinfection, can result in dengue hemorrhagic shock | As above | Vector control |
| YFV | Mosquito (*Aedes*) | Humans (monkeys) | Yellow fever: liver, kidney, heart, and GI (black vomit) damage | As above | Vector control/live, attenuated vaccine |

*Definition of abbreviations:* FUO, fever of unknown origin; SLE, St. Louis encephalitis virus; WNV, West Nile encephalitis virus; YFV, yellow fever virus.

| **Differential Diagnosis** | | | |
|------|------|------|------|
| SLE | WNV | Dengue | YFV |
| WNV, EEE, WEE, VEE | SLE, EEE, WEE, VEE | Coxsackie B, *R. rickettsii*, Ebola, YFV | HAV, HBV, HCV, HEV, EBV |

# TOGAVIRIDAE

**Family Characteristics**

- Enveloped, icosahedral
- Positive-sense ssRNA

**Figure II-4-19.** Togavirus

**Viruses of Medical Importance**

- **Alphaviruses (arboviruses)**
  - Eastern equine encephalitis virus (EEE)
  - Western equine encephalitis virus (WEE)
  - Venezuelan equine encephalitis virus (VEE)
- **Rubivirus**
  - Rubella

**Table II-4-14.** Summary of Togaviridae

| Virus | Vector | Host | Disease(s) | Diagnosis | Prevention |
|---|---|---|---|---|---|
| EEE, WEE, VEE | Mosquito | Birds, horses | Encephalitis | Cytopathology, immunofluorescence, RT-PCR, serology | Killed vaccines for EEE and WEE |
| Rubella | None | humans | German measles (erythematous rash begins on face, progresses to torso) | Serology | Live, attenuated vaccine |
| | | | CRS* | | |

*Definition of abbreviations:* CRS, congenital rubella syndrome; EEE, Eastern equine encephalitis virus; VEE, Venezuelan equine encephalitis virus; WEE, Western equine encephalitis virus.

*Congenital rubella syndrome—patent ductus arteriosis, pulmonary stenosis, cataracts, microcephaly, deafness. The effects are more serious if the maternal infection is acquired during the first 16 weeks' gestation.

| Differential Diagnosis | |
|---|---|
| EEE, WEE, VEE | Rubella |
| SLE, WNV | Measles, HHV-6, B19, echoviruses CMV, *T. gondii*, *L. monocytogenes* |

# CORONAVIRIDAE

## Family Characteristics

- Enveloped, helical
- Positive-sense ssRNA
- Hemagglutinin molecules make up peplomers on virus surface, which give shape like sun with corona

## Viruses of Medical Importance

- **Coronavirus**
- **Severe acute respiratory syndrome coronavirus (SARS-CoV)**

# Coronavirus

- Second most common cause of the common cold
- Winter/spring peak incidence

# SARS-CoV

**Reservoir**—birds and small mammals (civet cats)

**Transmission**

- Respiratory droplets
- Virus is also found in urine, sweat, and feces
- Original case is thought to have jumped from animal to human

**Disease**—severe acute respiratory syndrome (SARS)

- Atypical pneumonia
- Clinical case definition includes: fever of >100.4°F, flu-like illness, dry cough, dyspnea, and progressive hypoxia
- Chest x-ray may show patchy distribution of focal interstitial infiltrates

**Diagnosis**

- Includes clinical presentation and prior history of travel to endemic area or an association with someone who recently traveled to endemic area
- Lab tests: detection of antibodies to SARS-CoV, RT-PCR, and isolation of the virus in culture

**Treatment**

- Supportive
- Ribavirin and interferon are promising

## Key Vignette Clues

**SARS-CoV**

- Patient with acute respiratory distress
- Travel to Far East or Toronto
- Winter/spring peak incidence

## Differential Diagnosis

- *L. pneumophila*
- *S. pneumoniae*
- *C. pneumoniae*
- *M. pneumoniae*
- Influenza virus

## RETROVIRIDAE

### Family Characteristics

- Positive-sense ssRNA
- Virion-associated reverse transcriptase
- Enveloped

**Figure II-4-20.** Retrovirus

### Viruses of Medical Importance

- **Oncovirus group**
  - **Human T-cell leukemia/lymphotropic (HTLV)**
    - Adult T-cell leukemia
    - C-type particle (most oncoviruses, centrally located electron-dense nucleocapsid)
    - Japan, Caribbean, southern U.S.
- **Lentivirus group—human immunodeficiency virus (HIV);** acquired immunodeficiency syndrome

### Key Vignette Clues

**HIV**

- Homosexual male, IV drug user, sexually active adult
- Decreasing CD4 cell count
- Opportunistic infections
- Fatigue, weight loss, lymphadenopathy, low-grade fever

## Human Immunodeficiency Virus (HIV)

### Distinguishing Characteristics

- The HIV virion contains:
  - Enveloped, truncated, conical capsid (type D retrovirus)
  - Two copies of the ss(+)RNA
  - RNA-dependent DNA polymerase (reverse transcriptase)
  - Integrase
  - Protease

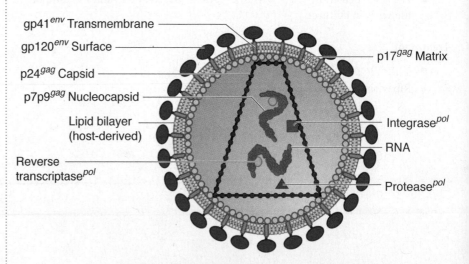

**Figure II-4-21.** Structure and Genes of HIV

**Table II-4-15.** Important HIV Genes and Their Functions

| Gene | Product(s) | Function |
|------|-----------|----------|
| **Structural Genes** | | |
| *Gag* | Group-specific antigens | Structural proteins |
| | p24 | Capsid protein |
| | p7p9 | Core nucleocapsid proteins |
| | p17 | Matrix protein |
| *Pol* | Reverse transcriptase | Produces dsDNA provirus (extremely error-prone, causes genetic drift of envelope glycoprotein |
| | Integrase | Viral DNA integration into host cell DNA |
| | Protease | Cleaves viral polyprotein |
| *Env* | gp120 | Surface protein that binds to CD4 and coreceptors CCR5 (macrophages) and CXCR4 (T cells); tropism; genetic drift |
| | gp41 | Transmembrane protein for viral fusion to host cell |
| **Regulatory Genes** | | |
| *LTR* (U3, U5) | DNA, long terminal repeats | Integration and viral gene expression |
| *Tat* | Transactivator | Transactivator of transcription (upregulation); spliced gene |
| *Rev* | Regulatory protein | Upregulates transport of unspliced and spliced transcripts to the cell cytoplasm; a spliced gene |
| *Nef* | **Regulatory protein** | **Decreases CD4 and MHC I expression on host cells; manipulates T-cell activation pathways; required for progression to AIDS** |

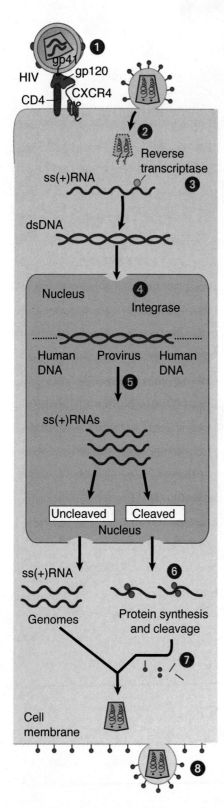

1. Surface gp120 of HIV binds to CD4 of T-helper cells, macrophages, microglia, and coreceptors (*CCR5* and *CXCR4*) found on macrophages and TH cells, respectively.

2. HIV is taken into the cell, losing the envelope; the RNA is uncoated.

3. The RNA is copied using the virion-associated reverse transcriptase; ultimately dsDNA with long terminal repeats is made.

4. The DNA and integrase migrate to nucleus and the DNA is integrated into host DNA forming the **provirus**.

   The provirus remains in the host DNA.

   The rate of viral replication is regulated by the activity of the regulatory proteins (*tat/rev*, *nef*, etc).

   *Tat* upregulates transcription.

   *Rev* regulates transport of RNA to cytoplasm.

   Co-infections (e.g., mycobacterial) stimulate the HIV-infected cells to produce more virus.

5. Transcription produces ss(+)RNA, some cleaved and some remain intact.
   - Cleaved RNA will be used as mRNA.
   - Uncleaved RNA is used as genomic RNA.

6. Translation produces the proteins some of which are polyproteins that are cleaved by the HIV protease.

7. Assembly

8. Maturation/release of virus

**Figure II-4-22.** Retrovirus Life Cycle: HIV

**Reservoir**—human TH cells and macrophages

**Transmission:**

- Sexual contact
- Bloodborne (transfusions, dirty needles)
- Vertical

**Disease**—acquired immunodeficiency syndrome (AIDS)

- Asymptomatic infection → persistent, generalized lymphadenopathy → symptomatic → AIDS-defining conditions
- Homozygous *CCR5* mutation → immune
- Heterozygous *CCR5* mutation → slow course
- The course of the illness follows the decline in CD4+ T cells (Figure II-4-23)
- Long-term survivors may result when virus lacks functional *nef* protein

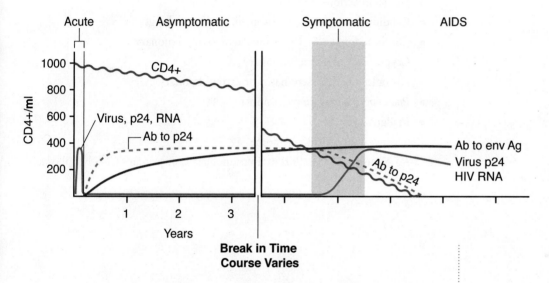

**Figure II-4-23.** Clinical Stages of HIV Infection

**COMLEX Note**

Viral and cellular details of the acute, asymptomatic, symptomatic and full blown symptoms of HIV infection are high yield.

**Conditions of Early Symptomatic Period**

- Bacillary angiomatosis (disseminated bartonellosis)
- Candidiasis (oral or persistent vulvovaginal)
- Cervical dysplasia or carcinoma in situ
- Constitutional symptoms (fever 38.5°C or diarrhea lasting >1 month)
- Hairy leukoplakia
- Idiopathic thrombocytopenic purpura
- Listeriosis
- Pelvic inflammatory disease (especially with abscess)
- Peripheral neuropathy

**Conditions Associated with AIDS**

- Encephalopathy, HIV-related
- Pneumonia, recurrent (leading cause of death)
- Fungal infections
- Candidiasis of esophagus, bronchi, trachea, or lungs
- Coccidioidomycosis, disseminated or extrapulmonary
- Cryptococcosis, extrapulmonary
- Histoplasmosis, disseminated or extrapulmonary
- *Pneumocystis jirovecii* pneumonia
- Malignancies
  - Invasive cervical carcinoma
  - Kaposi sarcoma; Burkitt, immunoblastic, or primary CNS lymphoma

- Viral infections
  - Cytomegalovirus retinitis (with loss of vision) or disease (other than liver, spleen, or nodes)
  - Herpes simplex: chronic ulcer(s) (>1 month); or bronchitis, pneumonitis, or esophagitis
  - Progressive multifocal leukoencephalopathy
  - Wasting syndrome due to HIV (TNF-α)
- Parasitic infections
  - Cryptosporidiosis, chronic intestinal (>1 month)
  - Isosporiasis, chronic intestinal (>1 month)
  - Toxoplasmosis of brain
- Bacterial infections
  - *Mycobacterium tuberculosis,* any site (pulmonary or extrapulmonary)
  - *Mycobacterium avium* complex or *M. kansasii* or other species or unidentified species, disseminated or extrapulmonary
  - *Salmonella* septicemia, recurrent

## Differential Diagnosis

- EBV for initial symptoms
- HTLV
- Mumps virus

**Table II-4-16.** Recommended Prophylactic Regimens During HIV Infection

| Disease Agent | Begin Prophylaxis | Distcontinue Pro-phylaxis |
|---|---|---|
| *Pneumocystis jirovecii* | ‹200 CD4 | ›200 CD4 for 3–6 mos |
| *Toxoplasma gondii* | ‹100 CD4 | ›100 CD4 for 3–6 mos |
| *Histoplasma capsulatum* | ‹100 CD4 (in endemic area) | continue |
| *Mycobacterium avium intracellulare* | ‹50 CD4 | ›100 CD4 for 3–6 mos |
| Cytomegalovirus | ‹50 CD4 | ›150 CD4 for 3–6 mos |
| *Cryptococcus neoformans* | ‹50 CD4 | continue |

**Table II-4-17.** Laboratory Analysis for HIV

| Purpose | Test |
|---|---|
| Initial screening | Serologic: ELISA (HIV1 and HIV2 antibodies, p24 antigen) |
| Confirmation | Serologic: Western blot |
| Detection of virus in blood (evaluate **viral load**) | RT-PCR* |
| Detect HIV infection in newborns of HIV+ mother **(provirus)** | PCR* |
| Early marker of infection | p24 antigen |
| Evaluate progression of disease | CD4:CD8 T-cell ratio |

*RT-PCR tests for circulating viral RNA and is used to monitor the efficacy of treatment. PCR detects integrated virus (provirus). Viral load has been demonstrated to be the best prognostic indicator during infection.

## COMLEX Note

- Screening test for HIV = ELISA
- Confirmatory test = Western Blot

**Table II-4-18.** Treatment

| Mechanism | Name | Resistance |
|-----------|------|------------|
| RT inhibitors<br><br>Nuceloside or non-nucleoside analogs | End in "ine" | Common, leads to cross-resistance |
| Protease inhibitors | End in "inavir" | Common via protease mutations, leads to cross-resistance |
| HAART* | 2 nucleoside analogs and 1 protease inhibitor | Increasing |
| Fusion inhibitors | Fuzeon, enfuvirtide | Not yet |
| CCR5 co-receptor antagonist | Maraviroc | Not yet |
| Integrase inhibitor | Raltegravir | Not yet |

*HAART—highly active anti-retroviral therapy

## Prevention

- Education/safe sex
- Blood/organ screening
- Infection control
- Vaccine development (currently none available)

# NEGATIVE-STRANDED RNA VIRUSES

**Table II-4-19.** Negative-Stranded RNA Viruses

| Virus | RNA Structure | Virion-Associated Polymerase | Envelope | Shape | Multiplies in | Major Viruses |
|---|---|---|---|---|---|---|
| Paramyxovirus | ss(−)RNA Linear Non-segmented | Yes | Yes | Helical | Cytoplasm | Mumps Measles Respiratory syncytial Parainfluenza |
| Rhabdovirus | ss(−)RNA Linear Non-segmented | Yes | Yes | Bullet-shaped helical | Cytoplasm | Rabies Vesicular stomatitis |
| Filovirus | ss(−)RNA Linear Non-segmented | Yes | Yes | Helical | Cytoplasm | Marburg Ebola |
| Orthomyxovirus | ss(−) RNA Linear 8 segmented | Yes | Yes | Helical | Cytoplasm & nucleus | Influenza |
| Bunyavirus | ss(−)RNA Pseudocircular, 3 segments, 1 is ambisense | Yes | Yes | Helical | Cytoplasm | California encephalitis La Crosse encephalitis Hantavirus |
| Arenavirus | ss(−)RNA Circular 2 segments 1 (−)sense 1 ambisense | Yes | Yes | Helical | Cytoplasm | Lymphocytic choriomeningitis Lassa fever |

Mnemonic for the ss(−)RNA viruses: Pain Results From Our Bunions Always. Gives them in order of size. You can remember these are the negative ones because pain is a negative thing. Another one: Bring a polymerase or fail replication.

Note that all are enveloped, all have virion-associated polymerase, and all have helical nucleocapsids. The oddballs are the last three:

- The orthomyxoviruses are linear (ortho) but with 8 (ortho/octo) segments, which is one of the reasons they can genetically "mix" it up. The orthomyxoviruses are also odd in that they replicate in both the nucleus and cytoplasm.

- The bunyaviruses are somewhat contortionists (circular): California playboy bunnies in a ménage à trois?

- The arenaviruses have one negative sense and one ambisense strand of RNA.

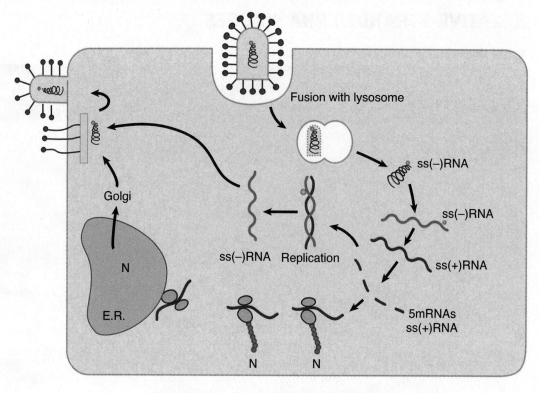

**Figure II-4-24.** Negative-Sense RNA Virus Life Cycle

**Abbreviations:**

H = Hemagglutinin—surface glycoproteins that bind to sialic acid (N-acetylneuraminic acid) receptors

N = Neuraminidase—clips off sialic acids, thus aiding in release of virus

M = Matrix protein—membrane stabilizing protein underlying the viral envelope

F = Fusion protein—destabilizes host membrane

P = Polymerase associated with virion

# PARAMYXOVIRIDAE

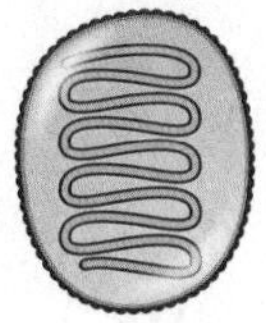

**Figure II-4-25.** Paramyxovirus

## Family Characteristics

- Enveloped, helical nucleocapsid
- Negative-sense ssRNA

## Viruses of Medical Importance

- Measles
- Mumps
- Parainfluenza
- Respiratory syncytial virus (RSV)
- Human metapneumovirus (human MNV)

# Measles Virus

### Distinguishing Characteristics

- Single serotype
- H glycoprotein and fusion protein; no neuraminidase

**Reservoir**—human respiratory tract

**Transmission**—respiratory route

### Pathogenesis

- Ability to cause cell:cell fusion → giant cells
- Virus can escape immune detection

### Disease

- Measles
  - Presentation generally the 3 C's (cough, coryza, and conjunctivitis) with photophobia
  - Koplik spots → maculopapular rash from the ears down → giant cell pneumonia (Warthin-Finkeldey cells)
- Subacute sclerosing panencephalitis
  - Rare late complication
  - Defective measles virus persists in brain, acts as slow virus
  - Chronic CNS degeneration

## Differential Diagnosis

- HHV-6
- Rubella virus
- B19
- VZV
- *R. rickettsii*

## COMLEX Note

Although measles and mumps are not common infections in the U.S. because of vaccination, they are board favorites.

**Diagnosis**—serology

## Treatment

- Supportive
- Ribavirin (experimental)

**Prevention**—live, attenuated vaccine, MMR

# Mumps Virus

## Distinguishing Characteristics

- Negative-sense ssRNA
- Helical
- Enveloped
- Single HN glycoprotein, also F protein
- Single serotype

**Reservoir**—human respiratory tract

**Transmission**—person to person via respiratory droplets

**Pathogenesis**—lytic infection of epithelial cells of upper respiratory tract and parotid glands → spread throughout body.

**Disease**—mumps

- Asymptomatic to bilateral parotitis with fever, headache, and malaise
- Complications include pancreatitis, orchitis (leads to sterility in males), and meningoencephalitis

## Differential Diagnosis

- HIV
- Influenza
- Coxsackie virus
- Parainfluenza virus

## Diagnosis

- Clinical
- Serology; ELISA, IFA, hemagglutination inhibition

**Treatment**—supportive

**Prevention**—live, attenuated vaccine, MMR

**Table II-4-20.** Summary of Additional Paramyxoviruses

| Virus | Transmission | Disease(s) | Diagnosis | Treatment/ Prevention |
|---|---|---|---|---|
| **Parainfluenza** | Respiratory | Older children and adults—subglottal swelling; hoarse, barking cough<br><br>Infants—colds, bronchiolitis, pneumonia, **croup** | RT-PCR | Supportive/none |
| **RSV** | Respiratory | Adults—colds; infants/**preemies**—bronchiolitis and necrosis of bronchioles, atypical pneumonia (low fever, tachypnea, tachycardia, expiratory wheeze) | IFA, ELISA, RT-PCR | Ribavirin and anti-RSV Abs/none<br><br>Palivizumab blocks fusion protein |
| Human MNV | Respiratory | Common cold (15% in kids), bronchiolitis, pneumonia | RT-PCR | Supportive/none |

*Definition of abbreviations:* IFA, indirect fluorescent antibody; ELISA, enzyme-linked immunosorbent assay; RSV, respiratory syncytial virus; MNV, metapneumovirus; RT-PCR, reverse transcriptase-polymerase chain reaction.

| Differential Diagnosis | | |
|---|---|---|
| Parainfluenza | RSV | Human MNV |
| RSV, parainfluenza, influenza, *B. pertussis*, *H. influenzae, C. diphtheriae* | Parainfluenza (croup); influenza | Parainfluenza, influenza, RSV |

# RHABDOVIRIDAE

## Family Characteristics

- Negative-sense ssRNA
- Bullet shaped
- Enveloped, helical

**Figure II-4-26.** Rhabdovirus

## Viruses of Medical Importance

- Rabies

# Rabies Virus

## Reservoir

- In the U.S., most cases sylvatic: bats, raccoons, foxes, and skunks
- Worldwide, dogs are primary reservoir

**Transmission**—bite or contact with a rabid animal

## Pathogenesis

- After contact, virus binds to peripheral nerves by binding to nicotinic acetylcholine receptor *or* indirectly into the muscle at the site of inoculation
- Virus travels by **retrograde axoplasmic** transport to dorsal root ganglia and spinal cord
- Once virus gains access to spinal cord, brain becomes rapidly infected

**Disease**—rabies

- Nonspecific flu-like illness followed by neurologic symptoms of **hydrophobia**, seizures, disorientation, **hallucination**, coma, and death
- With rare exception, rabies fatal unless treated by immunoprophylaxis

## Key Vignette Clues

### Rabies

- Patient bitten by bat or dog
- Influenza-like prodrome: hydrophobia, hallucination, coma, death

**Diagnosis**

- Clinical
- Negri bodies, intracytoplasmic inclusion bodies (brain biopsy)
- DFA (impression smears of corneal epithelial cells), PCR (usually too late)

**Treatment**

- If symptoms are evident: *none*
- If suspect:
  - Postexposure prophylaxis
  - One dose of human rabies immunoglobulin (hRIG)
  - Five doses of rabies vaccine (day of, 3, 7, 14, 28)
  - Killed virus vaccine

**Prevention**

- Vaccine for high-risk individuals
- Vaccination program for domestic animals (U.S.)

# FILOVIRIDAE

## Family Characteristics

- Negative-sense ssRNA
- Enveloped, helical
- Filamentous

## Viruses of Medical Importance

- Ebola virus
- Marburg virus

**Table II-4-21.** Summary of Filoviruses

| Virus | Reservoir | Transmission | Disease | Diagnosis | Treatment/Prevention |
|-------|-----------|--------------|---------|-----------|----------------------|
| Ebola, Marburg | Unknown | Direct contact (blood, secretions) | Fatal hemorrhagic fever | Level 4 isolation, ELISA, PCR | Supportive/quarantine |

| Differential Diagnosis | |
|------------------------|---|
| Ebola, Marburg | Dengue, YFV, *S. typhi* |

# ORTHOMYXOVIRIDAE

## Family Characteristics

- Negative-sense ssRNA
- Enveloped
- Segmented (8 segments)
- Helical

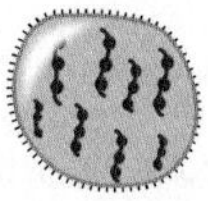

**Figure II-4-27.** Orthomyxovirus

## Viruses of Medical Importance

- Influenza A
- Influenza B

# Influenza Virus

## Distinguishing Features

- Envelope contains two glycoproteins, H and N
- Used to serotype virus

## Reservoir

- Influenza A (birds, pigs, humans)
- Influenza B (humans only)

## Transmission

- Direct contact
- Respiratory
- 1997 H5N1 strain jumped directly from birds to humans
- 2009 H1N1 strain—quadruple reassortment virus (North American swine, avian, human; Asian and European swine)

## Pathogenesis

- Antigenic drift
  - Influenza A and B
  - Slight changes in antigenicity due to mutations in H and/or N
  - Causes epidemics

**Key Vignette Clues**

**Influenza**

Patient with headache, malaise, fever, myalgia, cough

**COMLEX Note**

You must be able to differentiate between antigenic shift and antigenic drift.

## COMLEX Note

Antecedent illness to Guillain-Barre is high yield

- *C. jejuni* (most common)
- influeza
- EBV, CMV

## Differential Diagnosis

- Parainfluenza
- RSV
- Adenovirus
- Metapneumovirus

- Antigenic shift
  - *Influenza A only*
  - Rare genetic reassortment
  - Coinfection of cells with two different strains of influenza A (H5N1 and H3N2); reassortment of segments of genome
  - Production of a new agent to which population has no immunity
  - Responsible for pandemics

**Disease**—influenza

- Headache and malaise
- Fever, chills, myalgias, anorexia
- Bronchiolitis, croup, otitis media, vomiting (younger children)
- Pneumonia/secondary bacterial infections
- Can lead to Reye syndrome or Guillain-Barré syndrome

## Diagnosis

- Rapid tests (serology)
- Clinical symptoms plus season

## Treatment

- Amantadine/rimantadine (current isolates are commonly resistant)
  - Inhibit viral uncoating
  - Administer orally
- Zanamivir/oseltamivir
  - Neuraminidase inhibitors
  - Zanamivir is inhaled
  - Oseltamivir is given orally

## Prevention

- Killed vaccine
  - Two strains of influenza A (H3N2, H1N1, for example) and one strain of influenza B are incorporated into the vaccine
- Live, attenuated vaccine
  - Intranasal administration
  - Similar composition
  - Currently recommended for ages 2–49

# BUNYAVIRIDAE

## Family Characteristics

- Negative-sense ssRNA
- Enveloped viruses
- Three segments, one ambisense
- Mostly arboviruses, except Hantavirus

## Viruses of Medical Importance

- California encephalitis
- LaCrosse encephalitis
- Hantavirus (sin nombre)

**Table II-4-22.** Summary of Bunyaviridae

| Virus | Transmission | Disease | Diagnosis |
|---|---|---|---|
| California and LaCrosse encephalitis | Mosquito | Viral encephalitis | Serology |
| **Hantavirus** (sin nombre) | Rodent excrement, four-corners region, rainy season | Hantavirus pulmonary syndrome (cough, myalgia, dyspnea, tachycardia, pulmonary edema and effusion, and hypotension [mortality 50%]) | RT-PCR |

| Differential Diagnosis | |
|---|---|
| California and LaCrosse encephalitis | Hantavirus (sin nombre) |
| WNV, SLE, EEE, WEE, VEE, HSV | *L. interrogans, S. pneumoniae, K. pneumoniae, M. pneumoniae* influenza |

## Key Vignette Clues

### Hantavirus

- Patient with acute respiratory distress
- Four-corners region
- Exposure to rodent excrement
- Spring/early sumer incidence

# ARENAVIRIDAE

## Family Characteristics

- Negative-sense ssRNA
- Pleomorphic, enveloped
- Virions have a sandy appearance (ribosomes in virion)
- Two segments, one ambisense

## Viruses of Medical Importance

- Lymphocytic choriomeningitis virus (LCMV)
- Lassa fever virus

**Table II-4-23.** Summary of Arenaviridae

| Virus | Transmission | Disease | Diagnosis | Treatment |
|---|---|---|---|---|
| LCMV | Mice and pet hamsters (U.S.) | Influenza-like with meningeal signs | Serology, level 3 isolation | Supportive, ribavirin |
| Lassa fever | Rodents, human-to-human (West Africa) | Hemorrhagic fever with 50% fatality rate | Serology, level 4 isolation | Supportive, ribavirin |

*Definition of Abbreviations:* LCMV, Lymphocytic choriomeningitis virus

| Differential Diagnosis | |
|---|---|
| LCMV | Lassa fever |
| *S. typhi*, enteroviruses, arboviruses, *L. interrogans*, influenza, mumps | Ebola, Marburg, dengue, yellow fever |

# DOUBLE-STRANDED RNA VIRUSES

## REOVIRIDAE

**Table II-4-24.** Double-Stranded RNA Viruses

| | RNA Structure | Polymerase | Envelope | Shape | Major Viruses |
|---|---|---|---|---|---|
| Reovirus | Linear dsRNA 10-11 segments | Yes | Naked | Icosahedral<br>Double shelled | Reovirus<br>Rotavirus<br>Colorado Tick Fever Virus |

**Figure II-4-28.** Reovirus

**Table II-4-25.** Summary of Reoviridae

| Virus | Transmission | Disease | Diagnosis | Treatment/Prevention |
|---|---|---|---|---|
| Reovirus | Fecal-oral, respiratory | Common cold, gastroenteritis | Serology | Self-limiting/none |
| **Rotavirus** | Fecal-oral | Gastroenteritis, no blood or pus | ELISA (stool) | Live, attenuated vaccine, oral |

*Definition of Abbreviations:* ELISA, enzyme-linked immunosorbent assay.

| Differential Diagnosis | | |
|---|---|---|
| Reovirus | Rotavirus | CTFV (Western and Northwest U.S.) |
| Rhinovirus, coronavirus, (Norwalk, rotavirus) | Norwalk, adenovirus | *R. rickettsii,* EBV, influenza |

# ONCOGENIC VIRUSES

## Definitions

### Malignant transformation of cells

- Dedifferentiation
- Loss of growth control
- Immortalization
- Appearance of new surface antigens ("T" antigens)

### Provirus

Viral DNA inserted into host DNA

### Oncogenes

Genes with the potential to cause malignant transformation

### Cellular oncogenes (abbreviated c-onc)

These are normal cellular genes whose products control regulation of cell growth and division (e.g., kinases, growth factors and their receptors, G proteins and nuclear regulatory proteins).

### Viral oncogenes (abbreviated v-onc)

Genes carried by certain viruses causing cancer. Viral oncogenes are homologs of cellular oncogenes.

### Tumor suppressor genes

These genes suppress, or constrain, cell growth and replication.

## Major Concepts of Tumorigenesis

### Mutation of a c-oncogene or tumor suppressor gene

- Mutation in one of these control genes may result in unregulated growth of cells.
- Example of mutated oncogene—*ras*
- Retinoblastoma (Rb) is an example of mutation in tumor suppressor gene.

### Dosage effects

- Oncogenes in amplified DNA—increased number of copies results in overexpression of gene.
- **Translocation**, which links an oncogene with a more active enhancer and/or promoter, resulting in overexpression (Burkitt lymphoma)
- Provirus **insertional mutagenesis**—for example, a retrovirus with its very active transcriptional promoter/enhancer region, the LTR (long terminal repeat), may integrate (insert) near a cellular oncogene. This is one of the mechanisms by which retroviruses that do not have v-onc cause carcinoma.

- Infection with a virus carrying a v-onc: e.g., infection with a retrovirus carrying viral oncogenes such as *src*. The gene was probably picked up by a provirus inserted near a cellular oncogene picking up copies of c-onc. Viral progeny then contain the new oncogene now called v-onc. When a new cell is infected with the recombinant virus, the oncogene is now under the transcriptional control of the viral enhancer/promoter.

- Interaction between the products of oncogenes and tumor suppressor genes. Proteins E6 and E7 of the human papilloma virus combine with and inactivate the p53 and Rb, respectively.

## Specific Viruses Associated with Human Cancers

### EBV

- Burkitt lymphoma (BL) translocation t(8:14), nasopharyngeal, and thymic carcinoma
- BL occurs only in malarial regions; the plasmodia are thought to produce a slight immunosuppression.
- EBV stimulates B-cell replication and eventually, if a translocation of *c-myc* to the DNA region where genetic rearrangements involved in antibody synthesis occurs, BL develops.

### Chronic HBV

Primary hepatocellular carcinoma

### Chronic HCV

Primary hepatocellular carcinoma

### HPV

- Cervical carcinoma
- Mechanism: inactivation of tumor suppressor gene

### HTLV-1

- CD4+ T-cell leukemia/lymphomas
- Provirus insertion or capture

### HTLV-2

- Hairy cell leukemia

# PRION DISEASES

**Table II-4-26.** Prion Diseases

| Disease | Infectious agent | Host | Comments |
|---|---|---|---|
| Kuru | Prion | Human | Subacute spongiform encephalopathy (SSE); Fore Tribe, New Guinea; cannibalism |
| Creutzfeldt-Jakob disease (and variant) | Prion | Human | SSE <br><br> Genetic predisposition; ingestion of infected cow brains |
| Gerstmann-Sträussler-Scheinker | Prion | Human | SSE |
| Fatal familial insomnia | Prion | Human | SSE |
| Scrapie | Prion | Sheep | SSE—scraping their wool off on fences |

**Table II-4-27.** Slow Conventional Viruses (Viruses)

| Disease | Infectious agent | Host | Comments |
|---|---|---|---|
| Measles SSPE | Virus | Human having had measles | Subacute sclerosing panencephalitis |
| AIDS dementia | HIV | Human | Dementia |
| PML | JC virus | Human | Progressive multifocal leukoencephalopathy |

# VIRAL GENETICS

## Genetic Reassortment = Genetic Shift

- Two different strains of a segmented RNA virus infect the same cell.
- Major new genetic combinations are produced through "shuffling," resulting in stable and dramatic changes.

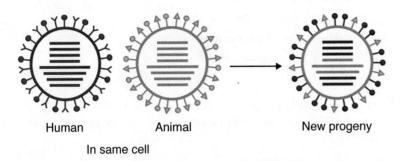

Human       Animal       New progeny

In same cell

**Figure II-4-29.** Genetic Reassortment in Influenza A

## Genetic Drift

- Minor antigenic changes from mutation
- Occurs in many viruses, particularly RNA ones
- Most noted in HIV and influenza

**COMLEX Note**

Antigenic shift and drift may be tested on the COMLEX, whereas the other mechanisms of viral genetics are not.

## Review Questions

1.  A 5-year-old presents to the pediatrician with complaints of a sore throat. Her mother also noticed that both of her eyes were slightly red. Examination reveals rhinopharyngitis with bilateral conjunctivitis. What activity likely led to the above illness?

    (A)  Hiking in a heavily wooded area

    (B)  Eating undercooked shellfish

    (C)  Playing with toys in a day care center

    (D)  Traveling to a developing country

    (E)  Swimming in a community pool

2.  Serologic test results from a hepatitis patient reveal: anti-HBc positive, HBsAg positive, and anti-HBs negative. The correct interpretation of the patient's status is

    (A)  No longer contagious

    (B)  Immune to hepatitis B virus

    (C)  Evidence of receiving hepatitis B vaccination

    (D)  Hepatitis B virus chronic carrier state

    (E)  Impossible to have both surface antigen and core antibody positive

3.  A 6-year-old girl presents to the emergency department with a fever and a lacy body rash. Her mother says that yesterday the rash was only on her face, but by this morning, had spread to her trunk and extremities. Which of the following agents is most likely?

    (A)  B19

    (B)  HHV-6

    (C)  Measles

    (D)  Rubella

    (E)  Varicella zoster virus

4.  The best prospects for treatment and cure of microbial diseases are always those unique factors of a pathogen's life cycle that can be altered without affecting the survival of the host's own cells. In HIV, one such therapeutic target would be the products of the *pol* gene, which codes for the reverse transcriptase unique to the retroviral life cycle. If it were possible to ablate expression of the HIV *pol* gene, what other aspect of the virus's life cycle would be directly altered?

    (A)  Transcription from proviral DNA

    (B)  Production of viral mRNA

    (C)  Integration of proviral DNA

    (D)  Nucleocapsid

    (E)  Viral maturation

5.  A 28-year-old male ER resident was accidentally stuck with a needle from a hepatitis B virus-positive patient. He was too embarrassed to tell his attending of his mistake. Two months later, he began to feel fatigued and lost his appetite. When he ordered a hepatitis B serologic panel, he received the results as follows:

    HBsAg   +

    HBsAb   −

    HBcAb   +

    HBeAg   +

    HBeAb   −

    What is the status of the resident?

    (A)  Acute infection

    (B)  Chronic infection

    (C)  Fulminant infection

    (D)  Immune

    (E)  Uninfected

6.  A prison inmate who was diagnosed with hepatitis 6 months ago is tested for his progress with the folllowing results:

    HBsAg   −

    HBsAb   +

    HBcAb   +

    HBeAg   −

    HBeAb   +

    What is the status of the patient?

    (A)  Acute infection

    (B)  Chronic infection

    (C)  Fulminant infection

    (D)  Immune

    (E)  Uninfected

7.  A 10-year-old boy is brought to the emergency department with a high fever, chills, headache, and nausea. He vomits at admission, where his temperature is 104.2°F, and he begins to hallucinate. A CT scan reveals encephalitis in one temporal lobe. Which of the following causal agents is most likely?

    (A)  California encephalitis

    (B)  Herpes simplex virus 1

    (C)  Polio virus

    (D)  St. Louis encephalitis

    (E)  West Nile virus

8. A 60-year-old woman who recently received a liver transplant develops a high fever and severe dyspnea with a dry hacking cough. Chest x-ray reveals bilateral interstitial infiltrates that are diffuse. Which of the following agents is most likely responsible for her condition?

   (A) Adenovirus

   (B) Cytomegalovirus

   (C) Influenza virus

   (D) Respiratory syncytial virus

   (E) Rhinovirus

9. An 8-year-old boy from India was brought to the emergency department while visiting the U.S. because of a flaccid paralysis in his lower extremities. His mother explains that the child had a flu-like illness a couple of weeks earlier. How was the agent in the above case likely acquired?

   (A) Fecal-oral

   (B) Mosquito

   (C) Respiratory

   (D) Sexual

   (E) Tick

10. A 5-year-old girl presents with a fever and a generalized macular rash that is most dense on the scalp and trunk of the body. Several waves of lesions appear, one after another, and evolve rapidly into vesicles and then pustules over several days. The most likely disease and causal agent is

   (A) Exanthem subitum due to cytomegalovirus

   (B) Chickenpox due to the varicella-zoster virus

   (C) Whitlow infection due to herpes simplex virus type 1

   (D) Herpetic gingivostomatitis due to the varicella-zoster virus

   (E) Infectious mononucleosis due to the Epstein-Barr virus

11. Infection of appropriate cells with a composite virus made up of Coxsackie virus capsid components and poliovirus RNA would yield progeny which would

   (A) Have the host cell range of Coxsackie virus

   (B) Also be composite viruses

   (C) Show phenotypic mixing

   (D) Have a recombinant genome consisting of both Coxsackie and poliovirus

   (E) React with Sabin-vaccine–induced antibodies

12. An epidemic of nausea, vomiting, and watery diarrhea breaks out on shipboard during a cruise to the Virgin Islands. Which of the following accurately describes the most likely causal agent?

   (A) Acid-fast oocysts

   (B) Enveloped DNA virus

   (C) Enveloped RNA virus

   (D) Nonenveloped DNA virus

   (E) Nonenveloped RNA virus

13. To design a vaccine against HIV infection, a logical goal would be to alter some native molecule or product of the virion in order to make it highly immunogenic. If you wished to prevent the attachment of the virus to helper T lymphocytes, which molecule or family of molecules might best be targeted?

    (A) gp41

    (B) gp120

    (C) nucleocapsid protein

    (D) p17

    (E) p24

14. A woman in her late twenties presents to the emergency department disoriented and confused. She is unable to remember where she lived or even her phone number. She is admitted for observation and testing and begins to hallucinate and salivate excessively. On the east coast of the United States, what is the most common reservoir of this disease?

    (A) Bat

    (B) Cat

    (C) Dog

    (D) Fox

    (E) Raccoon

15. An 11-month-old infant was brought to the emergency department with difficulty breathing and wheezing. History and physical examination reveal a slight fever, cough, and rhinorrhea that began about 2 days before. Analysis of the sputum reveals normal flora with the presence of giant multinucleated cells. Which of the following is the most likely cause?

    (A) B19

    (B) Influenza

    (C) Parainfluenza

    (D) Measles

    (E) Respiratory syncytial virus

16. A 37-year-old executive for a local Health Maintenance Organization comes to your office because he has developed multiple blister-like lesions on his penis over the last 1–2 days. They are somewhat painful, and he is worried that he has AIDS. He denies homosexuality and intravenous drug abuse and had an HIV test prior to his marriage 3 years ago. He reports several similar episodes several years ago when he worked as a photographer in Nepal. He was never told what they were, and they resolved over several days without any treatment. His physical examination is remarkable only for the presence of 6–8 vesicular lesions 3–4 mm in diameter on the glans of the penis. There is no crusting, drainage, or bleeding. The lesions are moderately tender and there is mild inguinal adenopathy bilaterally. How does the causal agent produce its messenger RNA?

    (A) By producing a positive sense intermediate

    (B) By direct translation from the genome

    (C) By transcription from proviral DNA

    (D) By producing a negative sense intermediate

    (E) By transcribing from the genomic DNA

    (F) By reverse transcription from the genome

    (G) By semi-conservative replication

17. Several individuals in the central United States from the ages of 5 to 25 have come down with symptoms of nausea, vomiting, and swelling of the parotid glands. Which of the following can be a complication of the above disease?

    (A) Guillain-Barré Syndrome

    (B) Glomerulonephritis

    (C) Orchitis

    (D) Multiple sclerosis

    (E) Reye syndrome

18. In the U.S., a baby has the greatest chance of acquiring which virus in utero?

    (A) Cytomegalovirus

    (B) Hepatitis B virus

    (C) Herpes simplex virus

    (D) Respiratory syncytial virus

    (E) Rubella virus

19. Which of these viruses has RNA for both its genome and replicative intermediate?

    (A) Cytomegalovirus

    (B) Hepadnavirus

    (C) Retroviruses

    (D) Togaviruses

    (E) Poxvirus

20. What is the most common lab testing method for diagnosing infectious mono-nucleosis?

    (A) The Monospot test to detect EBV-specific antibody

    (B) An assay for Epstein-Barr nuclear antigen

    (C) The presence of atypical lymphocytes in the blood establishes the etiology

    (D) A test for heterophile antibody, which cross-reacts with antigens found on a variety of animal red blood cells

    (E) A simple procedure is done to isolate EBV from saliva, blood, or lymphoid tissue

21. What virus is noted for genetic reassortment, which leads to major pandemics about once every 10 to 11 years?

    (A) Adenovirus

    (B) Herpes virus

    (C) Human immunodeficiency virus (HIV)

    (D) Influenza virus

    (E) Poliovirus

22. What virus is noted for such a high incidence of genetic drift that more than one antigenic variant can be isolated from most infected individuals who have high viral titers?

    (A) Adenovirus

    (B) Herpes virus

    (C) Human immunodeficiency virus (HIV)

    (D) Influenza virus

    (E) Poliovirus

23. A 19-year-old male college student reports sore throat and extreme fatigue following even normal non-taxing tasks like getting dressed and going down to breakfast. He tells you that he has been sick for several weeks, that he has been feverish, and that his girlfriend now appears to be getting the same thing. His tonsils are inflamed with a white exudate adhering; cervical lymphadenopathy is prominent, as is splenomegaly. The most likely causal agent is

    (A) ssDNA, naked icosahedral virus

    (B) dsDNA, naked icosahedral virus

    (C) dsDNA, enveloped complex virus

    (D) dsDNA, enveloped icosahedral virus

    (E) dsRNA, naked segmented virus

    (F) −ssRNA, segmented, enveloped and helical virus

    (G) −ssRNA, bullet-shaped, helical virus

    (H) −ssRNA, naked, helical virus

    (I) +ssRNA, naked, icosahedral virus

    (J) +ssRNA, enveloped, icosahedral virus

    (K) +ssRNA, enveloped, diploid virus

24. Cataracts and patent ductus arteriosus in a newborn suggest in utero infection with what viral family?

    (A) Adenovirus

    (B) Paramyxovirus

    (C) Parvovirus

    (D) Picornavirus

    (E) Reovirus

    (F) Togavirus

25. What is the primary means of spread for measles?

    (A) Animal bite

    (B) Fecal-oral

    (C) Fomite spread

    (D) Respiratory droplet spread

    (E) Sexual contact

    (F) Transfusion or intravenous drug abuse

    (G) Tick bite

26. How are human papilloma virus type 4 warts spread?

    (A) Animal bite

    (B) Fecal-oral

    (C) Fomite spread

    (D) Respiratory droplet spread

    (E) Sexual contact

27. A 15-year-old member of the high school swim team notices painless, umbilicated cutaneous lesions on the toes. Large eosinophilic cytoplasmic inclusions are present in the affected epithelia. What is the most likely causal agent?

    (A) Adenovirus

    (B) B19 virus

    (C) Molluscum contagiosum virus

    (D) Herpes simplex virus

    (E) Human papilloma virus

28. A bone marrow transplant recipient becomes febrile and hypoxic and chest films demonstrate diffuse interstitial pneumonia. What is the most likely causal agent?

    (A) BK virus

    (B) Cytomegalovirus

    (C) Herpes simplex virus

    (D) Molluscum contagiosum virus

    (E) Paramyxovirus

    (F) Varicella-zoster virus

29. A 6-month-old infant presents with painless verrucous growths on the laryngeal folds. What is the most likely causal agent?

    (A) B19 virus

    (B) Cytomegalovirus

    (C) Herpes simplex virus

    (D) Human papilloma virus

    (E) Molluscum contagiosum virus

## Answers and Explanations

1.  **Answer: E.** The disease is viral pharyngoconjunctivitis, caused by adenovirus, which is very commonly contracted through swimming pools. (Adenovirus is a naked virus and chlorination of pools does not inactivate it.) Hiking in a heavily wooded area (**choice A**) could be associated with a vector-borne disease, such as Rocky Mountain spotted fever. Eating undercooked shellfish (**choice B**) could be associated with hepatitis A or *Vibrio parahaemolyticus,* for example. Playing with toys in a day care center (**choice C**) and traveling to a developing country (**choice D**) both could begin the infection of a long list of agents.

2. **Answer: D.** The presence of hepatitis B surface antigen and the absence of the surface antibody (anti-HBs) indicate either an acute HBV infection (if patient has had the disease for only a short time) or a chronic carrier state (if the hepatitis has been going on for at least 6 months). Because acute HBV is not a choice, **choice D** then becomes the correct answer. **Choice B** would be a right answer if HBsAg had been negative and HBsAb positive. Core antibodies would not be present if the person is only vaccinated (**choice C**). Also, HBsAg should not be present in a detectable amount from vaccination. HBeAg and HBeAb are correlated to how contagious the patient might be, and these serologic results were not given (**choice A**).

3. **Answer: A.** The clues are lacy body rash preceded by a facial rash in a school aged child with fever. HHV-6 (**choice B**) is the causal agent of roseola, which is fever, followed by a lacy body rash in infants. Measles (**choice C**) is identified by cough, coryza, and conjunctivitis with photophobia, Koplik spots, and an exanthematous rash beginning below the ears then spreading to the trunk and extremities. Rubella (**choice D**) is the causal agent of German measles, which involves a rash beginning at the forehead and spreading down.

4. **Answer: C.** The *pol* gene codes for reverse transcriptase, integrase, and protease. Reverse transcriptase creates the provirus and integrase allows the proviral DNA to be integrated, apparently at a random site, into a chromosome in the host cell. Of the distractors, both **choices A and B** are accomplished using the host cell's RNA polymerase. **Choice D** is a function of the *gag* gene, and **choice E** is controlled by *tat* and *rev* genes.

5. **Answer: A.** The presence of HBsAg, HBcAb, and HBeAg are all indicators of an acute infection at 2 months postexposure. It is too early to identify a chronic infection (**choice B**), but the presence of HBsAg after 6 months is the main indication of a chronic infection. With a fulminant infection (**choice C**), the patient's symptoms are usually much more serious, likely a superinfection with hepatitis D or the delta agent. If he were immune (**choice D**), he would have had HBsAb in his serum. Since he has hepatitis B viral antigens in his blood, **choice E** is wrong.

6. **Answer: D.** The inmate is immune, as he has a complete complement of antiviral antibodies.

7. **Answer: B.** This patient has herpes simplex encephalitis, whch typically affects the temporal lobes. California encephalitis (**choice A**) affects older children in the middle and northwestern U.S. The polio virus (**choice C**) causes a flaccid paralysis with no sensory loss, and does not occur in the United States. St. Louis encephalitis (**choice D**) and the West Nile virus (**choice E**) usually affect older individuals.

8. **Answer: B.** The clues are transplant patient with interstitial pneumonia; CMV is the most common cause. Adenovirus (**choice A**) is associated with conjunctivitis and acute respiratory disease in military recruits, among other diseases. Although influenza (**choice C**) can cause pneumonia, there is no mention of season, and CMV is still the most common cause in transplant patients. Respiratory syncytial virus (**choice D**) is usually seen in children (especially premature infants), and rhinovirus (**choice E**) causes the common cold.

9. **Answer: A.** Polio is caused by the poliovirus. The clues are flaccid paralysis and India, and polio is transmitted by the fecal-oral route.

10. **Answer: B.** The clinical presentation is consistent with chickenpox caused by VZV. Exanthem subitum is caused by human herpes virus 6, not by CMV. Herpetic gingivostomatitis refers to herpes simplex type 1, not VZV. Infectious

mononucleosis is a lymphadenopathy and herpetic whitlow is a painful herpes infection of the nail bed.

11. **Answer: E.** The only nucleic acid in the composite parental virus is the RNA belonging to poliovirus. Thus, only poliovirus is made. The only role the Coxsackie virus would play in the infection is to bind to the host cell and stimulate the uptake of the composite virus. Once uncoating takes place, the Coxsackie components play no further role. A perfect poliovirus will have been made. The progeny will have the host-cell range of polio (**choice A**) because that is what they'll be. There is no genetic material coding for the Coxsackie components, so you cannot get a composite (**choice B**). No capsid components of Coxsackie will be made; there can be no mixing (**choice C**). There was only one type of RNA; there can never be recombination (**choice D**). Sabin is a polio-specific vaccine, and poliovirus will be produced.

12. **Answer: E.** A common cause of gastroenteritis on cruise ships is the Norovirus. Norovirus is a member of the Caliciviridae family and is a nonenveloped RNA virus. Acid-fast oocysts (**choice A**) refer to persistent diarrhea caused by *Cryptosporidium parvum* or *Isospora belli*, usually seen in AIDS patients. Enveloped DNA and RNA viruses (**choices B and C**) cannot be transmitted via the fecal-oral route or live in the gastrointestinal tract because of the instability of the envelope. A nonenveloped DNA virus (**choice D**) would be consistent with adenoviral gastroenteritis, which is not the most likely cause of cruise ship gastroenteritis.

13. **Answer: B.** Gp120 is the surface antigen of HIV that mediates its attachment to CD4 lymphocytes. Gp41 is a transmembrane glycoprotein, and p24, p17, and nucleocapsid protein are all internal molecules, which would rarely be accessible to the immune response.

14. **Answer: E.** This patient has rabies, which exhibits these neurologic symptoms. In the eastern United States, the primary reservoir is raccoons.

15. **Answer: E.** An infant with difficulty breathing, wheezing, and giant multinucleated cells (syncytia) is likely to have respiratory syncytial virus. B19 (**choice A**) and influenza (**choice B**) would not show giant multinucleated cells, and B19 does not usually cause breathing difficulty. Parainfluenza (**choice C**) causes croup, which exhibits the swelling of the larynx and the seal-like barking cough. There is no mention of rash or Koplik spots, which would indicate the measles (**choice D**).

16. **Answer: E.** The virus is HSV 2, a herpesvirus, which is a dsDNA virus that uses the mechanisms of our own cells to transcribe an RNA strand from its genomic DNA and use the transcribed RNA as a messenger RNA. Of the distractors: **choice A** is the technique used by the negative-sense RNA viruses; **choice B** is used by the positive-sense RNA viruses; **choice C** is used by the retroviruses; **choice D** is used during the genomic duplication of positive sense RNA viruses; **choice F** would not produce RNA; and **choice G** is used in genomic replication by most DNA viruses.

17. **Answer: C.** The disease is mumps. The complication often seen in adult males is orchitis, which can lead to sterility.

18. **Answer: A.** CMV is an extremely common virus and crosses the placenta oftentimes without causing obvious symptoms. Fortunately, rubella, which is highly teratogenic particularly in early pregnancy, is generally prevented by routine vaccination in childhood or at least 16 weeks prior to pregnancy. A small percentage of hepatitis B infections may occur in utero. HSV 2 will only cross the placenta if the mother acquires herpes for the first time during her pregnancy.

RSV and other respiratory viruses will not. Other viruses that can cross the placenta include coxsackie B, HIV, and B19.

19. **Answer: D.** Cytomegalovirus, hepadnavirus, and poxvirus are all dsDNA viruses and not RNA. Retrovirus is an RNA virus but replicates through a dsDNA, so it also is not the correct answer. Toga is a positive RNA virus that replicates through a negative RNA intermediate and has no DNA; therefore, it's the correct answer.

20. **Answer: D.** The monospot is the most commonly used test for the diagnosis of infectious mononucleosis caused by EBV. However, it does not detect EBV-specific antibody. It instead detects heterophile antibody, which is nonspecific in that it may be present in different organisms and individuals and it cross-reacts with many animal RBCs. Epstein-Barr nuclear antigen test is not routinely run in the diagnosis of mononucleosis. Atypical lymphocytes are found in mononucleosis caused by EBV and CMV, but CMV is heterophile antibody–negative. Isolation of EBV is cumbersome and laborious, and would not distinguish previous infections from current active ones.

21. **Answer: D.** The segmented influenza viruses may undergo recombination with a similar animal virus. This leads to drastic genetic change and pandemics result from the fact that there is no underlying "herd immunity" to the new viral entity.

22. **Answer: C.** HIV. It is this genetic drift that makes it difficult for the body to fight off HIV and has complicated the development of an effective vaccine. Genetic drift is due to minor mutational change, and is possible with any organism but best described in HIV.

23. **Answer: D.** Both the symptomology, length of infection, and the epidemiological clues (college student, age 19, has given it to his girlfriend) strongly suggest that this is EBV, which is a herpesvirus.

    **Choice A** = parvo; **choice B** = adeno, papilloma, polyoma; **choice C** = pox; **choice D** = herpes/hepadna because there's no distinction as to circular or partial dsDNA; **choice E** = reovirus; **choice F** = arena, bunya, and orthomyxo; **choice G** = rabies; **choice H** = none; **choice I** = calici, hepe, or picorna; **choice J** = flavi and toga; **choice K** = retro.

24. **Answer: F.** The description fits congenital rubella, a togavirus, which is an enveloped positive-sense RNA virus that is not segmented.

25. **Answer: D.** If you have any trouble, think about which of these viruses has respiratory symptoms (in this case, pneumonia).

26. **Answer: C.** Remember that type 4 strains cause common warts, and these are largely transmitted by fomites or direct contact.

27. **Answer: C.** This describes the typical presentation of molluscum contagiosum, which is commonly acquired through small breaks in the skin in environments where moisture keeps the virus viable (swimming pools, showers).

28. **Answer: B.** CMV is the most common viral cause of death in bone-marrow transplant patients, causing an interstitial pneumonia.

29. **Answer: D.** Perinatal infection with human papilloma virus can cause infantile laryngeal warts.

# Medically Important Fungi 5

## What the COMLEX Requires You To Know

- Basic morphology of fungi (hyphae, yeast, dimorphic, and various types of conidia)
- Basic chemistry, particularly that involved in antifungals or that distinguishes fungi from other groups
- Scientific names of fungal pathogens and opportunists found in the United States
  - What are the 4 dimorphic fungi?
    - Recognize their tissue and environmental forms.
  - What are the 3 dermatophytes and what tissues do they invade?
  - What is the most common cause of meningitis in AIDS patients?
    - What does it look like? How do you diagnose?
  - What is a common cause of interstitial pneumonitis in AIDS patients?
    - Why is it considered a fungus?
  - Which medically important fungus has a capsule?
  - Which is found most commonly inside cells of the reticuloendothelial system?
- The diseases they cause and:
  - How acquired (geography, route)
  - Common presenting symptoms, most common sites of dissemination (if they disseminate commonly)
  - What two fungi are a problem in IV lines?
  - Most common cause of fungal septicemia and the clues used in the cases (germ tube test positive, pseudohyphae and true hyphae as well as yeast forms)

## COMLEX Note

The basic morphology and geography of fungal diseases is high yield. Knowing these key details in case presentations, often will lead you to the correct answer.

## MYCOLOGY

**Mycology** is the **study of fungi (molds, yeasts, and mushrooms).**

**All fungi are**

- **Eukaryotic** (e.g., true nucleus, 80S ribosomes, mitochondria, as are humans).
- **Complex carbohydrate cell walls: chitin, glucan, and mannan.**
- **Ergosterol** = Major membrane sterol
  **Imidazole antifungals inhibit synthesis of ergosterol.**
  **Polyene antifungals bind** more tightly to **ergosterol** than cholesterol.

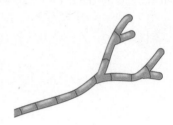

**Figure II-5-1.** Nonseptate Hyphae

**Figure II-5-2.** Septate Hyphae

**Figure II-5-3.** Yeasts

## Note

**Mnemonic**

**B**ody **H**eat **C**hanges **S**hape for the dimorphic fungi.

- *Blastomyces*
- *Histoplasma*
- *Coccidioides*
- *Sporothrix*

# FUNGAL MORPHOLOGY

Hyphae = filamentous cellular units of molds and mushrooms

## Nonseptate Hyphae

- No cross walls
- Broad hyphae with **irregular width**
- **Broad angle of branching**

## Septate Hyphae

- With **cross walls**
- Width is fairly regular (tube-like).

## Hyphal Coloration

- **Dematiaceous: dark colored** (gray, olive)
- **Hyaline: clear**

Mat of hyphae = mycelium

Yeasts = single celled (round to oval) fungi

## Dimorphic Fungi

- Fungi able to convert from hyphal to yeast or yeast-like forms.
- Thermally dimorphic: in the "cold" are the mold form.

**Key Dimorphic Fungi**

*Histoplasma*

*Blastomyces*

*Coccidioides*

*Sporothrix*

**Figure II-5-4.** Dimorphic Fungi

## *Pseudohyphae (Candida albicans)*

Hyphae with constrictions at each septum

**Figure II-5-5.**
Candida Pseudohyphae

## *Spore types*

### Conidia

- **Asexual spores**
- Formed off of hyphae
- Common
- Airborne

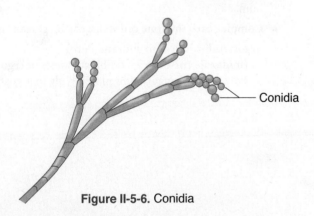

Conidia

**Figure II-5-6.** Conidia

**Blastoconidia:** "Buds" on yeasts (asexual budding daughter yeast cells)

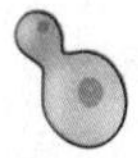

**Figure II-5-7.** Blastoconidia

**Arthroconidia:** Asexual spores formed by a **"joint"**

**Figure II-5-8.** Arthroconidia

**Spherules and Endospores (*Coccidioides*):** Spores inside the spherules in tissues

**Figure II-5-9.** Endospores and Spherules

# Diagnosis

**Table II-5-1.** Microscopic Methods/Special Fungal Stains

| Preparation | Fungal Color | Notes |
|---|---|---|
| KOH wet mount (KOH degrades human tissues leaving hyphae and yeasts visible) | Colorless (hyaline) refractive green or light olive to brown (dematiaceous) fungal elements | Heat gently; let sit 10 minutes; dissolves human cells |
| PAS | Hot pink | |
| **Silver** stain | Gray to black | *Pneumocystis* |
| Calcofluor white (can be done on wet mounts) | Bright blue-white on black | Scrapings or sections; fluorescent microscope needed |
| India ink wet mount of CSF sediment | Colorless cells with halos (capsule) on a black particulate background (*Cryptococcus neoformans*) | Only "rules in"; insensitive; misses 50% 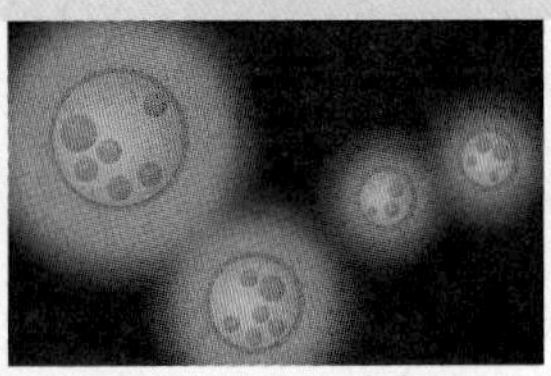 |

**Figure II-5-10.**
*Cryptococcus neoformans*

## Culture

(May take several weeks.) Special fungal media: inhibitory mold agar is modification of Sabouraud with antibiotics.

- **Sabouraud agar**
- Blood agar
- Both of the above with antibiotics

## Identification from cultures

- Fungal **morphology**
- PCR with nucleic acid probes

## Serology

(E.g., antibody screen, complement fixation, etc.) Looking for patient antibody.

## Fungal antigen detection: (CSF, serum)

Cryptococcal capsular polysaccharide detection by latex particle agglutination (LPA) or counter immunoelectrophoresis.

## Skin tests

- Most useful for **epidemiology** or **demonstration of anergy** to an agent you know patient is infected with (grave prognosis)
- Otherwise, like tuberculosis, a skin test **only indicates exposure** to the agent.

# NONSYSTEMIC FUNGAL INFECTIONS

## Superficial Infections (Keratinized Tissues)

### *Malassezia furfur*

**Normal skin flora (lipophilic yeast)**

Diseases

- **Pityriasis or tinea versicolor**
  - Superficial infection of keratinized cells
  - Moist, warm climates predispose
  - **Hypopigmented spots on the chest/back** (blotchy suntan)
  - KOH mount of skin scales: spaghetti and meatballs (bacon and eggs) **Yeast clusters & short curved septate hyphae**
  - Coppery-orange fluoresence under Wood lamp (UV)
  - Treatment is topical selenium sulfide; recurs.
- **Fungemia in premature infants** on intravenous lipid supplements

**Figure II-5-11.** *Malassezia furfur*

## Cutaneous Fungal Infections (Without Systemic Disease)

Yeast or dermatophytic infections.

### *Yeast skin infections*

- Commonly **cutaneous or mucocutaneous candidiasis**
- May disseminate in compromised patients
- Discussed with opportunistic fungi

### *Dermatophytes (group of fungi)*

- **Filamentous** fungi (**monomorphic**)
- **Infect only skin and hair and/or nails** (do not disseminate)
- Three genera:

  *Trichophyton*—Infects skin, hair and nails

  *Microsporum*—Infects hair and skin

  *Epidermophyton*—Infects nails and skin

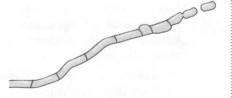

**Figure II-5-12.** Dermatophyte

Diseases

- Dermatophytic Infections = **Tineas** (Ringworms)
  - Itching is the most common symptom of all tineas.
  - If **highly inflammatory**, generally from **animals** (zoophilic)
  - If **little inflammation**, generally from humans

## Key Vignette Clues

*Malassezia furfur*

- Patient with blotchy hypopigmentation of skin
- KOH scraping shows "spaghetti and meatballs"

## Key Vignette Clues

**Dermatophytes**

- Patient with scaly, pruritic ring-like lesions of skin. May involve hair shaft or nails.
- KOH scraping shows arthroconidia and hyphae.

– Tinea capitis = ringworm of the scalp

– The most serious of the tineas capiti is **favus** (tinea favosa), which causes **permanent hair loss** and is very contagious.

– Tinea barbae = ringworm of the bearded region

– Tinea corporis = dermatophytic infection of the glabrous skin

– Tinea cruris = jock itch

– Tinea pedis = athlete's foot

– Tinea unguium = ringworm of the nails

## Differential Diagnosis

- *C. albicans*
- *S. pyogenes/S. aureus (impetigo)*

**Diagnosis**

- *Microsporum* fluoresces a bright yellow-green (Wood lamp)
- **KOH mount** of nail or skin scrapings should show **arthroconidia and hyphae.**

**Treatment**

- Topical imidazoles or tolnaftate
- Oral imidazoles or griseofulvin where hairs are infected, or skin contact hurts
- **Keep areas dry.**

**ID reaction**

(Dermatophy<u>id</u>) = Allergic response to circulating fungal antigens

## Key Vignette Clues

**Sporothrix schenckii**

- Patient with subcutaneous/lymphocu-taneous mycetoma
- Gardener, florist, basket weaver
- Cigar-shaped yeasts in pus

# Subcutaneous Mycoses

## *Sporothrix schenckii*

**Dimorphic Fungus**

- **Environmental form:** on **plant material**, worldwide as **hyphae with rosettes and sleeves of conidia**
- **Traumatic implantation** (rose or plum tree thorns, wire/sphagnum moss)
- **Tissue form: cigar-shaped yeast** in tissue

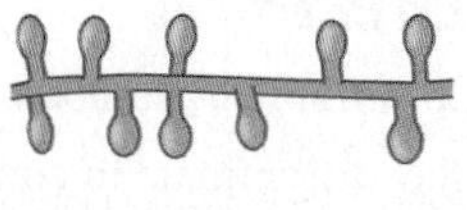

**Figure II-5-13.** *Sporothrix* Hyphae

**Diseases**

- **Sporotrichosis (rose gardener disease):** subcutaneous or lymphocutaneous lesions. Treatment: itraconazole or **potassium iodide in milk**
- **Pulmonary** (acute or chronic) **sporotrichosis.** Urban alcoholics, particularly homeless (**alcoholic rose-garden-sleeper disease**)

**Treatment:** Itraconazole or amphotericin B

## Differential Diagnosis

- *B. dermatitidis*
- *F. tularensis*
- Atypical mycobacteria

**Figure II-5-14.** *Sporothrix*

# DEEP FUNGAL INFECTIONS

## Classical Pathogens

Three important classical pathogens in the U.S.:

- *Histoplasma*
- *Coccidioides*
- *Blastomyces*

**All** 3 pathogens **cause**

- **Acute pulmonary** (asymptomatic or self-resolving in about **95%** of the cases)
- **Chronic** pulmonary, or
- **Disseminated** infections

### Diagnosis

(Most people never see a doctor.)

- Sputum cytology (calcofluor white helpful)
- **Sputum cultures** on blood agar and **special fungal media** (inhibitory mold agar, Sabouraud)
- Peripheral blood cultures are useful for *Histoplasma* since it circulates in RES cells.

## *Histoplasma capsulatum*

### Dimorphic Fungus

- **Environmental form: hyphae** with **microconidia** and **tuberculate macroconidia**
  - Endemic region: **Eastern Great Lakes, Ohio, Mississippi, and Missouri River beds**

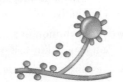

**Figure II-5-15.** *Histoplasma* Environmental Form

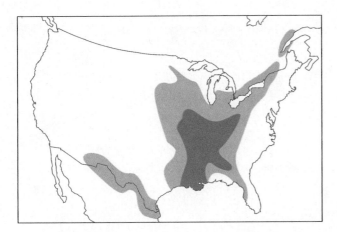

**Figure II-5-16.** *Histoplasma* Endemic Region

## Key Vignette Clues

*Histoplasma capsulatum*

- Normal patient with acute pulmonary; immunocompromised patient with chronic pulmonary or disseminated infection
- States following drainages of Great Lakes to Gulf of Mexico
- Exposure to bird or bat excrement
- Sputum or blood cultures with mononuclear cells packed with yeast cells

## COMLEX Note

Because all systemic fungal infections present similarly (acute pulmonary, chronic, disseminated), it is important to pay attention to tissue (diagnostic stage) and geographic location.

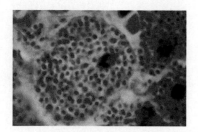

*Histoplasma capsulatum* yeast cells within an RES cell

## Differential Diagnosis

- *B. dermatitidis*
- *A. fumigatus*
- *H. capsulatum*
- *M. tuberculosis*
- *S. pneumoniae*

– Found in **soil (dust) enriched with bird or bat feces**

– Spelunking (cave exploring), cleaning chicken coops, or bulldozing starling roosts

- **Tissue form: small intracellular yeasts** with narrow neck on bud; **no capsule**
- **Facultative intracellular parasite** found in **reticuloendothelial (RES) cells** (tiny; can get 30 or so in a human cell)

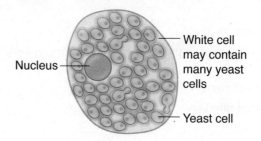

**Figure II-5-17.** Human RES Cell

### Disease

**Fungus flu** (a pneumonia)

- Asymptomatic or acute (but self-resolving) pneumonia with flu-like symptomatology
- **Hepatosplenomegaly may be present** even in acute pulmonary infections (facultative intracellular RES)
- Very common in summer in endemic areas: children or newcomers (80% of adults are skin-test positive in some areas)
- Lesions have a tendency to **calcify as they heal**.
- Relapse potential increases with T cell immunosuppression.
- **Disseminated infections:** Mucocutaneous lesions are common; also common **in AIDS** patients in endemic area.

**Treatment:** Itraconazole for mild, amphotericin B for severe

## *Coccidioides immitis*

**Dimorphic Fungus**

- **Environmental form: hyphae** breaking up into **arthroconidia** found **in desert sand**

**Figure II-5-18.**
*Coccicioides immitis*

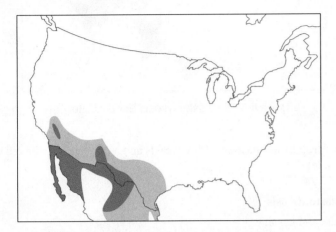

**Figure II-5-19.** *Coccidioides* Endemic Region

- Endemic region: **Southwestern United States**—Southern **California** (especially San Joaquin Valley), Arizona, New Mexico, Texas, Nevada

- Arthroconidia are inhaled, round up, and enlarged, becoming spherules inside which the cytoplasm walls off, forming endospores.

**Figure II-5-20.**
*Coccidioides immitis* Spherules

- **Tissue form: spherules with endospores**

**Disease: Valley fever** (asymptomatic to **self-resolving pneumonia**)

- **Desert bumps** (erythema nodosum) and arthritis are generally good prognostic signs.
- Very common in endemic region
- **Pulmonary lesions have a tendency to calcify as they heal.**
- **Systemic infections are a problem in AIDS and immunocompromised patients** in endemic region (meningitis, mucocutaneous lesions).
- Tendency to **disseminate in third trimester of pregnancy.**

**Treatment:** Azoles for mild to moderate (itraconazole, etc.), amphotericin B for severe

### Key Vignette Clues

*Coccidioides immitis*

- Normal patient with erythema nodosum or self-resolving pneumonia
- Immunocompromised patient with calcifying chronic pulmonary or disseminated infections
- Pregnant female in third trimester, disseminated infection
- Desert southwest
- Sputum has spherules with endospores

## *Blastomyces dermatitidis*

**Dimorphic Fungus**

Environmental form: **hyphae** with **nondescript conidia** (i.e., no fancy arrangements)

- Association not definitively known, **appears to be associated with rotting wood** such as beaver dams
- Endemic region: Upper Great Lakes, Ohio, Mississippi River beds, plus the southeastern seaboard of the U.S. and northern Minnesota into Canada

**Figure II-5-21.** *Blastomyces dermatitidis* Hyphae with Conidia

## Key Vignette Clues

*Blastomyces dermatitidis*

- Normal patient with acute pulmonary symptoms

- Immunocompromised patient with chronic pulmonary or disseminated infection

- North and South Carolina (otherwise coexists with *Histoplasma*)

- Sputum has broad-based, budding yeasts with double, refractile cell walls

## Differential Diagnosis

- *M. tuberculosis*

- *S. pneumoniae/K. pneumoniae*

- Influenza

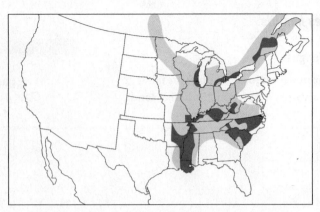

**Figure II-5-22.** Blastomycosis Endemic Region

**Tissue form: broad-based budding yeasts** and a double refractile cell wall (not capsule)

**Disease: Blastomycosis**

- Acute and chronic pulmonary disease

- Considered less likely to self-resolve than *Histoplasma* or *Coccidioides*, so many physicians will treat even acute infections.

- Disseminated disease

**Figure II-5-23.** *Blastomyces dermatitidis* Broad-Based Budding Yeasts

**Treatment:** Itraconazole for mild, amphotericin B for severe

# Opportunistic Fungi

## Aspergillus fumigatus

Monomorphic filamentous fungus

- **Dichotomously branching**
- **Generally acute angles**
- **Frequent septate hyphae with 45° angles**
- One of our **major recyclers:** compost pits, moldy marijuana

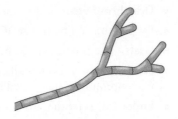

**Figure II-5-24.** *Aspergillus* Showing Monomorphic Filamentous Fungus

Diseases/Predisposing Conditions

- **Allergic bronchopulmonary aspergillosis**/asthma, cystic fibrosis (growing in mucous plugs in the lung but not penetrating the lung tissue)
- **Fungus ball**: free in preformed lung cavities (surgical removal to reduce coughing, which may induce pulmonary hemorrhage)
- **Invasive aspergillosis**/severe neutropenia, CGD, CF, burns
  - Invades tissues causing infarcts and hemorrhage.
  - Nasal colonization → **pneumonia or meningitis**
  - **Cellulitis**/in burn patients; may also disseminate

**Treatment:** Voriconazole for invasive and aspergilloma, glucocorticoids + itraconazole for ABPA

## Candida albicans (and other species of Candida)

- **Yeast** endogenous to our mucous membrane normal flora
- *C. albicans* yeasts form germ tubes at 37°C in serum.
- Forms **pseudohyphae** and **true hyphae** when it invades tissues (nonpathogenic *Candida* do not).

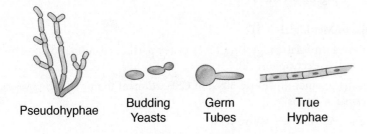

Pseudohyphae    Budding Yeasts    Germ Tubes    True Hyphae

**Figure II-5-25.** *Candida albicans*

## Key Vignette Clues

*Aspergillus fumigatus*

- Patient with asthma, cystic fibrosis—growing mucous plugs in lung
- Patient with cavitary lung lesions—fungus ball
- Patient with burns—cellulitis, invasion
- Immunocompromised patient—pneumonia, meningitis
- Septate hyphae branch at acute angles

## Differential Diagnosis

- *Nocardia* species
- *M. tuberculosis*
- *Mucor* species

*Aspergilus fumigatus*

## Key Vignette Clues

*Candida albicans*

- Immunocompromised patient, overuse of antibiotics—thrush, spread down GI tract, septicemia
- IV drug abusers—endocarditis
- Germ tube test demonstrates pseudohyphae and hyphae

## Diseases/Predisposing Conditions

- **Perlèche**: crevices of mouth/malnutrition
- **Oral thrush**/prematurity, antibiotic use, immunocompromised (IC) host, AIDS
- **Esophagitis**/antibiotic use, IC host, AIDS
- **Gastritis**/antibiotic use, IC host, AIDS
- **Septicemia** (with endophthalmitis and macronodular skin lesions)/immunocompromised, cancer and intravenous (IV) patients
- **Endocarditis** (with transient septicemias)/**IV drug abusers**
- **Cutaneous infections**/obesity and infants; patients with rubber gloves
- **Yeast vaginitis**/particularly a problem in diabetic women
- Chronic mucocutaneous candidiasis/endocrine defects; anergy to *Candida*

## Differential Diagnosis (a short list)

- *G. vaginalis*
- HSV
- *S. epidermidis/E. faecalis*

## Diagnosis

- KOH: pseudohyphae, true hyphae, budding yeasts
- Septicemia: culture lab identification: biochemical tests/formation of germ tubes

## Treatment

- Topical imidazoles or oral imidazoles; nystatin
- Disseminated: Amphotericin B or fluconazole

## Key Vignette Clues

### *Cryptococcus neoformans*

- Pigeon breeder with acute pulmonary symptoms
- Hodgkins/AIDS patient with meningitis
- India ink mount of CSF with encapsulated yeasts

## *Cryptococcus neoformans*

**Encapsulated Yeast (Monomorphic)**

**Environmental Source:** Soil enriched with pigeon droppings

**Diseases/Predisposing Conditions**

- **Meningitis/Hodgkin, AIDS (the dominant meningitis)**
- **Acute pulmonary** (usually asymptomatic)/**pigeon breeders**

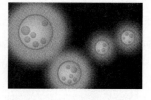

*Cryptococcus neoformans*

**Diagnosis of Meningitis: CSF**

- Detect capsular antigen in CSF (by latex particle agglutination or counter immunoelectrophoresis)
- India ink mount (misses 50%) of CSF sediment to find budding yeasts with capsular "halos"
- Cultures (urease positive yeast)

**Treatment:** AMB+5FC (flucytosine) until afebrile and culture negative (minimum of 10 weeks), then fluconazole

## Differential Diagnosis

- *H. capsulatum*
- *P. jiroveci*
- Atypical mycobacteria
- *M. tuberculosis*
- *Nocardia* species

## *Mucor, Rhizopus, Absidia (Zygomycophyta)*

Nonseptate filamentous fungi

**Environmental Source: Soil;** sporangiospores are inhaled

## Key Vignette Clues

### *Mucor, Rhizopus, Absidia*

- Ketoacidotic diabetic or leukemic patient with rhinocerebral infection
- Biopsy with nonseptate, irregular-width hyphae branching at 90-degree angles

**Figure II-5-26.** Nonseptate Hyphae with Broad Angles

**Disease**

- **Rhinocerebral infection** caused by *Mucor* (or other zygomycophyta)
- (Old names: Mucormycosis = Phycomycosis = Zygomycosis)
- Characterized by paranasal swelling, necrotic tissues, hemorrhagic exudates from nose and eyes, and mental lethargy
- Occurs in **ketoacidotic diabetic patients and leukemic patients**
- These fungi penetrate without respect to anatomical barriers, progressing rapidly from sinuses into the brain tissue

**Diagnosis:** KOH of tissue; broad ribbon-like nonseptate hyphae with about 90° angles on branches.

**Treatment**

- Debride necrotic tissue and start Amphotericin B fast
- High fatality rate because of rapid growth and invasion

## Differential Diagnosis

*A. fumigatus*

## Pneumocystis jirovecii (formerly P. carinii)

**Fungus** (based on molecular techniques like **ribotyping**)

- **Obligate extracellular parasite**
- **Silver stained cysts in tissues**

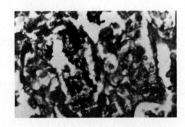

*Pneumocystis, silver stain, exudate*

### Key Vignette Clues

*Pneumocystis jirovecii*

- Premature infant or AIDS patient with atypical pneumonia
- Biopsy with honeycomb exudate and silver-staining cysts
- X-ray: ground glass

**Disease: Interstitial pneumonia**

- Pneumonia in AIDS patients even with prophylaxis (mean CD4+/mm$^3$ of 26), malnourished babies, premature neonates, and some other IC adults and kids
- Symptoms: fever, cough, shortness of breath; sputum nonproductive except in smokers
- Serum leaks into alveoli, producing an exudate with a foamy or **honeycomb appearance on H & E stain.** (Silver stain reveals the holes in the exudate are actually the cysts and trophozoites, which do not stain with H & E.)
- X-ray: **patchy infiltrative** (ground glass appearance); the lower lobe periphery may be spared.

**Diagnosis: Silver-staining cysts** in bronchial alveolar lavage fluids or biopsy

**Treatment:** Trimethoprim/sulfamethoxazole for mild; dapsone for moderate to severe

## Emerging Drug Resistances in Fungi

- Fungi are developing drug resistances by mechanisms analogous to those seen in bacteria.
- Resistance to azoles (clotrimazole, miconazole, ketoconazole, fluconazole) becoming widespread
- *Aspergillus, Candida, Cryptococcus*

## Differential Diagnosis

- *Nocardia* species
- *M. tuberculosis*
- Atypical mycobacteria
- *L. pneumophila*
- CMV
- *S. pneumoniae/K. pneumoniae*

## Review Questions

1. An obese 32-year-old diabetic woman presents with complaint of red and painful skin in her abdominal skin folds. Examination reveals a creamy white material at the base of the fold. It is erythematous underneath and extends beyond the creamy material. Microscopic examination of the exudate reveals oval budding structures (3 × 6 μm) mixed with more budding elongated forms. The most likely causal agent is

   (A) *Aspergillus fumigatus*
   (B) *Candida albicans*
   (C) *Epidermophyton floccosum*
   (D) *Microsporum canis*
   (E) *Sporothrix schenckii*

2. A 19-year-old migrant worker from the southwestern U.S. is brought to the family doctor complaining of cough, pleuritic chest pain, fever, and malaise. He also complains of a backache and headache. He is found to have an erythematous skin rash on his lower limbs. A chest radiograph reveals several calcifying lesions. Which of the following structures is most likely to be found?

   (A) Broad-based budding yeast
   (B) Monomorphic encapsulated yeast
   (C) Nonseptate hyphae with broad angles
   (D) Septate hyphae branching dichotomously at acute angles
   (E) Spherules with endospores

3. An 18-year-old high school student in rural north Mississippi develops fever, cough, and chest pain. The cough, associated with weight loss, persisted. Because of poor performance at football practice, he was advised to see a physician. Lymph node biopsies stained with H and E reveal granulomatous inflammation and macrophages engorged with oval structures measuring 2–4 μm. Cultures incubated at room temperature grow powdery white colonies, which on microscopic study have tuberculate spores. The high school student most likely acquired the infection from which of the following?

   (A) Desert sand
   (B) Cat feces
   (C) Soil enriched with bird excrement
   (D) Another human via respiratory secretions
   (E) Contaminated drinking water

4. A 32-year-old man from the southeastern U.S. is referred to a tertiary care center with chronic pneumonia. He also complains of malaise, weight loss, night sweats, chest pain, breathlessness, and hoarseness. Sputum smear revealed thick-walled, refractile, double-contoured yeast cells. What is the most common site of dissemination for the causal organism?

   (A) Heart
   (B) Liver
   (C) Mucocutaneous
   (D) Skin
   (E) Spleen

5. A 55-year-old man who recently recovered uneventfully from a heart valve transplant presents to the emergency room with pleuritic chest pain, hemoptysis, fever, and chills. While he is being examined, he has a myocardial infarction and the medical team is unable to revive him. An autopsy revealed septate, acutely branching hyphae in many tissues. Which of the following organisms is most likely to be identified?

(A) *Aspergillus fumigatus*

(B) *Blastomyces dermatitidis*

(C) *Cryptococcus neoformans*

(D) *Histoplasma capsulatum*

(E) *Mucor* species

6. A 33-year-old HIV-positive man complains of headache and blurred vision. Physical examination reveals papilledema and ataxia. A head CT scan is normal, but CSF obtained by lumbar puncture reveals encapsulated organisms visible by India ink. Which of the following is true concerning this organism?

(A) It can also be seen as "spaghetti and meatballs" on KOH stain

(B) It consists of branching septate hyphae

(C) It exists as a mycelial form at room temperature and a yeast at 37°C

(D) It is an encapsulated nondimorphic yeast found worldwide

(E) It is a nonencapsulated dimorphic yeast that reproduces by budding

7. A 32-year-old man who has AIDS presents to his physician with progressively increasing dyspnea over the past 3 weeks. He also complains of a dry, painful cough, fatigue, and low-grade fever. A chest x-ray reveals bilateral symmetrical interstitial and alveolar infiltration. Which of the following agents is the most likely cause of the above?

(A) *Cryptococcus neoformans*

(B) *Cryptosporidium parvum*

(C) *Histoplasma capsulatum*

(D) *Pneumocystis jiroveci*

(E) *Toxoplasma gondii*

## Answers and Explanations

1. **Answer: B.** Cutaneous candidiasis is a problem in skin folds of obese individuals. It is an even greater problem in diabetic patients because of the high sugar levels. Only the members of the genus *Candida* would produce a creamy surface growth. The erythematous base is due to the production of a cytotoxin. *Aspergillus, Epidermophyton,* and *Microsporum* are all monomorphic filamentous fungi and would not fit the description. *Sporothrix* is found as cigar-shaped budding yeasts but would not clinically present like this. It is traumatically implanted to start subcutaneous infections.

2. **Answer: E.** The causal agent is *Coccidioides immitis.* The clues are southwest U.S., migrant worker (works outside), erythematous skin rash (erythema nodosum). The diagnostic form of *C. immitis* in the sputum is a spherule. Broad-based budding yeast (**choice A**) describes *Blastomyces dermatitidis.*

Monomorphic encapsulated yeast (**choice B**) describes *Cryptococcus neoformans*. Nonseptate hyphae with broad angles (**choice C**) describes *Mucor* species. Septate hyphae dichotomously branching at acute angles (**choice D**) describes *Aspergillus fumigatus*.

3.  **Answer: C.** The clues here are the geography, weight loss, granulomatous inflammation, and macrophages engorged with oval structures (RES disease). The colonial appearance and tuberculate spores strongly suggest the causal agent to be *Histoplasma capsulatum*. *Histoplasma* is acquired from dusty environments containing bird (most often chicken or starling) or bat feces. The areas of highest endemicity are in the great central river beds with bat caves, chicken coops, and starling roosts having extremely high levels.

4.  **Answer: D.** The causal agent is *Blastomyces <u>dermatitidis</u>*. The clues are southeastern U.S. and a sputum smear revealing thick-walled, refractile, double-contoured yeast cells (another way to say broad-based budding). Remember that the name of the organism contains the site of dissemination.

5.  **Answer: A.** The clues are immunocompromised, myocardial infarction, and septate acutely branching hyphae in nearly every tissue. Remember, *Aspergillus* is extremely invasive in immunocompromised individuals.

6.  **Answer: D.** The causal agent is *Cryptococcus neoformans*. The clues are HIV, headache and blurred vision, encapsulated organisms in CSF. *C. neoformans* is the number one cause of meningitis in AIDS patients. You should know that it is monomorphic. "Spaghetti and meatballs" KOH (**choice A**) describes *Malassezia furfur*. Branching septate hyphae (**choice B**) describes *Aspergillus*. Mycelial form at room temperature and a yeast at 37°C (**choice C**) describes all of the dimorphic fungi. Nonencapsulated dimorphic yeast that reproduces by budding (**choice E**) describes *Blastomyces*.

7.  **Answer: D.** The clues are AIDS patient and atypical pneumonia. *Pneumocystis jirovecii* is the hallmark atypical pneumonia of AIDS.

# Medical Parasitology 6

## What the COMLEX Requires You To Know

- The COMLEX generally does not have many parasitology questions, but you will be expected to know the following:

- Name of organism (scientific and common) and major parasite type (e.g., nematode or flagellate)

- Name of disease (common names are frequently used)

- Route of spread, especially vector names and reservoir hosts

For the following organisms you should also know symptoms and understand the pathogenicity:

*Entamoeba*
*Giardia*
***Plasmodium***
*Toxoplasma*
*Cryptosporidium*
*Enterobius*
*Ascaris*
*Hookworms*
*Trichinella*
*Schistosoma*

- Review additional bolded material in the following tables.

# CLASSIFICATION OF PARASITES

Medical parasitology is the study of the invertebrate animals and the diseases they cause. Parasites are classified as protozoans or metazoans.

The most important organisms in the U.S. are identified in the following two tables in boldface type.

**Table II-6-1.** Protozoans

| Common Name | Amebae | Flagellates | Apicomplexa |
|---|---|---|---|
| Important Genera | ***Entamoeba***<br>*Naegleria*<br>*Acanthamoeba* | LUMINAL (GUT, UG)<br>***Trichomonas***<br>***Giardia***<br>HEMOFLAGELLATES<br>*Leishmania*<br>*Trypanosoma* | BLOOD/TISSUE<br>***Plasmodium***<br>***Toxoplasma***<br>*Babesia*<br>INTESTINAL<br>***Cryptosporidium***<br>*Isospora* |

*Pneumocystis*, which was formerly classified as a protozoan, has been determined to be a fungus through ribotyping and other molecular biologic techniques.

**Table II-6-2.** Metazoans: Worms*

| Phylum | Flat worms (Platyhelminthes) | | Roundworms |
|---|---|---|---|
| Classes:<br>Common name: | **Trematodes**<br>(flukes) | **Cestodes**<br>(tapeworms) | **Nematodes****<br>(roundworms) |
| Genera: | *Fasciola*<br>*Fasciolopsis*<br>*Paragonimus*<br>*Clonorchis*<br>*Schistosoma* | *Diphyllobothrium*<br>*Hymenolepis*<br>*Taenia*<br>*Echinococcus* | ***Necator***<br>***Enterobius***<br>*Wuchereria/Brugia*<br>***Ascaris*** and ***Ancylostoma***<br>*Toxocara, Trichuris &*<br>*Trichinella*<br>*Onchocerca*<br>*Dracunculus*<br>*Eye worm (Loa loa)*<br>*Strongyloides* |

\* Metazoans also include the Arthropoda, which serve mainly as intermediate hosts (the crustaceans) or as vectors of disease (the Arachnida and Insecta).

\*\*Nematodes mnemonic.

## Hosts

The infected host is classified as

- **Intermediate**—host in which **larval or asexual stages develop**.
- **Definitive** —host in which the **adult or sexual stages occur**.

## Vectors

Vectors are **living transmitters** (e.g., a fly) of disease and may be

- **Mechanical,** which transport the parasite but there is no development of the parasite in the vector.
- **Biologic,** in which some stages of the life cycle occur.

# IMPORTANT PROTOZOAN PARASITES

**COMLEX Note**

Chronic diarrhea in AIDS patients with Acid-Fast oocysts most likely = *Cryptosporidium* followed by *Isospora*

**Table II-6-3.** Protozoan Parasites

| Species | Disease/Organs Most Affected | Form/Transmission | Diagnosis | Treatment |
|---|---|---|---|---|
| *Entamoeba histolytica* | **Amebiasis:** dysentery **Inverted flask-**shaped lesions in large intestine with extension to peritoneum and liver, lungs, brain, and heart **Blood and pus** in stools **Liver abscesses** | Cysts Fecal-oral transmission— water, fresh fruits, and vegetables | Trophozoites: or cysts in stool: Serology: Nuclei have sharp central karyosome and fine chromatin "spokes". | Metronidazole followed by iodoquinol |
| *Giardia lamblia* | Giardiasis: Ventral sucking disk attaches to lining of duodenal wall, causing **a fatty, foul-smelling diarrhea** (diarrhea → *malabsorption* duodenum, jejunum) | Cysts Fecal (human, beaver, muskrat, etc.), oral transmission—water, food, day care, oral-anal sex | Trophozoites or cysts in stool or fecal antigen test (replaces "string" test) "Falling leaf" motility | Metronidazole |
| *Cryptosporidium* **sp.** *C. parvum* | Cryptosporidiosis: transient diarrhea in healthy, severe in immunocompromised hosts | Cysts Undercooked meat, water; not killed by chlorination | **Acid fast oocysts in stool:** Biopsy shows dots (cysts) in intestinal glands | Nothing is 100% effective; nitrazoxanide, puromycin, or azithromycin are the DOCs |
| *Isospora belli* | Transient diarrhea in AIDS patients; diarrhea mimics giardiasis malabsorption syndrome | Oocysts Ingestion Fecal-oral | **Acid-fast and elliptical oocysts in stool;** contain 2 sporocysts each with 4 sporozoites | TMP-SMX or pyrimethamine/ sulfadiazine |
| *Cyclospora cayetanensis* | Self-limited diarrhea in immunocompetent; prolonged and severe **diarrhea in AIDS** patients | Oocysts, water | Fecal; **acid-fast and spherical oocysts**; contain 2 sporocysts each with 2 sporozoites; UV fluorescence | TMP-SMX |

*(Continued)*

**Table II-6-3.** Protozoan Parasites (*Cont'd*)

| Species | Disease/Organs Most Affected | Form/Transmission | Diagnosis | Treatment |
|---------|------------------------------|-------------------|-----------|-----------|
| *Microsporidia* (6 genera) | Microsporidiosis: persistent, debilitating **diarrhea in AIDS** patients; other spp → neurologic, hepatitis, disseminated | Spores ingested | **Gram (+), acid-fast spores** in stool or biopsy material | None proven to be effective |
| *Trichomonas vaginalis* (urogenital) | Trichomoniasis: often asymptomatic or **frothy vaginal discharge** | Trophozoites **Sexual** | Motile trophozoites in methylene blue wet mount; **corkscrew motility** | **Metronidazole** |

**COMLEX Note**

Persistent diarrhea = Parasite

# Free Living Amebae

- Occur in water or soil (*Naegleria, Acanthamoeba*)
- Occur in contact lens saline solutions (*Acanthamoeba*): cysts from dust contaminate

**Table II-6-4.** Free Living Amoebae That Occasionally Infect Humans

| Species | Disease / Locale | Form / Transmission | Diagnosis | Treatment |
|---------|------------------|---------------------|-----------|-----------|
| *Naegleria* | **Primary amebic meningo-encephalitis** (PAM): severe **prefrontal headache**, nausea, high fever, **altered sense of smell**; often fatal | Free-living amebae picked up while swimming or **diving in very warm fresh water** | Motile trophozoites in CSF. Culture on plates seeded with gram-negative bacteria; amebae will leave trails | Amphotericin B (rarely successful) |
| *Acanthamoeba* | **Keratitis; granulomatous amebic encephalitis** (GAE) in immunocompromised patients: insidious onset but progressive to death | Free living amebae in contaminated **contact lens solution (airborne cysts)** Not certain for GAE: inhalation or contact with contaminated soil or water | Star-shaped cysts on biopsy; rarely seen in CSF. Culture as above | Keratitis: topical miconazole and propamidine isethionate GAE: ketoconazole, sulfamethazine (rarely successful) |

| Differential Diagnosis | |
|---|---|
| Naegleria | Acanthamoeba |
| *N. meningitidis, S. pneumoniae, H. influenzae* (bacterial meningitis) | *C. immitis, H. capsulatum, T. gondii, M. tuberculosis*, CMV, HSV |

## *Plasmodium* Species

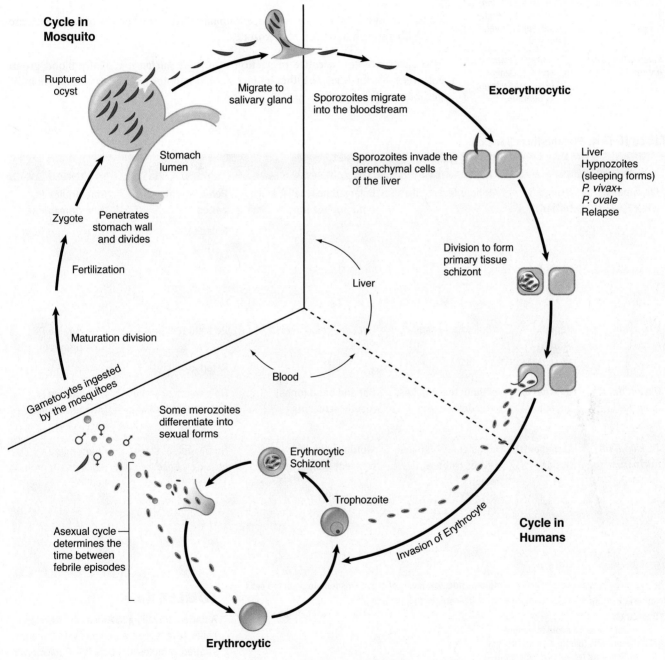

**Figure II-6-1.** *Plasmodium* Life Cycle

| Differential Diagnosis | |
| --- | --- |
| **Plasmodium vivax** | B. microti, Leishmania species, Dengue fever, yellow fever, C. burnetii |
| Plasmodium ovale | B. microti, Leishmania species, Dengue fever, yellow fever, C. burnetii |
| Plasmodium malariae | B. microti, Leishmania species, Dengue fever, yellow fever, C. burnetii |
| **Plasmodium falciparum** | B. microti, Leishmania species, Dengue fever, yellow fever, C. burnetii |

Each *Plasmodium* has two distinct hosts.

- A vertebrate such as the human where asexual phase (schizogony) takes place in the liver and red blood cells.
- An arthropod host (*Anopheles* mosquito) where gametogony (sexual phase) and sporogony take place.

Cause disease by a wide variety of mechanisms, including metabolism of hemoglobin and lysis of infected cells leading to anemia and to agglutination of infected RBC.

Cause paroxysms (chills, fever spike, and malarial rigors) when the infected RBC are lysed, liberating a new crop of merozoites.

HbS heterozygote—selective protection against *P. falciparum*. Duffy blood group Ag—receptor for *P. vivax*. Other abnormal hemoglobins (e.g., thalassemia) are indigestible to all *Plasmodium* spp.

## Table II-6-5. Plasmodium Species

| Species | Disease | Important Features | Blood Smears | Liver Stages | Treatment** |
| --- | --- | --- | --- | --- | --- |
| **Plasmodium vivax** | **Benign tertian** | 48-hour fever spikes | Enlarged host cells; ameboid trophozoites | Persistent **hypnozoites** **Relapse*** | Chloroquine $PO_4$ then **primaquine** |
| Plasmodium ovale | Benign tertian | 48-hour fever spikes | Oval, jagged, infected RBCs | Persistent hypnozoites Relapse | Chloroquine $PO_4$ then primaquine |
| Plasmodium malariae | **Quartan** or malarial | 72-hour fever spikes; recrudescence* | Bar and band forms; rosette schizonts | No persistent stage*; Recrudescence* | Chloroquine $PO_4$ (no radical cure necessary) |
| **Plasmodium falciparum** | **Malignant tertian** | Irregular fever spikes; causes **cerebral malaria** | **Multiple ring forms crescent-shaped gametes** | No persistent stage*; recrudescence | Chloroquine resistance a problem*** |

*Recrudescence is a reoccurrence of symptoms from low levels of organisms remaining in red cells.

Relapse is a return of clinical symptoms from liver stages (hypnozoites).

**Treatment:
1. Suppressive (to avoid infection)
2. Therapeutic (eliminate erythrocytic)
3. Radical cure (eliminate hypnozoites)
4. Gametocidal (destruction of gametocytes)
   Successful treatment is accomplished with chloroquine followed by primaquine. Chloroquine therapy is suppressive, therapeutic, and gametocidal, whereas primaquine eliminates the exoerythrocytic form.

***Use quinine sulfate plus pyrimethamine-sulfadoxine.

### COMLEX Note

A patient travelling to Africa who develops chills, fever spikes and rigors with banana shaped gametes in the rbc's = *P. falciparum*

# Hemoflagellates (Trypanosomes and Leishmanias)

Hemoflagellates infect blood and tissues.

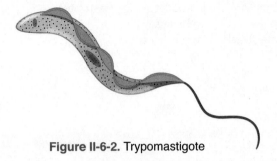

**Figure II-6-2.** Trypomastigote

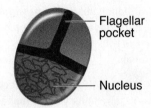

**Figure II-6-3.** Amastigote

Trypanosomes are found
- In human blood as trypomastigotes with flagellum and undulating membrane
- In tissues as **amastigotes (oval cells having neither the flagellum nor undulating membrane)**

*Leishmania* found always as amastigotes in macrophages.

**COMLEX Note**

For the hemoflagellates, try to recall the vector and one prominent disease symptom.

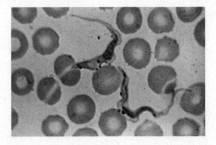

Trypomastigote in blood smear

## Table II-6-6. Hemoflagellates

| Species | Disease | Vector/Form/Transmission | Reservoirs | Diagnosis | Treatment |
|---|---|---|---|---|---|
| *Trypanosoma cruzi** | **Chagas disease** (American trypanosomiasis) Latin America Swelling around eye: (**Romaña sign**) common early sign Cardiac muscle, liver, brain often involved | **Reduviid bug (kissing or cone bug**; genus *Triatoma*) passes trypomastigote (flagellated form) **in feces**; scratching implants in mucosa | Cats, dogs, armadillos, opossums Poverty housing | Blood films, **trypomastigotes** | Benzimidazole |
| *Trypanosoma brucei gambiense Trypanosoma b. rhodesiense* | **African sleeping sickness** (African trypanosomiasis) **Antigenic variation** | Trypomastigote in saliva of **tsetse fly** contaminates bite | Humans, some wild animals | Trypomastigotes in blood films, CSF High immunoglobulin levels in CSF | Acute: suramin Chronic: melarsoprol |
| *Leishmania donovani*** complex | **Visceral Leishmaniasis** | **Sandfly** bite | Urban: humans Rural: rodents and wild animals | **Amastigotes in macrophages** in bone marrow, liver, spleen | Stibogluconate sodium (from CDC) |
| *Leishmania* (About 15 different species) | Cutaneous Leishmaniasis (Oriental sore, etc.) | **Sandfly** bite | Urban: humans Rural: rodents and wild animals | **Amastigotes in macrophages** in cutaneous lesions | Stibogluconate sodium |
| *Leishmania braziliensis* complex | Mucocutaneous Leishmaniasis | **Sandfly** bite | Urban: humans Rural: rodents and wild animals | Same | Stibogluconate sodium |

*T. cruzi: An estimated 1/2 million Americans are infected, creating some risk of transfusion transmission in U.S. In babies, acute infections often serious involving CNS.
  In older children and adults, mild acute infections but may become chronic with the risk of development of cardiomyopathy and heart failure.
**Leishmania all: Intracellular, sandfly vector, stibogluconate.

| Differential Diagnosis | | | | |
|---|---|---|---|---|
| *Trypanosoma cruzi** | *Trypanosoma brucei gambiense Trypanosoma b. rhodesiense* | *Leishmania donovani*** complex | *Leishmania* (About 15 different species) | *Leishmania braziliensis* complex |
| *T. gondii, Leishmania* species, *Plasmodium* species, *N. meningitidis/ S. pneumoniae* (meningitis) | *Plasmodium* species, *B. burgdorferi, M. tuberculosis, Brucella* species | *G.* lamblia, *I.* belli, Cyclospora | *Plasmodium* species and *M. tuberculosis* | *Plasmodium* species and *M. tuberculosis* |

# Miscellaneous Apicomplexa Infecting Blood or Tissues

**Table II-6-7.** Miscellaneous Apicomplexa Infecting Blood or Tissues

| Species | Disease/Locale of Origin | Transmission | Diagnosis | Treatment |
|---|---|---|---|---|
| **Babesia** (primarily a disease of cattle)<br><br>Humans: *Babesia microti*, WA1, & MO1 strains | Babesiosis (hemolytic, **malaria-like**)<br><br>Same range as lyme: NE, N Central, California, and NW U.S. | ***Ixodes* tick**<br><br>**Co-infections with *Borrelia*** | Giemsa stain of thin smear or hamster inoculation; small rings, maltese cross, tetrad in RBCs | Clindamycin + quinine |
| *Toxoplasma gondii* | See below | **Cat** is **essential definitive** host. Many other animals are intermediate host. Mode:<br>1) Raw meat in U.S. #1 = pork<br>2) Contact with cat feces | Serology<br><br>High IgM or rising IgM<br>acute infection | **Pyrimethamine + sulfadiazine** |

## *Toxoplasmosis*

**Diseases**

*Healthy individuals*

- *Toxoplasma* acquired after birth is most commonly asymptomatic or a mild, non-specific flu-like illness with lymphadenopathy and fever; heterophile-negative mononucleosis
- Once infected, as immunity develops, bradyzoites encyst, but generally remain viable as evidenced by a positive antibody titer.

*Pregnant patients*

- Women who acquire *Toxoplasma* as a primary infection during pregnancy present with flu-like illness/heterophile-negative mononucleosis.
- If primary maternal infection occurs during pregnancy, the fetus may be infected.
- If *Toxoplasma* crosses the placenta early, severe congenital infections (intracerebral calcifications, chorioretinitis, hydro- or microcephaly or convulsions) may occur.
- If *Toxoplasma* crosses the placenta later, infection may be inapparent, but may lead to progressive blindness in the child later in life (teens).
- Maternal antibodies (secondary infection) protect the fetus during pregnancy, even if the mother is re-exposed during pregnancy.

*AIDS patients*

- Leading cause of focal CNS disease in AIDS patients
- Brain scan will describe ring-enhancing lesions.
- Unless prophylactic drugs are given, AIDS patients who are seropositive for *Toxoplasma* will have reactivational infections.

## IMPORTANT METAZOAN PARASITES

### Trematodes

- Are commonly called flukes.
- Are leaf-shaped worms, which are generally flat and fleshy.
- Are hermaphroditic except for *Schistosoma*, which has separate male and female.
- Have complicated life cycles occurring in two or more hosts.
- Have operculated eggs (except for *Schistosoma*), which contaminate water, perpetuating the life cycle, and which are also used to diagnose infections.
- **The first intermediate hosts are snails.**

**Table II-6-8.** Trematode (Fluke) Diseases

| Organism | Common Name | Reservoir Host | Acquisition | Progression in Humans | Important Ova | Treatment |
|---|---|---|---|---|---|---|
| *S. mansoni Schistosoma japonicum* | **Intestinal schistoso-miasis** | Cats, dogs, cattle, etc. | Contact with water; **skin penetration** | Skin penetration (itching)→ mature in veins of mesentery → eggs cause granulomas in liver (liver enlargement in chronic cases) | | Praziquantel |
| *Schistosoma haemato-bium* | **Vesicular schistoso-miasis** | Primates | Contact with water; **skin penetration** | Skin penetration (itching) → mature in bladder veins; chronic infection has high association with **bladder carcinoma in Egypt and Africa** | | Praziquantel |
| **Non-human schisto-somes** | **Swimmer's itch** | Birds (Great Lakes U.S.) | Contact with water; **skin penetration** | Penetrate skin, producing **dermatitis** without further development in humans; itching is most intense at 2 to 3 days | | Trimeprazine Calamine Sedatives |
| *Clonorchis sinensis* | **Chinese liver fluke** | Dogs, cats, humans | Raw fish ingestion | Serum-like sickness | Operculated eggs | Praziquantel |

## Differential Diagnosis

| *S. mansoni Schistosoma japonicum* | *Schistosoma haematobium* | **Non-human schistosomes** | *Clonorchis sinensis* | *Fasciola hepatica* | *Fasciolopsis buski* | *Paragonimus westermani* |
|---|---|---|---|---|---|---|
| Hepatitis viruses (HAV, HBV, etc.), *Leishmania* species, *Plasmodium* species, *S. typhi* | *E. coli, M. tuberculosis* (renal), *Leishmania donovani* | *Trichophyton, Microsporum, Epidermophyton* species | Hepatitis viruses (HAV, HBV, etc.) | Hepatitis viruses (HAV, HBV, etc.), *E. histolytica* | *Leishmania* species, *S. typhi* | *M. tuberculosis, S. pneumoniae, K. pneumoniae* |

### COMLEX Note

Be prepared to differentiate between the schistosomes via the appearance of the eggs. *S mansoni* = subterminal spine, *S. hematobium* = terminal spine

## Cestodes

- Are the tapeworms.

- Consist of 3 basic portions: the head or scolex; a "neck" section, which produces the proglottids; and the segments or proglottids, which mature as they move away from the scolex. (The combination of the neck and pro-glottids is called the strobila.)

- Are hermaphroditic, with each proglottid developing both male and female reproductive organs, and mature eggs developing in the most distal proglottids.

- Adhere to the mucosa via the scolex, which is knobby looking and has either suckers or a sucking groove.

- Have no gastrointestinal (GI) tract; they absorb nutrients from the host's GI tract.

- Are diagnosed by finding eggs or proglottids in the feces.

- Have for the most part complex life cycles involving extraintestinal larval forms in intermediate hosts. When humans are the intermediate host, these infections are generally more serious than the intestinal infections with adult tapeworms.

# Gastrointestinal Cestodes (Tapeworms)

**Table II-6-9.** Gastrointestinal Cestodes (Tapeworms)

| Cestode* | Form/Transmission | Humans Are: | Disease/Organ Involvement/Symptoms (Sx) | Diagnosis | Treatment |
|---|---|---|---|---|---|
| *Taenia saginata* (beef tapeworm)<br><br>IH: cattle<br><br>DH: humans | Rare beef containing the **cysticerci** is ingested | DH* | **Intestinal tapeworm**/small intestine<br><br>Sx: Asymptomatic or vague abdominal pains | **Proglottids** or **eggs** in feces | Praziquantel |
| *Taenia solium* (pork tapeworm)<br><br>IH: swine; Rarely: humans | Water, vegetation, food contaminated with **eggs** **Autoinfection** | IH* | **Cysticercosis**/eggs → larva develop in brain, eye, heart, lung, etc.<br><br>Adult-onset epilepsy | Biopsy | Praziquantel: surgery in some sites |
| DH: humans; developing and Slavic countries | Rare/raw pork containing the **cysticerci** is ingested by humans | DH | **Intestinal tapeworm**<br><br>Sx: as for *Taenia saginata* | **Proglottids** or **eggs** in feces | Praziquantel |
| *Diphyllobothrium latum* (fish tapeworm)<br><br>IH (2): crustaceans → fish; rare: humans | Drinking pond water w/ → copepods (crustaceans) carrying the **larval** forms or frog/snake poultices | IH | **Sparganosis**/larvae penetrate intestinal wall and encyst | Biopsy | Praziquantel |
| DH: humans/mammals; cool lake regions | Rare, raw pickled fish → containing a **sparganum** | DH | **Intestinal tapeworm** (up to 10 meters)/small intestine **megaloblastic anemia** | Proglottids or eggs in feces | Praziquantel |
| *Echinococcus granulosus*<br><br>IH: herbivores; rare: humans<br><br>DH: carnivores in sheep-raising areas | Ingestion of eggs | IH | **Hydatid cyst disease**/liver & lung where cysts containing brood capsules develop | Imaging; serology | Surgery; albendazole |
| *Echinococcus multilocularis*<br><br>IH: rodents<br><br>DH: canines and cats; northern areas | Ingestion of eggs | IH | **Alveolar hydatid cyst disease** | As above | Surgical resection |

* Definitive host = adult tapeworm develops in; intermediate host = cysticerci or larvae develop in; cysticerci = encysted larvae found in intermediate host. Common name is in parentheses.

## Differential Diagnosis

| Taenia saginata (beef tapeworm)<br><br>IH: cattle<br><br>DH: humans | Taenia solium (pork tapeworm)<br><br>IH: swine; Rarely: humans<br><br>DH: humans; developing and Slavic countries | Diphyllobothrium latum (fish tapeworm)<br><br>IH (2): crustaceans → fish; rare: humans<br><br>DH: humans/mammals; cool lake regions | Echinococcus granulosus<br><br>IH: herbivores; rare: humans<br><br>DH: carnivores in sheep-raising areas | Echinococcus multilocularis<br><br>IH: rodents<br><br>DH: canines and cats; northern areas |
|---|---|---|---|---|
| D. latum, T. solium (DH) | C. neoformans, A. israelii, B. fragilis<br><br>D. latum, T. saginata | T. solium (DH), T. saginata | T. solium (IH), B. fragilis, M. tuberculosis, E. multilocularis | T. solium (IH), B. fragilis, M. tuberculosis, E. granulosis |

## Nematodes

- Are the roundworms
- Cause a wide variety of diseases (pinworms, whipworms, hookworms, trichinosis, threadworms, filariasis, etc.)
- Have round unsegmented bodies
- Are transmitted by:
  - ingestion of eggs (*Enterobius, Ascaris,* or *Trichuris*);
  - direct invasion of skin by larval forms (*Necator, Ancylostoma,* or *Strongyloides*);
  - ingestion of meat containing larvae (*Trichinella*); or
  - infection involving insects transmitting the larvae with bites (*Wuchereria, Loa loa, Mansonella, Onchocerca,* and *Dracunculus*).

**Table II-6-10.** Round Worms (Nematodes) Transmitted by Eggs

| Species | Disease/Organs Most Affected | Form/Transmission | Diagnosis | | Treatment |
|---|---|---|---|---|---|
| ***Enterobius vermicularis*** Most frequent helminth parasite in U.S. | **Pinworms**, large intestine, perianal itching | **Eggs**/person to person **autoinfection** | Sticky swab of perianal area Ova have flattened side with larvae inside | | Pyrantel, **mebendazole** Treat entire family (albendazole) |
| ***Trichuris trichiura*** | **Whipworm** cecum, appendicitis, and rectal prolapse | **Eggs** ingested | **Barrel-shaped eggs with bipolar plugs** in stools | | Albendazole |
| ***Ascaris lumbricoides*** Most common helminth worldwide Largest roundworm | **Ascariasis** Ingest egg → larva migrate thru lungs (cough) and mature in small intestine; may obstruct intestine or bile duct | **Eggs** ingested | **Bile stained, knobby eggs** Adults **6–12"** roundworms | | Supportive therapy during pneumonitis; surgery for ectopic migrations; mebendazole |
| ***Toxocara canis or cati*** (dog/cat ascarids) | **Visceral Larva Migrans** Larvae wander aimlessly until they die, cause inflammation | **Eggs** ingested/ from handling puppies or from eating dirt in yard (pica) | Clinical findings and serology | | Mebendazole; self-limiting in most cases (albendazole) |

| Differential Diagnosis | | | |
|---|---|---|---|
| *Enterobius vermicularis* Most frequent helminth parasite in U.S. | *Trichuris trichiura* | *Ascaris lumbricoides* Most common helminth worldwide Largest roundworm | *Toxocara canis or cati* (dog/cat Ascarids) |
| *A. lumbricoides, G. lamblia* | *A. lumbricoides, E. histolytica, E. vermicularis, T. saginata/solium, S. stercoralis* | *E. vermicularis, T. trichiura* | *A. lumbricoides, T. trichiura, A. duodenale* |

**Table II-6-11.** Roundworms (Nematodes) Transmitted By Larvae

| Species | Disease/Organs | Form/Transmission | Diagnosis | Treatment |
|---|---|---|---|---|
| *Necator americanus* New World hookworm | **Hookworm** infection Lung migration → pneumonitis bloodsucking → anemia | Filariform **larva penetrates intact skin of bare feet** | Fecal larvae (up to 13 mm) and ova: oval, transparent with 2–8 cell-stage visible inside Occult blood fecal may be present | **Mebendazole** and iron therapy (albendazole) |
| *Ancylostoma braziliense* *Ancylostoma caninum* (dog and cat hookworms) | **Cutaneous Larva Migrans**/intense skin itching | Filariform larva penetrates intact skin but cannot mature in humans | Usually a presumptive diagnosis; exposure | Thiabendazole Topical corticosteroids |
| *Strongyloides stercoralis* | **Threadworm** strongyloidiasis: Early: pneumonitis, abdominal pain, diarrhea Later: malabsorption, ulcers, bloody stools | Filariform **larva penetrates intact skin; Autoinfection** leads to indefinite infections unless treated | Larvae in stool, serology | Thiabendazole |
| *Trichinella spiralis* | Trichinosis: larvae encyst in muscle → pain | **Viable encysted larvae in meat** are consumed: wild game meat | Muscle biopsy; clinical findings: **fever, myalgia, splinter hemorrhages, eosinophilia** | Steroids for severe symptoms + mebendazole (albendazole) |

### Differential Diagnosis

| *Necator americanus* New World hookworm | *Ancylostoma braziliense* *Ancylostoma caninum* (dog and cat hookworms) | *Strongyloides stercoralis* | *Trichinella spiralis* |
|---|---|---|---|
| *E. histolytica, G. lamblia, S. stercoralis* | *B. burgdorferi* | *A. lumbricoides* | *N. americanus, S. stercoralis* |

**Table II-6-12.** Filarial Nematodes

| Species | Disease | Transmission/Vector | Diagnosis | Treatment |
|---|---|---|---|---|
| *Wucheria bancrofti; Brugia malayi* | Elephantiasis | Mosquito | Microfilariae in blood, eosinophilia | Surgery, ivermectin and diethylcarbamazine (DEC) |
| *Loa loa* (African eye worm) | Pruritus, calabar swellings | *Chrysops*, mango flies | Microfilariae in blood, eosinophilia | Surgical removal of worms; DEC |
| *Onchocerca volvulus* | River blindness, itchy "leopard" rash | Blackflies | Skin snips from calabar swellings | Surgical removal of worms; DEC or ivermectin |
| *Dracunculus medinensis* (guinea worm, fiery serpent) | Creeping eruptions, ulcerations, rash | Drinking water with infected copepods | Increased IgE; worm eruption from skin | Slow, cautious worm removal with stick; albendazole |

### Differential Diagnosis

| *Wucheria bancrofti; Brugia malayi* | *Loa loa* (African eye worm) | *Onchocerca volvulus* | *Dracunculus medinensis* (guinea worm, fiery serpent) |
|---|---|---|---|
| *S. schenkii, C. trachomatis* (L serotypes) | *O. volvulus* | *Loa loa* | *W. bancrofti, O. volvulus, Loa loa* |

## Review Questions

1.  A 44-year-old woman returns home to New York after a 2-week camera safari to East Africa. She started chloroquine antimalarial prophylaxis 2 weeks prior to her departure for Kenya and continued throughout her foreign travel. She stopped taking the pills on her arrival home because they made her nauseated. Two weeks after her return, she develops paroxysmal fever and diaphoresis and is quickly hospitalized with febrile convulsions, jaundice, and anemia. Blood smears reveal red blood cells multiply infected with delicate ring-like tropho-zoites and rare sausage-shaped gametocytes. The stage of the parasite life cycle that is responsible for the appearance of the parasites 2 weeks after departure from the malarious area is the

    (A)  hypnozoite

    (B)  sporozoite

    (C)  exoerythrocytic schizont

    (D)  erythrocytic schizont

    (E)  merozoite

2.  At a school nurse's request, a clinic in rural South Carolina sees a 9-year-old girl who appears listless and inattentive, although hearing and visual testing has been within normal limits. The physician finds the child thin, with the "potbelly" of malnutrition, and orders a fecal exam and CBC. The CBC reveals a microcytic, hypochromic anemia, and the fecal exam detects brown, oval nematode eggs approximately 65 microns in size, too numerous to count. What was the most likely means by which this child was infected?

    (A)  Ingestion of ova

    (B)  Ingestion of larvae

    (C)  Ingestion of cysts in muscle

    (D)  Skin penetration by larvae

    (E)  Mosquito transmission of sporozoites

3.  An HIV-positive patient with a CD4+ count of 47 presents with diarrhea. Acid-fast structures are found in the stool. From this finding, which of the following is true?

    (A)  Infection is short lasting and self-resolving and requires no treatment

    (B)  If treated with antibiotics, the infection should resolve in 3–6 days

    (C)  Infection will resolve only with a combination of antituberculous drugs, and then it may take weeks

    (D)  Infection could have been prevented by avoiding cat feces and under-cooked or raw meat

    (E)  Even with the best treatment, the infection may be unrelenting

4. A 24-year-old primiparous woman in her eighth month of gestation develops a positive IgM titer to *Toxoplasma gondii* for the first time. She should be advised by her physician that

   (A) this child and all future fetuses are likely to be infected

   (B) a newborn with a positive anti-*Toxoplasma* IgG response should be treated with anti-parasitics

   (C) future infections can be avoided by proper vaccination and worming of cats

   (D) retinochoroiditis can be prevented by drug treatment of an infant with a positive IgM response

   (E) major organ damage can be reversed by prompt treatment of the newborn

5. A 35-year-old captain in the army reserves has been plagued by a painful, erosive lesion near his ear lobe since his return from Operation Desert Storm several years ago. He denies exposure to the toxic by-products of burning oil fields. Punch biopsy of the leading edge of the erosion reveals macrophages distended with oval amastigotes. How was this infection acquired?

   (A) Contact with contaminated drinking water

   (B) Bite of *Anopheles* mosquito

   (C) Bite of reduviid bug

   (D) Fecal contamination of food

   (E) Direct human contact in barracks

   (F) Bite of sandfly

   (G) Bite of tsetse fly

6. A group of 6 college students undertake to climb Mt. Rainier outside Seattle on their spring break. They pack food and camping provisions except for water, which they obtain from the many fresh water mountain streams that arise at the summit. The adventure takes a little over a week to accomplish, and all return safely in good spirits to their classes the following week. Within the first week after their return, 5 of the 6 students report to the infirmary with profuse diarrhea and tenesmus. Each affected student experiences weakness and weight loss, and stool samples submitted to the lab are yellow, greasy, and foul smelling. What attribute of this parasite imparts its pathogenicity?

   (A) Lytic enzymes

   (B) Flagella

   (C) Ventral sucking disc

   (D) Encystment

   (E) Toxic metabolites

7. After one week vacationing in Mexico, a 14-year-old girl presents with abdominal pain, nausea, bloody diarrhea, and fever. Stool specimens are collected and sent to the laboratory for bacteriologic and parasitologic examination. Bacterial cultures are negative for intestinal pathogens. The laboratory report reveals organisms with red blood cells inside them. The most likely causal agent is

   (A) *Cryptosporidium parvum*

   (B) *Entamoeba histolytica*

   (C) *Giardia lamblia*

   (D) *Toxoplasma gondii*

   (E) *Shigella dysenteriae*

8. Four weeks after his arrival from Egypt, a 24-year-old graduate student presents with blood in his urine. Microscopic examination of his urine reveals the presence of eggs with terminal spines. In the interview he admits that he has been working on his family's rice field occasionally since his early childhood. The most likely etiologic agent of his complaint is

   (A) *Entamoeba histolytica*

   (B) *Fasciolopsis buski*

   (C) *Schistosoma haematobium*

   (D) *Schistosoma japonicum*

   (E) *Schistosoma mansoni*

9. A 30-year-old woman presents to her gynecologist with complaints of vaginal itching and a frothy, yellow discharge. She also complains of painful urination. She admits to being sexually active with several men in the past two weeks. Cultures are negative for bacterial growth, but organisms are visible via a wet prep on low power. The most likely causal agent is

   (A) *Candida albicans*

   (B) *Trichophyton rubrum*

   (C) *Chlamydia trachomatis*

   (D) *Trichomonas vaginalis*

   (E) *Giardia lamblia*

10. A 30-year-old missionary comes to the emergency department complaining of high fever, chills, severe headache, and confusion. He has recently returned from Africa. A peripheral blood smear reveals multiple ring structures and crescent-shaped gametes. Which of the following organisms is the most likely cause?

   (A) *Leishmania* species

   (B) *Plasmodium falciparum*

   (C) *Plasmodium malariae*

   (D) *Plasmodium ovale*

   (E) *Plasmodium vivax*

11. A 3-year-old girl presents to her pediatrician with intense perianal itching. Her mother explains that the child has also been extremely irritable during the day and has not been sleeping well at night. Eggs with a flattened side were identified by the laboratory technician from a piece of scotch tape brought in by the parent. Infection with which of the following organisms is most likely?

    (A) *Ascaris lumbricoides*

    (B) *Echinococcus granulosus*

    (C) *Entamoeba histolytica*

    (D) *Enterobius vermicularis*

    (E) *Trichuris trichiura*

12. A 12-year-old girl from Guatemala was brought to the emergency room with a prolapsed rectum. Examination of the rectum reveals small worms that resemble whips attached to the mucosa. A stool sample reveals eggs that are barrel shaped, with bipolar plugs. Which of the following is the most likely cause?

    (A) *Ascaris lumbricoides*

    (B) *Echinococcus granulosus*

    (C) *Entamoeba histolytica*

    (D) *Enterobius vermicularis*

    (E) *Trichuris trichiura*

## Answers and Explanations

1.  **Answer: C.** This patient is suffering from *Plasmodium falciparum* malaria acquired shortly before her departure from Kenya. Liver stages of *Plasmodium* are not susceptible to chloroquine killing. Because she did not continue the prophylaxis after her return to the States, those parasites were allowed to initiate all of the erythrocytic stages of the life cycle. Any erythrocytic stages generated out of the liver phase of the life cycle while she remained on prophylaxis would have been killed. Thus, the late onset of her symptoms was due to survival of exoerythrocytic stages that had not yet left the liver at the time she ceased prophylaxis. Hypnozoites **(choice A)** are responsible for relapse of symptoms in *P. vivax* and *P. ovale* malarias, but do not exist in *P. falciparum*, and it is clear that she has *falciparum* malaria due to the delicate ring forms multiply infecting erythrocytes and the sausage-shaped gametocytes. Sporozoites **(choice B)** are the infectious forms injected by mosquitoes and would not have been available in this country to initiate the symptoms on the time course described. Erythrocytic schizonts and merozoites **(choices D and E)** would have been killed by prophylaxis before she left Africa and could not be responsible for the late onset of symptoms.

2.  **Answer: D.** This child has the typical symptoms of hookworm disease, caused in this country usually by *Necator americanus*. The infection is acquired by penetration of the filariform larvae through the skin of the feet or buttocks, after contamination of soil with the eggs of the agent deposited in human feces. Of the other distractors, **choice A** would be most likely if the infection were due to ascarids, pinworms, or whipworms. **Choice C** would describe infection with either *Taenia* or *Trichinella*, and **choice E** would be the means of infection with *Plasmodium*.

3.  **Answer: E.** The described infection could be *Cryptosporidium*, *Isospora*, *Microsporidia*, or *Cyclospora*, which are very difficult infections in AIDS patients even though they are self-resolving in normal noncompromised individuals. In AIDS patients they are most commonly unrelenting, even with treatment. They are usually acquired from water. *Toxoplasma* (**choice D**) is from cats.

4.  **Answer: D.** The positive IgM titer arising in the eighth month means that this woman has become acutely infected with *Toxoplasma*. Infections acquired at this time have a high likelihood of infecting the fetus and are most likely to be manifested by the development of retinochoroiditis. A mother can transmit this parasite to her fetus only during an acute infection; therefore, all future fetuses will be protected from the disease (**choice A**). Because IgG antibodies cross the placenta (**choice B**), presence of the anti-*Toxoplasma* antibodies of this class in the neonate may simply reflect the infection of the mother—only a positive IgM response in the neonate is proof of the child's infection, which should therefore be treated. There is no way to reverse major organ damage (**choice E**) when it occurs in utero, but it would not be expected to occur with an acute infection beginning in the third trimester.

5.  **Answer: F.** *Leishmania* spp. are transmitted by the bite of sandflies. They cannot be transmitted from person to person by trivial means, so unless organ transplantation is occurring in the barracks, direct human contact (**choice E**) is not a possibility. To survive outside the human host, they must be in the vector (sandfly), so transmission by food or water (**choices A** or **D**) is not possible. Of the distractors that involve true vectors: *Anopheles* mosquitoes (**choice B**) transmit malaria; reduviid bugs (**choice C**) transfer American trypanosomiasis (Chagas disease); and tsetse flies (**choice G**) transmit African trypanosomiasis (sleeping sickness).

6.  **Answer: C.** *Giardia* is common in mountain streams throughout the U.S., and the presentation of prolonged fatty diarrhea and weight loss is pathognomonic. It causes its pathology by its adherence to the mucosa of the upper small intestine with its ventral sucking disc. No toxic metabolites or lytic enzymes are involved in the pathology, which apparently results from blockage of normal fat digestion. The organism is a flagellate, and thus has flagella, but migration into extraintestinal sites is not a well known problem associated with pathology. And although the organism does encyst as it passes along the intestine, this is not known to produce symptoms.

7.  **Answer: B.** The clues are bloody diarrhea, fever, bacterial cultures negative, organisms with RBCs inside them. *Cryptosporidium parvum* (**choice A**) is typically found in AIDS patients. *Giardia lamblia* (**choice C**) is associated with fatty, foul smelling diarrhea. *Toxoplasma gondii* (**choice D**) would likely cause a flu-like illness in this age group if acquired as primary infection; if acquired in utero, might cause blindness later in life. You can rule out *Shigella dysenteriae* (**choice E**), because bacterial cultures were negative.

8.  **Answer: C.** The clues are Egypt, blood in urine, eggs with terminal spines, working in rice field (indicates his possible exposure to contaminated water). Also, be aware that in Africa, *S. haematobium* is associated with bladder cancer. *Entamoeba histolytica* (**choice A**) would cause bloody stool, not urine. *Fasciolopsis buski* (**choice B**) is the intestinal fluke; eggs do not have terminal spines. *S. japonicum* and *S. mansoni* (**choices D** and **E**) are intestinal schistosomes and would not cause blood in urine; the egg for *S. mansoni* has a subterminal spine, whereas the egg for *S. japonicum* is fat and oval with one tiny lateral spine.

9. **Answer: D.** The clues are frothy, yellow discharge, itching, organisms identified on wet mount, bacterial cultures were negative. With *Candida albicans* (**choice A**), the discharge would have been white and creamy. *Trichophyton* (**choice B**) causes skin, hair, and nail infections and is a cutaneous fungus. *Chlamydia trachomatis* (**choice C**) would not be visible on wet mount and causes intracellular infection of epithelial cells. *Giardia lamblia* (**choice E**) is associated with diarrhea.

10. **Answer: B.** The clues are missionary, high fever, chills, Africa, multiple ring structures, and crescent-shaped gametes. *Leishmania* (**choice A**) produces amastigotes inside phagocytic cells and causes either visceral, cutaneous, or mucocutaneous pathology. *Plasmodium malariae* (**choice C**) clues might include bar and band forms in RBCs, and 72 hour fever spikes. In *P. ovale* and *P. vivax* (**choices D** and **E**) there will be Schüffner dots in RBCs.

11. **Answer: D.** The clues are perianal itching, irritable during the day, not sleeping at night, eggs with flattened side, and Scotch tape test.

12. **Answer: E.** The clues are tropical country, prolapsed rectum, worms resembling whips, barrel shaped eggs with bipolar plugs. The common name for *Trichuris* is whipworm.

# Clinical Infectious Disease

**7**

These charts are designed for self-study after the organisms have all been reviewed in class. They represent the basics used in clinical scenarios on the COMLEX.

Cover the last column on each chart and write the causal agent(s) on paper. Then think about how the organism causes disease. Is there a major virulence factor?

## Abbreviations Used

→ means progressing on to

~ means about or approximately

**HIV+** = patient with known human immunodeficiency virus infection; can be used for anyone who is infected but often used for those who are HIV+ but do not have full blown AIDS (in other words, CD4+ count >200)

**AIDS** = acquired immunodeficiency syndrome  (CD4+ count <200)

**abd** = abdominal

**CF** = cystic fibrosis

**CMI** = cell-mediated immunity

**CGD** = chronic granulomatous disease

**GU** = genitourinary

**IC** = immunocompromised

**Infl'd** = inflamed

**Infl'n** = inflammation

**IV** = intravenous

**mo** = month(s)

**NF** = normal flora

**occ** = occasional

**PMNs** = polymorphonuclear leukocytes

**pt** = patient

**RBCs** = red blood cells

**subQ** = subcutaneous

If there are multiple causal agents, at the end of the description there may be a # with the abbreviation "CA." This means you should be able to list that number. If it specifically says "species," you should give species.

**Table II-7-1.** Diseases of Skin, Mucous Membranes, and Underlying Tissues

| Type Infection | Case Vignette/Key Clues | Common Causal Agents |
|---|---|---|
| Furuncles, carbuncles | Neck, face, axillae, buttocks | *Staphylococcus aureus* |
| | Inflamed follicles from neck down | *Pseudomonas aeruginosa* (hot tub folliculitis) |
| Acne vulgaris | Inflammation of follicles and sebaceous glands | *Propionibacterium acnes* |
| Impetigo | Initially vesicular; skin erosion; **honey-crusted** lesions; catalase negative organism | *Streptococcus pyogenes* |
| | Initially vesicular but with longer lasting **bullae**; catalase-positive organism | *Staphylococcus aureus* |
| Vesicular lesions | Sometimes preceded by neurologic pain | Herpes |
| SubQ granulomas/ulcers/cellulitis | Tropical fish enthusiasts; granulomatous lesion | *Mycobacterium marinum* (fish tank granuloma) |
| | Cellulitis following contact with saltwater or oysters | *Vibrio vulnificus* |
| Mycetoma (swelling with pain, sinus tract formation, yellow granules in exudate) | Solitary or lymphocutaneous lesions, rose gardeners or florists, sphagnum moss | *Sporothrix schenckii* (rose gardener disease) |
| | Subcutaneous swelling (extremities, shoulders) multiple CA | Bacteria: *Actinomyces, Nocardia*, Fungi: *Madurella, Pseudallescheria, Sporothrix* |
| | Jaw area, associated with carious teeth, dental extraction, or trauma | *Actinomyces israelii* "lumpy jaw" |
| Malignant pustule | Pustule → dark red fluid-filled, tumor-like lesion → necrosis → black eschar surrounded by red margin | *Bacillus anthracis* |
| | Ecthyma gangrenosum (as above) | *Pseudomonas* septicemia |
| Cellulitis | Blue-green pus, grape-like odor, burns | *Pseudomonas aeruginosa* |
| | Dermal pain, edema, heat and rapid spread. Red, raised butterfly facial rash | *Streptococcus pyogenes* (Erysipelas) |
| | Hot inflamed tissues. Deeper tissues from extension of skin lesions or wounds including surgical | Variety of bacteria: *S. aureus, S. pyogenes*, gram (–) rods, *Clostridium* and anaerobes |

*(Continued)*

**Table II-7-1.** Diseases of Skin, Mucous Membranes, and Underlying Tissues (*Cont'd*)

| Type Infection | Case Vignette/Key Clues | Common Causal Agents |
|---|---|---|
| Wounds | Surgical wounds (clean) | *Staphylococcus aureus* |
| | Surgical wounds (dirty)—list groups | *S. aureus, Enterobacteriaceae*, anaerobes |
| | Trauma—list groups | *Clostridium,* Enterobacteriaceae, *Pseudomonas* |
| | Shallow puncture wound through tennis shoe sole | *Pseudomonas aeruginosa* |
| Animal bites | Various | *Pasteurella multocida* |
| | Human bites, fist fights | *Eikenella corrodens* |
| | Dog bites | *Capnocytophaga canimorsus* |
| | Rat bites | *Streptobacillus moniliformis and Spirillum minus* |
| | Cat scratches resulting in lymphadenopathy with stellate granulomas | *Bartonella henselae* |

(*Continued*)

**Table II-7-2.** Ear, Nose, Throat, Upper Respiratory System Infections

| Type Infection | Case Vignette/Key Clues | Common Causal Agents |
|---|---|---|
| Acute otitis media | Red, bulging tympanic membrane, fever 102–103; pain goes away if drum ruptures or if ear tubes are patent. 5 CA | *Streptococcus pneumoniae*<br>*H. influenzae* (often nontypeable, recurs)<br>*Moraxella catarrhalis*<br>RSV<br>Rhinovirus |
| Otitis externa | Ear pain—list of organisms | Normal flora often involved<br>Often mixed infections:<br>*Staph aureus* (from NF)*<br>*Candida albicans* (from NF)*<br>*Proteus* (water organism)<br>*Pseudomonas* (water) |
| Malignant otitis externa | Severe ear pain in diabetic; life threatening | *Pseudomonas aeruginosa* |
| Sinusitis | Sinus pain; low-grade fever | As for acute otitis media |
| Oral cavitary disease | Painful mouth—overgrowth of spirochetes and fusiform bacteria | *Fusobacterium* and treponemes (normal oral spirochetes) |
| | Sore mouth with thick white coating (painful red base under); increased risk: premature infants, AIDS, IC pts, pts on antibiotics, vitamin C deficiency | *Candida* |
| Sore throat | Inflamed tonsils/pharynx, which may be purulent and may develop abscesses; cervical lymphadenopathy, fever, stomach upset; sandpaper rash | *Streptococcus pyogenes* (group A strep) Rash indicates presence of erythrogenic exotoxin A |
| | White papules with red base on posterior palate and pharynx, fever | Coxsackie A |
| | Throat looking like Strep with severe fatigue, lymphadenopathy, fever, rash; heterophile (+); Downey type II cells | Epstein-Barr virus |
| | Low-grade fever with a 1–2 day gradual onset of membranous nasopharyngitis and/or obstructive laryngotracheitis; bull neck from lymphadenopathy; elevated BUN; abnormal ECG; little change in WBC (toxin). Exudate bleeds profusely when dislodged | *Corynebacterium diphtheriae* (diphtheria) |
| Common cold | Rhinitis, sneezing, coughing; list CA with seasonal peaks | Rhinoviruses (summer–fall)<br>Coronaviruses (winter–spring)<br>Human metapneumovirus<br>Adenovirus, many others |

*NF = normal flora

**Table II-7-3.** Eye Infections

| Type Infection | Case Vignette/Key Clues | Common Causal Agents |
|---|---|---|
| Eyelid | Bilateral eye lid swelling, >10% eosinophilia, fever, muscle pain; earlier GI Sx | *Trichinella* |
| | Stye; 2 CA | *Staphylococcus aureus*<br>*Propionibacterium acnes* |
| | Unilateral inflammation at bite site often around eye or mouth; travel to Mexico, Central or South America | *Trypanosoma cruzi* |
| Conjunctivitis neonate | Red itchy eye(s)/pus; onset 2–5 days<br>Red itchy eye(s)/pus; onset 5–10 days | Bacterial pink eye<br>*Neisseria gonorrhoeae*<br>*Chlamydia trachomatis* (serotypes D–K U.S.) |
| | Neonate with "sticky eye" | *Staphylococcus aureus* |
| Conjunctivitis (other age groups) | Red itchy eye(s), thin exudate; pain, photophobia | Viral pink eye: adenovirus (more common than bacterial pink eye) |
| | Red eye, pus; 4 CA | *S. aureus*, group A Strep, *Strep pneumoniae* (all gram [+])<br>*Haemophilus influenzae*, *H. aegyptius* |
| | Red eye, pus, presence of inclusion bodies in scrapings; CA with serotypes in U.S. | *Chlamydia trachomatis* serotypes D-K (inclusion conjunctivitis) |
| | Granulomas and inturned eye lashes, corneal scarring, blindness; CA with serotypes | *Chlamydia trachomatis* serotypes A, B, Ba, C (trachoma) |
| Chorioretinitis | Neonate or AIDS; 2 CA | *Toxoplasma*, CMV |
| Retinopathy with keratitis in baby | Mom IV drug abuser | *Treponema pallidum* (congenital syphilis) |

**Table II-7-4.** Cardiac Symptoms

| Type Infection | Case Vignette/Key Clues | Common Causal Agents |
|---|---|---|
| **Acute endocarditis:** Chills, fever, arthralgia, myalgia, back pain, acutely ill, Janeway lesions; emboli | Developing a heart murmur; IV drug user | *Staphyloccoccus aureus* |
| | Not IV drug user | *Staphyloccoccus aureus* |
| **Subacute endocarditis:** Fever with vague symptoms with insidious onset, fatigue, weakness, weight loss, night sweats, anorexia, myalgias; murmur may have been long present; emboli, splinter hemorrhages | Poor oral hygiene or dental work | *Viridans* streptococci (55% of cases in native hearts) |
| | Gram neg. endocarditis (normal oral flora) | HACEK organisms (**H**aemophilus aphrophilus **A**ctinobacillus actinomycetemcomitans **C**ardiobacterium hominis **E**ikenella corrodens **K**ingella kingae) |
| | Bilary or urinary tract infection GU manipulation in elderly men | *Enterococcus faecalis* |
| | IV drug user | *Staph. epidermidis* *Aspergillus* (branching <45) *Candida* (pseudohyphae) *Pseudomonas* *Viridans* streptococci |
| Dilated cardiomyopathy | Rural South America | *Trypanosoma cruzi* |

**Table II-7-5.** Middle and Lower Respiratory System Infections

| Type Infection | Case Vignette/Key Clues | Most Common Causal Agents |
|---|---|---|
| Respiratory difficulty or obstruction | Inflamed epiglottis; patient often 2–3 and unvaccinated | *Haemophilus influenzae* (epigottitis) |
| | Infant with fever, sharp barking cough, inspiratory stridor, hoarse phonation | Parainfluenza virus (Croup) |
| Bronchitis | Wheezy; infant or child ≤5 years | RSV |
| | >5 years | *Haemophilus influenzae, Mycoplasma pneumoniae, Chlamydophila pneumoniae* |
| | With cough >2 weeks, afebrile; >9 | *Bordetella pertussis* |
| Pneumonia <br><br>**Typical:** high fever, productive cough, diffuse infiltreates | Poorly nourished, unvaccinated baby/child; giant cell pneumonia with hemorrhagic rash | Measles: malnourishment ↑ risk of pneumonia and blindness |
| | Adults (including alcoholics) #1 CA <br> Rusty sputum, often follows influenza | *Streptococcus pneumoniae* |
| | Neutropenic pts, burn pts, CGD, CF | *Pseudomonas* |
| | Foul smelling sputum, aspiration possible | Anaerobes, mixed infection (*Bacteroides, Fusobacterium, Peptococcus*) |
| | Alcoholic, abscess formation, aspiration, facultative anaerobic, gram-negative bacterium with huge capsule, currant jelly sputum | *Klebsiella pneumoniae* |
| | Nosocomial, ventilator, post-influenza <br> Abscess formation <br> Gram +, catalase +, coagulase + <br> Salmon-colored sputum | *Staphylococcus aureus* |
| **Atypical:** low fever, dry cough, diffuse infiltrates | Pneumonia teens/young adults; bad hacking cough; initially non-productive cough | *Mycoplasma pneumoniae* (most common cause of pneumonia in school age children) |
| | Atypical with air conditioning exposure especially >50 yr, heavy smoker, drinker | *Legionella* spp. |
| | Atypical with bird exposure, hepatitis | *Chlamydophila psittaci* |
| | AIDS patients with staccato cough; "ground glass" x-ray; biopsy: honeycomb exudate with silver staining cysts, progressive hypoxia | *Pneumocystis jiroveci* |
| Acute respiratory distress | Travel to Far East, winter, early spring, hypoxia | SARS-CoV |
| | Spring, 4 corners region, exposure to rodents | Hanta virus |
| Acute pneumonia or chronic cough with weight loss, night sweats, calcifying lesions | Over 55, HIV+, or immigrant from developing country | *Mycobacterium tuberculosis* |
| | Dusty environment with bird or bat fecal contamination (Missouri chicken farmers), yeasts packed into phagocytic cells | *Histoplasma capsulatum* |
| | Desert sand, SW U.S. | *Coccidioides immitis* |
| | Rotting contaminated wood, North and South Carolina | *Blastomyces dermatitidis* |

**Table II-7-6.** Genitourinary Tract Infections

| Type Infection | Case Vignette/Key Clues | Most Common Causal Agents |
|---|---|---|
| Urethritis | Gram-negative diplococci in PMNs in urethral exudate | *Neisseria gonorrhoeae* |
| | Culture negative, inclusion bodies | *Chlamydia trachomatis* |
| | Urease positive, no cell wall | *Ureaplasma urealyticum* |
| | Flagellated protozoan with corkscrew motility | *Trichomonas vaginalis* |
| Cystitis | Frequent and painful urination, hematuria, and fever | #1 *E. coli*, other gram-negative enterics, *Pseudomonas*, *Proteus* |
| | Young, newly sexually active individual; gram-positive cocci | *Staphylococcus saprophyticus* |
| Pyelonephritis | As above, with flank pain and prominent fever | *E. coli*, *Staphylococcus* |
| Cervicitis | Friable, inflamed cervix with mucopurulent discharge; probes or culture to distinguish | *Neisseria gonorrhoeae* (gram-negative diplococci) *Chlamydia trachomatis* (non-staining obligate intracellular parasite) Herpes simplex (virus) |
| Vaginal itching, pain, discharge odor | Adherent yellowish discharge, pH >5, fishy amine odor in KOH, clue cells; gram-negative cells dominate | (Bacterial vaginosis) overgrowth of *Gardnerella vaginalis* and anaerobes |
| | Vulvovaginitis, pruritis, erythema, discharge: consistency of cottage cheese | *Candida* spp. |
| | Foamy, purulent discharge, many PMNs and motile trophozoites microscopically (corkscrew motility) | *Trichomonas vaginalis* |
| Pelvic inflammatory disease | Adnexal tenderness, bleeding, deep dyspareunia, vaginal discharge, fever; tenderness from cervical movement, possibly palpable inflammatory mass on bimanual exam, onset often follows menses | *Neisseria gonorrhoeae* or *Chlamydia trachomatis* or both or a variety of other organisms |
| Genital lesions | Genital warts | Human papilloma virus (most common U.S. STD), *Treponema pallidum*, molluscum contagiosum |
| | Multiple painful vesicular, coalescing, recurring | Herpes simplex virus |
| | Nontender, indurated ulcer healing spontaneously 2–10 weeks | *Treponema pallidum* |
| | Non-indurated, painful papule, suppurative with adenopathy, slow to heal | *Haemophilus ducreyi* |
| | Soft, painless ulcer, pt from Caribbean or New Guinea, gram negative intracellular bacilli | *Klebsiella granulomatis* (granuloma inguinale) |
| Genital elephantitis | Initial papule heals; lymph nodes enlarge and develop fistulas; genital elephantiasis may develop Tropics, microfilariae in bloodstream | *Chlamydia trachomatis* L1–L3 *Wuchereria* or *Brugia* (filarial nematodes) |

# Diarrhea

## Dysentery

- Abdominal cramps, tenesmus, and pus and blood in the stool
- Usually associated with invasive bacterial disease in the colon

## Diarrhea

- Refers to profuse watery feces
- Most commonly associated with increased secretion of fluid across the mucosal surfaces of the small intestine in response to a toxin or a viral infection
- No inflammatory cells, usually no fever

**Table II-7-7.** Diarrhea by Intoxication

| Most Common Sources | Common Age Group Infected | Incubation Period | Pathogenesis | Symptoms | Duration of Symptoms | Organism |
|---|---|---|---|---|---|---|
| **Ham, potato salad,** cream pastries | All | **1–6 hours** | **Heat stable enterotoxin is produced in food contaminated** by food handler; food sits at room temperature | **abd cramps, vomiting, diarrhea; sweating and headache may occur; no fever** | ‹24 hours | ***Staphylococcus aureus*** |
| **Rice** | All | ‹6 hours | **Heat stable toxin causes vomiting** | As above | 8–10 hours | ***Bacillus cereus:* emetic form** |
| **Meat, vegetables** | All | ›6 hours | Heat labile toxin causes diarrhea (similar to *E. coli* LT) | Nausea, abd cramps, diarrhea | 20–36 hrs | *Bacillus cereus:* diarrheal form |

**Table II-7-8.** Microbial Diarrhea: Organisms Causing Noninflammatory Diarrhea

| Common Age Group Infected | Most Common Sources | Incubation Period | Pathogenesis | Symptoms | Duration of Symptoms | Organism |
|---|---|---|---|---|---|---|
| **Infants and toddlers** | Day care, water, nosocomial, fecal-oral | 1–3 days (fall, winter, spring) | Microvilli of small intestine blunted; mononuclear infiltrate in lamina propria; disaccharidase activity down; glucose coupled transport normal; lactose intolerance may cause build up and osmotic influx creating watery diarrhea | Noninflammatory watery diarrhea, vomiting, fever, and dehydration | **5–7 days** | **Rotaviruses** |
| Young kids, IC | Nosocomial | 7–8 days | ? | Diarrhea, fever, and vomiting | 8–12 days | **Adenovirus 40/41** |
| Infants in developing countries | Food, water, fecal-oral | 2–6 days | **Adherence to enterocytes through pili causes damage to** adjoining microvilli | Watery to profusely watery diarrhea | 1–3 weeks | Enteropathogenic *E. coli* |
| **Older kids and adults** | Water, food, fecal-oral | 18–48 hours | Jejunal biopsy shows blunting of microvilli; cytoplasmic vacuolization is seen along with mononuclear infiltrates of tissue; virus appears to decrease brush border enzymes causing malabsorption | Diarrhea, nausea, and vomiting; fever in some | 12–48 hours | **Norwalk virus** |
| | Cruise ships | | | | | Noro-like virus |
| All | **Beef, poultry, gravies** Mexican food | 8–24 hours | Enterotoxin | Abd cramps and **watery diarrhea,** rarely fever or vomiting | <24 hours | *Clostridium perfringens* |
| All | Water, food, fecal-oral | 9–72 hours | **Toxin stimulates adenylate cyclase and causes increase in cAMP in the small intestine without inflammation or invasion** | **Profuse watery diarrhea with vomiting; fever may be present** (rice water stools) | 3–4 days | *Vibrio cholerae* |
| All | Raw or **undercooked shellfish** | 5–92 hours | Self-limited gastroenteritis mimicking cholera; there is a severe, rarer dysentery form, no clear enterotoxin; hemolysins, phospholipase and lysophospholipase; tests for invasiveness are negative | Explosive watery diarrhea along with headache, abdominal cramps, nausea, vomiting, and fever. | Up to 10 days | *Vibrio parahaemolyticus* |
| All | Water, uncooked fruits and vegetables | 12–72 hours | **Heat labile toxin (LT) stimulates adenylate cyclase resulting in efflux of water and ions into the small intestine;** stable toxin guanylate cyclase | Watery diarrhea with some vomiting and sometimes fever | 3–5 days | Enterotoxigenic *E. coli* |
| 50% <10 yrs., all | Food, fecal-oral **(hamburger)** | 3–5 days | **Verotoxin, which is a cytotoxin, causes bloody diarrhea** with no invasion of the organism | Abdominal cramps, watery diarrhea with blood **(no fever)** | 7–10 days | Enterohemorrhagic *E. coli.* |
| All | Water, day care, **camping,** beavers, dogs, etc. | 5–25 days | Cysts ingested; excyst in the duodenum and jejunum; **multiply and attach to intestinal villi by sucking disk** | **Loose, pale, greasy diarrhea; mild to severe malabsorption** syndrome | 1–2 weeks to years | *Giardia lamblia* |
| Children, AIDS patients | Day care, fecal-oral, animals, **homosexuals** | 2–4 weeks | Sporozoites attach to the epithelial surface of the intestine and replicate | Mild diarrhea in immunocompetent; severe chronic diarrhea in AIDS **Acid-fast** spores/oocysts in stool | 4 days to 3 weeks in **AIDS:** indefinite | *Cryptosporidium parvum Isospora belli; Cyclospora, Microsporidia* |

**Table II-7-9.** Microbial Diarrhea: Organisms Causing Inflammatory Diarrhea/Dysentery

| Common Age Group Infected | Most Common Sources* | Incubation Period | Pathogenesis | Symptoms | Duration of Symptoms | Organism |
|---|---|---|---|---|---|---|
| All, esp <1 year and young adults | **Poultry, domestic animals, water,** unpasteurized milk, day care, fecal-oral | 3–5 days | **Multiply in the small intestine; invades epithelium** resulting in inflammation and RBC and WBC in stools. | Diarrhea, abd pain, malaise; enteritis with diarrhea, malaise, fever | 1–2 days mild; <1 week normal self-limiting | *Campylobacter jejuni* |
| All, esp infants and kids | **Poultry, domestic animals,** water, day care, fecal-oral | 8–48 hours | Adsorb to epithelial cells in terminal small intestine; penetrate to lamina propria of ileocecal region causing **PMN response and PG response, which stimulates** cAMP and watery diarrhea | Diarrhea (occ bloody), abd cramps, abd tenderness, fever, and nausea w/occ vomiting; osteomyelitis in sickle cell anemia | 3–5 days; spontaneous resolution | *Salmonella* gastroenteritis |
| All, esp 6 mo to 10 yr. | Water, day care, no animal reservoirs, fecal-oral | 1–7 days | *Shigella* colonize the small intestine producing at first an enterotoxin-induced watery diarrhea; ultimately the *shigellae* penetrate the colon mucosa producing **shallow mucosal ulcerations and dysentery; septicemia rare** | Watery diarrhea at first → lower abdominal cramps, tenesmus and abundant pus and blood in the stools (dysentery) | 4–7 days; antibiotics can reduce spread | *Shigella* |
| All, esp older kids and young adults | Milk, wild **domestic animals** water, fecal-oral | 2–7 days | The terminal ileum is infected with enlargement of the mesenteric lymph nodes; produces focal necrosis difficult to distinguish from appendicitis; organism is able to grow in cold; produces heat insensitive enterotoxin. Arthritis may occur. | Fever, diarrhea (frequently with leukocytes & blood in stools), abdominal pain; also a noninflammatory gastroenteritis | 1 day – 3 weeks (avg. 9 days) | *Yersinia enterocolitica* |
| Pt on antibiotics | Associated with **antibiotic use (most common clindamycin)** | NA | Intense inflammatory response creates the friable yellow plaque-like colonic lesions (pseudo-membrane) associated with this disease | Mild diarrhea to severe **colitis;** abd cramps; spiking fever, systemic toxicity; blood, mucus, and pus in stools | Until antibiotic stopped; treat with metronidazole or change antibiotic | *Clostridium difficile* |
| Adults | Food, water, fecal-oral | 2–3 days | Similar to *Shigella* dysentery | Fever and cramps with blood and pus in the stools | 1–2 weeks; fluid and electrolyte replacement | Enteroinvasive *E. coli* |
| All | Food, water, fecal-oral, **tropical** generally | 2–4 weeks | Ingested cysts survive (trophozoites die) and multiply in the colon with invasion of the colon wall producing the **characteristic flask-like lesions and extra-intestinal abscesses** | Gen. acute diarrhea with cramping; sometimes dysentery; ulceration of colon may produce peritonitis | Weeks to months Rx with metronidazole followed by iodoquinol | *Entamoeba histolytica* |

*Sources:   Water = those listed are the most common diarrhea diseases spread through water

Day care = organisms listed are ones that have caused outbreaks in day care facilities, but note that any organism spread by the oral-fecal route may be a problem in this setting

Milk = unpasteurized milk or dairy products

**Table II-7-10.** Other Gastrointestinal or Liver Infections

| Signs and Symptoms | Case Vignette/Key Clues | Most Common Causal Agents |
|---|---|---|
| **Hepatitis:**<br>Jaundice, anorexia, nausea, right upper quadrant pain on palpation, cigarettes taste foul, elevated liver enzymes* | Food-borne (possibly contaminated raw oysters or clams); 14–45 days; without chronicity; sturdy naked RNA virus | Hepatitis A ("infectious" hepatitis) (picornavirus) |
| | IV drug abuse, needle stick; chronic carrier state, cirrhosis, primary hepatocellular carcinoma; DNA virus easily inactivated by alcohol | Hepatitis B ("serum" hepatitis) neonatal transmission (Hepadnavirus) |
| | Transfusion, IV drug abuse, or prison-acquired tatoos; acute illness is less severe than hepatitis B but chronicity is higher, with 60% of those infected having chronic active hepatitis; RNA, enveloped virus | Hepatitis C (Flavivirus) |
| | Enterically transmitted with high fatality in pregnant women, no chronic form | Hepatitis E (Hepevirus) |
| Acute abdominal pain | Intestinal blockage | *Ascaris lumbricoides* or *Diphyllobothrium latum* |
| Bile duct blockage | | *Ascaris lumbricoides* (following surgery)<br>*Fasciola hepatica* |
| Peritonitis | | Mixed flora often involving anaerobic normal flora: *Bacteroides fragilis* and facultative anaerobes such as *E. coli* |
| Cirrhosis | Travel history: Puerto Rico, Peace Corps, etc.; egg granulomas block triads → fibrosis | *Schistosoma mansoni* |
| | IV drug use | Hepatitis viruses |
| Pancreatitis | Generally with swelling of salivary glands | Mumps virus |

*Hepatitis may also occur with two other viruses: CMV and yellow fever virus or with toxoplasmosis or leptospirosis.

**Table II-7-11.** Changes in Blood Cells

| Symptoms and Signs | Case Vignette/Key Clues | Most Common Causal Agents |
| --- | --- | --- |
| Anemia | Megaloblastic | *Diphyllobothrium latum* |
| | Normocytic | Chronic infections |
| | Microcytic and hypochromic (iron deficiency anemia) | *Ancylostoma, Necator, Trichuris* |
| Patient with cyclic or irregular fever, decreased hemoglobin and hematocrit | Often foreign travel to tropics, rings or schizonts in RBCs | *Plasmodium* |
| Splenectomized patient, New England, hemolytic anemia, no travel history, summer months (tick exposure) | Multiple ring forms inside RBC | *Babesia microti* |
| Reduced CD4 cell count | | HIV |
| Increases in PMNs | | Generally found in many extracellular bacterial infections |
| Increases in eosinophils | | Allergy |
| | | Helminths during migrations |
| Increases in mononuclear leukocytes (monocytes or lymphocytes) | | Viruses and other intracellular organisms: *Listeria, Legionella, Leishmania, Toxoplasma* |
| | Infectious mononucleosis Heterophile (+)Downey type II cells (reactive T cells) sore throat, lymphadenopathy, young adult | Epstein-Barr virus (EBV) |
| | Heterophile negative | CMV *Toxoplasma* *Listeria* (Listeriosis) |
| Lymphocytosis with paroxysmal cough, stridor on inspiration | Unvaccinated child, hypoglycemic | *Bordetella pertussis* |

**Table II-7-12.** Central Nervous System Infections

| Signs and Symptoms | Case Vignette/Key Clues | Most Common Causal Agents |
|---|---|---|
| **Meningitis:** Headache, fever, vomiting, sepsis, seizures, irritability, lethargy, bulging fontanelles, nuchal rigidity | Neonate to 2 months | *Streptococcus agalactiae* #1 (gram-positive coccus)<br><br>*E. coli* (gram-negative rod)<br><br>More rarely: *Listeria monocytogenes* (motile gram-positive rod) |
| | 3 months to 2 years; unvaccinated child | *Haemophilus influenzae* type B* (gram-negative pleomorphic rod with polyribitol capsule) |
| | 3 mo to young adult. Prodrome may be very rapid; child may be properly vaccinated; rash | *Neisseria meningitidis* (gram-negative diplococcus with capsule; ferments maltose) |
| | <2 yrs<br>Young adults to elderly | *Streptococcus pneumoniae* (gram-positive coccus, catalase negative, alpha hemolytic, inhibited by optochin, lysed by bile |
| | Renal transplant patient | *Cryptococcus neoformans* (#1); encapsulated, urease (+) yeast<br><br>*Listeria monocytogenes* (motile gram-positive rod) |
| | Several month prodrome (except in severely compromised). Usually some underlying condition, endemic area | Fungal, e.g., Cryptococcal, or if in Southwestern U.S., *Coccidioides*<br><br>If near U.S. great river beds with exposure to bird, bat feces; *Histoplasma capsulatum* |
| | Patient with low CMI, nerve palsies in a patient with tuberculosis and low CSF glucose | *Mycobacterium tuberculosis* (Tuberculous meningitis) |
| **Meningoencephalitis:** | Swimming and often diving in very warm waters (hot springs). Prefrontal headache, high fever, disturbance of smell | *Naegleria* |
| | Immunocompromized patients | *Acanthamoeba* or *Toxoplasma* |

*By 1990, with day care centers and the dramatic increase in *Haemophilus* meningitis, *Haemophilus* meningitis became overall the most common. Since late 1990, when the conjugated vaccine went into use, there has been a dramatic decrease in *Haemophilus* meningitis in **vaccinated kids**.

(Continued)

**Table II-7-12.** Central Nervous System Infections (*continued*)

| Signs and Symptoms | Case Vignette/Key Clues | Most Common Causal Agents |
|---|---|---|
| **Encephalitis**: Headache, and fever → drowsiness, coma, hemiplegia, cranial nerve palsy, hallucinations, behavioral disturbances, and other focal neurological findings | Summer–fall, mosquito-borne from bird reservoirs (except for California encephalitis, which is a rodent reservoir) | Encephalitis with **arboviruses**: <br>**Western equine encephalitis** (midwest and west U.S.) <br>**St. Louis encephalitis** elderly blacks with hypertension, most severe infections <br>**West Nile Virus** (North America) <br>**California encephalitis** (entire U.S.) <br>**Eastern equine encephalitis** <br>all age groups, but most common in young and old; highest morbidity of viral CNS infections; with mental retardation, seizures, personality changes in survivors |
| | Focal uptake of radionucleotide, RBCs in CSF, high opening pressure, frontal temporal lobe involvement. | **Herpes simplex encephalitis** |
| **Mass lesion** | Generally following: sinus, ear, or dental infection, infection at distant site, head trauma, etc. (symptoms dependent on location of mass) and elevated intracranial pressure along with headache, mental changes, nausea, vomiting, fever with chills, and seizure | Don't do lumbar puncture; CT generally shows ring enhancing lesion; 45% mixed infections; Streptococci and *Bacteroides* are the two most commonly identified groups of bacteria |
| **Reye Syndrome** | Child following a viral illness with pernicious vomiting, lethargy and irritability, which may lead to brain swelling, indication of aspirin usage. | Influenza or varicella infection (Reye syndrome) |
| **Epilepsy** | Mexico, immigrant, onset after age 20 | *Taenia solium* (neurocysticercosis) |
| **Bell palsy** (acute facial nerve paralysis) | Systemic disease following bull's-eye rash | *Borrelia burgdorferi* |
| **Guillain-Barré** (acute inflammatory demyelinating polyneuropathy with ascending paralysis) | With GI tract problems <br><br> With respiratory problems | *Campylobacter jejuni* <br><br> *Influenza* |

**Table II-7-13.** Cerebrospinal Fluid Finding in Meningitis

| Pressure | CSF Appearance | Cell Count (cells/mm)³ | Dominant Cell Type | Glucose mg/dL | Protein mg/dL | Condition |
|---|---|---|---|---|---|---|
| <100 mm H2O | Clear | 0–5 | Lymphocytes | 40–70 | <40 | Normal |
| Normal or + | Clear | 0–500 | Early: PMNs<br>Late: lymphocytes | Normal or – | Normal or + | Viral infection |
| ++ | Opaque | 1–60,000 | PMNs | – | ++ | Bacterial infection |
| + | Clear | 10–500 | Early: PMNs<br>Late: lymphocytes | – | + to ++ | Fungal infection |

– Below normal range, + above normal range

**Table II-7-14.** Selected Rashes

| Type Rash | Progression | Other Symptoms | Disease | Causal Agent/Toxin |
|---|---|---|---|---|
| Erythematous maculopapular rash (sandpaper-like rash) | Trunk and neck → extremities | Sore throat, fever, nausea | Scarlet fever | *Strep. pyogenes* Exotoxin A-C |
| Diffuse erythematous, macular, sunburn-like rash | Trunk and neck → extremities with desquamation on palms and soles | Acute onset, fever >102°F, myalgia, pharyngitis, vomiting, diarrhea; hypotension leading to multi-organ failure | Toxic shock syndrome | *Staph. aureus* TSST-1 |
| Perioral erythema, bullae, vesicles, desquamation | Trunk and neck → extremities, except tongue and palate; large bullae and vesicles precede defoliation | Abscess or some site of infection | Staphylococcal skin disease: scalded skin disease & scarletina | *Staph. aureus* Exfoliatin |
| Petechiae → purpura | Trunk → extremities; spares palms, soles, and face | Fever, rash, headache, myalgias, and respiratory symptoms | Epidemic typhus | *Rickettsia prowazekii* ? Endotoxin |
| | Ankles and wrists → generalized with palms and soles | Fever, rash, headache, myalgias, and respiratory symptoms | Rocky Mountain spotted fever (most common on East Coast) | *Rickettsia rickettsii* ? Endotoxin |
| | Generalized | Abrupt onset, fever, chills, malaise, prostration, exanthem → shock | Early meningococcemia | *N. meningitidis* Endotoxin |
| Skin: maculopapular; mucous membrane: condyloma | Generalized involving the palms and soles, bronze or copper colored | Fever, lymphadenopathy, malaise, sore throat, splenomegaly, headache, arthralgias | Secondary syphilis | *Trep. pallidum* Endotoxin |
| Confluent erythematous maculopapular rash | Head → entire body | Cough coryza, conjunctivitis, and fever (prodrome), oral lesions (Koplik spots), exanthem, bronchopneumonia, and ear infections | Measles | Rubeola virus Rash from T cell destruction of virus-infected cells in capillaries |
| Erythematous concentric rings (Bull's eye) | Outward from site of tick bite | Fever, headaches, myalgias, Bell's palsy | Lyme disease | *Borrelia burgdorferi* |

**Table II-7-15.** Osteomyelitis

| Type Infection | Case Vignette/Key Clues | Most Common Causal Agents |
|---|---|---|
| Fever, bone pain with erythema and swelling, some patients (diabetic particularly) may have associated cellulitis | Adults, children, and infants without major trauma or special conditions | *Staphylococcus aureus* |
| | Neonates (<1 mo) | *Staphylococcus aureus*<br><br>Group B Streptococcus, Gram-negative rods (*E. coli, Klebsiella, Proteus, Pseudomonas*) |
| | Sickle cell anemia* | *Salmonella* |
| | Trauma | *Pseudomonas* |

* Sickle cell anemia patients are functionally asplenic and may have defective opsonic and alternate complement pathway activities. The most common bacterial infections include
  • Encapsulated organisms
    *Streptococcus pneumoniae*
    *Haemophilus influenzae*
    *Neisseria meningitidis*
    *Salmonella enterica* subsp.
  • Osteomyelitis due to *Salmonella enterica* subsp.
  • Pneumonia, bacteremia, and meningitis are all a problem.

**Table II-7-16.** Arthritis Related to Infections

| Type Infection | Case Vignette/Key Clues | Most Common Causal Agents |
|---|---|---|
| Pain, redness, low-grade fever, tenderness, swelling, reduced joint mobility | #1 overall except in the 15–40 age group where gonococcal is more prevalent | *Staphylococcus aureus* |
| | Multiple joints | From septicemia, e.g., staphylococci, gonococci |
| | 15–40 years; mono- or polyarticular | *Neisseria gonorrhoeae* |
| | Prosthetic joint | Coagulase negative staphylococci |
| | Viral | Rubella, hepatitis B, and parvovirus |
| | Chronic onset, monoarticular | *M. tuberculosis* or fungal |
| | Large joint resembling Reiter following tick bite or erythema migrans | *Borrelia burgdorferi* |
| Postinfectious (reactive arthritis) | Following gastrointestinal infection | *Salmonella, Shigella, Campylobacter,* or *Yersinia enterocolitica* |
| | Following sexual contact | *Chlamydia trachomatis* |

# CASE HISTORIES

**Case A:** A 28-year-old known alcoholic man presents with fever and productive cough. He was basically well until 3 days ago when he noticed perspiration, cough, shaking chills, and headache. His cough has been associated with the production of a yellowish-green sputum, which occasionally was tinged with brownish streaks, but was not foul smelling. A Gram stain shows Gram-positive cocci in pairs and short chains.

A. What laboratory tests could you use to identify the genus?

*Answer: Catalase test (negative) to genus.*

B. When plated on blood agar, what other bacterium might you isolate and confuse the causal agent with, and why? What test(s) could distinguish the two?

*Answer: Viridans strep; optochin and bile.*

C. What procedure would you perform to type the isolate?

*Answer: Quellung reaction with known antibodies to capsule (not antibodies to cell-wall antigens).*

**Case B:** The patient in Case A developed meningitis and died.

A. What would be the expected CSF cell count?

*Answer: High.*

B. What would be the expected CSF protein and sugar values?

*Answer: Protein high, sugar low.*

**Case C:** A 46-year-old, HIV-positive male complains of malaise, weight loss, fever, and night sweats of 6 weeks duration. More recently, he has developed a cough productive of bloody sputum. Physical exam reveals bronchial breath sounds with crepitant rales over the right upper chest. His CD4 cell count is 560 cells/mm$^3$. Auramine-rhodamine stain of the sputum is positive, and a chest radiograph reveals hilar lymphadenopathy with a small cavity and streaky infiltrates in the upper lobe.

A. What attribute of the most likely causal agent promotes its survival in reticuloendothelial cells?

*Answer: Sulfatides are sulfolipids which hydrolyze to make sulfuric acid. They impede the fusion of lysosomes with the phagosome.*

B. What attribute of the causal agent is injected in order to elicit a positive skin test?

*Answer: Tuberculin (outermost protein) plus mycolic acids (long-chain fatty acids in the envelope)*

C. What immune cells are most important in the response to this agent?

*Answer: TH1 cells and macrophages (granuloma formation)*

**Case D**: A patient presents with multiple, crusted and oozing, honey-colored lesions.

    A. What is the skin infection?

    *Answer: Impetigo.*

    B. What two bacteria would you expect to isolate on culture?

    *Answer:* Streptococcus pyogenes *(often honey-colored crusted) and/or* Staphylococcus aureus *(often longer-lasting vesicular or with bullae).*

    C. How would you separate the two?

    *Answer: Catalase test positive for* Staphylococcus, *negative for* Streptococcus.

**Case E**: A patient had intermittent bouts of general malaise, fever with weight loss, and progressive anemia. She presents also with a heart murmur.

    A. What additional physical sign might occur and what causes it?

    *Answer: Splinter hemorrhages are caused as septic emboli are thrown from heart valves. They are also seen in trichinosis and trauma.*

    B. What is her underlying condition and what are the most commonly involved bacteria?

    *Answer: Damaged heart valve;*
    *Viridans streptococci (associated with bad oral hygiene or dental work) or*
    Enterococcus faecalis *or* E. faecium *if she has had bowel surgery.*

    C. How would you distinguish the colony on blood agar?

    *Answer: Alpha hemolytic not inhibited by optochin; a viridans streptococcus.*

**Case F**: A family of Christian Scientists brings their youngest child to the emergency room because of fever and a stiff neck. The 18-month-old child is acutely ill with a temperature of 104°F. CSF is Gram stained, examined in a rapid test, and also cultured. A Gram stain shows pleomorphic, gram-negative rods.

    A. What laboratory test could confirm the identity of the isolate?

    *Answer: Meningitis screen, a series of immunologic rapid identification tests (usually EIAs using known antibodies), followed by growth of CSF sediment or filtrate on special media and drug susceptibilities.*

    B. What growth factors are required to grow the isolate on blood agar?

    *Answer: X = hemin and V = NAD.*
    *Chocolate agar provides both X and V.*

    C. What is the drug of choice?

    *Answer: Cefotaxime or ceftriaxone.*

    D. What is the mechanism of action of the vaccine which would have prevented this condition?

    *Answer: It is a conjugated vaccine containing the polyribitol phosphate capsular material of the most important serotype (the hapten) covalently coupled to the diphtheria toxoid (protein carrier). The hapten stimulates the B lymphocyte, the carrier stimulates the TH cell, and together, isotype switching becomes possible so that something other than IgM is made.*

**Case G**: A 23-year-old woman presents with lower back pain, fever, and dysuria of 3 days' duration. Urinalysis reveals many white blood cells (WBC) and WBC casts. Gram stain of the uncentrifuged urine reveals numerous Gram-negative bacilli per oil immersion field. On culture, extremely motile bacteria form waves of confluent growth.

A. What is the most important biochemical characteristic of this organism? Why?

*Answer: Proteus, urease-producing Enterobacteriaceae; kidney stones induced.*

**Case H**: A child developed a unilateral mucopurulent conjunctivitis 10 days after birth. A conjunctival specimen was sent to the laboratory and inoculated into tissue culture cells. Iodine-staining inclusion bodies were produced.

A. What is unusual about the chemical makeup of the organism?

*Answer: ATP defective mutant, also muramic acid missing from peptido-glycan.*

B. What are the two forms of the organism?

*Answer: Elementary bodies (extracellular) and reticulate bodies = repli-cating forms.*

C. What would you see on Gram stain?

*Answer: Nothing in the cells—poorly Gram staining.*

D. What serologic type caused the child's problem?

*Answer: If U.S. kid, serotypes D-K.*

**Case I**: A 27-year-old attorney is hospitalized. He was in excellent health until two days earlier when he noted malaise, fatigability, and profound anorexia. He remembers approximately 6–8 weeks ago receiving a tattoo while vacationing in the Caribbean.

A. How would you confirm your clinical diagnosis?

*Answer: HBsAg and IgM to HbcAg.*

B. What is meant by the "window"?

*Answer: A time period between the end of the detectable presence of HBsAg and the beginning of the production of HBsAb. HBcAb and HBeAb are present.*

C. What antigen's persistence beyond 6 months post-infection is indicative that the patient is entering a carrier state?

*Answer: HBsAg past 6 months.*

D. What antigen correlates with viral production?

*Answer: HBeAg.*

E. Does the virus carry a virion associated polymerase? If so, what kind?

*Answer: Yes, RNA-dependent DNA polymerase (Hepatitis B replicates through an RNA intermediate).*

**Case J:** A young man became ill with a sore throat and swollen tonsils, marked fatigue, cervical adenopathy, a palpable spleen, and a pruritic erythematous rash that started after self-administration of ampicillin.

A. What is the most likely disease? What are the most common laboratory diagnostic tests? What does the antibody test measure?

*Answer: Infectious mononucleosis; monospot test (measures heterophile antibody which is not specific to EBV antigen) plus CBC.*

B. What type of cells are the Downey type II cells?

*Answer: T lymphocytes. (Reactive cells, not infected.)*

C. What cells does the virus infect? Through what receptor does the lymphocytic infection begin?

*Answer: EBV infects epithelial cells and B lymphocytes, whose receptor is CD21 = CR2.*

**Case K:** A 35-year-old woman presents with a unilateral vesicular rash.

A. The most likely diagnosis is

*Answer: Shingles.*

B. Describe the virion's nucleic acid.

*Answer: Linear dsDNA.*

C. Patient had a previous history of what other disease?

*Answer: Chickenpox.*

**Case L:** A 27-year-old man presents to the hospital emergency room with a cough, chest pain, and fever. Two days before admission he developed a nonproductive cough. Rales are heard. Gram stain of sputum was negative. Sputum cultures on blood agar were also negative. Culture on a special medium containing cholesterol, purines, and pyrimidines produced colonies in 10 days. Serology 3 weeks later (when he returned because of persistent cough but feeling better) showed cold agglutinins.

A. What is the probable causal agent?

*Answer: Mycoplasma pneumoniae.*

B. Why did the organism not show up on the Gram stain?

*Answer: Organism does not have a cell wall and does not stain with either the primary or counterstain in the Gram stain.*

C. What antibiotics do you NOT use?

*Answer: Penicillin/cephalosporin.*

**Case M:** A 65-year-old retired male police officer reports to an emergent care facility complaining of fever, sore throat, shortness of breath, dry cough, and generalized muscle aches and pains. On examination the patient is pale, tachycardic, and tachypneic. His conjunctivae are congested and rales and wheezes are heard over both lung fields. A chest radiograph shows diffuse bilateral infiltrates and a hemagglutination inhibition antibody test is positive at high titer.

A. What is your diagnosis?

*Answer: Influenza*

B. What drugs are available to treat this disease?

*Answer: Amantidine/rimantidine (inhibit uncoating)*
*Zanamivir/ostelamivir (inhibit neuraminidase)*

C. To what viral family does it belong?

*Answer: Orthomyxovirus*

D. Where in the cell does it replicate?

*Answer: Cytoplasm and nucleus*

E. What vaccine might have prevented this?

*Answer: Killed, H3N2, H1N1 plus one strain of Influenza B*

F. What attribute of the agent causes pandemics?

*Answer: Segmented genome can be reassorted, causing genetic shift.*

**Case N:** A 4-year-old male is brought to the pediatrician by his mother, who is concerned by his lack of appetite and loss of weight. He has had diarrhea fairly constantly over the preceding two-week period, which occasionally has been associated with vomiting. On examination, the child is in the 60% percentile of weight for his age, and has mild epigastric tenderness. A fresh stool sample, collected rectally, is yellow, greasy and malodorous and contains motile organisms.

A. To what taxonomic group does this causal agent belong?

*Answer: (Giardia lamblia) Flagellated protozoan*

B. How was this child infected?

*Answer: Fecal/oral contamination with cysts*

C. What is the mechanism of pathogenesis?

*Answer: Organism adheres in the upper duodenum using a ventral sucking disk. This blocks common bile ducts, causes fat malabsorption and steattorhea*

**Case O:** A 35-year-old worker at a plant nursery seeks his physician for a suppurative lesion on one of his fingers. A smear is taken of the drainage and stained. Cigar-shaped yeasts are detected.

A. What is the causal agent?

*Answer:* Sporothrix schenckii.

B. Is the fungus dimorphic or monomorphic?

*Answer: This is DIMORPHIC FUNGUS consistent with Sporothrix. You can tell from cigar-shaped yeast (in tissues generally tough to visualize) and hyphae with sleeve and rosettes arrangement of conidia in culture.*

C. Treatment

*Answer: Itraconazole but oral KI given in milk will also clear up.*

**Case P:** A Christian missionary returns to the United States from Central America with high fever, chills, headache, and confusion. On examination his temperature is 39°C and he is pale and tachycardic. Both liver and spleen are enlarged and tender to palpation. Laboratory tests reveal microcytic anemia, thrombocytopenia, hyperbilirubinemia, and hypoglycemia, and a blood film is examined.

A. What is the diagnosis?

*Answer:* Plasmodium vivax *malaria*

B. What is the treatment?

*Answer: Chloroquine, quinine, amodiaquine, fansidar, halofantrine etc. (Lots of drug resistance is now occurring)*

C. Is primaquine required? Why or why not?

*Answer: Yes, to prevent relapse and kill hypnozoites. This is called "radical cure" and it is necessary for* P. vivax *and* P. ovale *malarias.*

D. How did the patient acquire this disease?

*Answer: Bite of female* Anopheles *mosquito injects sporozoites.*

**Case Q:** A 50-year-old Missouri farmer was referred to the hospital because of malaise, weakness, weight loss, fever, and a palpable spleen. Examination of the mouth reveals a painless ulcerated lesion. A punch biopsy of the lesion is obtained and submitted for laboratory study. Histologic study revealed oval structures measuring 2–5 μm, packing the macrophages.

A. What is the most likely causal agent, and what are the distinctive forms?

*Answer:* Histoplasma capsulatum *with the intracellular oval yeasts and the tuberculate macroconidia (and microconidia) in the hyphal state.*

B. Where in nature will you find the fungus in large numbers?

*Answer: Great central riverbed plains. Chicken coops in Missouri 100% infected. Indianapolis has had an ongoing outbreak and has major problems with it disseminating in their AIDS patients; NY City also high.*

**Case R:** A 75-year-old woman who has suffered chronic otitis media, is brought to the hospital by the staff of her long-term care facility. She has complained of dizziness and drowsiness, and preliminary examination reveals signs of meningismus. A CT scan is negative for parenchymal lesions of the brain, although the mastoid cavities are inflamed. A lumbar puncture reveals 2130 leukocytes/μl, 1.55 mm glucose/L (concomitant blood sugar 2.6 mmol/L), and 1582 mg protein/L. Gram staining organisms are absent, but filamentous forms are cultured.

A.  What is your diagnosis?

*Answer: Aspergillus fumigatus meningitis*

B.  How would you describe this organism?

*Answer: it is a monomorphic, dematiaceous fungus*

C.  What is the treatment of choice?

*Answer: Amphotericin B or itraconazole*

**Case S:** A 34-year-old accountant presents to the emergency room because of headache and fever of 3 days' duration. The day before admission his wife noted mild confusion and irritability. Lumbar puncture revealed an opening pressure of 300 mm, 200 red blood cells, 90% of the WBCs which are lymphocytes, sugar of 85 mg/dL (concomitant blood sugar of 110 mg/dL), and protein of 65 mg/dL. Bacteriologic smears (and ultimately also the bacterial cultures) were negative, as were India ink preparations. All latex particle agglutination tests for fungal and bacterial capsules done on the patient's CSF were also negative. The patient's condition did not improve despite appropriate therapy, and he died 10 days after hospitalization.

A.  What is the most likely diagnosis?

*Answer: Herpes simplex encephalitis*

B.  What is the virus's shape?

*Answer: Icosahedral with nuclear membrane envelope.*

C.  Where within the cell does the virus replicate?

*Answer: Nucleus for both DNA synthesis and assembly.*

D.  What other members belong to the same family?

*Answers: EBV, Varicella-Zoster, Cytomegalovirus.*

**Case T:** A 20-year-old male presents to the emergency department complaining of profuse bloody diarrhea of two days duration. On examination he has a purpuric rash over a large portion of his body, although his temperature is normal. The patient is dehydrated and weak, and lab values reveal an elevated blood urea nitrogen and creatinine, with thrombocytopenia. PT and PTT are within normal limits. Culture of the feces grew organisms which produced both colorless and colored colonies on sorbitol MacConkey medium.

A. What is your diagnosis?

*Answer: Enterohemorrhagic Escherichia coli, (EHEC)*

B. What is the most likely source of his infection?

*Answer: Hamburger, fecal contamination from bovine feces*

C. What is the most likely serotype in the United States?

*Answer: O157:H7*

D. What is the mechanism of pathogenesis?

*Answer: Toxin (verotoxin) is Shiga-like and inhibits the 60S ribosomal subunit, thereby stopping eukaryotic protein synthesis.*


**Case U:** A patient presents with anogenital warts.

A. What is the virus that probably caused the tumors?

*Answer: Human papilloma virus.*

B. What serotypes are most commonly associated with this clinical presentation?

*Answer: 6 and 11*

C. Are they premalignant?

*Answer: Rarely.*

D. What serotypes are most commonly associated with cervical intraepithelial neoplasia?

*Answer: 16, 18, and 31. These are sexually transmitted.*

E. What type of vaccine is now available that could have prevented this infection?

*Answer: 4 serotypes of capsid protein created by recombinant DNA technology.*

**Case V**: A girl received a bone marrow transplant for the treatment of leukemia. Nine weeks after the transplant her temperature rose, she became dyspneic, and died. Impression smears were taken from the cut surface of the lower lobe of the left lung. The smears were stained with H&E. Intranuclear inclusions with perinuclear clearing were found.

A. Why did the patient develop the pneumonia?

*Answer: Immunocompromised—No T cells.*

B. How would you describe what you would see (using only two words)?

*Answer: Owl's eyes: cells with prominent basophilic intranuclear inclusion bodies.*

C. What is the virion's nucleic acid type? To what viral family does it belong?

*Answer: dsDNA; Herpes viruses.*

**Case W**: A young woman developed a feverish illness with painful swelling of her knee, elbow, and wrist joints. She has a sparse rash on the distal parts of her limbs, consisting of small hemorrhagic pustules with an erythematous base. A smear was obtained from the exudate of the exanthem and Gram stained. The stain showed intracellular gram-negative diplococci.

A. What disease does she have?

*Answer: Disseminated gonococcal infection.*

B. What is the major mechanism of pathogenesis?

*Answer: Pili, for attachment to epithelial surfaces—colonizing factor along with outer membrane proteins. Also exhibit antigenic variation and protect from phagocytosis.*

## MORPHOLOGY/TAXONOMY

### Spore-Forming Bacteria (Have Calcium Dipicolinate)

*Bacillus*

*Clostridium*

### Non-motile Gram-Positive Rods

*Corynebacterium diphtheriae*

*Nocardia*

*Clostridium perfringens* (rest of the pathogenic *Clostridia* are motile)

*Bacillus anthracis* (most other *Bacillus* species are motile)

### Acid Fast Organisms

*Mycobacterium*

*Nocardia* (partially acid fast)

*Cryptosporidium* oocysts

*Isospora* oocysts

### Bacteria and Fungi That Characteristically Have Capsules

The "biggies" can be remembered by the mnemonic: <u>S</u>ome <u>K</u>illers <u>H</u>ave <u>P</u>retty <u>N</u>ice <u>C</u>apsules!

*Streptococcus pneumoniae*

*Klebsiella pneumoniae*

*Haemophilus influenzae*

*Pseudomonas aeruginosa*—slime producer especially in cystic fibrosis patients' lungs

*Neisseria meningitidis*

*Cryptococcus neoformans* (only encapsulated fungal pathogen)

*Bordetella pertussis*

#### Other Important Capsule Producers

*E. coli* meningeal strains have capsule, mostly $K_1$

*Bacillus anthracis*—poly D-glutamate capsule

*Salmonella enterica* subsp. *typhi*—(virulence; Vi) capsular antigen

*Streptococcus pyogenes* when first isolated; non-immunogenic (but anti-phagocytic) hyaluronic acid capsule

## Biofilm Producers

*Staphylococcus epidermidis* (catheter-related infections)

*Streptococcus mutans* (dental plaque)

## Pigment Production

*Pseudomonas aeruginosa* (**blue-green**)—**pyocyanin, fluorescein**

*Serratia*—red pigment

*Staphylococcus aureus*—yellow pigment

Photochromogenic and scotochromogenic *Mycobacteria*—Carotenoid pigments (yellow and orange)

*Corynebacterium diphtheriae*—black to gray

## Unique Morphology/Staining

**Metachromatic staining**—*Corynebacterium*

**Lancet-shaped diplococci**—***Pneumococcus***

**Kidney bean-shaped diplococci**—*Neisseriae*

Bipolar staining—***Yersinia pestis***

Gulls wings—*Campylobacter*

**Table II-8-1.** Viral Cytopathogenesis

| Inclusion Bodies | Virus |
|---|---|
| Intracytoplasmic (Negri bodies) | Rabies |
| Intracytoplasmic acidophilic (Guarnieri) | Poxviruses |
| Intranuclear (Owl eye) | Cytomegalovirus |
| Intranuclear (Cowdry) | Herpes simplex virus<br>Subacute sclerosing panencephalitis (measles) virus |
| **Syncytia formation** | **Virus**<br>Herpes viruses<br>Varicella-zoster<br>Paramyxoviruses (measles, mumps, rubella and respiratory syncytial virus)<br>HIV |

# PHYSIOLOGY

**Table II-8-2.** Metabolism*

| Aerobes | Anaerobes | Microaerophilic |
|---|---|---|
| *Mycobacterium* | *Actinomyces* | *Campylobacter* |
| *Pseudomonas* | *Bacteroides* | *Helicobacter* |
| *Bacillus* | *Clostridium* | |
| Nocardia | Fusobacterium | |
| Corynebacterium diphtheriae | Prevotella | |
| | Propionibacterium (aerotolerant) | |
| | Eubacterium | |
| | Lactobacillus (aerotolerant) | |

*Most others are considered facultative anaerobes.

# Enzymes

## Oxidase

- **All Enterobacteriaceae are oxidase negative.**
- **All *Neisseria* are oxidase positive** (as are most other Gram-negative bacteria).

## Urease Positive (mnemonic: PUNCH)

- All *Proteus* **species** produce urease; this leads to alkaline urine and may be associated with renal calculi.
- *Ureaplasma* (renal calculi)
- *Nocardia*
- *Cryptococcus* (the fungus)
- *Helicobacter*

## Catalase

$$H_2O_2 \xrightarrow{\text{catalase}} H_2O + 1/2\ O_2$$

*Staphylococci* have catalase, *Streptococci* do not.

Most anaerobes lack catalase.

Catalase positive organisms are major problems in chronic granulomatous disease (CGD):

- All staphylococci
- *Pseudomonas aeruginosa*
- *Candida*
- *Aspergillus*
- Enterobacteriaceae

### Coagulase positive

- *Staph. aureus*
- *Yersinia pestis*

# DETERMINANTS OF PATHOGENICITY

## Genetics

### Genes encoding pathogenic factors reside on:

- The bacterial **chromosome**

  Endotoxin
- A **plasmid**

  Most toxins and multiple drug resistances
- A **bacteriophage genome** stably integrated into the host DNA as a pro-phage. Virulence modified by the stable presence of phage DNA in bacterial cell = lysogenic conversion.

  ### Examples:

  **C** = cholera toxin

  **O** = *Salmonella* O antigen

  **B** = Botulinum toxin (phage CEβ and DEβ)

  **E** = Erythrogenic toxin of *Streptococcus pyogenes*

  **D** = Diphtheria toxin (Corynephage β)

  **S** = Shiga toxin

  Mnemonic: **COBEDS** (when 2 people share a bed somebody gets a little pregnant [with phage])

### Antigenic variation

*Neisseria gonorrhoeae (pili)*

*Borrelia recurrentis*

*Trypanosoma brucei*

HIV

# Toxins

## Table II-8-3. Disease Due to Toxin Production

| Bacterium | Disease | Activity of Toxin |
|---|---|---|
| *Corynebacterium diphtheriae* | **Diphtheria** | ADP ribosylation of eEF-2 results in inhibition of protein synthesis |
| *Clostridium tetani* | **Tetanus** | Binds to SV2 ganglioside protein receptor. SV2 enables internalization and cellular intoxication. |
| *Clostridium botulinum* | **Botulism** | Prevents release of acetylcholine |
| *Vibrio cholerae* | **Cholera** | Choleragen stimulates adenylate cyclase |
| *E. coli* (ETEC) | **Travelers' diarrhea** | LT stimulates adenylate cyclase |
| *Clostridium difficile* | Diarrhea | Toxin A and B inhibit protein synthesis and cause loss of intracellular K$^+$ |
| *Bordetella pertussis* | Whooping cough | Hypoglycemia due to activation of islets<br>Edema due to inhibition Gi<br>Lymphocytosis due to inhibition of chemokine receptors<br>Sensitivity to histamine |

eEF-2 = eukaryotic elongation factor-2

## *Heat stable toxins*

### *60°C*

- *Staphylococcus aureus* enterotoxin
- ST toxin of *E. coli*
- *Yersinia enterocolitica* toxin

### *100°C*

- Endotoxin

### Toxins with ADP-ribosylating activity

**Table II-8-4.** Toxins with A-B ADP-Ribosyl Transferase Activity

| Toxin | ADP-Ribosylated Host Protein | Effect on Host Cell |
|---|---|---|
| *Pseudomonas*<br>    Exotoxin A<br>    Exotoxin S | eEF-2<br>unknown | Inhibits translocation during protein synthesis |
| Diphtheria toxin | eEF-2 | Inhibits translocation during protein synthesis |
| *E. coli* heat-labile toxin (LT) | G-protein ($G_S$) | Increases cAMP in instestinal epithelium causing diarrhea |
| Cholera toxin | G-protein ($G_S$) | Increases cAMP in intestinal epithelium causing diarrhea |
| Pertussis toxin | G-protein ($G_i$) | Increases cAMP causing edema, lymphocytosis and increased insulin secretion |

A is the ADP-ribosyl transferase.
B binds to cell receptor and translocates the A subunit into the cell.

### Invasive factors

**Table II-8-5.** Invasive Factors

| Invasive Factor | Function | Bacteria |
|---|---|---|
| All capsules | Antiphagocytic | See earlier list with morphology |
| Slime layer (capsule or glycocalyx) | Antiphagocytic | *Pseudomonas* |
| M protein | Antiphagocytic | Group A Streptococci |
| A protein | Inhibits opsonization | *Staph. aureus* |
| Lipoteichoic acid | Attachment to host cells | All gram-positive bacteria |
| *N. gonorrhoeae* pili | Antiphagocytic | *N. gonorrhoeae* |

**Table II-8-6.** Extracellular Enzymes

| Enzyme | Function | Bacteria |
|---|---|---|
| Hyaluronidase | Hydrolysis of ground substance | Group A Streptococci |
| Collagenase | Hydrolysis of collagen | *Clostridium perfringens* *Prevotella melanino-genica* |
| Kinases | Hydrolysis of fibrin | *Streptococcus* *Staphylococcus* |
| Lecithinase (alpha toxin) | Damage to membrane | *Clostridium perfringens* |
| Heparinase | May contribute to thrombophlebitis | *Bacteroides fragilis* *Prevotella melanino-genica* |
| IgA Proteases | Colonizing factor | *Neisseria* *Haemophilus* *Strep. pneumoniae* |

# Ability to Survive and Grow in Host Cell

## Obligate Intracellular Parasites

Cannot be cultured on inert media. Virulence is due to the ability to survive and grow intracellularly where the organism is protected from many B-cell host defenses.

- Bacteria
  - All Rickettsiae
  - All Chlamydiaceae
  - *Mycobacterium leprae*
- Viruses
  - All are obligate intracellular parasites.
- Protozoa
  - *Plasmodium*
  - *Toxoplasma gondii*
  - *Babesia*
  - *Leishmania*
  - *Trypanosoma cruzi* (amastigotes in cardiac muscle)
- Fungi
  - None

### Facultative intracellular parasites of humans

- Bacteria
  - *Francisella tularensis*
  - *Listeria monocytogenes*
  - *Mycobacterium tuberculosis*
  - *Brucella* species
  - Non-tuberculous *mycobacteria*
  - *Salmonella enterica* subsp. *typhi*
  - *Legionella pneumophila*
  - *Yersinia pestis*
  - *Nocardia* species
- Fungi
  - *Histoplasma capsulatum*

### Obligate Parasites That Are Not Intracellular

(e.g., cannot be cultured on inert media but are found extracellularly in the body)

- *Treponema pallidum*
- *Pneumocystis jirovecii*

## EPIDEMIOLOGY/TRANSMISSION

## Bacteria That Have Humans as the Only Known Reservoir

*Mycobacterium tuberculosis*

**M. leprae** (armadillos in Texas)

**Shigella** species

**Salmonella enterica** subspecies *typhi*

**Rickettsia prowazekii** (epidemic typhus)

Group A β-hemolytic streptococcus

*Neisseria meningitidis* and *N. gonorrhoeae*

*Corynebacterium diphtheriae*

*Streptococcus pneumoniae*

*Treponema pallidum*

*Chlamydia trachomatis*

## Zoonotic Organisms

(Diseases of animals transmissible to humans)

*Bacillus anthracis*

*Salmonella enterica* all subspecies except *typhi*

*Leptospira*

*Borrelia*

*Listeria monocytogenes*

*Brucella* species

*Francisella tularensis*

*Pasteurella multocida* (cat bites)

*Vibrio parahaemolyticus* (from fish)

*Capnocytophaga canimorsus* (dog bites)

*Bartonella henselae* (cat scratches)

*Streptobacillus moniliformis* (rat bite fever)

*Mycobacterium marinum* (fish tank granuloma)

*Vibrio vulnificus* (oysters)

*Yersinia pestis, Y. enterocolitica, Y. pseudotuberculosis*

*Campylobacter fetus, C. jejuni*

Most Rickettsia

*Chlamydophila psittaci* (birds)

*Rabies virus*

# Arthropod Vectors in Human Disease: Insects

- Lice

    Epidemic or louse-borne typhus (*Pediculus h. humanus*)

    Epidemic relapsing fever

    Trench fever

- **True bugs**

    **Chagas' disease (American trypanosomiasis)—kissing bugs (Reduviidae)**

- Mosquitoes

    **Malaria (*Anopheles* mosquito)**

    **Dengue (*Aedes*)**

    **Mosquito-borne encephalitides: WEE, EEE, VEE, SLE, WNV**

    **Yellow Fever (*Aedes*)**

    Filariasis

- **Sandflies**

    **Leishmaniasis**

    Bartonellosis

- Midges

    Filariasis

- Blackflies

    Onchocerciasis

- Deerflies (*Chrysops*) and horse flies

    Loaloasis

    Tularemia

- **Tsetse flies**

    **African trypanosomiasis**

- **Fleas**

    **Plague**

    Endemic typhus

## Arthropod Vectors That Are Not Insects

- Ticks

  **Rocky Mountain spotted fever (*Dermacentor*)**

  **Colorado tick fever (*Dermacentor*)**

  **Lyme disease (*Ixodes*)**

  *Ehrlichia (Ixodes, Amblyomma)*

  **Babesiosis (*Ixodes*)**

  **Tularemia (*Dermacentor*)**

  **Recurrent fever or tick-borne relapsing fever (*Ornithodoros*, a soft tick)**

- Mites

  Scrub typhus (*Leptotrombium*) (transovarial transmission in vector)

  Rickettsialpox

## Parasitic Infections Transmitted by Ova

*Enterobius vermicularis* (pinworm)

*Ascaris lumbricoides* (roundworm)

*Toxocara canis (visceral larva migrans)*

*Trichuris trichiura* (whipworm)

*Echinococcus granulosus/multilocularis*

*Taenia solium (cysticercosis)*

All others are transmitted in larval stage.

## Bacterial and Fungal Infections That Are Not Considered Contagious

(i.e., no human-to-human transmission)

Nontuberculous mycobacterial infections, e.g., **Mycobacterium avium-intracellulare**

Non-spore forming anaerobes

**Legionella pneumophila**

All fungal infections except the dermatophytes

## Infections That Cross the Placenta

(**Mnemonic: TORCH**)

*Toxoplasma*

**O**ther (Syphilis)

**R**ubella

**C**MV

**H**erpes and **H**IV

<5% perinatal hepatitis B could possibly have been acquired by crossing placenta.

- Viruses

  *Cytomegalovirus*

  *Rubella*

  HSV 2 (in primary infection)

  Coxsackie B

  Polio

HIV

B19

- Parasites

  *Toxoplasma gondii*

- Bacteria

  *Treponema pallidum*

  *Listeria monocytogenes*

## Spread by Respiratory Droplet

*Streptococcus pyogenes* (Group A)

*Streptococcus pneumoniae*          Influenza

*Neisseria meningitidis*            Rubella

*Mycobacterium tuberculosis*        Measles

*Bordetella pertussis*              Chickenpox

*Haemophilus influenzae*            *Pneumocystis jirovecii*

*Corynebacterium diphtheriae*

*Mycoplasma pneumoniae*

## Spread by Inhalation of Organisms from the Environment

*Histoplasma*

*Coccidioides*

*Blastomyces*

**Nontuberculous mycobacteria, e.g., *M. avium-intracellulare* (*MAC*)**

*Legionella*

*Chlamydophila psittaci*

*Pseudomonas* (also spread by ingestion and contact)

## Spread by Oral/Fecal Route

(Infections may be spread by oral sex.)

*Salmonella*

*Shigella*

*Campylobacter*

*Vibrio*

*Yersinia enterocolitica*

*Yersinia pseudotuberculosis*

*Bacillus cereus*

*Clostridium*

*Staphylococcus* (also other routes commonly)

Enteroviruses, including poliovirus

Rotavirus

Norwalk agent

Hepatitis A

*Toxoplasma*—cat feces

*Entamoeba*

*Giardia*

All nematodes except filaria and *Trichinella*

All cestodes

## Contact: (Person-to-Person) Nonsexual

Impetigo (*Strep* and *Staph*)

*Staphylococcus*

Herpes I

Epstein-Barr (kissing)

Hepatitis B (all body fluids)

Molluscum contagiosum (wrestling teams)

## Contact: Sexual

| | | |
|---|---|---|
| *Chlamydia* | HPV | HBV |
| *Neisseria* | HIV | HCV |
| *Treponema* | HSV 2 | |
| *Trichomonas* | CMV | |

## PATHOLOGY

## Organisms that Produce Granulomas (most are intracellular, others have persistent antigen)

Fran Likes My Pal Bruce And His Blasted Cockerspaniel (in) Salt Lake City. (Mnemonic by M. Free.)

(ic) = intracellular organism

*Francisella* (ic)

*Listeria* (ic)

*Mycobacterium* (ic)

*Treponema pallidum*

*Brucella* (ic)

*Actinomyces*

*Histoplasma* (ic)

*Blastomyces*

*Coccidioides*

*Schistosoma* species

*Lymphogranuloma venereum* (ic)

Cat scratch fever

## Infections Causing Intracerebral Calcifications

*Toxoplasma*

CMV

Cysticercosis

*Cryptococcus neoformans*

Tuberculous meningitis

# LABORATORY DIAGNOSIS

## Special Stains

- Silver stains

    Dieterle—*Legionella*

    Gomori methenamine—*Pneumocystis*, fungi

- Acid fast (Ziehl-Neelsen or Kinyoun)

    *Mycobacterium, Nocardia* (partially AF), *Cryptosporidium, Isospora, Cyclospora,* and *Microsporidia* (oocysts in feces)

- India ink—*Cryptococcus* (if negative not a reliable diagnostic method)

- Calcofluor white—fungi

- Giemsa

    Blood protozoa (*Plasmodium, Babesia, Trypanosoma, Leishmania*)

    *Histoplasma capsulatum* in RES cells

## Name Tests

| Tests | Disease |
|---|---|
| PPD or Tuberculin (Mantoux) | TB |
| Lepromin | Leprosy |
| Fungal skin tests | Clinically valuable only to demonstrate exposure or anergy |
| CAMP test | *Strept agalactiae* carriers |
| Elek test | Toxin producing *C. diphtheriae* strains |
| Weil-Felix | Rickettsia (with *Proteus* strain OX antigens) |

## Unusual Growth Requirements

*Haemophilus* (most species require one or both)

- **X factor** = protoporphyrin IX, the precursor of **hemin**
- **V factor** = NAD (nicotinamide dinucleotide) or NADP

*Mycoplasma*

- **Cholesterol**

Salt (halophilic organisms)

- *Staph aureus* will grow on high salt media.
- Group D enterococci will grow on 6.5% NaCl.
- *Vibrio* species requires NaCl to grow and grows at 6.5%.

Cysteine requirement for growth

- Four Sisters Ella of the Cysteine Chapel (mnemonic by M. Free)
  *Francisella, Legionella, Brucella,* and *Pasteurella*

**Cultures that must be observed for a long time**

- *Mycobacterium tuberculosis* and all non-tuberculous mycobacteria except rapid growers
- *Mycoplasma pneumoniae*
- Systemic fungal pathogens (*Blastomyces, Histoplasma,* and *Coccidioides* in U.S.)

# TREATMENT/PREVENTION

## Treat Prophylactically

- *Neisseria meningitidis* (household and day care contacts—vaccination also used in outbreaks)
- *Mycobacterium tuberculosis* with a recent skin test conversion or known household (i.e., significant) exposure; or persons under 35 with a positive skin test who have never been treated
- *Haemophilus influenzae* B (unvaccinated household contacts <6 years old) —also vaccinate
- *Neisseria gonorrhoeae* (sexual contacts)
- *Treponema pallidum* (sexual contacts)
- *Yersinia pestis*
- Neonatal eyes (*Neisseria gonorrhoeae, Chlamydia trachomatis, Treponema pallidum*)

## Vaccines Available in the U.S.

### Inactivated vaccines (RIP-A; Rest In Peace Always)

- Rabies
- Influenza virus
- Salk polio (killed)—all primary vaccinations in U.S., including IC patients
- Hepatitis A
- Japanese encephalitis and several other encephalitis vaccines
- *Vibrio cholerae*

### Live, attenuated vaccines

- *Francisella tularensis*
- Measles (rubeola)
- Rubella
- Mumps (killed vaccine available for IC patients)
- Sabin polio (oral)
- Smallpox
- Yellow fever
- Varicella-Zoster
- Rotavirus

## Live, Pathogenic Virus (in enteric-coated capsules)

- Adenovirus

## Toxoid: Chemically Modified Toxin—-Vaccines

- Tetanus
- Diphtheria
- Pertussis toxoid (in DTaP)

## Subunit Vaccines

- *Haemophilus*—purified capsular polysaccharide conjugated to protein
- *Neisseria meningitidis*—capsular polysaccharides, pediatric version is conjugated to protein
- Pneumococcal—capsular polysaccharide (7 and 23 serotypes) (pediatric version is conjugated to protein)

## Recombinant Vaccines

- Hepatitis B—HBsAg (produced in yeast)
- Human papilloma virus vaccine, 4 capsid proteins

# Reference Charts and Tables

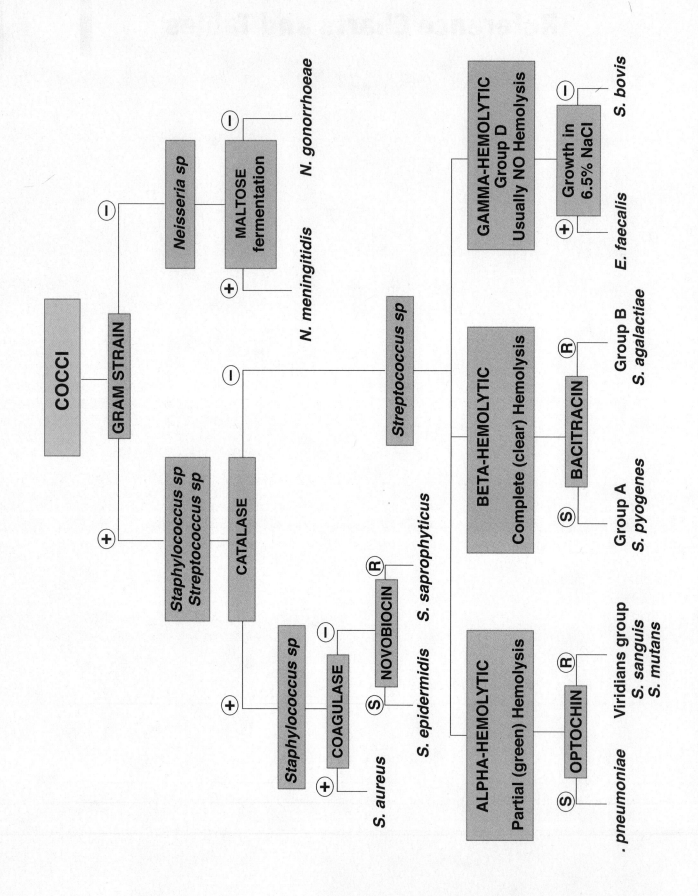

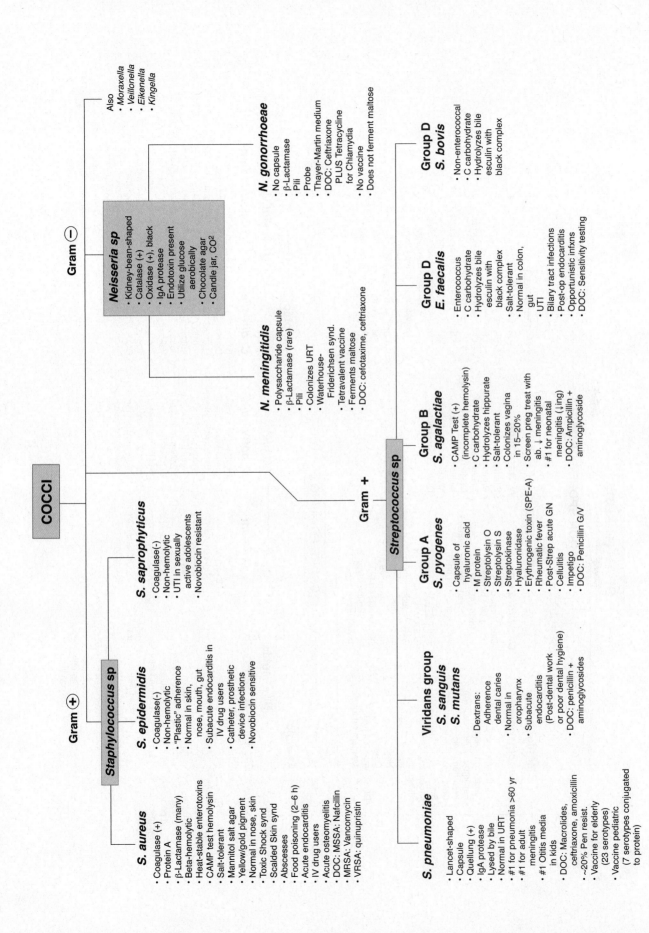

## COCCI

### Gram (+)

#### Staphylococcus sp

**S. aureus**
- Coagulase (+)
- Protein A
- β-Lactamase (many)
- Beta-hemolytic
- Heat-stable enterotoxins
- CAMP test hemolysin
- Salt-tolerant
- Mannitol salt agar
- Yellow/gold pigment
- Normal in nose, skin
- Toxic Shock synd
- Scalded Skin synd
- Abscesses
- Food poisoning (2–6 h)
- IV drug users
- Acute endocarditis
- Acute osteomyelitis
- DOC: MSSA: Nafcillin
- MRSA: Vancomycin
- VRSA: quinupristin

**S. epidermidis**
- Coagulase(-)
- Non-hemolytic
- "Plastic" adherence
- Normal in skin, nose, mouth, gut
- Subacute endocarditis in IV drug users
- Catheter, prosthetic device infections
- Novobiocin sensitive

**S. saprophyticus**
- Coagulase(-)
- Non-hemolytic
- UTI in sexually active adolescents
- Novobiocin resistant

### Gram (−)

#### Neisseria sp
- Kidney-bean-shaped
- Catalase (+)
- Oxidase (+), black
- IgA protease
- Endotoxin present
- Utilize glucose aerobically
- Chocolate agar
- Candle jar, $CO_2$

**N. meningitidis**
- Polysaccharide capsule
- β-Lactamase (rare)
- Pili
- Colonizes URT
- Waterhouse-Friderichsen synd.
- Tetravalent vaccine
- Ferments maltose
- DOC: cefotaxime, ceftriaxone

**N. gonorrhoeae**
- No capsule
- β-Lactamase
- Pili
- Probe
- Thayer-Martin medium
- DOC: Ceftriaxone PLUS Tetracycline for Chlamydia
- No vaccine
- Does not ferment maltose

Also
- *Moraxella*
- *Veillonella*
- *Eikenella*
- *Kingella*

### Gram +

#### Streptococcus sp

**S. pneumoniae**
- Lancet-shaped
- Capsule
- Quellung (+)
- IgA protease
- Lysed by bile
- Normal in URT
- #1 for pneumonia >60 yr
- #1 for adult meningitis
- #1 Otitis media in kids
- DOC: Macrolides, ceftriaxone, amoxicillin
- ~20% Pen resist.
- Vaccine for elderly (23 serotypes)
- Vaccine pediatric (7 serotypes conjugated to protein)

**Viridans group**
**S. sanguis**
**S. mutans**
- Dextrans:
  Adherence dental caries
- Normal in oropharynx
- Subacute endocarditis (Post-dental work or poor dental hygiene)
- DOC: penicillin + aminoglycosides

**Group A**
**S. pyogenes**
- Capsule of hyaluronic acid
- M protein
- Streptolysin O
- Streptolysin S
- Streptokinase
- Hyaluronidase
- Erythrogenic toxin (SPE-A)
- Rheumatic fever
- Post-Strep acute GN
- Cellulitis
- Impetigo
- DOC: Penicillin G/V

**Group B**
**S. agalactiae**
- CAMP Test (+) (incomplete hemolysin)
- C carbohydrate
- Hydrolyzes hippurate
- Salt-tolerant
- Colonizes vagina in 15–20%
- Screen preg treat with ab. ↓ meningitis
- #1 for neonatal meningitis (↓ing)
- DOC: Ampicillin + aminoglycoside

**Group D**
**E. faecalis**
- Enterococcus
- C carbohydrate
- Hydrolyzes bile esculin with black complex
- Salt-tolerant
- Normal in colon, gut
- UTI
- Biliary tract infections
- Post-op endocarditis
- Opportunistic infxns
- DOC: Sensitivity testing

**Group D**
**S. bovis**
- Non-enterococcal
- C carbohydrate
- Hydrolyzes bile esculin with black complex

# GRAM (+) RODS

## NON-SPORE-FORMING

### Aerobic

#### Motile

**L. monocytogenes**

- Tumbling motility
- "Jets" from cell to cell
- Fac intracellular organism
- Beta-hemolytic
- Cold enrichment
- Sepsis
- Crosses placenta
- Meningitis
  - Renal transplant
  - Neonatal
  - Cancer
- DOC: Ampicillin and Gentamicin for IC

#### Non-Motile

**C. diphtheriae**

- Club-shaped
- "Chinese Characters"
- Exotoxin (ADP-R of eEF-2) Heart, Nerves, epithelium
- Volutin granules on Loeffler's medium
- Tellurite: black colonies
- ELEK test
- Gray pseudomembrane
- Myocarditis
- Recrnt larngl nerve palsy
- DOC: Antitoxin PLUS Erythromycin
- Toxoid vaccine

**N. asteroides**

- Filaments to rods
- Urease (+)
- Partially acid-fast
- Cavitary bronchopulmonary
- Multiple brain abscesses
- Mycetoma (granules)
- DOC: Sulfonamides

### Anaerobic

**A. israelii**

- Rods with branching
- Non-motile
- Not restricted by anatomical boundaries
- Sulfur "granules" in exudates from sinus tract
- Normal in mouth and female genitourinary tract
- Cervicofacial (lumpy jaw)
- IUD-associated infections
- Solitary brain abscess
- Mycetoma
- Rx: Penicillin plus drainage

## SPORE-FORMING

### Aerobic

#### Motile

**B. cereus**

- Heat-stable exotoxin: vomiting increase cAMP
- Heat-labile toxin: diarrhea
- Fried rice
- Food poisoning (2–18 h)
- Symptomatic Rx

#### Non-Motile

**B. anthracis**

- Poly-D-glutamate capsule
- Spores
- In R-E cells
- Toxin:
  - Protective Ag
  - Lethal factor
  - Edema factor (an adenylate cyclase)
- Painless skin ulcer 95%
- Black eschar
- Striking local edema
- Woolsorter's disease Pneumonia
- DOC: Ciprofloxacin or doxycycline

### Anaerobic

#### Motile

**C. tetani**

- Terminal spores
- Exotoxin
  - Tetanospasmin Inhibits GABA Glycine
- Tetanus
  - Spastic paralysis
- DOC: hyperimmune globulin, Penicillin PLUS spasmolytic
- Toxoid vaccine

**C. botulinum**

- Neurotoxin heat-labile Blocks ACh release
- Flaccid paralysis
- Canned-food poisoning
- Trivalent antitoxin
- DOC: antitoxin PLUS Penicillin
- Infant botulism human hyperimmune serum, no drugs

#### Non-Motile

**C. difficile**

- Nosocomial
- Diarrhea to pseudomembranous colitis
- Antibiotic (Clindamycin) usage
- Yellow plaques
- Colon
- Toxins A + B
- DOC: Change or stop antibiotic

**C. perfringens**

- Subterminal spore
- Alpha lecithinase= Phospholipase C
- Enterotoxin
- Stormy fermentation
- Double-zone hemolysis
- Egg yolk agar
- Normal in colon
- Food poisoning
- Gas gangrene
- Myonecrosis
- High mortality
- DOC: Penicillin G ± Clindamycin PLUS debridement

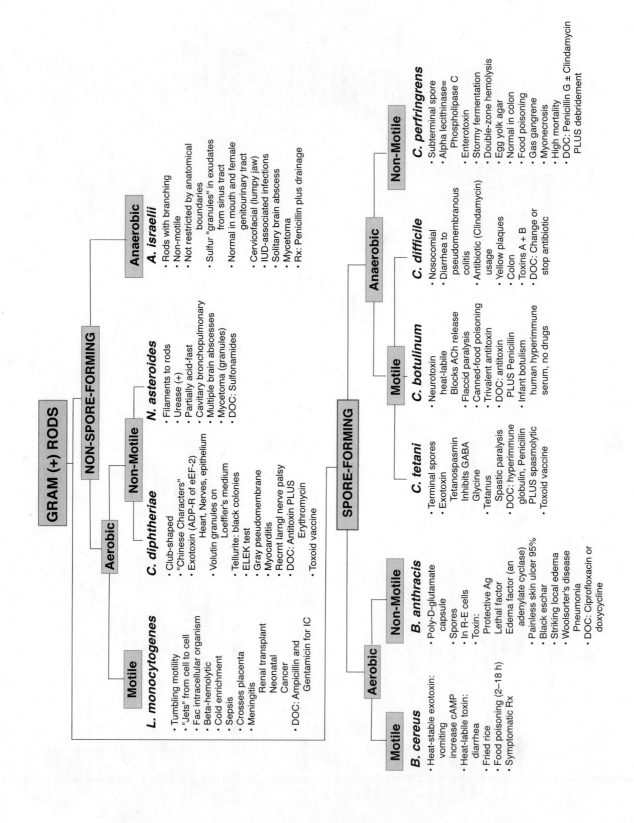

## GRAM (-) RODS & SPIROCHETES

Facultative Anaerobes →

### AEROBES

**B. pertussis**
- Adhesion to cell via hemagglutinin and pertussis toxin
- Adenylate cyclase txn (local edema)
- Tracheal toxin
- Dermanecrosis toxin
- Endotoxin - Lipid X, A
  ADP-R of GNBP
- Bordet-Gengou agar
- Regan-Lowe agar
- Whooping cough
- DOC: Erythromycin
- Vaccine toxoid and filamentous hemagglutinin

**Brucella sp**
- In R-E cells
- Endotoxin
- Requires CYS, CO₂
- Unpasteurized milk
- Undulant Fever
  Bang's disease
  Malta fever
- *B. abortus*
  cattle, mild
- *B. suis*
  pigs
  suppurative, chronic
- *B. melitensis*
  goats
  severe, acute
- DOC: rifampin and doxycycline

**F. tularensis**
- In R-E cells
- Requires CYS
- *Dermacentor* tick bite
  Transovarian trans.
- Aerosol
- Rabbits, rodents
- Granulomatous rxn
- Tularemia - AR, MO, TX
- Live, attntd vaccine
- DOC: Streptomycin

**L. pneumophila**
- Water-loving
  air conditioning
- Requires CYS & Fe
- Buffered Charcoal
  Yeast agar
- Dieterle silver stain
- Stains poorly Gram (-)
- Atypical pneumonia
- Mental confusion
- Diarrhea
- DOC: Erythromycin
- Not contagious

**P. aeruginosa**
- Slime-layer
- Grape-like odor
- Exotoxin A:
  ADP-R of eEF-2
  Liver
- Oxidase (+)
- Pigments
  pyocyanin, pyoverdin
- Transient colonization
  In 10% of normal pop
- Osteomyelitis in drug
  abusers
- Pneumonia in
  cystic fibrosis
- Nosocomial infections
  Burn patients
  Neutropenic patients
- Ecthyma gangrenosum
- DOC: Penicillin
  PLUS Aminoglycoside

### ANAEROBES

**Bacteroides sp**
- *B. fragilis* - obligate
- Modified LPS, capsules
- Predominant colonic flora
- Normal in oropharynx, vagina
- Predisposing factors:
  surgery, trauma
  chronic disease (cancer)
- Septicemia, peritonitis
  aspiration pneumonia
- *Prevotella melaninogenica*
  Human oropharynx
- *Fusobacterium* (combined w/
  *Treponema microdentium*)
  Vincent's angina
  Trench mouth
- DOC: Metronidazole OR
  Clindamycin OR Cefoxitin

### SPIROCHETES
- Thin-Walled
- Spiral-Shaped
- Axial Filaments
- Jarisch-Herxheimer Rxn

**Treponema sp**
- *T. pallidum* - Syphilis
  Obligate parasite
- 1° - PAINLESS chancre, infectious
- 2° - Rash infectious
- 3° - Gummas, CVS, CNS
- Congenital: stillbirths, malformed
- VDRL & RPR - Screening tests
- Reagin ab - xrxn with Cardiolipin
- FTA-ABS (immunofluorescence)
  specific test
- Dark-field microscopy
- DOC: Benzathine Penicillin

**Borrelia sp**
- Microaerophillic
- Giemsa stain
- *B. burgdorferi*
  Lyme disease
  (*I. scapularis*), *I. pacificus*
  Reservoirs: mice, deer
  CT, WI, CA
  Erythema Migrans
  Target lesions
- *B. recurrentis*
  Relapsing fever
  Vector: body louse
  Antigenic variation
- DOC: Penicillin or azithromycin

**Leptospira sp**
- Dark-field microscopy
- Contaminated water
  Animal urine
- Fever, jaundice, uremia
- Non-icteric Leptospirosis
  Meningitis - No PMN in CSF
  uveitis, rash
- Icteric Leptospirosis
  Weil's disease
  Renal failure, myocarditis
- DOC: Penicillin G or doxycycline

Gram (−) Rods

# FACULTATIVE ANAEROBES

## P. multocida
- Requires CYS
- Animal bites (cats & dogs)
- Cellulitis with Lymphadenitis
- DOC: Amoxicillin/Clav (prophylaxis)

## H. influenzae
- Polyribitol capsule
- Quellung (+)
- IgA protease
- Requires X (Hemin), V (NAD)
- Normal in nasopharynx and conjunctiva
- Pathogenic in kids: type B
- Meningitis in 1–2 yr
- Otitis media, pneumonia
- Acute epiglottitis
- DOC: Cefotaxime/Ceftriaxone
- Prev: HIB vaccine, Rifampin

## Vibrio sp
- Polar flagella, comma-shaped
- Enterotoxin (Choleragen) ADP-R, increase cAMP
- Catalase (+), Oxidase (+)
- Alkaline culture (TCBS)
- Classic cholera O₁
- Biotypes: El Tor, Cholerae
- Rice-water stools
- Most severe dehydration
- Rx: fluid & electrolytes tetracycline for contacts

- **V. parahaemolyticus**
  Catalase (−), salt-tolerant
  Raw seafood

- **V. vulnificus**
  Brackish water • Oysters
  Cellulitis, Septicemia
  DOC: tetracycline

## Campylobacter sp
## Helicobacter sp
- Microaerophilic
- Polar flagella
- Comma or S-shaped
- Oxidase (+), Catalase (+)
- Skirrow's agar CO₂
- Invasive
- **H. pylori**
  37°C, urease(+)
  gastritis, ulcers
  carcinoma
- DOC: omeprazole + amoxicillin + clarithromycin
- **C. jejuni**
  42°C enterocolitis
  #1 bacterial diarrhea U.S.A.
  "Gull-Wings"
- **C. fetus escapes GIT**
- DOC: Erythromycin, fluoroquinolones

Also:
- *Gardnerella*
- *Capnocytophaga*
- *Actinobacillus*
- *Cardiobacterium*

## ENTEROBACTERIACEAE
- Ferment Glucose
- Oxidase (−), Catalase (+)
- Reduce Nitrates to Nitrites

### Lactose-Fermenting

#### E. coli
- Normal in colon
- #1 for UTI
- P-pili, X-Adhesins
- Nosocomial infections
- Neonatal meningitis (K₁)
- ETEC • Traveler's Drha
  Toxins: LT, ST
- EIEC • Invasive
- EHEC • VTEC 0157:H7
  Hemorrhagic colitis
  Hemolytic uremic S
  Does not ferment Sorbitol
- EPEC
  Plasmid-coded EAF
- EAEC
  Fimbriae/biofilm
- DAEC
  Infants
  Bacteria in microvilli
- DOC: Ampicillin or
  Sulfonamides
  Cephalosporins

#### K. pneumoniae
- Capsule
- Quellung (+)
- Pneumonia
  Current jelly septum
  Chronic lung disease
  Alcoholism
  Aspiration
- UTI
  Nosocomial
  Catheterization
- DOC: Cephalosporin
  +/− aminoglycoside

### Motile and H₂S-Producing

#### Proteus sp.
- Swarming motility
- Indole (+), Urease (+)
- UTI, Septicemia
- Staghorn calculi
- DOC: Fluoroquinolones

#### Salmonella enterica subsp.
- Antigens: Vi, O, H
- EMB/MacConkey
- Predisposing factors
  High gastric pH
  Gastrectomy
- Widal test (O, H ag)
- Osteomyelitis in Sickle
  Cell disease

- **S. enterica subsp. typhi**
  No animal res.
  No H₂S produced
  Invasive (R-E) cells
  Rose spots
- DOC: fluoroquinolones
  or cephalosporins

- **S. enterica subsp. enteritidis**
  Poultry, reptiles
  Rx: Symptomatic
- DOC for invasive:
  ampicillin, cephalosporins

### Non-Lactose-Fermenting

### Non-Motile and Non-H₂S-Producing

#### Shigella sp
- No H Antigens
- Invasive
- Shigatoxin
  Nicks 60S SU
  Neurotoxin
  Cytotoxin
  Enterotoxin
- Enterocolitis
- Bloody diarrhea
- DOC: fluid and electrolytes
  FQ, Azithro

#### Y. pestis
- Coagulase (+)
- V&W antigens
- Safety-pin appearance
  (bipolar staining
  Wayson's stain)
- Wild rodents
- Flea bite
- Southwest U.S. (Sylvatic)
- Bubonic plague
  fever, buboes,
  conjunctivitis
- Pneumonic plague
- DOC: Aminoglycosides
  PLUS Quarantine (72 h)

- **Y. enterocolitica**
  Cold growth
- Heat-stable toxins

## Poorly Gram-Staining Organisms*

### ACID FAST

**Mycobacteria**

#### *M. tuberculosis*
- Gram (+) wall but doesn't stain due to waxy CW
- Acid fast, obligate aerobe
- Respiratory transmission
- Pathogen, contagious
- Cord factor-trehalose mycolate-inhib. WBC migration
- mitoch. resp./ oxid. phosphor
- Sulfatides-inhib. phagosome-lysosome fusion
- Niacin (+), catalase (+) at 37°C, (−) at 68°C
- Slow growing
- Drug resistance
- Lowenstein-Jensen medium
- DOC: isoniazid + rifampin + pyrazinimide (2 mo) then isoniazid + rifampin (4 mo)

#### *M. avium-intracellulare*
- Gram (+) wall but doesn't stain due to waxy CW
- Acid fast
- Obligate aerobe
- Soil organism
- Opportunist, non-contagious
- Pulmonary → diss infections CA pts, late AIDS pts

#### *M. leprae*
- Obligate intracellular bacterium
- Tuberculoid (CMI damage)
- Lepromatous leprosy (poor CMI)
- DOC: dapsone + rifampin + clofazimine

#### *M. marinum*
- Cutaneous lesions (fish tank granuloma)
- DOC: isoniazid, rifampin, ethambutol

### SOME ATP

**Rickettsias**

#### *R. rickettsii*
- Obligate intracellular bacteria
- Gram-negative envelope but stain poorly
- Rocky MT Spt'd Fever-rash on wrists/ankles → trunk, palms, soles
- Vector: *Dermacentor* tick
- Reservoirs: ticks, wild rodents
- Dx: serol: 4x incr indir Fl. Ab + Weil-Felix
- DOC: Doxycycline

#### *R. prowazekii*
- Obligate intracellular bacteria
- Epidemic typhus
- Vector: *Pediculus* louse
- Reservoir: humans, squirrel fleas, flying squirrels

#### *Bartonella henselae*
- Cat scratch fever
- Bacillary angiomatosis in AIDS

#### *Ehrlichia*
- Ehrlichiosis
- Morulae in WBC
- DOC: doxycycline
- *E. chafeensis*-monocytes + macrophages
- *E. phagocytophila* - PMNs
- *Ixodes* tick

### NO ATP, mod. peptidoglycan

**Chlamydiaceae**

#### *Chlamydia trachomatis*
- Obligate intracellular bacteria
- Gram-negative envelope but stain poorly; lack muramic acid
- Elementary body-transmitted
- Reticulate body-intracellular
- Dx: serology or tissue culture growth confirmed by inclusion bodies (Fl Ab, Giemsa, iodine)

**Serotypes D-K**
- U.S.-Most common bacterial STD (HPV and HSV2 more common)
- Neonatal/adult inclus. conjunct, neonatal. pneumo; urethritis cervicitis, PID, infertility

**Serotypes L1, 2, 3**
- Lymphogranuloma venereum
- STD in Africa, Asia, S. America

**Serotypes A, B, Ba, C**
- Trachoma-follic conjunctivitis → conj. scarring, entropion → corneal scarring
- Leading infectious cause blindness
- DOC: Doxycycline or azithromycin

#### *Chlamydophila pneumoniae*
- TWAR agent
- Respiratory infections
- Probably very common
- Potential association with atherosclerosis
- DOC: macrolides and tetracycline

#### *Chlamydophila psittaci*
- Atypical pneumonia
- Birds (parrots)
- DOC: tetracycline

### NO CELL WALL

**Mycoplasmas**

#### *M. pneumoniae*
- Lack cell wall peptidoglycan → non-Gram-staining
- Cholesterol (req'd) in membr.
- Atypical pneumonia in youth and young adults
- Free living (culturable, extracell.)
- Slow growth, special media: Myco-plasma, Eaton's or Hayflick's media-sterols+pur/pyrimidines: mulberry colonies
- Cold agglutinins in 65% cases
- No Penicillins nor Cephalosporins
- DOC: erythromycin, azithromycin

#### *Ureaplasma urealyticum*
- Urethritis, prostatitis
- Urease positive
- No cell wall
- DOC: erythromycin or tetracycline

*Also note that *Legionella* and the spirochetes (*Treponema, Leptospira,* and *Borrelia*)—all Gram-negative—do not show up reliably with Gram stain.

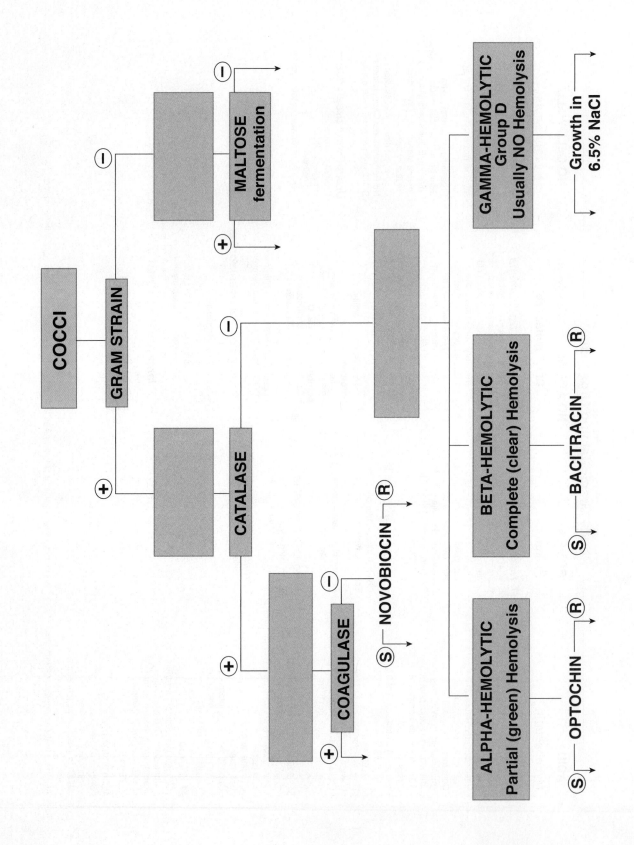

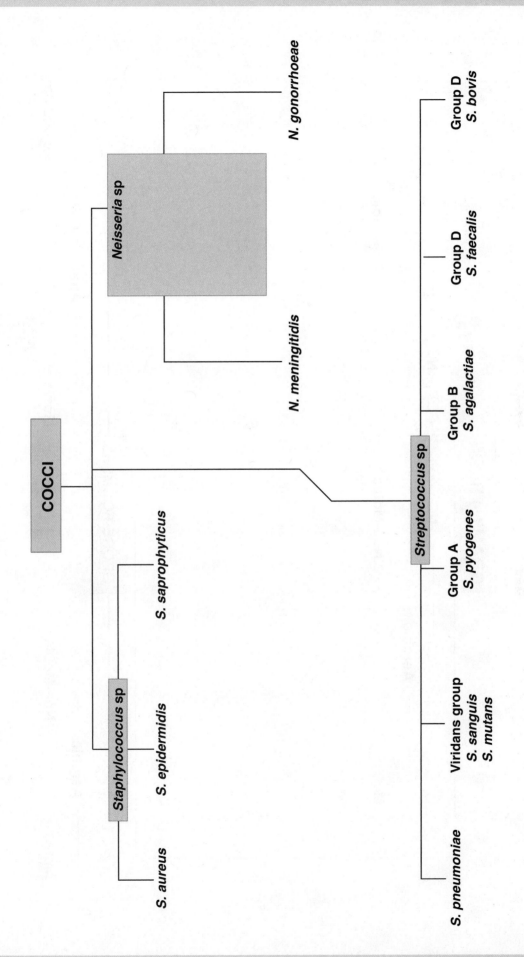

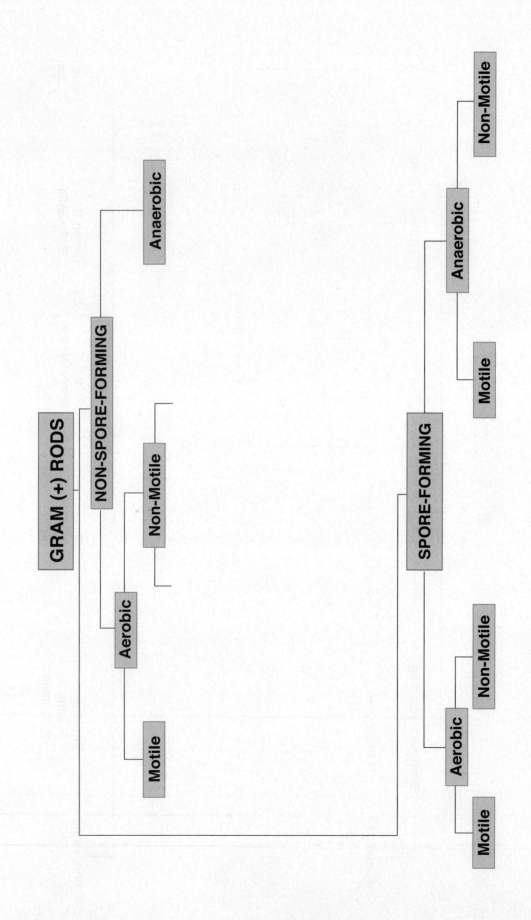

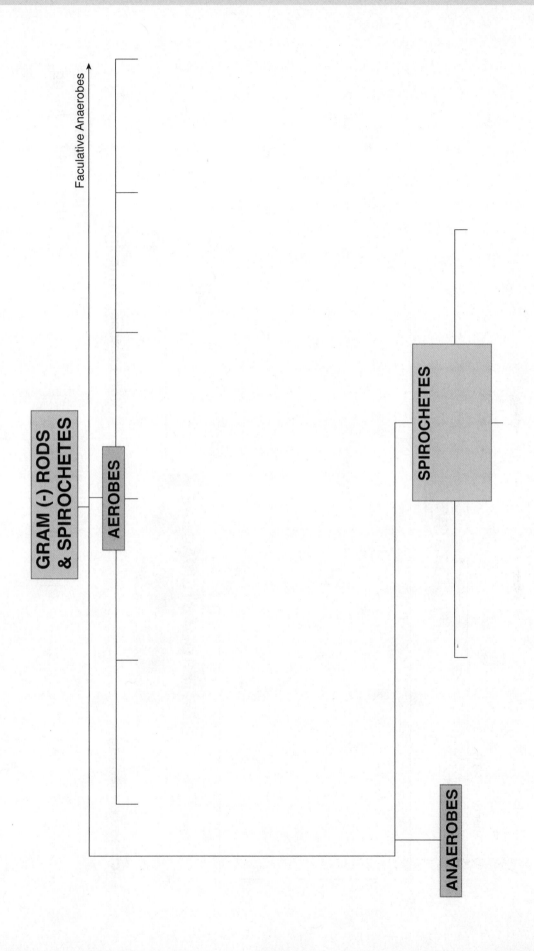

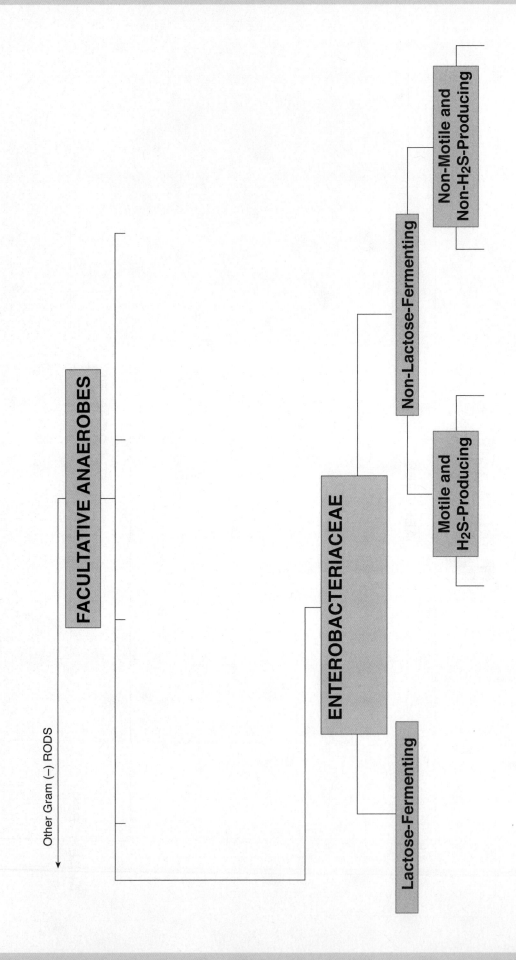

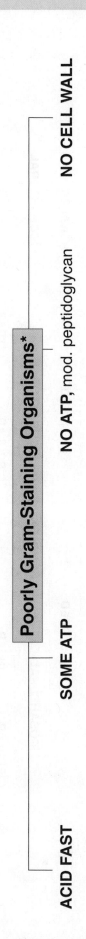

**Poorly Gram-Staining Organisms\***

ACID FAST

SOME ATP

NO ATP, mod. peptidoglycan

NO CELL WALL

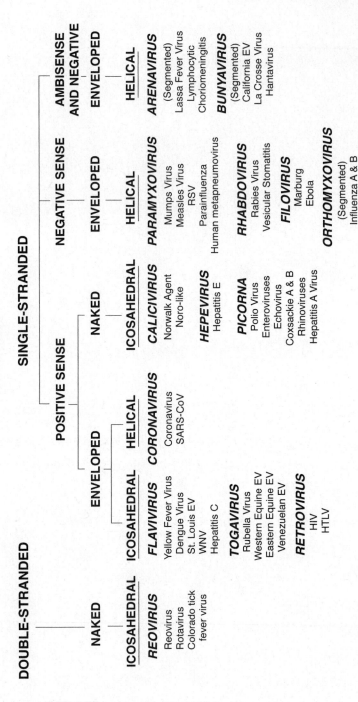

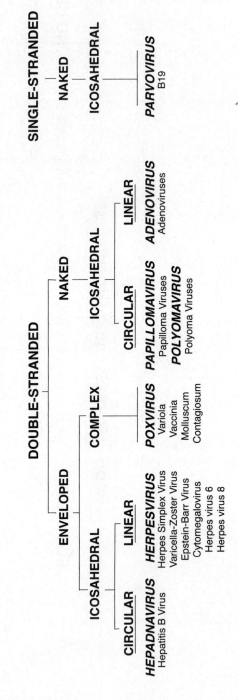

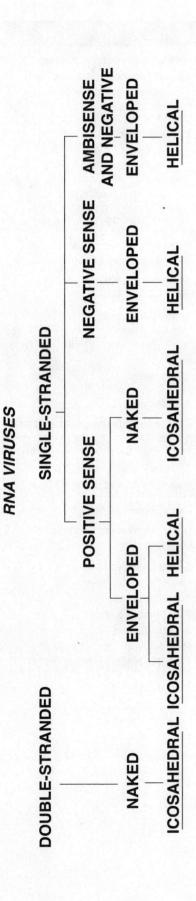

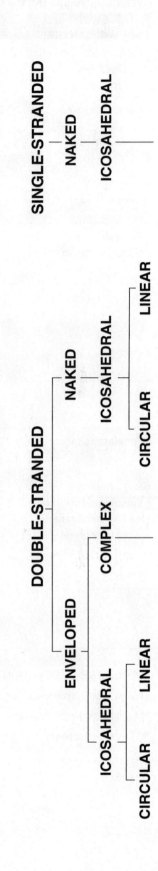

## Bacterial Envelope (All the Concentric Surface Layers of the Bacterial Cell)

| Envelope Structure | Gram + or – | Chemical Composition | Function |
|---|---|---|---|
| **Capsule** (Non-essential) = Slime layer = Glycocalyx | Both | Polysaccharide gel* | Pathogenicity factor protecting against phagocytosis until opsonized; immunogenic** |
| **Outer membrane** | Gram – only | Phospholipid/proteins: Lipopolysaccharide    Lipid A    Polysacccharide | Hydrophobic membrane: LPS = endotoxin    Lipid A = toxic moiety    PS = immunogenic portion |
| | | Outer membrane proteins | Attachment, virulence, etc. |
| | | Protein porins | Passive transport |
| **Cell wall** = peptidoglycan | Gram + (thick) Gram – (thin) | Peptidoglycan-open 3-D net of:    N-acetyl-glucosamine    N-acetyl-muramic acid    amino acids (DAP) | Rigid support, cell shape, and protection from osmotic damage; Synthesis inhibited by penicillins and cephalosporins; Confers Gram reaction |
| | Gram + only | Teichoic acids*** | Immunogenic, induces TNF-alpha, IL-1; Attachment |
| | Acid-fast only | Mycolic acids | Acid-fastness; Resistance to drying and chemicals |
| **Periplasmic space** | Gram – only | "Storage space" between the inner and outer membranes | Enzymes to break down large molecules, (β-lactamases); Aids regulation of osmolarity |
| **Cytoplasmic membrane** = inner membrane = cell membrane = plasma membrane | Gram + Gram – | Phospholipid bilayer with many embedded proteins | Hydrophobic cell "sack"; Selective permeability and active transport; Carrier for enzymes for: Oxidative metabolism, Phosphorylation, Phospholipid synthesis, DNA replication, Peptidoglycan cross linkage, Penicillin binding proteins (PBPs) |

*Definition of abbreviation:* DAP, diaminopimelic acid.

* Except *Bacillus anthracis*, which is a polypeptide of poly D-glutamate.

** Except *S. pyogenes* (hyaluronic acid) and type B *N. meningitidis* (sialic acid), which are nonimmunogenic.

*** Teichoic acid: polymers of ribitol or glycerol, bound to cell membrane or peptidoglycan.

## Outer Surface Structures of the Bacterial Cell

| | | | |
|---|---|---|---|
| Pilus or fimbria<br>1. Common<br>2. Sex<br>3. Virulence | Primarily Gram −* | Glycoprotein (pilin) | Adherence to cell surfaces, including attachment to other bacteria during conjugation |
| Flagellum | + and − | Protein (flagellin) | Motility |
| Axial filaments (internal flagellum) | Spirochetes gram − | Protein | Motility |

*M-protein of group A strep described as diffuse fimbriate layer or fimbriae.

## Internal Bacterial Structures*

| Structure | Cell Type | Chemical Composition | Function |
|---|---|---|---|
| Nucleoid region<br>No membrane<br>No histones<br>No introns | Gram + and gram − | DNA<br>RNA<br>Proteins | Genetic material (all essential genes)<br>Primers, mRNA<br>Linker proteins, polymerases |
| Plasmids | Gram + and gram − | DNA | Non-essential genetic material<br>Roles in conjugation, drug resistance, toxin production |
| Ribosomes | Gram + and gram − | 70S (protein/RNA)<br>30S (16S RNA)<br>50S (23 and 5S) | Protein synthesis |
| Granules (various types) | Gram + and gram − | Glycogen, lipids, polyphosphate, etc. | Storage: polymerization of molecules present in high numbers in cells reduces osmotic pressure. Volutin granules of *Corynebacterium diphtheriae* are used in clinical identification. |
| Endospores | Gram + *only* | Keratin coat, calcium dipicolinate | Resistance to heat, chemicals, and dehydration |

*Note that there are no mitochondria or membrane-bound structures, such as chloroplasts.

# Index

## A

A-B component toxins, 201
    diphtheria, 234, 479
A-B polypeptide neurotoxin, 228
Abciximab, 151
Abdominal pain, acute, 460
ABO blood typing, 170–171
    graft rejection and, 160–162
Abscesses
    *Klebsiella pneumoniae,* 260
    in nocardiosis, 237
    *Staphylococcus aureus,* 217
*Absidia* infection, 422–423
*Acanthamoeba* sp., 430
Accelerated acute graft rejection, 159
Acetylcholine receptor, in myasthenia gravis, 144, 147
Acid-fast organisms, 475
Acne vulgaris, 450
Acquired immunodeficiency syndrome (AIDS), 379.
            *See also* Human immunodeficiency virus (HIV)
    conditions associated with, 380–381
    dementia, 398
    toxoplasmosis in, 435
*Actinomyces* sp., 224, 236
*Actinomyces israelii,* 236
Actinomycosis, 236
Activation-induced cell death (AICD), 101
Activation phase, in apoptosis, 90
Active immunization, 107
Acute endocarditis, 454
Acute glomerulonephritis, 219
Acute graft rejection, 149, 159
Acute hemorrhagic cystitis, 358
Acute inflammatory response, 40–42
Acute lymphoblastic leukemia, 15
Acute respiratory disease, 358
Acute rheumatic fever, 144, 149
Acyclovir, for herpes simplex virus, 360
Adaptive immune response, regulation by helper T cells, 60
Adaptive immunity, 3–5
Addressins, 35
    characteristics of, 189
Adenosine deaminase deficiency, 120
Adenoviruses (Adenoviridae), 353, 358
    types 4 and 7, immunologic memory and, 102
Adenylate cyclase toxin, 249
Adherence, to cell surface, 198
Adhesins, for cell surface adherence, 198
Adhesion, in extravasation process, 40, 41
Adhesion molecules
    in acute inflammatory response, 40–42
    classification, 189–190
Adjuvants, immunogenicity, 112

ADP ribosylates eEF-2
    *Pseudomonas aeruginosa* and, 245
    toxin production and, 480
ADP ribosylation of G$_i$, *Bordetella pertussis* and, 249
Aerobic bacteria, 211, 212, 213, 477
Afferent lymphatics, lymphocyte recirculation and homing, 33–35
Affinity binding
    IgM pentamer, 71
    lymphatic receptors, 23–24
Affinity maturation, in humoral immunity, 73
Agammaglobulinemia, X-linked, 122
Agar diffusion test, 329, 414
Agglutinate/Agglutination, 69, 70
Agglutination tests
    for blood typing, 160, 170–171
    *Brucella,* 252
    latex bead, 170
    *Streptococcus pneumoniae,* 221
Albinism, 117
Alcohols, for disinfection/sterilization, 332
Allelic exclusion, cell function and, 15
Allergens, allergic disease associated with, 143
Allergic bronchopulmonary aspergillosis, 421
Allergic responses, in type I hypersensitivity, 141–143
Allergic rhinitis, 143
Allogeneic grafts, 157
    rejection prevention and treatment, 162
Alpha toxin, *Clostridium perfringens,* 230
Alphaviruses, 374
"Altered-self," transplantation immunology and, 157
Alternative complement pathway, 78
Amebae, 428, 430
Aminoglycosides, bacterial resistance to
    emerging, 326
    mechanisms, 325
Anaerobic bacteria, 211, 212, 213, 477, 495
    facultative. *See* Facultative anaerobes
Anaphylatoxins, 78
Anaphylaxis
    to drugs, 149
    systemic, 143
*Anaplasma phagocytophila,* 285
Anatomic barriers, immune system, 3
*Ancylostoma braziliense,* 441
*Ancylostoma caninum,* 441
Anemia, 461
    autoimmune hemolytic, 144, 145
    pernicious, 144
    phagocytic cell defects and, 117
Anergy, clonal, 24
Animal/human bites
    infection from, 451
    organisms associated with, 273
    *Pasturella multocida,* 272

Anogenital warts, human papilloma virus, 356–357

Anthrax toxin, 225

Anti-allotype antibodies, passive immunization, 108

Anti-phagocytic surface components, 199

Anti-RhD antibody, 145

Antibiotics

    *Clostridium difficile* and, diarrhea association in, 231

    emerging bacterial resistance to, 326–327

    susceptibility testing, 329–332

Antibody(ies)

    affinity, 73

    anti-RhD, 145

    antigen transport and, 54

    autoantibodies, 144

    B lymphocyte antigen receptor, 12–13

    bacteria-induced, tissue antigens and, 200

    excess, in infection, 170

    immune system, 4

    killed viral vaccines, 111

    linear deposits, 144

    maternal, vaccinations and, 111

    opsonization and, 43–44

    preformed, screening for, 162

    primary/secondary responses of, 73–77

    in syphilis diagnosis, 276

Antibody-dependent cell-mediated cytotoxicity (ADCC), 93

    IgE and, 93

    IgG and, 74

    IgM and, 72

Antibody-mediated (type II) hypersensitivity, 139, 144–147, 149

Antigen(s)

    blood-borne, 34

    bridging, 69

    Enterobacteriaceae, 257

    excess, in infection, 170

    foreign, hypersensitivity disease and, 139

    in fungal infection, 414

    in humoral immunity, 67–69

    immune system overview, 3

    memory cells and, 102

    receptors, mature lymphocytes, 11–13

    superantigens, 57

    thymus-dependent, 67

    thymus-independent, 68–69

    transportation to secondary lymphoid organs, 54

Antigen-antibody interactions, 169–170

Antigen-presenting cells (APCs)

    immune system, 3

    major histocompatibility complex and, 53–54

    T-cell receptor and, 24

Antigen recognition molecules, lymphocytes, 11–13

Antigenic drift, 199

    bacterial pathogenicity determinants, 478

    gp120, HIV and, 131

Antigenic specificity, 11–13

Antimicrobial agents, emerging bacterial resistance to, 326–327

Antitoxin, trivalent (A-B-E), 229

Apicomplexa parasites, 428, 435

Aplastic crisis, B19 parvovirus, 355

Apoptosis

    cell function and, 15

    cytoxic T cells and, 91

    phases in, 90

Arachidonic acid cascade, 143

Arboviruses, 342, 374

Arenaviridae, 383, 394

Arrest/adhesion, in acute inflammatory response, 40–42

Arthritis, 144

    infection and, 465

    reactive, 454

    rheumatoid, 148, 149

Arthroconidia, 413

Arthropod disease vectors, 483–484

Arthus reaction, 148, 149

Artificial immunization, 107

*Ascaris lumbricoides,* 440

Aspergillosis, 421

*Aspergillus fumigatus,* 421

Asplenia, susceptibility to blood-borne pathogens in, 54

Asthma, 143

Ataxia, 120

Atopic responses, in type I hypersensitivity, 141–143

Atopy, 118

Attachment, in apoptosis, 90

Attenuated vaccines, for infection treatment/prevention, 488

Auramine-rhodamine fluorescent stain, 238

Autoantibodies, 144

Autoclaving, for sterilization, 332

Autografts (autologous grafts), 157

Autoimmune diseases, 139, 149–150

    therapeutic strategies, 150–151

Autoimmune hemolytic anemia (HDNB), 144, 145

Autoimmune thrombocytopenic purpura, 144

Autoimmunity, 4

    mechanisms, 24

    pathogenesis, 149–150

    therapeutic strategies in, 150–151

Avidity

    decrease in, 71

    IgM molecule, 71

## B

B-cell conjugates, formation of, 67, 68

B lymphocytes

    antigen recognition molecules, 11–13

    antigens and, 39

    characteristics, 102

    contact with helper T cells, 67

    defects, 120

    differentiation, 23

    immune system function, 10

    immunodefiencies involving, 77, 119–120

    lumphoid follicles, 35

    memory cells, 101–103

    in type I hypersensitivity, 141

B19 parvovirus, 355

*Babesia* sp., 435

Babesiosis, 435, 484

Bacille Calmette-Guérin (BCG) vaccine, 240

Bacilli gram-negative bacteria, 245–256

*Bacillus* sp.

    function and resistance mechanism, 209

    morphology/taxonomy, 475

    pathogenicity, 225–226

*Bacillus anthracis,* 225–226

    morphology/taxonomy of, 475

*Bacillus cereus*, 226
Bacitracin, Streptococcal bacteria and, 218
Bacteremia, 197
Bacteria
  aerobic. *See* Aerobic bacteria
  anaerobic. *See* Anaerobic bacteria; Facultative anaerobes
  biofilm production by, 476
  capsule-producing, 475
  cell envelope, 208
  DNA rearrangement in, 309–310
  enzymes, 477–478
  epidemiology/transmission, 482–486
  genetic material, 308–309
  gram-staining reactions, 214
  growth and death, 210
  with human reservoirs, 482
  internal cell structures, 208, 507
  laboratory diagnosis, 487–488
  mating types, 314
  metabolism, 477
  microaerophilic, 212, 477
  morphology/taxonomy, 475–476
  nomenclature, 207
  non-gram-staining, 214
  non-spore-forming, 494
  opsonization, 44
  outer surface structures, 507
  oxygen requirements, 212
  pathogenicity determinants, 478–482
  pathology, 486–487
  physiology, 477–478
  pigment production by, 476
  spore-forming, 475, 494
  stains for, 212–213
Bacteria-induced antibodies, tissue antigens and, 200
Bacterial infections, resistance mechanisms in, 192–193
Bacterial vaccines, 109
Bacterial vaginosis, 271
Bacteriophage genome, 309
*Bacteroides fragilis*, 274
Bare lymphocyte syndrome, 120, 121
*Bartonella henslae*, 273
Basophil, immune system function, 10
Bell palsy, 463
Benzathine penicillin, in syphilis therapy, 276
Beta (T-cell) chain, lymphocyte antigen receptors, 14–16
 -lactamases, 246
  antibiotic susceptibility testing, 330
  emerging bacterial resistance to, 326
Bile duct blockage, 460
Binding peptides, rough endoplasmic reticulum and, 52, 53
Biofilm, bacteria producing, 476
  partial adherence to, 198
Biowarfare agents
  *Brucella*, 251
  *Francisella tularensis*, 248
  *Yersinia pestis*, 263
Bipolar staining, 476
BK polyomavirus, 357
Blackflies, 483
Blastoconidia, 413
*Blastomyces dermatitidis*, 417, 419–420
  endemic region for, 420

Blastomycosis, 420
Blood, normal flora of, 198
Blood-borne antigens, 34
Blood cells, changes in infectious disease, 461
Bone marrow, lymphocyte development in, 10, 23
Bordet-Gengou media, *Bordetella pertussis*, 250
*Bordetella pertussis*, 249–250
*Borrelia burgdorferi*, 277–278
Botulinum toxin, 228, 479
Botulism, 228–229
  toxin production and, 479
Bradykinin-induced vasodilation, 200
Bronchitis, 455
  *Haemophilus influenzae*, 269
*Brucella* sp., 251–252
*Brugia malayi*, 441
Bruton X-linked hypogammaglobulinemia, 118
Bubonic plague, 263
Bunyaviridae, 383, 393
Burkitt lymphoma, 362, 397
Bystander activation, autoimmune failure and, 150

## C

C3b complement, opsonization with, 43–44
Calcifications, intracerebral, infections causing, 486
Calciviridae, 368, 370
California encephalitis, 393
CAMP test, Streptococcal bacteria, 220
*Campylobacter jejuni*, 253
Cancer
  nasopharyngeal, 362, 397
  of stomach, 254
  of thymus, 397
  viruses associated with, 254, 397
*Candida albicans*, 412, 421–422
Candidiasis, cutaneous/mucocutaneous, 415, 422
*Capnocytophaga canimorsus*, 273
Capsid proteins, component vaccines, 112
Capsular bacteria, 475
Capsular vaccines, 111–112
Capsule, bacterial envelope, 506
Carbuncles, 450
Carcinoma. *See* Cancer
Cardiac symptoms, of infection, 454
Cardiolipin, in syphilis diagnosis, 276
Carrier, 197
Caspases, cytotoxic T-lymphocytes and, 90
Catalase-negative bacteria, 218, 223, 477
Catalase-positive bacteria, 215, 477–478
  chronic granulomatous disease and, 45
  immunodeficiency disease and, 117
Cavitary bronchopulmonary nocardiosis, 237
CCR5 chemokine receptor, HIV and, 131, 132
CD markers, 183
CD4+ cells, 27
  HIV and, 132
  in type IV hypersensitivity, 139, 148
CD4 molecules
  T-cell activation and, 55
  thymocyte expression, 26–27
CD4 receptors, HIV attachment to, 131
CD4+ T cells
  effector mechanisms and, 58
  in immunodeficiency diseases, 120

CD4oL deficiency, 118
CD8+ cells, 27
    cytotoxic, HIV and, 132
CD8 molecules
    T-cell activation and, 55
    thymocyte expression, 26–27
    in type IV hypersensitivity, 148
CD8+ T cells
    cytotoxic, cell-mediated immunity and, 89. *See also* Cytotoxic T
        cells (CTLs)
    in immunodeficiency disease, 120
    major histocompatibility class antigens and, 51–52
CD16 molecule, NK cell killing, 92
CD18 molecule, absence in leukocyte adhesion deficiency, 41, 117
CD28 molecules, T-cell activation, 55, 56
CD56 molecule, NK cell killing, 92
Cefotaxime, *Streptococcus pneumoniae* and, 221
Ceftriaxone, *Streptococcus pneumoniae* and, 221
Celiac disease, 148, 149
Cell(s). *See also* Bacteria; *specific cell types*
    immune system function, 9–10
    lymphocyte antigen recognition molecules, 11–13
    malignant transformation, 396
    ontogeny, 8
    origins, immune system, 7
    receptor diversity generation, 13–16
    receptor signaling, 26–27
    virus-infected, NK cell killing mechanisms and, 92
Cell-bound peptides, B lymphocyte antigen receptor, 12–13
Cell-mediated immunity (CMI), 59–60
    effector cells in, 95
    effector mechanisms, 89–95
    evasion of, viral strategies for, 95
    leprosy, 241
    live viral vaccines, 111, 112
    *Mycobacterium tuberculosis,* 239
    overview, 94
    pre-B stage, 118
Cell wall
    bacterial drug resistance and, 326
    in bacterial envelope, 506
Cellular oncogenes *(c-onc),* 396
Cellulitis, 450
    in nocardiosis, 237
    *Pasturella multocida,* 272
Central nervous system, infections of, 462–463
Cephalosporins, bacterial resistance mechanisms, 325
Cerebrospinal fluid (CSF), findings in meningitis, 464
Cervicitis, 281, 456
Cestodes, 428, 438–439
Chediak-Higashi syndrome, 117, 122
Chemoattractants
    in acute inflammatory response, 40–42
    in extravasation process, 40, 41
Chemokines
    in acute inflammatory response, 42
    in AIDS, 132
    in extravasation process, 41
Chickenpox, 361
*Chlamydia trachomatis,* 280–281
Chlamydiaceae, 280–282
    staining process in, 214
*Chlamydophila sp.,* 282

*Chlamydophila pneumoniae,* 282
*Chlamydophila psittaci,* 282
Chloramphenicol, bacterial resistance to
    emerging, 326
    mechanisms, 325
Chlorine, in protein modification, 332
Cholera enterotoxin, 255
    production, 479
Chorioretinitis, 453
Chromosomes
    bacterial, 308
    in drug resistance mediation, 324, 327
Chronic graft rejection, 159
Chronic granulomatous disease (CGD), 117, 122, 478
    intracellular killing in, 45
    *Pseudomonas aeruginosa,* 245
Chronic intracellular infections, type IV hypersensitivity and, 148
Ciprofloxacin, for *Bacillus anthracis,* 225
Cirrhosis, 460
Class switching, in humoral immunity, 67
Classical complement pathway, 78–79
    deficiencies in, 119
Clonal anergy, 24
Clonal deletion, 24
Clonal expansion, in T cell activation, 55
Clonal selection, in humoral immunity, 73
*Clonorchis sinensis,* 437
*Clostridium* sp., 224, 227
    function and resistance mechanism, 209
    morphology/taxonomy, 475
*Clostridium botulinum,* 228–229
*Clostridium difficile,* 231
*Clostridium perfringens,* 229–230
*Clostridium tetani,* 227–228
Clue cells, *Gardnerella,* 271
Coagulase
    *Staphylococcus aureus,* 216
    *Yersinia,* 263
COBEDS, lysogenic conversion, 320–323
Cocci
    gram-negative bacteria, 242–244, 492–493
    gram-positive bacteria, 215–223, 492–493
*Coccidioides immitis,* 417, 419
    endemic region for, 419
Codominance
    class I molecules, 25
    class II molecules, 25–26
    in graft rejection, 157–158
Cold sores, herpes simplex virus type 1, 359
Colitis, *Clostridium difficile,* 231
Colon, normal flora of, 198
Colonization, 198
Colorado tick fever, 484
Common cold, 452
Common variable immunodeficiency, 118
    hypogammaglobulinemia, 122
Complement
    genetic deficiencies in, 79
    opsonization and, 43–44
    split product C5a, in acute inflammatory response, 42
Complement system, 77–80
    activation pathways, 77
        alternative, 78
        classical, 78–79

deficiencies in, 79, 119
functions, 78
immune system overview, 4–5
type III hypersensitivity and, 139, 147–148
Component vaccines, 110–111
Conidia, in fungal morphology, 412–413
Conjugal crosses, 315, 317
Conjugates, B- and T-cell, 67, 68
Conjugation
DNA exchange, 313–314
drug resistance and, 327–328
gene transfer, 311
and transformation and transduction compared, 323
Conjunctivitis, 453
Contact, infectious disease transmisison through, 486
Contact dermatitis, 148, 149
Coombs test, 171
Cord factor, *Mycobacterium tuberculosis,* 239
Coronaviridae, 375
*Corynebacterium* sp., 224, 234
*Corynebacterium diphtheriae,* 234–235
morphology/taxonomy, 475
Coxsackie A virus, 372
Coxsackie B virus, 372
Creutzfeldt-Jakob disease, 398
Crohn disease, 148, 149
Crosslinking, of antigens, 39
Cryptococcal capsular polysaccharide, 414
*Cryptococcus neoformans,* 422
in HIV infection, prophylactic regimen, 381
morphology/taxonomy, 475
*Cryptosporidium* sp., 429
oocysts, 475
CTLA-4, in TH cell stimulation, 56
Cultures, in fungal infection, 414
Cutaneous anthrax, 225
Cutaneous fungal infections, 415–416
*Candida albicans,* 422
Cutaneous surfaces
diseases of, 450–451
normal flora of, 198
Cutaneous warts, human papilloma virus, 356–357
CXCR4 chemokine receptor, HIV and, 131
Cyclic adenosine monophosphate (cAMP) inducers, 202
*Cyclospora cayetanensis,* 429
Cyclosporin A, for graft rejection prevention and treatment, 162
Cysteine, in *Legionella pneumophila* culture, 247
Cystic fibrosis, *Pseudomonas aeruginosa* and, 246
Cystitis, 456
acute hemorrhagic, 358
Cytochrome C oxidase, Enterobacteriaceae, 257
Cytokines
in acute inflammatory response, 40–42
in cell-mediated immunity, 89–95
classification, 185–187
recombinant forms, 188
cytotoxic T-lymphocytes and, 90
in helper T cell classification, 58–60
immune system, 4
isotype switching and, 73
T cell activation and, 55
T cell proliferation and, 55
viral infection resistance and, 349

Cytolysins, 201
exotoxins, 201, 202
Cytomegalovirus (CMV), 363–364
cytotoxic T cells and, 95
in HIV infection, prophylactic regimen, 381
Cytopathogenesis, viral, 476
Cytoplasmic membrane, 208
bacterial envelope, 506
Cytotoxic T cells (CTLs), 27
in cell-mediated immunity, 89–92, 95
killing mechanisms, 90–91
Cytotoxicity, antibody-dependent cell-mediated. *See* Antibody-dependent cell-mediated cytotoxicity (ADCC)

## D

Dacliximab, 151
Dapsone, in leprosy prevention, 241
"Death domain," cytotoxic T-lymphocytes and, 90
Deerflies, 483
Defensins, in intracellular killing, 44
Delayed-type hypersensitivity (type IV) (DTH), 139, 148–149
cell-mediated immune response and, 89
pathogenicity and, 200
Deletion, clonal, 24
Dementia, AIDS-related, 398
Dendritic cells
HIV and, 132
immune system function, 9, 53
Dengue virus, 373
Dental caries, *Viridans streptococci* and, 222
Dermatophytes, 415–416
Desert bumps, 419
Detachment, in apoptosis, 90
Detergents, for disinfection/sterilization, 332
Diabetes mellitus
insulin-dependent (type I), 148, 150
insulin-resistant (type II), 144, 149
Diarrhea
*Clostridium difficile,* 231
by intoxication, 457
microbial organisms causing, 457–459
inflammatory diarrhea/dysentry, 459
noninflammatory diarrhea, 458
toxin production and, 479
DiGeorge syndrome, 120, 122
Digestion, in phagocytosis, 43
Dimorphic fungi, 412, 416–420
*Diphillobothrium latum* (fish tapeworm), 439
Diphtheria toxin (A-B component), 234
production of, 479
Diplococci, morphology of, 476
Direct fluorescent antibody test (DFA), 171–172
Direct repeats, multiple drug-resistance plasmids and, 324–325
Disinfection, 332
Disseminated intravascular coagulation (DIC), 200
Diversity
immune system, 3, 4
receptor, generating, 15–16
DNA
exchange mechanisms, 312–314
rearrangement within a bacterium, 309–310
transfer between bacteria, 311

DNA viruses, 353–367, 504. *See also specific viruses and families by name*
    characteristics, 353–354
Donors, transplant, 157
Double-stranded RNA viruses, 395–397
Doxycycline, *Bacillus anthracis* and, 225
*Dracunculus medinensis,* 441
Drug allergies, haptens and, 40
Drug resistance
    *Bacillus* sp., 209
    chromosome-mediated, 324
    *Clostridium* sp., 209
    in fungal infections, 423
    intrinsic, 323
    mechanisms
        plasmid-related, 325
        transfer factor, 325
    methicillin-resistant *Staphylococcus aureus,* 218
    multiple drug-resistance plasmids and, 324–325
    overview, 323
    plasmid-mediated, 324
    *Pseudomonas aeruginosa,* 246
    transfer, 327–328
    vancomycin-resistant bacteria
        *Enterococcus faecium/faecalis,* 223
        *Staphylococcus aureus,* 218
Drug resistance genes (DRGs), 328
DTaP vaccine, *Bordetella pertussis,* 249, 250
DTH skin test, 89
Duodenal ulcer, *Helicobactor pylori,* 254
Dysentry, 457
    microbial organisms causing, 459

**E**

E-test (agar diffusion), 329
Ear infections, 452
Eastern equine encephalitis virus (EEE), 374
Ebola virus, 390
*Echinococcus granulosus,* 439
*Echinococcus multilocularis,* 439
Echoviruses, 372
Ecthyma grangenosum, 246
Eczema, 120
Edema factor, anthrax toxin, 225
Effector lymphocytes, characteristics, 102
Effector mechanisms
    cell-mediated, 59–60, 89–95
    humoral, 59–60
        overview, 80
    in hyperensitivity diseases, 139
    T-cell activation, 55, 58–60
Effector phase, in graft rejection, 158
Effector T cells
    antigen transport and, 54
    costimulatory molecules and, 55
*Ehrlichia chaffeensis,* 285
Ehrlichiosis, 283
*Eikenella corrodens,* 273
Elek test, *Corynebacterium diphtheriae,* 234, 235
Emetic toxin, 226
Encephalitis, 463
    herpes simplex virus type 1, 360
    meningoencephalitis, 385
    subacute sclerosing panencephalitis, 385
    viral causes, 373–374, 393
Endarteritis, 275
Endemic typhus, 283
Endocarditis
    acute, 454
    infective, 217, 222, 422, 454
    subacute, 454
Endogenous pathway, major histocompatibility class antigens and, 51–52
Endosomal (exogenous) pathway, major histocompatibility class antigens and, 52
Endospores
    in fungal morphology, 413
    structure and function, 209
Endotoxin, 200
    *Brucella,* 251
    Enterobacteriaceae, 257
    heat stability, 479
    *Klebsiella pneumoniae,* 260
    *Pasturella multocida,* 272
    *Pseudomonas aeruginosa,* 245
    *Yersinia pestis,* 263
*Entamoeba histolytica,* 429
Enterobacteriaceae, 257–274
*Enterobius vermicularis,* 440
*Enterococcus* sp., 215, 223
*Enterococcus faecalis/faecium,* 223
    resistance to drugs, 327
Enterocolitis
    *Salmonella enterica* subsp. other than *typhi,* 267, 268
    *Yersinia enterocolitica,* 264
Enterotoxin, *Clostridium perfringens,* 230
Enteroviruses, 371, 372
*env* gene, 377
Envelope, bacterial, 506
Envelope antigen, *Yersinia pestis,* 263
Enveloped viruses
    naked viruses vs., 343
    release, 345
Environmental factors
    in autoimmune failure, 149
    in infection transmission, 485
Enzyme-linked immunoabsorbent assay (EIA/ELISA), 173
    in Lyme disease diagnosis, 277
Enzymes
    bacterial, 477–478
    extracellular, 481
Eosinophil
    antibody-dependent cell-mediated cytotoxicity, 93
    chemotactic factor A, in type I hypersensitivity, 143
    immune system function, 9
Epidemic typhus, 283
Epidermophyton, 415
Epiglottitis, *Haemophilus influenzae,* 269
Epilepsy, 463
Episomes, 308
Epitope, antigen, 39
Epstein-Barr virus (EBV), 362
    and cancer association, 397
Equivalence/Equivalence zone, in antigen-antibody interactions, 169–170
Erythroblastosis fetalis. *See* Hemolytic disease of the newborn (HDNB)

Erythromycin, *Corynebacterium diphtheriae* and, 235
*Escherichia coli*, 258–259
 as capsule producer, 475
Esophagitis, *Candida albicans*, 422
Ethambutol, emerging bacterial resistance to, 326
Ethylene oxide, in protein modification, 332
Excision error, lysogenic phage, 321–322
Exocytosis
 in apoptosis, 90
 in phagocytosis, 43
Exogenotes, 309
Exotoxins, 201–202
 bacterial plasmids, 308
 *Pseudomonas aeruginosa*, 245
Exposure, immune system activity and, 3
Extracellular enzymes, 481
Extracellular microbes, in humoral immunity, 67
Extravasation, steps in, 40–42
Eye infections, 453

**F**

Facultative anaerobes, 212, 496
 Enterobacteriaceae, 257
Facultative intracellular parasite, 482
 *Histoplasma capsulatum*, 418
 *Listeria monocytogenes*, 232
Fas ligand (FasL), cytotoxic T-lymphocytes and, 90, 91
Fatal familial insomnia, 398
Fc receptor, in type I hypersensitivity, 141
Fertility factor(s)
 conjugation, 313–314
 integrated, 316–317
 in site-specific integration, 310
Fever, cyclic/irregular, 461
Filarial nematodes, 441
Filoviridae, 383, 390
Filtration, for sterilization, 332
Flares, 143
Flaviviridae, 373
Fleas, 483
Floppy baby syndrome, 228
Flora, normal, 197–198
Flow cytometry analysis, 175
Flukes, 428, 436–437
Fluorescence-activated cell sorter, 175
Fluorescent antibody tests, 171–172
Fluoroquinolones, emerging bacterial resistance to, 327
Folate inhibitors, emerging bacterial resistance to, 327
Follicles. *See* Lymphoid follicles
Follicular conjunctivitis, 281
Food allergies, 143
Food poisoning, *Clostridium perfringens*, 229–230
Foreign antigens, hypersensitivity disease and, 139
Formaldehyde, in protein modification, 332
Formyl methionyl peptides, in acute inflammatory response, 42
Fragments, proteolytic cleavage of immuniglobulin and, 69, 70
*Francisella tularensis*, 248
Fungal infection
 deep
  classical pathogens, 417–420
  opportunistic pathogens, 421–423
 diagnostic methods, 413–414
 epidemiology and transmission, 484

 in immunodeficiency diseases, 119–120
 morphology, 412–414
 mycology, 411
 nonsystemic, 415–416
 resistance mechanisms, 194
Fungemia, 415
Fungus ball, 421
Fungus flu, 418
Furuncles, 450
Fusion protein, 384

**G**

*gag* gene, 377
Ganglioside receptors, *Clostridium tetani*, 227
*Gardnerella* sp., 271
Gas gangrene, *Clostridium perfringens*, 230
Gastritis, *Candida albicans*, 422
Gastritis, *Helicobactor pylori*, 254
Gastroenteritis
 adenovirus, 358
 *Bacillus cereus*, 226
 *Campylobacter*, 253
 *Escherichia coli*, 259
 *Salmonella enterica* subsp. other than *typhi*, 267, 268
 *Staphylococcus aureus*, 217
Gastrointestinal anthrax, 225
Gastrointestinal infection/infectious diseases, 118, 457–458
Gene products, class I and II, 24–25
Gene rearrangement, failure, clinical outcomes, 16
Gene transfer, 311
Generalized transduction, 318–319
 and specialized transduction compared, 323
Genetic drift/shift, 399
Genetics
 bacterial, 308–309, 478–482
 viral, 399
Genital elephantitis, 456
Genital infections, herpes simplex type 2, 360
Genital lesions, 456
Geniturinary tract infections, 456
Genome
 bacterial chromosome, 308
 bacteriophage, 309
Genomic nucleic acid, replication of, 344
Germinal centers, in primary/secondary antibody responses, 73
Gerstmann-Strässler-Scheinker, 398
Ghon complex, 239
*Giardia lamblia*, 429
Gingival crevices, normal flora of, 198
Gingivostomatitis, herpes simplex virus type 1, 359
Glomerulonephritis
 acute, 219
 poststreptococcal, 148, 149
Glucose-6-phosphate dehydrogenase (G6PD) deficiency, 117
Glycopeptides, emerging bacterial resistance to, 326
Glycosylation, HIV and, 131
Gonococcal infection, complement system deficiency and, 119
Goodpasture syndrome, 144, 149
gp120 antigenic drift, HIV and, 131
Graft rejection
 acute, 148
 mechanisms, 157–160
 prevention and treatment, 162
 types and tempo, 159

Graft-versus-host disease, 149, 160
Gram-negative bacteria, 214
   *Bacteroides fragilis*, 274
   *Bordetella pertussis*, 249–250
   *Brucella*, 251–252
   *Campylobacter*, 253
   Enterobacteriaceae, 257–274
   *Escherichia coli*, 258–259
   *Francisella*, 248
   *Gardnerella*, 271
   *Haemophilus*, 269–270
   *Helicobacter*, 254
   *Klebsiella*, 260
   *Legionella pneumophila*, 247
   *Neisseria*, 242–244
   *Pasteurella*, 272
   *Proteus mirabilis/Proteus vulgaris*, 265
   *Pseudomonas*, 245–246
   rods, 495
   *Salmonella*, 266–268
   *Shigella*, 261–262
   *Vibrio*, 255–256
   *Yersinia*, 263–264
Gram-positive bacteria, 214–241
   *Actinomyces*, 224, 236
   *Bacillus*, 224, 225–226
   *Clostridium*, 224, 227–231
   *Corynebacterium*, 224, 234–235
   *Enterococcus*, 215, 223
   *Listeria*, 224, 232–233
   *Mycobacterium*, 224, 238–241
   *Nocardia*, 224, 237
   non-motile rods, 475
   rods, 224, 494
   *Staphylococcus* sp., 215, 216–218
   *Streptococcus* sp., 215, 218–220
Gram-staining organisms
   gram-negative, 214
   gram-positive, 214
   non-gram-staining, 214
   poorly gram-staining, 497
Gram stains, 212
Granule enzyme deficiency, 117
Granulocyte colony-stimulating factor (G-CSF), 187
Granulocyte-macrophage colony-stimulating factor (GM-CSF), 187
Granulomatous response, 200
   pathology, 486
Granzymes
   cytotoxic T-lymphocytes and, 90, 91
   NK cell killing mechanisms, 92
Graves disease, 144, 149
   antibodies to TSH receptor in, 144, 146
Group A streptococci (GAS), 215, 218–220
Group B streptococci (GBS), 220
Growth requirements, in infectious disease diagnosis, 487–488
Guillain-Barré syndrome (GBS), 148, 253, 463
Gulls wings morphology, 476

# H

HACEK group infections, 273
*Haemophilus ducreyi*, 270
*Haemophilus influenzae*, 269–270
   as capsule producer, 475
   pediatric vaccines for, 111

Hageman factor activation, 200
Hairy oral leukoplakia, 362
Hantavirus, 393
Haplotypes, in graft rejection, 157–158
Hapten-carrier conjugate, drug allergies and, 40
Haptens
   characteristics, 39
   drug allergies and, 40
Hashimoto thyroiditis, 148, 149
Hay fever, 149
Heat stable toxins, 479
Heavy chain
   B lymphocyte antigen receptor, 11–13
   secondary immune responses and, 74
   T cell receptor, 13–16
Heavy chain switching, immunoglobulin, 72
Heavy metals, in protein modification, 332
*Helicobacter pylori*, 254, 477
Helper T cells (TH), B-cell contact with, 67
   in antigen processing, 56
   classification, 58–59
   effector mechanisms and, 58–59
   regulation of adaptive immune response by, 60
   in tuberculoid *vs.* lepromatous leprosy, 61
Hemagglutinin, 384
Hemoflagellates, 428, 433–434
α-Hemolytic bacteria, 222
β-Hemolytic bacteria
   *Listeria monocytogenes*, 232
   *Staphylococcus aureus*, 216
   *Streptococcus agalactiae*, 220
   *Streptococcus pyogenes*, 218
Hemolytic disease of the newborn (HDNB), 144, 145, 149
Hemorrhagic cystitis, acute, 358
Hepadnaviridae. *See* Adenoviruses (Adenoviridae)
Heparin, in type I hypersensitivity, 143
Heparnavirus, 371, 372
Hepatitis A virus (HAV), 350, 372, 460
   vaccine, 109
Hepatitis B virus (HBV), 350, 460
   acute, 352
   and cancer association, 397
   chronic, 352
   serology, 351
   terminology and markers, 351
   vaccine, 110
Hepatitis C virus (HCV), 350, 373, 460
   and cancer association, 397
Hepatitis D virus (HDV), 350
Hepatitis E virus (HEV), 350, 460
Hepatosplenomegaly, 418
Hepeviridae, 368, 370
Hereditary angioedema, complement deficiences in, 79, 119
Herpes simplex virus (HSV)
   type 1, 361
   type 2, 360
Herpesviruses (Herpesviridae), 353, 358–365
   cytomegalovirus, 363–364
   Epstein-Barr virus, 362
   HHV-6, 364
   HHV-8, 364
   HSV-1 and HSV-2, 358–360
   life cycle, 354
   varicella zoster virus, 361

Heterophile-negative mononucleosis, 363
Heterophile-positive mononucleosis, 362
Hfr chromosome, 316–317
Hib vaccine, 111
High endothelial venules (HEVs), 35
Highly active anti-retroviral therapy (HAART), 382
Hilum, lymphocyte recirculation and homing, 33–35
Hinge region, B lymphocyte antigen receptor, 11–13
Histamine, in type I hypersensitivity, 143
*Histoplasma capsulatum,* 417–418
    endemic region for, 417
    in HIV infection, prophylactic regimen, 381
Hodgkin lymphoma, 362
Homing, lymphocyte, 33–35
Homologous recombination, 309
    conjugation, 313
    gene transfer, 317
    in specialized transduction, 322
    transduction, 318–323
Hookworms, 441
Hormonal triggers, of autoimmune failure, 149
Host defense system, 199
    obligate intracellular parasites, 481
    parasitic infections, 428
    viral entry, 343
    viral infection resistance, 348–349
Human herpesviruses (HHV) 6 and 8, 364
Human immunodeficiency virus (HIV), 131–133, 376–382. *See also*
    Acquired immunodeficiency syndrome (AIDS)
    clinical stages of infection, 379
    conditions associated with, 380
    global effects on immune response, 133
    laboratory analysis for, 381
    life cycle, 378
    macrophage-tropic nature, 131
    prophylactic regimens, 381
    structure and genes, 376–377
    T cell-tropic nature, 131
    treatment and prevention, 382
    Western blot test for, 174
Human leukocyte antigens (HLA)
    autoimmune failure, 150
    tissue compatibility, 161
Human metapneumovirus (hMNV), 387
Human papilloma virus (HPV), 356–357
    and cancer association, 397
    vaccine, 110
Human T-cell leukemia/lymphotropic virus (HTLV), 376
    and cancer association, 397
Humoral immunity (HMI), 59–60. *See also* Antibody(ies)
    defects, 118
    effector mechanisms, overview of, 80
    goals, 67–70
    isotype switching in, 69, 72–73
    live viral vaccines, 111, 112
    primary response in, 70–72
"Hunting and gathering" nutrients, 199
Hyaluronic acid, *Streptococcus pyogenes* and, 218
Hydatid cyst disease, 439
Hydrogen peroxide, in protein modification, 332
Hydrolytic enzymes, in intracellular killing, 44
Hydrolyze hippurate, Streptococcal bacteria and, 220
Hyper IgM syndrome, 122
    X-linked, 74, 118

Hyperacute graft rejection, 159
Hyperimmune human globulin (TIG), 228
Hypermutation, somatic, 73
Hypersensitivity diseases, 139
    therapeutic strategies, 150–151
    type I (immediate) hypersensitivity, 139, 140–143, 149
    type II (antibody-mediated) hypersensitivity, 139, 144–147, 149
    type III (immune complex) hypersensitivity, 139, 147–148, 149
    type IV (T-cell-mediated) hypersensitivity, 139, 148–149
Hyperthyroidism, Graves disease, 144, 146
Hyphae, in fungal morphology, 412, 421
Hypopigmentation, 415
Hypothyroidism
    Graves disease, 144, 146, 148
    Hashimoto thyroiditis, 148

**I**

Idiotype
    antigen recognition molecule, 11–13
    antigens, 39
    receptor diversity, 13–16
Imipenem, *Pseudomonas aeruginosa* resistance to, 328
Immediate (type I) hypersensitivity, 139, 140–143, 149
    development, 141
    late-phase reaction in, 143
    mediators, 142
Immune complex-mediated (type III) hypersensitivity, 139, 147–148, 149
    passive immunization, 108
    pathogenicity, 200
Immune defense, to viral infection, 348
Immune response
    disease caused by, 139–151
    effects of HIV on, 131–133
    primary and secondary, 103
    type I hypersensitivity and, 139, 140–143
    type II hypersensitivity and, 139, 144–147
    type III hypersensitivity and, 139, 147–148
    type IV hypersensitivity and, 139, 148–149
Immune system
    antibodies, 74–76
    cell ontogeny, 8
    cell origins, 7
    destruction by HIV
        mechanisms of, 131
        sequence in, 132
    overview, 3–5
Immunization. *See also* Vaccines
    recommended schedules, 108
Immunoblot test, 174
Immunocompromised patients
    *Klebsiella pneumoniae* and, 260
    *Listeria monocytogenes* and, 232
    live viral vaccine contraindications in, 110
Immunodeficiency diseases
    bare lymphocyte syndrome, 121
    complement defects, 119
    and developmental blocks, association between, 122
    humoral immunity defects, 118
    involving B lymphocytes, 77, 119–120
    involving T lymphocytes, 119–120
    major histocompatibility complex class I deficiency, 121
    phagocyte defects, 117

T lymphocyte defects and severe combined immunodeficiencies, 119–120
Immunogen, 39. *See also* Antigen(s)
Immunogenicity, adjuvants, 112
Immunoglobulin(s)
    antigen receptors, 11–13
    in fetus and neonate, 111
    heavy chain
        DNA, 16
        switching, in humoral immunity, 72–73
    heavy chain DNA, 16
    proteolytic cleavage with papain and pepsin, 69
Immunoglobulin A (IgA)
    biologic functions, 77
    as dimer, 74–75
    memory B cells, 101
    production deficiency, 120
    proteases, 199
        for cell surface adherence, 198
        *Haemophilus influenzae* and, 269
    in secondary immune responses, 74–76
Immunoglobulin cellular adhesion molecules (IgCAMs)
    in acute inflammatory response, 40–42
    classification, 190
    in extravasation process, 40–41
    T-cell activation and, 55, 56
Immunoglobulin D (IgD)
    B lymphocyte receptor, 11–13
    biologic functions, 77
Immunoglobulin E (IgE)
    biologic functions, 77
    immunologic diseases and, 139
    memory B cells, 101
    passive immunization, 108
    production deficiency, 120
    in secondary immunie responses, 76
    type I hypersensitivity and, 140–141
Immunoglobulin G (IgG)
    antibody-dependent cell-mediated cytotoxicity, 93
    basic structure, 74
    biologic functions, 77
    memory B cells, 101
    neonatal infection, 111
    opsonization with, 43–44
    in secondary immune responses, 74–76
    type II hypersensitivity and, 144–148
Immunoglobulin M (IgM)
    B lymphocyte receptor, 11–13
    biologic functions, 77
    humoral immunity defects, 118
    isotype switching and, 72–73
    neonatal infection, 111
    pentamer, 70–72
    in primary immune responses, 72
    in secondary immune responses, 74–76
    transfusion reaction, 144
    type II hypersensitivity and, 139, 144–147
Immunologic diseases, classification of, 139. *See also*
        Hypersensitivity diseases
Immunologic memory
    dissemination, 102
    generation, 101–103
Immunology, laboratory techniques in, 169–175

Immunopropylaxis, active immunization for, 109–112
Immunosuppression
    for graft rejection prevention and treatment, 162
    *Legionella pneumophila* and, 247
Impetigo, 450
    *Staphylococcus aureus,* 217
    *Streptococcus pyogenes,* 219
Inactivated vaccines, for infection treatment/prevention, 488
Inclusion conjunctivitis, 281
Inclusion disease, cytomeaglic, 363
Indirect fluorescent antibody test (IFA), 172
Indirect repeats, multiple drug-resistance plasmids and, 324–325
Induction process, in transduction, 321–322
Infection. *See also specific infectious disease and/or pathogen*
    arthritis related to, 465
    bacterial, resistance mechanisms in, 192–193
    blood cell changes in, 461
    case histories in, 466–474
    of central nervous system, 462–463
    crossing placenta, 484–485
    epidemiology/transmission, 482–486
    granulomatous response to, 486
    intracerebral calcifications caused by, 487
    laboratory diagnosis, 487–488
    mechanisms, 198–200
    osteomyelitis and, 465
    pathology, 486–487
    treatment/prevention, 488–489
    viral. *See* Viral infections
Infectious disease. *See also specific infectious disease and/or pathogen*
    cardiac symptoms, 454
    case histories, 466–474
    of ear, nose, throat, and upper respiratory system, 452
    of eyes, 453
    of gastrointestinal tract, 460
        diarrhea, 457–459
    of genitourinary tract, 456
    of liver, 460
    of middle and lower respiratory system, 455
    rashes in, 464
    of skin, mucous membranes, and underlying tissues, 450–451
Infective endocarditis, 217, 222, 422, 454
Infectivity mechanisms, 198–200
Inflammation
    acute, 40–42
    autoimmune failure, 150
    complement system and, 77
    effector cells and, 102
    immune system, 3
    pathogenicity and, 199
    type IV hypersensitivity and, 148–149
Inflammatory diarrhea, microbial organisms causing, 459
Infliximab, 151
Influenza
    vaccine, 109
    virus, 391–392
Inhalation, infection transmission through, 485
Initial binding leukocyte, 189
Innate immunity, overview, 3–5
Insect disease vectors, 483
Insect venom sensitivity, 149
Insertional mutagenesis, in tumorigenesis, 396
Insomnia, fatal familial, 398

Insulin-dependent diabetes mellitus (type I), 148, 150
Insulin-resistant diabetes (type II), 144, 149
Integrated fertility factor, 316–317
Integrins
    in acute inflammatory response, 40–42
    characteristics, 189
    in extravasation process, 40–41
    T-cell activation and, 55, 56
Interferons
    classification, 186–187
    IFN-α
        innate/adaptive immunity, 4
        NK cell killing mechanisms, 92
        therapeutic use, 349
    IFN-β
        innate/adaptive immunity, 4
        K cell killing mechanisms, 92
        therapeutic use, 349
    IFN-γ
        in cell-mediated immunity, 89–95
    cytotoxic T cells and, 90
        helper T cell differentiation and, 58–60
        therapeutic use of, 349
        type IV hypersensitivity and, 148
    production, 348–349
    therapeutic use, 349
Interleukins
    classification, 186
    IL-2, cytotoxic T cells and, 90
    IL-4
        helper T cell differentiation and, 58–60
        type I hypersensitivity and, 141
    IL-8, in extravasation process, 40–41
    IL-10, helper T cell differentiation and, 58–60
    IL-12
        helper T cell differentiation and, 58–60
        NK cell killing, 92
    IL-13, type I hypersensitivity and, 141
Internal organs, normal flora of, 198
Interstitial pneumonia/pneumonitis
    cytomegalovirus, 363
    Pneumocystis jirovecii, 423
Intoxication, diarrhea by, 457
Intracellular killing, 44–45
    in chronic granulomatous disease, 45
Intracellular survival, 199
Intracerebral calcifications, infections causing, 486
Intrauterine device infection, 236
Intrinsic defenses, immune system, 3
Intrinsic drug resistance, 323
Invariant chain, synthesis of, 52
Invasins, pathogenicity and, 199
Invasive aspergillosis, 421
Invasive factors, bacterial pathogenicity, 480
Iodine/iodophors, in protein modification, 332
Iron, in Legionella pneumophila culture, 247
Isografts (syngeneic grafts), 157
Isoniazid
    emerging bacterial resistance to, 326
    for tuberculosis, 240
Isospora sp., oocysts, 475
Isospora belli, 429

Isotypes
    antibody, biologic functions of, 77
    antigen recognition molecule, 11–13
    in humoral immunity, 69
    switching, in humoral immunity, 69, 71–73
Ixodes scapularis/Ixodes pacificus, 277

J
J chain, 70
Jarisch-Herxheimer reaction, to syphilis therapy, 276
JC polyomavirus, 357, 398
Job's syndrome, 117

K
Kaposi sarcoma, 364
Keratinized tissues, superficial fungal infection of, 415
Keratoconjunctivits, herpes simplex virus type 1, 359
Killed vaccines, 109
Kinyoun stain, 213
Kirby-Bauer agar disk diffusion test, 329
Klebsiella pneumoniae, 260
    as capsule producer, 475
Kuru, 398
K constant domain, light chain production and, 15–16

L
LaCrosse encephalitis, 393
Lactoferrin, in intracellular killing, 44
Lactose fermenters
    Enterobacteriaceae, 257, 496
    Klebsiella pneumoniae, 260
Lag phase, in bacterial growth and death, 210
λ constant domain, light chain production, 15–16
Lambda phage, lysogenic conversion and, 320–323
Lassa fever virus, 394
Late-phase reaction, in type I hypersensitivity, 143
Latex bead agglutination tests, 170, 414
Lecithinase, Clostridium perfringens and, 230
Legionella sp., staining process in, 214
Legionella pneumophila, 247
Legionnaires disease, 247
Leishmania sp., 433–434
Leishmania braziliensis, 434
Leishmania donovani, 434
Lentivirus, 376. See also Human immunodeficiency virus (HIV)
Lepromatous leprosy, 61
Lepromin skin test, 241
Leprosy, 241
    tuberculoid vs. lepromatous, 61
Leptospira interrogans, 279
Leptospirosis, 279
Lethal factor, anthrax toxin, 225
Leukemia, acute lymphoblastic, 15
Leukocyte adhesion deficiency (LAD), 41, 117
Leukoencephalopathy, progressive multifocal, 398
Leukotriene B$_4$
    in acute inflammatory response, 42
    in type I hypersensitivity, 143
Leukotrienes, in type I hypersensitivity, 143
Lice, 483
Light chain
    B lymphocyte antigen receptor and, 11–13
    variable domain amino acids, 14–16

Limited diversity, 3
Limited specificity, 3
Lincosamides, emerging bacterial resistance to, 326
Lipid A, toxicity, 200
Lipopolysaccharide (LPS), 200
*Listeria* sp., 224, 232
*Listeria monocytogenes,* 232–233
Listeriolysin O, 232
Listeriosis, 232
Live vaccines, 110–111, 488–489
*Loa loa,* 441
Log phase, in bacterial growth and death, 210
Lower respiratory tract infection, 455
*LTR* (U$_3$, U$_5$) gene, 377
Lyme disease, 277–278, 484
Lymph nodes
    antigen exposure in, 23
    compartmentalization, 34
    lymphocyte recirculation and homing, 33–35
Lymphadenitis
    mediastinal hemorrhagic, 225
    *Pasturella multocida,* 272
Lymphocytes. *See also* B lymphocytes; T lymphocytes
    antigen recognition molecules, 11–13
    immune system function, 3, 10
    recirculation and homing, 33–35
    selection and differentiation, 23–28
Lymphocytic choriomeningitis virus (LCMV), 394
Lymphocytosis, 461
Lymphogranuloma venereum, 281
Lymphoid cells, immune system function, 9, 10
Lymphoid follicles
    in humoral immunity, 67
    lymphocyte recirculation and homing, 34, 35
Lymphoid organs, 23–24
    lymphocyte recirculation and homing, 33–35
    secondary, antigen transportation to, 54
Lymphopoiesis, 23
Lymphoproliferative disease, 362
Lysis, in complement system, 77
Lysogenic conversion, 309
    excision error, 321–322
    specialized transduction as sequelae to, 320–323
Lysogeny, 320–321
    in specialized transduction, 322
Lysozyme, in intracellular killing, 44
Lytic enzymes, antibody-dependent cell-mediated cytotoxicity, 93
Lytic infection, transduction and, 318–319
Lytic virus life cycle, 319

**M**
M-protein, *Streptococcus pyogenes* and, 218
Macrolides, emerging bacterial resistance to, 326
Macromolecular synthesis, in viral replication, 341, 343–344
Macrophage
    adhesion, helper T cell and, 56
    antibody-dependent cell-mediated cytotoxicity, 93
    in cell-mediated immunity, 89, 95
    HIV and, 132
    in immune system, 4, 9
    immunodeficiency diseases and, 122
    T helper cell differentiation and, 58
    in type IV hypersensitivity, 139, 148–149

Major histocompatibility complex (MHC)
    class I, 24–25, 53
        cytotoxic T cell differentiation, 90
        gene products, 24–25
        molecule deficiency, 120
        NK cell killing, 92
    class II, 25–26, 53
        autoimmune disease development, 150
        gene products, 24–25
        molecule deficiency, 120, 121
        tissue typing, 162
    endogenous pathway, 51–52
    endosomal (exogenous) pathway, 52
    thymocyte exposure to, 24
Malaria, 431–432
*Malassezia furfur,* 415
Malignant otitis externa, 452
Malignant pustule, 450
Mannitol, *Staphylococcus aureus* and, 216
Mantoux test, 239
Marburg virus, 390
Mass lesion, 463
Mast cells
    in immune system, 10
    in immunologic diseases, 139
    mediators, in type I hypersensitivity, 143
Mastitis, 217
Maternal antibodies, vaccinations and, 111
Matrix protein, 384
Mature lymphocytes, characteristics of, 33–35
Measles virus, 385–386, 398
Mediastinal hemorrhagic lymphadenitis, 225
Medullary sinus, lymphocyte recirculation and homing and, 33–35
Membrane-bound immunoglobulin, B lymphocyte antigen
        receptor and, 11–13
Membrane pore formation, complement system and, 77
Membranes, agents damaging, 332
Memory, immune system, 4
Memory cells
    antigen transport and, 54
    characteristics, 102
    in immunologic memory, 101–103
    immunologic memory and, 101–102
    T-cell activation and, 55, 56
Meningitis, 462
    cerebrospinal fluid findings in, 464
    *Cryptococcus neoformans,* 422
    *Haemophilus influenzae,* 269
    *Listeria monocytogenes,* 232
    *Streptococcus pneumoniae,* 221
Meningococcal infection, complement system deficiency and, 119
Meningoencephalitis, 462
    herpes simplex virus type 1, 360
Metabolic stimulation, in phagocyte, 44
Metabolism, bacterial, 477
Metachromatic staining, 476
Metazoans, 428, 436–441
Methicillin-resistant *Staphylococcus aureus* (MRSA), 218, 328
Metronidazole, 228
    *Clostridium difficile* and, 231
Microaerophilic bacteria, 212, 477
Microbial infections
    diarrhea caused by, 458–459

epidemiology, 197–198
resistance mechanisms, 191–194
Microcytotoxicity test, 161–162
Microorganisms, culture of, 210–211
*Microsporidia,* 430
Microsporum, 415
Middle respiratory tract infection, 455
Midges, 483
Minimal bacterial concentration (MBC), 330, 331
Minimal inhibitory concentration (MIC), 330, 331
Mites, 484
Mitogens, B-cell, 68
Mixed lymphocyte reaction, 162
Mobile genetic elements, multiple drug-resistance plasmids and, 324–325
Mobilization process, in drug resistance, 328
Molecular mimicry, autoimmune failure and, 150
Molluscum contagiosum, 367
Monoclonal antibodies, clinical applications, 151
Monocytes
    antibody-dependent cell-mediated cytotoxicity, 93
    immune system function, 9
Mononucleosis
    heterophile-negative, 363
    heterophile-positive, 362
*Moraxella catarrhalis,* 244
Mosquitoes, 483
mRNA molecules, variable domain sequence, 14
Mucinase-positive *Helicobacter pylori,* 254
Mucocutaneous candidiasis, 122
*Mucor* infection, 422–423
Mucosal-associated lymphoid tissues (MALT)
    antigen exposure, 23
    lymphocyte recirculation and homing, 33–35
    in secondary immune responses, 75
Mucous membranes, infectious dieases of, 450–451
Multiple drug-resistance plasmids, 324–325
Multiple sclerosis, 148, 149
Mumps virus, 386
Muromonab, 151
Mutagenesis/Mutations
    insertional, in tumorigenesis, 396
    multiple drug-resistance plasmids and, 324–325
Myasthenia gravis, 144, 149
    acetylcholine receptor antibodies in, 144, 147
Mycetoma, 450
    *Actinomyces israelii,* 236
    *Nocardia,* 237
Mycobacteria other than tuberculosis (MOTTS), 240–241
*Mycobacterium* sp., 224, 238–241
    morphology/taxonomy, 475
    staining process in, 214
*Mycobacterium avium-intracellulare,* 240
    in HIV infection, prophylactic regimen, 381
*Mycobacterium kansasii,* 240
*Mycobacterium leprae,* 61, 241
*Mycobacterium marinum,* 240
*Mycobacterium scrofulaceum,* 240
Mycology, 411
*Mycoplasma pneumoniae,* 286–287
Mycoplasmataceae, 280, 286–287
Mycoses, subcutaneous, 416

Myeloid cells
    immune system function, 9–10
    immunodeficiency diseases and, 122
Myeloperoxidase
    deficiency in, 117
    in intracellular killing, 44
Myocarditis, 144
Myonecrosis, *Clostridium perfringens,* 230

**N**
N-nucleotide addition, light chain production, 15
NADPH oxidase
    chronic granulomatous disease and, 45
    deficiency, 117
    in intracellular killing, 44
*Naegleria* sp., 430
Nafcillin/oxacillin, for *Staphylococcus aureus* infection, 218
Nagler reaction, in *Clostridium perfringens* infection, 230
Naive lymphocytes, 33–35, 102
Naked viruses, enveloped viruses vs., 343
Name tests, in infectious disease diagnosis, 487
Nasal infections, 452
Nasopharyngeal carcinoma, 362, 397
Natural immunization, 107
Natural killer (NK) cells
    activation, 92
    in cell-mediated immunity, 89, 92, 95
    in immune system function, 10
    mechanisms, 92
    T helper cell differentiation and, 58
*Necator americanus,* 441
*nef* gene, 377
    product, in HIV, 131
    in retrovirus life cycle, 378
Negative selection, T-cell receptor signaling, 26–27
Negative-stranded RNA viruses, 383–394
*Neisseria* sp., 242
*Neisseria gonorrhoeae,* 199, 243–244
    pediatric vaccines for, 111–112
    resistance to drugs, 328
*Neisseria meningitidis,* 242–243
    as capsule producer, 475
Nematodes, 428, 440–441
Neonatal disease
    herpes simplex type 2, 360
    *Listeria monocytogenes* and, 232
    meningitis, 220
Nephritis
    type I hypersensitivity and, 144
    type III hypersensitivy and, 148
Neuraminidase, 384
Neurotoxins, 202
Neutrophil(s)
    in acute inflammatory response, 40–42
    antibody-dependent cell-mediated cytotoxicity and, 93
    immune system function and, 9
    in immunodeficiency diseases, 122
    substances chemoattractive to, 42
Neutrophil oxidative index (NOI), 45
Newborn, hemolytic disease of (HDNB), 144, 145
Nitroblue tetrazolium (NBT) reduction test, 45
*Nocardia* sp., 224, 237
    morphology/taxonomy, 475

*Nocardia asteroides/Nocardia brasiliensis,* 237
Nocardiosis, 237
Non-gram-staining bacteria, 214
Non-lactose fermenters, 257, 496
Non-self peptides, cytotoxic T cells, 89–90
Non-spore-forming bacteria, 494
Nonconjugative plasmids, 328
Nongonococcal urethritis, 281
Noninflammatory diarrhea, microbial organisms causing, 458
Nonsupperative sequelae, in *Streptococcus pyogenes* infection, 219
Nontransducting phage, in induction process, 321
Norwalk virus, 370
Nose, normal flora of, 198
Nosocomial infection, *Klebsiella pneumoniae,* 260
Nucleic acids
    genomic, replication of, 344
    modification, 332
    synthesis inhibitors, 327

**O**

Obligate aerobes/anaerobes, 212
Obligate parasites, 481, 482
Omenn syndrome, gene rearrangement in, 16
Omeprazole, *Helicobactor pylori* and, 254
*Onchocerca volvulus,* 441
Oncogenes, 396
Oncogenic viruses, 396–397
Oncovirus, 376
One-way isotype switching, 72–73
Opportunistic fungal infections, 421–423
Opsonins, 43–44
Opsonization, 4, 43–44
    in complement system, 77
    in *Staphylococcus aureus,* 44
    type II hypersensitivity and, 139, 144
Optochin resistance, *Viridans streptococci,* 222
Oral cavitary disease, 452
Oral/fecal transmission, of infectious disease, 485–486
Origin of transfer *(oriT),* conjugation, 313
Oropharynx, normal flora of, 198
Orthomyxoviridae, 383, 391–392
Osteomyelitis, 217, 465
    *Salmonella enterica* subsp. other than *typhi* and, 267, 268
Otitis externa, 452
    malignant, 452
Otitis media
    acute, 452
    *Haemophilus influenzae,* 269
    *Streptococcus pneumoniae,* 221
Outer membrane, bacterial envelope, 506
Oxidase, bacterial, 477
Oxidase (cytochrome C oxidase) test, 242
Oxygen, bacteria requirements for, 212

**P**

Pain, acute abdominal, 460
Palivizumab, 151
Pancreatitis, 460
Panencephalitis, subacute sclerosing, 385
Papain, proteolytic cleavage with, 69, 70
Papillomaviridae, 353, 356–357
Paracortical areas, lymphocyte recirculation and homing, 35

Parainfluenza virus, 387
Paralysis
    botulinum toxin, 228
    tetanus toxin, 227
Paramyxoviridae, 383, 385–387
Parasites
    antibody-dependent cell-mediated cytotoxicity, 93
    classification, 428
    host cell growth and survival, 481–482
    metazoans, 428, 436–441
    protozoans, 428, 429–435
Parasitic infections
    resistance mechanisms, 193
    transmission, 484
Parvoviridae, 353, 355
Passive immunization, 107
Pasteurization, 332
*Pasturella multocida,* 272
Pathogenicity mechanisms, 198–200, 478–482. *See also specific bacteria*
Pathogens
    complement system activation and, 77–79
    immunologic memory and, 101–103
Pelvic inflammatory disease (PID), 281, 456
Penicillin-binding protein mutations, 328
Penicillins
    bacterial resistance mechanisms, 325
    for tetanus, 228
    *Viridans streptococci* and, 222
Pentamer, IgM molecule as, 70–72
Pepsin, proteolytic cleavage with, 69, 70
Peptide-binding groove, MHC
    class I, 25
    class II, 26
Peptides
    B lymphocyte antigen receptor, 12–13
    formyl methionyl, in acute inflammatory response, 42
Peptidoglycan, bacterial envelope, 208, 506
Peptidoglycan-teichoic acid, inflammation and, 200
Perforin
    antibody-dependent cell-mediated cytotoxicity, 93
    in cytotoxic T-lymphocytes, 90, 91
    NK cell killing mechanisms, 92, 93
Periarteriolar lymphoid sheaths (PALS), 35
Periplasmic space, 208
    bacterial envelope, 506
Peritonitis, 460
Perlèche, *Candida albicans* infection, 422
Pernicious anemia, 144
Person-to-person contact, infectious disease transmisison through, 486
Pertactin, *Bordetella pertussis* and, 249
Pertussis toxin, 249. *See also* Whooping cough
    production, 479
Phages
    in lysogenic life cycle, 320–323
    in transduction, 318, 319
Phagocyte extravasation, 40–42
Phagocytes
    immunodeficiency disease and defects, 117
    metabolic stimulation and killing within, 44
    rolling, 40, 41
    tight binding, 40, 41

Phagocytic cells, 4
    defects, 117
    immune system defenses, 3
Phagocytosis
    enhancement (opsonization), 43–44
    immune system overview, 3–5
    intracellular killing and, 44–45
    mechanisms, 43
    respiratory burst in, 44
    type II hypersensitivity and, 139, 144
    *Yersinia pestis,* 263–264
Phagolysome formation, 43
Phagosome, in phagocytosis, 43
Pharyngitis, *Streptococcus pyogenes* and, 219
Pharyngoconjuctivitis, 358
Phenols, for disinfection/sterilization, 332
Physiologic barriers, in immune system, 3
Picornaviridae, 368, 371–372
Pigment production, viral, 476
Pili/fimbriae, for cell surface adherence, 198
Pityriasis, 415
Placenta, infections crossing, 484–485
Plantar warts, 356
Plaque, *Viridans streptococci,* 222
Plasma cell
    in humoral immunity, 67
    in immune system function, 10
Plasmids
    bacterial genetics, 308
    drug resistance, 324–325
*Plasmodium* sp.
    hosts for, 432
    life cycle, 431
*Plasmodium falciparum,* 432
*Plasmodium malariae,* 432
*Plasmodium ovale,* 432
*Plasmodium vivax,* 432
*Pneumocystis jirovecii,* 74, 423
    in HIV infection, prophylactic regimen, 381
Pneumonia, 455
    adenovirus, 358
    anthrax toxin, 225
    *Haemophilus influenzae,* 269
    *Klebsiella pneumoniae,* 260
    *Pseudomonas aeruginosa,* 245
    *Staphylococcus aureus,* 217
    *Streptococcus pneumoniae,* 221
    walking pneumonia, 282, 286
Pneumonic plague, 263
*pol* gene, 377
Polio picornavirus, 372
Polio vaccine, 109
Polyarteritis nodosa, 148, 149
Polymerases, negative-stranded RNA viruses, 384
Polyomaviridae, 353, 357
Polysaccharide capsule/vaccine
    *Haemophilus influenzae,* 269
    *Streptococcus pneumoniae,* 222
Pontiac fever, 247
Positive selection, T-cell receptor signaling, 26–27
Positive-stranded RNA viruses, 368–382
Poststreptococcal glomerulonephritis, 148, 149
Poxviridae, 353, 366–367

PPD skin test, 239
Precipitate/Precipitation, 69, 70
Preformed antibodies, screening for, 162
Pregnancy
    hemolytic disease of newborn, 144, 145
    infections that cross the placenta, 484–485
    *Listeria monocytogenes,* 232, 233
    Rh factor and, 144, 145
    toxoplasmosis in, 435
Primary defense, to viral infection, 348
Primary immune responses, 72–73, 103
    and secondary immune responses compared, 103
Prion diseases, 398
Progeny viruses, genomic nucleic acid sequence, 344
Progressive multifocal leukoencephalopathy, 398
Prophage coding
    bacteriophage genome, 309
    botulinum toxin, 228
    *Corynebacterium diphtheriae,* 234
    in lysogenic conversion, 320–323
Prophylaxis
    in HIV infection, 381
    for infection treatment/prevention, 488
Prostaglandins, in type I hypersensitivity, 143
Protective antigen, anthrax toxin, 225
Protein toxins, 201
Proteins
    agents modifying, 332
    synthesis inhibitors, 202, 326
Proteolytic cleavage, of immunoglobulin, 69
*Proteus mirabilis/Proteus vulgaris,* 265, 477
Protozoans, 428, 429–435
Provirus, 381, 396
Pseudohyphae, 412, 421
Pseudomembranous colitis, 231
*Pseudomonas aeruginosa,* 245–246
    as pigment producer, 476
    resistance to drugs, 328
Pseudopodia
    in extravasation process, 40
    in phagocytosis, 43
Pulmonary anthrax, 225
Pulmonary sporotrichosis, 416
Punch biopsy, leprosy, 241
Pustule, malignant, 450
Pyelonephritis, 456
Pyoderma, *Streptococcus pyogenes* and, 219
Pyrrolidonyl arylamidase (PYR) positive bacteria
    *Enterococcus faecalis/faecium,* 223
    *Streptococcus pyogenes,* 218

Q
Quellung reaction, *Streptococcus pneumoniae,* 221

R
Rabies
    vaccine, 109
    virus, 388–389
Radiation, for disinfection/sterilization, 332
Radioimmunoassay (RIA), 173
*rag*1/2 genes, nonsense mutations, 120
"Rapid" methods, antibiotic susceptibility testing, 330

Rashes, in infectious disease, 464
Reactivational tuberculosis, 239
Reactive arthritis, 454
Receptors, viral, 343
Recirculation, lymphocyte, 33–35
Recombinant cytokines, 188
Recombinant vaccines, for infection treatment/prevention, 489
Recombinase A, 309
Recombination
    homologous, 309
    site-specific, 310
Red pulp, 34
Reduvlid bug, 434, 483
Regan-Lowe media, 255–256
    *Bordetella pertussis* and, 250
Rejection. *See* Graft rejection
Reoviridae, 395
Replication, viral. *See* Viral replication
Resistance mechanisms
        to drugs. *See* Drug resistance, mechanisms
        to microbial infection, 191–194
        to viral infection, 346
Respiratory burst, intracellular killing and, 44
Respiratory disease, acute, 358
Respiratory distress/difficulty, 455
Respiratory droplet, infection spread by, 485
Respiratory syncytial virus (RSV), 387
Respiratory tract infection, 452, 455
Restriction endonucleases, 310
Reticuloendothelial (RES) cell, *Histoplasma capsulatum,* 418
Retinopathy with keratitis, 453
Retroviridae, 376–382
*rev* gene, 377
    in retrovirus life cycle, 378
Reye syndrome, 463
Rh factor, type II hypersensitivity and, 144, 145
Rh incompatibility, Coombs test for, 171
Rhabdoviridae, 383, 388–389
Rheumatic fever
    acute, 144, 149
    *Streptococcus pyogenes* pathogenicity, 219
Rheumatoid arthritis, 148, 149
Rhinocerebral infection, 423
Rhinoviruses, 371, 372
*Rhizopus* infection, 422–423
RhoGAM™, 145
*Rickettsia rickettsii,* 283–284
Rickettsiaceae, 280
    infections caused by, 283
    staining process in, 214
Rickettsial pox, 484
Rifamycins, emerging bacterial resistance to, 327
Ringworm infection, 415–416
Rituximab, 151
RNA viruses
    charactersistics, 367
    double-stranded, 395–397, 504
    negative-stranded, 383–394, 504
    postive-stranded, 368–382, 504
Rocky Mountain spotted fever (RMSF), 283, 484
Rolling, in extravasation process, 40, 41
Roseola, 364
Rotavirus, 395

Rough endoplasmic reticulum (RER), binding peptides and, 52, 53
Roundworms, 428, 440–441
Rubella
    vaccine, 110
    virus, 374
Rubivirus, 374

S

*Salmonella enterica* subsp. *typhi,* as capsule producer, 475
*Salmonella enteritidis,* 267–268
*Salmonella typhi,* 266–267
*Salmonella typhimurium,* 267–268
Sandflies, 434, 483
"Sandpaper" rash, *Streptococcus pyogenes,* 219
SARS-coronavirus, 375
Sbouraud agar, 414
Scalded skin syndrome, 217
Scarlatiniform rash, *Staphylococcus aureus,* 217
Scarlet fever, *Streptococcus pyogenes* and, 219
*Schistosoma haematobium,* 437
*Schistosoma mansoni/japonicum,* 437
Scrapie, 398
Scrub typhus, 283, 484
Secondary immune responses, 103
    antibodies, 74–77
    and primary immune response compared, 103
Secretion systems, type III, 199
Secretory IgA, in secondary immune responses, 75–76
Selectin-type adhesion molecule, in acute inflammatory response, 40–42
Selectins
    characteristics, 189
    E-selectins, in extravasation process, 40, 41
    L-selectins
        initial binding leukocyte, 189
        lymphocyte recirculation, 35
Selective IgA deficiency, 118, 122
Self-limitation, immune system, 3, 4
Self/non-self recognition, immune system, 3, 4
Self-tolerance
    clonal anergy and deletion producing, 23–24
    failure, 139, 149. *See also* Autoimmune diseases
Septicemia, 197
    *Brucella,* 251
    *Candida albicans* infection, 422
    *Escherichia coli,* 259
    *Klebsiella pneumoniae,* 260
    *Listeria monocytogenes,* 232
    *Pseudomonas aeruginosa,* 245
    *Salmonella enterica* subsp. other than *typhi,* 267, 268
    *Streptococcus agalactiae,* 220
Serology
    in fungal infection, 414
    Leptospirosis, 279
    Lyme disease, 277
    syphilis, 276
*Serratia* sp., as pigment producer, 476
Serum sickness, 148, 149
Severe acute respiratory syndrome (SARS), 375
Severe combined immunodeficiency (SCID), 119–120, 121
    gene rearrangement in, 16
Sex pili, conjugation, 313

Sexually transmitted diseases (STDs), 486
    *Chlamydia trachomatis*, 280–281
    *Haemophilus ducreyi*, 270
    *Neisseria gonorrhoeae*, 243–244
    *Treponema pallidum*, 275–276
Shiga toxin, 261
*Shigella* sp., 261–262
Shingles, 361
Shock, toxic reactions in, 200
Sickle cell anemia
    B19 parvovirus and, 355
    susceptibility to blood-borme pathogens in, 54
Siderophores, 199
Signal transduction complex, antigen recognition molecule, 12–13
Sinopulmonary infection, 118
Sinusitis, 452
    *Streptococcus pneumoniae* and, 221
Sinusoids, vascular, 34
Site-specific recombination, 310
Skin. *See also* Cutaneous *entries*
    infectious dieases, 450–451
    normal flora, 198
Skin test, in fungal infection, 414
Smallpox, 366–367
Somatic hypermutation, in humoral immunity, 73
Sorbitol MacConkey screen, 258
Sore throat, 452
Spasmolytic drugs, 228
Specialization, immune system, 4
Specialized transduction, 320–323
    and generalized transduction compared, 323
Specific defenses, immune system, 3
Specificity, immune system, 4
Spherules, in fungal morphology, 413
Spirochetes, 275–279, 495
    staining process and, 214
Spleen. *See also* Asplenia
    antigen exposure, 23
    lymphocyte recirculation and homing, 33–35
    structure, 34
Spore-forming bacteria, 475, 494
Spore types, in fungal morphology, 412–413
*Sporothrix schenckii*, 416
Sporotrichosis, 416
St. Louis encephalitis virus, 373
Stains
    bacterial, 212–213
    in infectious disease diagnosis, 487
    leprosy diagnosis, 241
*Staphylococcus* sp., 215, 216
*Staphylococcus aureus*, 215, 216–218
    opsonization in, 44
    as pigment producer, 476
    A protein, 199
    resistance to drugs, 327, 328
*Staphylococcus epidermis*, 215, 216
    as biofilm producer, 476
*Staphylococcus mutans*, as biofilm producer, 476
*Staphylococcus saprophyticus*, 215, 216
Stationary phase, in bacterial growth and death, 210
Sterilization, 332
Stimulator cells, tissue compatibility, 162
Stomach, normal flora of, 198

Stomach cancer, *Helicobactor pylori* and, 254
Strawberry tongue, 219
Streptococcal cell-wall Ag, 144
*Streptococcus* sp., 215, 217
*Streptococcus agalactiae*, 215, 220
*Streptococcus bovis*, 215
*Streptococcus mutans*, 215, 222
*Streptococcus pneumoniae*, 215, 220–222
    as capsule producer, 475
        pediatric vaccines for, 111–112
        penicillin-binding protein mutations, 328
*Streptococcus pyogenes*, 215, 218–220
    as capsule producer, 475
    M protein, 199
*Streptococcus sanguis*, 215, 222
Streptolysin O, 218
Streptolysin S, 218
Streptomycin, tularemia, 248
Stromal cells, thymic, 27
*Strongyloides stercoralis*, 441
Structural toxins, 200
Subacute endocarditis, 454
Subacute sclerosing panencephalitis, 385, 398
Subcapsular sinus, lymphocyte recirculation and homing, 33–35
Subcutaneous mycoses, 416
Subunit vaccines, for infection treatment/prevention, 489
Sulfatides, *Mycobacterium tuberculosis* and, 239
Sulfonamides, bacterial resistance mechanisms, 325
Sulfur granules, in actinomycosis, 236
Superantigens, 57, 202
    *Streptococcus pyogenes* and, 219
    toxic shock syndrome toxin-1, 217
Survival, intracellular, 199
Syncytia formation, 476
Syngeneic grafts, 157
    rejection prevention and treatment, 162
Syphilis, stages of, 275
Systemic anaphylaxis, 143
Systemic lupus erythematosus (SLE), 148, 149

## T

T-cell activation, 55
T-cell conjugates, formation of, 67, 68
T-cell function, 10
    in autoimmune and hypersensitivity diseases, 150–151
T-cell-mediated (type IV) hypersensitivity. *See* Delayed-type
        hypersensitivity (type IV) (DTH)
T-cell receptor (TCR), 11–13
    binding to MHC class-II peptide, 55–56
    $\alpha/\beta$ chains, 12–13
T lymphocytes
    activation, 54
    activation and differentiation of, antigen transport and, 54
    antigen recognition molecules, 11–13
    antigen transport and, 54
    characteristics, 102
    defects, 119–120
    differentiation, 26–28, 54
    Hib vaccine, 111
    immune system function and, 4, 10
    memory cells, 101–103
    periarteriolar lymphoid sheaths, 35
T regulatory cell ($T_{Reg}$), helper T cell differentiation and, 58–60

*Taenia saginata* (beef tapeworm), 439
*Taenia solium* (pork tapeworm), 439
Tapeworms, 428, 438–439
Target recognition, antibody-dependent cell-mediated
 cytotoxicity, 93
*tat* gene, 377
 product, in HIV, 131
 in retrovirus life cycle, 378
Teichoic acids, 200
 for cell surface adherence, 198
Telangiectasia, 120
Tellurite medium, 211, 494
Temperate phage, 318, 320
 in specialized transduction, 322
Terminal deoxyribonucleotidyl transferase (Tdt), light chain
 production, 15
Tetanospasmin, 227
Tetanus, 227–228
 toxin production and, 479
Tetracyclines, bacterial resistance to
 emerging, 326
 mechanisms, 325
TH17 cell, helper T cell differentiation and, 58–60
Thiosulfate citrate bile salt (TCBS), *Vibrio*, 255
Thoracic duct, lymphocyte recirculation and homing, 33–35
Throat infections, 452
Thrombocytopenia, 120
Thrush, 422
Thymus
 cancer of, Epstein-Barr virus association with, 397
 lymphocyte development, 23
 structure, 24
 T-cell selection in, 26–27
 T lymphocyte development, 10, 24
 thymocyte development, 26
Thymus-dependent antigens, 67
Thymus-independent antigens, 68–69
Ticks/tick bites
 disease vectors for, 484
 *Francisella tularensis*, 248
Tinea (ringworm), 415–416
Tinea versicolor, 415
Tissue, infectious dieases of, 450–451
Tissue-borne antigens
 bacteria-induced antibodies with, 200
 lymphocyte recirculation and homing, 33–35
Tissue compatibility/typing, in transplant immunology, 160–162
Togaviridae, 374
Tolerance, clonal anergy and deletion, 24
Toll-like receptor (TLR), 55, 56
Toxic shock syndrome, 217
Toxic shock syndrome toxin-1 (TSST-1) superantigen, 217
Toxicity mechanisms, 198–200
Toxicosis, botulism, 229
Toxins, 200–202
 with ADP-ribosylating activity, 480
 *Clostridium difficile*
  toxin A, 231
  toxin B, 231
 pathogenicity, 479–481
*Toxocara canis/cati*, 440
Toxoid vaccine, for *Bacillus anthracis*, 226
Toxoid vaccines, for infection treatment/prevention, 489

*Toxoplasma gondii*, 435
 in HIV infection, prophylactic regimen, 381
Toxoplasmosis, 435
Tracheal cytotoxin, *Bordetella pertussis* and, 249
Trachoma, 281
Trafficking
 lymphocyte recirculation and, 35
 of memory lymphocytes, 102
Transducing phages, 319
 specialized, 322
Transduction
 bacterial transfer, 318–323
 and conjugation and transformation processes compared, 323
 drug resistance, 328
 gene transfer, 311
 specialized, 320–323
Transendothelial migration, in extravasation process, 40, 41
Transformation
 and conjugation and transduction processes compared, 323
 DNA exchange, 312
 drug resistance, 328
 gene transfer, 311
Transforming growth factor β, 187
Transfusion, 157
 reaction to, 144
Transient hypogammaglobulinemia of infancy, 118
Translocation, in tumorigenesis, 396
Transplantation immunology, 157–162
Transposases, multiple drug-resistance plasmids and, 324–325
Transpositional insertion, plasmid-mediated drug resistance, 324–325
Transposons, 310
 multiple drug-resistance plasmids, 324–325
Trastuzumab, 151
Travelers' diarrhea, 479
Trehalose dimycolate, *Mycobacterium tuberculosis* and, 239
Trematodes, 428, 436–437
*Treponema pallidum*, 275–276
*Trichinella spiralis*, 441
*Trichomonas vaginalis*, 430
Trichophyton, 415
*Trichuris trichiura*, 440
Trivalent (A-B-E) antitoxin, 229
*Trypanosoma brucei gambiense/rhodesiense*, 434
*Trypanosoma cruzi*, 434
Trypanosomes, 433–434
Tsetse flies, 434, 483
TSH receptor, in Graves disease, 144, 146
Tuberculin, *Mycobacterium tuberculosis* and, 239
Tuberculin test, 148, 149
Tuberculoid leprosy, 61
Tuberculosis, primary pulmonary, 239
Tularemia, 248, 484
Tumbling motility, *Listeria monocytogenes*, 232
Tumor cells, NK cell killing mechanisms, 92
Tumor necrosis factor(s)
 antibody-dependent cell-mediated cytotoxicity, 93
 classification, 187
 TNF-α, in cell-mediated immunity, 89–95
  cytotoxic T-lymphocytes and, 90
 TNF-β, in cell-mediated immunity, 89–95
  cytotoxic T-lymphocytes and, 90
 type IV hypersensitivity and, 148
Tumor suppressor genes, 396

Tumorigenesis, 396–397
Typhoid fever, 266–267
Typhus, 283
Tyrosine kinase deficiency, 118
Tzanck smear, 361

## U

Ulceroglandular disease, 248
Upper respiratory tract infection, 452
*Ureaplasma urealyticum,* 287
Urease-positive bacteria, 477
    *Helicobacter pylori,* 254
Urethritis, 456
    nongonococcal, 281
Urinary tract infections
    *Escherichia coli,* 259
    *Klebsiella pneumoniae,* 260
    *Proteus mirabilis/Proteus vulgaris,* 265
    *Pseudomonas aeruginosa,* 246

## V

Vaccines. *See also* Immunization
    for active and passive immunization and, 107, 109–112
    *Bacillus anthracis,* 226
    bacterial, 109
    component, 110–111
    contraindications, 110
    *Corynebacterium diphtheriae,* 235
    immunologic memory and, 102
    for infection treatment/prevention, 488–489
    killed, 109
    live viral, 110, 112
    *Streptococcus pneumoniae,* 222
    tetanus, 228
    toxoid production, 201
    tuberculosis, 240
    viral, 109–110, 112
Vagina, normal flora of, 198
Vaginal itching/pain, 456
Vaginitis, *Candida albicans,* 422
Vaginosis, bacterial, 271
Valley fever, 419
Vancomycin
    bacterial resistance mechanisms, 325
    *Enterococcus faecalis/faceium* resistance to, 223, 327
    for *Streptococcus pneumoniae,* 221
Vancomycin-intermediate *Staphylococcus aureus* (VISA), 218
Vancomycin-resistant *Enterococcus faecalis/faecium,* 223, 327
Vancomycin-resistant *Staphylococcus aureus* (VRSA), 218
Variable domains, receptor diversity, 14–16
Varicella zoster virus (VZV), 361
Variola, 366–367
VDJ rearrangement, heavy chain diversity, 14–16
Vectors
    arthropod, 483–484
    parasitic, 428
Venezuelan equine encephalitis virus (VEE), 374
Vesicular lesions, 450
*Vibrio* sp., 255–256
*Vibrio cholerae,* 255–256
*Vibrio parahaemolyticus,* 256

Viral hepatitis, 350–352. *See also specific viruses by name*
    symptoms of, 350
Viral infections
    by age group, 347
    cellular effects, 346
    host resistance to, 348–349
    in immnodeficiency disease, 119–120
    patterns, 346–347
    resistance mechanisms, 191–192
Viral oncogenes *(v-onc),* 396
Viral receptors, 343
Viral replication, 341
    attachment, 342–343
    by genomic nucleic acid replication, 344
    in herpes virus life cycle, 354
    by macromolecular synthesis, 343–344
    spread, 342
    viral entry into host cell, 343
    and viral release, 345
Viral vaccines, 109–110, 112
*Viridans streptococci,* 215, 222
Virulent phage, in transduction, 318
Virus-infected cells, NK cell killing mechanisms, 92
Viruses. *See also* Viral infections
    and cancer association, 397
    cytopathogenesis, 476
    DNA viruses, 353–367, 504. *See also individual viruses and families by name*
    genetics, 399
    oncogenic, 396–397
    prion diseases, 398
    release, 345
    replication. *See* Viral replication
    RNA viruses. *See also individual viruses and families by name*
        double-stranded, 395–397, 504
        negative-stranded, 383–394, 504
        positive-stranded, 368–382, 504
    slow conventional, 398
    structure and morphology, 339–341
Volutin (granules), *Corynebacterium diphtheriae,* 238

## W

Walking pneumonia, 282, 286
Warts
    human papillomavirus, 356–357
    molluscum contagiosum, 367
Weil disease, 279
Weil-Felix test, *Proteus mirabilis/Proteus vulgaris,* 265
West Nile encephalitis virus, 373
Western blot test, 174
Western equine encephalitis virus (WEE), 374
Wheals, 143
Whiff test, *Gardnerella,* 271
White pulp, 34
Whooping cough
    stages, 250
    toxin production and, 479
Window perid (equivalence zone), in antigen-antibody interactions, 170
Wiskott-Aldrich syndrome, 120
Wool sorter's disease, 225

Wound management, infection in, 451
    *Clostridium perfringens*, 230
    *Clostridium tetani*, 228
*Wucheria bancrofti*, 441

## X

X-linked agammaglobulinemia, 122
X-linked hyper-IgM syndrome, 74, 118
Xenogeneic grafts, 157

## Y

Yeast infections
    *Candida albicans*, 421–422
    of skin, 415
Yellow fever
    vaccine for, 110
    virus, 373
*Yersinia enterocolitica*, 264
*Yersinia pestis*, 263–264

## Z

Ziehl-Neelsen acid fast stain, 213
Zoonosis
    *Brucella*, 251
    *Francisella tularensis*, 248
    *Yersinia enterocolitica*, 264
    *Yersinia pestis*, 263
Zoonotic organisms, 251, 482–483